CORPORATE HEDGING IN THEORY AND PRACTICE

Lessons from Metallgesellschaft

CORPORATE HEDGING IN THEORY AND PRACTICE

Lessons from Metallgesellschaft

Edited by Christopher L. Culp and Merton H. Miller

RISK
BOOKS

Published by Risk Books, a specialist division of Risk Publications.

Haymarket House
28–29 Haymarket
London SW1Y 4RX
Tel: +44 (0)171 484 9700
Fax: +44 (0)171 930 2238

ISBN 1 899 382 391

British Library Cataloguing in Publication Data
A catalogue record for this book is available from the British Library

Risk Books Commissioning Editor: William Falloon
Project Editor: Lisa Carroll
Pre-press: Lindsey Hofmeister and Bridie Selley
Typesetter: Marie Doherty

Printed and bound in Great Britain by Bookcraft (Bath) Ltd, Somerset

CONTENTS

THE MGRM CONTROVERSY – HEDGING OBJECTIVES DO MATTER

THE MATHEMATICS OF HEDGING LONG-DATED OBLIGATIONS WITH SHORT-DATED FUTURES

AUTHORS

Nicolas P. Bollen is an assistant professor at the David Eccles School of Business, University of Utah. He received his BA from Cornell University and MBA and PhD from Duke University. His research encompasses a wide range of topics in investments, including derivative valuation in regime-switching models, the interactions between stock and option markets, and mutual fund performance. He is currently studying the volatility smile of index options.

Michael J. Brennan holds the Irwin and Goldyne Hearsh Chair in Banking and Finance at the University of California, Los Angeles, and is a professor of finance at the London Business School. He has served as president of the American Finance Association, the Society for Financial Studies and the Western Finance Association, and has been Editor of both the *Journal of Finance* and the *Review of Financial Studies*. His current research interests include the study of international capital flows and the analysis of optimal dynamic portfolio strategies under incomplete information.

Michael S. Canter joined AIG Risk Finance as a senior vice president, head of the Insurance Securitisation Group, in 1998. At AIG his roles include originating, structuring and marketing insurance securitisation transactions. Prior to joining AIG, Dr Canter was a vice president of trading at Hedge Financial Products, Inc, a wholly-owned subsidiary of CNA Financial Corporation. At Hedge Financial, his responsibilities involved securitisation as well as the structuring of insurance products that integrate financial risks and insurance risks into one policy. He has published scholarly articles on derivatives and securitisation in *Derivatives Handbook*, the *Journal of Futures Markets*, the *Journal of Applied Corporate Finance*, the *Journal of Derivatives* and other publications. Dr Canter received a BA in economics and mathematics from Northwestern University and a PhD in finance from the Columbia University School of Business.

Nicholas I. Crew currently works for Analysis Group/Economics, a business and litigation consulting firm specialising in economics and finance. He received his PhD from the Anderson School at UCLA.

Christopher L. Culp is director of risk management services at CP Risk Management LLC in Chicago and is also Adjunct Associate Professor of Finance at The University of Chicago. At CPRM he is the practice director for consulting on matters of financial risk management control, risk-adjusted capital allocation and asset/liability management. He was previously president of Risk Management Consulting Services, Inc, prior to which he served as a senior examiner in the Supervision & Regulation Department of the Federal Reserve Bank of Chicago, as research economist at G.T. Management (Asia) Ltd and as currency options trading strategist at TradeLink LLC. He has published widely in the areas of derivatives, risk management and financial regulation and is a managing editor of *Derivatives Quarterly*. Dr Culp is also Senior Fellow in Financial Regulation with the Competitive Enterprise Institute in Washington, DC. He holds a PhD in finance from the Graduate School of Business of the University of Chicago and a BA in economics from The Johns Hopkins University.

Louis H. Ederington is Associate Dean for Research and Graduate Programs and Oklahoma Bankers Professor of Finance at the Michael F. Price College of Business, University of Oklahoma. He is a specialist in financial markets, derivative securities and banking. Professor Ederington earned a BA from Hendrix College in Arkansas and an MA and a PhD from Washington University in St Louis. From 1970 to 1983 he was employed at Georgia State University in Atlanta, where he rose to the rank of Professor of Finance, Senior Research Scholar and Director of the Institute of Banking and Financial Studies. In 1989 he joined the University of Oklahoma as Oklahoma Bankers Professor of Finance. In 1993–94 he served as Senior Economic Adviser to the Deputy Prime Minister of the Republic of Georgia, a USAID-funded project. He has also been a Fulbright lecturer in Romania.

Professor Ederington has written widely cited articles on hedging, corporate bonds, market incorporation of macroeconomic information, default risk and market microstructure in the *Journal of Finance*, *Journal of Financial and Quantitative Analysis*, *Journal of Financial Economics*, *Journal of Business*, *Journal of Money, Credit and Banking*, *Journal of Financial Research*, *Financial Review*, *Financial Management* and the *Journal of Banking and Finance*. Several of his articles have won awards. He has served as associate editor of the *Journal of Financial and Quantitative Analysis*, the *Journal of Financial Research* and *Financial Management*.

Professor Ederington has held several offices in the Southern Finance Association and the Financial Management Association, including serving on both boards of directors.

Franklin R. Edwards is a professor at the Graduate School of Business at Columbia University and holds the Arthur F. Burns Chair in Free and Competitive Enterprise. He is also Chairman of the Finance and Economics Division of the Columbia Business School and Director of the Center for the Study of Futures Markets at Columbia University. Professor Edwards holds a PhD in Economics from Harvard University and a JD from New York University Law School. His areas of expertise are financial markets and institutions, investment management, financial regulation and derivatives markets, and he currently teaches MBA courses related to institutional funds management and derivatives markets. He is the author of *The New Finance: Regulation and Financial Stability and Futures and Options*. In addition, he is the author of more than a hundred professional articles in the areas of banking, financial regulation, investment management and derivatives.

Professor Edwards' recent work focuses on mutual funds, hedge funds and commodity funds. His most recent publications include "Hedge Funds and the Collapse of Long-Term Capital Management" in the *Journal of Economic Perspectives* and "Hedge Funds and Managed Futures as Alternative Asset Classes" in the *Journal of Derivatives*.

David Fite is managing director of Westpac Financial Services (WFS). He will continue in this key role and assume responsibility for the Global Transaction and Treasury Solutions business, which currently sits within the institutional bank. He joined Westpac in 1994 as Assistant Chief Financial Officer and Group Treasurer before being appointed to head WFS in 1996. He formerly worked with Bankers Trust United States in senior strategic planning and business roles.

Kenneth A. Froot is The Industrial Bank of Japan Professor of Finance and Director of Research at Harvard University's Graduate School of Business. He teaches courses in capital markets, international finance and risk management. From 1991 to 1993 he held the Thomas Henry Carroll–Ford Foundation Visitor's Chair at Harvard while on leave from MIT's Sloan School of Management. At MIT he held the Ford International Development Chair. He has taught executive education programmes at MIT, Harvard, Princeton, Dartmouth and for many corporations and institutions in addition to his regular teaching of MBAs and PhDs.

Professor Froot received his BA from Stanford University and PhD from the University of California at Berkeley. He spent the academic year 1988–89 as an Olin Fellow at the National Bureau of Economic Research, where he is now Research Associate. His research on a wide range of topics in finance and international economics has been published in many journals and books. He is editor of the *Journal of International Financial Management and Accounting*, associate editor of the *Journal of International Economics* and has edited *The Financing of Catastrophe Risk*, *Foreign Direct Investment* and volumes 1 and 2 of *The Transition in Eastern Europe*. He is a member of the American Finance Association, the American Economics Association and the Behavioral Finance Working Group and has served as a term member of the Council on Foreign Relations.

Professor Froot is a founding partner of Emerging Markets Finance, LLC, an investment management and advisory firm. He has also been a consultant to many companies, countries and official institutions, including the IMF, the World Bank and the Board of Governors of the Federal Reserve. He has worked with a number of financial intermediaries and other financial corporations on international financial, risk management and investment management issues. He serves on the boards and policy review committees of several financial institutions. He has also acted as a Financial Adviser to the Prime Minister of the Republic of Slovenia and the Finance Minister of Poland and has served on the staff of the US President's Council of Economic Advisers and the Economic Advisory Board of the Export–Import Bank of the US.

Jimmy E. Hilliard holds a C. Herman and Mary Virginia Terry Chair of Business Administration at the University of Georgia. His research interests include investment management, international financial markets, pricing of options and futures and managing foreign exchange, commodity and interest-rate risk. Dr Hilliard has published his research in several scholarly journals, including the *Journal of Finance*, the *Journal of Financial and Quantitative Analysis* and the *Journal of Business and Management Science*. He has taught and lectured in Austria, France, Slovakia, Poland, Bulgaria and Moldova. He is past president of the Southern Finance Association and a past director of the Financial Management Association and he serves on the editorial boards of several journals. Dr Hilliard has also directed and lectured in executive education programmes on financial risk management and international markets.

Leland L. Johnson, a consultant in telecommunications economics, retired in 1993 from RAND, Santa Monica, California, where he was employed, with two interruptions for government service, from 1957. In 1978–79 he was associate administrator for Policy Analysis and Development in the National Telecommunications and Information Administration in Washington, DC. In that capacity he was director of an office that, as adviser to the White House, focused on issues of reducing government regulation in the domestic telephone and broadcasting fields, expanding competitive pressures in the international communications industry and making more effective use of the radio spectrum. During 1967–68 he was research director of the President's Task Force on Communications Policy in Washington. There the author directed the staff activities and preparation of the final report (the *Rostow Report*) delivered to the President in 1968. The report and accompanying staff papers addressed a wide range of issues in the telephone, cable and broadcasting fields, with numerous specific recommendations for national policy.

Dr Johnson's subsequent studies at RAND spanned a wide range of telecommunications areas, including the development of high-definition television, subsidies for telephone services to encourage universal coverage, development of technical compatibility standards and international trade in telecommunications equipment. In recent years he has focused on telephone company entry into video, including the effects of advances in fibre optics and other technologies. Dr Johnson has presented numerous seminars and briefings and has testified before congressional subcommittees and government administrative agencies. He is the author of the recent book *Toward Competition in Cable Television* (MIT Press and AAEI Press, 1994). He received his PhD in economics from Yale University in 1957.

Antonio S. Mello is an associate professor of finance at the University of Wisconsin–Madison. Prior to that he was in charge of research at the Central Bank of Portugal. He has also taught at MIT and INSEAD. Dr Mello holds an MA and an MBA from Columbia University and a PhD from the University of London.

Merton H. Miller is the Robert R. McCormick Distinguished Service Professor of Finance Emeritus at the Graduate School of Business, University of Chicago. Professor Miller was awarded the Nobel Prize in Economic Science in 1990 for his work in the area of corporate finance. A graduate school of business faculty member since 1961, Professor Miller has written extensively on a variety of topics in economics and finance. Along with Franco Modigliani of MIT, he developed the M&M theorems on capital structure and dividend policy that are the foundations of the theory of corporate finance.

Professor Miller received an AB from Harvard University in 1944 and a PhD from The Johns Hopkins University in 1952. He began his career as an economist in 1943 with the US Treasury, Division of Tax Research. In 1947 he joined the staff of the Board of Directors of the Federal Reserve System, where he remained until 1949. Following a term as an assistant lecturer at the London School of Economics, he joined the faculty of the Graduate School of Industrial Administration at the Carnegie Institute of Technology in 1953. He taught economics and industrial administration there until his appointment at The University of Chicago in 1961.

Professor Miller was appointed by the CME as Chairman of the Committee of Inquiry to examine events surrounding the market drop of October 19, 1987. He was appointed a distinguished fellow by the American Economic Association in 1990, a fellow by the American Academy of Arts and Sciences in 1989 and a senior fellow of the American Association of Financial Engineers in 1992. He has received honorary doctor's degrees from the University of Leuven (Belgium), the University of Karlsruhe (Germany) and many US universities.

Professor Miller is the author of numerous publications, including *Macroeconomics: A Neoclassical Introduction* (with C. Upton, 1974), *The Theory of Finance* (with E. F. Fama, 1972), *Financial Innovations and Market Volatility* and, most recently, *Merton Miller on Derivatives* (1997).

Anthony Neuberger is an associate professor of finance at the London Business School, where he is Associate Dean of the full-time Masters in Finance programme. Prior to joining LBS, he worked for the UK Government on its Central Policy Review Staff and at the Department of Energy. His research interests include the pricing and use of derivative securities and also the microstructure of securities markets. He has published extensively in these areas and consults widely for financial firms.

John E. Parsons is a vice president at the economics consulting firm Charles River Associates. He holds an AB degree from Princeton University and a PhD in economics from Northwestern University. He has taught finance at MIT, CUNY and Columbia University. Dr Parsons is an expert in the field of corporate finance and has extensive experience in designing specialised securities and financial contracts, including derivative instruments and hedging programmes.

Paul Pfleiderer has been the William F. Sharpe Professor of Financial Economics, Graduate School of Business, Stanford University, since 1996. His more recent research interests include estimation techniques of equity factor models, the pricing consequences of home bias and market segmentation and the modelling of liquidity. He has published over 25 papers in academic journals and was awarded the prize for the best paper published (with Anat Admati) in the first volume of the *Review of Financial Studies* in 1987.

He holds a BA and PhD in economics from Yale University.

Stephen Craig Pirrong is Assistant Professor of Finance at the Olin School of Business at Washington University and is a principal at the consulting firm Electrapartners.com. Prior to that he was at the University of Michigan Business School and the University of Chicago. He holds a PhD in business economics from the University of Chicago. Dr Pirrong's research focuses on the economics of commodity markets, the relation between market fundamentals and commodity price dynamics and the implications of this relation for the pricing of commodity derivatives. His recent research is concentrated on the power markets. He has created a power derivatives pricing model that links observable fundamentals (eg, temperature, loads) to power derivatives prices. He has published over 25 articles in professional publications and is the author of three books. Dr Pirrong has consulted widely, his clients including electric utilities, major commodity processors and consumers, and commodity exchanges around the world.

Stephen A. Ross is co-chairman of Roll and Ross Asset Management Corporation (Roll and Ross) and is the Franco Modigliani Professor of Finance and Economics at MIT. He was previously the Sterling Professor of Economics and Finance at Yale University and, before that, a professor of economics and finance at the Wharton School of the University of Pennsylvania. Professor Ross is the author of more than 75 articles in economics and finance and is the co-author of an introductory textbook on finance. Although he has worked on a variety of topics in economics and finance, he is probably best known for having invented the arbitrage pricing theory (APT) and the theory of agency and as the co-discoverer of risk-neutral pricing and the binomial model for pricing derivatives. Models developed by him and co-workers, including term structure models and option pricing models, are now standards for pricing in major securities trading firms. He has been the recipient of numerous prizes and awards, including the Graham and Dodd Award for financial writing, the Pomerance Prize for excellence in the area of options research, the University of Chicago's Leo Melamed Prize for the best research by a business school professor and the 1996 IAFE Financial Engineer of the Year Award. A fellow of the Econometric Society and a member of the American Academy of Arts and Sciences, he currently serves as an associate editor of several economics and finance journals and in 1988 was president of the American Finance Association. Roll and Ross is one of the leading quantitative financial management firms in the world and is the leading firm applying the APT invented by Ross and developed in collaboration with the other principal of the firm, Professor Richard Roll of UCLA. Its clients include major international corporations, government groups and mutual funds.

He received a BS in physics from CalTech and PhD in economics from Harvard.

David S. Scharfstein is the Dai-Ichi Kangyo Bank Professor of Finance and Management at MIT's Sloan School of Management. Prior to joining the Sloan faculty in 1987, he was an Assistant Professor of Finance at Harvard Business School. He received an AB in public and international affairs from Princeton University in 1982 and a PhD in economics from MIT in 1986.

Professor Scharfstein is the author of numerous articles on topics in corporate finance and industrial organisation, including work on financial distress, risk management, financial intermediation, corporate resource allocation and the economics of health care. In recognition of this work he has been awarded an Olin Fellowship by the National Bureau of Economic Research, a Batterymarch Research Fellowship and a Sloan Foundation Research Fellowship. Professor Scharfstein serves on the editorial boards of the *Journal of Finance* and *Economics Letters* and was editor of the *RAND Journal of Economics* and associate editor of the *Review of Financial Studies*. He is also a research associate of the National Bureau of Economic Research.

Eduardo S. Schwartz is the California Professor of Real Estate and Professor of Finance, Anderson Graduate School of Management at the University of California, Los Angeles. He holds an engineering degree from the University of Chile and a Masters and PhD in finance from the University of British Columbia. He has been on the faculty at the University of British Columbia and visiting professor at the London Business School and the University of California at Berkeley. His wide-ranging research has focused on different dimensions in asset and securities pricing. Topics in recent years have ranged from interest rate volatility and asset allocation issues to evaluating natural resource investments. His collected works include more than 80 articles in finance and economic journals, two monographs and many monograph chapters, conference proceedings and special reports. He is the winner of a number of awards for both teaching excellence and the quality of his published work. He is associate editor for at least a dozen journals, including the *Journal of Finance* and the *Journal of Financial and Quantitative Analysis*. He is past president of the Western Finance Association and the American Finance Association. He has also been a consultant to governmental agencies, banks, investment banks and industrial corporations.

Clifford W. Smith received his PhD from the University of North Carolina–Chapel Hill. He is the Louise and Henry Epstein Professor of Business Administration at the William E. Simon Graduate School of Business Administration at the University of Rochester, where he has taught since 1974. His research interests in the fields of corporate financial policy, financial institutions and derivative securities have resulted in 14 books and over 80 articles in leading finance and economics journals.

Students on the Executive Development Program gave Professor Smith their Superior Teaching Award 15 times and those on the MBA programme have voted him their Superior Teaching Award 10 times. He gained the first Special Award for a Perfect Teaching Rating by the School and was made a University Mentor in recognition of his scholarship and teaching.

He has held visiting professor positions at the Graduate School of Business, The University of Chicago; School of Law, George Mason University; City University Business School, London; and Faculdade de Economica, Universidade do Porto, Portugal. In addition, he has taught courses on "Corporate Governance and Financial Markets" and "Insurance and Risk" to Federal judges.

Professor Smith has served as president of the Financial Management Association National Honor Society, vice president of the International Economics and Finance Society, president of the Risk Theory Society and as a member of the Board of Advisors of the International Association of Financial Engineers. He is also an advisory editor of the *Journal of Financial Economics*, an associate editor of the *Journal of Financial Engineering, Financial Management*, *Financial Practice and Education* and *Review of International Economics* and is a member of the advisory board of the *Journal of Applied Corporate Finance*, *The Financier*, *Contemporary Finance Digest* and *The Arbitrageur*.

Charles W. Smithson is a managing director of CIBC World Markets, where he is responsible for the CIBC School of Financial Products. His career has spanned the gamut, with positions in academia and government as well as in the private sector. He is the author of numerous articles in professional and academic journals.
Dr Smithson is best known as the originator of the "building block approach" to financial products. He is the author of five books, including *Managing Financial Risk*, the third edition of which was published in 1998. He served as a member of the Working Group for the Global Derivatives Project sponsored by the Group of Thirty. He currently serves on the

boards of directors of the International Swaps and Derivatives Association and the International Association of Financial Engineers, as well as the US Commodity Futures Trading Commission's Financial Products Advisory Committee and the Financial Accounting Standards Board's Financial Instruments Task Force.
Dr Smithson received his PhD in economics from Tulane University in 1976.

Jeremy C. Stein is the J. C. Penney Professor of Management at MIT's Sloan School of Management, where he teaches finance in the MBA, PhD and executive education programmes. Prior to joining the Sloan faculty in 1990, he was an assistant professor of finance at the Harvard Business School. He received his AB in economics from Princeton University and PhD in economics from MIT. Professor Stein spent the 1989–90 academic year as a senior staff economist on the President's Council of Economic Advisers in Washington, DC, where he specialised in issues relating to financial markets and banking. In 1987 he served as a staff member of the Presidential Task Force on Market Mechanisms (aka the Brady Commission). In 1986–87 he worked at the investment banking firm Goldman Sachs and Co. He has done consulting or executive education work for many major organisations, including Andersen Worldwide, Citicorp, IBM, Merck, Phillips Petroleum, ThermoElectron and the World Bank. Professor Stein is the author of a number of articles on finance and macroeconomics, covering such topics as stock market trading, options pricing, corporate investment and financing decisions, takeovers and highly leveraged transactions, risk management, financial intermediation and monetary policy. In recognition of this work he was granted a Batterymarch Research Fellowship for the academic year 1991–92. He is also a four-time recipient of the Sloan School's Excellence in Teaching prize, and in 1998 was elected winner of Sloan's Alumni Award for Excellence in Management Education ("Teacher of the Year").

Professor Stein serves or has served on the editorial boards of several leading economics and finance journals, including the *American Economic Review*, the *Quarterly Journal of Economics* and the *Journal of Finance*. He is also a Research Associate at the National Bureau of Economic Research.

René M. Stulz is the Everett D. Reese Chair of Banking and Monetary Economics and Director of the Dice Center for Research in Financial Economics at Ohio State University. He previously taught at the University of Rochester and held visiting appointments at MIT and the University of Chicago. He was also a Marvin Bower Fellow at the Harvard Business School.

Dr Stulz is currently the editor of the *Journal of Finance* and was formerly an editor of the *Journal of Financial Economics*. He is also associate editor of several other academic and practitioner journals. Further, he is a member of the asset pricing and corporate finance programmes of the National Bureau of Economic Research.

He has published more than 50 papers in finance and economics journals, including the *Journal of Political Economy*, the *Journal of Financial Economics*, the *Journal of Finance* and the *Review of Financial Studies*. His research addresses issues in international finance, corporate finance and investments. He is currently working on a textbook entitled "Financial Engineering, Risk Management, and Derivatives".

He received his PhD from MIT and holds an honorary doctorate from the University of Neufchatel in Switzerland.

Robert E. Whaley is the T. Austin Finch Foundation Professor of Business Administration at the Fuqua School of Business, Duke University, and is Director of the Futures and Options Research Center (FORCE). He received his bachelor of commerce degree from the University of Alberta and his master of business administration and doctorate degree from the University of Toronto. His current research interests are in the areas of the predictability of market volatility, market microstructure, valuation of exotic options, stock splits, executive stock option valuation and volatility futures and option contracts. Much of his past work focused on investigations of the effects of programme trading on stock prices, the expiration day effects of index futures and options, and the valuation of option and futures option contracts and the efficiency of the markets in which they trade.
Dr Whaley has recently published three books, and his work has been printed in the top academic and practitioner journals and is frequently presented at major conferences and seminars. He holds a number of editorial positions, including co-editor of *The Review of Futures Markets* and associate editor of the *Journal of Financial Economics*, *Journal of Finance*, *Journal of Futures Markets*, *Journal of Derivatives*, and *Advances in Futures and Options Research*. He also serves as a referee for more than 40 journals and granting agencies. In addition, he is a member of the Board of Directors of the Western Finance Association and the American Finance Association. Dr Whaley is an established expert in derivative contract valuation and market operation. He has been a consultant for many major investment houses, security (futures, option and stock) exchanges, governmental agencies and accounting and law firms.

Born in 1895, **Holbrook Working** received his AB from the University of Denver in 1915, an MA from Cornell in 1919 and a PhD from the University of Wisconsin in 1920. He was an instructor in economics at Cornell in 1916, assistant and associate professor of agricultural economics at the University of Minnesota from 1920 to 1925, visiting professor at the University of Chicago in the summer of 1928, and acting professor at the University of Michigan in 1934–35. From 1925 to 1952 Professor Working taught prices and statistics at Stanford and was an economist at the Food Research Institute. He served as associate director of the Institute from 1952 to 1960, when he became emeritus. His non-academic positions included: consultant to the Commodity Exchange Administration, 1939; statistical consultant to the Fourth Air Force, 1942–43; chief statistical consultant, Office of Production Research and Development, War Production Board, 1943; chief of the office's Production Economy Branch, 1945; and director of its Quality Control Program at Carnegie Institute of Technology, 1945. Dr Working was a former director of the Social Science Research Council, a member of the American Economic Association and a fellow of the American Agricultural Economics Association, the American Statistical Association and the American Association for the Advancement of Science. He was also a founding member of the Econometric Society.

Dr Working's interest in futures markets began with his appointment as an economist at the Food Research Institute. The Institute, founded in 1921, had been directed to study the world wheat economy with particular emphasis on its relationship to US agriculture. *Wheat Studies*, a 20-volume publication begun in 1924, was the published record of those investigations. Dr Working's contributions were many and varied, but most dealt with some aspect of futures markets and the role they performed in the wheat economy. Contained in these early studies are the empirical foundations for his later writings on the theory of intertemporal prices relationships on futures markets. From his empirical analyses of futures market data, Dr Working developed the theory of price storage to explain observed relationships between cash and futures prices. This theory has become fundamental to understanding the markets and the role they perform in commodity marketing.
Holbrook Working died in 1985.

Prologue: A Timely Debate That is Proving Timeless

Charles W. Smithson

CIBC Wood Gundy School of Financial Products

In 1993, Metallgesellschaft AG (MG AG) managed to lose in excess of a billion dollars, and this loss was somehow related to derivatives transactions. While a billion dollars is a lot of money, there have been a lot of derivatives-related losses since then - and some of the more recent losses have been larger than MG AG's. Why should we care about an event that occurred more than five years ago?

The first reason is that there are important lessons to be learned from the MG AG debacle. Indeed, were it not so hard for a non-German-speaker to pronounce the phrase "Metallgesellschaft risk", it might become a shorthand way of referring to a particular type of risk - in the same way that "Herstatt risk"[1] is used to refer to settlement risk and "Barings risk" is used to refer to risks associated with inadequate internal controls on trading (or risk-taking) activities. After all, the billion dollars that MG AG lost was lost *while MG AG was supposedly hedging*. If such an outcome is possible, other firms will want to guard against making the errors that MG AG made.

A second reason for revisiting the MG AG debate is that it was a great spectacle, and the modern-day gladiators involved deserve our praise for being willing to take the field. I have often wondered about the necessity these days of "tenure" and all the rest in the name of academic freedom. The heat that was at times felt by the gladiators in this spectacle showed me the importance of having the protagonists not bound financially to one or other side of the debate. Indeed, the protection provided by academe carries with it the responsibility for academics to express their convictions regardless of whether or not the views are universally popular. The protagonists in this debate did precisely that.[2]

A third reason for revisiting the debate is that it benefited the academic community (and will eventually benefit the market) in the sense that it reinvigorated the discussion about corporate hedging.

The history of the case

In 1993, the story of MG AG (at the time, Germany's fourteenth-largest corporation) seemed to be black-and-white. Sylvia Nasar summarised the conventional wisdom in *The New York Times*:[3]

> ... when Deutsche Bank whisked Metallgesellschaft ... from the brink of ruin, most observers accepted the bank's version of events: a bunch of financial cowboys at MG AG's American subsidiary, MG Refining and Marketing, were making hugely risky bets with oil futures. When an unexpected plunge in oil prices threatened staggering losses, Deutsche Bank, Metallgesellschaft's biggest shareholder and creditor and the power behind the company's supervisory board, did what it had to: it fired the old management, brought in a SWAT team to liquidate the bets, installed a new management and lent the company money to cover the losses.

However, as is so often the case, conventional wisdom left out a few things.

THE EVENTS OF 1992–93[4]

In 1992, MG Refining & Marketing (MGRM) began to sell five- and ten-year contracts to supply buyers with gasoline, heating oil, jet fuel and diesel fuel at fixed prices. Buyers also had the option to terminate the contract at a profit if the spot price rose above the fixed price.

MGRM decided to hedge the fixed-price contracts and the "buy-out option" with a "stack-and-roll" strategy: it bought near-month futures and rolled them into the next contract at the end of each month. There were two reasons for employing this strategy:

1. The strategy provided a hedge for the "buy-out option" that MGRM had sold to its customers. If the spot price rose dramatically, MGRM would be faced with customers cashing in immediately; and so MGRM hedged everything in the near-month and rolled over all of its positions at the expiry date.
2. If the futures market remained in "backwardation" (ie, if the price for future delivery were lower than that for immediate delivery), MGRM stood to make a profit on the rollover.

But this strategy involved a risk: if futures prices fell unexpectedly, MGRM would experience cash drains as they made variation margin payments.

In September 1993 the situation in the oil market changed dramatically so that the price for future delivery was higher than that for immediate delivery – a situation that is referred to as "contango". The market remained in contango for the remainder of the year, meaning that MGRM's positions were continuously losing value. The New York Mercantile Exchange (Nymex) called for additional margin – apparently more than the parent MG AG could provide without going to its bankers. Once the over-the-counter market got wind of MGRM's difficulties, counterparties would not roll over their contracts without collateral – preferably a letter of credit from one of MG AG's banks.

On December 3, 1993, Deutsche Bank and Dresdner Bank agreed to put in DM1.5 billion of liquidity. But, nine days later, KPMG came up with an estimate of DM800 million for the losses incurred by MG Corp (MG AG's oil-trading unit in New York) from oil derivatives for the year ended September 30, 1993. Ronaldo Schmitz, chairman of MG AG's supervisory board and a board member of Deutsche Bank, called oil trader Nancy Kropp out of retirement to sort out the mess. On December 16 Siegfried Hodapp, chief executive of MG Corp, resigned and the next day MG AG's CEO, Heinz Schimmelbusch, was fired. Turnaround specialist Kajo Neukirchen was named to be MG AG's new chief executive.

By January 5, 1994, the new CEO presented a rescue concept to the 120 or so creditor banks – which included all but one of the major German banks and almost every big international bank. Neukirchen put losses for the year ended September 30, 1993, at DM1.87 billion and potential further losses over the following two to three years at DM1 billion. He asked the banks to convert DM1.3 billion of their outstanding claims into junior convertible stock and to put in new equity of DM1.4 billion and fresh credits of DM700 million. Deutsche and Dresdner agreed to put in an extra DM100 million each to make the new credit up to DM700 million; they also agreed to put an extra DM50 million each into the DM1.3 billion of junior convertible stock.

EARLY 1994: TWO ACADEMICS SET OFF A FIRESTORM

Christopher Culp and Merton Miller found the press accounts of MGRM's "excessively risky" hedging strategy troublesome. They began work on a paper that was subsequently published in *Derivatives Quarterly*.[5] Culp and Miller argued that "stacking and rolling over short-term futures *can* provide an effective hedge against price risk". They went on to observe that "the supervisory board and creditors of [MG AG's] parent may not have fully understood the nature and risks of the hedging strategy it chose". The risks that Culp and Miller were alluding to were the "substantial cashflow requirements" of a stack-and-roll hedge. They concluded that the supervisory board's "lack of understanding, along with MGRM's failure to lock in the cash funding requirements of the hedge, led to a premature liquidation of the hedge".

The Culp and Miller paper was not the only academic paper assigning blame for MG AG's problems to parties other than the company's CEO and MGRM and implicitly defending the legitimacy of MGRM's marketing and hedging strategies. Franklin Edwards (Columbia University) expounded a similar view: "MGRM's hedging strategy went wrong because of misleading hedge accounting and disclosure principles, funding rigidities, and lack of understanding at the level of the (MG) supervisory board (or board of directors)." (Edwards, 1994) It was, however, the Culp and Miller paper that became the lightning rod for the MG AG hedging debate.

According to Culp and Miller, one of MG AG's problems was the cashflow requirements of the strategy: when oil prices began to decline significantly, MGRM faced massive cash requirements to keep its Nymex positions open – requirements *not* offset by cash inflows on its fixed-price delivery contracts. They suggested that MG AG's other problem was the *operational risk* that arises from failure in the oversight and internal control process:

> MGRM's problem was not with its derivatives group, but with its supervisory board and supporting banks, who may not have understood the hedging strategy and forced the liquidation of MGRM's hedge positions. Unwinding MGRM's futures positions, though later widely applauded in the press, proved unfortunate on several counts. By the time MGRM began to unwind its positions in mid-December [1993], the price of oil had fallen to roughly $14 per barrel. The premature liquidation of MGRM's futures hedge thus turned "paper losses" into realized losses. It also left MGRM unprotected against market risk on its flow delivery contracts. After MGRM liquidated its futures positions, the price of oil rebounded, as did the prices of No. 2 heating oil and unleaded gasoline, thus "whipsawing" MGRM.

As the debate heated up, *Risk* reported on the opinions of market participants and observers (Falloon, 1994). Several of the traders to whom *Risk* spoke felt that Culp and Miller had assumed zero "basis risk" between the short-term futures and the long-term supply contracts.[6] The traders to whom *Risk* spoke also observed that price movements are generally more pronounced in short-term contracts than in the longer-term contracts; hence, the potential movement in prices in the five-to-ten-year sector was quite small relative to the huge move being experienced in the nearby futures hedge. Traders agreed that the Miller–Culp effect as a whipsaw does indeed exist and that some MGRM paper losses may well have been recouped if management had waited for the market to recover. However, traders also noted that, until the front end of the price curve recovered, there would have been monthly rollover losses that could have reached several hundred millions of dollars.

Culp and Miller were quick to respond to their critics. They argued that rollover costs "do not vitiate a stack strategy". Instead, those rollover costs are equivalent to the "storage and interest costs" that would exist in a pure buy-and-hold physical hedge. When the market is in backwardation the interest and storage costs are being offset by the convenience yield. However, Culp and Miller noted that, if fixed prices are being set in the future, the price should be based on the *expected* rollover cost. Finally, they noted: "Both theory and empirical evidence suggest that the long-run … average rollover costs will be negative, which is a further reason for not panicking on the few occasions (like the second half of 1993) when the basis happens to turn positive." (Culp and Miller, 1994.)

AUTUMN 1994: THE MARKET AND MG AG'S MANAGEMENT REACT

The Culp–Miller paper had an electric effect. When it surfaced in the autumn of 1994, investors hammered MG AG stock (Nasar, 1994). MG AG's new management, along with Ronaldo Schmitz, chairman of MG AG's supervisory board, fired back. At a news conference in Frankfurt in September 1994, senior executives of MG AG argued that "where Miller and Culp go wrong is moving from theory to reality". Their view was that MG AG would have faced a US$50 billion loss if it hadn't liquidated the hedges (Nasar, 1994).

On September 26 and 27, 1994, MG AG's stock nose-dived, falling more than 20% to DM118. Schmitz talked to reporters to rebut the professors personally. "The quick unwinding of the futures positions was the correct professional move", he told reporters (Nasar, 1994).

On October 12 Hutchinson, an MG AG board member and the head of its metals trading company in London, delivered a detailed rebuttal.[7] The company asserted that Culp and Miller's arguments were based on incomplete data[8] and that they had ignored significant costs and risks – for instance, had MG AG not unwound its futures contracts, it might have spent US$20–40 million per month to roll over the futures positions. MG AG also argued that Culp and Miller ignored the possibility that an unforeseen change in the composition of the gasoline futures contract, scheduled to take effect in 1995, could have cost another several hundred million dollars. More significantly, MG AG disputed the hedge nature of the structure, raising two issues: first, there existed credit risk because the long-term contracts with consumers might not have been watertight; and, second, MGRM had contracts to deliver a particular slate of refined products and had hedged this with futures based on related commodities – in effect gambling that the various commodities' relative prices would remain stable for up to 10 years. MG officials also took sharp issue with the economists' assertion that the company had left itself vulnerable to a jump in energy prices by liquidating its hedge positions while maintaining the fuel-delivery contracts. In fact, said Hutchinson, MG AG "eliminated a large volume of its customer contracts" and was safely managing the rest.

NOVEMBER 1994: YET ANOTHER SHOE DROPS

On November 23, 1994, MG AG announced that huge losses had virtually wiped out its capital, forcing it to seek additional funds from its shareholders. CEO Neukirchen disclosed that fiscal year 1994's net loss was DM2.7 billion (US$1.75 billion), citing MG Corp as having a loss of US$2.86 billion. Neukirchen stated that the loss had eaten up most of the company's capital. An equity write-down, or "capital cut", is a standard German accounting method to compensate for losses. In this case, it would prove to be the equivalent of a two-for-one reverse stock split but without the doubling of the share price that would normally follow. Some analysts were skeptical that the company could be salvaged: "If one takes a cynical view, this is essentially an orderly liquidation of the company", said Robert Willis, an analyst at Schroder Securities in London.[9]

EARLY 1995: AN EXTERNAL AUDIT IS RELEASED AND MORE CASH IS REQUESTED

In January 1995 the results of a special audit of MGRM were released. The audit had been commissioned by the shareholders of the parent company MG AG and undertaken by auditors C&L Treuarbeit Deutsche Revision and Wollert-Elmendorff Industrie Treuhand. The auditors' report absolved MG AG's supervisory board of responsibility for the oil-trading losses and declared that Heinz Schimmelbusch, MG AG's former CEO, and Meinhard Forster, previously chief financial officer, had "gravely neglected their duties". The report accused Schimmelbusch and Forster of having had "inadequate coordination and control" over their duties and accused Schimmelbusch of deliberately misleading the board as to the risks involved in oil-futures trading.

Writing in the April 1995 issue of ***Risk***, Culp and Miller noted that the auditors' estimate of MGRM's total losses from June 1, 1992, to December 31, 1993, was US$1.277 billion gross (US$1.06 billion net). In contrast, the authors' calculation of the net 1993 loss for MGRM as the initial capital asset value of the programme less unexpected rollover costs and the change in conditional expected rollover costs was US$170 million – a fifth of the auditors' estimate.

On February 2, 1995, MG AG's supervisory board announced that MG Corp was deeper in the red than previously estimated. The unit's pre-tax loss widened to DM3.32 billion (US$2.19 billion) in the year ended September 30, 1994, from the estimate of DM2.86 billion announced in November 1994.[10] MG AG's board asked shareholders and creditors for concessions and fresh cash – for the second time in just over a year. The measures called for creditor banks to waive their conversion rights for half of the convertible profit-sharing certificates created in the 1994 bail-out. The plan also included a capital write-down that wiped out half of the existing MG AG stock.

The ongoing academic debate

Culp and Miller published an expanded argument about the MG AG situation in the Winter 1995 issue of the *Journal of Applied Corporate Finance* (a paper that is included in the present collection). They argued in that article (Culp and Miller, 1995b) that the transactions undertaken by MGRM were to hedge its business risk rather than to speculate:

> MGRM's derivatives were part and parcel of its marketing program, under which it offered long-term customers firm price guarantees for up to ten years on gasoline, heating oil and diesel fuel purchased from MGRM. The firm hedged its resulting exposure to spot price increases to a considerable extent with futures contracts. Because futures contracts must be marked to market daily, cash drains must be incurred to meet variation margin payments when futures prices fall. After several consecutive months of falling prices in the autumn of 1993, MGRM's German parent reacted to the substantial margin calls by liquidating the hedge.

Culp and Miller continued to argue that the real problem began when MG decided to liquidate its futures contracts:

> Whatever the reason, the decision to liquidate the futures leg proved unfortunate on several counts, turning "paper losses" into realized losses, sending a distress signal to MGRM's over-the-counter (OTC) derivatives counterparties, and leaving MGRM exposed to rising prices on its remaining fixed-price contracts.

And they laid the blame on MG AG's senior management:

> [A] synthetic storage program like MGRM's ... is neither inherently unprofitable nor fatally flawed, provided top management understands the program and the long-term funding commitments necessary to make it work.
>
> ... the supervisory board may not have understood that MGRM was hedging and not speculating. ... the team the supervisory board called in to liquidate the futures positions had also been used to resolve the Klockner speculative episode for Deutsche Bank. The supervisory board may have interpreted MGRM's appeals for more cash as "doubling-up" or, at least, as the all-too-typical symptom of an imminent business failure. Or perhaps the supervisory board, in light of the power struggles then going on within MG AG, may have deliberately chosen not to understand MGRM's program.
>
> In any case, unwinding MGRM's futures positions, though widely applauded in some parts of the press then and now, proved unfortunate on several counts. By the time MGRM began to unwind its positions in mid-December [1993], the price of oil had fallen to its low of roughly $14 per barrel. The precipitous liquidation of MGRM's futures hedge thus turned "paper losses" on that leg into realized losses and left MGRM exposed to rising spot prices on its still-outstanding flow delivery contracts. ... when the new management awakened to its naked price exposure following the liquidation, it began negotiating unwinds of its flow contracts without demanding any compensation for its positive expected future cashflows.
>
> If MGRM had not unwound its futures, the positive daily pays received when prices recovered in 1994 would have given it a substantial positive cash inflow. MGRM's forced liquidation, moreover, sent a signal to MGRM's OTC derivatives counterparties that its credit standing might be in jeopardy, thereby increasing calls for collateral to keep its OTC positions open.[11]

Antonio Mello and John Parsons entered the debate in the May 1995 issue of *Risk* and in the Spring 1995 issue of the *Journal of Applied Corporate Finance*. (The latter paper is included as chapter 12 of this volume.) In *Risk*, Mello and Parsons (1995a) argued that the "rolling stack" hedge strategy was flawed:

> The critical problem with this strategy was the mismatch in the maturity structure of MG's delivery obligations and its futures portfolio. This had two consequences.
>
> First, the rolling stack can dangerously increase the variability of a company's cash-flow at the start of the programme, even if it succeeds in locking in the programme's total value. ... a small movement in oil prices within a month produces enormous losses or gains on the entire stack, which are realised immediately. In contrast, counter-balancing losses or gains on the delivery contracts are largely unrealised until scheduled deliveries are made, months or years later. The result for MG was a much greater variability of monthly cashflows initially than if it had been completely unhedged. ... As the MG case demonstrates, the short-run consequences of a cashflow deficit this large can be disastrous, even if delivery contracts generate a compensating but unrealised gain of an equal amount.
>
> Second, since long- and short-term oil prices are only imperfectly correlated, the rolling stack hedge does not guarantee that the company has locked in the value of the delivery contracts.

Thus, "basis risk" has been introduced. More importantly, Mello and Parsons also argued that the transactions undertaken by MG Corp were indeed intended as a speculation on the shape of the oil-price term structure (opposite to the Culp–Miller argument):

> Why did MG's New York subsidiary run a hedge with a mismatched maturity structure? Certainly the management was aware that the long- and short-term prices of oil do not always move in step and therefore that it would be exposed to basis risk.
>
> The answers to these questions reveal the real source of MG's blunder. Not only did the management appreciate the difference between long- and short-term oil prices but the motivation for its entire strategy was to profit from this difference, including signing up customers for the long-term delivery contracts.
>
> ... it was a set of profitable delivery contracts that motivated MG to buy one-month futures as a hedge ... it was the profitability of holding one-month futures contracts that made oil delivery over the long term appear to be a sensible business. ... this is a ques-

tion about whether or not the speculation is a good speculation and not about whether or not the rolling stack is a good hedge. ...

If the company's business exposes it to short-term oil price movements, then the right hedge is a set of securities tied to movements in the short-term oil price, whether futures or swaps. If the company's business exposes it to long-term oil price movements, then the right hedge is a set of securities tied to movements in the long-term oil price. If the company's business exposes it to long-term oil price movements and it hedges with securities tied to short-term oil prices, then it has bought a combination of a hedge and a bet on the yield curve of oil. ...

By management's own calculations, if the delivery contracts had been hedged with long-term instruments, the entire programme would have been unprofitable. In retrospect this is clear since it is impossible to think of the New York subsidiary as a company with competitive advantage in the costs and techniques of oil supply and delivery. The physical assets at its disposal were minimal and generally inefficient. The subsidiary's only claim to competitive advantage was in its financial trading skills.

The front-to-back hedging strategy developed at MG's New York office was the oil market equivalent of riding the yield curve. When the curve shifted unfavorably, the company lost its shirt. Whether it was a good bet when it started can be debated indefinitely. But what is clear is that it was not a hedge in the proper sense.

Miller and Culp (1995c) issued a direct reply to Mello and Parsons in the next issue of the *Journal of Applied Corporate Finance* (a paper also included in this collection). They disagreed with the premise that the only real "hedge" is one that eliminates basis risk, arguing that hedging is a much richer concept. Referring to the much earlier work of Holbrook Working, Miller and Culp argued that many firms seek out basis risk, in effect seeking profit from superior information about the relationship of prices to each other rather than the level of prices:

> That carrying-charge hedging may be undertaken by value-maximizing firms principally if not wholly to exploit perceived informational advantage does *not* [emphasis theirs] mean that carrying-charge hedging is "speculation". And Working argues that risks are, in fact, reduced by carrying-charge hedging even though its primary motivation need not be risk reduction.

The authors went on in the same article to cite excerpts from MG AG's 1991/92 Annual Report, aiming to show that supervisory board members understood MGRM's hedging strategy as one of seeking attractive "arbitrage" opportunities in the basis between a commodity's spot price, its own forward curve or the forward curve of other commodities or markets:

> MGRM's strategy of carrying-charge hedging, rather that standard finance risk-avoidance hedging, makes perfect sense under the assumption that basis risk exposed MGRM to no real threat of bankruptcy, while naked spot price exposure might well have. ...
>
> As a standalone firm MGRM and its outside creditors might well have been concerned with the costs of bankruptcy or depleted cash for investment expenditures, especially after the large margin calls of late 1993. But MGRM was *not* [emphasis theirs] a standalone firm. Deutsche Bank was not only the principal inside creditor and principal shareholder of MG AG, but thanks to cross-holdings, it was also effectively the *controlling* [emphasis theirs] shareholder.
>
> With Deutsche Bank thus standing *in loco parentis*, as it were, what sense does it make to assume that MGRM could be brought to ruin by the cash margin calls on the futures leg of a combined program *hedged* against spot price risk?

As for the assertion that the MGRM's entire programme would have been unprofitable had it been hedged by a strip of futures rather than a stack, Miller and Culp responded:

> A pure strip, even if it had been available (which it was not), would not only have been inconsistent with MGRM's business objectives, but would have made it unnecessary for customers to turn to MGRM for fixed-price forward-delivery contracts in the first place. After all, the customers could have strip-hedged their purchase requirements directly.

The four parts to this book

I am grateful to Chris Culp and Merton Miller for collecting some of the classic papers dealing with "The Foundations of Hedging in Futures Markets" (Part I of the book), the "Rationales for Corporate Hedging" (Part II) and "The Mathematics of Hedging Long-Dated Obligations with Short-Dated Futures" (Part IV). However, as they point out in their introduction, the real focus of this collection of articles is on two of the several different debates that were going on in 1994 and 1995 about the "MG fiasco".

The first debate surveyed in this volume is "Why was MGRM hedging and how would those motives have affected the implementation of its hedging programme?" Critics of MGRM argued that the company's marketing programme was "unhedgeable" because of the maturity mismatch between the short-dated futures and the long-dated customer contracts. The papers collected in Part III of the book explore that issue. The second debate surveyed in this volume is "How best to hedge long-dated commodity swaps with short-dated futures?" The papers collected in Part IV consider this topic.

Final thoughts

At the outset of this prologue I suggested that were it not so hard for a non-German-speaker to pronounce "Metallgesellschaft risk" it might become a shorthand phrase for a type of risk. In this case, the risk is a form of liquidity risk.

For me, the primary lesson of the MG AG experience is that, for some hedging strategies using derivatives, it is essential to consider in advance how much it might cost to finance the hedge. MGRM's strategy entailed large cash outflows to finance the hedge; and, in advance, senior management could have - and should have - considered how bad the outflow could become and whether they would be willing to stay with the strategy.

In this context I would argue that one of the elements that led to the widely publicised losses experienced by Long Term Capital Management (LTCM) in 1998 was "Metallgesellschaft risk". Even if we accept the contention that LTCM's investment strategies were true "convergence plays", the fact remains that LTCM would have needed enough capital to finance the position until the convergence occurred. LTCM thought that they had enough capital and lines of credit, but it turned out that they did not. And I don't think that LTCM will be the last to experience "Metallgesellschaft risk".

1 *This refers to the 1974 failure of Bankhaus Herstatt.*

2 *I am convinced that neither Culp nor Miller was paid by either side of the debate. And, although the* Wall Street Journal *reported that Professor Parsons was hired by Charles River Associates as a consultant to MG AG, that hiring was subsequent to writing the articles that were part of this debate.*

3 *Nasar (1994).*

4 *Adapted from Shirreff (1994).*

5 *Culp and Miller (1994a).*

6 *Culp and Miller refer to this as "covariance risk". They argue that they did not assume zero basis risk.*

7 *"MG AG - Answering Back",* The Economist, *October 15, 1994.*

8 *But MG did not tell the full story, citing a legal dispute with Arthur Benson, former boss of MGRM, which was scheduled to begin on October 14, 1994.*

9 *"German Metals Giant Plans to Reduce its Share Value",* The New York Times, *November 24, 1994.*

10 *The larger-than-expected loss at MG Corp grew because more reserves were set aside and because of foreign-exchange movements. For the year ended September 30, 1993, MG Corp had a loss of DM770 million.*

11 *Writing in* Risk *in April 1995, Culp and Miller (1995a) used the auditors' report to quantify the loss that MG suffered by closing out its programme inappropriately: "That MG AG in effect blundered into this worst case for a substantial fraction of its programme is now a matter of record in the auditors' report. The supervisory board ordered a substantial unwinding of the futures positions, and subsequently began cancelling many of its forward contracts with no payment required from customers. How much money MGRM threw away in the process cannot be estimated with exactitude. The US$788 million it might have received from the sale of its programme was clearly forgone."*

Culp, C. L., and M. H. Miller, 1994a, "Hedging a Flow of Commodity Deliveries with Futures: Lessons from MG AG", *Derivatives Quarterly* Fall, pp. 7-15.

Culp, C. L., and M. H. Miller, 1994b,"Slaughter Those Sacred Cows", *Risk* November.

Culp, C. L., and M. H. Miller, 1995a, "Auditing the Auditors" *Risk* April, pp. 35-9; reprinted as Chapter 10 of the present volume.

Culp, C. L., and M. H. Miller, 1995b, "Metallgesellschaft and the Economics of Synthetic Storage", *Journal of Applied Corporate Finance* 7(4), pp. 62-76; reprinted as Chapter 9 of the present volume.

Culp, C. L., and M. H. Miller, 1995c, "Hedging in the Theory of Corporate Finance: A Reply to Our Critics", *Journal of Applied Corporate Finance* 8(1); reprinted as Chapter 14 of the present volume.

Edwards, F., 1994, "Systematic Risk in OTC Derivative Markets: Much Ado About Not Too Much", Working paper, Columbia University.

Falloon, W., 1994, "MG's Trial by Essay", *Risk* October.

Mello, A. S., and J. E. Parsons,1995a, "Rolling the Dice", *Risk* May, pp. 49-50.

Mello, A. S., and J. E. Parsons, 1995b, "Maturity Structure of a Hedge Matters: Lessons from the Metallgesellschaft Debacle", *Journal of Applied Corporate Finance* 8(1); reprinted as Chapter 12 of the present volume.

Nasar, S., 1994, "The Oil-Futures Bloodbath: Is the Bank the Culprit?", *The New York Times* October 16.

Shirreff, D., 1994, "In the Line of Fire", *Euromoney* March.

Introduction: *Why* a Firm Hedges Affects *How* a Firm Hedges

Christopher L. Culp and Merton H. Miller
The University of Chicago

Metallgesellschaft AG (MG AG) is a century-old, industrial conglomerate owned largely by institutional investors, including Deutsche Bank, Dresdner Bank, Daimler-Benz and the Kuwait Investment Authority. At the end of 1992, MG AG had 251 subsidiaries, with activities ranging over trade, engineering and financial services. Its subsidiary responsible for petroleum marketing in the United States was MG Refining and Marketing, Inc (MGRM).

In December 1991 MGRM recruited, from Louis Dreyfus Energy Corp., Arthur Benson and his management team. The team's key marketing strategy was to offer firm price guarantees to retail customers (largely) for a period of 5–10 years on gasoline, heating oil and diesel fuel purchased from MGRM. By September 1993, MGRM had sold forward the equivalent of over 160 million barrels of petroleum products in these contracts. The company hedged its resulting exposure to spot oil price increases with futures contracts and futures-equivalent commodity swaps. The bulk of MGRM's futures positions were on the New York Mercantile Exchange, in the most liquid contracts of between one and three months to maturity.

MGRM's hedging strategy was called a "one-for-one stack-and-roll hedge". This meant that, at any given time, an amount equivalent to the total remaining delivery obligation on the customer contracts was stacked in short-dated futures – in other words, the hedge ratio of futures to underlying oil sold forward was unity. When the futures contracts matured each month, the total position (less current-month deliveries) was rolled forward into the next-listed contract maturities. Because the term structure of oil futures prices is normally downward-sloping (unlike other commodity markets), the monthly rollovers were expected to generate steady "backwardation gains".

But when futures prices fall unexpectedly, cash drains must be incurred to meet variation margin payments. After OPEC failed to reach production-quota agreements in late 1993, oil prices did indeed plunge. Faced with rising margin calls, in December of that year the supervisory board of MG AG ordered the liquidation of substantial portions of MGRM's futures hedge and subsequently cancelled up to 40 million barrels of its customer contracts. The early termination of the hedge and the cancelling of the customer contracts resulted in an estimated net loss of about $1.08 billion, earning MGRM its place as one of the largest "derivatives-related" disasters.[1]

This unfortunate outcome to MGRM's marketing and hedging activities has given rise to many questions. What led MGRM to enter into such a large programme of long-dated marketing contracts? Did the programme make economic sense when it was first started? Why did the firm choose a one-for-one hedge ratio? Why did MGRM opt for a stack-and-roll hedge with short-dated futures rather than a maturity-matched commodity-swap hedge? Could MGRM have better addressed the funding risk of its programme? When the programme was wound up, was it terminated in an appropriate manner? How much of MGRM's loss came from the forgiven customer contracts, and how much from "rollover costs" associated with a shift in the oil-price yield curve from backwardation to contango? Did senior management in Germany understand all the risks of the programme? Did senior management rationally put an end to a speculative gamble, or did it panic in ending a viable programme too soon? Or was the whole episode just an excuse for a change in corporate control of MG AG in Germany?

The answers to most of the questions above are explored - often contentiously - in the essays reproduced in this book. But these answers are in some ways less interesting than the major disagreement that the debate provoked in the academic finance literature on the relation between why and how firms hedge.

The genesis of the academic controversy

Practitioners, journalists, policy-makers and academics alike originally perceived the MGRM fiasco as just another derivatives-related loss. Yet, unlike the other derivatives disasters (for example, Barings with its rogue trader, Nick Leeson, and Procter & Gamble with its leveraged interest-rate bet), a feature of the MGRM episode that immediately distinguished it from the rest was that this firm had apparently lost over a billion dollars *while hedging*. That struck many observers at the time, including us, as odd.

Our original goal in analysing the MGRM episode was twofold. The first goal - and still the most important - was to create teaching materials on the mechanics of hedging long-dated contracts with short-dated futures. The second goal was to shed light on the events of MGRM in the hope of discouraging legislators and regulators from overreacting to the string of derivatives disasters with unwarranted new regulations. We thus sought to explain that long-dated commitments *could* be hedged using short-dated futures - though readers should note that *could* is not the same as *should*.

As we undertook our original analysis of hedging long-dated commodity obligations with short-dated futures (Culp and Miller, 1994), the facts quickly called into question the conventional wisdom - namely, that MGRM's former management was speculating recklessly on oil prices. We concluded that Benson and his team, contrary to press accounts, seemed to have known exactly what they were doing, but that the supervisory board and creditors of MG AG may not have fully understood the nature and risks of the strategy.

We subsequently undertook a more detailed account of the MGRM programme (Culp and Miller, 1995e), reproduced here as chapter 9. In that article, our conclusion that MGRM's hedging programme was viable did not change, but our hypothesis about why the programme was terminated early did. A number of detailed accounts in the German financial press began to reveal a contentious power struggle that had been going on for some time between MG AG's two boards of directors. Under German corporate governance, the "management board" is charged with oversight of the day-to-day operations of the company, and the "supervisory board" is responsible for management board oversight. A supervisory board is precluded from interfering in the normal operations of the company, unless certain extenuating circumstances require it. As more facts about MGRM's problems unfolded, suspicions arose that MGRM's supervisory board and creditors did not misunderstand MGRM's programme but, rather, may have been using the large margin calls as an excuse for the ousting of the management board.

Academics also stepped into the debate over whether MGRM's programme was fatally flawed - a disaster waiting to happen. This academic debate has seemed so confusing to so many because several *different* debates were actually occurring - all at the same time, all involving the same events at the same company and all with a bearing on the current theory and practice of corporate hedging. This book focuses on two of those "sub-debates". The first is why MGRM was hedging and how those motives affected the implementation of its hedging programme. The second is the more technical issue of how best to hedge long-dated commodity swaps with short-dated futures.

The importance of strategic risk management objectives

The Modigliani-Miller capital-structure irrelevance propositions imply that corporations maximising shareholder wealth should be indifferent to hedging; stockholders can manage risks on their own through normal diversification decisions. Why firms hedge, then, is far from obvious and is the subject of a large body of theoretical and empirical work. Furthermore, the strategic objectives that lead a company to hedge can affect the design of any hedge. Parts I–III of this book illustrate why this happens, taking account of the experiences at MGRM.

EARLY THEORIES OF HEDGING[2]

In Part I, the "early classics" of hedging in futures markets are presented, all of which assume that the hedger is a trader or investor whose behaviour is dictated by the maximisation of expected utility. Johnson's 1960 article "The Theory of Hedging and Speculation in Commodity Futures", reproduced here as chapter 1, argues that hedgers are like risk-averse investors.[3] His formulation of the hedging problem treats variance as a sufficient summary measure of *all* risks with which the trader is concerned. As in Markowitz, the goal of a traditional Johnson-style mean–variance efficient hedger is thus to minimise the variance of a hedged portfolio for a given target return. The solution to Johnson's hedging problem is the classic "variance-minimising hedge ratio". Ederington (1979), reproduced here as chapter 2, provides an alternative formulation of the same mean–variance hedging concept.

Working's "Futures Trading and Hedging" (chapter 3), first published in 1953, and his 1962 paper, "New Concepts Concerning Futures Markets and Prices" (chapter 4), come at the problem in an entirely different way. In those articles, Working explains that not all traders view specific types of risk in the same way. He argues that some traders manage risk *selectively*, choosing to bear risks in which they perceive themselves as having a comparative informational advantage and opting to hedge risks in which they perceive no such informational superiority.[4]

EXTENSIONS TO CORPORATIONS

The papers in Part II of the book represent the modern corporate finance analogues of early hedging theories. Most of these theories are, at their core, not much different from the early model of Johnson. But because corporations have *profit* functions rather than *utility* functions, the conventional mean–variance hedging paradigm only works for firms when the profit function is somehow "concave" in shape. Once a concavity is introduced into the profit function, corporate hedging can be addressed as if the firm were a risk-averse investor. In chapters 5 and 6, Fite and Pfleiderer (1995) and Smith and Stulz (1995) summarise the main sources of these potential concavities, including taxation, the cost of financial distress, agency costs and signalling. The hedging theories discussed generally assume that the firm is concerned with changes in its market value over specific intervals of time.

A somewhat different picture of corporate hedging is presented by Froot, Scharfstein and Stein in their 1993 work, reproduced as chapter 7. Motivated by the agency cost of debt, the authors paint a picture of a firm concerned with hedging the volatility of its cashflows. Their typical cashflow hedger is not so much a value variance minimiser as a cashflow variance *eliminator* – as, for example, with a maturity-matched swap.

Despite differences in detail, the models in Fite and Pfleiderer, Smith and Stulz and Froot and colleagues all agree that the firm should pay no attention to the specific risks that it reduces to achieve its objectives. No distinction is drawn, for example, between market and credit risk, or different types of market risk (such as spot-price risk and basis risk). All risk is treated as homogeneous, as in Johnson and Ederington.

Working's early theory of hedging, by contrast, was a theory of *selective* risk management, in which traders had defined preferences over which risks to manage. Building on this idea, Stulz (1996) attempts to generalise selective risk management to the level of the corporation. In his article "Rethinking Risk Management", reproduced as chapter 8, he shows how firms may choose to hedge some risks and not others to exploit informational asymmetries.[5] One obvious implication of Working's theory is that *total* variance-minimising value or cashflow hedge ratios are not usually, if ever, optimal for corporations whose objective is the management of selected risks.

STRATEGIC HEDGING OBJECTIVES AND MGRM

Critics of MGRM were quick to argue that the company's marketing programme made little economic sense given its seemingly "unhedgeable" risks – most notably the basis risk arising from the maturity mismatch between the short-dated futures and long-dated customer contracts. These general criticisms took more specific forms, including some of the following: the one-to-one hedge exposed MGRM to too much basis risk; the lack of any present-value adjustment to the hedge ratio exaggerated the funding risk of the programme; and the size of the programme was too big to allow MGRM to engage in the one-for-one stack-and-roll hedge without incurring significant transaction costs – as well as rollover costs when the term structure moved from backwardation to contango. Part III of the book explores these issues.

In chapter 9, Culp and Miller (1995e) address many of the above criticisms. The paper argues that these criticisms make little sense in the context of MGRM's apparent corporate hedging objectives. MGRM was exploiting a perceived informational marketing advantage while remaining insulated from changes in the level of spot prices that could suggest to customers an inability to honour long-dated physical delivery contracts. The design of MGRM's customer contracts (including an early termination provision) is also considered in the chapter, and a method for determining the economic value of MGRM's "synthetic storage" programme is presented.

In chapter 10, the valuation method from Culp and Miller (1995e) is employed to quantify the sources of MGRM's stated accounting loss. Of the estimated $1.08 billion in net losses calculated by MGRM's auditors, Culp and Miller (1995a) conclude that about $800 million was attributable to the cancellation in 1994 of valuable customer contracts by the new MGRM management. The remaining $200 million or so was allocated to rollover costs arising from unfavourable changes in the calendar basis, much of which would have eventually been recouped had the programme not been terminated early.[6]

In chapter 11, Bollen and Whaley (1998) undertake a simulation analysis of MGRM's hedged marketing programme. They conclude that the programme was economically viable throughout and would ultimately have been profitable in almost all situations, notwithstanding the heavy cash drains very early in the life of the programme. Bollen and Whaley also argue that the traditional variance-minimising hedge ratio would *not* have made sense for MGRM.

Mello and Parsons (1995) take the other side of the debate in chapter 12, arguing that MGRM's programme was fundamentally flawed. Viewing MGRM as a hedger in the sense of Froot, Scharfstein and Stein (1993), they contend that cashflow risk should have been virtually the only risk with which MGRM's management was concerned. Accordingly, they argue that the one-for-one stack-and-roll hedge subjected the firm to extreme funding and basis risk and should not have been undertaken. Mello and Parsons conclude that the only sensible hedge for MGRM would have been maturity-matched commodity swaps.

Edwards and Canter (1995) are also critical of MGRM's hedging strategy and set out their (albeit different) arguments in chapter 13. They implicitly adopt the value-hedging paradigm (as opposed to the Froot–Scharfstein–Stein cashflow model). By that standard, they contend that MGRM was overhedged by at least a factor of two when variance-minimising hedge ratios are estimated using ordinary least-squares regression.

Culp and Miller (1995d) respond to these two papers in chapter 14 by emphasising that neither maturity-matched cashflow hedging nor variance-minimising value hedging properly described MGRM's commercial business objectives.[7] MGRM was a marketing firm that was set up precisely to exploit its informational advantage using "basis trading" strategies. When viewed as such in the selective risk-management tradition of Working, Culp and Miller argue in the chapter that MGRM's programme made a great deal of sense.

Technical hedging issues raised by MGRM

Chapters 15 through 19 in Part IV of the book deal mainly with *how* to hedge rather than *why* to hedge. In particular, the issue of optimal hedge ratio estimation is considered in some detail, taking particular account of the stochastic properties (for example, mean-reversion) of the time series being hedged. Almost all of these essays accept variance minimisation or some other total risk management objective.

The essay by Schwartz (1997) reproduced in chapter 20 is the only paper in Part IV that was not written as part of the MGRM debate. We include this paper because of its usefulness as a thorough summary of the theories of commodity contract valuation on which several of the other papers in Part IV are based.

1 *For a discussion of the social costs of the so-called derivatives disasters, see chapter 2 of Miller (1997).*

2 *One other early classic that space considerations prevent us from including in this book is Stein (1961).*

3 *In this sense, Johnson is building on earlier literature, including Kaldor and Keynes.*

4 *Working's theories are summarised and expanded in Williams (1986).*

5 *For a similar line of argument, see Schrand and Unal (1998).*

6 *See also Culp and Miller (1995c).*

7 *See also Culp and Miller (1995b).*

BIBLIOGRAPHY

Bollen, N., and R. Whaley, 1998, "Simulating Supply", *Risk* September; reprinted as Chapter 11 of the present volume.

Brennan, M. J., and N. I. Crew, 1997, "Hedging Long Maturity Commodity Commitments with Short-Dated Futures Contracts", in M. A. H. Dempster and S. R. Pliska (eds), *Mathematics of Derivative Securities* (New York: Cambridge University Press).

Culp, C. L., and M. H. Miller, 1994, "Hedging a Flow of Commodity Derivatives with Futures: Lessons from Metallgesellschaft", *Derivatives Quarterly* 1(1).

Culp, C. L., and M. H. Miller, 1995a, "Auditing the Auditors", *Risk* 8(4); reprinted as Chapter 10 of the present volume.

Culp, C. L., and M. H. Miller, 1995b, "Basis Risk and Hedging Strategies: Reply to Mello and Parsons", *Derivatives Quarterly* 1(4).

Culp, C. L., and M. H. Miller, 1995c, "Blame Mismanagement, Not Speculation, for Metall's Woes", *Wall Street Journal, Europe* April 25.

Culp, C. L., and M. H. Miller, 1995d, "Hedging in the Theory of Corporate Finance: A Reply to Our Critics", *Journal of Applied Corporate Finance* 8(1); reprinted as Chapter 14 of the present volume.

Culp, C. L., and M. H. Miller, 1995e, "Metallgesellschaft and the Economics of Synthetic Storage", *Journal of Applied Corporate Finance* 7(4); reprinted as Chapter 9 of the present volume.

Ederington, L. H., 1979, "The Hedging Performance of the New Futures Markets", *Journal of Finance* 34(1); reprinted as Chapter 2 of the present volume.

Edwards, F. R., and M. S. Canter, 1995, "The Collapse of Metallgesellschaft: Unhedgeable Risks, Poor Hedging Strategy, or Just Bad Luck?", *Journal of Applied Corporate Finance* 8(1); reprinted as Chapter 13 of the present volume.

Fite, D., and P. Pfleiderer, 1995, "Should Firms Use Derivatives to Manage Risk?", in W. H. Beaver and G. Parker (eds), *Risk Management: Problems & Solutions* (New York: McGraw-Hill); reprinted as Chapter 5 of the present volume.

Froot, K. A., D. S. Scharfstein and J. C. Stein, 1993, "Risk Management: Coordinating Investment and Financing Policies", *Journal of Finance* 48(5); reprinted as Chapter 7 of the present volume.

Hilliard, J. E., 1999, "Analytics Underlying the Metallgesellschaft Hedge: Short-Term Futures in a Multi-Period Environment", *Review of Quantitative Finance and Accounting* 12(3); reprinted as Chapter 15 of the present volume.

Johnson, L. L., 1960, "The Theory of Hedging and Speculation in Commodity Futures", *Review of Economic Studies* 26; reprinted as Chapter 1 of the present volume.

Mello, A. S., and J. E. Parsons, 1995, "Maturity Structure of a Hedge Matters: Lessons from the Metallgesellschaft Debacle", *Journal of Applied Corporate Finance* 8(1); reprinted as Chapter 12 of the present volume.

Miller, M. H., 1997, *Merton Miller on Derivatives* (New York: John Wiley & Sons).

Neuberger, A., 1999, "Hedging Long Term Exposures with Multiple Short Term Futures Contracts", *Review of Financial Studies* 12(3); reprinted as Chapter 18 of the present volume.

Pirrong, S. C., 1997, "Metallgesellschaft: A Prudent Hedger Ruined, or a Wildcatter on NYMEX?", *Journal of Futures Markets* 15(5); reprinted as Chapter 17 of the present volume.

Ross, S. A., 1997, "Hedging Long Run Commitments: Exercises in Incomplete Market Pricing", *Economic Notes* 26(2); reprinted as Chapter 19 of the present volume.

Schrand, C., and H. Unal, 1998, "Hedging and Coordinated Risk Management: Evidence from Thrift Conversions", *Journal of Finance* 53(3).

Schwartz, E. S., 1997, "The Stochastic Behavior of Commodity Prices: Implications for Valuation and Hedging", *Journal of Finance* 52(3); reprinted as Chapter 20 of the present volume.

Smith, C. W., Jr, and R. M. Stulz, 1995, "The Determinants of a Firm's Hedging Policies", *Journal of Financial and Quantitative Analysis* 20(4); reprinted as Chapter 6 of the present volume.

Stein, J. L., 1961, "The Simultaneous Determination of Spot and Futures Prices", *American Economic Review* 51.

Stulz, R. M., 1996, "Rethinking Risk Management", *Journal of Applied Corporate Finance* 9(3); reprinted as Chapter 11 of the present volume.

Williams, J., 1986, *The Economic Function of Futures Markets* (New York: Cambridge University Press).

Working, H., 1953, "Futures Trading and Hedging", *American Economic Review*, 43; reprinted as Chapter 3 of the present volume.

Working, H., 1962, "New Concepts Concerning Futures Markets and Prices", *American Economic Review*, 52; reprinted as Chapter 4 of the present volume.

THE FOUNDATIONS OF HEDGING IN FUTURES MARKETS

1

The Theory of Hedging and Speculation in Commodity Futures*

Leland L. Johnson

Although significant contributions have appeared in the literature in recent years, the present-day theory of hedging and speculation appears to account inadequately for certain market practices. In particular, the motivation of the trader who undertakes hedging activities, the role that hedging plays in his overall market operations and the distinction between a trader who hedges and one who speculates have given rise to difficulties in the literature. My purposes here are: (1) to outline briefly the purposes and mechanics of a commodity futures market, (2) to discuss and appraise the theory of hedging and speculation as it exists today, (3) to present a reformulated concept of hedging and (4) to construct a model that may both assist in clarifying the concepts of hedging and speculation and contribute to a better understanding of certain market phenomena.

The nature of futures trading

Organised commodity futures trading facilitates two kinds of activity – speculation and hedging. When futures trading in a given commodity exists, the speculator generally finds it advantageous to deal in futures contracts rather than either (1) buying a quantity of the commodity at the current "spot" price and holding it in the hope of a rise in the spot price or (2) selling the commodity short by promising in private negotiations with a buyer to deliver at a specified later date, at a price which he expects to be above the spot price that will prevail at that date. Equally important, if not more so, futures markets are useful for hedging operations. An essential feature of commodity hedging is that the trader synchronises his activities in two markets. One is generally the "cash" or "spot" market (the market for immediate delivery); the other is generally the futures market.

A future contract, being merely a promise of the seller to deliver within a specified month and a promise of the buyer to take delivery of a *standard* quantity and quality of the commodity at an agreed price is readily adaptable by its homogeneous character to being traded on an exchange. The commodity exchange provides a central location where potential buyers and sellers make bids and offers for contracts covering delivery in various later months. Each delivery month in which trading takes place is referred to as a "future". Because of the centralised nature of the market and the rapidity and ease with which sales and purchases can be made, the price of any sale in a given future during the trading day is a near-perfect reflection of supply and demand conditions existing at that instant of time for contracts of that particular future.

In most futures markets, only a small fraction of contracts sold is closed out by delivery of the actual commodity. Because nearly all participants are motivated by the desire to trade on price movements, they liquidate by undertaking offsetting transactions. The buyer (seller) can liquidate his position in the futures market *prior to actual delivery* of the commodity by merely *selling* (buying) on the exchange contracts of the *same* future. The second transaction offsets and cancels the previously existing commitment. For each contract purchased or sold and subsequently liquidated the trader takes a total profit or loss equal to the difference between his buying and selling price multiplied by the number of units of the commodity specified in the contract.

**Originally published in the* Review of Economic Studies *27 (1960), pp. 139–51. The author is indebted to Richard R. Nelson and Richard N. Rosett for many helpful comments on earlier drafts of the manuscript.*

The theory of hedging

Most commodity trading theorists have visualised the hedger as a dealer in the "actual" commodity who desires "insurance" against the price risks he faces. For example, if he purchases a unit of the commodity at a given spot price and the price falls (rises) prior to his reselling it, he is exposed to a capital loss (gain), in addition to whatever merchandising profit he receives, by the amount of that price change. According to these theorists he would typically protect his inventory position of x units from the risk of such price fluctuation by simultaneously *selling* a sufficient number of future contracts to cover delivery of x units;[1] when he resells his inventory he would simultaneously liquidate his position in futures by *purchasing* the same number of contracts (of the same future) as before. If the net change in spot price is equal to the net change in the price of his future, ie, if the price movements are parallel to each other, the gain he enjoys in one market offsets the loss in the other and he would be left with only his "normal" merchandising profit.[2] Otherwise he would be left with a residual capital gain or loss.

As an illustration assume a hedge carried in a future from time t_1 to time t_2 (where the future specifies delivery at t_3) against x units of inventory purchased at t_1, and sold at t_2. Let S_1 and S_2 denote the spot price and F_1 and F_2 the price of the future that exist at t_1 and t_2 respectively. The hedger will take a total gain (loss) arising from price movements from t_1 to t_2 equal to the positive (negative) value of $x[(S_2 - S_1) - (F_2 - F_1)]$. The hedge is perfectly effective if $[(S_2 - S_1) - (F_2 - F_1)]$ is equal to 0.

A major role of the speculator in futures, according to the bulk of the literature, is to assume the risks that hedgers desire to transfer from their own shoulders;[3] the futures market is visualised as a convenient mechanism through which price risk can be transferred from one group to another. The hedger is often described as an apparently unsophisticated participant in futures dealings who, in the words of Hawtrey, "regards the making of price as a whole-time occupation for experts [speculators?], and, in general, will not pit his fragmentary information against the systematic study at the disposal of the professional dealers."[4] Expanding upon this thesis, J. M. Keynes, in his *A Treatise on Money*, deduced the theory of "normal backwardation" in which he asserted that hedgers are willing to pay a "risk premium" to relieve themselves of price risk, while speculators are willing to enter the futures market only if they have the expectation of collecting a premium. Therefore, since hedgers are predominantly short in futures and speculators are predominately long, the current future or "forward" price must fall *below* the future price expected to prevail at any later time by the amount of this risk premium. If the expected future price is equal to the current spot price, the current future price must fall below the current spot price by the amount of the premium. The existence of a discount of a future below the current spot price by an amount equal to the premium is a condition of normal backwardation.[5]

In recent years Holbrook Working has written a series of articles that run counter to the older, "traditional" concept of the nature of hedging and the function of a futures market. He envisages the hedger as one who does not seek primarily to avoid risk but one who hedges because of an expected return arising from anticipations of favourable *relative* price movements in the spot and futures markets. The trader does not somehow find himself with a given size inventory that has to be hedged against, but he takes positions in *both* markets as a form of "arbitrage".

> The role of risk-avoidance in most commercial hedging has been greatly overemphasised in economic discussions. Most hedging is done largely, and may be done wholly, because information on which the merchant or processor acts leads logically to hedging. He buys the spot commodity because the spot price is low *relative to* the futures price and he has reason to expect the spot premium to advance; therefore he buys *spot* and sells the future.[6]

Since the hedger is not motivated primarily by desire to reduce risk it is also misleading, Working asserts, to judge the effectiveness of hedging according to the degree to which futures price and spot price movements are parallel.

> ... the basic idea that complete effectiveness of hedging depends on parallelism of movement of spot and futures prices is false, and an improper standard by which to test the effectiveness of hedging. The effectiveness of hedging intelligently used with commodity storage, depends on *inequalities* between the movements of spot and futures prices and on reasonable predictability of such inequalities.[7]

An appraisal

On the basis of personal interviews with representatives of 20 firms in one particular commodity market - the New York coffee trade - I have concluded that the present-day body of theory outlined above does not account adequately for certain market phenomena. On the basis of interviews with several representatives of brokerage firms dealing in a wide range of commodities, there is reason to believe that this situation extends to trading in other commodities as well.

On one hand, it is true that hedgers in the coffee market sometimes at least act on the basis of expected relative price movements between spot and futures and adjust both their stockholdings and their positions in futures somewhat as described by Working. The price of a given future is almost always at a large discount relative to spot at the time trade in it begins a year prior to its delivery period, and this discount tends to diminish as the delivery month approaches. According to our previous terminology, $(S_1 - F_1)$ and $[(S_2 - S_1) - (F_2 - F_1)]$ tend to be positive and negative respectively. Therefore, the trader tends to take a loss, aside from merchandising profit, on his hedged inventory. For this reason most of the traders contacted who claim to hedge at all stated that they often carry very small inventories ("buy hand-to-mouth") and thereby maintain only small positions in futures. At the same time, however, they claim to be motivated to hedge primarily in order to reduce price risk. The importance of the price "insurance" factor in coffee hedging most clearly manifests itself in the fact that one group of traders, the roasters, who face little price risk in holding inventory, almost never hedge, while another group, the importers, who *do* face large price risks, make extensive use of the futures market for hedging purposes.[8]

Furthermore, the traders in the survey take cognisance not only of expected relative price movements but of expected *absolute* price movements as well. Generally, if traders expect spot prices to rise they tend to remove hedges and increase their inventory holdings. In some cases they take long positions in both the spot and futures markets as a more obvious speculative venture. On the other hand, if they are bearish they increase their short futures positions in excess of hedging requirements. In other words, hedging activities get mixed in very closely with speculative operations in the accounts of the individual trader.

In general, hedging activities appear to be motivated by the desire to reduce risk, as described in traditional theory, but levels of inventory held appear to be not independent of expected hedging profits, as emphasised by Working. Furthermore, that an individual may hold a mix of hedged and speculative positions in response to his expectations concerning *absolute* price changes is a practice not well explained in either traditional theory or in Working's theory. In the former the tendency, as illustrated by Keynes' "normal backwardation", is much more to speak of the hedger and the speculator as if they were entirely separate individuals with entirely different motivations.[9] In the latter, there is no treatment of the conditions under which the trader may speculate in lieu of or in combination with hedging. In fact, the very distinctions between hedging and speculation is fuzzy when the trader takes market positions on the basis of expectations concerning *relative* price changes, he is speculating insofar as he is not betting on a "sure thing".

In view of the disparities between theory and these market phenomena one could well ask: "Precisely what is a hedge? Can a hedge be meaningfully defined in the case in which the trader acts on the basis of absolute price expectations? Can hedging be treated theoretically as an activity conducted simultaneously with speculation?"

A reformulation of the theory of hedging

First, a reformulated definition and analysis of hedging in commodity futures is in order. Given a position consisting of a number, x_i, of physical units held in market i, a "hedge" is defined as a position in market j of size x_j^* units such that the "price risk" of holding x_i and x_j^* from time t_1 to time t_2 is *minimised*. The scope of the term "market" is restricted in this definition to include trading in a commodity of sufficiently exact specification so that its price may be considered a scalar magnitude.

"Price risk" can be considered a reflection of the variance (or standard deviation) of a subjective probability distribution (or a subjective probability density function) for price change from t_1 to t_2 that the trader holds at time t_1, where *actual* price from t_1 to t_2 is treated as a random variable. The variance of price change, denoted by σ_i^2 in the i market is equal to the *variance of return* or "price risk" of holding one unit in the i market from t_1 to t_2, since the (absolute) value of actual return attributed to price change from t_1 to t_2 is equal to the (absolute) value of the actual price change itself. The variance of return or the price risk of holding x_i units is equal to $x_i^2\sigma_i^2$. Likewise, the price risk of holding one unit in the j market can be considered as the variance, denoted by σ_j^2, of a subjective probability distribution of price change in the j market. The variance of return of holding x_j units, when these units are considered alone, is equal to $x_j^2\sigma_j^2$. Where cov_{ij} denotes the covariance of price change (or covariance of return due to price change) between market i and market j, a *combination* of positions in i and j has a total variance of return V(R) due to price change given by:

$$V(R) = x_i^2\sigma_i^2 + x_j^2\sigma_j^2 + 2x_ix_j cov_{ij} \tag{1}$$

The combination also has an actual return R and an expected return E(R) due to price change given respectively by

$$R = x_iB_i + x_jB_j \tag{2}$$

and

$$E(R) = x_iu_i + x_ju_j \tag{3}$$

where B_i and B_j denote the *actual* price changes from t_1 to t_2 in i and j, and u_i and u_j denote the price changes from t_1 to t_2 *expected at* t_1. As such, u_i and u_j are the mean values of the probability distributions of return existing in the i and j markets respectively at time t_1.[10]

Differentiating equation (1) with respect to x_j and setting the derivative equal to 0, we have the value x_j^* minimising the variance of return for the combination x_i, x_j^*.

$$x_j^* = -\frac{x_i\, cov_{ij}}{\sigma_j^2} \tag{4}$$

Substituting the value x_j^* for x_j in equation (1) and letting $V(R)^*$ denote the total variance of return of the combination x_i, x_j^*, we have:

$$V(R)^* = x_i^2\sigma_i^2 + \frac{x_i^2\, cov_{ij}^2}{\sigma_j^2} - \frac{2x_i^2\, cov_{ij}^2}{\sigma_j^2}$$

or

$$V(R)^* = x_i^2\left(\sigma_i^2 - \frac{cov_{ij}^2}{\sigma_j^2}\right)$$

Since the coefficient of correlation, ρ, estimated by the trader is equal to $cov_{ij}/\sigma_i\sigma_j$, then $V(R)^* = x_i^2\sigma_i^2(1 - \rho^2)$. Generally speaking the larger the (absolute) value of the coefficient of correlation, the greater the reduction in price risk of holding x_i that can be effected by carrying the hedge x_j^*. If the trader believes at time t_1 that price movements are perfectly correlated between t_1 and t_2, ρ is equal to 1 and overall price risk is reduced to 0. If he believes that there is no correlation whatever, $V(R)^*$ is equal to $x_i^2\sigma_i^2$ – the variance of x_i held alone. The effectiveness e of the hedge is measured by considering the variance of return, $V(R)^*$ associated with the combination x_i,x_j^* in a ratio with the variance $x_i^2\sigma_i^2$ associated with the position x_i held alone so that

$$e = \left(1 - \frac{V(R)^*}{x_i^2\sigma_i^2}\right) \quad \text{or} \quad e = \rho^2$$

Although this reformulated concept resembles the traditional theory insofar as the hedge is considered as a mechanism to reduce price risk, the concept of price risk itself is quite different. In traditional theory price risk is measured by the size of *actual* gain or loss due to price change that the trader incurs. The effectiveness of the hedge is measured by considering the gain or loss due to price changes incurred in an unhedged position relative to that incurred in a hedged position. If price movements in i and j from t_1 to t_2 were equal to each other, any loss in one market would be exactly offset by the gain in the other; price risk would therefore be reduced to zero, and the hedge would be considered perfectly effective.

However, in the reformulated framework both price risk and the effectiveness of the hedge are treated quite apart from the effects of *actual* price change. Price risk is something that exists in the mind of the trader at t_1; namely it is the variance of his probability distribution of return due to price change. Hence, it is treated only in subjective terms – not in terms of *ex post* price changes. The effectiveness of the hedge is likewise considered only in subjective terms – it is measured by the extent to which the trader believes at t_1, that the variance of return of holding x_i is reduced by simultaneously holding x_j^*.

Parallelism of actual price movements should be indicative of a perfectly effective hedge only if the trader believed with certainty at t_1 that any change in one price would be equal to the change in the other, but the condition of actual parallelism itself would be neither a necessary nor a sufficient condition to make possible a perfectly effective hedge. It is not a necessary condition because if the trader believed with certainty that *any* relationship held perfectly between price movements in i and j he could take a perfectly effective hedge. If, for example, he believed with certainty that the price in the j market would fall from t_1 to t_2 by c cents relative to the price in the i market, he could take a long position x_i in combination with short position in j of the same number of units, and be certain of achieving a return equal to $c(x_i)$, and no price risk as such would be involved. In other words, neither the expected return nor the actual return of the combination need be equal to zero to make possible a perfectly effective hedge.

The reformulated theory is similar to the traditional theory in that a "primary" market is postulated, the primary market visualised here as one in which the trader in some sense "makes his living". More specifically, the primary market is defined as one in which the trader (assumed to be normally efficient) is able to obtain a net merchandising profit by carrying positions in that market. As such he can most generally be considered a middleman in the handling of a commodity. References to the middleman role played by the hedger are frequently found in the literature, although the "primary" market condition is generally not defined explicitly. Here it is essential to postulate the primary market within the definition of hedging because the market in which the risk of a given position is to be minimised *must be specified in advance*. Only if the (subjective) coefficient of correlation were equal to 1 would the x_j^* that minimises the risk of holding x_i be of a value such that the x_i^* which would in reverse minimise the risk of holding x_j^* be equal to x_i.[11]

A model of hedging and speculation

With this general concept of hedging in mind we shall consider a model within which a wide range of trading activities may be examined. Given a framework of particular assumptions about the trader and the nature of his world, it will be possible to demonstrate under what conditions various market phenomena arise.

As to the nature of the trader himself, he is postulated to have an indifference map illustrated in Figure 1. The total expected net return $E(R)$ generated by all of his market positions together from t_1 to t_2 is plotted on the X-axis. As a direct measure of price risk, the standard deviation $\sqrt{V(R)}$ of return is plotted on the Y-axis. Curves 1 and 2 represent indifference curves among which the trader has ranked all possible combinations of $\sqrt{V(R)}$ and $E(R)$. The shape and positions of the curves indicate that to remain on a given indifference level the incremental ratio of $\sqrt{V(R)}$ to $E(R)$ must fall as he moves to a higher $E(R)$. With a given level of $E(R)$ he moves to a higher (lower) indifference curve as $\sqrt{V(R)}$ decreases (increases). His optimum overall market position is defined as that position or combination of positions which generates an $E(R)$ and $\sqrt{V(R)}$ such that he attains the highest indifference curve that he is able to attain under given constraints.

1.

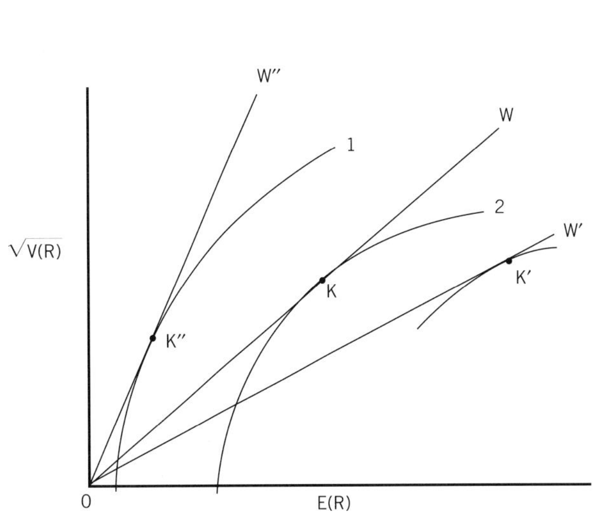

I shall assume further that the trader can engage in one or more of the following activities:

- He can take a long position in the *spot or* i *market* at t_1 by purchasing a stock of the commodity at the spot price prevailing at t_1 and reselling it at t_2 at the spot price prevailing at t_2; he receives for this operation, in addition, a net merchandising profit (m) equal to a fixed markup per unit held from t_1 to t_2. This profit is simply a net return for services rendered as a middleman. The institutional environment is assumed to be such that the size of this return is known with certainty. The total risk faced by the trader is confined to "price risk". In this case equation (3) must be modified to

$$E(R) = x_i(u_i + m) + x_j u_j \quad \text{where} \quad x_i > 0 \tag{3a}$$

The spot market is, therefore, regarded as the primary market.

- He can take a long position in a *given future of the* j *market* at t_1 by purchasing contracts of a given future at the price prevailing at t_1 and liquidate them at t_2 at the price prevailing at t_2.
- He can take a *short* position in the given future by selling contracts at t_1, and liquidating them at t_2, also at the relevant prevailing prices. In all cases future contracts are assumed to be completely divisible – he can take positions in a future representing any number of units of the commodity he chooses.

The coordinate system in Figure 2 illustrates geometrically the market positions he can take at t_1. The number of units *purchased* in the spot or i market is measured along the positive X-axis, the number *sold* in the given future or j market along the negative Y-axis and the number *purchased* in the same future along the positive Y-axis.

Iso-expected return lines of slope $(u_i + m)/u_j$ appear in Figure 2 to denote combinations of market positions for which total expected return remains constant.[12] Suppose, first, that the trader expects no price changes in either the spot or the future markets, ie, u_i and u_j are both equal to 0. Vertical iso-expected return curves such as AB and CD in Figure 2 would be appropriate in this case to denote the fact that positive expected return for any combination is generated solely by merchandising profit. m, from positions in the spot market on the X-axis.

Iso-variance of return ellipses (which are centred as 0) are drawn on the basis of equation (1) to connect combinations for which variance of return remains constant. Because short positions in the spot market are not postulated, only quadrants 1 and 4 of the coordinate systems are relevant. The locus of tangencies OZ indicates the combinations of positions such that for any given level of total expected return E(R), variance (or standard deviation) of return V(R) is minimised. Each such combination of E(R) and standard deviation of return $\sqrt{V(R)}$ is in turn plotted in Figure 1; the opportunity line OW which is necessarily linear, connects these points. The trader's optimum combination of E(R) and $\sqrt{V(R)}$ is at point K where he attains his highest indifference curve; therefore he would take the market combination in Figure 2, let us say X_1 and $-Y_1$ read from point L, which generates this combination of E(R) and $\sqrt{V(R)}$.

According to the earlier definition of hedging, $-Y_1$ represents a hedge against X_1 because this is the short position in the future which minimises the variance of holding X_1. It can be seen that any combination read from the line OZ would represent a position in spot against which a hedge in the future is held. By substitution in equation (4), the position $-Y_1$ is equal to $-(X_1 \text{cov}_{ij}/\sigma_j^2)$. Therefore, the slope of OZ is equal to $-\text{cov}_{ij}/\sigma_j^2$ or to $-\rho(\sigma_i/\sigma_j)$. OZ, then, indicates the appropriate value along the Y-axis that constitutes a hedge against any given value along the X-axis.

2.

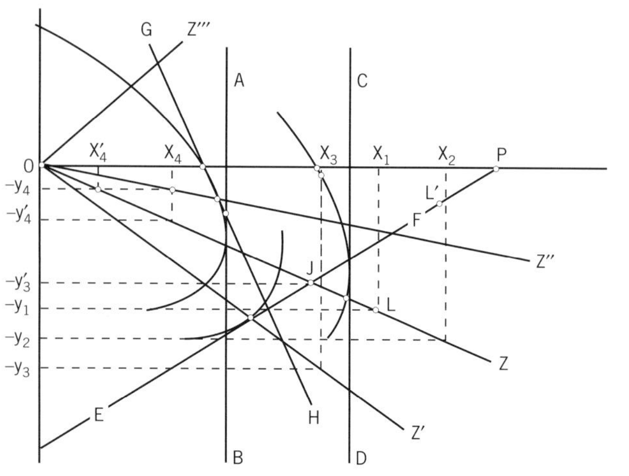

The empirical observation that the individual trader may assume market positions representing a mixture of hedging and speculative activity can be analysed in this model by comparing various alternative market combinations with the one that the trader would take if he engaged in no speculative activity. Letting α_0 denote a position held in either the spot or future market under conditions in which both u_i and u_j are equal to 0, and letting α_1 denote the position in the same market when either u_i or u_j is non-zero, I shall define a "speculative element" of a market position as $\alpha_1 - \alpha_0$. The value of $\alpha_1 - \alpha_0$ will be called a *direct* speculative element if it arises because of an expected non-zero price change in the *same* market to which the value $\alpha_1 - \alpha_0$ refers; it will be called an *indirect* speculative element if it arises because of an expected non-zero price change in the *other* market. Under these definitions the combination X_1, $-Y_1$ read from point L in Figure 2 involves no speculative element since both u_i and u_j are equal to 0. The trader in this situation may be considered a "pure" hedger because he takes a position in spot on the basis of an expected return composed entirely of merchandising profit and he takes a position in the future only to minimise the price risk of holding his position in spot. Suppose, however, that u_i is positive, and u_j remains equal to 0. The iso-expected return lines would still be vertical and the locus of tangencies would remain along OZ, but AB and AC would indicate higher levels of expected return for given levels of variance than before. A new opportunity line, OW′ in Figure 1, indicates that for any given level of $\sqrt{V(R)}$, E(R) is higher than before. The trader's optimum combination of $\sqrt{V(R)}$ and E(R) is at K′; the corresponding market combination is, say, at X_2 and $-Y_2$. Because of an expected spot price rise the trader carries a larger position in spot than if no price rise had been expected. The increase in spot from X_1 to X_2 is a direct speculative element. He maintains a hedge against X_2 by increasing his short position in the future to $-Y_2$. He is motivated to increase his short position only to minimise the risk of holding a now larger position in spot, and not because of any return expected in the future itself; nevertheless, the gap between $-Y_1$ and $-Y_2$ is in some sense a speculative element because it arises in response to an expected price rise although it is one in the other market. Therefore, the change in the future may be termed an *indirect* speculative element. In the case of an expected price *fall* in spot by less than the amount of merchandising profit ($u_i + m > 0$) and an expected constant future price, iso-expected return lines remain vertical and the locus of tangencies remains along OZ. For any $\sqrt{V(R)}$, E(R) is *lower* than in the pure hedge case and a new opportunity line OW″ in Figure 1 is generated. The market combination is calculated from K″ in the same manner as before, and deviations from X_1 and Y_1 are respectively regarded as direct and indirect speculative elements.

If, instead, he expects a price fall in the future and no price change in spot, the iso-expected return lines such as EF would have a positive slope and a new locus of tangencies OZ′ would be generated. On the basis of a corresponding opportunity line in Figure 1, the trader would pick a market combination, say X_3, $-Y_3$ indicated in Figure 2. Because of the expected price fall in the future, the trader increases his position in the future beyond that required for a hedge against X_3 by the distance $-Y_3'$ to $-Y_3$. The movement from X_1 to X_3 is an indirect speculative effect; the movement from $-Y_1$ to $-Y_3$ is a direct speculative effect. Or suppose he expects a price *rise* in the future and a constant price in spot. In this case the iso-expected return lines such as GH are negatively sloped, a new locus of tangencies OZ″ is generated, and a market combination, say X_4, $-Y_4$ is taken. In this case the trader would go short in the future, even though he would expect a negative return in the future in so doing, for the sake of reducing the risk of holding X_4 in spot. This situation is illustrative of Keynes' "normal backwardation" – the trader is willing to pay a risk premium (in the form here of an expected loss in the future) for the sake of reducing the risk of holding a position in another market. However, he would not carry a full hedge against X_4, which would require a position of $-Y_4'$ in the future; owing to the effect of the expected price rise in the future the trader carries a hedged position X_4' in spot and leaves X_4 to X_4' unhedged. In this case the hedge is partially withdrawn. The reduction in spot from X_1 to X_4 is an indirect speculative element, the reduction in the short future from $-Y_1$ to $-Y_4$ a direct speculative element. If the expected price rise in the future is of sufficient magnitude, the slope of the iso-expected return curves will move the locus of tangencies, say OZ‴ to quadrant 1. In this case the trader would withdraw his hedge completely and go long in the future.

Both expected prices could be allowed to vary simultaneously from 0, but in this case it would be impossible to distinguish in Figure 2 between direct and indirect speculative elements. Market combinations could be derived as before, however, and deviations from X_1 and Y_1 could be considered simply as a mixture of direct and indirect speculative elements.

In general, this model appears to account to some degree for the phenomena mentioned earlier that I have observed in the New York coffee market – traders may well undertake hedging activities but these activities are not independent of expected price changes. A hedge may be lifted, a long position taken in the future, inventories adjusted, all on the basis of price expectations. This model explains how price expectations can affect market positions in a like manner.

Hedging and relative price changes

What about the case of Working, however, in which the trader may have expectations only about *relative* price changes? Suppose it is true at least in some instances that the trader takes position in one market to offset a position in another market because of the expected gain in so doing and not primarily in order to avoid risk. So long as it can be assumed that the trader has an indifference map between *overall* $E(R)$ and $\sqrt{V(R)}$ as illustrated in Figure 1, the concept of hedging as a form of arbitrage fits into the present model as a special case – a case in which the model collapses from a two-market to what is in effect a one-market analysis. Since the trader has no price expectations in the separate markets, he has no subjective probability distribution of return in each of the two markets and, therefore, faces no price risk as defined previously in terms of a variance of return. But since he takes a unit-for-unit hedge, his expectations concerning relative price changes can form the basis of a probability distribution whose mean u_h and variance σ_h^2 measure the expected return and price risk respectively of holding the hedged commodity. Both expected return and variance can be defined only in terms of a unit of hedged commodity consisting of one unit in spot and one unit in a future *taken together and inseparably*. Where X_h denotes the number of units held long in spot and hedged, $E(R)$ is equal to $X_h(u_h + m)$ and $V(R)$ is equal to $X_h^2 \sigma_h^2$. The hedger, since he is dealing here in a one-to-one ratio in two markets, can be considered to be dealing in one market – the market for the hedged commodity. A non-zero mean and variance of the probability distribution of return have the same significance here as they would for any commodity normally considered in one market. Figure 3 represents a coordinate system identical to that in Figure 2. There are no iso-variance or iso-expected return curves, however, since expected return and variance of return are not computed from spot and futures positions taken singly. The only combinations the trader can take fall along OH which necessarily has a slope of -1. Each point along OH has an $E(R)$ and a $\sqrt{V(R)}$ combination which can be plotted in Figure 1, say along OW. The optimum combination at K corresponds to the combination at L in Figure 3. If u_h is equal to 0, the combination at L would represent a "pure" hedge. If u_h is greater than 0, the trader might take a combination other than L on the basis of a new opportunity line. The difference, measured along the X-axis, between this combination and the one at L is what I would call the direct speculative effect on stocks held and hedged. For a u_h less than 0 the analysis runs symmetrically in reverse as long as $m + u_h > 0$. If $m + u_h \leq 0$, the trader would take no position at all. Since there is only one market to consider, no indirect speculative effects can be analysed.

This one-market model illustrates the reason why the theory of hedging has not been satisfactorily integrated with the general theory of speculation and why the tendency has been to speak of the hedger as one kind of trader and the speculator as another. Since the trader has no expectations of absolute price level movements, $E(R)$ and $V(R)$ can be expressed in quantitative terms only along OH. Although we may speak of the direct speculative effect that may exist in a hedge as deviations from L in Figure 3, there is no way to demonstrate under what conditions the trader would alter his positions in the two markets in other than a one-to-one ratio, or under what conditions he would move to a combination in quadrant 1.

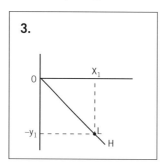

3.

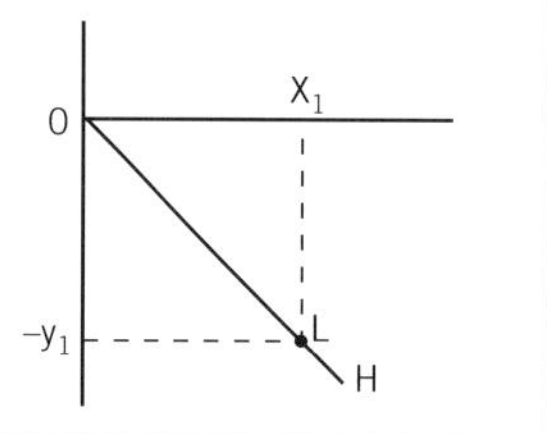

Concluding remarks

In conclusion, the major points of this analysis can be summarised as follows: if a trader has expectations regarding only relative price changes, he necessarily takes a unit-for-unit position in the two markets. However, this hedge may contain a speculative element, depending on his reaction to expected non-zero relative price changes. If he has expectations regarding absolute price changes, his activities can be analysed on a general iso-variance, iso-expected return coordinate systems; however, a hedge can be meaningfully defined only in terms of "given a position in one market", ie, one market must be regarded as his primary market. With this definition of hedging, the pure hedge and the deviations from it generated by expected non-zero price changes can be geometrically analysed. There is no distinction between the hedger and the "ordinary" speculator insofar as both are motivated by a desire to obtain a for-them optimum combination of $E(R)$ and $V(R)$ as determined by their respective utility functions. The only essential distinction between them is that the hedger has a primary market which in this model gives rise to a merchandising profit. A necessary condition for a full hedge to be taken against the position in the primary market is that u_j be equal to 0. The ordinary speculator could also work within the framework of Figure 2. But unless we postulate the primary market condition (conceptually it could be either the spot or futures market) nothing can be said about a hedging element within his combination of market positions.

This model is expressed under quite simple assumptions: only the effects of expected price changes and a fixed rate merchandising profit enter into (net) expected return; all business risk is confined to a price risk. No money budget constraints, imputed interest costs or brokerage commissions are postulated.

Analysis is confined to two narrowly defined markets. If a budget constraint were postulated, the principal effect would be that the trader could be pushed off the locus-of-tangency curve in Figure 2 because of a preference for some other combination along the budget line. For example, letting the budget constraint be represented in quadrant 4 by EF, and considering vertical iso-expected return curves (u_i and u_j both equal to 0) we can see that he might prefer L′ to J.[13]

Several markets, both primary and futures markets, could be included in a multidimensional analysis in which the trader selects an optimum combination on the basis of his indifference map again in terms of E(R) and V(R). In this case the hedge would be defined as "given the combination found in the primary markets, what is the combination in the futures which would minimise overall variance".

Finally, the "marginal convenience yield", a concept which has appeared on occasion in the literature, could be introduced into the model.[14] This yield is a "convenience" return enjoyed by the trader who holds an inventory. The marginal yield is a declining function of the size of inventory held. The effect of its inclusion here would be to make convex to the origin non-vertical iso-expected return lines.

1 *This abstracts from the problem of indivisibility which arises from the fact that a contract covers a fixed quantity of the commodity.*

2 *In a case where he carries a permanent stock he could also carry a "perpetual" hedge by liquidating his contracts prior to delivery and simultaneously selling contracts of a later future to maintain the hedge. This procedure, however, does not alter the basic principles of hedging outlined above.*

3 *See, for example, Samuelson (1958), p. 425.*

4 *Hawtrey (1940), p. 203.*

5 *Keynes (1930), Vol. 2, Chap. 29. This theory has been elaborated by Hicks (1946), pp. 137–9, and has been extensively treated by Kaldor (1939). An interesting recent analysis of the financial results of speculation in commodity futures is contained in Houthakker (1957).*

6 *"Futures Trading and Hedging",* American Economic Review, *1953, 43 (June), p. 325. Italics in the original.*

7 *"Hedging Reconsidered",* Journal of Farm Economics, *1953, 35 (November) pp. 547–49. Italics in the original.*

8 *For a detailed discussion of this point, see my article, "Price Instability, Hedging and Trade Volume in the Coffee Market".*

9 *Telser (1955–56) demonstrates the rationality of holding hedged and unhedged positions simultaneously but operates under the highly restrictive assumption that the trader maximises expected income under the constraint that the probability of the occurrence of a given "disaster" level of income not exceed a given value. Brennan (1958) mentions briefly the simultaneous holding of both hedged and unhedged stocks on the basis of risk above a "critical" level being transferred to speculators via hedging.*

10 *Equations (1), (2) and (3) are based on the general equations involving the actual return, expected return, and variance of return of a linear combination of random variables. Given a number* n *markets in which actual return* B_t *in each is a random variable, total return* R *is a weighted sum of random variables such that* $R = \sum_{i=1}^{n} x_i B_t$ *where each weight is the size of position* x_i *held in each market. The expected return* $E(R)$ *is given by* $E(R) = \sum_i^n x_i u_i$ *and the variance of return* $V(R)$ *is given by* $V(R) = \sum_{i=1}^{n} x_i^2 \sigma_i^2 + \sum_{i=1}^{n} \sum_{j>1}^{n} x_i x_j \, cov_{ij}$.

11 *The value of* x_j^* *is* $(x_i^* \, cov_{ij}/\sigma_i^2)$. *By substitution in equation (4) the value of* x_i, *denoted here by* x_i^* *that minimises the risk of holding* x_j^* *is given by* $(x_i \, cov_{ij}^*/\sigma_i^2\sigma_j^2)$. x_i^* *is equal to* x_i *only if* $(cov_{ij}^*/\sigma_i^2\sigma_j^2)$ *is equal to 1.*

12 *According to equation (3a)* $E(R) = x_i(u_i + m) + x_j u_j$. *Therefore,*

$$x_j = -\frac{x_i(u_i + m) + E(R)}{u_j} \quad \text{and} \quad \left.\partial x_j/\partial x_i\right|_{E(R)} = -\frac{u_i + m}{u_j}.$$

13 *The opportunity line in Figure 1 would be kinked upward at the point corresponding to market combination at* J *in Figure 2, and the upper segment would represent combinations of* $E(R)$, $\sqrt{V(R)}$, *attainable along the constraint segment* JP.

14 *Kaldor (1939) and Brennan (1958).*

BIBLIOGRAPHY

Brennan, M. J., 1958, "Supply of Storage", *American Economic Review* 48.

Hawtrey, R. G., 1940, "Mr. Kaldor on the Forward Market", *Review of Economic Studies* 7 (June).

Hicks, J. R., 1946, *Value and Capital,* 2nd edn (Oxford).

Houthakker, H. S., 1957, "Can Speculators Forecast Prices?" *Review of Economics and Statistics* 39, pp. 143–51.

Johnson, L., 1957, "Price Instability, Hedging and Trade Volume in the Coffee Market", *Journal of Political Economy* 45 (August), pp. 319–21.

Keynes, J. M., 1930, *A Treatise on Money* (London).

Kaldor, N., 1939, "Speculation and Income Stability", *Review of Economic Studies* 7, pp. 1–27.

Samuelson, P. A., 1958, *Economics, An Introductory Analysis,* 4th edn (New York).

Telser, L. G., 1955–6 "Safety First and Hedging", *Review of Economic Studies,* 23, no. 60, pp. 1–16.

2

The Hedging Performance of the New Futures Markets*

Louis H. Ederington

University of Oklahoma

Organised futures markets in financial securities were first established in the US on October 20, 1975 when the Chicago Board of Trade opened a futures market in Government National Mortgage Association 8% pass-through certificates. This was followed in January, 1976, by a 90-day Treasury bill futures market on the International Monetary Market of the Chicago Mercantile Exchange. In terms of trading volume both have been clear commercial successes and this has led to the establishment, in 1977, of futures markets in long-term government bonds and 90-day commercial paper and, in 1978, of a market in one-year Treasury notes and new GNMA markets.

The classic economic rationale for futures markets is, of course, that they facilitate hedging, ie, they allow those who deal in a commodity to transfer the risk of price changes in that commodity to speculators more willing to bear such risks. The primary purpose of this chapter is to evaluate the GNMA and Treasury bill futures markets as instruments for such hedging. Obviously it is possible to hedge by entering into forward contracts outside a futures market, but, as Telser and Higinbotham (1977) point out, an organised futures market facilitates such transactions by providing a standardised contract and by substituting the trustworthiness of the exchange for that of the individual trader.

In the futures market, price change risk can be eliminated entirely by making or taking delivery on futures sold or bought, but few hedges are concluded in this manner.[1] The major problem with making or taking delivery is that there are only four delivery periods per year for financial security futures so it is often impossible to hedge in this manner over the desired time period. Moreover, the desired time period may change or may be uncertain. The most common hedge, therefore, is one in which the seller (buyer) of the futures contract cancels his delivery commitment by buying (selling) a contract of the same future prior to delivery. It is this type of hedge, in which futures positions are liquidated by offsetting trades, that has received the most attention in the hedging literature and is examined in this chapter.

In order to illustrate such a hedge and the potential of the new markets for risk avoidance, let us suppose that on September 16, 1977 a mortgage lending institution committed itself to a future loan at a set interest rate. Suppose, further, it was the lender's intention to finance this loan by issuing or selling US$100,000 of 30-year GNMA pass-through certificates with an 8% coupon rate, which were selling at that time (September 16, 1977) at US$99,531 or an effective yield of 8.02%.[2] Fearing that interest rates would rise and GNMA prices would fall by the time it actually sold its certificates, the mortgagor decided to hedge against this risk by selling December 1977 GNMA futures, which were trading at US$98,219 or an effective yield of 8.20% on September 16.[3] This transaction is summarised in the top half of Table 1.

In this particular case, our firm's fears of an interest rate rise were realised and the hedge was successful. By October 14, 1977, when the firm closed its loan and sold the GNMA certificates, cash market yields had risen 17 basis points to 8.19%. However, futures market yields had also risen 15 basis points to 8.30% so, as shown in Table 1, the futures market gain largely offset the cash market loss. This is a short hedge. If an individual or firm plans to purchase GNMAs, Treasury bills or some other security in the future, it could attempt to

**Originally published in the* Journal of Finance *34(1) (1979), pp. 157–70, reproduced with permission of Blackwell Publishers. The author would like to acknowledge the helpful comments of Bruce Fielitz, Ed Ulveling and Jerome Stein. This research was supported in part by the Bureau of Business and Economic Research of Georgia State University.*

protect against the contingency of a decline in interest rates by buying GNMA or Treasury bill futures, ie, entering a long hedge. In this particular example, the hedge was successful because cash and futures prices both fell, but this may not always be the case.

There is not perfect agreement in the futures market literature as to what hedging is or why it is undertaken. This chapter begins, therefore, with a survey of three major theories of hedging: the traditional theory, the theories of Holbrook Working and the portfolio theory. The portfolio theory, which the author finds superior to the other two, suggests a method for measuring the hedging effectiveness of a futures market and this measure is then used to evaluate the GNMA and Treasury bill futures markets. These financial security futures are compared with each other and with two more established and heavily traded futures markets: corn and wheat. The portfolio theory also provides a method for measuring the costs of hedging and these costs are examined for the two financial security futures. The chapter closes with a summary of the conclusions and some observations on possible future research in futures.

Theories of hedging

TRADITIONAL HEDGING THEORY

While traditional hedging theory predates the work of Working and the application of portfolio theory to hedging, it continues to be important. Indeed, it is the traditional theory underlying almost all the early "How To" articles on hedging that accompanied the establishment of the GNMA and Treasury bill futures markets.[4]

Traditional hedging theory emphasises the risk avoidance potential of futures markets. Hedgers are envisioned as taking futures market positions equal in magnitude but of opposite sign to their position in the cash market, as in the example in Table 1. For instance, holders of an inventory of X units would protect themselves against the loss from a decline in the cash price by selling X futures of the same commodity or security. When the inventory is sold, futures contracts would be purchased cancelling both positions.

If the cash or spot prices at times t_1 and t_2 are P_s^1 and P_s^2, respectively, the gain or loss on an unhedged position, U, of X units is $X[P_s^2 - P_s^1]$, but the gain or loss on a hedged position, H, is $X\{[P_s^2 - P_s^1] - [P_f^2 - P_f^1]\}$ where the f subscript denotes the futures price. Traditional theory argues that spot and futures prices generally move together so that the absolute value of H is less than U or that $\mathrm{Var}(H) < \mathrm{Var}(U)$. This question is often discussed in terms of the change in the cash price versus the change in the "basis", where the basis is defined as the difference between the futures and spot prices so that the change in the basis is $\{(P_f^2 - P_s^2) - (P_f^1 - P_s^1)\}$ or $\{(P_s^2 - P_s^1) - (P_f^2 - P_f^1)\}$. A hedge is viewed as perfect if the change in the basis is zero. It is commonly argued that the basis and changes in the basis are small because of the possibility of making or taking delivery, hence $\mathrm{Var}(H) < \mathrm{Var}(U)$. The question of smallness is, of course, relative. While it is true that delivery possibilities limit changes in the basis, a range for variation obviously remains.

Certainly, the familiar theory of adaptive expectations implies that if futures prices reflect market expectations they should not normally match changes in cash prices. According to the theory of adaptive expectations

$$E_n^2 - E_n^1 = a[P_s^2 - E_2^1] + u$$

Table 1. A possible short hedge based on actual prices

Cash market	Futures market
September 16, 1977 Makes mortgage commitment and makes plan to sell US$100,000 face value of GNMA 8% certificates	Sells one December futures contract at US$98,219
Current price US$99,531	
October 14, 1977 Sells GNMA 8% certificates (US$100,000 face value)	Buys one December futures contract at US$97,156
Current price US$98,281	
Results: Loss from delay on cash market	US$1,250
Gain on futures market	US$1,063
Net loss	US$187

where E_n^2 and E_n^1 represent the cash prices expected to prevail in period n as of periods 2 and 1, respectively, and E_2^1 represents the price which in period 1 had been expected to prevail in period 2. If one assumes that $P_f^2 = E_n^2$ and $P_f^1 = E_n^1$, one obtains

$$P_f^2 - P_f^1 = a[P_s^2 - P_s^1] - a[E_2^1 - P_s^1]$$

If, therefore, no change in spot prices is expected between periods 1 and 2 $(E_2^1 - P_s^1)$ and $a \neq 1$, this theory implies that any change in the spot price will be accompanied by a proportional but unequal movement of the futures price. If, on the other hand, cash prices change in exactly the manner expected $(P_s^2 = E_2^1)$, then certainly there will be no change in futures prices.

While it is clear that the basis changes so that most traditional hedges are not perfect, Working (1953) complained that many writers of the time were conveniently ignoring this fact:

> A major source of mistaken notions of hedging is the conventional practice of illustrating hedging with a hypothetical example in which the price of the future bought or sold as a hedge is supposed to rise or fall by the same amount that the spot price rises or falls. (pp. 320–1)

In perusing articles and pamphlets on hedging in GNMAs and Treasury bills, I have been surprised to note that many continue to follow the same practice almost 25 years later. This includes not only publications of the exchanges and brokerage houses and articles in trade publications, such as *Savings and Loan News* (Smith, 1976) and *The Mortgage Banker* (Jacobs and Kozuch, 1975), but also articles in the *Review of the Federal Reserve Bank of St. Louis* (Stevens, 1976) and the *Federal Home Loan Bank Board Journal* (Sandor, 1975). In these articles, any caveat that cash and futures price changes may not be equal is relegated to a footnote or a discussion of cross-hedging.

WORKING'S HYPOTHESIS

Working (1953, 1962) challenged the view of hedgers as pure risk minimisers and emphasised expected profit maximisation. In his view hedgers functioned much like speculators, but, since they held positions in the cash market as well, they were concerned with relative, not absolute, price changes. Instead of expecting cash and futures prices to move together, he argued that "most hedging is done in expectation of a change in spot-futures price relations". Holders of a long position in the cash market would, according to Working, hedge if the basis was expected to fall and would not hedge if the basis was expected to rise.

PORTFOLIO AND HEDGING THEORY

By viewing hedging as a simple application of basic portfolio theory, Johnson (1960) and Stein (1961) were able to integrate the risk avoidance of traditional theory with Working's expected profits maximisation. Johnson and Stein argued that one buys and sells futures for the same risk-return reasons that one buys any other security. While traditional theory argued that hedgers should always be completely hedged and Working's hypothesis indicated (though he realised such was not always the case) that hedgers would be completely hedged or unhedged, the application of portfolio theory allowed Johnson and Stein to explain why hedgers would hold both hedged and unhedged commodity stocks.

While the portfolio model of hedging may contain nothing that is new to those in the finance field, it is less familiar to analysts of commodity futures markets and has experienced a somewhat slower acceptance in this field. Since we will use this model to evaluate the GNMA and Treasury bill futures as hedging instruments in the next section, let us briefly summarise its important characteristics.

One difference between this and the more familiar portfolio model is that cash and futures market holdings are not viewed as substitutes. Instead, spot market holdings, X_s, are viewed as fixed and the decision is how much of this stock to hedge. Following Johnson and Stein, let us restrict our attention to the case in which the potential hedger holds only one spot market commodity or security. Since spot market holdings are exogenous, any interest payments may also be viewed as predetermined and therefore irrelevant to the hedging decision. Letting U represent once again the return on an unhedged position,

$$E(U) = X_s E[P_s^2 - P_s^1] \tag{1}$$

$$Var(U) = X_s^2 \sigma_s^2 \tag{2}$$

Let R represent the return on a portfolio that includes both spot market holdings, X_s, and futures market holdings,[5] X_f.

$$E(R) = X_s E[P_s^2 - P_s^1] + X_f E[P_f^2 - P_f^1] - K(X_f) \tag{3}$$

$$Var(R) = X_s^2 \sigma_s^2 + X_f^2 \sigma_f^2 + 2X_s X_f \sigma_{sf} \tag{4}$$

where: X_s and X_f represent spot and futures market holdings; $K(X_f)$ are brokerage and other costs of engaging in futures transactions, including the cost of providing margin; and σ_s^2, σ_f^2 and σ_{sf} represent the subjective variances and the covariance of the possible price changes from time 1 to time 2.

Note that the portfolio, whose returns are represented by R, may be a portfolio that is either completely or partially hedged. There is no presumption, as in traditional theory, that $X_f = -X_s$ (in which case $R = H$). Indeed cash and futures market holdings may even have the same sign.

Let $b = -X_f / X_s$ represent the proportion of the spot position that is hedged. Since in a hedge X_s and X_f have opposite signs, b is usually positive.

$$\mathrm{Var}(R) = X_s^2\{\sigma_s^2 + b^2\sigma_f^2 - 2b\sigma_{sf}\} \tag{5}$$

and

$$E(R) = X_s\{E(P_s^2 - P_s^1) - bE(P_f^2 - P_f^1)\} - K(X_s, b)$$

$$= X_s\{(1-b)E(P_s^2 - P_s^1) + bE(P_s^2 - P_s^1) - bE(P_f^2 - P_f^1)\} - K(X_s, b) \tag{6}$$

or, letting $E(\Delta b) = E\{P_f^2 - P_s^2 - (P_f^1 - P_s^1)\}$ represent the expected change in the basis,

$$E(R) = X_s[(1-b)E(S) - bE(\Delta B)] - K(X_s, b) \tag{7}$$

where $E(S) = E(P_s^2 - P_s^1)$ is the expected price change on one unit of the spot commodity.

If the expected change in the basis is zero, then clearly the expected gain or loss is reduced as $b \to 1$. It is also obvious that expected changes in the basis may add to or subtract from the gain or loss which would have been expected on an unhedged portfolio $\{E(U) = X_s E(S)\}$.

Holding X_s constant, let us consider the effect of a change in b, the proportion hedged, on the expected return and variance of the portfolio R.

$$\frac{\partial \mathrm{Var}(R)}{\partial b} = X_s^2\{2b\sigma_f^2 - 2\sigma_{sf}\} \tag{8}$$

1.

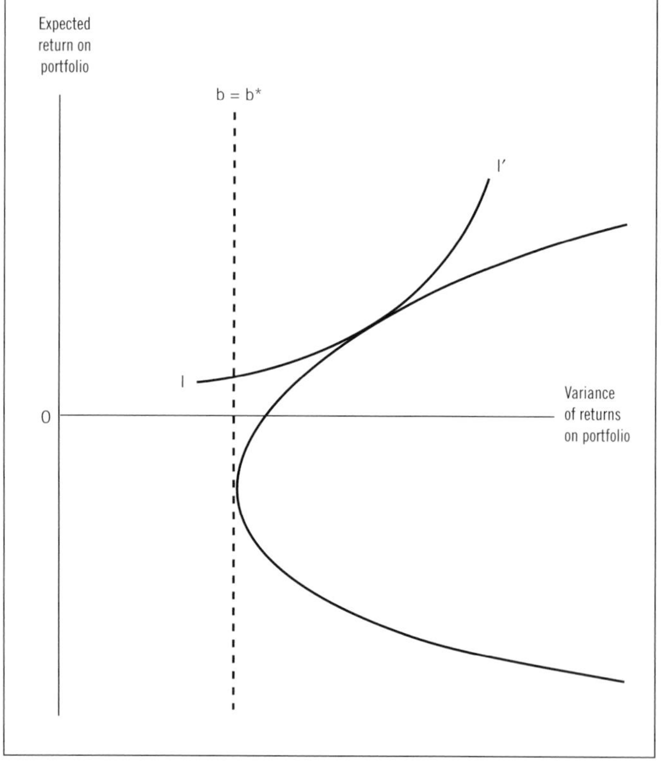

so the risk minimising b, b*, is

$$b^* = \frac{\sigma_{sf}}{\sigma_f^2} \tag{9}$$

$$\frac{\partial E(R)}{\partial b} = -X_s[E(\Delta B) + E(S)] - \frac{\partial K(X_s, b)}{\partial b} \tag{10}$$

Since $E(\Delta B)$ and $E(S)$ may be either positive or negative, the opportunity locus of the possible combinations of E(R) and Var(R), which are shown in Figure 1, may lie in either the first or second quadrant or both. Moreover, as b increases one moves either clockwise or counterclockwise around the locus depending on the sign of equation (10).

In this model there is no riskless asset. Treasury bills, which are usual candidates for a riskless asset, are themselves being hedged. One may wish to liquidate a position in bills prior to maturity, in which case there is a price risk, however small. Consequently, the optimal b, $\hat{b}$, will be that associated with the point on the indifference curve that is just tangent to the highest indifference curve, II′. Not only need $\hat{b}$ not equal one as traditional hedging theory presumed, but $\hat{b}$ may be greater than one, in which case one takes a greater position in the futures than in the cash market, or $\hat{b}$

may be less than zero, in which case one takes the same position (either short or long) in both the spot and futures markets.[5]

Evaluating the GNMA and Treasury bill futures markets

The purpose of this section is to estimate the effectiveness of the new futures markets in reducing the risk associated with a cash position in GNMAs or Treasury bills based on the market experience to date and to estimate the costs of hedging (the impact on expected returns).

While traditional theory indicates that the risk reduction to be achieved by hedging can be measured by comparing the variance of the change in the basis to the variance of the change in the cash price, this presumes that $b = 1$, which, as shown above, may not be the case. Fortunately, portfolio theory also provides a measure of hedging effectiveness. While the risk reduction achieved by any one hedger depends on the chosen b, the futures markets' potential for risk reduction can be measured by comparing the risk on an unhedged portfolio with the minimum risk that can be obtained on a portfolio containing both spot and forward securities. This minimum risk is represented by the left-most point of the opportunity locus in Figure 1 and corresponds to the variance of the return on a portfolio where b equals the b^* defined in equation (9). The measure of hedging effectiveness used in this study is, therefore, the per cent reduction in the variance or

$$e = 1 - \frac{\text{Var}(R^*)}{\text{Var}(U)}$$

where $\text{Var}(R^*)$ denotes the minimum variance on a portfolio containing security futures.

Substituting equation (9) into equation (5) yields

$$\text{Var}(R^*) = X_s^2\left\{\sigma_s^2 + \frac{\sigma_{sf}^2}{\sigma_f^2} - 2\frac{\sigma_{sf}^2}{\sigma_f^2}\right\} = X_s^2\left(\sigma_s^2 - \frac{\sigma_{sf}^2}{\sigma_f^2}\right)$$

Consequently

$$e = \frac{\sigma_{sf}^2}{\sigma_s^2\sigma_f^2} = \rho^2$$

where ρ^2 is the population coefficient of determination between the change in the cash price and the change in the futures price.

In order to judge the market's effectiveness at reducing risk, we estimated e using the sample coefficient of determination, r^2, for hedges of two arbitrary lengths (two and four weeks) and using the sample variances and sample covariance of the two- and four-week price changes over the observed period to estimate b^* as well as σ_s^2, σ_f^2 and σ_{sf}. As noted above, the GNMA and Treasury bill markets were established in October 1975 and January 1976, respectively. Since it seemed prudent to allow the markets to gain some depth before analysing them, weekly data collection for the GNMA market began in January 1976 and for the Treasury bill market in March 1976. Both data sets were continued until the end of December 1977. For comparison purposes we also collected data (January 1976–December 1977) and calculated e for two established and heavily traded futures: corn and wheat.[6]

For Treasury bill cash prices, 90-day Treasury bill prices were consistently used because they were readily available. This ignores the fact that over the hedge period the term to maturity of any Treasury bills held will decline. Actual hedgers would need to adjust their b according to the term of the Treasury bills held and the length of the hedge (Duncan, 1977).

Since a hedger can buy futures with near or distant delivery dates, hedges in futures with a delivery date in three months or less (the nearby contract), in three to six months, in six to nine months and in nine to 12 months were evaluated separately.[7] It could be argued that one's expectations of the near future will be affected more by unexpected changes in the cash price than one's expectation of the more distant futures, and this is supported by some work on adaptive expectations using forward rates from the term structure (Michaelsen, 1973). Consequently, we hypothesise that e will decline as one considers more distant contracts.

In addition, it is hypothesised that e will be greater for four-week than for two-week hedges because absolute changes in cash prices should generally be greater and futures prices would have more time to respond (if there is a lag) over the longer period.

The results for two-week hedges are shown in Table 2 and the results for four-week hedges in Table 3. The most striking result is the marked superiority of the GNMA market to the Treasury bill market particularly for the shorter hedges. While it appears less effective than the wheat market, the GNMA market compares quite favourably with the corn market as a hedging instrument. With the puzzling exception of hedges in the nearby contract for a four-week period, the Treasury bill market appears rather ineffective in reducing exposure to price change risk, particularly over the shorter period. Indeed, if one followed the prescription of traditional theory and set b = 1, the hedged Treasury bill portfolio would have been more risky than the unhedged portfolio in all cases except for four-week hedges in the nearby contract. The author feels that this may be due to the fact that the Treasury bill rate is closely related to the federal funds rate which, given current Federal Reserve operating procedures, is basically controlled by the Fed over short periods. If short-run changes in Treasury bill rates are viewed as induced by monetary authorities, market participants may see no need to adjust their expectations of future rates.

While the author is unaware of any way to statistically test this hypothesis, the results in Tables 1 and 2 are certainly consistent with the hypothesis that e will be larger for the longer hedges. This difference in hedging effectiveness appears particularly pronounced for the financial security futures.

The hypothesis that short-term hedges in nearby contracts are more effective than hedges in more distant contracts appears to hold for all except the GNMA market.

In estimating e we also estimated b*.[8] These estimates, which are also reported in the Tables, are themselves of interest since traditional theory implies that b* = 1. In most cases b* was significantly different from 1 and in general was less than 1. The hypothesis that b* = 1 is therefore rejected.

Since these are *ex-post* estimates of b* and since hedgers may be unable because of the individuality of the futures contract to achieve the desired b, the question of the sensitivity of e to the chosen b is one of some importance. To address this question, we calculated e or r^2 for bs 10% greater and lower than those shown in Tables 1 and 2. For hedges in either GNMAs or Treasury bills, in either the nearby or the next closest contract, and over either a two- or four-week period, raising or lowering b 10% from the estimated b* resulted in a reduction in e of approximately 1%. We conclude, therefore, that these results are not very sensitive to small deviations in b.

While real cross-hedging was not considered, the effectiveness of the GNMA futures market in hedging positions in $6\frac{1}{2}$% and 9% certificates was examined. As mentioned earlier, one can deliver these certificates to satisfy a futures contract, and an earlier study (Ederington and Plumly, 1976) indicated that, at least in 1976, it would have been cheaper to deliver 9% certificates than 8% certificates and more expensive to deliver $6\frac{1}{2}$% certificates. For this reason we expected e to be higher for 9% than for either 8% or $6\frac{1}{2}$% certificates. This proved to be the case for all two-week hedges. Indeed, for all futures contracts e was highest for a hedge against 9% certificates, lower for 8% certificates and lowest for $6\frac{1}{2}$% certificates. For hedges in the nearby contract over a two-week period, for instance, the measures of e were 0.820, 0.664 and 0.662, respectively.

Table 2. Two-week hedges

The futures contract	Estimated e	Estimated b*
8% GNMAs (46 observations)		
The nearby contract	0.664	0.801*
Three- to six-month contract	0.675	0.832
Six- to nine-month contract	0.677	0.854
Nine- to 12-month contract	0.661	0.852
90-day Treasury bills (41 observations)		
The nearby contract	0.272	0.307*
Three- to six-month contract	0.256	0.237*
Six- to nine-month contract	0.178	0.143*
Nine- to 12-month contract	0.140	0.116
Wheat (45 observations)		
The nearby contract	0.898	0.864*
Two- to six-month contract	0.889	0.815*
Four- to eight-month contract	0.868	0.784*
Six- to 10-month contract	0.841	0.778*
Corn (45 observations)		
The nearby contract	0.649	0.915
Two- to six-month contract	0.605	0.905
Four- to eight-month contract	0.541	0.868
Six- to 10-month contract	0.450	0.764

* Significantly different from 1 at 0.05 level.

Table 3. Four-week hedges

The futures contract	Estimated e	Estimated b*
8% GNMAs (23 observations)		
The nearby contract	0.785	0.848
Three- to six-month contract	0.817	0.993
Six- to nine-month contract	0.799	1.019
Nine- to 12-month contract	0.780	1.035
90-day Treasury bills (21 observations)		
The nearby contract	0.741	0.651*
Three- to six-month contract	0.571	0.427*
Six- to nine-month contract	0.406	0.242*
Nine- to 12-month contract	0.369	0.228*
Wheat (21 observations)		
The nearby contract	0.918	0.917
Two- to six-month contract	0.921	0.862*
Four- to eight-month contract	0.909	0.840*
Six- to 10-month contract	0.887	0.843*
Corn (21 observations)		
The nearby contract	0.725	1.021
Two- to six-month contract	0.666	1.011
Four- to eight-month contract	0.608	0.969
Six- to 10-month contract	0.560	0.887

* Significantly different from 1 at 0.05 level.

Table 4. Average change in the basis over four-week periods: January 1976 (March for Treasury bills) to December 1977

	Average change in the basis as a percentage of the cash price	
Futures contract	GNMA certificates	Treasury bills
The nearby contract	0.271	0.184
Three- to six-month contract	0.162	0.220
Six- to nine-month contract	0.133	0.161
Nine- to 12-month contract	0.098	0.164

Having found that, at least for GNMAs, one can lower the risk (as measured by the variance) associated with holding securities by holding futures, attention is now turned to the impact of hedging on expected returns. Two points are clear from equation (7). Firstly, expected returns are lowered by the amount of the brokerage and other costs associated with the futures. Secondly, if the expected change in the basis is zero and $0 < b < 1$, partial hedging reduces the gain or loss associated with an unhedged position $\{X_s E(S)\}$. Attention is therefore centred on the term, $E(\Delta B)$. The important question is whether over the long run $E(\Delta B)$ will tend to be consistently negative or positive, ie, whether the expected value of the expected change in the basis is positive or negative. Since the basis must be approximately zero at the delivery date,[9] $E(\Delta B)$ will generally be positive if the current cash price exceeds the current futures price and will generally be negative if the futures price exceeds the cash price.

The longer the hedge and the closer the delivery date, the closer this relationship between $E(\Delta B)$ and the initial basis should be. The question basically reduces, therefore, to whether there is any reason to anticipate that in the long run futures prices will generally be above or below cash prices.

Over the observed period, cash prices on GNMAs and Treasury bills consistently exceeded futures prices (except occasionally at delivery). To provide an idea of what changes in the basis might have been expected during this period, the average change in the basis as a percentage of the cash price (for comparison) was calculated for four-week hedge periods.[10] The results are shown in Table 4.[11] As expected, the average change in the basis was positive so that over this period the change in the basis tended to add to (subtract from) the expected returns of those taking a long (short) position in the futures market.[12] In addition, it is interesting to note that for GNMAs the average change in the basis tended to vary inversely with the length of the futures contract. Since the risk reduction was approximately the same for all four contracts, this suggests that long (short) hedgers would have been well advised to hedge in the nearby (distant) contract.

While over the observed period cash prices on GNMAs and Treasury bills consistently exceeded futures prices so that positive changes in the basis could generally be expected, this was not always the case in 1978 and may not be the case in the future. The author is much more reluctant to accept Table 4 as a guide to the future than Tables 2 and 3. The crucial question is whether futures prices are unbiased measures of market expectations of future spot rates or whether they are biased downward by "normal backwardation". There are not enough data to answer this question since the lower futures prices to date could simply reflect consistent expectations of rising interest rates.

There continues to be a theoretical and empirical debate over "normal backwardation", the Keynes–Hick argument from which the liquidity premium theory of the term structure was developed.[13] However, it is questionable whether evidence from other futures markets is applicable to GNMA and Treasury bill markets. Hicks's argument (Hicks, 1946, pp. 136–9) was that most hedgers of agricultural commodities maintain a long position in the cash and a short position in the futures market, so that there is a weakness on the demand side of the futures market which speculators will not step in and absorb until the futures price is sufficiently low for the expected favourable price change to compensate for the risk. Since it is an open question whether hedgers in GNMAs and Treasury bills are generally long or short, the existence and sign of any liquidity premium in these markets is less certain.

For the Treasury bill market there is an additional consideration. Since one can satisfy the delivery commitment by delivering longer Treasury bills on which all but three months have elapsed, the possibility of riskless arbitrage should theoretically keep the futures rates close to the forward rates implicit in the term structure.[14] If, therefore, there are liquidity premiums in the term structure, they should be reflected in the futures market. While there is still debate on this point, the bulk of recent evidence indicates that the term structure does contain liquidity premiums (Fama, 1976 and Holland, 1965). For Treasury bills, therefore, it may be that futures prices normally tend to be below cash prices so that $E(\Delta B)$ is generally positive.

Conclusions and observations

The conclusions of this study may be summarised as follows:

- ❑ The decision to hedge a cash or forward market position in the futures market is no different from any other investment decision – investors hedge to obtain the best combination of risk and return. Basic portfolio theory, which best explains when and how much holders of financial portfolios will wish to hedge, encompasses both the traditional hedging theory and Working's theory as special cases.
- ❑ The implication of many "How To" articles in the popular financial press that hedges in GNMAs and Treasury bills are perfect because cash and futures prices change by equal amounts is completely indefensible.
- ❑ Contrary to traditional hedging theory (but consistent with the theory of adaptive expectations), our empirical results indicate that even pure risk minimisers may wish to hedge only a portion of their portfolios. In most cases the estimated b^* was less than one.
- ❑ Based on the experience to date, the GNMA futures market appears to be a more effective instrument for risk avoidance than the Treasury bill market, particularly for short-term (ie, two-week) hedges.
- ❑ Both the GNMA and the Treasury bill market appear to be more effective in reducing the price-change risk over long (four-week) than over short (two-week) periods.
- ❑ While changes in the basis were generally positive over the observed period (adding to the return on long hedges and subtracting from that on short hedges), the financial futures markets have not been in existence long enough to tell whether this is the usual case because of "normal backwardation" or whether it merely reflects expectations during the observed period.

A number of unanswered questions and topics for future research regarding futures markets in financial securities obviously remain. One which the author regards as particularly important is the effectiveness of the new futures markets for cross-hedging, ie, for reducing the risk of portfolios containing securities other than GNMAs or Treasury bills. Since mortgage lenders must often commit themselves months before the funds are lent, the effectiveness of the GNMA future in hedging against changes in conventional mortgage rates (or in the cost of funds) seems to be an important unanswered question. However, our results are appropriate if the lender plans to finance the mortgages by issuing GNMA pass-through certificates as in Table 1. Unfortunately, the only data series for local mortgage rates of which the author is aware – the Federal Home Loan Bank Board series – measures the rate on loans made and these loans may reflect commitments made months ago. What are needed are localised data on new commitments.

1 *It should perhaps be noted that in the GNMA market there would, however, be some uncertainty regarding the amount one would need to hold to make delivery. The futures contract is for US\$100,000 of GNMA 8% pass-through certificates. Since prepayment on these certificates might occur prior to delivery, there is some uncertainty regarding the quantity one would need to hold at present in order to deliver US\$100,000 of certificates. This is mitigated by the fact that one can deliver certificates of between US\$97,500 and US\$102,500 face value with the deficiency or excess to be settled in cash, but some uncertainty remains. In addition, the person who accepts delivery of GNMA futures faces uncertainty regarding the type and relative market value of the certificates to be received. While trading is in 8% certificates, certificates of any mortgage rate can be delivered as long as the quantity delivered is equivalent to US\$100,000 of 8% certificates assuming a thirty-year certificate with total prepayment at the end of 12 years. Since the market doesn't always accept such arbitrary prepayment assumptions, it may be cheaper to deliver 6.5% or 9% or some other certificates. Indeed, it has generally been cheaper to deliver 9% certificates (Ederington and Plumly, 1976). Consequently, those accepting delivery may not receive US\$100,000 of 8% certificates or their market equivalent. This also means that at delivery the futures price for GNMAs will generally remain somewhat below the cash price.*

It should also be noted that over the observed period, January 1976 to July 1977, futures prices were below cash prices except for a few occasions within a few weeks of delivery. Purchasers of GNMA or Treasury bill futures could therefore lock in a lower price as well as a certain price but sellers of futures would have to be willing to lock in a loss. On GNMAs, for example, the futures price averaged 1.9% below the cash price two months before delivery over the observed period and ranged from 1.1% below the cash price to 2.5% below.

2 *GNMA yields are calculated on the assumption of a prepayment after 12 years. The published market yields also take into account, as the face yields do not, that there is an interest-free delay of 15 days in payments of principal and interest.*

3 *Note that if the firm were to wait until December and make delivery, it would lock in exactly this price and yield but if it closes the hedge prior to delivery the price and yield are still somewhat uncertain.*

At the present time there are no good data on what sort of firms are hedging in the market so this example is hypothetical. In addition, there are regulatory constraints on the participation of banks and S & Ls (See Ederington and Plumly, 1976).

4 *Examples are the Chicago Board of Trade's "Hedging in GNMA Interest Rate Futures" (1975) and articles by Smith (1976), Jacobs and Kozuch (1975), Sandor (1975), Stevens (1976) and Duncan (1977).*

5 *Since one would normally assume that* $\sigma_{sf} > 0$, $b^* > 0$ *but since* b *may be either increasing or decreasing as one moves counterclockwise around the opportunity locus, the portion of the locus above* b^* *may represent either* $b < b^*$ *or* $b < b^*$.

6 *The futures prices were weekly closing prices as reported in the* Wall Street Journal. *For the spot price of wheat, we used the price of No. 2 Kansas City hard and for corn we used the price of No. 2 Chicago yellow as reported in the* Journal.

7 *Two- or four-week periods in which the nearby contract expired were dropped from the sample. During the harvest season, futures contracts are available for every other month for corn and wheat, so the time periods for these differ somewhat from those for GNMAs and Treasury bills.*

8 *Let us note again that hedgers in Treasury bills must adjust these estimates of* b^* *to reflect the term to maturity and the hedging period of their own portfolio.*

9 *If it is cheaper to deliver GNMA certificates with a mortgage rate other than 8%, the basis for GNMAs will not be eliminated completely. A negative basis remains depending on the difference in costs.*

10 *The average change for four weeks is not exactly double the change for two weeks because the periods do not completely overlap since periods in which the nearby contract matured were eliminated.*

11 *The author does not feel that corn and wheat provide a meaningful comparison in this case because the basis on these varies with the time till harvest and storage costs.*

12 *Note that when the basis is negative, those who take a long position in the futures market and take delivery lock in the lower buying price and higher interest rate. Those who are short and make delivery lock in a selling price which is below the current selling price.*

13 *See Peck (1977), Burger, Lang and Rasche (1977), Fama (1976) and Cornell (1977).*

14 *While this should theoretically be the case, surprisingly large differences between future and forward rates have been observed (Branch, 1978).*

BIBLIOGRAPHY

Bacon, P. W., and R. E. Williams, 1976, "Interest Rate Futures: New Tool for the Financial Manager", *Financial Management*, pp. 32–8.

Branch, B., 1978, "Testing the Unbiased Expectations Theory of Interest Rates", paper presented at annual meeting of the Eastern Finance Association.

Burger, A. E., R. W. Lang and R. H. Rasche, 1977, "The Treasury Bill Futures Market and Market Expectations of Interest Rates", *Review of the Federal Reserve Bank of St. Louis* 59(6), pp. 2–11.

Cornell, Bradford, 1977, "Spot Rates, Forward Rates and Exchange Market Efficiency", *Journal of Financial Economics*, pp. 55–60.

Duncan, W. H., 1977, "Treasury Bill Futures – Opportunities and Pitfalls", *Review of the Federal Reserve Bank of Dallas*.

Ederington, L. E., and W. E. Plumly, 1976, "The New Futures Market in Financial Securities", *Futures Trading Seminar Proceedings* IV, Chicago Board of Trade.

Fama, E. F., 1976, "Forward Rates as Predictors of Future Spot Rates", *Journal of Financial Economics*, pp. 361–78.

Hicks, J. R., 1946, *Value and Capital*, 2nd edn (London: Oxford University Press).

Holland, T. E., 1965, "A Note on the Traditional Theory of the Term Structure of Interest Rates on Three- and Six-Month Treasury Bills", *International Economic Review*, pp. 330–6.

Jacobs, S. F., and J. R. Kozuch, 1975, "Is there a Future for a Mortgage Futures Market?", *The Mortgage Banker*.

Johnson, L. L., 1960, "The Theory of Hedging and Speculation in Commodity Futures", *Review of Economic Studies* 27(3), pp. 139–51.

Michaelsen, J. B., 1973, *The Term Structure of Interest Rates* (New York: Interest Educational Publishers).

McCulloch, J. H., 1975, "An Estimate of the Liquidity Premium", *Journal of Political Economy*, pp. 95–119.

Peck, A. E., 1977, *Selected Writings on Futures Markets* II (Chicago: Board of Trade of the City of Chicago).

Sandor, R. L., 1975, "Trading Mortgage Interest Rate Futures", *Federal Home Loan Bank Board Journal*, pp. 2–9.

Smith, B., 1976, "Trading Complexities, FHLBB Rules Impede Association Activity", *Savings and Loan News*.

Stein, J. L., 1961, "The Simultaneous Determination of Spot and Futures Prices", *American Economic Review* LI(5).

Stevens, N. A., 1976, "Mortgage Futures Market: Its Development, Uses, Benefits and Cost", *Review of the Federal Reserve Bank of St. Louis*.

Telser, L. G., and H. N. Higinbotham, 1977, "Organized Futures Markets: Costs and Benefits", *Journal of Political Economy* 85, pp. 969–1,000.

Working, H., 1953, "Futures Trading and Hedging", *American Economic Review*, pp. 314–43; reprinted as Chapter 3 of the present volume.

Working, H., 1962, "New Concepts Concerning Futures Markets and Prices", *American Economic Review*, pp. 431–59.

3

Futures Trading and Hedging*

Holbrook Working†

A good deal of difference of opinion on the utility of futures trading persists even among economists who have studied the subject rather closely. Some, at least, of this disagreement is traceable to imperfect concepts that emerged in connection with early academic studies of futures trading. Such concepts have tended to survive on the strength of their partial validity, despite shortcomings evident to the well-informed. Businessmen and others who are intimately acquainted with futures trading and its consequences tend to realise (often unconsciously) the defects of such imperfect concepts, to employ the concepts so far as they are valid and useful, and to avoid drawing any seriously mistaken conclusions from them. People who have little direct knowledge of futures trading and its observable results have no such protection against false inferences. If, like most economists, they are accustomed to rely on deductions from what seem to be well-established premises, they are especially vulnerable to the imperfections of basic concepts.

Origin and nature of futures trading

Much of the popular suspicion of futures trading stems from a sense of mystery associated with it. It is in this respect, and some others, rather like bank credit. Futures trading, like banking, is an institution that developed as a contribution to efficiency of a relatively free competitive economy. A primitive form of futures trading emerged spontaneously in various market centres at least as early as 1850. Only in the grain trade at Chicago, however, was the demand for a means of hedging commercial risks then strong and persistent enough to permit this unconventional form of trade to survive the fluctuations in speculative interest, overcome conservative opposition, and live through the stormy period of experimentation necessary to put it on a firm footing. When that had been accomplished at Chicago, the new form of trading was soon adopted at other market centres and for other commodities than grains.[1]

Futures trading in commodities may be defined as *trading conducted under special regulations and conventions, more restrictive than those applied to any other class of commodity transactions, which serve primarily to facilitate hedging and speculation by promoting exceptional convenience and economy of the transactions.*

This may seem to some an inadequate definition. It does not say that futures trading is buying and selling for deferred delivery; it draws only a slender line of distinction between futures transactions and "cash" transactions (dealings in the "actual commodity"); and it makes the distinction between futures trading and other sorts of trading turn primarily on *purpose* rather than on more easily and objectively recognisable criteria. All of these characteristics are in fact merits of the definition.

It would be inaccurate to define futures trading as always involving purchase and sale for deferred delivery. Trading in the September wheat future, for example, is done in the month of September as well as in earlier months, and in that month it often happens that some sellers of September wheat intend to make immediate delivery, and the purchaser knows that he may expect to receive immediate delivery. The price of the future is then in fact a

Originally published in the American Economic Review *(June 1953); reproduced with permission of the American Economic Association. The paper was prepared under a research grant from the Merrill Foundation for Advancement of Financial Knowledge.*
†*Holbrook Working, 1895–1985.*

spot price. One might, of course, qualify the statement by saying that *most* futures trading is for deferred delivery. The statement would then be true, but objectionable in a definition because it would focus attention on a characteristic (deferred delivery) that has little distinguishing value. A great deal of buying and selling that is *not* futures trading involves delivery at some later time. In international commodity trade in staples, purchases calling for delivery two or three months or more in the future are commonplace, quite apart from true futures trading, and independently of whether or not futures trading exists in the commodity. Much of the trade in manufactured products as diverse as flour, steel rails, and machine tools (none of which has futures trading) involves purchase on contracts entered into several months in advance of the specified delivery date; in the case of machine tools, the interval may sometimes be measured in years. Because the people who turn for enlightenment to a definition of futures trading are often unaware of the wide prevalence of forward purchases (except in retail trade), the characterisation "usually for deferred delivery" would fail to be generally recognised as only slightly narrowing the area of reference, and would divert attention from more sharply distinguishing characteristics.

The definition given above does in fact distinguish clearly between futures transactions and other transactions – so clearly that there need never be any problem of identification except in such cases as appeared when futures trading was taking its first steps in evolution from other trading and was not yet clearly differentiated. The definition lacks sharpness only in the sense that it does not make futures trading appear very different from other trading. That is a merit, because futures trading in fact has no distinguishing economic characteristics except those stated in the definition, or resulting from them (such as exceptional volume of trading, frequency of transactions, and publicity of quotations).

If a reader feels that the foregoing definition does not distinguish strongly enough between futures trading and other trading in commodities, it may be either because he underestimates the remarkable convenience and economy which are the primary distinguishing characteristics of futures trading, or because he mistakenly believes it to have peculiar characteristics that it does not have. Its extraordinary economy is illustrated by data cited below, in another connection, indicating that a trader in cotton futures could make a very satisfactory net income on the basis of a *gross* profit margin of about 23 cents per thousand dollars worth of transactions – a gross profit of one-fortieth of one per cent.

Mistaken impressions of the difference between futures trading and other trading have been furthered by a language difficulty that arises in connection with the frequent need to speak collectively of all-other-sorts of trading, as against futures trading. There is no good and convenient word for the purpose – and perhaps there cannot be, simply because the need is to designate all of a heterogeneous category except one special, narrow segment of it. "Non-futures" would be an accurate and transparent term for the purpose, but an awkward one. In this situation, convenience has been served most commonly by using the word "cash" to mean "non-futures". The practice probably originated in the Chicago grain trade, contemporaneously with the origin of sustained futures trading. Its application involved two shifts of meaning: (1) use of "cash" to designate, not immediate *payment*, as is usual, but immediate *delivery*; and (2) extension of the altered meaning to cover all terms of delivery except those involved in futures contracts. These changes left the word with no logical merit for the purpose except its brevity. In the cotton trade, the common word for "non-futures" is "spot". This is inherently more confusing than use of the term "cash", because "spot" continues to be used in the trade also in its specific sense of "immediate delivery"; but the grain trade has lost such potential relative advantage of clarity as it might have had, by using "cash" also as equivalent to "spot" in the sense of "immediate delivery".[2] Most seriously misleading is the frequent resort to use of "actual" to mean "non-futures", as when purchases on terms other than those of futures contracts are distinguished as purchases of the "actual commodity". That expression is used to *include* forward purchases other than on futures contracts, even though all forward purchases are alike in the fact that there is no acquisition of the actual commodity at the time of purchase.[3] Like the other expressions used for the same purpose, it is a verbal expedient only vaguely defensible in terms of the normal meaning of the expression. Futures contracts involve transactions in the actual commodity as truly as do any other forward transactions.

As regards failure of the definition to give easily and objectively recognisable criteria for identifying futures trading, it should be noted that there is no practical problem of identification except in cases of primitive futures trading, and in such cases purpose is the only available criterion;[4] otherwise, futures trading has always gone under that name, or the equivalent in another language. The definition should indicate the essential distinguishing nature of futures trading, and that is not done by mere listing of superficial technical characteristics, specified in regulations intended to promote convenience and economy. Reliance on these superficial characteristics for definition encounters also the difficulty that they have varied widely from time to time and from place to place. Consequently, definitions based on such characteristics show a historical trend toward increasing complexity and obscurity as later writers tried to remedy technical shortcomings found in earlier definitions.[5]

Hedging as a basis for futures trading

An interesting conflict of evidence has emerged regarding the comparative roles of speculation and hedging in sustaining futures trading. Most of the available information prior to about 1920 encourages the view that futures trading rests primarily on an urge for speculation. Hedging is rarely mentioned except in arguments justifying the continuation of futures trading. One gains the impression that hedging, like a hitchhiker, seized the chance for a ride since speculation presented the opportunity. But as statistics have been accumulated that give appropriate quantitative information on futures markets, year in and year out, hedging begins to look like the driver, and speculation in futures like a companion going where hedging gives it opportunity to go.

The first conspicuous evidence in this direction came in studies of the Grain Futures Administration (predecessor of the present Commodity Exchange Authority) that showed the volume of open (outstanding) futures contracts in each commodity rising and falling each year in rough correspondence with the volume of the commodity in commercial hands and likely to be hedged.[6] Speculators tend to be most heavily committed in futures, not during the growing season of a crop, when prices are most variable, but some time after harvest, when large stocks have moved into commercial storage and been hedged.

As between commodities, the volume of open contracts varies likewise with the amount of the commodity that is hedged. The volume of open contracts in wheat futures in the US during recent years has averaged about 90 million bushels, while the volume in corn futures has averaged not much over 50 million, though corn has been produced in nearly three times the volume of wheat. The reason is that much less corn than wheat gets into commercial hands (farmers rarely or never hedge the stocks that they hold). Oats, produced in volume less than half that of corn and, like corn, stored mainly on farms, has had an average volume of open futures contracts less than half that of corn.[7] So one may go through the list of commodities in which there is futures trading and find, wherever there is information on the amount of hedging use of futures markets, an unmistakable connection between size of the futures market and the amount of hedging that the market is called on to carry.[8]

Though the amount of speculation on a futures market seems to depend so much on the volume of hedging, there is also a connection in the other direction. As between different exchanges dealing in the same commodity, there is a strong tendency for hedgers to prefer to use the exchange that has the largest volume of speculative trading. We shall examine the reason for this later. As regards commodities, it may be observed that in some the volume of hedging has, at times at least, been restricted by absence of sufficient speculative interest to carry the hedges.[9] In the US, no futures market for a commodity which is chiefly imported has flourished like the markets for the more important domestically produced commodities. This may be not entirely because the imported commodities give less occasion for hedging, but partly because there are relatively few people in the US who have acquired an interest in those commodities sufficient to inspire speculation in them.

When one reviews evidence on the earlier history of futures trading, making allowance for the tendency for sporadic news and comment to concentrate on the unusual, and for exceptional outbursts of speculation to draw special attention, one can find reason to think that a desire for hedging opportunities may have always provided the primary support for futures trading. It seems reasonable to suppose that a primitive form of futures trading in grains was able to survive and develop to maturity in Chicago in the middle of the last century, whereas similar trading tried somewhat earlier in Europe was abandoned, because there was much more occasion for hedging the large stocks of grain that came into commercial hands in the Chicago area than for hedging the much smaller stocks of European markets. It seems quite clear that the first successful futures trading in wheat in the UK was based on contracts for Californian wheat because that was the wheat which importers found most need to hedge, on account of the long periods over which importers held ownership while the wheat travelled by sailing vessel around Cape Horn to Britain.[10]

One can imagine existence of futures trading purely on the basis of desire of people to speculate; but apparently futures trading cannot long persist except on the basis of conditions that create speculative risks which somebody must carry, and which some people are led to transfer to others by hedging. The reasons for choosing thus to transfer risks deserve our attention next.

Misapprehensions about hedging

It is common to suppose that hedgers exercise no part in determining the price of the commodity in which they deal, and this supposition is substantially valid as regards those who practise hedging uniformly.[11] But most hedgers are engaged in a business that requires them to keep informed on many aspects of the commodity situation, with the result that many hedgers often form quite definite opinions on price prospects. Except in firms that have a strict rule against taking hedgeable risks, it is common, therefore, for stocks to be carried unhedged at times, when the responsible individual expects a price advance, and for stocks of the commodity to be hedged at other times. Some individuals and firms hedge stocks only when they are particularly fearful of price decline.

Such discretionary hedging, involving a firm in the practice of both hedging and speculation, seems to be especially prevalent among dealers and processors who handle commodities such as wool and coffee, which have relatively little public speculation in their futures markets.[12] When hedge selling in such a futures market becomes heavy, the price may readily be depressed to a point where a good many dealers and processors are attracted by the possibilities of profit through speculative holding of the commodity. Even among handlers of commodities that attract broad public participation to their futures markets, such as wheat, discretionary hedging is not uncommon.[13] Consequently, the existence of futures trading in a commodity and widespread use of futures for hedging do not in fact mean that the responsibilities of price formation are shifted entirely, or even mainly, to people who deal only in the commodity futures.

A major source of mistaken notions of hedging is the conventional practice of illustrating hedging with a hypothetical example in which the price of the future bought or sold as a hedge is supposed to rise or fall by the same amount that the spot price rises or falls. Let us instead consider hedging realistically in terms of some actual prices. The prices to be used will be those for wheat at Kansas City on the first trading day of each month in which futures matured during the crop-year 1951–52.[14]

On the first business day of July 1951, a merchant or processor[15] considering the purchase of the cheapest quality No. 2 Hard Winter wheat (the quality represented by quotations on Kansas City wheat futures) found such spot wheat selling at three cents per bushel under the price of the September future. If he bought spot wheat, hedged it in the September future, and carried the wheat until the first business day of September, the results, in cents per bushel, would have been as shown in Table 1.

The profit of two cents per bushel in Table 1 is calculated, in what may seem an awkward way, from the change in spot premium (a negative premium, or discount, on each of these dates). It is awkward, however, only for those to whom it is unfamiliar. The hedger tends to calculate his profits in this way because he would buy the wheat on July 2 primarily for the reason that he could get it at discount of three cents per bushel under the price of the September future. In fact, the bargaining which preceded the purchase would normally proceed in terms of discount rather than of price, the price being ascertained by reference to the latest futures price quotation, after sale at a mutually satisfactory discount had been agreed on.[16]

Table 1

Quotation	Date and price: July 2	Date and price: September 4	Gain or loss
Spot No. 2 hard (low)	229¼	232½	...
September future	232¼	233½	...
Spot premium	–3	–1	+2 (gain)

Table 2

Quotation	Date and price: September 4	Date and price: December 1	Gain or loss
Spot No. 2 hard (low)	232½	252	...
December future	238¼	252	...
Spot premium	–5¾	0	+5¾ (gain)

The fact that on September 4 No. 2 Hard Winter wheat sold at a discount under the September future, though it is the grade of wheat currently deliverable on the future, is accounted for the by the fact that the spot price applies to wheat "on track", requiring additional expenditure to get it into a warehouse.[17] Wheat was then moving into commercial storage on a large scale because of heavy marketing by producers.

On September 4 our grain merchant or processor would probably not have sold the wheat he bought earlier but instead would have bought more wheat. If he did that, and held until December 1, the results, in cents per bushel, would have appeared as shown in Table 2.

In this case the spot price of the cheapest deliverable wheat came, on December 1, to exact equality with the price of the December future, and the gross return for storing the wheat was exactly what might have been expected, on September 4, from the fact that such wheat was then selling at a discount of $5\frac{3}{4}$ cents under the price of the December future.

In these calculations we have left out of account the possibility that a merchant who bought at a discount of $5\frac{3}{4}$ cents on September 4 might have got wheat of a little better than minimum No. 2 quality - wheat which might have been sold on September 4 at a discount of say, $5\frac{1}{2}$ cents, rather than $5\frac{3}{4}$ cents, if the seller had been willing to look farther for a buyer. And we have ignored the possibility that on December 1 the merchant might have sold at a premium of $\frac{1}{2}$ cent over the December future by virtue of the slightly superior quality of the wheat, and by finding a buyer who did not choose to shop around enough to get the best bargain possible. In other words, we have left out of account sources of normal *merchandising* profits.

On December 1 a merchant or processor may seem to have had no incentive for longer holding of wheat for which he had no immediate need. The spot price then was on a par with the December future, and at a premium of one cent over the price of the May future. But let us suppose that he continued to hold, with a hedge in the May future, and see what would have happened if he held until May 1. Though we imagine that the wheat is already in storage, we may make the next calculation as though it concerned a new purchase (see Table 3).

This time a merchant would have gained a gross return of eight cents per bushel from storage. It would have been in part a windfall profit, since he had no advance *assurance* of obtaining it; but he would have gained it on a quite conservative venture. He was well assured of not losing more than one cent per bushel (because the spot wheat that he held would surely sell at as high a price as the May future at some time in May), and he could count with virtual certainty on spot wheat going to a substantial premium over the price of the May future at some time between December and May.[18]

As of May 1 there remained no prospect of profit from continued storage of wheat during that crop-year, unless perhaps for a few days more. Before the end of the month, the spot premium, based on the May future, would have to fall from nine cents to near zero.[19] Moreover, the spot price on May 1 was at a premium of 18 cents over the July future, and that premium should be expected to fall to zero or below by July 1. The outcome, if a merchant in fact held any wheat in storage from May 1 to July 1, was as shown in Table 4.

Probably some merchants did store a little wheat from May 1 to July 1, hedged in the July future, and did take the loss per bushel indicated by the calculation in Table 4. Grain merchants, like operators of retail stores, must try to keep adequate stocks on their shelves to serve their customers. But a merchant who hedged would have seen clearly on May 1 that any wheat that he might continue to hold until July would involve a loss, as surely, though not so completely, as would Christmas trees held until December 26.

The foregoing examples of hedging tend in one respect to be a little misleading: spot premiums do not always follow so obviously logical a pattern through the course of a crop year as they did in 1951-52. If spot wheat in July were regularly, in all years, at a moderate discount under the September future, and if spot wheat in September were always at a large discount under the December future, and spot wheat in May always at a large premium over the July future, merchants and processors would have less need than they do for futures markets.[20] They would then have no need to watch spot-future price relations in order to judge when to accumulate stocks, and when

Table 3

Quotation	Date and price: December 1	Date and price: May 1	Gain or loss
Spot No. 2 hard (low)	252	$247\frac{1}{4}$	...
May future	261	$238\frac{1}{4}$	...
Spot premium	+1	+9	+8 (gain)

Table 4

Quotation	Date and price: May 1	Date and price: July 1	Gain or loss
Spot No. 2 hard (low)	$247\frac{1}{4}$	$218\frac{1}{2}$	...
July future	$229\frac{1}{4}$	225	...
Spot premium	+18	$-6\frac{1}{2}$	$-24\frac{1}{2}$ (loss)

to draw them low. But our purpose at the moment is merely to see how hedgers use spot-futures price relations as a guide in inventory control, thereby earning a return for holding stocks that must be stored by someone. We may reasonably avoid being led here into discussion of the frequent effects on spot premiums produced by exceptional export demand, by governmental price supports, or by unusual holding disposition on the part of producers.

We should now note three facts concerning hedging. First, contrary to a common impression, hedging of the sort here considered is not properly comparable with insurance. It is a sort of arbitrage. We shall consider later an example of conditions under which hedging may in fact be profitably compared with insurance, but such conditions obtain for only a small proportion of the hedging that is done on futures markets. Most hedging is done in the expectation of a change in spot-future price relations, the change that is reasonably to be expected being often indicated quite clearly by the current spot-future price relation.

Secondly, hedging does not eliminate risks arising from price variability. Risk is less than on stocks held unhedged, but it still exists. When the commodity involved is of quite different quality than that represented by the future, or in a location remote from that to which the futures price relates, the risks assumed by hedgers tend to be much larger than is suggested by the examples given here.

And thirdly, hedging is not necessarily done for the sake of reducing risks. The role of risk-avoidance in most commercial hedging has been greatly overemphasised in economic discussions. Most hedging is done largely, and may be done wholly, because the information on which the merchant or processor acts leads logically to hedging. He buys the spot commodity because the spot price is low *relative to* the futures price and he has reason to expect the spot premium to advance; therefore he buys spot *and* sells the future. Or in the case of a flour miller, he sells flour for forward delivery because he can get a price that is favourable *in relation to* the price of the appropriate wheat future; therefore he sells flour *and* buys wheat futures. (Here the arbitrage, it may be noted, is between two forward prices, that for flour and that for wheat.)[21]

Incidentally, recognition of the fact that hedging may be done purely as a logical consequence of the reasoning on which the hedger acts (reasoning, for example, that the spot price is low relative to the future) rather than from any special desire to minimise risks helps to explain why many dealers and processors sometimes hedge and sometimes do not. As we have remarked, merchants and processors, even though they hedge, have need to keep informed on conditions that affect the price of the commodity, and they may often have opinions on prospective price changes. If a merchant is accumulating stocks at a time when spot premiums are low – his most reliable basis for such action – and if at the same time he is fairly confident of an advance in futures prices as well as in spot premiums, why should he not carry the stocks unhedged, if he can afford to take some extra risk?

Perhaps the main reason that hedging, as commonly practised on futures markets, has been so widely misunderstood and misrepresented is that economists have tried to deal with it in terms of a concept that seemed to cover all sorts of hedging. This would be desirable if it were feasible, but the general concept of hedging as taking offsetting risks wholly, or even primarily, for the sake of reducing net risk, serves so badly as applied to most hedging on futures markets that we need another concept for that most common sort of hedging. To put it briefly, we may say that hedging in commodity futures involves the *purchase or sale of futures in conjunction with another commitment, usually in the expectation of a favourable change in the relation between spot and futures prices.*

An unfortunate consequence of the prevalent misconception of hedging has been that, while it has correctly credited futures markets with allowing merchants and processors to curtail their risks, it has diverted attention from a service of probably larger economic importance. Merely by supplying simultaneous quotations applying to various subsequent dates, futures trading tends to promote economically desirable control of stocks; and futures markets, through their use for hedging, make the holder of stocks sharply aware of any losses that must be expected from carrying unnecessary stocks in times of relative shortage of supplies, and provide assured[22] returns for storage over periods when there is a surplus to be carried. A merchant or processor with warehouse facilities will undertake storage in response to prospect of a 10 cents per bushel gain from carrying hedged stocks about as readily as he will undertake storage in response to an offer of 10 cents per bushel as a fee for storing government-owned grain. Indeed he may undertake storage for the return promised by hedging more willingly than for the fee, because the stocks that he holds hedged need be carried only as long as he wishes, and can be a source of convenience or of profit in connection with his merchandising or processing business. The argument often made that management of reserve stocks of commodities should be a governmental function rests in large part on ignorance of the effectiveness with which the hedging facilities of futures markets assure private carrying of stocks in about as large a volume as can be justified on purely economic grounds.[23]

The claim sometimes made by able economists[24] that prices of such storable commodities as wheat, corn and cotton fluctuate excessively because stocks are accumulated at wrong times, and not accumulated when they should be, seems also a consequence, indirectly, of the prevalent misconception of hedging. Mismanagement of stocks by non-hedgers would have to be on a very large scale to produce an overall tendency toward perverse stockholding in any commodity with a futures market much used for hedging.[25]

Price fluctuations

Futures trading tends to emerge and persist especially in commodities which are subject to exceptionally large price fluctuations, arising from unpredictable variations in production, from other supply uncertainties and from relative inelasticity of consumption demand.[26] Susceptibility of a price to large and unpredictable changes tends to stimulate hedging, and therefore futures trading, whether handlers of the commodity seek insurance against the risks of price change, or are led into hedging merely because they find spot premiums a more reliable guide to inventory control than are the prices themselves. (The relative superiority of spot premiums as such a guide depends of course on the price variability.) On this account, the fact that prices of commodities which have futures trading are found to be more variable than most other prices gives no ground for supposing that futures trading is a *cause* of the exceptional price variability.[27] It is none the less pertinent to raise the question whether existence of futures trading has a stabilising or destabilising influence on prices, and to seek some objective evidence on the question.

The results of attempts to determine whether prices of commodities that have futures trading fluctuate more or less than they would in the absence of futures trading have been generally inconclusive. Even if clear proof were given that futures trading tended somewhat to restrict price fluctuations, it might still be true that futures prices fluctuate too much. Some criterion is needed for an absolute test by which to determine whether the price fluctuations that occur are excessive, or are, in the main, rational and desirable responses to changing economic conditions and information.

A few years ago I suggested that such a test might be developed from the consideration that prices of durable goods (and especially futures prices) reflect expectations.[28] These expectations are always subject to error, but the errors of expectation might, in an *ideal* market, be only such as must arise from uncertainties inherent in the economic situation. That is, the price of May wheat, for example, might fluctuate, and yet be always the best estimate that could be made at the moment of what the price of wheat should be next May. *Excessive* price fluctuations might be measurable as the amount of fluctuation that occurred over and above the amount attributable to unpredictable changes in the economic situation. Unpredictability of change would thus be taken as the ideal in price behaviour.

This idea has been pursued, and appropriate statistical methods have been devised for making the suggested tests.[29] For technical reasons the new approach to the problem of testing price behaviour has been applied first to appraisal of the frequent and sometimes large price fluctuations that occur on active futures markets during the course of a day. The results indicate some departure of actual price behaviour from the ideal, as was to have been expected, but only slight departures; the observed price fluctuations were for the most part such as should occur purely from unpredictable changes in price prospects.[30]

In an ideal futures market in which the price of May wheat, for example, was at all times the best possible estimate of what the price would be next May, no speculator would be able to consistently make money, and the speculation necessary to maintain even an approximation to ideal price behaviour would tend to vanish. Speculative profits that are not purely the result of chance must rest on ability to anticipate price changes with some degree of reliability, whereas if a futures price were always the best estimate of a price at a later date, its changes would be entirely unpredictable.[31] Since many professional traders do make money in actual markets with some degree of consistency, it is evident that they are able to anticipate price changes with some approach to reliability and hence that the price behaviour is not ideal. Study of the nature of the price fluctuations that professional traders

Table 5

Month	Number of transactions[a] Total	Per day	Average daily sales (million pounds)	Gross profit[b] Cents per lb	Per cent	Number of days with Gain	Loss
February	1701	77.4	4.9	0.0167	0.042	15	7
March	1343	64.0	4.2	(c)	(c)	13	8
Total	3044	70.8	4.6	0.0093	0.023	28	15

[a] Purchases and sales.
[b] Per pound or per dollar of sales.
[c] Infinitesimal; a gross profit of $187.00 on $35 million of sales.

are able to anticipate may therefore give the best clue to the nature of the imperfections of actual speculative markets – the predictable price fluctuations that would be absent in an ideal futures market, but that are present in actual markets.

Perhaps the largest class of professional traders is that of "day traders" – those who operate primarily on intraday price fluctuations, and who end each day neither net long nor net short in appreciable amount.[32] Table 5 shows the record one such trader in cotton had over a two-month period chosen substantially at random.[33]

During the two months of the record, this man averaged nearly 70 trades per day, which is at the rate of about one every four minutes. His purchases were not bunched during the parts of the day when prices were low, nor were his sales bunched during the parts of the day when prices were high, but purchases and sales were distributed throughout the price range of the day.[34] He made money simply by managing to have his purchases, on the average, at prices a little lower than the prices of his sales. On the days on which he made money, his gross profits averaged 1/30 cent per pound. Since the cotton price was about 39 cents per pound, his gross profit on the days when he made money was about 82 cents per thousand dollars worth of cotton that he bought and sold. Net profits, after paying commissions and other business expenses, were substantially less.

The gross profits calculated in Table 5 are on trading during only the 28 days out of 43 on which he made money. On 15 out of 43 trading days during the two months he lost money. Such a result might not be surprising in the case of a man who made only a few trades each day, but 70 trades per day – about 35 purchases and 35 sales – gave much opportunity for successes and errors to offset within a day. Nevertheless, he lost money on more than one day out of three, on the average. This is not the sort of experience that most people imagine successful professional traders as having.

Because profits were so uncertain and variable, a calculation of the average rate of profit of this trader over even a two-month period may not give a very reliable indication of the normal profit expectation for such a trader. The figures, for whatever they may be worth, show that in the first of the two months, his gross profit averaged 1/60 cent per pound; in the second of the two months, losses nearly equalled gains – his total gross profit for the month would not have covered the commission charges he often paid on a single day's trading. For the two months together, his gross profits averaged about 23 cents per thousand dollars worth of cotton sold – less than one-fortieth of one per cent. Doing such business, he could make a living only by dealing in great quantities of the commodity; he bought and sold an average of over nine thousand bales of cotton – 4.6 million pounds – per day.[35]

Another day trader, who was not primarily a true scalper, but sought principally to trade on larger price fluctuations within a day than those on which pure scalpers operate, found that his gross profits during the previous seven months, on the Chicago Board of Trade, averaged 70 cents per thousands dollars of sales – seven hundredths of one per cent. The period beginning with January 1952 was one that he described as especially successful. Giving particular attention, as he did, to somewhat larger price fluctuations than occupy the pure scalper, he made relatively few trades per day in any one commodity, but a considerable total number because on most days he did trading in five or six different commodities.[36]

One might seek to get a large number of records such as those summarised in Table 5, and for longer periods, in order to arrive at a conclusion regarding *typical* behaviour and profits of day traders, but it is clear from this and other evidence, that the typical day trader and his profits would prove about as elusive as the typical insurance salesman and his income. These records, by themselves, serve as warning that some popular concepts of the manner in which professional traders operate, and of the source of their profits, may be quite mistaken. With other and more detailed records, they give valuable aid in interpreting results of statistical measurements or price behaviour, made on the principle outlined above.[37] All of the evidence converges toward the conclusions that: (1) the price movements that day traders are able to anticipate with even moderate reliability are usually small relative to the total price range for the day; (2) the reliability of their judgement is rather low; and (3) the overall effect of their trading operates strongly toward "smoothing" the course of prices, helping to make intraday price fluctuations conform closely to our criterion of ideal behaviour.

These conclusions bear directly on the question whether the price fluctuations that occur in futures markets within the day tend to be excessive or not. The question is not inherently a very important one because, though price fluctuations in the two months of the illustration covering cotton resulted in an average price difference of 0.4 cents per pound between the lowest price and the highest price each day, it would not matter greatly if fluctuations of such magnitude did occur without good reason. The conclusions reached are more important than the specific question to which they apply, because they indicate reasonableness in just that trading and those price fluctuations which may be thought most likely to be unwarranted.

On the question whether the larger price fluctuations that occur over longer periods are in the main warranted, the best evidence that I can yet cite[38] is essentially subjective and inconclusive. It is the evidence that led me to question the common assumption, and to try to measure the amount of "excessive" fluctuation that is present in "speculative" prices. During the 20 years of publication of *Wheat Studies* by the Food Research Institute, members of the research staff periodically studied the recent fluctuations of wheat prices and sought to interpret them as warranted by current developments, or unwarranted. For much of that period we sought three times a year to appraise price prospects for the next several months. Everyone concerned with these efforts gained a great respect for the rationality of the price behaviour observed. During 20 years some price movements occurred which it seemed possible to appraise at the time as ill-founded or excessive, but these were exceptional. Only rarely did it seem possible to anticipate subsequent price movements with confidence on the ground that the current price appeared unjustifiably high or low.

As regards price changes from year to year, it is entirely clear, as noted in the previous section, that futures markets contribute substantially toward desirable adjustment of stocks carried from one year to another. Whether or not they produce as much flexibility of storage as is desirable they at least operate in that direction.

Costs of hedging

We turn now from topics on which there has existed major disagreement, springing largely from imperfect or mistaken concepts, to examine a new, or at least largely neglected, idea that illuminates hitherto obscure aspects of futures trading. The idea came to me through puzzling over two questions:[39] Why does futures trading in a commodity tend to concentrate largely or wholly in one exchange? And why is futures trading on any one exchange usually confined to a single set of contract specifications for a commodity, rather than distributed among several contracts, representing different qualities of the commodity? Hedgers, it may seem, would be best served by having numerous futures exchanges, and several different futures contracts in each, so that hedges could be placed always in a future that applied to a quality of the commodity corresponding closely with that being hedged, and to a location at or near that of the hedged stocks. The answer seems to lie in a cost of hedging.[40]

There are at least two significant elements to be considered as parts of the cost of hedging.[41] The most obvious one is the commission charge that must be paid on futures transactions.[42] Futures trading must operate with great efficiency to keep this charge so low as not to discourage hedging seriously, since much of the advantage that a hedger gains, as we have seen, comes from a guidance in inventory control that is available without actually placing hedges. In addition to commissions, there is a cost of hedging that can be much larger, arising from what may be called the bivalence[43] of market price. The contribution of price bivalence to costs of hedging declines sharply, as we shall see, with increase in the volume of business done on an exchange, and it declines also with increase in the volume of business in a particular futures contract. It has, therefore, just the characteristics needed to explain observed tendencies in the concentration of futures trading.

Our awareness of the fact that there are usually two (or more) prices for a commodity unit of specific quality in any market at a given time is dulled by the convention of treating wholesale and retail prices as though they were registered in separate markets. But of course they are in fact two separate prices within the same market, differing because of a service that (at least presumptively) goes with the commodity when it is sold at retail.

When, as in the case of houses, for example, the circumstances of trade do not favour distinction between wholesale and retail prices, there remain price differences according to the conditions of sale. Even under stable and well-known market conditions the man who chooses to sell without much search for someone who particularly wants a house like his takes one price, and the man who chooses to buy without much "shopping" pays a higher price. The difference between the two prices need not represent any exploitation of bargaining weakness, but only a fair margin for an intermediary. Or in a country grain market, a merchant may buy wheat from a farmer at one price and sell it almost immediately to a poultry raiser at a higher price. The difference, again, is likely to represent only a return for service, small in this case because a poultry raiser who had reason to believe that the difference would be large would seek out the farmer and buy from him directly.

In terminal commodity markets (and in security markets) there appears the same sort of price differences, though smaller, that provide the margin on which merchants in such markets principally operate. In large central markets the small price differences which provide these margins cannot be realistically treated as differences between a wholesale and a retail price. They tend then to be clearly reflected in price quotations only through differences between "bid" and "asked" prices.

A merchant who hedges usually finds his situation in the futures market the opposite of that which he enjoys in the spot market. In his spot dealings, he buys at bid prices and sells at the higher asked prices (a fact that we ruled out of consideration in our illustrations of hedging, because we were there concerned with storage and its returns). In his futures dealings, on the contrary, he tends to buy at asked prices and to sell at the lower bid prices. At least he prefers to do so, unless the margin between bid and asked prices is so wide that he is forced to "shop" in the futures market, as well as in the spot market. The merchant is paid for his services to processors and exporters by *receiving* an asked price, and he in turn is willing to pay for corresponding services of dealers in futures by buying often from them at asked prices.

The dealers in futures from whom a hedger often[44] buys at asked prices, or to whom he sells at the lower bid prices, are the so-called scalpers, or other day traders.[45] We saw in the last section some evidence on the very narrow margin that such dealers in futures take. From that evidence it would appear that their margin is of the order of $\frac{1}{14}$ to $\frac{1}{40}$ of 1%. Those figures, however, represent averages that are somewhat "watered down" by the effects of transactions between day traders themselves.[46]

Another way of estimating the dealer's margin that a hedger tends to pay on his futures transactions is from the profit margin that scalpers try for. In wheat on the Chicago Board of Trade this has been typically $\frac{1}{8}$ cent per bushel, or a little over $\frac{1}{20}$ of 1% at recent prices. An estimate so derived, however, tends slightly to overstate the margin actually paid by a hedger, because hedgers benefit from scalpers' mistakes of judgement.

A third basis for estimating the margin that hedgers pay on their futures transactions is afforded by data showing that a loss of 0.21 cents per bushel was taken by processors and terminal grain merchants on 109 million bushels of wheat futures bought (and sold) over a nine-year period.[47] If the futures transactions were virtually all hedging transactions, as may reasonably be assumed, this indicates a hedging cost, in addition to commissions, of slightly over $\frac{1}{5}$ cent per bushel, or less than one-fifth of 1% of the average wheat price over the time period. This is a cost figure, however, that includes speculative profits forgone[48] (or, to put the same thing in another light, that includes any return to speculators for carrying the hedges). And it is in any case a cost per bushel bought and sold, whereas the foregoing estimates of scalpers' margins might tend to be paid on purchases and on sales alike. So there is at least no evident inconsistency between these data and the previous estimates of scalpers' margins.

Whether scalpers' margins are less than $\frac{1}{10}$ per cent, or as much as $\frac{1}{5}$ per cent, a merchant or processor can afford that cost in addition to commission charges of, say, $\frac{1}{10}$ of 1%.[49] His own dealer's or processor's margin, though small, is usually several times the total of these costs of hedging.

In small and relatively inactive futures markets, however, scalpers must take much wider margins than in the circumstances to which the foregoing data apply.[50] They must do so primarily because their volume of business is restricted to perhaps half-a-dozen transactions per day, or less, as compared with the 70 transactions per day of the cotton trader cited. And, secondly, they must do so because their risks are greater. In an active futures market, a scalper can usually buy and resell within the space of a few minutes, running little risk that some change in news will involve him in a serious loss. In inactive markets, purchase and sale may be separated by hours, or the scalper may buy today and have to wait until tomorrow to sell, running correspondingly large risks of loss from unpredictable developments. And because scalpers must take wider margins on inactive markets, hedging on them is more costly than on active futures markets.[51] Consequently, if a hedger has two futures markets to choose between he tends to do his hedging in the more active one.[52]

The element of hedging cost that arises from scalpers' margins, or from the inconvenience and price disadvantages incurred in the absence of scalpers, explains the restriction of trading almost universally to a single futures contract on one exchange, in the same way that it explains the tendency for futures trading in a commodity to concentrate mainly or wholly on some one exchange. When two futures contracts are offered for trading applying to different descriptions of the commodity, trading tends to become more active in one of them than in the other; scalpers' margins then rise on trading in the less active contract, leading to further concentration of hedging, and of other trading, in the more active contract. For example, after five years of use of the Californian wheat contract for futures trading at Liverpool, trading was initiated also (in 1891) in an American Red wheat contract. The latter proved the more popular, and in spite of the important difference between the two kinds of wheat, quickly drew trade away from the Californian contract to such an extent that trading in the Californian was presently abandoned.[53] Maintenance of futures trading in two descriptions of a commodity on any one exchange was found generally impractical early in the history of futures trading, and has rarely been tried in recent years.

These conclusions have some interesting implications. If we are correct in inferring, as seems necessary, that hedgers' responses to cost differentials account for the observed tendency toward concentration of futures trading dominantly or wholly in some one exchange, and wholly in some one contract on each exchange, it follows that hedgers are as a rule unwilling to pay for superior hedging facilities. Does this mean that hedging is usually considered worthwhile only if it is very cheap - that its advantages are really not very great? Or does it mean something else?

"Insurance" hedging

The question posed above may well be considered in a concrete situation. Grain merchants and flour millers in the Pacific Northwest of the US have long sought to gain and hold the advantages of futures trading in a contract well suited to their needs. Largely because of the great distance between that area and the main wheat-producing regions of the country, wheat prices in the Pacific Northwest are only loosely tied to prices at Chicago or Kansas City. When the Chicago futures price represents hard wheat, as has commonly been the case,[54] the important quality difference between hard wheat and the soft wheat typical of the Pacific Northwest contributes to disparity of movement between Chicago and Pacific Northwest wheat prices. No. 1 Soft White wheat in Portland or Seattle may sell at 20 to 30 cents per bushel under the spot price of contract wheat at Chicago, or it may sell at 10 cents per bushel, or more, above the Chicago price. Chicago futures consequently afford a very imperfect hedge for soft wheat in the Pacific Northwest.

Efforts to provide good hedging facilities for Pacific Northwest wheat have included maintenance, over many years, of futures trading at Seattle and, until 1942, at Portland also. These markets did not flourish,[55] and in 1950 the experiment was tried of providing for trading in the North Pacific Coast wheat futures on the Chicago Board of Trade (with delivery on the Pacific Coast). The special Chicago contract failed to attract enough business to warrant its continued use; it seemed to serve only to draw business away from Seattle.

The volume of hedging in a Pacific Northwest wheat futures contract must necessarily be a fairly small fraction of total wheat hedging in the US, because total wheat production in the area is only some 10–12% of the national wheat crop.[56] Moreover, there is relatively less occasion for hedging in the Pacific Northwest than in most other areas of concentrated wheat production in the US, because of abundant "country" storage facilities and a widespread disposition of growers to retain ownership of their wheat for considerable periods after delivery.[57] But even so, there could have been a lively business in Pacific Northwest wheat futures if commercial stocks of wheat in that area had not been held to such a large

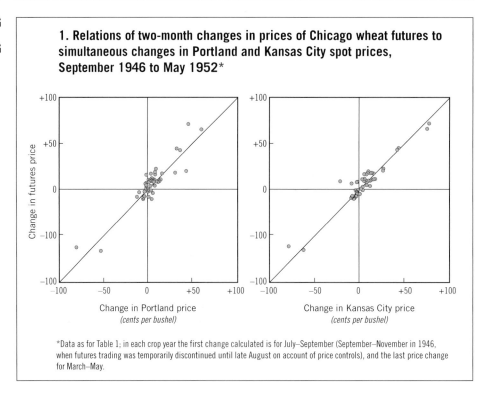

1. Relations of two-month changes in prices of Chicago wheat futures to simultaneous changes in Portland and Kansas City spot prices, September 1946 to May 1952*

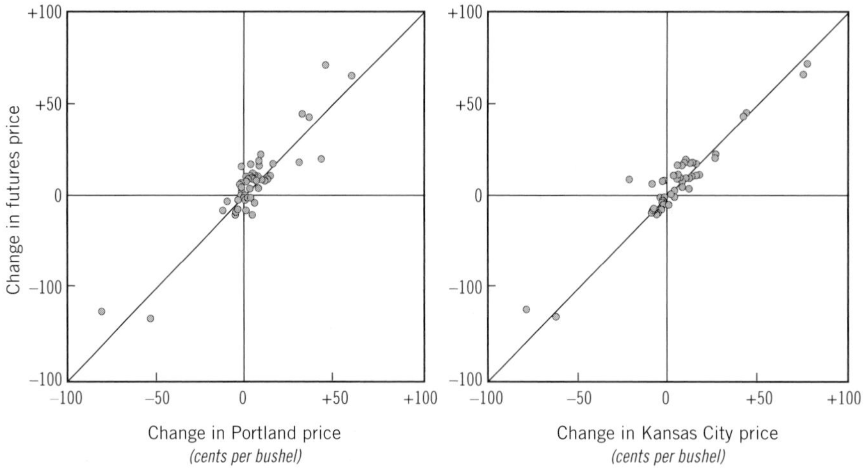

*Data as for Table 1; in each crop year the first change calculated is for July–September (September–November in 1946, when futures trading was temporarily discontinued until late August on account of price controls), and the last price change for March–May.

extent either unhedged, or hedged in futures markets of the Middle West, especially Chicago (and in the standard contract there).

Decision of a wheat merchant or processor in the Pacific Northwest to hedge in Chicago futures rather than in a Pacific Northwest futures contract is only a rather extreme example of the sort of decision often made by hedgers – to take inferior risk protection for the sake of a saving in cost. Even though he hedges in Chicago futures, a merchant or processor in the Pacific Northwest can still rely on prices of the Seattle futures for guidance in deciding whether to buy for storage or not to buy.[58] If he buys because the relation between the spot price and a Seattle futures price promises a return for storage, he may still decide to hedge in a Chicago future with only the result that he will take more risk, but not so much risk as though he held the wheat unhedged. In other words, the decision on where to place the hedge concerns only the insurance aspect of hedging.[59]

A merchant or processor choosing between Seattle and Chicago futures as the medium for hedging that he has decided to do is in much the same position as though he were taking out casualty insurance, and choosing whether to take full coverage or coverage only for losses above some stated minimum. The choice he makes is whether to take coverage on all insurable risks, at a fairly high cost, or to insure only against serious loss, at a considerably lower cost. The chief function of insurance is to give protection against serious, crippling, loss. Carrying insurance against small losses that occur frequently is ordinarily poor business because the holders of the insurance have to pay the losses, through the insurance premiums, and to pay also the overhead costs of writing policies and adjusting losses. Hedging, as we saw earlier, is not ordinarily done primarily for its insurance value, but because it is a logical consequence of the information on which the hedger acts. The fact that business risks attending such hedging are very small is nonetheless a valued consequence of such hedging; and when the costs of hedging in the futures contract logically indicated are excessive, businessmen naturally consider the possibilities of obtaining at least the insurance values of hedging at a moderate cost. The principal insurance value of hedging wheat stocks in the Pacific Northwest is supplied about as well by Chicago futures as by Seattle futures.

This interpretation of hedging deserves empirical support. Is a "poor" hedge reasonably comparable with insurance that covers losses above some stated minimum? Or is it more properly comparable with insurance covering only a *fraction* of the total loss; or with insurance carried with a company of uncertain financial status, that may turn out to be no insurance at all? The facts are well illustrated by Figure 1.

The meaning of the points plotted in the figure may be grasped readily by considering their relation to the illustrative data in Table 6. The point, for example, that appears at the

Table 6. Spot and futures prices of wheat and two-month price changes, July 1947 to May 1948* (cents per bushel)

	Chicago futures[a]		Spot prices		Two-month price changes		
Date	December	May	Kansas City[b]	Portland[c]	Chicago Futures	Kansas City	Portland
1947							
July 16	237	...	234	219	...	...	...
August 16	237	...	231	222	...	...	...
September 15	279	...	275	256	+42	+41	+37
October 16	302	...	306	281	+64	+75	+59
November 15	299	286	301	300	+19	+26	+44
December 16	309	296	304	293	+07	–02	+12
1948							
January 16	...	305	311	291	+18	+10	–09
February 14	...	235	235	212	–62	–79	–81
March 16	...	239	249	237	–66	–62	–54
April 16	...	252	249	243	+17	+14	+31
May 17	...	244	240	235	+05	–09	–02

* Prices for that trading day nearest the middle of the month on which quotations are available in all three markets, rounded to the nearest cent.
[a] Means of highest and lowest prices during the day, from Chicago *Journal of Commerce.*
[b] Weighted average of reported spot sales of No. 2 Hard and Dark Hard Winter wheat, compiled by US Department of Agriculture from Kansas City *Grain Market Review.*
[c] Spot prices of No. 1 Soft White wheat, compiled by US Department of Agriculture.

extreme lower left of each section of the figure is plotted from the data for "two-month price changes" appearing in the table opposite "February 14". These are price changes from December 16, 1947, to February 14, 1948. Over this two-month interval, the spot price at Portland fell 81 cents; that at Kansas City fell 79 cents; and the price of the Chicago May future fell 62 cents. Despite these severe price declines holders of wheat stocks of the indicated qualities at Portland and Kansas City, hedged in the Chicago future, would have lost only 19 and 17 cents per bushel, respectively.

Points on the diagonal line across the centre of each section of the figure represent instances in which the spot and the futures prices changed equally. Points to the left of this line represent instances in which the spot price fell more than the future price, or rose less. These were instances in which hedged stocks would have been carried at a loss, as in the specific case just considered. Conversely, points to the right of the diagonal represent instances in which a gain would have resulted from the carrying of hedged stocks. Nothing further need be said here about the way in which hedgers use futures quotations to judge in advance where the carrying of stocks is likely to prove profitable, but it is pertinent to note that Table 6 includes evidence that a hedger anywhere in the Middle West, at least, had reason to expect a loss if he carried stocks of wheat from December 16, 1947, to February 14, 1948. This prospect was indicated by the fact that on December 16 the price of the Chicago May future was 13 cents under the price of the December future.[60]

Amounts of gain or loss from carrying hedged stocks of wheat are indicated in Figure 1 by the horizontal (or vertical) distances of the plotted points from the diagonal line. The scatter of the points is greater, and therefore gains and losses were greater, for Portland wheat than for Kansas City wheat, though perhaps not so much greater as some would have expected. But the important fact for present purposes is that the points in the figure cluster as closely around (or are no more widely dispersed around) the diagonal lines near their ends than near their midpoints. There is no evident tendency for gains and losses on hedged stocks to have been larger when price changes were large than when price changes were small. Hedgers take some risks even though they can estimate fairly well the prospective gain or loss from storage, and a good deal more risk on wheat stored in Portland and hedged in Chicago than on wheat stored in Kansas City and hedged in Chicago. But in either case the amount of risk is substantially *independent* of the amount of price change. Hedging limits the amount of risk in substantially the same sense that insurance covering losses above a stated amount limits risk.

In the light of these facts, it is understandable that many hedgers should prefer a "poor" hedge that is cheap to a more nearly perfect hedge that is relatively expensive. The tendency for most futures trading in any commodity to converge in some one exchange, and to concentrate in some one contract there, is explained. There is even an implied suggestion that trading in barley futures, for example, may have died out in the US because grain dealers chose commonly to hedge their barley stocks in corn futures, at low cost, in preference to hedging in the small and relatively inactive barley futures market, where the costs of hedging were relatively high. And the fact that merchants and processors make such choices does not necessarily indicate that they put a low estimate on the value of hedging. Their valuation of hedging must be judged from cases where the only choice open is to hedge in a market where hedging is expensive, or not to hedge at all. In such cases the common choice is to hedge, as is evidenced by the vitality of small futures markets that have no larger competitor.

Summary

To summarise, we began with a definition of futures trading that related it intimately to other commodity transactions, and emphasised economy as its major distinguishing feature. A language problem, we found, has promoted a false idea of contrast between futures trading and other commodity trading. Looking at the bases of futures trading, we saw them to lie more in utilisation of the advantages of futures markets by merchants and processors, for hedging, than in the desires of others to speculate.

Hedging we found to be not primarily a sort of insurance, nor usually undertaken in the expectation that spot and futures prices would rise or fall equally. It is a form of arbitrage, undertaken most commonly in expectation of a favourable change in the relation between spot and futures prices. The fact that risks are less with hedging than without is often a secondary consideration. The prevalent tendency to regard curtailment of business risks as the main service of futures markets has diverted attention from their probably more important service of promoting economically desirable adjustment of commodity stocks, thereby reducing price fluctuations. The argument for governmental stockpiling rests heavily on a consequent false appraisal of the causes of price fluctuations.

In further consideration of the subject of price fluctuations, we stated an ideal of behaviour of a futures price that permits objective statistical tests, and put in one sentence the gist of conclusions arising from application of such tests to the intraday behaviour of futures prices. The statement of conclusions was prefaced by some data on the operations of two professional traders that reveal characteristics far from those usually imagined to exist. Pending further research based on the stated concept of ideal price behaviour, inferences on the reasonableness of the larger fluctuations of futures prices, beyond the limits of one trading session, must still rest largely on subjective judgement, but there is considerable evidence that these large price fluctuations may usually reflect substantially accurate appraisals of changing economic facts that should be accompanied by such price changes.

Finally, we inquired into the causes of some puzzling characteristics of futures trading and found them explained by hedgers' responses to cost differentials associated with the "bivalence" of market price. The responses themselves depend largely on the fact that even a "poor" hedge affords good protection of the sort for which insurance is mainly needed. It is like casualty insurance covering losses above some stated minimum.

1 *This, in two sentences, is the story that can be read from scattered comments in Taylor (1917). Passages in volume 1, pp. 146–7, 192, 217, 317 and 332, among others, cover the main developments through 1865, when the Board of Trade at last assumed responsibility for aiding and governing the conduct of futures trading.*

Emery (1896) traces the history of trading that had at least some essential characteristics of that done in futures, from institution of the use of warrants by the East India Company in 1733 (p. 35), and says that "Futures were sold in some kinds of grain in Berlin by 1832, and some years earlier in France and Holland" (footnote, p. 41).

2 *This is not to say that anybody in either the cotton or the grain trade is confused by these practices any more than initiates are confused by the colloquial uses of "buck", "date" and "doll" (all words with the same brevity as "cash" and "spot"); but the usage is a bit frustrating, and even misleading, to an inquiring novice.*

3 *Whether use of the expression has its foundation directly in this characteristic, or in the related fact that* speculators *use futures contracts, as they may any forward contracts, to avoid necessity for* handling *of the actual commodity, is a matter of surmise.*

4 *The characteristics of convenience and economy being not well developed at that stage.*

5 *See, for example, the evolution of definitions from Emery (1896), p. 46, through Smith (1922), p. 44; Hardy (1923), pp. 205–6; Baer and Saxon (1949), pp. 132–4.*

6 *See, for example, the summary of much earlier work in Hoffman (1941), pp. 33-8.*

7 *Data are conveniently available in* Agricultural Statistics *(Washington) for any recent year.*

8 *Size of a futures market is better judged by volume of open contracts than by volume of trading because of the wide variation between markets in proportion of trading contributed by "scalping" and by other trading that involves holding a commitment for only a few minutes or hours, with correspondingly small speculative risk and small economic significance.*

9 *For example, such an inference seems to follow from information in Stewart (1941), pp. 16-26.*

10 *See Working and Hoos (1938), pp. 125, 142-4. I would now attach less importance than is done there to the uniformity of the quality of the Californian wheat, judging that factor to have been important mainly in the preference for the Californian over the Indian wheat contracts, in which also there was effort for a time to maintain futures trading.*

11 *Not entirely valid because hedgers are the active agents in determining the* relation *of spot to futures prices, and to that extent they play a major role in formation of the spot price.*

12 *The case of wool has been documented* (cf. *Stewart, 1941); the inference that similar situations exist in certain other commodities is based on fairly reliable trade reports.*

13 Cf. *the Federal Trade Commission's* Report on the Grain Trade *(Washington), vol. I (1920), pp. 213-27; vol. VII (1926), pp. 38-57; and Working (1931).*

14 *Kansas City is used rather than Chicago because changes in the major wheat-producing areas and in the normal lines of movement of the commodity have left Chicago with a vestigial spot wheat market that no longer affords a good source of spot price quotations.*

15 *The case of a merchant or processor deserves to be considered rather than that of someone not in such a business, who might buy merely for storage, because merchants and processors gain auxiliary benefits from having stocks on hand that give them a competitive advantage in storing. Their competition for the returns available from storage leaves little opportunity for profitable storing as an independent enterprise.*

16 *This is the normal procedure in connection with spot sales of wheat at Kansas City and at other markets with active futures trading. The actual bargaining on July 2, however, would have been in terms of premium or discount in relation to the price of the* July *future, the prospective hedger bearing in mind the prevailing discount of the July future under the September.*

Since the gain or loss from hedging calculated in such tabulations as that in the text above depends only on the spot premiums, the prices included in the tabulations are no more than interesting collateral information. The spot premium or discount for a specified quality of the commodity rarely changes much during the course of a day or even a week. With regard to the futures prices, however, it is pertinent to note the time of day. Those used here are the closing prices for the day. The spot prices are closing prices of the future currently being used as a basis for spot sales, plus the quoted premium for lowest quality No. 2 Hard Winter wheat. The source is the Kansas City Grain Market Review, *which quotes also daily high and low spot prices for the various grades, in which the low quotation for each grade is obtained by adding the premium for lowest-quality wheat in that grade to the lowest price of the future for that day.*

17 *Sometimes the spot price on track in a delivery month falls to a considerable discount under the near future because of lack of warehouse space for economical storage. The spot price on track tends to be at a* discount *under the price of a current-month future, which is then also effectively a spot price, when the prevailing direction of movement of the commodity is into storage; it tends to stand at a premium over the future when the prevailing direction of movement is out of storage. Moreover, the spot quotations for the cheapest wheat of deliverable grade may represent wheat of slightly better quality than that which will be delivered on futures contracts. To be graded No. 2, wheat must meet all of several requirements; the wheat delivered on futures contracts may be at or near the minimum in all respects when the cheapest wheat on which spot quotations are available is close to the minimum in only one of the grade requirements.*

18 *One of the indications of this prospect was the fact that spot wheat had already reached a premium of one cent over the May future by December 1. The cause, of which any holder of large wheat stocks would have been well aware, was the holding by growers of some 300 million bushels or more under non-recourse loans offered by the Commodity Credit Corporation.*

19 *Not necessarily to zero, because deliveries on futures contracts would consist of wheat in public elevators; in May, wheat on track tends to be worth more than the same quality of wheat in a public elevator because it is already loaded in a freight car and ready to be moved to wherever it is wanted.*

20 *When spot wheat in May is at a premium over the July future, it is not because the new wheat crop - coming to market in large volume by July - is expected to be large, but because current supplies of old wheat are scarce. (In May 1952 the scarcity applied only to commercially available supplies, being a result of the large holdings of wheat by the Commodity Credit Corporation in connection with its price-support operations.) On the subject of "inverted" intertemporal price relations in general, see Working (1948, 1949a and 1949b).*

21 *Two instructive explanations of hedging written by hedgers themselves, such as are not often found, are those by English (1952) and Wiese (1952).*

22 *Though subject to some risk, as we have seen.*

23 *If considerations of national defence warrant the carrying of commercially uneconomic stocks of a commodity, government should of course assume the responsibility and the financial burden of carrying such excess stocks.*

24 *For example, Schultz (1919), pp. 172–4.*

25 *The hypothesis of perversity of stockholding tendencies is not supported by any statistics that I know, but is contradicted by them. Of particular interest is the fact that in the years when one could speak realistically of a world wheat market, the countries in which year-end (June 30) stocks of wheat varied in rational correspondence with world wheat supplies were the countries where hedging was practised on a substantial scale. In most countries, year-end stocks of wheat varied little, and primarily with size of the previous* domestic *crop. Britain, with a futures market but with only small storage facilities, contributed little to the carrying of world wheat surpluses. Canada contributed more; and the country that most consistently carried large stocks at the end of any year of world wheat surplus, and reduced stocks to a minimum in times of world wheat shortage, was the US.* Cf. *Working (1930).*

26 *No reference is made here to changes in demand as a cause of* exceptional *price variability, because those demand changes which contribute to price instability of staple commodities are mainly of the sort that affect all sensitive prices similarly.*

27 *It appears sometimes to be so taken, nevertheless, even by economists who would be expected to see the fallacy of such an inference.*

28 *Working (1949c), p. 158* ff.

29 *The tests involve in principle the measurement of serial correlation among price* changes, *which in practice must be present to some extent. If price changes are predictable (that this is so may seem obvious, but the proof requires more space than is available here). The statistical measures used have been especially devised to be more sensitive than serial correlation coefficients to the sorts of departure from randomness of change that are to be expected in price series. They have also an advantage of economy in use.*

30 *The relative amount of departure from ideal behaviour has been measure numerically, but it is not possible to summarise the results meaningfully in brief.*

31 *Price changes would always be consequences of new information, unavailable as a basis for prediction before the price change occurred.*

32 *Professional traders specialise to such an extent as to make classification meaningful, and the intraday traders especially tend to concentrate on one type of trading.*

33 *The record was obtained for this individual because he was regarded as a representative, successful day trader. The period was simply the two months ending at the time (in 1952) when he was interviewed.*

34 *This was ascertained by separately tabulating purchases and sales each day in frequency distributions according to price.*

35 *Incidentally, the fact that a gross profit of 23 cents per thousand dollars worth of purchases and sales could permit any net profit at all is striking evidence of the main technical characteristic of futures trading – the economy with which transactions can be made.*

36 *A feat comparable to that of playing several games of chess simultaneously, blindfolded.*

37 *A full report on the research will be published shortly.*

38 *Pending completion of research under way.*

39 *And also from what we learned in the study of intraday price behaviour referred to above.*

40 *I thought at first that the answer lay in a somewhat capricious behaviour of speculators, coupled with a necessity for hedgers to use those exchanges and contracts in which there was sufficient speculation to carry the hedges. But, when this argument was advanced in a paper dealing with a special case ("Western Needs for Futures Markets," mimeo., Food Research Institute, 1952) it drew objections that seem fatal.*

41 *One might choose to regard potential speculative profits forgone as a cost of hedging; but though a potential hedger may wisely take account of potential profits from speculation in deciding whether to hedge or not, I think that treating forgone speculative profits as a cost of hedging would not be the best way of taking them into account.*

42 *And if the hedger maintains an exchange membership for the sake of the consequent saving in commissions, there are membership expenses to be counted as part of the cost.*

43 *Using "bivalent" to mean "two-valued" rather than, as in chemistry, "having a value of two".*

44 *"Often", because the purchase or sale of futures made by a hedger does not necessarily go through the hands of an intermediary scalper.*

45 *A scalper, in the strict sense, may be characterised as always willing either to buy at one-eighth of a cent below the last price or to sell at one-eighth of a cent above the last price (or at such other difference from the last price as market conditions permit); he operates purely on the difference between bid and asked prices, as ordinarily understood. Other professional day traders perform an essentially similar function, but at least partially with respect to somewhat larger price differences. Bid and asked prices tend to be farther apart for large quantities than for small quantities of a commodity.*

46 *The first of any pair of transactions by a scalper is made in the belief that he is buying "below the market" from an urgent seller, or selling "above the market" to an urgent buyer. But scalpers often find that they have misjudged the market, or that it has turned against them immediately after such an initial transaction. Then they seek to make the offsetting transaction quickly, often at a loss, and often to another day trader.*

47 *The data, from Stewart (1949), Table 27 (the calculations of loss per bushel are mine), are as follows:*

Business	No. of firms	Transactions (thousand bushels)	Loss (thousand bushels)	Loss per bushel (cents)
Terminal grain merchants	45	76,054	174	0.23
Processor	44	33,407	55	0.17
Total	89	109,461	229	0.21

Similar data, from the same source, on hedging transactions amounting to 9.6 million bushels by 33 country and subterminal grain merchants, show a loss of 2.6 cents per bushel on their transactions in futures. The magnitude of this loss indicates that more of the hedges against wheat stocks by this group of dealers were carried in periods of rising prices than in periods of declining prices. The classes of grain merchants involved commonly practise discretionary hedging, and those represented in the data apparently chose to hedge at such times that they "protected" themselves against profits from price increase somewhat more than against losses from price decreases. The results tabulated above for terminal grain merchants and processors may also be affected to some extent by the practice of discretionary hedging, though it is much less prevalent among such wheat handlers than among country and subterminal merchants.

48 *Which we wish to leave out of account here, as previously noted. It is scarcely possible to deal with them in general terms, except in such a global average as the one just given, because their magnitude depends so much on special circumstances, including the knowledge and judgement of the hedger.*

49 *Commission charges are not fixed as a percentage of the price; expressed so, they depend on the price, and they vary rather widely among commodities and exchanges, and according to whether the transaction is for a member of the exchange or a non-member. The figure of one-tenth of 1% is representative of commissions for commodities and exchanges with a fairly large volume of business and low commission rates, and is therefore applicable to most of the hedging that is done.*

50 *Part of the difference in gross profit obtained per $100 of transactions by the two day traders for whom data were given is accounted for by the fact that the second trader operated mainly in commodities which have only moderately active trading.*

51 *At some point not very far down on a scale of diminishing market activity, it becomes impossible to conduct scalping as a specialised form of trading and to make a living at it. Then the scalping function is performed by some speculators, and the distinction between scalping and speculation becomes blurred.*

52 *The preference, as commonly expressed in trade circles, is for a "broad" market as against a "thin" market. This terminology expresses the fact that size as well as frequency of transactions is important. On the supposition that most readers would understand "active" to mean about what a trader calls "broad", I have thought it unnecessary to introduce the trade terminology into the exposition.*

53 Cf. *Working and Hoos (1938), p. 144.*

54 *Though during the last few years the Chicago future has most of the time been effectively a soft winter wheat future because the deliverable soft wheat was cheaper than deliverable hard wheat.*

55 *See data on open contracts in wheat futures, by exchanges, in* Commodity Futures Statistics, *US Department of Agriculture, Statistical Bulletin No. 107 (1952), pp. 5 and 10, and earlier publications in the series.*

56 *Opinions differ as to how the "Pacific Northwest" wheat area should be defined, but on any reasonable definition it does not follow the boundaries of states, which are the units for wheat production statistics; consequently the production of the area can be stated only roughly.*

57 Cf. *Davis (1934), p. 377.*

58 *Though, of course, if too little hedging is left for the Seattle market, even the guidance afforded by its prices will be lost.*

59 *Unless he expects a change in the relation between Seattle and Chicago prices, in which case the hedging problem becomes entangled with one of intermarket arbitrage.*

60 *This relation reflected a current high premium on spot wheat over the May future, indicative of prospective declines in spot prices relative to the May future throughout the US east of the Rocky Mountains, but not necessarily on the Pacific Coast.*

BIBLIOGRAPHY

Baer, J. B., and O. G. Saxon, 1949, *Commodity Exchanges and Futures Trading* (New York).

Davis, J. S., 1934, "Pacific Northwest Wheat Problems and the Export Subsidy", *Wheat Studies* X (August).

Emery, H. C., 1896, *Speculation on the Stock and Produce Exchanges of the United States* (New York).

English, E. D., 1952, "The Use of the Commodity Exchange by Millers", *Proceedings, Fifth Annual Symposium,* Chicago Board of Trade, mimeo, pp. 22-9.

Hardy, C. O., 1923, *Risk and Risk Bearing* (Chicago).

Hoffman, G. W., 1941, *Grain Prices and the Futures Market,* USDA Technical Bulletin No. 747, January.

Schultz, T. W., 1919, *Production and Welfare of Agriculture* (New York).

Smith, J. G., 1922, *Organized Produce Markets* (London).

Stewart, B., 1941, "Trading in Wool Top Futures", USDA Circular No. 604, August, pp. 16-26.

Stewart, B., 1949, "An Analysis of Speculative Trading in Grain Futures", USDA Technical Bulletin No. 1001, October.

Taylor, C. H., 1917, *History of the Board of Trade of the City of Chicago* (Chicago).

Wiese, V. A., 1952, "Use of Commodity Exchanges by Local Grain Marketing Organizations", *Proceedings, Fifth Annual Symposium,* Chicago Board of Trade, mimeo, pp. 108-16.

Working, H., 1930, "The Changing World Wheat Situation", *Wheat Studies* VII (September), pp. 433-52.

Working, H., 1931, "Financial Results of Speculative Holding of Wheat", *Wheat Studies* VII (July), pp. 417-28.

Working, H., 1948, "Theory of the Inverse Carrying Charge in Futures Markets", *Journal of Farming Economics* XXX, pp. 1-28.

Working, H., 1949a, "Professor Vaile and the Theory of Inverse Carrying Charges", *Journal of Farming Economics* XXXI, pp. 168-72.

Working, H., 1949b, "The Theory of Price of Storage", *American Economic Review* XXXIX, pp. 1254-62.

Working, H., 1949c, "The Investigation of Economic Expectations", *Papers and Proceedings, American Economic Review* XXXIX (May).

Working, H., and S. Hoos, 1938, "Wheat Futures Prices and Trading at Liverpool since 1886", *Wheat Studies of the Food Research Institute* XV (November), pp. 125, 142-4.

4

New Concepts Concerning Futures Markets and Prices*

Holbrook Working†

Research on futures markets during the last 40 years has produced results that have required drastic revision or replacement of a great part of the previously accepted theory of futures markets and of the behaviour, not only of futures prices, but of the general class of prices that may be called "anticipatory". New light has been thrown on the behaviour of businessmen, including speculators, and on the functioning of the price system.

To say that new theory has been required poorly expresses the consequences of the research, because the main results have not been "theory" in the usual economic sense of that term. One may better follow an example set by Conant when he faced a similar problem in undertaking to explain the nature of science, and said, "... science emerges from the other progressive activities of man to the extent that new concepts arise from experiments and observations, and the new concepts in turn lead to further experiments and observations" (Conant, 1947, p. 24). The chief results of the research to be considered here has been the emergence of a series of new concepts arising from observation and statistical analysis. They are listed in Table 1, with a parallel statement of the concepts that they partially or wholly displace, and their emergence is traced in succeeding sections of the chapter, where the main evidence on which the new concepts rest is summarised.

Empirical research has played a leading role in the advancement of economic knowledge and understanding that is described here, but the role has been a different one than economists have ordinarily thought that such research would play in advancing their science - if economics be a science.[1] In the final section we re-examine some prevalent views on the function of empirical research in economics, and conclude that such research can serve economics in the same way that Conant describes it as serving the natural sciences.

The practical question of economic usefulness of future markets is only incidentally referred to in the present chapter, inasmuch as our concern here is to trace the advance of economic understanding rather than to discuss the practical uses of such understanding. It will be readily observable, however, that the improved understanding contributed by each of the new concepts except the first, which bears only on the technical question of correct measurement, tends either toward refuting common criticisms of futures markets or toward indicating greater usefulness than has ordinarily been attributed to them, or both.

The open-contract concept

First of the six new concepts to emerge, and a necessary precursor of much that was to follow, was the concept that the business of futures markets should be measured primarily in terms of volume of contracts outstanding - so-called "open contracts". This was a revolutionary concept, carrying with it recognition that the traditional main function of markets, transfer of ownership, is not a significant function of a futures market. In futures markets there is little buying and selling in the usual sense, with its connotation of transfer of ownership. Instead, futures markets exist chiefly to facilitate the holding of contracts; the making and offsetting of those contracts, misleadingly called buying and selling,[2] is only incidental to the main function of such markets.

The revolutionary character of this concept was so little recognised at the outset that the concept was accepted in its original form without controversy,[3] and without explicit record

Originally published in the American Economic Review *(June 1962), reproduced with permission of the American Economic Association.*

†Holbrook Working, 1895-1985.

Table 1. Concepts concerning futures markets

New concepts*	Displaced concepts
1. *Open-contract concept:* Futures markets serve primarily to facilitate contract holding (1922).	Futures markets serve primarily to facilitate buying and selling. (Disproved.)
2. *Hedging-market concept:* Futures markets depend for their existence primarily on hedging (1935; 1946).†	Futures markets depend for their existence primarily on speculation. (Disproved.)
3. *Multipurpose concept of hedging:* Hedging is done for a variety of different purposes and must be defined as the use of futures contracts as a temporary substitute for a merchandising contract, without specifying the purpose (1953).	Hedging is done solely to avoid or reduce risk. (Disproved.)
4. *Price-of-storage concept:* Storage of a commodity is a service supplied often at a price that is reflected in intertemporal price spreads, and because the holding of commodity stocks can afford also a "convenience yield", the price for storing small stocks is often negative (1933; 1949).	Storage of a commodity is a service that is supplied only in response to an assured or expected financial return equal to or greater than the cost, the latter calculable ordinarily without regard to the quantity of stocks to be stored. (Disproved.)
5. *Concept of reliably anticipatory prices:* Futures prices tend to be highly reliable estimates of what should be expected on the basis of *contemporarily available information* concerning present and probable future demand and supply; price changes are mainly appropriate market responses to changes in information on supply and demand prospects (1934; 1949).	Futures prices are highly unreliable estimates of what should be expected on the basis of existing information; their changes are largely unwarranted. (A wholly unproved inference; accumulating evidence mainly supports the new concept.)
6. *Market-balance concept:* A significant tendency for futures prices to rise during the life of each future is not uniformly present in futures markets, and when it exists is to be attributed chiefly to lack of balance in the market (1960).	Aversion to risk-taking, leading to risk premiums, produces a general tendency toward "normal backwardation" in futures markets, statistically measurable as a tendency for the price of any future to be higher in the delivery month than several months earlier.

*Dates shown in parentheses are years in which the concepts may be said to have emerged. Where two dates are shown, the earlier one is the date of publication of evidence recognised as challenging the older concept; the later date, that of first-known publication of at least the substance of the new concept.
†A statement of this concept was first prepared for publication by H. S. Irwin about 1946, but actual publication was delayed until 1954 (see endnotes 5–8).

of who deserves credit for the innovation. The concept emerged effectively about 1922 during consideration of what data should be collected by the newly created Grain Futures Administration. Credit for it belongs chiefly, I think, to J. W. T. Duvel, who was shortly to become the first administrator of that federal agency, and during his long occupancy of that position gave research a prominent place in the work of that regulatory body.[4]

Directing attention to open contracts in the study of futures markets had an effect similar to that produced on the study of medicine and related science by Pasteur's discovery of bacteria; it led to study of the *causes* of phenomena, and thus toward true understanding, where previously only symptoms had been considered and understanding had been frustrated. And, incidentally, terms new to economics were required, such as "long position" and "short position" and "long hedging" and "short hedging".

The main fruits thus far of adoption of the open-contract concept have flowed from the fact that it led to quantitative study of hedging, which was obviously not significantly measurable in terms of trading statistics. It thus led directly to a new understanding of the parts played by hedging and speculation, respectively, in the origin and functioning of futures markets – a new understanding reflected in the hedging-market concept to be considered next; and it contributed significantly to emergence of the multipurpose concept of hedging. Studies of speculation have not benefited so much from the open-contract concept, partly at least because persistence of the mistaken idea that speculation is well measured by trading has considerably retarded study of speculation in terms of open contracts; but studies of the statistics of open contracts, as we shall see in the next section, have recently raised questions that bear especially on speculative behaviour.

The hedging-market concept

Futures markets have usually been regarded, in the past, as essentially *speculative* markets. Although they rather early won recognition as useful for hedging, their hedging use was treated as a fortunate by-product, neither necessary to the existence of such a market, nor very closely related quantitatively to the amount of speculation on the market. At Chicago, where dealings in forward contracts first took on the essential characteristics of a modern futures market, dealing in futures was initially regarded in the grain trade itself as a disreputable speculative business; for more than a decade the Chicago Board of Trade refused to allow such transactions in its quarters.[5] The opinions of economists are reflected in familiar treatments of the theory of futures markets that begin by supposing the only participants in the market to be speculators.

The first step toward a radically altered view of futures markets came with the discovery of what might justly be called Irwin's Law. After statistics of open contracts had been collected by the Grain Futures Administration for only a few years, a staff member of that agency, H. S. Irwin, noted that the volume of open contracts varied seasonally in accordance with seasonal changes in the volume of commercial stocks subject to hedging (Irwin, 1935). Irwin was not then willing to conclude that speculation tended to enter and leave a market in direct response to variation in the amount of hedging, and sought explanation otherwise.[6] Hoffman (1941, pp. 33–41) later studied additional evidence on the correspondence between commercial stocks and open futures contracts, and found it observable in year-to-year variations as well as within the year. With the aid of statistics of hedging, available for the last three years of the period that he studied, he brought to light the fact that the net amount of hedging (short minus long), which he supposed was the hedging variable logically to be considered, did not always vary in close correspondence with commercial stocks.

Presently Irwin undertook a study of the origins of futures markets in butter and eggs, taking advantage of the fact that there were then people still alive who had witnessed the early stages of emergence of futures markets in those commodities. Verbal accounts by such people, supplemented by extensive study of contemporary published information, convinced Irwin that the prime incentive to emergence of those futures markets came from hedgers rather than from speculators. This conclusion, though consistent with the statistical evidence noted above, ran contrary to an established belief, and Irwin was unable to get publication for his original paper. By the time he resorted to private publication in 1954, in expanded form (Irwin, 1954), the present writer had profited from a reading of Irwin's original manuscript in 1946, had found that his conclusion conformed with a great and varied mass of other information, and had argued that futures markets ought not to be regarded as primarily speculative, but as primarily hedging markets (Working, 1953a, pp. 318–19[7]; 1954a).

The statistical data on hedging and speculation, as they accumulated, produced evidence that the relationship was not a simple one connecting speculation with net hedging, as it had seemed natural to assume. Statistical analysis presently revealed that long hedging serves only in part to offset short hedging, and in part creates a need for short speculation. With this circumstance taken into account, the amount of speculation was shown to vary in much closer correspondence with the amount of hedging than had been evident previously. Figure 1 illustrates the correspondence found for variations through time in one market.[8] A similarly close correspondence was found for variations between markets, using five-year averages (Working, 1960b, p. 198).

The multipurpose concept of hedging

According to the traditional concept, hedging consists in matching one risk with an opposing risk, and hedging in futures is effective because changes in spot prices of a commodity tend to be accompanied by like changes in the futures price. The fact that hedging usually involves more than risk avoidance has long been known to hedgers themselves and to some economists. Wiese, a businessman, seems to have been the first person to criticise the traditional concept as seriously misleading (Wiese, 1952, p. 113). An attempt by Graf (1953) to test the efficacy of hedging produced the first evidence which was recognised as showing that the simple risk-avoidance concept was seriously misleading to economists (Working, 1953b, pp. 544–5).

Quantitative studies, perhaps surprisingly, have contributed more to understanding of hedging than have verbal inquiries concerning business motivation. Particularly noteworthy among these were studies of the quantitative relation between hedged stockholding and

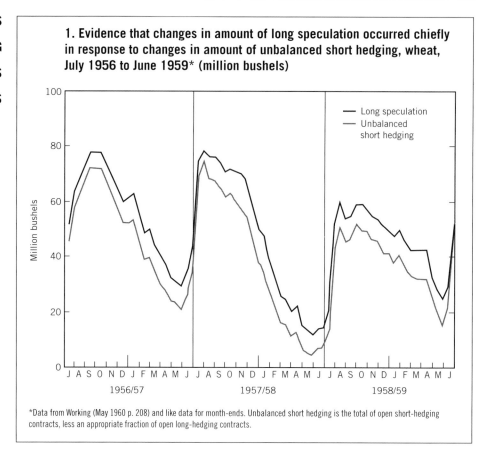

1. Evidence that changes in amount of long speculation occurred chiefly in response to changes in amount of unbalanced short hedging, wheat, July 1956 to June 1959* (million bushels)

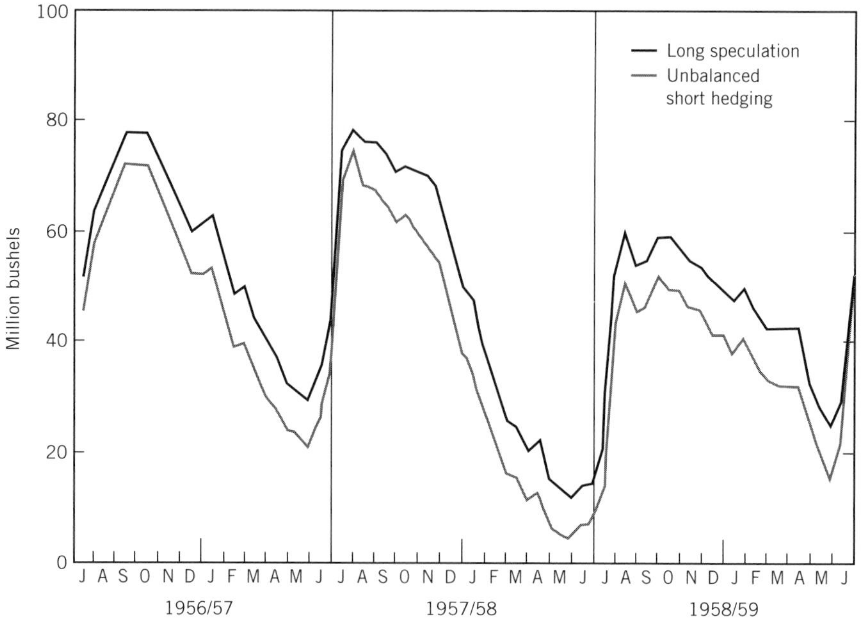

*Data from Working (May 1960 p. 208) and like data for month-ends. Unbalanced short hedging is the total of open short-hedging contracts, less an appropriate fraction of open long-hedging contracts.

market "carrying charges", which brought recognition that much hedging was done to assure profits, not merely to avoid risk (Working, 1953b, pp. 556–7); studies of flour-mill practice in maintaining a rough inventory balance involving the three items, physical stocks, forward merchandising contracts and futures contracts (Working, 1953b, p. 549), which produced evidence that risk avoidance was inadequate as an explanation of flour-mill hedging;[9] and statistical inquiries intended to test the efficacy of hedging, which as noted above, produced demonstrably false conclusions explicable only on the ground that acceptance of the pure risk-avoidance concept of hedging had led to the making of a test that grossly misrepresented the effects of hedging as actually practised. And even non-quantitative inquiry has been sufficient to establish that some hedging is practised with neither the intent nor the effect of reducing risk.

Business hedging is done for a variety of reasons, which differ according to circumstances. Consequently it is necessary to recognise the existence of several different categories of hedging and to consider them separately with respect to business purposes and economic effects.

Carrying-charge hedging is done in connection with the holding of commodity stocks for direct profit from storage (rather than merely to facilitate the operation of a producing or merchandising business). Whereas the traditional concept implies that hedging is merely a collateral operation that, in this application, would influence the stockholding only through making it a less risky business, the main effect of carrying-charge hedging is to transform the operation from one that seeks profit by anticipating changes in price level to one that seeks profit from anticipating changes in relations. Whether a businessman regards such a transformation of the operation as desirable or not depends less on differences between inherent riskiness of the two sorts of operation than on whether he personally feels better able to predict changes in price levels or changes in price relationships. In general, producers of a commodity and those who use it as a raw material, when they undertake storage for profit, prefer to seek the profit by anticipating changes in price level, and therefore either do not hedge, or hedge selectively (see below): it is chiefly merchants, whose merchandising business requires close attention to price differences according to grade, quality and location, who choose to seek storage profits by anticipating changes in price relations, thus using to best advantage their special knowledge concerning price relations.

Whereas the traditional hedging concept represents the hedger as thinking in terms of possible loss from his stockholding being offset by gain on the futures contracts held as a hedge, the carrying-charge hedger thinks rather in terms of change in "basis" - that is, change in the spot-future price relations. And the decision that he makes is not primarily whether to hedge or not, but whether to store or not.[10]

Operational hedging is done chiefly to facilitate operations involved in a merchandising or processing business. It normally entails the placing and "lifting" of hedges in such quick succession that expectable changes in the spot-future price relation over the interval can be largely ignored; and it is this fact that chiefly distinguishes operational hedging from carrying-charge hedging. Because the intervals over which individual operational hedges are carried tend to be short, the amount of risk reduction accomplished tends to be small - quite insufficient to explain the observed prevalence of operational hedging. Besides reducing risk, to an extent that the hedger may or may not consider significantly advantageous, it leads to economies through simplifying business decisions and allowing operations to proceed more steadily than otherwise.

Illustrations of the principal advantages of operational hedging may well be drawn from flour-milling because it was study of flour-mill hedging that first led to recognition of the special characteristics of operational hedging. In this industry buying and selling decisions are facilitated because it is easier for the mill buyer to judge prices on particular lots of wheat in terms of their relation to other wheat prices than in terms of absolute level. And similarly it is easier to judge the price offered by a potential flour buyer in relation to a present wheat price than in relation to the price that may have to be paid on a later wheat purchase. When hedging is practised, it becomes logical to make these buying and selling judgements on the easier basis. And wheat buying in particular can be carried on more steadily than otherwise because the basis is subject to less fluctuation than is the price.

These business advantages of operational hedging, however, depend on the existence of a high correlation between changes in spot prices and changes in futures prices over short intervals - day to day and even within the day. Such correlation of short-interval price changes is not always present, and in its absence there tends to be little operational hedging even though the broader correspondence between changes in spot and futures prices be close enough to permit effective risk reduction through hedging. Flour mills west of the Rocky Mountains in the US usually do not hedge, because spot wheat prices in that area do not move in sufficiently close day-by-day correspondence with future prices in mid-western markets to permit satisfactory operational hedging.[11]

Selective hedging is the hedging of commodity stocks under a practice of hedging or not hedging according to price expectations. Because the stocks are hedged when a price decline is expected, the purpose of the hedging is not risk avoidance, in the strict sense, but avoidance of loss. Published studies of hedging in the grain trade of the US have indicated the presence of selectivity in hedging, through reports that hedging was done "to some extent" or "occasionally", chiefly among country elevators (Mehl, 1931; US Federal Trade Commission, 1, pp. 213, 214). Efforts on the part of such firms to gain profits from appraisal of price prospects, as is implied by selectivity in hedging, appear ordinarily ill-advised. But personal inquiry among large and well-managed firms in the grain trade has revealed that, though hedging is their standard practice in most parts of the country, they sometimes hedge incompletely. To the extent that they allow circumstances in individual instances to influence the decision whether to hedge unsold stocks or not, they hedge selectively. Outside the grain and cotton trades, which appear to be the principal ones in which routine hedging is accepted as standard practice in most parts of the country, selectivity in hedging is so common as to suggest that in a considerable number of futures markets the greater part of the short hedging done may be selective.[12]

When hedging is done selectively, the advantage of the hedging to the individual firm may often (perhaps usually) be measured approximately by the amount of loss avoided directly by the hedging. Though curtailment of the amount of unsold stocks is an alternative means of restricting loss at a time of expected price decline, it is a means that few firms are able to use freely, owing to operating needs for carrying stocks. Selective hedging almost inevitably yields large advantages to any merchandising or processing firm that is able to anticipate price changes reasonably well. From an economic standpoint selective hedging deserves appraisal as simply one aspect of the use of futures markets as a means by which handlers of a commodity increase the efficiency of their participation in the price-forming process, instead of largely withdrawing from such participation, as they do when they practise routine carrying-charge or operational hedging. Futures markets that receive a large amount of selective hedging tend also to have a considerable amount of "speculation" by handlers of the commodity. Inasmuch as selective hedging must come chiefly from those handlers of the commodity who commonly hold substantial stocks, and who therefore take along position by merely refraining from hedging, it is to be presumed that the "speculative" use of futures by handlers of the commodity comes mainly from dealers whose business requires relatively little holding of physical stocks.

Anticipatory hedging, which also is ordinarily guided by price expectations, differs from selective hedging in that the hedging contract is not matched by either an equivalent stock of goods or a formal merchandising commitment that it may be said to offset. It takes either of two principal forms: (a) purchase contracts in futures acquired by processors (or manufacturers) to cover raw material "requirements",[13] or (b) sales contracts in futures by producers, made in advance of the completion of production. In either of these forms the anticipatory hedge serves as a temporary substitute for a merchandising contract that will be made later. In the one case it serves as a substitute for immediate purchase of the raw material on a merchandising contract; in the other case it serves as a substitute for a forward sale of the specific goods that are in course of production. The purpose of the hedge may be said to be to take advantage of the current price; or bearing in mind the usual availability of an alternative means of doing that, merely to gain some advantage in convenience or economy through the choice made between alternatives.

The best presently available statistics that give some indication of the prevalence of anticipatory hedging are those on long hedging, which reflect also the similarly motivated forward merchandising contracts, to the extent that they are hedged, that many processors use as a means of anticipating requirements. Nearly all long hedging consists either of anticipatory hedging or of hedging of forward merchandising contracts (often called unfilled orders) that are themselves anticipatory in the same sense as the anticipatory hedging. On the latest date (September 28, 1956) for which there are statistics of open contracts in cotton that allow accurately segregating "matching" contracts from those that were purely speculative, long-hedging contracts totalled 1,001 thousand bales, as compared with 268 thousand bales of long-speculative contracts (Working, 1960b, p. 192). This was at a time when the amount of short hedges to be carried was near its peak.

Pure *risk-avoidance hedging*, though unimportant or virtually non-existent in modern business practice, may have played a significant part in the early history of futures markets. In the absence of records concerning the uniformity of hedging by firms using the early futures markets, however, it is impossible to know to what extent early hedging, described as done "to reduce risk", actually had that purpose in the strict sense, or was selective hedging, done to avoid incurring loss from an expected price decline.

Recognition of the fact that hedging is done for a variety of purposes requires defining hedging otherwise than has been customary. The verb "to hedge", in the sense of avoidance or shelter, has no general connotation of avoidance especially of risk; the gambling practice of hedging bets is perhaps as often used to offset an expected loss as to reduce risk in the strict sense; and there is in any case no good reason why the word "hedging" as applied to business practices should be restricted to operations such as gamblers call hedging. For present purposes we need to define only hedging in futures. All the uses of futures that are commonly called "hedging" will be comprised, and all other uses excluded, if we characterise hedging as the use of futures contracts as a temporary substitute for a merchandising contract that is to be made later.[14]

Inclusion as hedging of the practices characterised above as selective hedging and anticipatory hedging requires either regarding hedging as sometimes closely akin to speculation,[15] or defining speculation otherwise than has been usual in economics texts. In ordinary usage and in much economic discussion the word "speculation" refers to buying and selling (or, more accurately, holding) property purely for the sake of gain from price change, and not merely as an incident to the normal conduct of a producing or merchandising business or of investment. So it is usual to distinguish between speculation in securities and the holding of securities for capital gain; many people tend to think it a strained use of the term when speculation in commodities is defined to include the holding by a farmer of part of his crop for a few weeks after harvest; and business purchasing agents object to being said to speculate when they seek to time their buying, within reasonable limits, in accordance with their judgement of price prospects. If speculation is defined in accordance with ordinary usage of the term, hedging and speculation in futures are always distinguishable.[16]

The price-of-storage concept

Though much uncertainty has existed about the relations of futures prices to spot prices, one proposition long stood unquestioned: there seemed to be no generally necessary relationship between prices that depend on the abundance or scarcity of currently available supplies - spot prices for example - and prices on futures contracts applying to supplies from a subsequent harvest. To be more specific, it was regarded as clear that, in the presence of a current relative scarcity of wheat, prospects for an abundant harvest in the following summer would have no significant bearing on prices paid for existing supplies.

Statistical studies published in 1933, supplemented by further evidence later, showed this belief to be untrue.[17] What happens in fact is that any change in price of a distant, new-crop, wheat future tends to be accompanied by an equal change in prices paid for wheat from currently available supplies.[18] A comparative shortage of currently available supplies of wheat has its direct effect on the spread between the spot price and the futures price, causing wheat from current supplies to sell at a premium over the expected future price of new-crop wheat. In effect, then, the spot price is determined as the sum of the futures price, dependent primarily on expectations, plus a premium dependent on the shortage of currently available supplies.

These observed facts of price behaviour were contrary to what was logically deducible from the prevalent concept. Introduction of the concept that intertemporal price differences constitute prices of storage (Working, 1949c) provided a key to understanding the observed facts and served in effect as a summary of the facts. The most significant of these facts from the standpoint of economic theory is that spot prices of storable commodities tend to respond sensitively to changes in distant expectations. Figure 2 illustrates this tendency. The great price advance that it shows in the new-crop December corn future, owing to crop deterioration in July and August 1947, was accompanied throughout by a like advance in the price of the old-crop September future. If the traditional concept of price dependence on currently available supplies were valid, the price of the September future, comparatively high in June because of shortage of old-crop supplies, would have held fairly steady during June and early July, until deterioration in new-crop prospects caused the December future to rise to and above the price of the September future, and thereafter would have followed the course of the December future, but at a slightly lower level.

The main reason for listing the price-of-storage concept as marking a significant step in the advance of economic science is that it seems capable of displacing the belief that spot prices are commonly little affected by changes in distant expectations. That opinion is not founded on any factual observation, but has its basis in an assumption embedded in the conventional exposition of price formation, an exposition that is ordinarily taken to mean that "supply", as a determinant of spot price, means currently available physical supplies. A belief so derived will not be corrected merely by citing observational evidence to the contrary,[19] but only through providing an evidently valid conceptual scheme that requires bringing expectations into account as determinants of spot prices.[20]

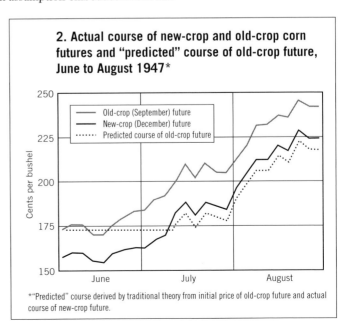

2. Actual course of new-crop and old-crop corn futures and "predicted" course of old-crop future, June to August 1947*

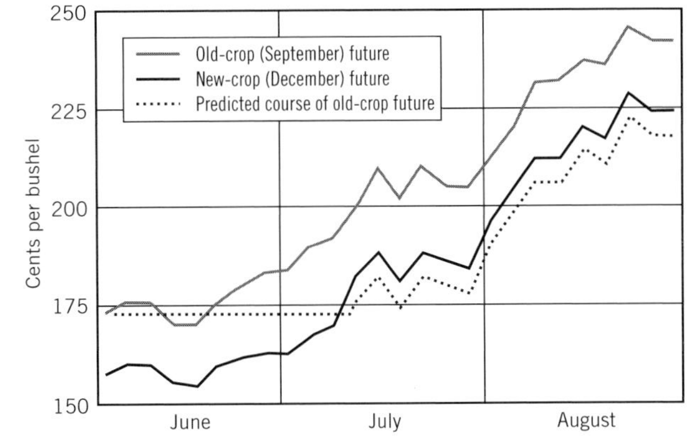

*"Predicted" course derived by traditional theory from initial price of old-crop future and actual course of new-crop future.

The concept of reliably anticipatory prices

Prices on futures markets (and also spot prices of many commodities and prices on the stock market) are observed to change frequently and in an apparently erratic manner. These price changes have traditionally been conceived to be in large part random fluctuations, with some degree of cyclicality impressed upon them. Evidence of the substantial falsity of that concept has long been widely known, but the conflict between concept and evidence could be visible only to a person who was well aware of the distinction between random variation and random walk.[21] The so-called "fluctuations" of futures prices, of some other commodity prices, and of stock prices, exhibit close approximations to pure random walk.[22]

When attention was drawn to that characteristic of certain prices, about a quarter-century ago, the discovery aroused no comment and no apparent lasting interest on the part of either statisticians or economists.[23] It was a factual observation that carried no economic meaning, even to people who understood the technical distinction between random variation and random walk. But presently the economic meaning of the discovery was found: Pure random walk in a futures price is the price behaviour that would result from perfect functioning of a futures market, the perfect futures market being defined as one in which the market price would constitute at all times the best estimate that could be made, from currently available information, of what the price would be at the delivery date of the futures contracts (Working, 1949b, p. 160).

The observation that the behaviour of futures prices corresponded closely to random walk thus led to the economic concept that futures prices are *reliably* anticipatory; that is, that they represent close approximations to the best possible current appraisals of prospects for the future (Working, 1958). Conceiving the "fluctuations"[24] of futures prices to be mainly appropriate responses to valid changes in expectations produces a great change in thought regarding them, as compared with regarding the price movements as mainly lacking economic justification.

Further discussion of the evidence that futures prices are reliably anticipatory requires dealing with a problem of the meaning of "reliability" in this context. Custom has established the idea that reliability of uncertain expectations is to be tested by correspondence between the expectation and the event, but we need here to consider reliability of expectations in the sense of correspondence between the actual expectations and what ought to be expected in the light of available information. At times, in order to avoid confusion, I shall speak of the latter as *anticipatory reliability*.

The inference, from evidence of approximate randomness of change in futures prices, that those prices have a high degree of anticipatory reliability was initially open to serious question on the ground of suspicion that the price changes were in fact much less nearly random than early statistical tests seemed to indicate. Randomness of walk in a statistical series is not a specific characteristic detectable by any one specific test, but a term that designates absence of any systematic characteristic – absence of any sort of "structure", as Cowles and Jones aptly expressed it (Cowles and Jones, 1937). Because the kinds of structure commonly believed present in futures prices and in stock prices are trends and cycles (in a somewhat loose usage of those terms), those kinds of structure were the first looked for as evidence of non-randomness; and the statistical tests used were familiar ones that had been proved appropriate for revealing structure of those sorts in other data, namely, tests for the presence of simple autocorrelation.[25] Failure of those tests to reveal an appreciable degree of structure in futures prices, however, left open the question whether other sorts of structure might not be present.

Two principal lines of inquiry have been followed in the search for kinds of structure that would not be revealed by simple autocorrelation analysis, or equivalent methods. One line of inquiry has reasoned that the price movements to be correlated should be selected according to magnitude of the movement, without regard to the time taken to accomplish a movement of that amount. By proceeding thus, Alexander (1961) has recently shown the presence of an appreciable tendency for stock-price movements of 5% or more (in an index of industrial stocks) to be followed by further price movement in the same direction.[26] Houthakker (1961, p. 166) has published results that, though calculated and presented from a point of view different from that of Alexander, can be interpreted as indicating presence of the same sort of tendency in prices of wheat and corn futures that Alexander found in the stock-price index.

Another line of attack involved the design of a new type of statistical test that appeared capable of revealing any such tendency toward continuity of movement in futures prices, if it were present, and also capable of revealing a tendency for a price movement in one direction to be followed by an opposite movement (reaction), but without uniformity in timing of the reaction, which might sometimes be prompt and sometimes considerably delayed. A test devised for this purpose promptly yielded statistically significant evidence of structure in futures prices (Brinegar, 1954), but further research was required to determine the kind of structure that was indicated.[27] The principal component of the structure was presently identified as such as would be produced by a tendency for the price effects of new market information to be partially dispersed over a considerable time interval rather than all concentrated within the day on which the new information became available (Working, 1956 and 1958). Later it was found possible to determine approximately the fraction of the average price effect that was so dispersed and the average time span of dispersal, and also to derive similar approximations for a secondary sort of structure, involving excessive price movement on individual days, with reaction dispersed on the average over a period of a few adjacent days (Larson, 1960). The latter, rather weak, tendency was found to be associated with relatively small price movements, and the former tendency, mainly with the larger price movements.

The results produced by the two lines of inquiry summarised above appear at present to be entirely consistent. Those from the first approach are the more readily interpretable, up to a certain point. Those from the second approach lend themselves the more readily to appraisal of the degree of anticipatory reliability that can be attributed to futures prices, or to such other prices as deserve similar appraisal. The most notable feature of the evidence from these two lines of inquiry, however, is not quantitative but qualitative. Each has indicated that the main kind of structure present in anticipatory (speculative) prices is roughly the opposite of that which has been chiefly charged against such prices. Whereas these prices commonly have been thought to "fluctuate" too much, showing large movements up or down that tended to be followed by reaction, in a roughly wave-like pattern, the evidence is that reaction is common only from very small movements, of short duration, which may be regarded as caused by minor accidental disturbances; that in the main the imperfection of behaviour in futures markets takes the form of retardation of price response to information that warrants price change. This retardation, being an effect similar to that of shock-absorbers on an automobile, tends toward the avoidance of excessive initial movement and subsequent reaction.

The concept that futures prices are reliably anticipatory, in the full sense of that term, evidently does not correspond wholly to the facts. In that respect it is like the concept that gases are perfectly elastic, as represented by Boyle's Law, $VP = C$. If the economic concept of anticipatory reliability of futures prices is subject to a good deal more supplementary qualification than is the physical concept of perfect elasticity of gases, it appears nevertheless to correspond more closely to full reality than does any other concept that might be used for fairly simple representation of the main facts. It avoids the gross misrepresentation involved in the concept that the variations in futures prices are in large part unwarranted, wave-like, fluctuations; and its own misrepresentation is of a sort that is inevitable in a concept that, for the sake of simplicity, must fall short of representing the full facts.

Risk premiums versus the market-balance concept

The concept that risk-bearing commands a reward has been applied at several related points in the theory of futures markets, but has recently attracted attention principally in connection with discussion of J.M. Keynes' "theory of normal backwardation". The market-balance concept, recently proposed by Gray (1960, 1961) as a substitute for the risk-premium concept in that context, has been advanced on the basis of evidence that may be thought inconclusive,[28] and has been applied only to explaining differences in seasonal trends[29] of future prices in different markets - not obviously a matter of great importance. The reasons for nevertheless discussing the market-balance concept in the company of the better-proved and more demonstrably fruitful concepts discussed previously are, first, that the grounds for considering the merits of the market-balance concept are stronger than appears from the statistical evidence alone; and secondly, that there is evident need for taking other considerations into account, along with risk, at several points in the theory of futures markets where the tendency has been to consider only the risk aspect.

The earlier studies that sought to test Keynes' theory of normal backwardation took seasonal trend in futures prices to be a measure of risk premium (as Keynes apparently had done), and focused on the question whether the statistics gave evidence of a tendency to such seasonal trend or not. Telser at first denied that they did (1958), whereas Houthakker (1957, 1961) and Cootner (1960) found evidence of seasonal trends consistent with the Keynesian hypothesis. Gray, meanwhile, had been making studies of some of the smaller futures markets, which had previously received little attention from economists, and was thus led to put together the pertinent evidence for a considerable number of different markets, large and small. The diversity in magnitude, and even in direction, of apparent seasonal trend that he found among the various markets appeared to him not explainable on the basis of difference between risk premiums in different markets (Gray, 1961, p. 258), whereas the differences did appear explainable on other grounds that could be comprised by the term "market balance". The term was suggested by the evidence that the differences in seasonal trend were largely associated with differences between markets in amount of speculation relative to hedging – or, more strictly, relative to the potential amounts of hedging, inasmuch as a shortage of speculation in a futures market must restrict the amount of hedging actually done.

The market-balance concept thus emerged because examination of a wider range of observational data than had been considered before posed a new question for answer. Viewed as bearing only on the original question – whether futures prices tend to show an upward seasonal trend – the new data could be interpreted as supporting an affirmative answer, in agreement with the general tenor of previous evidence; but the new data posed also the question of how to account for the occurrence of seasonable trends that in some markets and circumstances appeared to be significantly positive, and in others, significantly negative. The answer that was suggested, in the form of the market-balance concept, does not require rejecting the risk-premium concept, but regarding it as providing at best only a partial explanation of the tendencies to seasonal trend observable in futures prices.

Speculators' earnings have received significant direct study only by Stewart (1949), and his inquiry, based on detailed records for nearly 9,000 speculators in grain futures, and covering a time period of nine years, was singularly unproductive of positive conclusions. Such unproductiveness in a large-scale investigation by an able economist skilled in statistical analysis and with a wealth of data at his command must indicate need for reconsidering prevalent economic ideas about the bases of speculative profits, which Stewart sought to explore. The "sample" of speculators that he dealt with showed a strong overall tendency for them to incur losses, and though many among them gained profits, Stewart was unable to find an objective characteristic by which to classify speculators into groups with appreciably different profit experience.

If speculation be regarded as a skilled occupation (not mere risk-taking), in which the making of profits depends both on special skills and on continuously maintained knowledge of current economic conditions and prospects relevant to prices of particular commodities, Stewart's results become understandable. He had no information by which to classify speculators according to special speculative skills, or according to the amount and quality of their pertinent knowledge; hence his study could throw no direct light on the relations of speculative rewards either to special speculative skills or to amounts of pertinent economic information that they used.[30]

In order that speculation should contribute to economically desirable price formation, speculators must keep well informed concerning the pertinent economic facts, and must be able to appraise those facts properly. The evidence considered earlier that futures prices are reliably anticipatory, to a fairly high degree, indicates that a large proportion of speculation in futures markets has been based on sound information, properly appraised. Such speculation deserves to command a wage, and that fact is ignored when the returns from speculation are viewed solely as a reward for risk-bearing.

Data published by the Commodity Exchange Authority in recent years concerning some of the smaller futures markets have revealed that much of what is classed by the CEA as speculation in them comes from persons and firms dealing in the commodity, such as are ordinarily expected to be hedgers.[31] If one accepts the argument that speculation should be defined as suggested earlier[16] this raises the question whether a considerable part of the contract holdings that have been classed as "speculative", in those markets, might not more properly be treated as anticipatory hedging. In any case the evidence reveals that, for those commodities, the futures markets have served in important degree to allow dealers in the commodity to exercise their price-forming function more freely than they otherwise could. In the absence of a futures market, price formation is almost wholly in the hands of dealers (using that term to comprise all handlers of the commodity); and many of them must exercise that function under the handicap that their need to accumulate stocks in order to maintain their position as merchandisers may force them to act in support of a price that they regard as too high, or obstacles to stock accumulation at a given time may bar effective market expression of an opinion that the current price is unduly low.[32] The presence of a futures market permits dealers to exercise price judgement without such restraints. The dealer who must accumulate stocks at a certain time for merchandising reasons may sell futures in equivalent amount and thus avoid exerting a price-supporting influence when he expects a price decline; and the dealer who expects a price advance, but cannot well accumulate physical stocks of the commodity at the time, can buy and hold futures instead.

Thus the introduction of a futures market could result in substantially improved price behaviour even though the futures market were used only by the dealers in the commodity, the better price behaviour being attributable to the opportunity given dealers to exert price influence strictly in accordance with price judgement instead of exerting price influence, or refraining from doing so, largely in response to immediate merchandising or processing needs. Existence of a futures market may tend toward better support of prices during rapid marketing of a crop shortly after harvest, not primarily because speculators demand a lower risk premium than do dealers (if that be true), but chiefly because the futures market allows stocks to be "carried" either as physical stocks held unhedged or through the holding of long futures contracts that offset short hedging. This tends to change the balance of the market in the sense of the market-balance concept.

Because potential carriers of stocks have differing opinions regarding the price at which they can afford to buy for carrying, there exists at any time a demand curve for stock-carrying such as is represented by DD in Figure 3. Introducing the opportunity for stocks to be carried through the holding of futures contracts tends to move this curve rightward to a position such as D′D′, giving an intersection at P′ with the vertical, representing total stocks to be carried, at a higher level than before. Such a rightward shift clearly tends to occur if the futures market attracts many speculators who would not otherwise deal in the commodity, and it might occur also if the futures market were patronised only by dealers in the commodity.[33]

The conclusion, considered in an earlier section, that hedging is done for a variety of reasons, not merely to reduce risk, carried no necessary implication that speculation should be regarded as other than pure risk-bearing; but here we have seen further evidence that futures markets are viewed much too narrowly when they are regarded as serving merely to allow transfer of risk from hedgers to speculators: the risk-premium concept has appeared inadequate, by itself, to account for observed differences in seasonal trends of futures prices. Direct consideration of returns to speculators has produced evidence that seems to require regarding the returns as mainly a wage, often negative, that varies greatly according to ability and knowledge of the speculator. And information that has become available concerning futures markets in which much of the hedging is selective, and much of the "speculation" comes from persons who deal in the commodity otherwise, suggests that they serve in large part as means by which dealers take risks discriminatingly, and make their price judgements bear more effectively on price formation.

The place of empirical research in economics

Around 1920 and subsequently, when economics was turning strongly toward doing more empirical research, it was common for economic theorists to say that the function of empirical research was to verify theory. One may still sometimes hear that opinion expressed. It is an opinion that has its foundations in the philosophy of science that was elaborated by John Stuart Mill (1900) or else in reasoning similar to that of Mill. The feature of Mill's philosophy that gave grounds for that view had been widely recognised as fallacious before the end of the nineteenth century, and Marshall, in his *Principles*, recorded dissent from the view that economics is peculiarly a deductive science (1922, p. 29). Economic theorists have in fact rarely shown a strong feeling of need for empirical verification of theory. More typical of their attitude, at least prior to recent years, has been the aphorism, "If statistics conflict with theory, so much the worse for the statistics".

3.

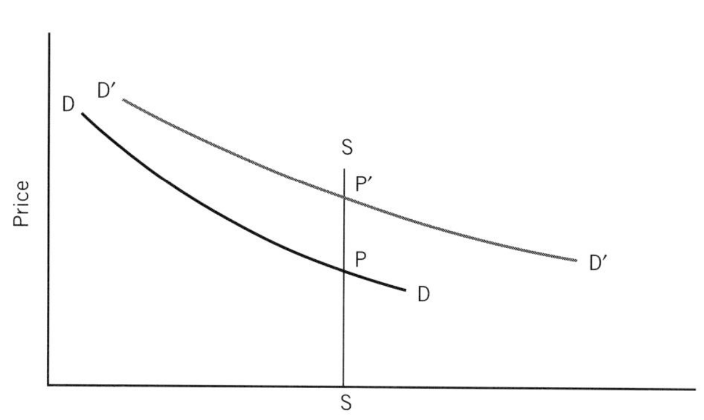

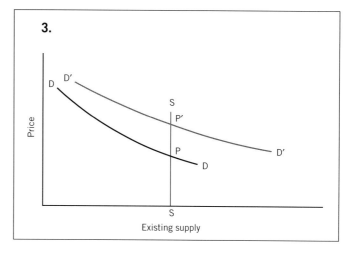

Empirical research has long been recognised as serving to clothe theory in a body of realistic circumstance that is necessary, or at least advantageous, for the practical application of theory to specific economic problems. But that use of empirical research is concerned with applied economics, not with advancing economics as a science. Though Marshall rejected Mill's classification of the sciences according to method, which had permitted regarding economics as peculiarly a deductive science with correspondingly limited opportunity for effective use of empirical research, Marshall accepted the nineteenth century view that the accomplishments of a science are to be measured by the laws of nature that it has discovered (see below); and he failed to discriminate between practical art and science. Predicting the tides "at London Bridge or at Gloucester", to which Marshall likened the tasks of economics (Marshall, 1922, p. 32), is not an undertaking that advances science.

A third view, which has had much influence in guiding empirical research on the part of economists aiming to advance economics as a science, stems from the opinion that the chief shortcoming of economics has been a failure to quantify its laws. One of the grounds for that view has been the recognised value in natural science of quantitative investigation. The research that we have been considering here offers many examples of the values of quantitative work in economics also. But the argument for quantifying economic theory depends more particularly on acceptance of the view, prevalent in natural science as well as in economics until about the beginning of the twentieth century, that the substance of science is the body of "laws of nature" that it has discovered. Marshall's statement that, "A science progresses by increasing the number and exactness of its laws..." (Marshall, 1922, p. 30) is a representative expression of the view. The turn of thinking in the natural sciences toward the conception of science that Conant has expressed particularly well may have been started by observation that the Darwinian concept of evolution continued to stand and to mark a great advance in biological science even though Darwin's "laws" of evolution became in considerable part discredited. In physical science, the results of the Michelson–Morley experiment (1887) posed an evidently severe conceptual problem, and those results were followed by a series of other discoveries that focused attention similarly on the role of concepts in science (Jeans, 1948, chapter 8).

Quantifying economic theory can produce clear advantages for applications of theory to practical economic and business problems, but it is not so clear that quantifying received theory leads often to advancing understanding of economic phenomenon. In the research considered here, the main useful results of attempts to quantify received theory have come through demonstration that the theory was fallacious - fallacious because of having started from wrong assumptions. The extreme example of such demonstration arose from an attempt to quantify the theory that price relations between old-crop and new-crop futures depended on expectations regarding the size of the new crop, which proved wholly untrue. After the price-of-storage concept had provided the basis for a new theory, quantification of the price-of-storage function involved in it produced some significant new information in the initial case, most fully revealed in Working (1953b, p. 556), where changes in the function from period to period are shown. Thereafter, though numerous additional quantifications of the function in specific instances could be useful for purposes of practical application, additional quantifications seemed not to offer promise of yielding further advances in understanding.[34]

Economics has been forced to go through a difficult process of learning how to make effective use of observation as a continuing means of advance, after having become accustomed to rely principally on deduction from a body of observational information that remained comparatively static because it was limited largely to what could be learned from "common observation" and from introspection. The difficulty of the learning process has been enhanced by a tradition in economics of accepting problems of evident practical importance as the ones at which research should be directed. Economists have been slow to recognise the error in Mill's attempt to explain the relatively primitive state of economics as a science on the ground that, "In every department of human affairs, practice long precedes Science: systematic inquiry into the modes of action of the powers of nature, is the tardy product of a long course of efforts to use those powers for practical ends" (Mill, 1898, p. 1).

Natural science did not develop out of practice. That route led to the empirical accomplishments of Watt, Burbank and Edison, not to the accomplishments of Newton, Darwin, Mendel or Heisenberg. Science has advanced by attacking manageable problems of acquiring understanding of observed phenomena with little or no immediate regard to evident practical importance of the problems. Seeking support for their efforts, scientists have often laid stress on the practical usefulness of scientific advance. Not infrequently they have chosen to push a particular line of inquiry because of hope that it would service such a practical end as unlocking the mystery of cancer. But the route of science toward such an end is always that of acquiring information that promises to yield greater understanding. For example, the research economist with a scientific viewpoint who may be considering the study of futures markets does not ask himself whether futures markets are economically important institutions, concerning which conclusions are needed for practical purposes; he asks instead whether study of futures markets offers favourable opportunity for gaining understanding of the behaviour of businessmen, including speculators, and of the behaviour of prices of the class that we have called anticipatory. He makes his decision on principles like those that govern the decision of a geneticists considering the study of fruit flies.

The place of empirical inquiry in economic science, it appears to me, is that of making observations, statistical or otherwise, and conducting analysis such that one may be able to say, paraphrasing Conant, that in economics new concepts arise from observation and analysis, and the new concepts in turn lead to further observation and analysis.

1 *Most natural scientists, including Conant (1947, pp. 26–7), have felt during at least the past half century that economics did not fully qualify as a science. Conant (1947, pp. 118–9) reserved judgement on the possibilities of economics becoming a science.*

2 *Futures contracts, used chiefly as purely financial rather than as merchandising contracts, are executed under terms that provide explicitly for settlement by financial transfer rather than by any transfer of commodity ownership (though allowing the latter as an alternative means of settlement). If the execution of such contracts went under an appropriately distinctive name instead of being called "buying and selling", people would not so often think it a perversion of sound business practice that transfer of commodity ownership occurs only infrequently under those contracts. In fact, it is excessive forcing of settlement by transfer of commodity ownership, in connection with corners and squeezes, that is a perversion of the use of futures contracts.*

3 *This was probably because of the evident significance of open contracts for the theory of hedging and because initial acceptance of the importance of open contracts did not require granting open contracts a central position in consideration of futures markets, such as they were eventually to command, but only granting them attention. Collection of the data on open contracts was indeed opposed by those who sought to avoid the expense entailed in supplying data, and even more vigorously opposed on the ground that the statistics of open contracts revealed information that, it was alleged, should not be made public. The latter contention, it should be noted, implied recognition of the pertinence of the data to study of market functioning.*

4 *The decision to collect statistics of open contracts is recorded in US Department of Agriculture (1923, p. 691). Preparation of the US Federal Trade Commission's monumental* Report on the Grain Trade *was then in progress and economists of the Commission, promptly adopting the idea that open contracts should be studied, undertook compilation of open-contract data for some earlier years* (Report on the Grain Trade, *vol. 7, pp. 8–89, 124ff). W. H. S. Stevens, who, with Francis Walker, was in general charge of the Federal Trade Commission inquiry, has told me that G. P. Watkins, of the Commission staff, may have been responsible for the idea that statistics of open contracts should be collected; but the fact that Watkins, instead of presenting an argument of his own for use of open-contract statistics, quotes Duvel on the subject (vol. 7, p. 134) leads me to think that principal credit belongs to Duvel.*

5 *Irwin (1954, pp. 69ff), dates futures trading in Chicago from near the beginning of the 1850s, and my reading of Taylor's History (Taylor, 1917) leads me to a similar conclusion. Dealings in futures were first admitted to the Chicago Board of Trade in 1865 (Taylor, 1917, 1, p. 331).*

6 *His suggestion was that the seasonal increase in amount of speculative buying of wheat at harvest time "arises chiefly from the wheat-growing sections tributary to each market, and that is done largely when the wheat is sold", and he was able to cite some evidence in support of the hypothesis (Irwin, 1935, p. 45); but the hypothesis subsequently proved inadequate to account for the observed facts.*

7 *Inadvertent omission from that paper of due credit to Irwin was corrected in Working (1955).*

8 *Further research seeking interpretation of the evidence in Figure 1 has led the author to two conclusions that deserve to be noted, though they cannot be elaborated here. The estimation procedure used to arrive at the data for the figure assumes fairly complete reporting of hedging, both short and long, and in the absence of that condition tends to produce a spurious degree of stability in the ratio between estimated amounts of long speculation and of short hedging, hence to exaggerate the closeness of response of speculation to hedging. The condition for reliability of the estimates in this respect is probably better met for wheat than for any other commodity, and is met best in periods when the amount of short hedging is large. Secondly, theoretical study of the mechanism by which one may suppose that the adjustment between amounts of speculation and of hedging is accomplished seems to make the concept of incomplete balancing between short and long hedging appropriate theoretically only in connection with comparatively long-time adjustments; its use in the accompanying figure to exhibit evidence on short-time adjustment is then to be regarded as only a graphic device. Statistical analysis of the data on lines that now seem theoretically appropriate have shown a degree of correspondence between estimated amounts of speculation and of hedging broadly similar to that indicated in the figure above.*

9 *This led presently to at least a partial explanation of the ineffectiveness of verbal inquiry into the motivation of hedging: after conclusions concerning the reasons for mill hedging had been published, a mill manager, asked why millers say that they hedge to avoid risk instead of giving the real reasons, promptly replied, "Because it is hard to explain the real reasons to a person who doesn't understand the milling business".*

10 *In consequence, the term "carrying-charge hedging" tends to be used sometimes to designate the combined operation of storage and hedging for profit. In trade usage the combined operation is sometimes called "earning the carrying charge". It is an operation not properly divisible into two parts, for without the hedging the storage becomes a quite different operation, from the business point of view, requiring use of different information to conduct it successfully, and leading often to a different choice of intervals over which storage is undertaken.*

11 *Mills in the area tributary to Seattle make little use of the alternative of hedging in the Seattle futures market because that is a very "thin" market, with consequent high costs of hedging.*

12 *The prevalence of selectivity in hedging on the smaller futures markets has at least two possible explanations. One, attributing smallness of the futures market to lack of speculative interest in the commodity would explain the prevalence of selective hedging on the ground that the market lacks enough speculation to support routine hedging by any large proportion of potential hedges, thus discouraging the development of much operational hedging and making storage for profit from expected price increases, with hedging when price decrease is expected seem more profitable than carrying-charge hedging.*

Another possibility is that the smaller futures markets have as little business as they do because of circumstances apart from the futures market that lead potential hedgers to prefer to rely on price judgements rather than on judgements concerning spot-future price relationships. Recognition of the multiple purposes of hedging should open the way to research that would give better evidence than we now have to explain why some futures markets are as little used as they are.

13 *Such use of futures contracts was first given legal status as hedging under the Commodity Exchange Act by an amendment enacted in 1956 (70 Stat. 630).*

14 *This definition was originally given with slightly different wording in Working (1953b), p. 560.*

15 *For administrative purposes of distinguishing between anticipatory hedging of raw material requirements and speculation, the Commodity Exchange Act, as amended in 1956, restricts such anticipatory hedging to "… an amount of such commodity the purchase of which for future delivery shall not exceed such person's unfilled anticipated requirements for processing or manufacturing during a specified operating period not in excess of one year: Provided, that such purchase is made and liquidated in an orderly manner and in accordance with sound commercial practice …" In effect this provision draws the same line between hedging and speculation as does the definition of speculation given in note 16.*

16 *For this purpose, speculation in commodities may be defined as the holding of a net long or a net short position, for gain, and not as a normal incident to operating a producing, merchandising or processing business. The reference to net position in this definition, proposed in Working (1960b), p. 187, serves to exclude arbitrage from speculation. Though the two have something in common, they need to be distinguished, and that is done more conveniently by defining speculation to exclude arbitrage than by adopting a new term to mean "speculation other than arbitrage".*

17 *See especially Working (1933), pp. 188–203 and Working (1934a), pp. 199–205. These studies, dealing with prices in a single exporting country, were later supplemented by a similar inquiry into price behaviour in the major import market for the same commodity (Hoos and Working, 1940). Comparisons of behaviour between these two widely differing sorts of markets helped to indicate which behaviour characteristics were special to a particular sort of market and which were more generally observable. In both markets prices of the near future responded sensitively to distant price expectations, but the influences that bore particularly on the price of the near future, causing its price movement to diverge more or less from that of the distant future, were appreciably different in the two markets (Hoos and Working, 1940, esp. pp. 102–5, 110–26, 136–8).*

18 *This statement is true also for most other commodities that have futures markets, but is inapplicable to prices of a commodity, like potatoes or onions, that is incapable of economical interseasonal storage. Gray (1960, pp. 305ff) has noted that it seems not to apply to coffee in the US Interpretation of his evidence requires recognition that the "price of storage", reflected in the price difference between futures for different dates, is dependent on the expected level of stocks during the interval between those dates, and that such expectations regarding future domestic stocks of an imported commodity may be affected by some of the same circumstances that influence the price of a distant future.*

19 *One evidence of this fact appears in the short-lived controversy that developed between the present author and Roland P. Vaile (Working, 1948; Vaile, 1948; Working, 1949a).*

20 *Two recent expositions by leading economists (Samuelson, 1957 and Houthakker, 1959) that may seem to ignore or reject the price-of-storage concept were not so intended. They sought to present a theory of price formation under conditions of certainty, leaving the effects of uncertainty to be treated in later elaboration of the theory, and assumed that under conditions of certainty stocks would be carried only in the expectation of a direct return for storage equal to the "costs" of storage, the latter treated as being invariant with respect to the quantity to be stored. In fact, however, the observed willingness of dealers and processors to carry stocks of wheat, for example, at the end of a crop year for a negative price of storage arises only in small part from the presence of uncertainty. Each of three other considerations has more influence, namely: costs of abnormal acceleration of the movement of new-crop wheat from harvest field to mill rollers; temporal dispersion of harvest times; and geographical dispersion of flour mills among areas with different harvest times.*

If convenience of exposition is well served by proceeding in two stages, the first of which assumes that stocks will fall to zero in the absence of an expected return from storage equal to the full "costs" of storage, the simplifying assumptions involved at the first stage should include instantaneous harvest of the entire crop, and costs of movement from producer to consumer that are invariant with respect to rate of movement. The supposed advantage of the two-stage exposition, with price of storage ignored at the first stage, will be found illusory, I think, when economists have fully assimilated the price-of-storage concept.

21 *A familiar illustration of random variation is the variation in number of spots that turn up when a pair of "true" dice is thrown after being thoroughly shaken each time. By proceeding from that illustration, one may illustrate random walk by drawing on a chart a line that moves forward one space for each throw of the pair of dice, and up or down by a number of units equal to the number of spots minus seven (seven being the "expected" number of spots on each throw). Randomness, in the statistical sense, however, does not necessarily involved absence of known causes for the events designated as random, but only that individual events are unpredictable from knowledge of previous events in the series. Thus prices may change from known causes, but if the changes are unpredictable from any knowledge of previous prices and price changes, as the exchanges in the curve drawn on the basis of dice-throwing are unpredictable from the previous course of the curve, the price series exhibits random walk.*

22 *This appears to be true of commodity prices only within time spans not longer than about one year, but true of stock prices over much longer time spans.*

23 *The two early papers on the subject were complementary in nature. Mine (1934b) stressed the difference between random variation and random walk, and presented a 2,400-term random-walk series as a device both for illustrating the close conformity of actual price series with the random-walk model and for testing such evidences of departure from that model as might be observed. Cowles and Jones (1937) gave a great amount of statistical evidence in the course of exploring the question whether appreciable non-randomness of stock-price change might be found at some difference-intervals though not at others. See also Cowles (1960), in which Cowles gave revised results that eliminated the effects of inadvertent use in Cowles and Jones (1937) of one index number series that had employed undesirable averaging. Kendall (1953), much later and in apparent ignorance of earlier work, provided a test of the hypothesis that non-randomness of change might be revealed by serial correlations of orders higher than the first, using a constant difference-interval. The only substantial indication of significant serial correlation that Kendall found was in a first-order coefficient for cotton prices; and that, as shown in Working (1960c), was a correlation attributable to averaging in the construction of the cotton price series used, hence invalid as evidence that cotton prices showed any departure from random walk.*

24 *The quotation marks are repeated here as a reminder that the price changes referred to do not have a dominantly wave-like character such as tends to be implied by calling them fluctuations.*

25 *By "simple" autocorrelation I mean autocorrelation in the sense in which that term has been commonly understood, namely, correlation between items uniformly spaced in time, or in the case of correlation of first differences, differences taken over uniform time intervals, uniformly spaced. It would be reasonable to regard any form of structure in a time series as involving some form of autocorrelation.*

26 *Price moves of 5% were the smallest ones considered by Alexander. In an earlier work of mine, I applied the same principle as did Alexander to study of very small price movements of futures, and found in the smallest movements, of which there may be several hundred within a day, a substantial tendency to negative (rather than positive) correlation (Working, 1954b, p. 11). Like Alexander, I found that the evidence of structure that was revealed by considering movements of given size tended to become invisible under consideration of movements over given time intervals.*

Analysis of correlation by movement size is laborious (my work along that line was done before electronic computers became widely available), and partly for that reason I turned to another approach, described below, that seemed to hold as good, or perhaps better, possibilities of uncovering the presence of obscure sorts of structure in price "fluctuations".

27 *The difficulty in identifying the kind of structure indicated arose partly from inherent difficulty in predicting how a new sort of test, designed to be responsive to a variety of different sorts of structure, would respond to particular sorts of structure; but that inherent difficulty was complicated by the fact that the kind of structure indicated was of an unexpected sort.*

28 *The purely statistical evidence in Gray (1961), p. 257, for example, did not include a specific test of the hypothesis that the observed variation among apparent seasonal trends might be explainable as consistent with existence of a uniform tendency toward positive seasonal trend in all the markets and periods considered.*

29 *I speak of "seasonal trends" rather than "bias", which has been the term more commonly used, because it designates what is actually measured, and then interpreted as evidence of bias; and I mean the term to comprise trends measured with respect to some pertinent seasonal variable such as Cootner (1960, pp. 400–1) has suggested should be used, as well as trends measured with respect to calendar dates.*

30 *The overall tendency toward losses by the speculators in Stewart's sample must be attributed chiefly to lack of full representativeness of the sample; it included relatively few, if any, professional speculators, and may have been unrepresentative otherwise.*

31 *Such data appear in Stewart (1941, p. 22), and subsequently in a number of CEA "surveys" for several markets and dates.*

32 *Particularly clear examples are afforded by the onion market, which is one of those in which a large proportion of the futures contracts classed as speculative was found to be held by dealers in the commodity (Working, 1960a, p. 7). Onions from the late summer crop, which are stored for use over a period extending into April, are sold by growers to "country shippers", who store them. In order to maintain his competitive position as a dealer, the country shipper must buy when growers want to sell, and he is thus severely limited in opportunity to adjust his stock-holding in accordance with expectations of price change. Country shippers sell in turn to "dealers" in the large cities, who cannot economically accumulate large stocks because refrigerated storage, on which they would ordinarily need to rely, is much more expensive*

than "common storage" in the cold climates where most of the onions are produced. Consequently the city dealer, who may be better informed about the nationwide supply and demand situation for onions than most country shippers, and financially better able to carry risks of price change, is handicapped in expressing his price opinions through adjustment of stockholdings.

33 *The effect in the case of a futures market used only by dealers is not necessarily to move the curve to the right because* DD, *representing amounts of stock that dealers are willing to hold unhedged in the absence of opportunity for hedging, cannot be taken to represent also the amounts that they would be willing to hold unhedged, at the same prices, in the presence of opportunity for hedging. The possibility that such a rightward shift might occur even in the case of a futures market used only by dealers was suggested to me by the great apparent effect of the onion futures market in supporting the post-harvest price level for that commodity, which seemed difficult to explain solely on the ground of price support given by pure speculators (persons not connected with the industry) in view of the fact that, according to the available information, such speculations accounted for only about half of the long "speculative" holdings of onion futures at the times when such support was principally needed (Working, 1960a, p. 7).*

There is a general tendency for performance of the storage function for any seasonally produced commodity to concentrate largely at some one stage of the marketing process. The concentration is most commonly at terminal markets, but it may be at country points, as for onions, or in the hands of processors of the commodity, as appears to be the case with rubber; but in any case, such concentration tends to restrict opportunity for exerting price influence through the holding of physical stocks mainly to those handlers of the commodity who operate at that stage. Existence of a futures market, allowing the many other handlers of the commodity to readily "carry" stocks by holding futures contracts against hedged stocks, would tend therefore to produce such a rightward shift as is illustrated in Figure 3, even though only handlers of the commodity used the futures market.

34 *The further quantifications provided in Brennan (1958) may nevertheless be regarded as useful for corroboration of the original findings.*

BIBLIOGRAPHY

Alexander, S. S., 1961, "Price Movements in Speculative Markets: Trends or Random Walks", *Industrial Management Review* (May), pp. 7–26.

Brennan, M. J., 1958, "The Supply of Storage", *American Economic Review* 47 (March), pp. 50–72.

Brinegar, C. S., 1954, "A Statistical Analysis of Speculative Price Behavior", doctoral dissertation, Stanford.

Conant, J. B., 1947, *On Understanding Science* (New Haven).

Cootner, P. H., 1960, "Returns to Speculators: Telser versus Keynes", *Journal of Political Economy* 48 (August), pp. 396–404, 415–18.

Cowles, A., and H. E. Jones, 1937, "Some a Posteriori Probabilities in Stock Market Action", *Econometrica* 5 (July), pp. 280–94.

Cowles, A., 1960, "A Revision of Previous Conclusions Regarding Stock Price Behavior", *Econometrica* 28 (October), pp. 909–15.

Graf, T. F., 1953, "Hedging – How Effective is It?" *Journal of Farm Economics* 35, August pp. 398–413.

Gray, R. W., 1960, "The Characteristic Bias in Some Thin Futures Markets", *Food Research Institute Studies* 1 (November), pp. 296–312.

Gray, R. W., 1961, "The Search for a Risk Premium", *Journal of Political Economy* 69 (June), pp. 250–60.

Hoffman, G. W., 1941, *Grain Prices and the Futures Market*, USDA Tech. Bull. no. 747.

Hoos, S., and H. Working, 1940, "Price Relations of Liverpool Wheat Futures", *Wheat Studies* (Food Research Institute, Stanford) 17 (November), pp. 101–43.

Houthakker, H. S., 1957, "Can Speculators Forecast Prices?" *Review of Economics and Statistics* 39, pp. 143–51.

Houthakker, H. S., 1959, "The Scope and Limits of Futures Trading", in Moses Abramovitz *et al*, *The Allocation of Economic Resources* (Stanford).

Houthakker, H.S., 1961, "Systematic and Random Elements in Short-Term Price Movements", *American Economic Review* 51 (May), pp. 164–72.

Irwin, H. S., 1935, "Seasonal Cycles in Aggregates of Wheat-Futures Contracts", *Journal of Political Economy* 43 (February), pp. 34–9.

Irwin, H. S., 1954, *Evolution of Futures Trading* (Madison, Wisconsin).

Jeans, J., 1948, *The Growth of Physical Science* (New York).

Kendall, M. G., 1953, "The Analysis of Economic Time Series", *Journal of the Royal Statistical Society* 116, pp. 11-34.

Larson, A. B., 1960, "Measurement of a Random Process in Future Prices", *Food Research Institute Studies* 1 (November), pp. 313-24.

Marshall, A., 1922, *Principles of Economics*, 8th edn (London). (First edn, 1890.)

Mehl, J. M., 1931, *Hedging in Grain Futures*, USDA Circular no. 151.

Mill, J. S., 1900, *Principles of Political Economy*, Revised edn (New York). (First edn, 1848.)

Mill, J. S., 1898, *A System of Logic, People's edition* (London). (First edn, 1843.)

Samuelson, P. A., 1957, "Intertemporal Price Equilibrium: A Prologue to the Theory of Speculation", *Weltwirtschaft. Archiv* 79 (December), pp. 181-221.

Stewart, B., 1941, *Trading in Wool Top Futures*, USDA Circular no. 604.

Stewart, B., 1949, *An Analysis of Speculative Trading in Grain Futures*, USDA Technical Bulletin no. 1001.

Taylor, C. H., 1917, *History of the Board of Trade of the City of Chicago* (Chicago).

Telser, L. G., 1958, "Futures Trading and the Storage of Cotton and Wheat", *Journal of Political Economy* 66 (June), pp. 233-55.

Telser, L. G., 1960, "Rejoinder", *Journal of Political Economy* 68 (August), pp. 404-15.

Vaile, R. S., 1948, "Inverse Carrying Charges in Futures Markets", *Journal of Farm Economics* 30 (August), pp. 574-5.

Wiese, V. A., 1952, "Use of Commodity Exchanges by Local Grain Marketing Organisation", Proceedings, Chicago Board of Trade Annual Symposium, pp. 108-16.

Working, H., 1933, "Price Relations Between July and September Wheat Futures at Chicago Since 1885", *Wheat Studies* (Food Research Institute, Stanford) 9 (March), pp. 217-38.

Working, H., 1934a, "Price Relations Between May and New-Crop Wheat Futures at Chicago Since 1885", *Wheat Studies* (Food Research Institute, Stanford), 10 (February), pp. 183-228.

Working, H., 1934b, "A Random-Difference Series for Use in the Analysis of Time Series", *Journal of American Statistics Association* 29 (March), pp. 11-24.

Working, H., 1948, "Theory of the Inverse Carrying Charge in Futures Markets", *Journal of Farm Economics* 30 (February), pp. 1-28.

Working, H., 1949a, "Professor Vaile and the Theory of Inverse Carrying Charges", *Journal of Farm Economics* 31 (February), pp. 168-72.

Working, H., 1949b, "The Investigation of Economic Expectations", *American Economic Review, Proc.* 39 (May), pp. 150-66.

Working, H., 1949c, "The Theory of Price of Storage", *American Economic Review* 39 (December), pp. 1254-62.

Working, H., 1953a, "Futures Trading and Hedging", *American Economic Review* 43 (June), pp. 314-43, reprinted as Chapter 3 of the present volume.

Working, H., 1953b, "Hedging Reconsidered", *Journal of Farm Economics* 35 (November), pp. 544-61.

Working, H., 1954a, "Whose Markets? Evidence on Some Aspects of Futures Trading", *Journal of Marketing* 29 (July), pp. 1-11.

Working, H., 1954b, "Price Effects of Scalping and Day Trading", *Proceedings of Chicago Board of Trade Annual Symposium* (September), pp. 114-39.

Working, H., 1955, "Review of Irwin, Evolution of Futures Trading", *Journal of Farm Economics* 37 (May), pp. 377-80.

Working, H., 1956, "New Ideas and Methods for Price Research", *Journal of Farm Economics* 38 (December), pp. 1427-36.

Working, H., 1958, "A Theory of Anticipatory Prices", *American Economic Review, Proc* 48 (May), pp. 188-99.

Working, H., 1960a, "Price Effects of Futures Trading", *Food Research Institute Studies* 1 (February), pp. 3-31.

Working, H., 1960b, "Speculation on Hedging Markets", *Food Research Institute Studies* 1 (May), pp. 185-220.

Working, H., 1960c, "Note on the Correlation of First Differences of Averages in a Random Chain", *Econometrica* 28 (October), pp. 916-18.

US Department of Agriculture, 1923, Annual Report Department of Agriculture (Washington, D.C.).

US Federal Trade Commission, 1920-26, *Report on the Grain Trade,* 7 vols (Washington, D.C.).

RATIONALES FOR CORPORATE HEDGING

5

Should Firms Use Derivatives to Manage Risk?*

David Fite and Paul Pfleiderer

Westpac; Stanford University

Over the past few decades, the performance of financial markets has been greatly improved by the development of new technologies in communications and information processing. Some argue that financial market performance has also been improved by the creation of new types of securities, especially the financial instruments known as derivatives. The creation and widespread use of derivatives has been brought about in large measure by conceptual advances that have allowed various financial institutions to value and hedge these complex instruments. While the use of derivatives has become widespread, it has also become controversial. Some question the value of derivatives and call for restrictions on their use and new regulations. In this article we consider the economic role played by derivatives. We focus in particular on the use of derivatives by corporations to hedge risks. Should corporations hedge risks; and if so, which ones and why?

Before addressing the issue of corporate hedging, it is useful to consider the general role derivatives can play in financial markets. Financial markets create value in free market economies by performing a number of important functions. One is the allocation of scarce capital to its most productive uses. Should a billion-dollar electric power plant be built, or should the billion dollars be spent instead on the development of a new commercial aircraft? Any elementary textbook on finance or economics shows that financial markets, by establishing the cost of capital for different types of projects, help direct investment to its most productive applications. Financial markets also create value by facilitating an efficient distribution of risks among risk bearers. If the power plant is built and the demand for electricity falls, who should suffer the consequences? Should this be the same party that bears the risk of increases in the price of the coal that fuels the plant? These functions of allocating capital and risks are obviously closely related. In general, the optimal allocation of capital depends on how efficiently risks can be shared among investors. In particular, if the risks created by a given investment can be more efficiently allocated among risk bearers, then the cost of capital for that investment may be reduced and the investment becomes more attractive.

Derivatives have generally lowered the cost and increased the precision with which the market is able to unbundle and distribute risks among risk bearers. However, from this it does not immediately follow that corporations should use derivatives to hedge risks. After all, it might be argued that the ultimate bearers of risk are individuals and not corporations. Corporations can trade risks among themselves, but would such trading have any consequences for how these risks affect individual investors? Since individual investors typically hold positions in many corporations and can themselves alter their risk exposure by trading in derivatives, the case for corporate hedging is not immediately obvious.

We argue below that various "market imperfections" create a solid case for corporate hedging. It is not correct to view corporations as simply passing risks through the corporate structure to individuals who then adjust their positions to attain their optimal risk exposure. Some risks affect corporate earnings in ways that individual investors cannot offset by

* *This paper was first published in W. Beaver and G. Parker (1995),* Risk Management: Problems and Solutions, *and is reproduced with permission of The McGraw-Hill Companies. The authors thank Anat Admati and Howard Mason for helpful comments.*

altering their own financial positions. Because of this, there are several valid reasons for corporations to hedge risks. At the same time, there are some reasons that have been given for corporate hedging that do not make economic sense. We do not intend to provide an exhaustive list of valid reasons for hedging. Undoubtedly many readers can think of specific cases for hedging that do not fall neatly in the taxonomy we present. Our hope is that we have identified most of the major justifications for corporate hedging as well as some of the more dubious ones.

The question as to whether or not a corporation should hedge is not well posed. To have a meaningful discussion, we must specify an objective for the corporation and then ask if and how hedging advances the corporation toward this objective. The standard objective used in a context such as this one is the maximisation of shareholder value or shareholder wealth. For most of the following discussion we assume that this is the goal; but in some cases this is problematical - especially where significant differences exist among a firm's shareholders. For example, if some shareholders hold diversified portfolios while others have concentrated holdings in a firm, the two groups will not necessarily agree on the value of a hedging programme. In such a case there will not be a clear, unambiguous measure of shareholder value.

Three views of corporate hedging

To frame our discussion of corporate hedging, we begin by examining three frequently encountered views about the value of hedging programmes. Our arguments against these lead us to conclude that the only valid justifications for hedging on corporate account are those based on "market imperfections."

HEDGING, SINCE IT REDUCES RISK, IS GOOD

Financial markets provide a wealth of evidence supporting the notion that investors are risk-averse and demand a premium (in terms of a higher expected return) when they hold risky positions.[1] Hedging, it might be argued, reduces the volatility of a firm's earnings and by doing so makes the cashflow stream delivered by a company to its investors less volatile and therefore more valuable. According to this line of argument, the firm reduces volatility through hedging, which reduces the risk premium investors demand to hold its stock and bonds. This, in turn, raises the value of the future cashflows delivered by the firm since they will be discounted at a lower rate, and this increases the value of the firm and shareholders' wealth.

HEDGING, SINCE IT REDUCES RISK, IS BAD

This polar view of hedging is based on the argument that value is generally created by taking on risk and not by avoiding it. A firm that wants to reduce risk can always do so by not investing in risky projects. In the extreme, it can reduce all risk by investing only in short-term government securities. Obviously this course of action produces no value for the shareholders. Thus it is argued that a firm must take on reasonable risks to create value; and if it avoids or transfers these risks, it gives up this value.

Both these arguments are based on incorrect views of how the market "prices" risk. Some risks are priced in the financial markets in the sense that investors require a higher rate of expected return to bear those risks. Other risks are not priced in the sense that investors require no adjustment in expected return. A firm generates value for its investors only when it makes an investment that has a higher expected return than investors require as compensation for the risk.

HEDGING IS NEITHER GOOD NOR BAD; IT IS IRRELEVANT

Unlike the first two views, which rely on simplistic notions of the relations between risk and value, this view is based on a more subtle understanding of the alternatives available to investors and how these investors view various risks.

Part of this argument for the irrelevancy of hedging is based on the fact that many sources of volatility within a firm are not risks that investors care about since these risks nearly vanish in a diversified portfolio.[2] In particular, an investor who holds a diversified portfolio is not affected in any significant way by sources of volatility that affect only one or a few firms. Such "idiosyncratic" risks are inconsequential for investors. Consider a well-diversified investor who holds stock in Ford. Even though Ford is a large firm with a market capitalisation of US$18.854 billion (as of December 1992), its capitalisation is only 0.47% of the total value of New York Stock Exchange (NYSE) stocks and an even smaller fraction of the total value of all US stocks.

Assume there is a risk that affects only Ford and that this risk either adds 10% to Ford's return or subtracts 10% from it. Then a diversified investor who holds Ford in same proportion as its value in the NYSE stock portfolio will see his return vary by at most 0.047% due to this risk. To put this into perspective, note that a diversified investor with a total investment of US$100,000 loses only US$4.70 as a result of a 10% decline in Ford stock. Such an investor would see little value in Ford's removing this risk and would oppose its removal if there were a significant cost involved. The diversified investor is only concerned with *pervasive* risks – ie, risks that affect a large number of firms. The idiosyncratic risk at Ford has virtually no effect on any investor who has allocated his wealth across many firms.

Even when we consider pervasive risks, it is not immediately clear that a firm can gain by hedging these risks. Oil price shocks are good examples of pervasive risks that affect many firms. Note, however, that unexpected changes in the price of oil affect firms in different ways. An increase in the price of oil will generally increase the earnings of the oil companies but will reduce those of the airlines. A diversified investor who holds both oil and airline stocks is therefore at least partially hedged in his portfolio against oil price shocks. Such a diversified investor's risk exposure is essentially unchanged if the airlines take long positions in oil futures contracts and obtain them from the oil companies who take the offsetting short sides. Of course, there are pervasive risks that affect most firms in the same way. These risks do not "cancel out" in a diversified portfolio, and it is reasonable to assume that diversified investors will be sensitive to them. Does this mean that a firm is better off if it reduces these risks? Not necessarily.

Assume that an unexpected increase in energy costs affects almost all firms adversely. This, then, is a pervasive risk that does not cancel out in diversified portfolios.[3] Assume that because energy cost risk cannot be diversified away, diversified investors require a higher expected return on securities with a high sensitivity to energy costs than they do for securities with lower sensitivity. If a firm could change its real operations in some costless way that reduced its exposure to energy costs, then its value would increase. However, if that firm reduced its energy cost exposure by hedging, it would pass energy risk on to some counterparty who would demand compensation for bearing this risk. In an efficient market, that compensation is precisely equal to the increase in the value of the firm's cashflows due to the energy risk reduction. The shareholders will be neither better nor worse off. Thus it is irrelevant what the firm does to "manage" this risk.

Even if one is unwilling to accept the arguments made above for the irrelevancy of corporate hedging policies, one still must contend with another argument for irrelevancy – this one based on the well-known and important insights contained in Modigliani and Miller's analysis of a firm's capital structure.[4] Modigliani and Miller considered changes in a firm's financing policy that do not alter the firm's investment policy. They showed that such changes neither increase nor reduce the firm's value when there are no transactions costs, no taxes and no information asymmetries. Their argument was based on the observation that any financial position that the firm can achieve by altering the set of claims it issues can also be achieved by holders of the firm's debt and equity if they adjust their "own account" positions. At the same time, any investors unhappy with the change can undo it by trading on their own accounts.

In their original analysis, Modigliani and Miller focused on the corporation's debt/equity ratio (ie, its use of leverage), but their arguments clearly apply with equal force to a firm's hedging strategy. Under the assumptions made by Modigliani and Miller, there is no reason for a firm to hedge since investors can do it on their own accounts if this is something they desire. For example, a US export firm that sells in Germany can reduce its exposure to exchange risk by taking a position in the US$/DM forward market. However, any of the firm's shareholders who value this risk reduction can achieve the same result without the firm's hedging by taking a similar (but smaller) position in the forward market on their own account. However, some of the shareholders might actually prefer the export firm's exposure to exchange risk – perhaps because they are importers of German goods and their risk is offset to some extent by the exporter's position. If the exporter does hedge its exposure, these shareholders can undo the result by taking the opposite and offsetting position on their own accounts. In all cases, it makes no difference what the exporter does as long as the shareholders know the exporter's hedging positions and can trade in the same instruments.

The general conditions for corporate hedging to benefit shareholders

If value is created by altering risk exposure through derivatives, it must be because one or more of the assumptions used by Modigliani and Miller do not hold. It is clear that at least two conditions must be met by any worthwhile corporate hedging strategy: (1) it must change the firm's cashflows in a way that shareholders value and the benefit to shareholders must be greater than the cost of hedging; and (2) hedging on corporate account must be the least expensive way to bring about the beneficial change in cashflows. In particular, the firm must be at least as efficient in adjusting the risk exposure and creating the improvement as shareholders would if they hedged on their own account.

One might think that the second condition hardly merits serious attention. Doesn't the firm always have a cost advantage over individual shareholders since it can take advantage of scale economies and therefore pay lower transactions costs? In fact, there are many situations in which shareholders have a distinct advantage over firms in controlling risk exposure. For example, in the 1960s, a large number of conglomerate mergers occurred in the US. At the time one of the justifications given for these mergers was that, by creating a diversified company, a conglomerate merger lowered the risk experienced by shareholders. While there may have been good reasons for the formation of conglomerates, this almost certainly was not one of them. Individual shareholders could on their own accounts achieve the benefits of diversification simply by buying shares in a number of companies in different industries. This could be accomplished at far lower cost (especially if it were done through mutual funds) than that of "physically" merging several companies. Corporations are *high-cost* producers of diversification – at least when they do it through mergers. It is therefore reasonable for us to ask whether the second condition is met by corporate hedging strategies. As we show below, for many of the benefits produced by hedging the corporation is likely to be the lowest-cost producer. In fact, we argue that several benefits of hedging cannot be produced at all by the shareholders' hedging on their own accounts and that only corporate hedging can bring about these gains.

Since we measure the value of corporate hedging in terms of the effects hedging has on shareholder wealth, we must now consider how shareholders value the cashflows produced by a firm. Many approaches break the problem of valuing a firm's shares into two parts. In the first step, future cashflows that will be produced by the firm and paid to shareholders are forecast. In the second step, these expected cashflows are discounted to the present using the appropriate risk-adjusted discount rate. This discount rate is the rate of return shareholders require as compensation for the riskiness of the firm's cashflows. It follows that hedging can affect the firm's value by changing the expectation of its future cashflows, by changing the discount rate shareholders use to discount these cashflows, or by doing both. Since corporate hedging policies alter the firm's risk exposure, it would seem that the most profound effects of hedging would be felt through changes in the firm's risk-adjusted discount rate.

We argue below that, paradoxically, most of the gains produced by corporate hedging for shareholders are due to increases in expected cashflows and not to reductions in the discount rate. Along these lines, we divide the remaining discussion into two parts. First we discuss the effects of corporate hedging on the risks shareholders actually bear. This relates mainly to the discount rate. Then we discuss how risk actually affects the firm and, more specifically, how corporate hedging affects the expected cashflows the firm can generate and deliver to shareholders.

Risks shareholders bear, and benefits of corporate hedging

Does corporate hedging produce any gain to shareholders by changing the risk they experience? Much of the foregoing discussion leads one to be sceptical that it does. Since shareholders tend to hold well-diversified portfolios through intermediaries such as mutual funds and pension funds, many corporate risks are diversified away in the typical shareholder's portfolio. In addition, the Modigliani–Miller argument reminds us that shareholders have the ability to control their risk exposure on their own account and do not necessarily require that corporations do it for them. Do these arguments for the irrelevance of corporate hedging hold up after we explicitly consider transactions costs and other market imperfections?

First, note that not all shareholders hold well-diversified portfolios. Many US corporations have shareholders who own fairly large stakes in the firm and for whom this stake is a large portion of their net worth. In many cases, these are founders or others who for control reasons have acquired a significant number of shares. These undiversified shareholders will quite likely differ from diversified shareholders in the way they view the risks faced by the corporation. We have already noted that in this case it is somewhat problematic to talk about the effects of hedging on shareholder value. Shareholders will not value corporate hedging in the same way.

For example, assume that a firm has one large shareholder who holds 30% of the firm's shares and that this stake represents almost all of his wealth. The remaining shares (70%) are held by diversified investors. Now assume that the firm faces foreign exchange risk since it is a net importer from Canada, but also assume that the diversified shareholders *on net* have no foreign exchange exposure. This can come about if the diversified shareholders hold stock in both exporters to and importers from Canada. In terms of their risk exposure, the diversified shareholders will not benefit if the corporation hedges the exchange rate risk, but clearly the undiversified shareholder will see his risk reduced. Should the firm hedge?

Assume that the firm can *costlessly* eliminate the foreign exchange risk by trading a futures contract with a firm that exports to Canada but that the cost of the undiversified shareholder's hedging on his own account is greater than zero. An argument can be made for the firm to hedge since the diversified shareholders are no worse off and the large shareholder is better off.[5] Now assume that it is somewhat costly for the firm to hedge the exchange rate risk due to transactions costs, but that this cost is less than the cost the undiversified shareholder pays if he hedges on his own account. Should the firm hedge? If it does, the diversified shareholders are worse off since they pay 70% of the cost of hedging but receive no gain. The diversified shareholder potentially gains, however, since he pays only 30% of the costs of hedging but benefits from the lower risk exposure. Given the assumptions we have made, it is clear that if we put the matter to a shareholder vote and everyone votes in his or her own interest, the vote will go against hedging.

Before concluding that hedging will always be rejected by shareholders when the majority of shareholders are diversified, we should ask if the large shareholder's presence in any way benefits the diversified shareholders. Several arguments have been made to support the notion that the presence of a large shareholder does benefit the other shareholders. Many of these are based on "free-rider" problems that occur when shareholding is widely diversified. It is clear that when each shareholder holds a very small stake in each firm, none has much of an incentive to monitor the performance of the firm or to pressure its management into making value-improving changes. A diversified shareholder who pays the substantial costs of time and effort involved in monitoring and lobbying for changes receives only a tiny fraction of the gain. He prefers that others pay these costs and that he "free ride" on their efforts. Of course, the free-rider problem exists even when there is a shareholder who holds a stake of, say, 30%, but in this case it is not as severe. A shareholder with a 30% stake has some incentive to monitor since he receives 30% of the gains rather than the minuscule part a diversified investor receives. In fact, the larger the stake, the greater the incentive to monitor.

Since this monitoring produces a gain for all of the shareholders, diversified shareholders may want to encourage a few shareholders to maintain large positions in the firm. One way to do this is to lower the costs paid by those investors who take large stakes. Obviously one of the major costs borne by these investors is the added risk exposure due to the loss of diversification. A corporate hedging programme reduces this cost and encourages the undiversified investors to maintain larger stakes than they otherwise would. Ultimately this increases expected cashflows since, with more concentrated ownership, more monitoring occurs.[6]

Now we turn to the diversified investors' exposure to risks. Again, diversified investors include a large number of securities in their portfolios and put a small weight on each. Although investors who hold well-diversified portfolios are hardly affected by risks that are felt by only one or two firms, they generally have reason to be concerned with risks that are pervasive – ie, risks that are felt by many firms. Pervasive risks typically do not vanish in diversified portfolios.[7] Diversified investors will therefore prefer that firms hedge pervasive risks rather than non-pervasive risks.[8] It must be emphasised, however, that diversified investors as a class gain only if the pervasive risks are transferred "out of the system." This means that when corporation A hedges a risk, it is not absorbed by corporation B, a company in which the diversified shareholders also hold stock. If risk is not transferred out of the system, the risk exposure of the *average* diversified investor remains the same. If, however, corporation A hedges the risk by transferring it to a privately held company or to a foreign company in which the diversified investors do not hold shares, then the average diversified shareholder may gain.

Hedging that transfers risk "out of the system" is one way to expand the set of securities over which investors diversify. Consider international diversification. The gains to international diversification appear to be quite large, yet most investors continue to concentrate their portfolio holdings in their domestic markets. Under certain circumstances, hedging can provide a way for these investors to realise some (but by no means all) of the gains of international diversification. For example, if the average firm in the country of Sellpetrol has positive exposure to the risk of changes in oil prices (returns increase when oil prices rise) while the average firm in the country of Buypetrol has negative exposure, the inhabitants of both countries can reduce the variance of their portfolios' returns by buying diversified portfolios consisting of shares in Sellpetrol *and* Buypetrol. If, for some reason, the inhabitants of each country do not diversify in this fashion but instead hold only portfolios diversified over their domestic stocks, then risk can still be reduced if the companies in each country hedge their risk of oil price exposure. This might be done by having the companies in Sellpetrol take short positions in oil futures and the companies in Buypetrol take the offsetting long positions. It could also be done if the investors of Sellpetrol issue short futures contracts to the investors of Buypetrol.

Given resistance or impediments to international diversification, hedging is potentially valuable to the shareholders of each country; but at this point there is no reason for it to be done at the corporate level. The obvious justification for corporate-level hedging is the savings in transactions costs. The potential sources of these savings are obvious. If fixed costs are associated with a hedge, it is better for a firm to pay these costs once on behalf of all shareholders than for each shareholder to pay these costs individually. A major component of these fixed costs is the cost of acquiring the information about the firm's risk exposure. Clearly there are also possibilities of reducing trading costs, legal costs and so on when hedging is done at the corporate level.

It would seem that the transactions cost advantages that firms possess would always decide in favour of hedging on corporate account. Surprisingly, this is not always true. The question of who should hedge - the corporation or shareholders - becomes much more complicated once we acknowledge that not all diversified investors are alike. This is because diversified investors are exposed to risks that affect them outside of their investment portfolios.

An airline pilot, for example, is exposed to oil price risk by virtue of his occupation.[9] If the pilot is a savvy investor, he skews his investment portfolio away from stocks that are negatively affected by oil price risk (ie, have low returns when oil prices increase) and toward those that are positively affected. This reduces his overall exposure to oil price risk. If the pilot holds a stock in a firm that has a *negative* exposure to oil price risks, he prefers that the firm hedge the risk if it is not too costly to do so. At the same time, an Exxon employee who holds stock in a company with a *negative* exposure to oil price risk prefers that the company bear this risk. The negative exposure to oil price risk is a valuable hedge for the Exxon employee since it tends to offset his positive exposure to oil price risk resulting from his employment in the oil industry. Thus even shareholders who hold diversified portfolios may disagree over what a particular firm's hedging policy should be.

This disagreement among shareholders may mean that the best policy for the firm is not to hedge even if a majority of its shareholders benefit and if the firm's transactions costs are lower than those of its shareholders. For example, consider a firm with 100 shares and assume that it has a negative exposure to oil prices. Suppose that 60 of its shares are held by airline pilots and the remaining 40 by oil company employees.[10] Finally, assume that it costs twice as much for shareholders to hedge a unit exposure to oil price risk as it does for the company to hedge the same unit of exposure. If the company hedges its negative exposure to oil price risk, it pays $100c$, where c is the cost the company pays per *share* to hedge. The oil company employees are, however, worse off than they were before since they have lost the risk reduction produced by the company's negative exposure to oil price risk. As a consequence, they must unwind the hedge on their own accounts. This costs them $40(2c) = 80c$. (Recall that individual shareholders pay twice the transactions costs that the firm pays.) Thus the total transactions cost spent when the firm hedges is $180c$. If the firm does not hedge, the airline pilots must hedge on their own. This will cost $60(2c) = 120c$, which is less than $180c$.

Of course this is only a partial analysis of the problem. If the company does hedge, it becomes more attractive to airline pilots and less attractive to oil company employees. The mix of shareholders may change from the 60/40 mix we assumed. The point remains that if shareholders have differing risk exposures due to such factors as their occupations (their human capital) and their undiversified real estate holdings, they will have conflicting preferences about corporate hedging programmes. Hedging to meet some of the shareholders' needs may be worse than not hedging at all.

This brings us to the final consideration concerning shareholder risk exposure. Since shareholders have differing risk exposures outside of their security market portfolios (again consider the pilot and the oil company worker), they form "clienteles" for various stocks that serve as good hedges for these non-market risks. These shareholders want the risk exposure of the stocks they are buying to remain relatively constant over time. If the risk exposures of firms' shares were subject to frequent and major changes, then investors would need to closely follow the firms in which they invest. If exposures were changing significantly, these investors would often find it necessary to trade their shares to re-establish their optimal positions. This places a burden on the shareholders that can be avoided if companies follow a hedging policy that keeps the exposure of their shares relatively constant even if their operational exposure to risks is changing. This argument for stabilising a stock's risk exposure in the interest of a clientele resembles arguments made concerning dividend policy. It is suggested that some investors desire dividends and form a natural clientele for high-yield stocks; others prefer "growth" and seek low-yield stocks. Firms do not necessarily gain by following a high-yield or low-yield strategy. What is important is that the firm not vary its payout significantly quarter to quarter or even year to year.

We have argued that there are justifiable reasons for corporate hedging based on its effects on shareholder risk-bearing. However, in all of these cases, the gain is probably modest (at least for investors that hold well-diversified portfolios). The biggest gains may come when hedging substitutes (partially) for international diversification or allows shareholders to share risk with privately held firms or other firms in which diversified shareholders cannot trade. The issue is complicated by the fact that there are cases where a hedging programme might benefit some shareholders but make others worse off.

Even if the gains created by corporate hedging and the lowering of shareholders' risk are typically small, this does not mean that hedging is not worthwhile. After all, the costs of hedging are often also small. We could attempt to quantify these gains and costs in particular situations; but this would not be easy - nor is it necessary. Most of the value of corporate hedging is not due to how it alters the risks experienced by shareholders but rather to how it alters the risks experienced by the firm itself. We now turn to this issue.

The effects of risk on the firm and the benefits of corporate hedging

In considering the effects of risk on the firm itself, we do not want to fall into the trap of assuming that the firm should be treated as a separate individual with preferences of its own. We recognise that the firm is owned by the shareholders and that the firm's behaviour is determined by the interaction of a number of individuals who may have conflicting interests. It has been argued that since the firm is not an individual with preferences, it is inappropriate to characterise the firm as risk-averse. In some cases, this has been interpreted to mean that the firm should be considered "risk-neutral". Discussions along these lines are generally not very fruitful and are often misleading. Nevertheless, we argue that often the firm should, from the perspective of its shareholders, behave as if it is risk-averse. This risk-aversion on the firm level creates the demand for corporate hedging and risk management.

Individuals are risk-averse if they value the gain of any given dollar amount less than they value the loss of the same dollar amount. A risk-averse individual rejects a gamble that gives an equal chance of winning and losing US$10,000; the 50% chance of having an extra US$10,000 does not make up for the 50% chance of having US$10,000 less. Now consider a firm that accepts the following gamble: with 50% probability, its earnings (before interest and taxes) will be US$20 million higher than otherwise; and with 50% probability they will be US$20 million lower. Does this gamble increase, reduce or leave unchanged the *expected* amount the firm can deliver to its investors? Suppose that the increase of US$20 million results in only US$13 million in additional cash for the investors but that the investors feel the full effect of the US$20 million loss: when the company loses US$20 million, the investors receive US$20 million less cash than they would have received if the company had not gambled. In this case, the investors are clearly worse off with the gamble than they are without it.

We emphasise that the investors are worse off *not* because this gamble added risk to their portfolios. The gamble could be decided by the flip of a coin, in which case it would be purely diversifiable risk. A diversified investor essentially would not care about this risk as it affects the risk of his portfolio holdings. Rather, the investors lose because the gamble reduces the expected amount of cash the firm delivers to them. From an investor's perspective, the value of the extra US$20 million in corporate earnings measured *in terms of the extra cash delivered to the investors* is less than the value of the US$20 million loss in corporate earnings *measured in terms of cash lost to the investors*. This means that even if an investor were risk-neutral, he would want the firm to behave as if it were risk-averse when it considered this gamble.

This raises the key question: do a firm's investors lose more when a dollar of earnings is lost than they gain when an extra dollar is earned? Note that this asymmetry does not occur when investors buy shares in an open-end mutual fund. Within a mutual fund, gains and losses are generally symmetric. A dollar earned is one more dollar available to the fund's investors, and a dollar lost is one less dollar. The amount the mutual fund can distribute to its investors is a linear function of the amount it earns.[11] If there are asymmetries in gains and losses within a corporation, it will be because of some *non-linear* relation between earnings and what investors receive. We now explore some of these, starting with taxes.

CORPORATE TAXATION AND HEDGING

Consider a firm with a corporate tax rate of 40%. Assume that if this firm does not hedge any of its operating risks, it will each year either earn US$250 million with probability 75% or lose US$50 million with probability 25%. Given these probabilities, the firm's expected earnings each year are US$175 million. Assume that the company has the opportunity to fully and costlessly hedge its risks away. This means that the company will receive US$175 million per year for certain. Should this company hedge?

Assume that it does not. Then when the firm earns US$250 million, it will have US$150 million after taxes to distribute to shareholders. (To simplify matters, we assume that the company has no debt so that all after-tax earnings are paid to shareholders.) When the company loses US$50 million, it pays no taxes. If we assume that it can carry these losses forward (with interest) and use them fully to offset future taxes, then the loss to shareholders is not US$50 million but only US$30 million since future tax liability is reduced by US$20 million. Thus the expected cash available to shareholders is 0.25 × (– US$30,000,000) + 0.75 × (US$150,000,000) = US$105,000,000. If the company hedges, the cash available is also US$105,000,000 since this is 60% of US$175,000,000. Hedging has not changed the expected amount of cash available to shareholders.

Hedging did not have any effect because we assumed a uniform tax structure which treats losses and gains symmetrically by allowing the firm to take full advantage of losses carried forward or backward. In actuality, most tax structures are not linear. Tax rates often rise as income increases, and corporations cannot fully realise the tax benefits of losses as we assumed. This creates a role for hedging. Assume that when a US$50 million loss is incurred, future tax liability is only reduced by US$10 million, not by US$20 million as we assumed above. This could be due to limitations on the ability to carry losses forward or backward, reductions in value of these offsets due to the time value of money, and so on. If the firm does not hedge, the expected amount available to shareholders is only 0.25 × (– US$40,000,000) + 0.75 × (US$150,000,000) = US$102,500,000. This is US$2.5 million less than the amount available to shareholders when the firm hedges. Even if hedging is costly, as long as the cost is under US$2.5 million, shareholders are better off with corporate hedging. Hedging is valuable here because with the asymmetric tax structure, shareholders lose more when the company's before-tax income falls by a given amount than they gain when it rises by an equal amount. In a sense, the tax structure makes the corporation risk-averse.[12]

Finally and importantly, this gain can *only* be produced by hedging on the corporate level; shareholders cannot hedge on their own accounts and reduce the corporation's tax liability in the manner shown above.[13]

HEDGING AND THE COSTS OF BANKRUPTCY AND FINANCIAL DISTRESS

Any good corporate finance textbook has a long disquisition on the costs of bankruptcy and financial distress. These costs are usually cited as one of the reasons why firms do not fully exploit the tax advantages of increasing leverage. Since these costs are described in such detail elsewhere (Brealey and Myers, 1991; Ross, Westerfield and Jaffe, 1993; and Van Horne, 1992), we summarise them briefly here and then discuss the obvious role hedging plays in reducing these costs. When a levered firm defaults on its debt or enters bankruptcy proceedings, direct costs are incurred through the increased need for legal, accounting and other professional services. While these direct costs are not necessarily trivial, it is usually claimed that the *indirect* costs of financial distress and bankruptcy are the most significant. These indirect costs take many forms.

For example, in situations of financial distress, the attention of upper management may be diverted from managing the firm's operations. This generally results in a loss of value. Due to uncertainties in how bankruptcy proceedings will be resolved, customers may be more reluctant to buy and suppliers may be more reluctant to make costly supply commitments when the value of these transactions depends on how long and in what form the firm remains in business.[14] Conflicts among various claimholders may cause the firm to pass up profitable investment opportunities. These conflicts occur when a firm is near bankruptcy and any new investment by shareholders will mainly benefit the bondholders. The simple solution to this problem is to reorganise the firm in such a way that the conflict no longer exists and then raise the funds necessary to undertake the profitable investment. In practice, such reorganisation takes time and may not be achievable. These are just a few examples of indirect costs.

While some of the costs of bankruptcy and financial distress are subtle, the role hedging can play in reducing these costs is obvious. Hedging generally lowers the probability of financial distress and bankruptcy. By lowering the probability, hedging lowers the expected costs of distress and increases the expected cashflows available for shareholders. Again, the gain produced by hedging is due to an asymmetry. If earnings are low or negative, the shareholders must pay the costs of financial distress and perhaps bankruptcy.[15] If earnings are high, the shareholders do not get any extra bonus (eg, a reverse payment from bankruptcy lawyers) to make up for the costs on the downside. Finally, note that when hedging reduces the cost of financial distress, it also increases debt capacity. Thus the gain due to hedging may show up through the firm's ability to increase its degree of leverage and realise the tax advantages or other benefits of a higher debt-to-equity ratio.[16]

HEDGING AND THE COST OF FUNDING NEW INVESTMENT

The simple rule often given for choosing investment projects is the net present value rule: choose those and only those projects with *positive* net present values (NPVs). A project has a positive NPV if the present value of the cashflows it produces is greater than the investment required to undertake the project. Value is left lying on the table whenever a positive net present value project is not undertaken.[17] Unfortunately, a firm's current shareholders may find that they are better off passing up a positive NPV project. This occurs when the project cannot be funded out of retained earnings and outside financing is required.[18] Consider a firm that has 100 shareholders, each of which owns one share. The firm's management knows that the total value of the firm's assets is US$1,000,000. Thus each shareholder currently has a claim worth US$10,000. Now assume that the firm can undertake an investment project that costs US$500,000 but which will produce cashflows worth US$700,000. The net present value of this project is therefore US$200,000. The firm, however, has not retained earnings to fund the project, so it must issue new shares to raise the capital. The firm's problem is that the outside market only values the assets the firm has in place at US$500,000, not US$1,000,000.

What could give rise to this discrepancy in valuations? Those who firmly believe in efficient markets would probably conclude that the management is mistaken and that it overestimates the value of the firm by US$500,000. This, of course, is possible. But it is also possible that the management has information about the value of assets in place that the market does not have. For example, the company might be a biotech firm that is developing an experimental drug. The management could have some information relating to the prospects for success that cannot be quantified and is not subject to disclosure requirements. Indeed, the management may have compelling strategic reasons to keep the information secret. Thus, even if the management could voluntarily disclose the information, it might find it too costly to do so.

Assume that the management's valuation of US$1,000,000 is correct, and consider what happens if the management raises capital to undertake the project. To do this, an additional 100 shares must be issued to raise US$500,000. This means that each of the original shareholders will own 1/200 of the firm. The true value of the firm will be US$1,000,000 + US$700,000 = US$1,700,000. Each of the original shareholder's stakes thus falls in value to US$8,500. Recall that if the project is not undertaken, the value of each stake is US$10,000. Quite simply, the dilution that occurs when shares are issued at prices below their true value overwhelms the increase in value brought about by the positive NPV project. The shareholders are forced to leave money on the table.

This problem would not have occurred had the firm possessed sufficient internal funds to undertake the project without raising capital on the outside. For example, if the firm had US$500,000 in retained earnings in addition to its US$1,000,000 in fixed assets, it could undertake the project and increase its value from US$1,500,000 to US$1,700,000. The original shareholders would not be hurt by dilution and would capture the full US$200,000 increase created by the positive NPV project. All of this points to another valid reason for hedging on corporate account. Consider a firm that will over the years have a sequence of valuable investment projects to undertake, and assume that in a typical year it will have sufficient internal funds to finance the projects available that year. However, in those years when earnings fall to very low levels, the firm will not have sufficient internal funds to undertake positive NPV projects and may find itself in the predicament described above. A hedging strategy that stabilises earnings and lowers the likelihood of the firm's needing outside capital is valuable since it reduces the chance that profitable investment projects will be foregone. In fact, any additional cost associated with outside financing (underwriters' fees, market price impact, etc) creates a rationale for stabilising earnings through hedging.[19]

HEDGING AND AGENCY COSTS

We have shown that in many circumstances, reducing the volatility of earnings increases the expected amount of cash shareholders will receive. One should not conclude from this that shareholders always desire lower volatility. In fact, when the firm has substantial leverage (ie, a high debt-to-equity ratio), shareholders have strong incentives to increase volatility. Additional risk or volatility tends to raise the value of the shareholders' position in a levered firm whenever the shareholders receive the benefits of the "upside" while the debtholders suffer the consequences of the "downside".

The possibility of the shareholders' taking advantage of the debtholders with a "heads I win, tails you lose" gamble is one of the sources of what has come to be termed "the agency costs of debt." The following example illustrates these agency costs and shows how hedging might be used to reduce them. Assume that a firm has a single debt liability of US$700 million which is due in one year. Suppose that, if the firm continues to operate in its current manner, it will have assets worth US$600 million when the debt comes due. This means that the firm will be bankrupt, shareholders will receive nothing and debtholders will receive only US$600 million of the US$700 million owed to them.

Now assume that the company can change its operations and follow a risky strategy. If the risky strategy pays off, the firm will be worth US$800 million; if the strategy fails, the firm will only be worth US$400 million. If these two outcomes (success and failure) are equally likely, the expected payout to shareholders will be US$50 million (50% chance of receiving US$100 million – which is the residual from the US$800 million once the US$700 million in debt is paid – and 50% chance of receiving zero). The expected payout to bondholders is US$550 million (50% chance at US$400 million and 50% at US$700 million). The risky strategy has not increased the expected value of the firm's assets (this remains US$600 million), but it has transferred US$50 million in expected payout from the bondholders to the shareholders. Of course, the bondholders are well aware of this possibility when they purchase the bonds and use bond covenants to restrict shareholders from following risky strategies.

Assume that the shareholders are prevented by covenants from taking a risky strategy of the sort described above. Is this a problem? Consider again the above example but with one change: assume that if the risky strategy pays off, the value of the firm is US$1,200 million, not US$800 million. The risky strategy has now increased the expected value of the firm from US$600 million to US$800 million (the average of US$400 million and US$1,200 million). This strategy is clearly worth pursuing.[20] However, unless the terms of the debt are renegotiated, the debtholders will not favour the strategy and will be unwilling to waive the covenants even though doing so would increase the firm's value. This is because the debtholders continue to have a claim that pays either US$400 million or US$700 million with equal probability. Since the expectation of this claim is US$550 million, they will prefer that the company do nothing since this gives them US$600 million for sure. The problem is solved if the terms of the debt contract can be easily renegotiated; but in many cases, especially those of publicly placed debt, this may be costly or impossible. Can hedging solve this problem?

Assume that the risk of the proposed risky strategy can be hedged away. For example, it may be that the risky strategy involves the firm's selling in a foreign market and that much of the risk is due to foreign exchange uncertainties. Assume that when this risk is hedged away, the 50/50 gamble of US$400 million or US$1,200 million becomes US$800 million with certainty. Then, without the debt being renegotiated, the debtholders will receive US$700 million instead of US$600 million, and the shareholders will receive US$100 million instead of nothing. By hedging the risk, the firm captures the value of the risky strategy; if the risk had not been hedged and the debt could not be renegotiated, the bondholders would have blocked the firm from obtaining the increase in value.

The example is admittedly simplistic, but the point it illustrates carries over to more realistic and complicated settings. When the capital structure includes debt, shareholders and debtholders may take opposite positions as to the firm's operations since such matters affect the riskiness of the firm's value. Hedging allows risks to be controlled and thus gives the shareholders more flexibility in altering the firm's operations without substantially changing the firm's overall risk. As we have shown, this added flexibility may mean that the firm can make value-improving changes in the way the firm operates – changes which otherwise would have been blocked by the bondholders.[21]

HEDGING, INCENTIVES AND EMPLOYEE COMPENSATION

In most cases, the compensation of employees is positively related to the performance of the firms that employ them. If a firm does well, its employees generally receive higher levels of compensation than if the firm does badly. There are at least three reasons that justify this positive relation: risk sharing, constraints on the firm, and incentives.

First, we consider risk sharing. A small shopkeeper with a single employee would probably find it advantageous to pay the employee more when business is good and less when it is bad. This is because the shop owner absorbs all of the risk if the employee is paid a wage that is independent of the level of business in the shop. Unless the shop owner is risk-neutral, it is generally better for the owner and the employee to share the risk. This means that, on *average*, the employee must be paid more since the employee must be compensated for bearing some of the risk. However, a risk-averse shop owner will gladly pay a little more to the employee (on average) for bearing some risk since this reduces the shop owner's risk. The employee's variable compensation is basically a hedge for the shop owner.

While risk sharing along these lines makes sense in a small business, it is a less compelling reason for the variable compensation of employees in large corporations with diversified shareholders. The risk of a large corporation is shared extensively among its shareholders and other financial claimholders; there is minuscule advantage in employees' bearing a portion of the risk.[22] In fact, if risk sharing is the only consideration, a substantial loss occurs when employees bear significant risk since they must be compensated for it through higher average compensation. This increased cost is worth much less than the meagre benefit the shareholders receive when risk is shifted to the employees.[23]

This brings us to the second reason employee compensation might vary with the firm's fortunes: in bad times, the firm may be constrained to pay employees less because of market imperfections. Consider a firm that has a wage bill of US$50 million and revenues that vary between US$25 million and US$100 million. We have argued that, from a risk-sharing point of view, it is generally optimal for the shareholders to absorb most of the risk of variations in revenues or earnings. If the firm has several bad years of revenues at the US$25 million level, the shareholders should contribute to make up the shortfall between the wage bill and revenue. If the money is not available in retained earnings, then the firm should raise more capital. But this may be excessively costly if it is even possible. Recall our discussion about hedging and the cost of funding new investment where the issuance of new shares involved substantial dilution. In such a situation, the company may cut back on employee compensation rather than raise funds externally. The employees are forced to bear a risk created by the company's funding constraints. Obviously, hedging can play a role here. If the risk of the revenue stream can be reduced, the company is less likely to have to reduce employee compensation. This means that employees will have more stable incomes and will not require additional compensation for risk. This savings in the wage bill accrues to the shareholders.

The third and final reason for employee compensation to be tied to the firm's performance concerns incentives, especially those for upper management. Over the last two decades, economists have extensively studied incentive contracting issues. This research considers the problems faced by a principal who hires an agent to act on the principal's behalf. It is generally assumed that the principal cannot observe all the agent's actions and, in particular, cannot observe the agent's level of effort. The optimal incentive contract for a principal to offer an agent can be quite complicated. Among other things, it depends on what the principal can observe, how the agent can affect the principal's welfare, and what degree of risk the principal and the agent can tolerate. In the context of our discussion, the principals are the shareholders of a firm and the agents are the firm's managers. As we have pointed out above, the shareholders are generally well-diversified investors and are much better able than the employees to bear the firm's risks. A number of results in the incentive contracting research concern cases where the principal is risk-neutral (or nearly so) and the agent is risk-averse. In these cases, the optimal incentive contract for the agent does not expose the agent to a risk unless it creates an incentive for the agent to work harder.

For example, assume that in January a US company sends an employee to negotiate a one-year supply contract with a French company. Assume that the contract will specify the quantity to be delivered each month and that the monthly payment will be denominated in French francs and fixed up front. Clearly, it is not sensible for the company to pay the employee a bonus in December that is inversely related to the *dollar* cost of the goods purchased over the year. If the French franc unexpectedly appreciates relative to the dollar over the year, the dollar cost of the good will increase, but it is not sensible to penalise the employee for this since the exchange rate is completely outside of his control. Of course, if the French franc depreciates instead, the dollar cost falls and the employee is rewarded. But again there is no reason for this since the gain was due to an exchange rate change and not to the employee's efforts. Exposing the employee to the risk of exchange rate movements that occur after the contract is negotiated serves no purpose at all in motivating the employee at the beginning of the year to negotiate a better price in French francs.

It would seem that these incentive contracting considerations provide another rationale for hedging on the corporate level. The compensation of the upper-level managers of a corporation is typically tied to various measures of corporate performance, such as earnings and stock price appreciation. Stock options, for example, provide an obvious incentive for managers to increase shareholder value since many things affecting the stock price are under the managers' control. However, for almost every company, many determinants of the stock price are beyond the managers' control. If the company is a multinational corporation, *unexpected* changes in exchange rates can affect the company's profitability and its stock price; but just as in our example above, these typically fall outside the control of managers. It would seem that corporate hedging, since it removes some of these risks, makes stock options more effective in motivating the manager. If exchange rate fluctuations, oil price changes and similar risks are hedged, then changes in the stock price are less likely to arise from factors not under management control and more likely to result from actions taken by the management.

There is a problem with this incentive-based argument for corporate hedging. It provides a reason for hedging certain risks insofar as they affect the amount paid to managers, but it provides no reason for hedging to be done for the entire firm. Assume that a multinational firm faces exchange rate risk beyond the control of management. One way to establish the appropriate incentives for managers is to base their compensation on the firm's future stock price performance and then hedge the exchange rate risk for the entire company. Call this Plan A. The same effect, however, can be achieved by Plan B. Under Plan B, the company does not hedge the exchange rate risk but instead adjusts the manager's compensation to remove the effects of unexpected exchange rate movements. Doing this involves determining what the stock price would have been had the company hedged and what the manager's compensation would have been had this been the stock price and had the company adopted Plan A. The manager could then receive this amount. The company would not need to hedge its entire risk to remove this risk from the managers' compensation. (Note that Plan B involves no trading at all by the firm in outside markets. All hedging is done internally by adjusting accounts.)

One could argue that the compensation committee of the board of directors would not have all the information needed to make these adjustments. The risk exposure of the company might frequently change, and at any time of the year the managers would be the best informed about the need for hedging. It could be argued that managers should be given the opportunity to take the appropriate hedging positions on corporate account throughout the year as opposed to letting a committee guess an appropriate year-end adjustment. While this might seem to justify using Plan A and hedging for the entire corporation, it does not. Plan B can still be implemented if during the year the managers report daily the hedging they would do under Plan A. These reports can then be used at the end of the year to make the appropriate adjustments.

Is there any reason to adopt Plan A over Plan B? One possible justification for the use of corporate-wide hedging over hedging only for the managers is more "political" than economic. Consider what might happen if Plan B is used and the company experiences a large loss due to a risk beyond the managers' control. Even though the shareholders suffer this major loss, the compensation required for the managers under Plan B might be quite high. This would be true if the managers had performed quite well in terms of those things under their control. In other words, losses would have been even higher had the managers not performed so well. In such a circumstance, managerial compensation (under Plan B) might be higher than it typically is in years when earnings are high. This outcome might seem perverse to shareholders who do not fully understand the incentive considerations behind the compensation contract. Under Plan A, the compensation of managers would appear to be more closely tied to shareholder wealth and would perhaps generate less controversy.

HEDGING AND THE MARKET'S SIGNAL EXTRACTION PROBLEM

As noted earlier, a firm can be hurt if the market undervalues its assets. This occurs, for example, when the firm has a valuable investment opportunity and needs to raise external funds. Corporate hedging has the potential to reduce these "information asymmetries" existing between the firm's managers and the market by improving the "signal-to-noise" ratio in corporate earnings. This can be illustrated by a rather fanciful example. Imagine that a charitable organisation hires a fundraiser to solicit donations but is unsure of the fundraiser's ability. Assume that all the organisation observes is the amount of money the fundraiser turns in each day. Over time, the organisation will gather data to help it resolve the uncertainty concerning the fundraiser's ability. Obviously, a good fundraiser will on average turn in more than a poor one.

Now imagine that each day the fundraiser, before turning in the money, goes to the track and wagers some of the day's proceeds on the horses. The fundraiser then turns in the amount raised plus or minus the winnings or losses at the track. The betting has clearly made it more difficult for the charitable organisation to determine the fundraiser's ability. For several days a good fundraiser could turn in little due to losses at the track while a poor fundraiser might look good due to some lucky bets. In making its assessment of the fundraiser's ability, the organisation will put less weight on the daily amounts turned in when these are influenced by the noise of the wagers at the track. A fundraiser who knows he is good and who wants to have this revealed as soon as possible has a clear incentive to avoid the noise added by gambling.

Hedging, to the extent that it removes noise, seems to allow security analysts and others in the market to obtain some precise estimates of the value of a firm's assets. Of course, a key assumption here is that the security analysts do not know all of the risk exposures the firm would face if it did not hedge. If the charitable organisation in the example above knows all of the bets placed by the fundraiser at the track and the outcome of each race, then the gambling does not produce noise. Similarly, if the analysts know precisely the foreign exchange exposure, interest rate risk exposure and oil price risk exposure of the company at each moment, then the company gains nothing in terms of eliminating noise by hedging these risks. Of course, if the analysts do not know the company's exposure, the firm's management has the alternative strategy of removing the noise – not by hedging but by publicly disclosing the firm's exposure. In a similar manner, the fundraiser need not avoid the track altogether to remove the noise; instead, he could give the charitable organisation his track receipts and disclose his betting for the day. The hedging approach might be preferred to the disclosure approach since it puts less of a burden on the market. For many investors, it may be difficult to process all of the information necessary to describe the risk exposures of a large company.[24]

REWARDS FOR SUPPLYING HEDGING SERVICES

Our final reason for hedging on corporate account is based on all the above reasons for hedging. These show that corporations can gain by hedging and should in many circumstances be willing to pay another firm or institution to take the counterparty position if necessary. Consider a company, Company A, that is exposed to a particular risk which it has no compelling reason to hedge. This company is in a natural position to provide a hedging contract to another firm, Company B, that is exposed to the same risk but in the opposite way. If Company B derives significant benefit from hedging its exposure, then Company A may be in a position to demand favourable terms of the contract. Whether it can depends on whether there are other potential suppliers of the hedging contract that can compete on the same terms as Company A. The simple point here is that even if the firm has no demand for hedging, its operating exposures may place it in a privileged position to supply hedging services and to receive value for doing so.

Conclusion

We have shown a number of ways in which hedging on corporate account can increase shareholder value. While a firm that hedges on corporate account can change the risk borne by shareholders in their portfolios, the gains from this are likely to be small. The substantial gains produced by hedging are due to the fact that risk affects the expected cashflows corporations can deliver to their shareholders because of taxes, bankruptcy costs, flotation costs for externally generated funds and other "market imperfections." These considerations make the firm behave as if it were risk-averse when it acts in the interest of shareholders and creates a need for hedging. Moreover, for most of these market imperfections, hedging on shareholders' accounts does not substitute for hedging on a corporate account. A shareholder's hedging on his own account cannot lower the firm's expected costs of bankruptcy or financial distress. Nor can a shareholder take a position in a futures market and change the firm's expected tax liability. The firm itself must hedge to capture these advantages of risk reduction. We have not described in any detail how derivatives can be used to hedge since this is done elsewhere. Instead of looking at how derivatives can used by corporations, we have asked the prior questions of whether they should be used at all and why. The justifications given above for hedging on corporate account show that corporations have a legitimate demand for instruments such as derivatives that they can use to control risk.

1 *For example, Ibbotson and Sinquefield report that from 1926 to 1991, the average return on common stocks was 8.5% higher than the return on US Treasury bills. This is an estimate of the risk premium that investors require to hold risky common stocks. The estimated risk premium for small company stocks over this period is even higher: 14.6%.*

2 *A diversified portfolio is one that is composed of many securities. Moreover, the value of each security in a diversified portfolio is a small portion of the total value of the portfolio. With the growth of large institutional investors such as pension funds and mutual funds, a large portion of corporate liabilities is now held by diversified investors.*

3 *It is possible for some investors to hold some stocks long and others short in such a way that energy cost risk disappears. The average investor, however, must hold a portfolio that is sensitive to energy cost risk.*

4 *See Modigliani and Miller (1958).*

5 *We assume that the diversified shareholders also hold shares in the firm that exports to Canada and that took the other side of the futures contract. If this is true, the diversified shareholders' exposure to foreign exchange risk remains neutral.*

6 *We have not provided a full argument for why large shareholders exist. Corporate hedging lowers the cost of a large shareholder's taking an undiversified position, but it does not remove that cost entirely. Some other explanation must be provided for large shareholders. It is often suggested that there are benefits to holding controlling stakes in a corporation beyond the cashflows paid out to shares and that this compensates the large shareholder for the disadvantages of a large position. Another explanation is that large shareholders are caught in undiversified positions by historical circumstances and it is too costly for them to sell their shares and diversify. This is because large shareholders who sell out might be required to pay significant capital gains taxes. It is also possible that the sale of their shares might have a large negative impact on the market price due in part to the market's recognition that they will no longer monitor the firm as closely. Note also that if the diversified shareholders use corporate hedging to lower the cost of a large shareholder's taking a larger position in the firm, there must be some way that the firm can commit to maintaining a hedging policy in the future. An exploration of these issues is beyond the scope of this article.*

7 *As we mentioned above, it is possible to construct portfolios that are unaffected by pervasive risks. This is done by carefully choosing portfolio weights so that those securities having positive exposures to the pervasive risk exactly offset those having negative exposures. For example, one balances the positive exposure of oil companies to oil price risk with the negative exposure of airlines. If all securities have the same exposure (eg, they are all affected positively), then this is still possible if one is willing to take short positions. The point is that diversification alone is not sufficient to remove pervasive risks. Moreover, although any individual investor can construct a portfolio that removes a pervasive risk, not all investors can do so.*

8 *One might think that, from a* diversified *investor's point of view, it makes no difference whether a particular firm hedges away a pervasive risk or a non-pervasive risk. It would seem that in both cases the effect on the diversified investor's portfolio is roughly proportional to the weight the firm's stock receives in*

the portfolio, and in a diversified portfolio this weight is small. This intuition is not correct. Assume, for example, that an investor holds 100 stocks and puts 1% of his wealth in each. (Dividing the investment equally among the 100 firms is generally not the optimal way to diversify. We make this assumption only to simplify the illustration.) Assume that firm i*'s return is equal to* $\tilde{F} + \tilde{e}_i$, *where* $\tilde{F}$ *measures the effect of the pervasive risk on returns (in this case, the pervasive risk affects all of the firms in the same way), and* $\tilde{e}_i$ *captures the risk that affects only firm* i. *For simplicity, assume that the variance of each of the* $\tilde{e}_i$*s is equal to* V *and the variance of the pervasive risk is equal to* W. *Then, if no firm hedges any of its risks, the variance of the diversified investor's portfolio is* W + V/100. *If the first firm hedges its non-pervasive risk component (ie,* $\tilde{e}_1$*) the variance of the diversified investor's portfolio falls to* W + 99V/100. *If instead the first firm hedges its exposure to the pervasive risk* ($\tilde{F}$) *and this risk is not transferred to any of the other 99 firms in the diversified investor's portfolio, then the variance of the diversified investor's portfolio falls to* $(99/100)^2W + V/100$. *If* W *is roughly equal to* V *(the variances of the pervasive and the non-pervasive risks are roughly equal), the hedging of the pervasive risk reduces the variance of the diversified investor's portfolio by 199 times the amount hedging the non-pervasive risk does. As* N *(the number of stocks in the diversified investors portfolio) grows, so does the difference between the effects of hedging pervasive and non-pervasive risks.*

9 *We implicitly assume that the pilot's employer is not fully hedged against oil price risk and that when oil prices increase the pilot's compensation falls. This occurs, for example, if the pilot is temporarily laid off due to a decline in air travel. Issues concerning employee compensation and corporate hedging are discussed below.*

10. *The reader may object that we have assumed that the majority of shareholders are pilots and not oil company employees. After all, pilots are the ones who should shy away from companies with negative exposure to oil price risk. Even though this seems perverse, it could occur if there were many more pilots in the economy than oil industry employees or, more to the point, if pilots had greater wealth to invest.*

11 *We ignore transactions costs and other fees associated with the mutual fund since these are generally small. Moreover, these only invalidate our assertion about the symmetry of gains and losses in a mutual fund if these costs have a non-linear relation to the fund's returns.*

12 *For more discussion on the effects of a convex tax structure on the value of corporate hedging, see Smith and Stulz (1985).*

13 *Of course, given the progressive nature of personal taxation in many countries, individual taxpayers who have volatile incomes might reduce their expected tax liability by hedging on personal account. This does not in any way reduce the need for the corporation to hedge on corporate account as a way of reducing corporate tax liability.*

14 *Note that we need to distinguish between what is caused directly by bankruptcy or financial distress and what is caused by general market conditions. The proverbial firm that manufactured buggy whips in the 1920s went out of business because the market for its product changed – not because of its financial structure. Even if the buggy whip firm had no debt at all, it still would go out of business. We are concerned here with what happens when a firm has debt; and because of the failure of the firm's creditors to reorganise the firm quickly and efficiently, the firm follows a different (and lower-value) trajectory than it would have followed if it had no debt.*

15 *It might be argued that the shareholders do not completely absorb the costs of bankruptcy and financial distress but instead that they share them with the bondholders. After all, the bondholders have expenses; and even if these are paid out of the firm's assets, this is money they might otherwise have received. This argument is wrong because it focuses only on what occurs at the time of financial distress. At the time the bonds are issued, the price is set to compensate bondholders for their expected losses due to these costs. The shareholders thus receive less from the bond issue, and the shareholders pay the expected costs of the bondholders at the time of issuance.*

16 *Some additional discussion of the ability of hedging to increase debt capacity can be found in Smith and Stulz (1985).*

17 *This statement is a bit too strong. The NPV rule looks at investment in a "static" environment where investing in a project is a take-it-or-leave-it matter. In a more dynamic context, firms may find it optimal to delay initiating a project with a positive net present value since over time more information becomes available. In this sense, investment projects are like call options for which early exercise is not necessarily optimal. Even if we consider investment in a dynamic context, the story we tell below does not change in any major way.*

18 *This example is based on Myers and Majluf (1984).*

19 *For a more detailed discussion of this rationale for hedging, see Froot, Scharfstein and Stein (1993).*

20 *We implicitly assume here that the risk of success or failure is diversifiable risk, so it is appropriate to consider only the expected outcome. In other words, we assume no need to adjust for risk.*

21 *Some additional discussion on the ability of hedging to reduce agency problems can be found in Stulz (1990).*

22 *See Stulz (1984) for a discussion of the differences between the diversified position of shareholders and the undiversified position of managers and other employees. Stulz argues that this creates an incentive for the managers to hedge on corporate account if they are free to do so.*

23 *If all investors in the economy are equally averse to risk, then, for optimal risk sharing, each employee of a company should bear a fraction of the company's risk that is equal to the fraction of his wealth to the*

total wealth in the economy. To illustrate in a very rough *way the magnitude of this account, we consider an employee of a company who has US$100,000 to invest. Since the total value of the US stock market is approximately US$4 trillion, the investor should bear something on the order of 1/4,000,000 of the company's risk. (This fraction actually overestimates the exposure the employee should face if risk is shared completely since we ignore international diversification and investment in bonds. Since the total value of the world capital market is estimated to be well over US$20 trillion, complete risk sharing would put the fraction closer to 1/20,000,000. However, if we also account for non-investable wealth, such as human capital, the employee's wealth increases as does world wealth. Since we only want to establish a rough order of magnitude here, we do not consider these other factors and take the lower value of 1/4,000,000 to obtain a conservative estimate.) Now, assume that the company is a US$500 million company and suppose that it loses 10% of its value. If risk is efficiently shared, the employee should suffer a loss of only US$12.50 (= US$50,000,000/4,000,000). This means that a 10% loss for the company is only a 0.0125% loss for the employee. It might be argued that it makes no difference how much risk the employee faces in his compensation since the employee can always hedge on his own account to remove this risk. Here we must again distinguish between pervasive risks and company-specific risks. For the former, the employee can potentially make adjustments in his portfolio to balance his exposure. For example, the Exxon employee who is exposed to oil price risk through his compensation can adjust by holding very little investment in stocks that have positive exposure to oil prices and by increasing his holdings in those that have negative exposure. In some cases, the employee can also use derivatives and other hedging instruments to control these risks, but for many employees this is costly. If employees are forced to do this, then efficient risk sharing is in all likelihood not being achieved in the least costly manner. While the employee has some ability to manage his exposure to pervasive risks, he has much less ability to control his exposure to company-specific risks. The only effective way for the employee to remove a significant exposure to these risks is through shortselling his employer's stock. When this is allowed, it is generally quite costly for the employee. Of course, the shareholders of a company clearly have legitimate concerns about employees' taking short-sale positions in the stock, especially if these employees are upper-level managers. This means that employees will face restrictions on shortselling. When these restrictions are enforced, employees cannot hedge exposures to company-specific risk in their compensation.*

24 *For models of the use of hedging in improving the outside market's signal-extraction problem, see Breeden and Viswanathan (1990) and Demarzo and Duffie (1992).*

BIBLIOGRAPHY

Brealey, R. A., and S. Myers, 1991, *Principles of Corporate Finance* (New York, NY: McGraw-Hill).

Breeden, D., and S. Viswanathan, 1990, "Why Do Firms Hedge? An Asymmetric Information Model", Working paper, Duke University.

DeMarzo, P., and D. Duffie, 1992, "Corporate Incentives For Hedging and Hedge Accounting", Working paper, Northwestern University.

Froot, K. A., D. S. Scharfstein and J. C. Stein, 1993, "Risk Management: Coordinating Corporate Investment and Financing Policies", *Journal of Finance* 48(5), pp. 1629–58; reprinted as Chapter 7 of the present volume.

Modigliani, F., and M. H. Miller, 1958, "The Cost of Capital, Corporation Finance, and the Theory of Investment", *American Economic Review* 48, pp. 261–97.

Myers, S., and N. Majluf, 1984, "Corporate Financing and Investment Decisions When Firms Have Information That Investors Do Not Have", *Journal of Financial Economics* 13(2), pp. 187–221.

Ross, S. A., R. W. Westerfield and J. F. Jaffe, 1993, *Corporate Finance* (Homewood, IL: Irwin).

Smith, C. W., and R. M. Stulz, 1985, "The Determinants of a Firm's Hedging Policies", *Journal of Financial and Quantitative Analysis* 20(4), pp. 391–405; reprinted as Chapter 6 of the present volume.

Stulz, R. M., 1984, "Optimal Hedging Policies", *Journal of Financial and Quantitative Analysis* 19(2), pp. 127–40.

Stulz, R. M., 1990, "Managerial Discretion and Optimal Financing Policies", *Journal of Financial Economics* 26, pp. 3–27.

Van Horne, J. C., 1992, *Financial Management and Policy* (Englewood Cliffs, NJ: Prentice Hall).

6

The Determinants of Firms' Hedging Policies*

Clifford W. Smith and René M. Stulz

University of Rochester; Ohio State University

There is a considerable literature on the hedging practices of firms;[1] however, the focus is generally on risk-averse producers who use forward or futures markets to reduce the variability of their income.[2] Although this literature provides a useful basis for the analysis of hedging in closely-held corporations, partnerships or individual proprietorships, it is not as applicable to large, widely-held corporations whose owners, the stockholders and bondholders, have the ability to hold diversified portfolios of securities.[3] In this chapter, we develop a positive theory of hedging by value-maximising corporations in which hedging is part of overall corporate financing policy.

Modigliani and Miller (1958) show that, with fixed investment policy and with no contracting costs or taxes, corporate financing policy is irrelevant. Their argument implies that if a firm chooses to change its hedging policy, investors who hold claims issued by the firm can change their holdings of risky assets to offset any change in the firm's hedging policy, leaving the distribution of their future wealth unaffected.[4] Thus, if the hedging policy affects the value of the firm, it must do so through (1) taxes, (2) contracting costs or (3) the impact of hedging policy on the firm's investment decisions. We examine each of these potential explanations of the observed diversity of hedging practices among large widely-held corporations.[5] Our analysis provides answers to the following questions: (1) Why do some firms hedge while others do not? (2) Why do firms hedge some risks, but not others? (3) Why do some firms hedge accounting exposure, while others hedge economic values?

A definition of hedging. A firm can hedge by trading in a particular futures, forward or options market even though it has no identifiable cash position in the underlying commodity. Furthermore, a firm can hedge by altering real operating decisions; for instance, a merger can produce effects similar to those of hedging through financial contracts. Thus, we adopt a fairly general definition of hedging in terms of the market value of the firm. Let $V(\underline{S})$ be the value of a firm if it does not hedge, where $\underline{S}$ is a vector of state variables. Consider two firms, "A" and "B", that differ from the firm with value $V(\underline{S})$ only in their hedging policies. We say that "firm A" hedges more with respect to state variable i than "firm B" if the absolute value of the covariance of the value of "firm A" with state variable i is less than or equal to that of "firm B". Therefore, hedging reduces the dependence of firm value on changes in the state variable. Alternatively, we say that "firm A" hedges more than "firm B" if the absolute value of the covariance of the value of "firm A" with the value of an unhedged firm with the same production policy and capital structure is less than or equal to that of "firm B".

Taxes and hedging

The structure of the tax code can make it advantageous for firms to take positions in futures, forward or options markets. If effective marginal tax rates on corporations are an increasing function of the corporation's pre-tax value, then the after-tax value of the firm is a concave function of its pre-tax value. If hedging reduces the variability of pre-tax firm values, then the expected corporate tax liability is reduced and the expected post-tax value of the firm is increased, as long as the cost of the hedge is not too large (see Figure 1).

**Originally published in the* Journal of Finance and Quantitative Analysis *20(4) (1995), pp. 391–405. The authors thank P. Meyers, L. Wakeman and two anonymous* Journal of Finance and Quantitative Analysis *referees for their comments and suggestions. Clifford Smith receives support from the Managerial Economics Research Center, Graduate School of Management, University of Rochester, USA.*

HEDGING AND CORPORATE TAX LIABILITIES

To analyse the effect of hedging on the present value of the firm's after-tax cashflow, we employ a state-preference model of firm value. We assume that there are S states of the world, with V_i defined as the pre-tax value of the firm in state of the world i. States of the world are numbered so that $V_i \leq V_j$, if $i < j$. Let P_i be the price today of one dollar to be delivered in state of the world i and $T(V_i)$ be the tax rate if the before-tax value of the firm is V_i. In the absence of leverage, the value of the firm after taxes, $V(0)$, is given by

$$V(0) = \sum_{i=1}^{S} P_i(V_i - T(V_i)V_i) \tag{1}$$

Hedging can increase the value of the firm if there are two states of the world, j and k, such that $T(V_j) < T(V_k)$. To demonstrate this, suppose that the firm holds a hedge portfolio such that $V_j + H_j = V_k + H_k$, and that the hedge portfolio is self-financing in the sense that $P_jH_j + P_kH_k = 0$. (Such a portfolio is feasible if it is possible to create a portfolio that pays one dollar in state j and a portfolio that pays one dollar in state k.) Let $V^H(0)$ be the value of the hedged firm. It follows that

$$\begin{aligned} V^H(0) - V(0) = {} & P_j(T(V_j)V_j - T(V_j + H_j)(V_j + H_j)) \\ & + P_k(T(V_k)V_k - T(V_k + H_k)(V_k + H_k)) > 0 \end{aligned} \tag{2}$$

(The inequality is implied by the definition of a concave function.) Therefore, costless hedging increases the value of the firm. This analysis also implies that incomplete hedging (ie, hedging that does not eliminate all uncertainty in future cashflows) also raises firm value.

The previous analysis must be modified if hedging is costly. If transactions costs of hedging do not exceed the benefits identified in (2), ie, $V^H(0) - V(0)$, hedging increases firm value. The amount of hedging undertaken by the firm depends on the transactions cost structure of hedging. If transactions costs exhibit scale economies, then the firm either hedges completely, if the cost is low enough, or hedges nothing.

Hedging can be costly because the firm purchases before-tax cashflows from investors who receive after-tax cashflows. If the marginal investor's tax function is linear in the payoffs of the hedging instruments, our analysis still holds; the self-financing hedge portfolio analysis is still valid. However, if investors' tax functions are non-linear and investors face different tax rates across states, the analysis is more complex. It could be the case that the decrease in the firm's expected tax liability from hedging is offset by an increase in the expected tax liability of the investors who enable the firm to hedge. Thus, there may be no impact on expected taxes. Hedging instruments would be priced accordingly and there would be no benefit from hedging. However, in this case, it would pay firms that expect to face a constant tax rate to offer hedging instruments to firms that expect their tax rate to be an increasing function of their cashflow. This mechanism tends to produce hedging instrument prices as if the marginal investor faces a linear tax function.[6]

1. Corporate tax liability and post-tax firm value as a function of pre-tax firm value

(if costless hedging reduces the variability of pre-tax firm value, then the firm's expected tax liability falls and its expected post-tax value rises)

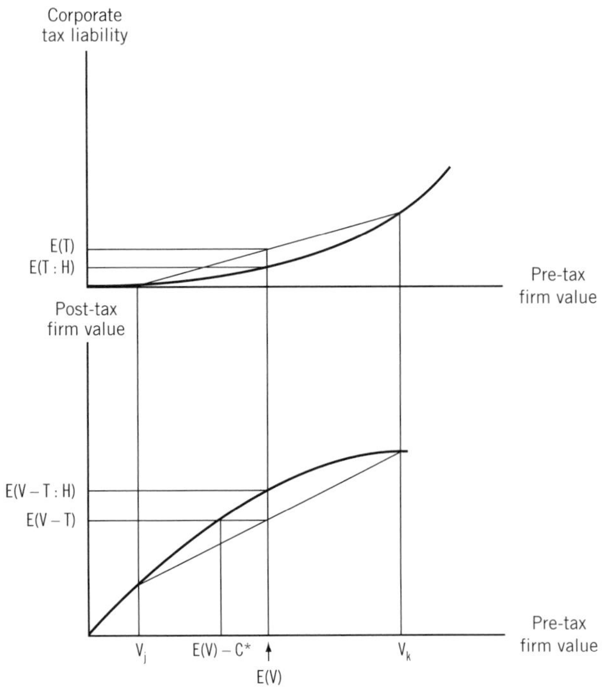

$V_j[V_k]$: pre-tax value of the firm without hedging if state j[k] occurs
E(V): expected pre-tax value of firm without hedging
E(T): expected corporate tax liability without hedging
E(T : H): corporate tax liability with a costless, perfect hedge
E(V – T): expected post-tax firm value without hedging
E(V – T : H): post-tax firm value with a costless, perfect hedge
C*: maximum cost of hedging where hedging is profitable

EMPIRICAL IMPLICATIONS

The basic provisions of the corporate tax code (a zero tax rate on negative taxable income, moderate progressivity for taxable income under US$100,000 and a constant rate thereafter) yield a convex statutory tax function. The convex region is extended by tax preference items like the investment tax credit that offset a stated maximum fraction, x, of a corporation's tax liability.[7] The effective marginal tax rate is constant only if taxable income exceeds $1/x$ times the corporation's accumulated investment tax credits – a number that can substantially exceed US$100,000. DeAngelo and Masulis (1980) report that, over the period 1964–73, in any year an average of 27% of the firms filing tax returns paid no taxes; for the largest corporations, the average was between 10% and 20%.

The tax-reducing benefits of hedging increase if the function that yields after-tax income becomes more concave. Thus, if excess-profits taxes or investment-tax credits increase the convexity of the tax function, then such a tax will induce firms to hedge more. Conversely, allowing trading in tax credits reduces the convexity of the tax function and reduces the tax benefits of hedging.[8]

The three-year carry-back, 15-year carry-forward provision and the progressivity provisions of the tax code produce local concavities in the tax function.[9] A firm that faces concavities in the tax function finds it profitable to "reverse-hedge", increasing the variability of its taxable income over that range of outcomes.

Debt and hedging policies

TRANSACTIONS COSTS OF BANKRUPTCY

Transactions costs of bankruptcy can induce widely-held corporations to hedge.[10] Consider a levered firm that pays taxes on its cashflows net of interest payments to the bondholders. Let F be the face value of debt. If the value of the firm is below F at maturity, the bondholders receive F minus the transactions costs of bankruptcy. Otherwise, the shareholders receive firm value minus both taxes paid and the bondholders' payment, F. The lower are expected bankruptcy costs, the higher the expected payoffs to the firm's claimholders. By reducing the variability of the future value of the firm, hedging lowers the probability of incurring bankruptcy costs. This decrease in expected bankruptcy costs benefits shareholders. Figure 2 illustrates this point. If transactions costs of bankruptcy are a decreasing function of firm value and the tax rate is either constant or an increasing function of firm value, expected after-tax firm value net of bankruptcy costs is higher if the firm can costlessly hedge.

To extend our analysis, we consider a simple model in which a firm issues debt to create a tax shield. Again, let P_i be the price today of one dollar delivered in state i and $T(V_i)$ be the tax rate, if the before-tax value of the firm is V_i. In the absence of leverage, the after-tax value of the firm is $V(0)$. We assume a leveraged firm issues pure discount bonds with face value F and pays taxes on its before-tax value net of its payment to the bondholders. The after-tax value of a levered firm with the same investment policy as the unlevered firm is $V(F)$. For simplicity, it is assumed that $V_j < F < V_k$. If $V_i < F$, bankruptcy costs are given by $C(V_i) \le V_i$. The difference in the value of the levered firm and the unlevered firm is given by

$$V(F) - V(0) = \sum_{i=1}^{j} P_i(T(V_i)V_i - C(V_i)) + \sum_{i=k}^{S} P_i T(V_i)F \tag{3}$$

where F corresponds to the payment to the bondholders in the absence of bankruptcy. By inspection, the value of the levered firm equals the value of the unlevered firm minus the present value of bankruptcy costs plus the present value of the tax shield from interest payments.[11] From equation (3), the value of the levered firm increases with decreases in the present value of expected bankruptcy costs.[12]

To analyse the effects of hedging on expected bankruptcy costs, we examine an unlevered firm whose shareholders plan to issue debt. Since potential bondholders have no market power, shareholders capture any increase in firm value from bond issuance. We

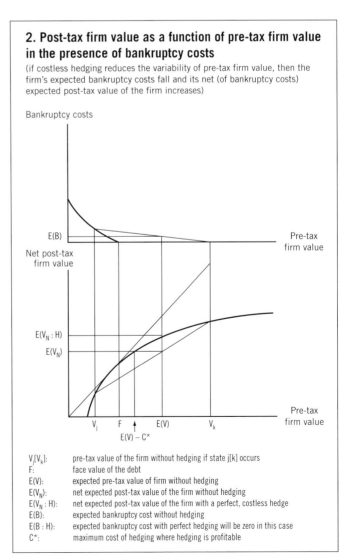

2. Post-tax firm value as a function of pre-tax firm value in the presence of bankruptcy costs

(if costless hedging reduces the variability of pre-tax firm value, then the firm's expected bankruptcy costs fall and its net (of bankruptcy costs) expected post-tax value of the firm increases)

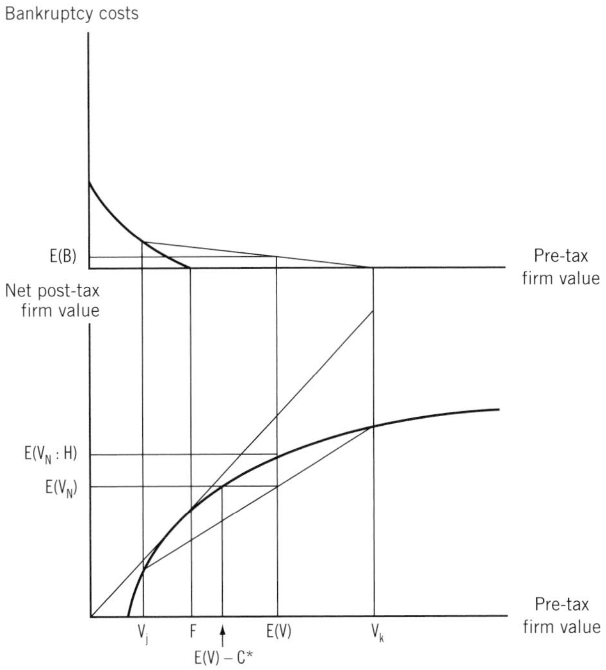

$V_j[V_k]$:	pre-tax value of the firm without hedging if state j[k] occurs
F:	face value of the debt
E(V):	expected pre-tax value of firm without hedging
$E(V_N)$:	net expected post-tax value of the firm without hedging
$E(V_N : H)$:	net expected post-tax value of the firm with a perfect, costless hedge
E(B):	expected bankruptcy cost without hedging
E(B : H):	expected bankruptcy cost with perfect hedging will be zero in this case
C*:	maximum cost of hedging where hedging is profitable

assume that investment policy is fixed, ($V_i(0)$ is given for all is) and any proceeds of a debt issue are distributed to the shareholders as a dividend.

The firm can reduce bankruptcy costs by holding a hedge portfolio that pays positive amounts when the firm would be bankrupt without hedging. To analyse the benefits of hedging, consider a hedge that pays $H_g < 0$ in state g and $H_m > 0$ in state m. We assume the hedge portfolio involves no current cashflows (ie, $P_g H_g + P_m H_m = 0$) and that $V_g + H_g > F$ and $V_m + H_m > F$. By construction, $V_g < F$. Let $V^H(F)$ be the value of the leveraged firm if the firm hedges. Then, assuming a constant tax rate T, we have

$$V^H(F) - V(F) = P_g C(V_g) + P_g T(F - V_g) \tag{4}$$

Since $C(V_g) > 0$ and $V_g < F$, $V^H(F) - V(F)$ is always positive. Thus, the hedge decreases the present value of bankruptcy costs and increases the present value of the tax shield of debt. (With a constant tax rate, expected tax payments from the hedge are zero unless the firm is bankrupt when the hedge pays off.) Shareholders benefit from hedging only because bankruptcy involves real costs to stockholders and bondholders: the direct bankruptcy costs and the loss of debt tax shields.

Again, with costly hedging it is still generally profitable to hedge. However, shareholders must account for hedging costs when they decide among alternative hedging strategies.

BOND COVENANTS AND COSTS OF FINANCIAL DISTRESS

For hedging to increase shareholder wealth, the firm must convince potential bondholders that it will hedge after the bond sale and, hence, that expected bankruptcy costs are not as high as the firm's investment policy would otherwise suggest. But potential bondholders recognise that hedging after the sale of the debt is not in the stockholders' best interests. Although hedging increases the value of the firm, it also redistributes wealth from shareholders to bondholders in a way that makes shareholders worse off.[13] Without an incentive to hedge, despite promising to do so, it will be difficult for the firm to make a credible announcement that it will hedge.[14]

There are at least two ways that market forces create incentives for shareholders to pursue a hedging policy. First, if the firm borrows frequently, it benefits from a reputation for hedging since that reputation increases the price for its new debt. Yet such a reputation is not likely to be sufficient to insure that the firm will hedge when the probability of bankruptcy is large. Then, the gain from no longer hedging is likely to outweigh the cost of lost reputation, since the reputation is valuable only if the firm successfully avoids bankruptcy. Second, hedging provides a means whereby the firm can reduce the costs of financial distress imposed by bond covenants that constrain the shareholders to take actions they would otherwise avoid. For instance, binding bond covenants can force the firm to alter its investment policy; hedging can reduce the likelihood that covenants become binding.

EMPIRICAL IMPLICATIONS

Warner (1977) suggests that transactions costs of bankruptcy are a small fraction of large firms' assets. Yet small bankruptcy costs can be sufficient to induce large firms to hedge, if the reduction in expected bankruptcy costs exceeds the costs of hedging. Warner also indicates that the bankruptcy costs are less than proportional to firm size. If hedging costs are proportional, the reduction in expected bankruptcy costs is greater for the small corporation, and, hence, small firms are more likely to hedge.

A firm can hedge to reduce the expected costs of financial distress. Because bond covenants use accounting numbers to define states where the firm's activities are restricted,[15] a firm that wants to decrease the probability of financial distress must manage its accounting numbers so that bond covenants do not become binding. It is thus possible for a value-maximising firm to choose to reduce the variance of its accounting earnings, even if this increases the variance of economic earnings.[16]

Managerial compensation, risk-aversion and hedging

The corporation's managers, employees, suppliers and customers are frequently unable to diversify risks specific to their claims on the corporation. Because they are risk-averse, these individuals require extra compensation to bear the non-diversifiable risk of the claims.[17] With limited liability, the amount of risk that can be allocated to the stockholders is restricted by the company's capital stock. But the firm can reduce the risk imposed on other claimholders by hedging. Thus, as long as the reduction in compensation of managers and employees and other suppliers plus the increased revenues from customers exceed the costs of hedging, hedging increases the value of the firm.

MANAGERIAL RISK-AVERSION AND HEDGING

Shareholders hire managers because they have specialised resources that increase the value of the firm. Managers cannot use their expertise unless they have some discretion in the choice of their actions. Yet, unless faced with proper incentives, managers will not maximise shareholder wealth. The managerial compensation contract must be designed so that when managers increase the value of the firm, they also increase their expected utility. Frequently observed provisions of managerial compensation contracts make the manager's total current compensation an increasing function of firm value.[18]

The managers' expected utility depends on the distribution of the firm's payoffs. Hedging changes the distribution of the firm's payoffs and, therefore, changes the managers' expected utility. To analyse the managers' hedging choices, we define hedging as the acquisition of financial assets that reduce the variance of the firm's payoffs. The firm is assumed to acquire a hedge portfolio that creates neither a cash inflow nor outflow at acquisition. Let H_i be the payoff of the hedge portfolio in state of the world i so that

$$H_i = \sum_j N_j \cdot Q_{ij} \tag{5}$$

where N_j is the number of shares of asset j purchased and Q_{ij} is the payoff of one share of asset j in state of the world i.

To derive the optional hedge portfolio, we assume a two-period world in which the manager's end-of-period wealth equals the sum of his pecuniary compensation plus the payoff of his non-tradeable investment in the firm. This implies that the manager's indirect utility function in state i is a function only of his end-of-period wealth in state i, written W_i; and his wealth is an increasing function of the total value of the firm in state i, ie, $V_i + H_i$,

$$U_i = U(W(V_i + H_i)); \quad i = 1,\ldots, S \tag{6}$$

The indirect utility function of wealth is assumed to be strictly concave; thus, the manager is risk-averse. With these assumptions, the manager maximises expected utility:

$$U = \sum_i P_i \cdot U(W(V_i + H_i)) \tag{7}$$

where p_i is the probability of state i occurring, subject to the budget condition that

$$\Sigma_j N_j \cdot Q_{0j} = 0 \tag{8}$$

where Q_{0j} is the price at the beginning of the period of a share of asset j. To obtain the optimal number of shares of each security, N_j, the first-order conditions are:

$$\sum_i P_i \frac{\partial U}{\partial W} W' \frac{Q_{ij}}{Q_{0j}} = \sum_j P_i \frac{\partial U}{\partial W} W' \frac{Q_{ik}}{Q_{0k}}, \quad \text{for all j and k} \tag{9}$$

where W' is the first derivative of function $W(\cdot)$. The first-order conditions state that the marginal increase in expected utility per dollar of security j purchased must equal the marginal increase in expected utility per dollar of security k purchased. To simplify, we assume that all financial assets have equal expected rates of return and that the firm incurs no transactions costs when it purchases or sells financial assets.

The solution to the hedging problem has several interesting properties. First, if the manager's end-of-period wealth is a concave function of the end-of-period firm value, the optimal hedging strategy is to hedge the firm completely, if this is feasible. The expected income of the manager is maximised if the firm is completely hedged, because the expected value of a concave function of a random variable is smaller than the value of the function evaluated at the expected value of the random variable (Jensen's Inequality). As the manager is risk-averse, he will choose to bear risk only if he is rewarded for doing so by higher expected income. Since his expected income is maximised when the firm is completely hedged, the manager will choose to bear no risk.[19]

Second, if the manager's end-of-period wealth is a convex function of the end-of-period firm value, but the manager's expected utility is still a concave function of the end-of-period value of the firm, the optimal strategy generally will be to eliminate some, but not all, uncertainty through hedging. In this case, the expected income of the manager is higher if the firm does not hedge, since his income is a convex function of the value of the firm. However, because the manager is risk-averse, he will want to give up some expected income to reduce risk. Faced with a trade-off between expected income and risk of income, the manager will not, in general, choose a policy that makes his income riskless.

Third, if the manager's end-of-period utility is a convex function of the end-of-period firm value, Jensen's Inequality implies that the manager's end-of-period utility has a higher expected value if the firm is not hedged at all. Bonus or stock option provisions of compensation plans can make the manager's expected utility a convex function of the value of the firm. If the manager's expected utility is a convex function of the value of the firm, the manager will behave like a risk-seeker even though his expected utility function is a concave function of his end-of-period wealth.

An example of a situation in which a firm does not hedge even though the manager is risk-averse can make this point clearer. We assume that the compensation contract promises a payment equal to $\mathcal{T} + \text{Max}(V_i - K_i, 0)$. The option-like feature of this contract can be found in many compensation contracts. For simplicity, we assume that $S = 2$ and $V_2 > K > V_1 > \mathcal{T}$. The manager is assumed to maximise an expected utility function of the form

$$U = P_1 \frac{1}{d} W_1^d + P_2 \frac{1}{d} W_2^d; \quad d < 1 \tag{10}$$

The firm hedges if it purchases financial assets that pay a positive amount in state 1 and a negative amount in state 2. Given our assumptions, the expected payoff of the hedge portfolio must equal zero, which implies that $H_2 = (-p_1/p_2)H_1$. By eliminating H_2 in equation (7) and taking the partial derivative of the manager's expected utility with respect to H_1, one can easily verify that U is a decreasing function of H_1 for positive values of H_1 equal to or smaller than the value of H_1 required to hedge the value of the firm completely. Thus, the structure of the manager's compensation package can induce him not to hedge the firm at all.

Frequently, compensation packages make the manager's end-of-period wealth a concave function of the firm value in some regions and a convex function in others. This suggests that hedging will take place for some values of the firm and not others. Furthermore, for values of the firm that make the manager's end-of-period wealth a convex function of firm value, the manager may choose to "reverse-hedge" (make the value of the firm even more dependent on the realisation of some state variable).

We have assumed that the expected rates of return on all financial assets are equal and that transactions costs are negligible.[20] If expected returns to financial assets vary, the manager faces a trade-off between expected income and risk of income. In such cases, he will hedge less if hedging involves going short in a portfolio with a high expected return. If transactions costs increase, the firm will hedge less, as hedging decreases the manager's expected end-of-period wealth. We also must assume that the firm has a comparative advantage in hedging over the manager. In other words, it should not pay for the manager to hedge his end-of-period wealth on his personal account. The combination of transactions costs, economies of scale and the large number of managers within any firm make this comparative advantage likely.[21]

MANAGERIAL COMPENSATION AND HEDGING

Our analysis has, thus far, taken as given the form of the management compensation contract. This analysis is interesting in itself since it produces positive statements about the firm's hedging policies. In reality, however, shareholders choose the management compensation package and, thereby, affect the hedging that managers undertake. Making managerial wealth a concave function of firm value bonds the firm to a hedging policy. This should be important for a firm with debt or other fixed claims as it offers greater assurance that the firm will hedge as long as that compensation policy is followed.

Managers whose compensation is a concave (or not too convex) function of firm value have incentives to reduce firm cashflow variability. Hence, such managers might reject variance-increasing positive net present value (NPV) projects. If hedging costs are negligible, it pays to let managers hedge as this increases incentives to take variance-increasing positive NPV projects. If shareholders instead try to prohibit hedging, managers will focus more on non-priced risks. Still, as long as their compensation depends on firm value, managers have incentives to consider market valuation in evaluating projects.

With costly hedging, shareholders have incentives to devise a compensation plan that discourages managers from devoting excessive resources to hedging. This can be accomplished when computing the manager's compensation by filtering out those changes in firm value that are not under the manager's control and by making the manager's compensation a more convex function of firm value. However, it will generally not be efficient to eliminate all incentives to hedge. Earlier sections have demonstrated that hedging can be profitable. Moreover, a compensation plan that eliminates all hedging incentives would be costly to negotiate and implement.[22]

EMPIRICAL IMPLICATIONS

A manager's compensation often includes a payment whose value depends on accounting earnings. It follows that the manager's expected utility depends on both the firm's market value and its accounting earnings. If the manager's expected utility depends heavily on accounting earnings and is a concave function of accounting earnings, one would expect the firm to principally hedge accounting earnings even if doing so increases the variance of the firm's economic value.

Managers' risk-aversion can lead them to hedge, but it does not necessarily do so. If the compensation package of the manager is such that his income is a convex function of the value of the firm, it can be the case that the manager is better off if the firm does not hedge. Hence, the more option-like features in a firm's compensation plan, the less the firm is expected to hedge. For instance, bonus plans that make a payment to managers only if accounting earnings exceed some target number will induce managers to hedge less since this payment is a convex function of accounting earnings.

If the manager owns a significant fraction of the firm, one would expect the firm to hedge more, as the manager's end-of-period wealth is more a linear function of the value of the firm. This reinforces the incentive for closely-held firms to hedge since the owners are unlikely to hold well-diversified portfolios and, thus, have incentives to induce managers to reduce the variance of the firm's returns.

Summary and conclusions

This chapter presents an analysis of the hedging behaviour of firms that differs fundamentally from the existing literature. Rather than assuming that the firm is risk-averse, we follow modern finance theory and assume that incentives exist within the contracting process to maximise the market value of the firm. We then show that a value-maximising firm can hedge for three reasons: (1) taxes, (2) costs of financial distress and (3) managerial risk-aversion. Our analysis offers a framework within which the wide diversity of hedging practices among firms can be understood.

Further research should focus on empirical tests of the implications of our analysis. To implement the tests, however, more detailed data are required than are available from sources such as CompuStat, in which firms' hedging activities are aggregated with other contingent outcomes such as insurance contracts and outstanding lawsuits. Transactions, such as mergers, also accomplish some of the same results as hedging, although it is likely to be difficult to appropriately control for other changes in investment and financing policy to focus on these hedging characteristics.

1 *A recent review of papers on hedging foreign exchange risks by Jacques (1981) contains 80 references.*

2 *References that consider the hedging problems for risk-averse agents includes Anderson and Danthine (1980, 1981), Feder, Just and Schmitz (1980), Ho and Saunders (1983), Holthausen (1979), Makin (1978) and Rolfo (1980).*

3 *Notice that the literature on the demand for insurance addresses a problem that is similar to the problem discussed by the literature on hedging. However, for corporations, the determinants of the demand for insurance differ crucially from the determinants of hedging policies. For a corporation, the purchase of insurance provides real services due to the expertise of insurance companies in evaluating some types of risks and administering claims settlement procedures (for an analysis of these services, see Mayers and Smith, 1982), while forward or futures contracts provide no apparent real services.*

4 *If markets are perfect and complete, the value of the firm is independent of its hedging policy for other reasons, as well. For example, if a firm hedges the value of an input by purchasing forward contracts and*

that input price rises, the firm's pricing and production policies should not be affected by the existence of the hedge. The opportunity cost of the input is its current price, not the (sunk) cost of the forward contract.

5 *This diversity has been well documented in the case of foreign exchange risks. See, for instance, Rodriguez (1980).*

6 *Cornell (1981) offers some supporting evidence for this conjecture.*

7 *For tax years 1983 and 1984, the maximum tax offset by the investment tax credit is 85%. It was 50% in 1978 and increased by 10% per year until it reached 90% in 1982.*

8 *Regulations are equivalent to in-kind taxes. For example, if unexpectedly large changes in firm value lead politicians to impose additional constraints on the firm, then these additional regulatory costs are like taxes even though they do not result from the filing of a tax form. Note also that if regulations typically impose constraints on firms expressed in terms of accounting numbers, then this establishes incentives for firms to hedge accounting rather than economic values.*

9 *The 15-year carry-forward provision applies only for operating losses. Notice that the existence of a minimum tax introduces further complications. However, the minimum tax tends to make after-tax income more of a concave function of before-tax income, as it implies that some taxes will be paid on positive cashflows. Cordes and Sheffrin (1983) present evidence on the use of these provisions.*

10 *Diamond (1984) also argues that bankruptcy costs lead to hedging. In his model of financial intermediaries, financial intermediaries hedge all systematic risks, ie, all risks that have no incentive effects. His inclusions are stronger than ours because in his model there are no cases in which it does not pay to hedge, either because of transaction costs or for other reasons discussed in this chapter.*

11 *The model we employ is similar to those developed by Kraus and Litzenberger (1973) and Brennan and Schwartz (1978). While our treatment of taxes is not very sophisticated, it is important to understand that the role played by taxes in this analysis is simply to justify the existence of debt. A more realistic treatment of taxes would not add important insights to our analysis.*

12 *Note that with a more sophisticated treatment of taxes the analysis becomes more complex. As the probability of bankruptcy decreases, the promised yield of the debt decreases and so does its tax shield.*

13 *In this context, the decision not to hedge after debt has been sold has the same effect on the shareholders' wealth as a decision by the firm to substitute a more risky asset for a less risky asset. See Smith and Warner (1979).*

14 *Note that this is an example of a time-inconsistent optimal policy. See Kydland and Prescott (1977).*

15 *See Smith and Warner (1979) for a description and analysis of bond covenants.*

16 *One also would expect firms to hedge more if accounting rules are changed to increase the variance of accounting earnings. Thus, firms will hedge less under FASB 52 than under FASB 8, as translation gains and losses are not recognised in earnings when they occur under FASB 52 while they were under FASB 8.*

17 *Employees demand higher wages if the probability of layoff is greater. Managers demand higher salaries (or perhaps even an equity stake in the company) if the risks of failure, insolvency and financial embarrassment are great. Suppliers set more unfavourable terms in long-term contracts with companies whose prospects are more uncertain. And customers, concerned about a company's ability to service their products in the future or fulfil warranty obligations, will be reluctant to buy its products. Reagan and Stulz 1983 provide an analysis of risk-sharing when one party of the contract has a comparative advantage in using capital markets to diversify risks away.*

18 *See Smith and Watts (1982) for a description and analysis of the provisions of management compensation contracts and see Healy (1983) for a discussion of the specification of bonus plans. Note also that we assume the manager's marginal tax rate is constant. Progressive tax rates only make managerial wealth a more concave function of firm value and thus reinforce our results based on risk-aversion alone.*

19 *This result is equivalent to Arrow's (1963) proposition that a risk-averse individual offered fairly priced insurance fully insures. See also Huberman, Mayers and Smith, 1983.*

20 *Stulz (1984) derives optimal hedging strategies in a continuous-time framework when holding costs for forward contracts are positive and when expected rates of return differ across assets for the case of foreign exchange exposure.*

21 *If there is a single manager, scale economies can still induce the manager to hedge through the firm. Note that the size of most future contracts is too large to make them useful to hedge a manager's income.*

22 *The Diamond and Verrecchia (1982) analysis suggests that bonus schemes would filter out the effect of variables over which management has no control. However, the difficulty in administering such a scheme must explain why they are rarely observed.*

BIBLIOGRAPHY

Anderson, R. W., and J. P. Danthine, 1980, "Hedging and Joint Production: Theory and Illustrations", *Journal of Finance* 35, pp. 487–97.

Anderson, R. W., and J. P. Danthine, 1981, "Cross Hedging", *Journal of Political Economy* 89, pp. 1,182–96.

Arrow, K. J., 1963, "Uncertainty and the Welfare Economics of Medical Care", *American Economic Review* 53, pp. 943–73.

Brennan, M., and E. Schwartz, 1978, "Corporate Income Taxes, Valuation, and the Problem of Optimal Capital Structure", *Journal of Business* 51, pp. 103–14.

Cordes, J. J., and S. M. Sheffrin, 1983, "Estimating the Tax Advantage of Corporate Debt", *Journal of Finance* 38, pp. 95–105.

Cornell, B., 1981, "Taxes and the Pricing of Treasury Bill Futures Contracts: A Note", *Journal of Finance* 36, pp. 1,169–76.

DeAngelo, H., and R. Masulis, 1980, "Optimal Capital Structure under Corporate and Personal Taxation", *Journal of Financial Economics* 8, pp. 3–29.

Diamond, D. W., 1984, "Financial Intermediation and Delegated Monitoring", *Review of Economic Studies* 51, pp. 393–414.

Diamond, D., and R. Verrecchia, 1982, "Optimal Managerial Contracts and Equilibrium Security Prices", *Journal of Finance* 37, pp. 275–87.

Feder, G., R. E. Just and A. Schmitz, 1980, "Futures Market and the Theory of the Firm under Uncertainty", *Quarterly Journal of Economics* 94, pp. 317–28.

Healy, P., 1983, "The Impact of Accounting Bonus Schemes on the Selection of Accounting Principles", unpublished PhD dissertation, University of Rochester.

Ho, T. S. Y., and A. Saunders, 1983, "Fixed Rate Loan Commitments, Take-Down Risk, and the Dynamics of Hedging with Futures", *Journal of Financial and Quantitative Analysis* 18, pp. 499–516.

Holthausen, J. M, 1979, "Hedging and the Competitive Firm under Uncertainty", *American Economic Review* 69, pp. 989–95.

Huberman, G., D. Mayers and C. W. Smith, 1983, "Optimal Insurance Policy Indemnity Schedules", *Bell Journal of Economics* 14, pp. 415–26.

Jacques, L., 1981, "Management of Foreign Exchange Risk: A Review Article", *Journal of International Business Studies* 11, pp. 81–101.

Jagannathan, R., 1984, "Call Options and the Risk of Underlying Securities", *Journal of Financial Economics* 13, pp. 425–34.

Kraus, A., and R. Litzenberger, 1973, "A State Preference Model of Optimal Financial Leverage", *Journal of Finance* 28, pp. 911–22.

Kydland, R. E., and E. C. Prescott, 1977, "Rules Rather than Discretion: The Inconsistency of Optimal Plans", *Journal of Political Economy* 85, pp. 513–48.

Makin, J. H., 1978, "Portfolio Theory and the Problem of Foreign Exchange Risk", *Journal of Finance* 33, pp. 517–34.

Mayers, D., and C. Smith, 1982, "On the Corporate Demand for Insurance", *Journal of Business* 55, pp. 281–96.

Modigliani, F., and M. Miller, 1985, "The Cost of Capital, Corporation Finance and the Theory of Investment", *American Economic Review* 48, pp. 261–97.

Reagan, P. B., and R. M. Stulz, 1983, "Risk Sharing, Labor Contracts and Capital Markets", unpublished manuscript, University of Rochester.

Rodriguez, R., 1980, *Foreign Exchange Management in US Multinationals* (Lexington, Massachusetts: D. C. Heath).

Rolfo, J., 1980, "Optimal Hedging under Price and Quantity Uncertainty: The Case of a Cocoa Producer", *Journal of Political Economy* 88, pp. 100–16.

Smith, C., and J. Warner, 1979, "On Financial Contracting: An Analysis of Bond Covenants", *Journal of Financial Economics* 7, pp. 117–61.

Smith, C., and R. Watts, 1982, "Incentive and Tax Effects of US Executive Compensation Plans", *Australian Journal of Management* 7, pp. 139–57.

Stulz, R., 1984, "Optimal Hedging Policies", *Journal of Financial and Quantitative Analysis* 19, pp. 127–40.

Warner, J., 1977, "Bankruptcy Costs: Some Evidence", *Journal of Finance* 32, pp. 337–48.

7

Risk Management: Coordinating Corporate Investment and Financing Policies*

Kenneth A. Froot, David S. Scharfstein and Jeremy C. Stein

Harvard Business School; MIT; MIT

Corporations take risk management very seriously – recent surveys find that risk management is ranked by financial executives as one of their most important objectives.[1] Given its real-world prominence, one might guess that the topic of risk management would command a great deal of attention from researchers in finance, and that practitioners would therefore have a well-developed body of wisdom from which to draw in formulating hedging strategies.

Such a guess would, however, be at best only partially correct. Finance theory does do a good job of instructing firms on the implementation of hedges. For example, if a refining company decides that it wants to use options to reduce its exposure to oil prices by a certain amount, a Black–Scholes-type model can help the company calculate the number of contracts needed. Indeed, there is an extensive literature that covers numerous practical aspects of what might be termed "hedging mechanics", from the computation of hedge ratios to the institutional peculiarities of individual contracts.

Unfortunately, finance theory has had much less clear-cut guidance to offer on the logically prior questions of hedging strategy: What sorts of risks should be hedged? Should they be hedged partially or fully? What kinds of instruments will best accomplish the hedging objectives? Answering these questions is difficult because, paradoxically, the same arbitrage logic that helps the refining company calculate option deltas also implies that there may be no reason for it to engage in hedging activity in the first place. According to the Modigliani–Miller paradigm, buying and selling oil options contracts cannot alter the company's value, since individual investors in the company's stock can always buy and sell such contracts themselves if they care to adjust their exposure to oil prices.

It is not that there are no stories to explain why firms might wish to hedge. Indeed, a number of potential rationales for hedging have been developed recently, by, among others, Stulz (1984), Smith and Stulz (1985), Smith, Smithson and Wilford (1990), Stulz (1990), Breeden and Viswanathan (1990) and Lessard (1990). However, it seems fair to say that there is not yet a single accepted framework that can be used to guide hedging strategies.[2] In part this gap arises precisely because previous work has focused on why hedging can make sense, rather than on how much or what sort of hedging is optimal for a particular firm. Indeed, much of the previous work has the extreme implication that firms should hedge fully – completely insulating their market values from hedgeable risks.

In this chapter we illustrate how optimal risk management strategies can be designed in a variety of settings. To do so, we build on one strand of the previous work on hedging – that

**Originally published in the* Journal of Finance *48(5) (1993), pp. 1,629–58, reproduced with permission of Blackwell Publishers. We thank Don Lessard, Tim Luehrman, André Perold, Raghuram Rajan, Julio Rotemberg and Stew Myers for helpful discussions. We are also grateful to the IFSRC and the Center for Energy Policy Research at MIT, the Department of the Research at Harvard Business School, the National Science Foundation and Batterymarch Financial Management for generous financial support.*

which examines the implications of capital market imperfections. Broadly speaking, this work argues that if capital market imperfections make externally-obtained funds more expensive than those generated internally, they can generate a rationale for risk management.

The basic logic can be understood as follows. If a firm does not hedge, there will be some variability in the cashflows generated by assets in place. Simple accounting implies that this variability in internal cashflow must result in either: (a) variability in the amount of money raised externally, or (b) variability in the amount of investment. Variability in investment will generally be undesirable, to the extent that there are diminishing marginal returns to investment (ie, to the extent that output is a concave function of investment). If the supply of external finance were perfectly elastic, the optimal *ex-post* solution would thus be to leave investment plans unaltered in the face of variations in internal cashflow, taking up all the slack by changing the quantity of outside money raised. Unfortunately this approach no longer works well if the marginal cost of funds goes up with the amount raised externally. Now a shortfall in cash may be met with some increase in outside financing, but also some decrease in investment. Thus variability in cashflows now disturbs both investment and financing plans in a way that is costly to the firm. To the extent that hedging can reduce this variability in cashflows, it can increase the value of the firm.

A prominent example of this line of reasoning is Lessard (1990).[3] Lessard writes: "...the most compelling arguments for hedging lie in ensuring the firm's ability to meet two critical sets of cashflow commitments: (1) the exercise prices of their operating options reflected in their growth opportunities (for example, the R&D or promotion budgets) and (2) their dividends... The growth options argument hinges on the observation that, in the case of a funding shortfall relative to investment opportunities, raising external capital will be costly."

The model that we develop below is very much in the spirit of this verbal argument. However, it takes the argument a couple of steps further: rather than simply demonstrating that there is a role for hedging, we are able to show how a firm's optimal hedging strategy – in terms of both the amount of hedging and the instruments used – depends on the nature of its investment and financing opportunities. Or, put differently, we illustrate how a well-designed risk management programme can enable a firm to optimally coordinate its investment and financing policies.

The chapter starts by briefly sketching several other explanations of corporate risk management that have been offered. Following this, we present our model in its most elemental form and use it to demonstrate the basic rationale for hedging, examining a series of practical applications of our framework. Further on in the chapter, we extend the model to show how optimal hedge ratios can be calculated as a function of shocks to investment and financing opportunities. Next, we consider the question of optimal currency hedging by multinationals that have investment opportunities in more than one country. We then examine "non-linear" hedging strategies that make use of options and other complex hedging instruments. Finally, a few further extensions are outlined briefly, and the chapter concludes with an examination of the empirical implications of the theory.

Other rationales for corporate risk management

MANAGERIAL MOTIVES

Stulz (1984) argues that corporate hedging is an outgrowth of the risk aversion of managers. While outside stockholders' ability to diversify will effectively make them indifferent to the amount of hedging activity undertaken, the same cannot be said for managers, who may hold a relatively large portion of their wealth in the firm's stock. Thus managers can be made strictly better off (without costing outside shareholders anything) by reducing the variance of total firm value.

One weakness of the Stulz theory is that it implicitly relies on the assumption that managers face significant costs when trading in hedging contracts for their own account – otherwise they would be able to adjust the risks they face without having to involve the firm directly in any hedging activities. At the same time, unless one also introduces transactions costs to hedging at the corporate level, the Stulz theory makes the extreme prediction that firms will hedge as much as possible – that is, until the variance of stock prices is minimised.

A very different managerial theory of hedging, based on asymmetric information, is put forward by Breeden and Viswanathan (1990) and DeMarzo and Duffie (1992). In both of these models, the labour market revises its opinions about the ability of managers based on their firms' performance. This can lead some managers to undertake hedges in an attempt to influence the labour market's perception.

TAXES

Smith and Stulz (1985) argue that if taxes are a convex function of earnings, it will generally be optimal for firms to hedge. The logic is straightforward - convexity implies that a more volatile earnings stream leads to higher expected taxes than a less volatile earnings stream. Convexity in the tax function is quite plausible for some firms, particularly those that face a significant probability of negative earnings and are unable to carry forward 100% of their tax losses to subsequent periods.

COSTS OF FINANCIAL DISTRESS AND DEBT CAPACITY

For a given level of debt, hedging can reduce the probability that a firm will find itself in a situation where it is unable to repay that debt. Thus if financial distress is costly, and if there is an advantage to having debt in the capital structure (say due to taxes or agency problems associated with "free cashflow"), hedging may be used as a means to increase debt capacity. The simplest variant of this argument, put forth by Smith and Stulz (1985), simply assumes that bankruptcy involves some exogenous transactions costs.

CAPITAL MARKET IMPERFECTIONS AND INEFFICIENT INVESTMENT

A more sophisticated version of the argument invokes Myers's (1977) "debt overhang" underinvestment effect to endogenise the costs of financial distress. This rationale for hedging (or equivalently, for using debt indexed to exogenous sources of risk) is given by Froot, Scharfstein and Stein (1989) in the context of highly indebted less-developed countries. The same basic point is made in a corporate finance setting by Smith, Smithson and Wilford (1990). Stulz (1990) also argues that hedging can add value by reducing the investment distortions associated with debt finance.[4]

We view these debt overhang explanations for hedging to be very close cousins of those presented both in Lessard (1990) and in our model below. Although the exact mechanism is somewhat different, all the theories rely on the basic observation that, without hedging, firms may be forced to underinvest in some states of the world because it is costly or impossible to raise external finance.

The basic paradigm

A SIMPLE MODEL OF THE BENEFITS TO HEDGING

As stated above, hedging is beneficial if it can allow a firm to avoid unnecessary fluctuations in either investment spending or funds raised from outside investors. To illustrate this point, it is best to begin with a very simple and general framework. Afterwards, we demonstrate how this simple framework corresponds to a well-known optimising model of costly external finance.

Consider a firm that faces a two-period investment/financing decision. In the first period the firm has an amount of liquid assets, w. At this time the firm must choose its investment expenditures and external financing needs. In the second period, the output from the investment is realised and outside investors are repaid.

On the investment side, let the net present value of investment expenditures be given by

$$F(I) = f(I) - I \tag{1}$$

where I is investment, $f(I)$ is the subsequent expected level of output, $f' > 0$ and $f'' < 0$.[5] For notational simplicity we assume the discount rate is equal to zero.

As will become clear, the company prefers to finance investment with internal funds first before turning to external sources. Therefore, the company will raise from outside investors an amount e, so that

$$I = w + e \tag{2}$$

Given the discount rate of zero, outside investors require an expected repayment of e in the second period.

We assume, however, that there are additional (deadweight) costs to the firm of external finance, which we denote by C. (Per dollar raised, these funds therefore cost C/e above the riskless rate.) These costs could arise from a number of sources. First, they could originate in costs of bankruptcy and financial distress, which include direct costs (eg, legal fees) as well as indirect costs (eg, decreased product-market competitiveness and underinvestment). Second, such costs could arise from informational asymmetries between managers and outside investors. Or, to the extent that managers are not full residual claimants, there may be agency costs associated with motivating and monitoring managers who resort to certain types of outside finance. Finally, managers may obtain private benefits from limiting their dependence on external investors. Thus even if there are no observable costs to external finance, management may *act* as though external financing has real economic costs.[6]

Regardless of which interpretation one chooses, the deadweight costs should be an increasing function of the amount of external finance. We represent these costs as $C = C(e)$ and note that $C_e \geq 0$.[7]

The issue of hedging arises when first-period wealth, w, is random. To the extent that there are marketable risks that are correlated with w, the firm may attempt to alter the distribution of w by undertaking hedging transactions in period zero. For simplicity, we make the extreme assumption that all the fluctuations in w are completely hedgeable, and furthermore that hedging has no effect on the expected level of w.[8] Given this assumption, complete hedging will clearly be beneficial if, and only if, profits are a concave function of internal wealth.[9]

To explore the impact of hedging on optimal financing and investment decisions, we solve the model backwards, starting with the firm's first-period investment decision. The firm enters the first period with internal resources of w and chooses investment (and thereby the amount of external financing, $e = I - w$) to maximise net expected profits:

$$P(w) = \max_{I} F(I) - C(e) \tag{3}$$

The first-order condition for this problem is

$$F_I = f_I - 1 = C_e \tag{4}$$

where we have used the fact that, in the second period when w is given, $de/dI = 1$. Equation (4) implies that there is underinvestment – the optimal level of investment, I^*, is below the first-best level, which would set $f_I = 1$.

Moving to period zero, the firm chooses its hedging policy to maximise expected profits. As noted above, random fluctuations in w reduce expected profits if $P(w)$ is a concave function. Using the first-order condition in (4), the second derivative of profits is given by

$$P_{ww} = f_{II}\left(\frac{dI^*}{dw}\right)^2 - C_{ee}\left(\frac{dI^*}{dw} - 1\right)^2 \tag{5}$$

where f_{II} and C_{ee} are evaluated at $I = I^*$. If this expression is globally negative, then hedging raises average profits. Equation (5) can be rewritten by applying the implicit function theorem to (4) to yield[10]

$$P_{ww} = f_{II}\frac{dI^*}{dw} \tag{6}$$

Equation (6) clarifies the sense in which hedging activity is determined by the interaction of investment and financing considerations. If hedging is to be beneficial, two conditions must *both* be satisfied: (i) marginal returns on investment must be decreasing, and (ii) the level of internal wealth must have a positive impact on the optimal level of investment. The latter condition is a ubiquitous feature of models of external finance in the face of information and/or incentive problems. Furthermore, there is substantial empirical evidence suggesting that corporate investment is indeed sensitive to levels of internal cashflow.[11]

Two simple examples may help to develop further the intuition behind equations (5) and (6). In the first, assume that a company has no access at all to financial markets. In this case, C is always equal to zero in equilibrium, and any variation in w is reflected one-for-one in changes in investment, $dI^*/dw = 1$. Equations (5) and (6) then tell us that $P_{ww} = f_{II}$: the concavity of the profit function comes solely from the concavity of the production technology.

In the second polar example, investment is completely fixed (eg, the company has only one indivisible investment project with high returns). Now any fluctuations in internal funds translate one-for-one into fluctuations in the amount of external funds that must be raised, $dI^*/dw = 0$. Equation (5) then says that the concavity of the profit function comes exclusively from the convexity of the C function, ie, $P_{ww} = -C_{ee}$.

Clearly, for intermediate cases – those in which $0 < dI^*/dw < 1$ – the concavity of the profit function will come from both the concavity of the investment technology and the convexity of the financing cost function. Another way to see this is to substitute out dI^*/dw from equation (5), yielding

$$P_{ww} = \frac{-f_{II}C_{ee}}{f_{II} - C_{ee}} \tag{7}$$

Equation (7) illustrates again that hedging is driven by an interaction between investment and financing considerations (as represented by f_{II} and C_{ee}, respectively).

Thus far we have used an arbitrary specification for the C function to establish conditions under which hedging is value-increasing. However, it is unclear whether those conditions (ie, the requirement that $C_{ee} \geq 0$) would emerge naturally if we derived the C function from an optimising model with rational agents. Next, we examine an important class of such models and demonstrate that the required convexity in C obtains under a wide range of parameterisations.

HEDGING IN AN OPTIMAL CONTRACTING MODEL

The model we adopt is a variant of the costly-state-verification (CSV) approach developed by Townsend (1979) and Gale and Hellwig (1985). As we shall see, the prescription that companies should hedge takes the form of a simple and fairly weak restriction on the specification of this CSV model. Moreover, we are able to rewrite the $C(e)$ function explicitly in terms of parameters of the CSV model.

As before, we assume that in the first period a firm can invest an amount I, which yields a gross payoff of $f(I)$ in the second period. Also in the second period, the firm generates *additional* random cashflows of x from its pre-existing assets. The cumulative distribution and density of x are given by $G(x)$ and $g(x)$, respectively.

As in the Townsend and Gale–Hellwig models, we assume that cashflows are costlessly observable to company insiders, but are observable to external creditors only at some cost. In particular, we suppose that the cashflows from the *existing* assets can be observed at a cost, c, but that it is infinitely costly to observe the cashflows from the new investment project. As is well known, when $c > 0$, the optimal contract between outside investors and the company will be a standard debt contract. In return for receiving e in the first period, the company is required to repay in the second period a state-invariant amount D. If the company fails to perform, creditors pay the monitoring costs, then observe - and keep for themselves - company profits. States in which monitoring occurs can be interpreted as bankruptcy.

Our formulation of the CSV model is slightly different from that in Townsend and Gale–Hellwig: we suppose that a set of pre-existing assets entirely determines the firm's capacity for external finance, so that this capacity is unaffected by the current investment spending. This parallels our set-up in the section above, where we assume that new investment spending has no independent effect on deadweight costs for a given level of external finance. That is, in both models C can be represented simply as $C(e)$. This assumption simplifies our analysis but does not affect the basic results.[12]

Under these circumstances, the company chooses investment and outside financing to maximise

$$L \equiv \max_{I,D} f(I) + \int_D^X (x - D)g(x)dx \tag{8}$$

subject to a non-negative profit constraint for outside investors:

$$\int_{-X}^D (x - c)g(x)dx + \int_D^X Dg(x)dx \geq I - w \tag{9}$$

The first-order conditions for this constrained optimisation problem are

$$\frac{\partial L}{\partial D} = (\lambda - 1)(1 - G(D)) - \lambda c g(D) = 0 \tag{10}$$

$$\frac{\partial L}{\partial I} = f_I - \lambda = 0 \tag{11}$$

where λ is the Lagrange multiplier on constraint (9).

Equations (10) and (11) together imply that the firm sets I^* such that

$$f_I = \frac{1 - G(D)}{1 - G(D) - cg(D)} \geq 1 \tag{12}$$

If there are no deadweight costs ($c = 0$) the firm sets investment efficiently ($f_I = 1$). However, if $c > 0$, then the firm underinvests, setting $f_I > 1$.[13] Underinvestment occurs in this model because an increase in I necessitates an increase in D, which raises the probability of bankruptcy. At the optimum, the firm reduces investment from the first-best level in order to economise on deadweight costs.

In this set-up, there is a direct correspondence between expected deadweight costs of external finance and the probability of bankruptcy:

$$C(e) = cG(D) \tag{13}$$

where equation (9) implicitly defines the function $D = D(e)$.

One can verify that the first-order condition, $F_I = C_e + 1$, derived above (equation (4)), is identical to (12) above. From equation (11) it is clear that the expected shadow value of an additional dollar of internal wealth ($L_w = \lambda$) is equal to the marginal return on investment, which is given by f_I.

As before, hedging raises the value of the company if profits are concave in internal wealth, ie, $L_{ww} = d\lambda/dw = F_{II}dI^*/dw < 0$. (Note this is the same condition we derived in equation (6) for our reduced form model.) Totally differentiating equations (9) to (11) and solving for dI^*/dw, we can show that a sufficient condition for $dI^*/dw > 0 \forall x$ is that the hazard rate $g(x)/1 - G(x)$ is strictly increasing in x. This is a fairly weak condition, and is satisfied for the normal, exponential, and uniform distributions, among others.[14] Thus, when $f_{II} < 0$ and the hazard rate of $G(\ )$ is increasing, hedging is optimal in this CSV framework.

Optimal hedging with changing investment and financing opportunities

So far our results create a very simplistic picture of optimal hedging policies - firms with increasing marginal costs of external finance should always fully hedge their cashflows. In this section, we extend our analysis to incorporate randomness in both investment and financing opportunities. As will be seen, these considerations lead to a richer range of solutions to the optimal hedging problem.

CHANGING INVESTMENT OPPORTUNITIES

In the discussion above, we have assumed that a firm's investment opportunities were non-stochastic, and thus independent of the cashflows from its assets in place. In many cases, however, this assumption is unrealistic. For example, a company engaged in oil exploration and development will find that both its current cashflows (ie, the net revenues from its already developed fields) and the marginal product of additional investments (ie, expenditures on further exploration) decline when the price of oil falls. For such a company, hedging against oil price declines is less valuable - even without hedging, the supply of internal funds tends to match the demand for funds.

It is straightforward to extend the analysis of the previous section to address the question of the optimal hedge ratio in a world of changing investment opportunities. If we focus for the moment on linear hedging strategies (ie, forward sales or purchases), the hedging decision can be modelled by writing internal funds as[15]

$$w = w_0(h + (1 - h)\epsilon) \tag{14}$$

where h is the "hedge ratio" chosen by the firm, and ϵ is the primitive source of uncertainty.[16] To keep things simple, we assume that ϵ - the return on the risky asset - is distributed normally, with a mean of 1 and a variance of σ^2.[17]

To model changing investment opportunities, we redefine profits as

$$F(I) = \theta f(I) - I \tag{15}$$

with $\theta = \alpha(\epsilon - \bar{\epsilon}) + 1$. In this formulation, α is a measure of the correlation between investment opportunities and the risk to be hedged.

In period zero, the firm must choose h to maximise expected profits:

$$\max_h E[P(w)] \tag{16}$$

where the expectation is taken with respect to ϵ. The first-order condition for this problem is

$$E\left[P_w \frac{dw}{dh}\right] = 0 \tag{17}$$

Equation (17) simplifies to

$$E[P_w(1 - \epsilon)] = 0 \tag{18}$$

which can be written as

$$\mathrm{cov}(P_w, \epsilon) = 0 \tag{19}$$

Equation (19) says that the optimal hedge ratio insulates the marginal value of internal wealth (P_w) from fluctuations in the variable to be hedged. Notice that this is *not* necessarily the same as insulating the total value of the firm, P, from such fluctuations.

To simplify the covariance term, we use a second-order Taylor series approximation (which is exact if the asset's return, ϵ, is normally distributed) with respect to h around $\epsilon = 1$.[18] Equation (19) and a little algebra then yield the optimal hedge ratio

$$h^* = 1 + \alpha \frac{E\left[f_I P_{ww} / \theta f_{II}\right]}{w_0 \bar{P}_{ww}} \tag{20}$$

where a bar over a variable implies that an expectation has been taken with respect to ϵ, for example, $\bar{P}_{ww} = E[P_{ww}]$.

The last term in equation (20) takes account of the direct effect of ϵ on output. Clearly, if $\alpha = 0$ (ie, there is no correlation between investment opportunities and the availability of internal funds), it is optimal to hedge fully (ie, $h^* = 1$), as described above.

If $\alpha > 0$, the firm will not want to hedge as much. To see why, note that when ϵ is low, the firm may be low on cash, but doesn't need much since it has few attractive investment opportunities. Conversely, when ϵ is high the firm has good investment opportunities and therefore needs the additional cash generated internally. This logic implies that there is less to be gained from a hedge, which transfers funds from high ϵ states to low ϵ states. Thus, the more sensitive investment opportunities are to ϵ, the smaller the optimal hedge ratio.

It should be emphasised that in this case ($\alpha > 0$), the firm chooses *not* to insulate fully either its cashflows or market value from fluctuations in ϵ. In the example of the oil company mentioned above, the optimal hedging strategy would involve leaving the stock price exposed to oil price fluctuations. This conclusion differs from that of many other papers, which often imply complete insulation.

It should also be noted that according to equation (20), h^* need not necessarily be between zero and one. The possibility of $h^* < 0$ arises when investment opportunities are extremely sensitive to the risk variable. In that case it may make sense for a firm to actually *increase* its exposure to the variable in question in order to have sufficient cash when ϵ is high and very large investments are required. Conversely, optimal hedge ratios greater than one will arise when investment opportunities are negatively correlated with current cashflows. In this case it makes sense to "overhedge", so as to have more cash when ϵ is low.[19]

To build some further intuition for why companies with different investment opportunities might implement different hedging strategies, consider the following example. Suppose there are two companies engaged in natural resource exploration and extraction. Company g is a gold company. It currently owns developed mines that produce 100 units of gold in period one at zero marginal cost. Thus company g's period one cashflows are $100\tilde{p}_g$, where $\tilde{p}_g$ is the random price of gold.

Company g also has the opportunity to invest in additional exploration activities in period one. If it spends an amount I on exploration, it discovers undeveloped lodes containing $f_g(I)$ units of gold. Before the gold can be extracted, however, a further *per unit* development cost of c_g must be paid in period two. Thus, the net returns to an exploration investment of I are given by $(\tilde{p}_g - c_g)f_g(I) - I$.

Company o is an oil company. In most respects it is very similar to company g. Its period one cashflows are $100\tilde{p}_o$, and it is assumed that $\tilde{p}_o$ has the same distribution as $\tilde{p}_g$. Thus both companies face exactly the same risks with regard to the nature of their period one cashflow.

Company o can also uncover undeveloped reserves containing $f_o(I)$ units of oil by spending an amount I on exploration in period one. Company o's development costs are higher than company g's - it must pay $c_o > c_g$ in period two to develop the new reserves before they can be extracted. Thus, the net returns to an exploration investment of I are given by $(\tilde{p}_o - c_o)f_o(I) - I$. To preserve comparability across the two companies, it is further assumed that $f_o(I) = (\bar{p} - c_g/\bar{p} - c_o)f_g(I)$, where $\bar{p}$ is the mean of both price distributions. This implies that in the "base case", where commodity prices equal their means, both companies have the same marginal product of capital at any given level of investment.

The key difference between company o and company g is the fact that higher development costs make company o's investment opportunities *more leveraged* with respect to commodity prices. For example, if $c_g = 0$ and $c_o = 50$, the marginal product of capital for the gold company drops by 10% when gold prices fall from 100 to 90. However, the marginal product of capital for the oil company falls by 20% when oil prices fall from 100 to 90.

In the terminology of the above model, this difference in technology can be represented as a higher value of the parameter α for the oil company. Thus, the two companies should pursue different hedging strategies, with company g hedging more than company o. In other words, company o should leave its market value more exposed to fluctuations in oil prices than company g because its investment opportunities are more sensitive to the price of oil.

CHANGING FINANCING OPPORTUNITIES

Up to now we have assumed that the supply schedule for external finance - given by the $C(e)$ function - is exogenously fixed and insensitive to the risks impacting the firm's cashflows. However, it seems quite possible that negative shocks to a firm's current cashflows might also make it more costly for the firm to raise money from outside investors. If this is the case, it may make sense for the firm to hedge more than it otherwise would. This will allow the firm to fund its investments while making *less* use of external finance in bad times than in good times.[20]

We can formalise this insight by generalising the C function to be $C(e,\phi)$, where ϕ is given by $\delta(\epsilon - \bar{\epsilon}) + 1$. Such a generalisation emerges naturally from the CSV model sketched above. Suppose that instead of yielding x the assets already in place yield ϕx. That is, the eventual proceeds from assets in place are correlated with the risk variable ϵ, and δ measures the strength of this correlation. As long as the distribution of x satisfies the increasing hazard rate property, then the $C(e,\phi)$ function that emerges from the CSV setting has the feature that $C_{e\phi} < 0$ (for fixed first-period wealth). This simply means that marginal costs of external finance, C_e, are lower for higher realisation of ϵ.

If we assume for the moment that α - which measures the correlation of *investment* opportunities with ϵ - is zero, we can derive an expression that gives us the pure effect of changing financing opportunities on the hedge ratio. The methodology is the same as before. In particular, the first-order condition in (19) still applies. But now the optimal hedge ratio is given by

$$h^* = 1 + \delta \frac{\bar{C}_{e\phi}}{w_0 P_{ww}} \tag{21}$$

Given that $C_{e\phi} < 0$, the optimal hedge ratio is greater than one, the effect being greater the more sensitive assets in place become to the risk variable ϵ. Again, the intuition is that hedging must now allow the firm to fund its investments and yet conserve on borrowing at those times when external finance is most expensive.[21]

However, even with a non-stochastic production technology (ie, $\alpha = 0$), it is no longer true that investment is completely insulated from shocks to ϵ. This is purely a consequence of the fact that we are restricting ourselves to linear hedging strategies. Non-stochastic investment would (by the firm's first-order conditions) require that, once the hedge is in place, C_e be independent of ϕ. This generally cannot be accomplished using futures alone. In the section below on non-linear hedging strategies, we argue that if options are available, the firm will indeed wish to construct a hedging strategy that leads to non-stochastic investment.

Risk management for multinationals

Our framework also has implications for multinational companies' risk management strategies.[22] Multinationals have sales and production opportunities in a number of different countries. In addition, the goods that they produce at any given location may either be targeted for local consumption (ie, non-tradeable goods, such as McDonald's hamburgers) or for worldwide markets (ie, tradeable goods, such as semiconductors). These factors complicate the hedging problem for multinational corporations.

We begin with a quite general framework which builds on that of the previous sections. Assume that the multinational can invest in two locations, "home" and "abroad", and that profits are given by

$$P(w) = f^H(I^H) + \theta f^A(I^A) - I^H - \gamma I^A - C(e) \tag{22}$$

where $\theta = \alpha(\epsilon - \bar{\epsilon}) + 1$, $\gamma = \beta(\epsilon - \bar{\epsilon}) + 1$, and the production functions, $f^i(I^i)$, $i = A, H$ are increasing and concave. In this expression, ϵ now represents the home currency price of the foreign currency, and α and β are parameters (between zero and one) which index the sensitivity of foreign revenues and foreign investment costs to the exchange rate.[23] Implicitly, equation (22) treats the domestic currency as the numeraire.[24]

It is easiest to build an understanding of equation (22) by examining several special cases:

Case 1: Exchange rate exposure for both investment costs and revenues from foreign operations, $\alpha = \beta = 1$. This case might correspond to situations where both the outputs and the investment inputs are non-traded goods.[25] An example might be Euro-Disney in France, since local factors are required to begin operations.

Case 2: Exchange rate exposure for foreign investment costs but no exchange rate exposure for foreign or domestic revenues, $\alpha = 0$ and $\beta = 1$. This case might correspond to a situation where the output from both plants is sold at the same price on the domestic market.[26] An example might be ball bearings, which can be produced using primarily local factors, but which are sold on a global market.

Case 3: No exchange rate exposure for investment costs but exchange rate exposure for foreign revenues, $\alpha = 1$ and $\beta = 0$. This might correspond, as above, to a situation where the outputs are non-traded goods. However, now the investment inputs used in both locations are purchased on a single domestic market at the same price. An example might be a construction company, like Bechtel, which makes heavy use of construction equipment that is sold on a global market.

In order to finance these different investments, the firm requires external finance of an amount

$$e = I^H + \gamma I^A - w \tag{23}$$

Maintaining our focus on linear hedging strategies, w continues to be given by equation (14) above. In this formulation, a hedge ratio of one means that period zero wealth, w_0, is held entirely in the domestic currency. In contrast, a hedge ratio of zero means that wealth is held entirely in the foreign currency.

Using arguments analogous to those developed above, we can solve for the optimal hedge ratio. (See the Appendix for a sketch of the derivation.)

$$h^* = 1 + \frac{E\left[(\alpha\gamma - \beta\theta)\, f_I^A P_{ww}/\theta f_{II}^A\right]}{w_0 \bar{P}_{ww}} - \beta \frac{E\left[I^A P_{ww}\right]}{w_0 \bar{P}_{ww}} \tag{24}$$

where

$$P_{ww} = \frac{f_{II}^H \theta f_{II}^A C_{ee}}{C_{ee}(\gamma^2 f_{II}^H + \theta f_{II}^A) - \theta f_{II}^H f_{II}^A} < 0 \tag{25}$$

There are two basic components of the optimal hedge ration in (24). First, there is a slightly more complex version of the "changing investment opportunity set" term,

$$\frac{E\left[(\alpha\gamma - \beta\theta) f_{II}^A P_{ww}/\theta f_{II}^A\right]}{w_0 \bar{P}_{ww}}$$

which effectively captures the *net* exchange rate exposure of foreign investment profitability. Second, there is a new "lock-in" term, $\beta(E[I^A P_{ww}]/w_0 \bar{P}_{ww})$, which is, loosely speaking, driven by the expected size of the foreign investment relative to internal wealth.

We can understand this lock-in term better by focusing on Case 1 above, where $\alpha = \beta = 1$. In this case (or in any case with $\alpha = \beta$), (24) can be simplified considerably – the changing investment opportunity set term disappears completely and the lock-in term itself becomes easier to interpret. In particular, we demonstrate in the Appendix that:

PROPOSITION 1: *If $\alpha = \beta$, then the optimal hedging strategy is such that investment in both locations is independent of the exchange rate: $I^H(\epsilon) = \bar{I}^H$, and $I^A(\epsilon) = \bar{I}^A \forall \epsilon$. This hedging strategy is given by $h^* = 1 - \beta \bar{I}^A / w_0$.*

To understand the intuition behind the proposition, imagine that the company did not hedge at all but that the actual realisation of the exchange rate coincided with its expectation, $\epsilon = \bar{\epsilon}$.[27] One could then solve for the optimal first-period levels of investment. What hedging does is to *assure* that domestic and foreign investment will always be at exactly these levels, regardless of the actual realisation of the exchange rate. In other words, hedging *locks in* the ability to carry out a predetermined (as of period zero) investment plan, where that plan is based on the expected future exchange rate.

In Case 2, with $\alpha = 0$ and $\beta = 1$, the lock-in term remains. However, it takes on a more complicated form, since I^A and P_{ww} are now random variables, and it is no longer generally true that $E[I^A P_{ww}] = \bar{I}^A \bar{P}_{ww}$. In addition, the hedge ratio is increased by the changing investment opportunity set term,

$$\frac{-E\left[f_I^A P_{ww}/f_{II}^A\right]}{w_0 P_{ww}}$$

This term implies that it is optimal to hold relatively *more* of the domestic currency than in Case 1. The logic is similar to that developed in the section above on optimal hedging with changing investment and financing opportunities. When the domestic currency depreciates, investments abroad become less attractive due to higher input costs. Thus, less foreign investment is warranted, and there is less need to hold foreign currency as a hedge against such an outcome.

Finally, in Case 3, with $\alpha = 1$ and $\beta = 0$, there is no lock-in effect. Because the price of foreign investment is insensitive to the exchange rate, it is unnecessary to hold foreign currency to guarantee a given level of foreign investment. At the same time, it is still worthwhile to hold *some* wealth in the form of foreign currency. This is because the correlation of net investment opportunities with the value of the domestic currency is now *negative* - when the domestic currency depreciates, returns on foreign investment are now *high*.

Non-linear hedging strategies

Thus far we have restricted our attention to hedges that employ only forward or future contracts. With these instruments the sensitivity of internal wealth to changes in the risk variable to be hedged is constrained to be a constant. That is, $dw/de = (1 - h)w_0$, which is independent of the realisation of ϵ. While such linear hedges can add value, they generally will not *maximise* value if other, non-linear instruments, such as options, are available. Options effectively create the possibility for hedge ratios to be "customised" on a state-by-state basis.

To see why a firm might want its hedge ratios to be sensitive to the realisation of ϵ, let us return to our oil company example. We argued that the oil company's investment opportunities become less attractive when the price of oil falls, and that this militated in favour of leaving its cashflows somewhat exposed to these fluctuations. But suppose we use futures to pick a single, state-independent hedge ratio and that this hedge ratio results in the oil company cutting capital investment expenditures by 2% for every 1% decline in the price of oil. This might make good sense for small fluctuations in oil prices - perhaps the company's level of investment *should* be cut by 20% when oil prices fall by 10%. But it may not make equally good sense for the company to completely eliminate its investment spending when oil prices fall by 50%.

If this is the case, the oil company may wish to do some of its hedging with options. For example, by adding out-of-the-money puts on oil to its futures-hedging position, the company can give itself relatively more protection against large decreases in the price of oil than against small decreases. (Similarly, the company might also write out-of-the-money calls on oil, if a linear hedging strategy results in "too much" cash for very large increases in the price of oil.)

We can develop the general logic for non-linear hedging strategies using the same basic set-up as in the previous section. We denote the frequency distribution of the random variable, ϵ, by $p(\epsilon)$. If we assume complete markets, the firm's hedging problem now becomes one of choosing a profile for wealth across states of nature, $w^* = w^*(\epsilon)$, to maximise expected profits:

$$\max_{w(\epsilon)} \int_{\epsilon} P(\epsilon, w(\epsilon))p(\epsilon)d\epsilon \tag{26}$$

subject to the "fair pricing" constraint that hedging cannot change the expected level of wealth,

$$\int_{\epsilon} w(\epsilon)p(\epsilon)d\epsilon = w_0 \tag{27}$$

and to the first-order conditions for domestic and foreign investment (which are given in equations (A1) and (A2) of the Appendix).[28]

The first-order condition for the constrained optimisation problem in (26) is given by

$$P_w = \lambda \tag{28}$$

where λ is the Lagrange multiplier on the constraint (27). Equation (28) says that the optimal hedging policy equalises the shadow value of internal wealth across states. By smoothing the impact of costly external finance in this way, the firm has optimally matched the cash demand of investment with the supply of internal funds.

Equation (28) implicitly defines an optimal level of internal wealth across states. Note that because λ is constant, the implicit function theorem can be applied to (28), which after some algebra yields an expression for the optimal hedge ratio in each state:

$$\frac{dw^*(\epsilon)}{d\epsilon} = \frac{P_{w\epsilon}}{-P_{ww}} = -(\alpha\gamma - \beta\theta)\frac{f_I^A}{w_0\theta f_{II}^A} + \frac{\beta I^A}{w_0} \tag{29}$$

where $w^* = w^*(\epsilon)$ describes the optimal level of wealth for every value of ϵ. The expression of the right-hand side of (29) can be shown to be a function (denoted by $\ell = \ell(w(\epsilon), \epsilon)$), of both internal wealth and ϵ:

$$\frac{dw^*(\epsilon)}{d\epsilon} = -(\alpha\gamma - \beta\theta)\frac{f_I^A}{w_0\theta f_{II}^A} + \frac{\beta I^A}{w_0} = \ell(w^*(\epsilon),\epsilon) \tag{30}$$

This expression defines the basic differential equation which the optimal level of wealth must satisfy. The constraint (27) provides the restriction that ties down the constant of integration.

One can use (29) to see when the first-best hedge can be attained using only futures contracts. In such cases, it must be that $(dw^*/d\epsilon)$ is a constant. Thus, making use of the results of Proposition 1, we have:

PROPOSITION 2: *With* $\alpha = \beta$, *futures contracts alone can provide value-maximising hedges. In all other cases, options may be required to obtain the value-maximising hedge.*

Futures hedging alone is thus optimal: (i) in the simple models of the earlier section on the basic paradigm with fixed investment and financing opportunities (ie, with α, δ and β equal to zero); and (ii) in our multinational set-up in the section on risk management for multinationals whenever there is the complete lock-in described in Proposition 1. In contrast, options will be needed for implementing the optimal hedges when either $\alpha \neq \beta$ or when there are state-dependent financing opportunities ($\delta \neq 0$), as above in the part of the optimal hedging section that deals with changing financing opportunities. In the latter case, the use of options allows investment to be completely insulated from shocks to financing opportunities.[29]

For those cases in which options are required, equation (29) implicitly yields a recipe for the number of options to be purchased at different strike prices. While the first derivative of wealth, $(dw^*/d\epsilon)$, gives us the optimal exposure to ϵ, it is the *second* derivative, $(d^2w^*/d\epsilon^2)$, that describes the "density" of the options position at each strike price in the optimal hedge portfolio. Intuitively, an option at a strike price of $\hat{\epsilon}$ is indispensable for *changing* the degree of exposure at the point where $\epsilon = \hat{\epsilon}$. Thus, for example, if there are regions in which $(d^2w^*/d\epsilon^2)$ is large and positive, a substantial number of call options with strike prices in that region should be added. In contrast, for regions in which the hedge ratio is constant, $(d^2w^*/d\epsilon^2) = 0$, no additional options are required.

To see the role for options more concretely, consider the following numerical example. Suppose that there are three equally probable states of nature, 1, 2 and 3, and that a firm's first-best levels of investment (ie, that for which $f_I = 1$) are 6, 9 and 15, in each state respectively. Suppose also that at any level of investment below 6 the firm will be unable to compete and will be forced into bankruptcy, and that the firm has no access to external finance.

Table 1. Hypothetical hedging strategies and investment spending (with initial wealth of 10)

			Net funds available for investment			
State	Probability	Optimal investment spending	No hedging (1)	Optimal futures hedge (2)	Payoffs to first-best options (3)	First-best hedge with options (2) + (3) – cost
1	1/3	6	5	6	1	6 + 1 – 1 = 6
2	1/3	9	10	10	0	10 + 0 – 1 = 9
3	1/3	15	15	14	2	14 + 2 – 1 = 15

Total cost of options: –1/3 – 2/3 = –1

Finally, suppose that internal wealth is initially equal to 10, and that a no-hedging strategy yields 5, 10 and 15 of internal funds available for investment. (See Table 1 for a schematic.)

If the firm has only futures contracts available to it, it can increase state one internal wealth only through an equivalent reduction in state three wealth. Its optimal hedge will therefore be predicated on protecting revenues in the lowest state, and will lead to an internal wealth configuration of something like 6, 10 and 14. This is a better profile than without hedging, but it does not generate first-best levels of investment.

Now suppose that options become available. With its futures hedge in place, the firm has excess cash in state two and insufficient cash in state three. The value-maximising hedging strategy therefore involves buying 1 state one "put" option (which pays 1 in state one and zero otherwise) and 2 state three "call" options (each of which pay 1 in state three or zero otherwise). Because each option costs 1/3, their total cost is 1, which exactly eliminates the previously existing excess cash balance in state two (see Table 1). Options are therefore valuable when value-maximising hedge ratios are not constant.[30]

Further extensions

Although we have explored a number of applications of our basic risk management paradigm, several interesting questions remain. In this section, we briefly sketch some additional extensions, focusing on the basic intuition and leaving the formal development for future work.

INTERTEMPORAL HEDGING CONSIDERATIONS

Since the model developed above is essentially a static one – there is only a single period during which investment takes place – we have not addressed any of the potentially important intertemporal issues associated with risk management.

To see how intertemporal considerations can complicate matters, suppose that at each of N dates, the firm has a random cashflow and *a non-stochastic* investment opportunity. (The simplest model of the benefits of hedging given earlier is just a special case of this with N = 1.)

Since investment opportunities are non-stochastic, a first guess might be – following the logic set out above – that the optimal strategy is to hedge *all* of the N random cashflows. For example, if the cashflows represent revenues from oil wells that will deliver 100 million barrels in each of the next ten years, it might seem that the best thing to do is to sell short 100 million barrels-worth of futures with delivery one year hence, 100 million barrels-worth with delivery two years hence, and so on, with contract maturities running out to 10 years.

However, this raises a problem, at least if futures contracts are used in the hedge. If oil prices rise in the first year, the margin call on the aggregate futures position – representing 10 years' worth of production – will be very large, and will much more than offset the positive impact of oil prices on first-year revenues. In other words, hedging the whole future stream of production leads to enormous margin fluctuations and hence to enormous variations in the year-by-year level of cash available for investment.

This suggests that if futures are indeed to be used, the aggregate size of the position will have to be lowered somewhat. The optimal hedge will have to trade off insulating the present value of all cashflows versus insulating the level of cash at each point in time.

An alternative possibility might be for the firm to structure its hedge using a series of forward contracts (or other "forward-like" instruments, such as swaps or indexed debt) rather than futures contracts. In an intertemporal setting, forwards might represent a more desirable instrument, since they do not have to be settled until maturity and hence do not entail interim margin calls. However, there are reasons to believe that forward contracts, while potentially useful, may not completely "solve" the problem sketched above. Precisely because they are not settled until maturity, forwards can involve substantially more credit risk than futures.[31]

In effect, one can think of a forward contract as (loosely speaking) a combination of futures plus borrowing. In the context of our model, this means that a decision to use forwards may lower the firm's ability to raise external financing at any point in time. As a practical matter, it may simply be impossible for many firms to take very large positions in forwards because of the credit risks involved.

CAPITAL BUDGETING WHEN RISKS ARE NOT MARKETABLE

We have assumed throughout that all risks impacting a firm's cashflows are marketable and can therefore be hedged. However, this will not in general be true. For example, a firm's cashflows will be abnormally low if its new product introduction fails, but there may be no futures market in which this risk can be laid off.

If this is the case, such unmarketable idiosyncratic risks will (in a world with costly external finance) impose real costs on the firm. Capital-budgeting procedures should therefore take these costs into account. Consequently, the CAPM (or any other standard asset-pricing model) will no longer be universally valid as a capital-budgeting tool. In other words, when investment projects impose large idiosyncratic risks that cannot be directly sold off, a second-best risk management strategy will involve reducing the level of investment in these projects below that implied by a CAPM-type discounting procedure.

The *magnitude* of the deviation from traditional capital-budgeting principles should depend on the same sorts of factors that we identified above as determinants of the optimal hedging strategy. For example, if the unmarketable idiosyncratic risk on the investment currently being evaluated is closely correlated with the availability of future investment opportunities, then the logic developed in the earlier section on changing investment opportunities suggests that there is relatively less reason to "hedge" by skimping on this investment. In contrast, if the investment in question is uncorrelated with the availability of future investment opportunities, it should be evaluated more harshly.

HEDGING AND PRODUCT-MARKET COMPETITION

Our framework also has the implications for how companies' hedging strategies should depend on both (1) the nature of product market competition, and (2) their competitors' hedging strategies.[32] To see this, suppose that there are two firms and they compete à la Cournot - they each choose production quantities, q_i, $i = 1,2$, holding fixed the other's quantity decision. One can interpret the quantity decision as investment I_i, so that $I_i = cq_i$, where c is the marginal cost of a unit of capacity.

Assume that both firms have no access to external finance, so that investment can never exceed cashflow. Suppose further that cashflow is perfectly correlated across firms and that its mean is equal to I^*, which we define as the investment level that would prevail in an unconstrained Cournot equilibrium.

The important feature of the Cournot model is that investment is less attractive the more a rival firm invests. In the terminology of Bulow, Geanakoplos and Klemperer (1985), investment is a "strategic substitute". This contrasts with other models in which the strategic variables are "strategic complements" - firms want to invest more when their rivals invest more. Such might be the case in a research and development (R&D) model in which there are informational spillovers across firms.

Suppose that neither firm hedges. When their cashflows exceed I^*, the unconstrained Cournot equilibrium prevails - both firms invest I^*. However, when cashflow is less than I^*, both firms invest what they have. Both would like to increase their investment in these states - since investment/output is relatively low and prices are high - but cannot because of liquidity constraints.

Now suppose that just firm 1 hedges, locking in a cashflow of I^*. When firm 2's cashflows exceed I^*, the unconstrained Cournot equilibrium is achieved - just as it would be without hedging. But, when firm 2's cashflows are less than I^*, firm 2 invests only what it has, while firm 1 (which has hedged) gets to invest more. Because investment is a strategic substitute, the additional investment that hedging makes possible is particularly attractive to firm 1 in these states: firm 2 is not investing much; prices are high; and so are the marginal returns to the investment. Thus firm 1 is clearly better off hedging. Indeed, firm 1 would like to go even further - adopting a hedge ratio greater than one - because the returns to investments are now higher when cashflow is low than when it is high. In the context of our model with changing investment opportunities, this is analogous to the case of $\alpha < 0$.

One can also show that there are benefits to firm 1 from hedging in this model if firm 2 *does* hedge, but they are not as high as in the previous example. The reasoning is that if firm 2 hedges - ensuring that it can invest I^* in all states - its generally stronger position makes investment less appealing to firm 1. Thus, there is less reason for firm 1 to use hedging to lock in a high level of investment.

There are two related implications that follow from this example. First, hedging policy inherits the strategic substitutability feature of the product-market game - a firm will want to hedge more when its rival hedges less. Second, the overall industry equilibrium will involve some hedging by both firms.

We conjecture that we might get very different results if investment were a strategic complement, such as in the R&D example mentioned above. In this framework, if firm 2 does not hedge, the marginal returns to firm 1 R&D are low when cashflow is low and high when cashflow is high. This is because when cashflow is low, firm 2 is constrained and does little R&D. And when cashflow is high, just the opposite is true. This is analogous to the case of a positive α - a positive correlation between investment opportunities and cashflow - so that less than full hedging is optimal.

Thus it would seem that hedging is generally less attractive when investment is a strategic complement. One might also conjecture that, as in the previous model, hedging policy inherits the strategic character of the product-market game. In this case, that would imply that hedging policies are strategic complements: a firm will want to hedge *more* when its rival hedges more.

Empirical implications

In this section we discuss some of the model's empirical implications. However, before doing so we should note two points. First, it is not at all clear that our theory should be interpreted solely as a positive one, ie, as an accurate description of the actual status of corporate hedging policy. Even if empirical work were to find that few firms currently hedge according to our theory, we nevertheless think that the theory has a number of useful *prescriptive* implications.

Second, empirical work in this area is made difficult by the fact that most hedging operations are off balance sheet (and thus are not included in databases such as CompuStat). This lack of a well-developed database has led researchers to collect survey data on firms' hedging policies. We begin with a review of some of this evidence. Next, we propose a new type of test for optimal hedging, one that has the advantage of not requiring direct measurement of hedging positions.

ANECDOTAL AND SURVEY EVIDENCE

That the coordination of financing and investment is the basis for at least some managers' hedging strategies seems evident from what they say. For example, a Unocal executive, Matthew Burkhart, argues that "one possible added value of hedging is to continue on a capital programme without funding and defunding".[33] And Lewent and Kearney (1990), in explaining Merck's philosophy of risk management, note that a key factor in deciding whether to hedge is the "potential effect of cashflow volatility on our ability to execute our strategic plan - particularly, to make the investments in R&D that furnish the basis for future growth".

It is, of course, far more difficult to say whether the considerations we outline are those that drive hedging strategies more broadly. A recent study by Nance, Smith and Smithson (1993) uses survey data to compare the characteristics of firms that actively hedge with those that do not. Some of their findings are consistent with our framework, while others cut less clearly. One noteworthy result is that high R&D firms are more likely to hedge. There are a couple of reasons why this might be expected in the context of our model. First, it may be more difficult for R&D-intensive firms to raise external finance either because their (principally intangible) assets are not good collateral (see Titman and Wessels (1988)) or because there is likely to be more asymmetric information about the quality of their new projects. Second, R&D "growth options" are likely to represent valuable investments whose appeal is *not correlated* with easily hedgeable risks, such as interest rates. Thus, the logic of the section on changing investment opportunities would imply more hedging for R&D firms.

Nance, Smith and Smithson (1993), as well as Block and Gallagher (1986) and Wall and Pringle (1989), also find weak evidence that firms with more leveraged capital structures hedge more. To the extent that such firms have fewer unencumbered assets, and hence more difficulty raising large amounts of external finance, this finding also fits with our model.

Finally, Nance, Smith and Smithson (1993) also find that high-dividend-paying firms are more likely to hedge. It is not obvious how this fact squares with our model. One interpretation - which is inconsistent with our model - is that high-dividend payers are not likely to be liquidity constrained since they have chosen to pay out cash rather than use it for investment.[34] However, a second interpretation would be that high-dividend firms need to hedge more if they are to maintain both their dividends *and* their investment. This interpretation is more consistent with our model.[35]

A NEW TEST FOR OPTIMAL HEDGING

The broadest implication of our model is that firms use hedging to lower the variability of the shadow value of internal funds. In the model of the section above on changing investment opportunities, this was accomplished by choosing the hedge ratio, h, such that $\text{cov}(P_w, \epsilon) = 0$ (equation 19); in the model described in the section on non-linear hedging strategies, it was done by setting P_w equal to a constant (equation (28)). Either way, the first-order condition of our model generates a clear testable restriction: that the shadow value of internal funds and ϵ ought to be uncorrelated.

Consider, then, the first of these two models, in which firm value is a function $P = (w(\epsilon), \epsilon)$. This means that the risk variable, ϵ, may affect P directly through its impact on investment opportunities *given* internal funds, w, and indirectly through its effect on w *given* investment opportunities. In addition, there is a third possible effect on P: changes in w that are unrelated to ϵ. This suggests a simple empirical specification of the form

$$P_{t,i} = \alpha + w_{t,i}(\alpha_1 + \alpha_2 \epsilon_t) + \alpha_3 \epsilon_t + \nu_{t,i} \qquad (31)$$

where t denotes time and i denotes firm i. The error term, $\nu_{t,i}$, is interpreted as all other exogenous shocks to firm value. To get unbiased estimates of the coefficients involving ϵ, we would require that any unobserved shocks to P are independent of ϵ.

To implement this regression, we need to consider the choice of actual data. Take, for example, a gold-mining firm. In this case we would interpret: P as the market value of the firm; w as the amount of contemporaneous cashflow; ϵ as the price of gold. One also might want to scale value and cashflow by the book value of assets, or some other indicator of size, in order to facilitate cross-firm comparisons.

Equation (31) says that the marginal value of internal funds, P_w, is given by $\alpha_1 + \alpha_2 \epsilon_t$. The cross term thus allows ϵ_t to have an effect on the *marginal* value of internal funds. As discussed above, optimal hedging should eliminate this effect. Thus, according to the model's first-order condition, the null hypothesis that the firm is hedging optimally is given by $\alpha_2 = 0$.

To understand the intuition behind the test, imagine that we estimated α_2 to be significantly negative. This would mean that firm value is more sensitive to cashflow in low ϵ states, or, put differently, that liquidity constraints are more costly when ϵ is low. In this case, the firm could be made better off by shorting the source of ϵ risk.

Note that the model does *not* predict that α_3 should be zero. This is the point we made earlier: firm value should generally *not* be completely insulated from ϵ.

One possible problem with using firm value as a dependent variable in a regression of this sort is that firm value may respond to cashflow for reasons outside our model. For example, even if there are no liquidity constraints, α_1 is likely to be positive simply because cashflow is serially correlated and the dependent variable is forward-looking. This will not create a problem in the estimation of α_2, however, unless the degree of serial correlation is a function of ϵ. For example, if current cashflows are a better predictor of future cashflows when ϵ is low, we will estimate a negative α_2 even when the firm is hedging optimally. Thus, a key identifying assumption of our methodology is that other exogenous variables that simultaneously drive w and P are independent of ϵ.

If this identifying assumption is not appropriate, a second-best alternative might be to use investment, rather than firm, value as the dependent variable and to add Tobin's Q as another explanatory variable. Here too, the test would involve checking to see whether α_2 is equal to zero. The benefit of such an approach is that it would be harder to argue here that a non-zero α_2 was spurious. The drawback, however, is that investment is not quite the right variable to be measuring. Such a specification implies that the impact of liquidity constraints on the *quantity* of investment should not vary with ϵ. In contrast, the theory implies that the impact of liquidity constraints on the *value* of investment should not vary with ϵ.

In fact, regressions very much like the latter set that we propose have been implemented in the literature. Gertler and Hubbard (1988), Hoshi, Scharfstein and Singleton (1993) and Kashyap, Lamont and Stein (1993) all find that investment spending is more sensitive to liquidity during episodes of tight monetary policy, ie, that liquidity constraints are more binding at these times. Subject to the above caveats, these regressions would seem to suggest that the firms in these samples could have benefited by hedging more actively against the risk of tight monetary policy, say by using interest rate futures.

Conclusion

When external finance is more costly than internally generated sources of funds, it can make sense for firms to hedge. While this basic point seems to have already been recognised in the literature, its implications for optimal hedging strategy have not been fully developed. In this chapter, we have argued that there is a rich set of such implications:

- Optimal hedging strategy does not generally involve complete insulation of firm value from marketable sources of risk.
- Firms will want to hedge less, the more closely correlated their cashflows are with future investment opportunities.
- Firms will want to hedge more, the more closely correlated their cashflows are with collateral values (and hence with their ability to raise external finance).
- In general, multinational firms' hedging strategies will depend on a number of additional considerations, including the exchange rate exposure of both investment expenditures and revenues. In some special cases, multinationals will want to hedge so as to "lock in" a fixed quantity of investment in each country in which they operate.
- Non-linear hedging instruments, such as options, will typically allow firms to coordinate investment and financing plans more precisely than linear instruments, such as futures and forwards.
- In an intertemporal setting, there is a meaningful distinction between futures and forwards as hedging tools. In particular, the use of futures will involve a difficult trade-off between insulating the present value of all cashflows versus insulating the level of cash at each point in time.
- Optimal hedging strategy for a given firm will depend on both the nature of product market competition and on the hedging strategies adopted by its competitors.

Appendix

DERIVATION OF EQUATION (24)

First, note that at the moment when the investments are made, ϵ has already been realised. It follows that the first-order condition of (22) with respect to domestic investment is

$$f_I^H = \frac{\theta}{\gamma} f_I^A \tag{A1}$$

which says that the firm equalises the marginal revenue product of an additional unit of domestic currency across investments. Second, note that the marginal return on domestic investment will always be set equal to the marginal cost of an additional unit (in domestic currency terms) of external finance

$$f_I^H = C_e + 1 \tag{A2}$$

Together these equations, along with the budget constraint in (23), tie down the optimal choices for domestic and foreign investment, *for given wealth* of w. By applying the implicit function theorem to them, one can determine the sensitivity of optimal investment plans to changes in ϵ, $(dI^H/d\epsilon)$ and $(dI^A/d\epsilon)$.

Moving back to the initial period when the hedging decision is made, equation (22) must be maximised with respect to h. The first-order condition for this problem is identical to that given in equations (17) to (19). Applying the formula for covariance given in footnote 18, equation (19) can be rewritten

$$E\left[C_{ee}\left(\frac{dI^H}{d\epsilon} + \gamma\frac{dI^A}{d\epsilon} + \beta I^A - (1-h)w_0\right)\right] = 0 \tag{A3}$$

Substituting in the expressions for $(dI^H/d\epsilon)$ and $(dI^A/d\epsilon)$ derived above and simplifying yields equation (24).

Proof of Proposition 1: We start by hypothesising that I^H and I^A are non-stochastic, and $h = 1 - \beta \bar{I}^A/w_0$. We then verify that this is optimal, ie, that the first-order conditions for both hedging (equation (24)) and investment (equations (A1) and (A2) above) are satisfied.

First, note that I^H and I^A constant and $h = 1 - \beta \bar{I}^A/w_0$ together imply, from the budget constraint in (23), that $(de/d\epsilon) = 0$ - external financing is independent of the exchange rate. This implies that C_e is independent of ϵ. But, given the first-order condition in (A2), this in turn implies that it is optimal for I^H to be independent of ϵ. Similarly, when $\alpha = \beta$, the first-order condition in (A1) reduces to $f^H_I = f^A_I$. So if it is optimal for I^H to be constant, then it is optimal for I^A to be constant also.

This establishes that a constant I^H and I^A are optimal, given

$$h = \frac{1 - \beta \bar{I}^A}{w_0}$$

We now must check that this hypothesised hedge ratio is itself optimal. This now follows immediately from (24), once we note that $E[I^A P_{ww}]$ can be simplified to $\bar{I}^A \bar{P}_{ww}$ when I^A is non-stochastic.

1 *See Rawls and Smithson (1990).*

2 *This gap in knowledge is illustrated in the most recent edition of Brealey and Myers's (1991) textbook. Brealey and Myers do devote an entire chapter to the topic of "Hedging Financial Risk", but the chapter focuses almost exclusively on questions relating to hedging implementation. Less than one page is devoted to discussing the potential goals of hedging strategies.*

3 *Closely related rationales for hedging include Froot, Scharfstein and Stein (1989), Smith, Smithson and Wilford (1990) and Stulz (1990). These papers are discussed in detail below.*

4 *A somewhat related paper is Diamond (1984). In his model of financial intermediation, "hedging" (actually diversification) mitigates incentive problems associated with debt finance.*

5 *The most natural interpretation of the concavity of* $f(I)$ *is that there are technological decreasing returns to scale. However, if the corporate tax system is progressive, then* $f(I)$ *will be concave even with constant technological returns to scale. Of course, taxes will impact the hedging decision in other ways since they affect not only the returns on* new *investment (* $f(I)$*), but also the returns on existing assets; see the discussion under "Taxes" in the first section of this chapter.*

6 *On costs of external finance, see, eg, Townsend (1979), Myers and Majluf (1984), Jensen and Meckling (1976) and Myers (1977) among many others.*

7 *A more general formulation of these costs would allow them to depend also on the scale of the investment project undertaken,* $C = C(I,e)$. *This would make it possible for a firm to lower its per dollar costs of external finance by undertaking larger investment projects. The qualitative nature of our results is unaffected (although the exposition is somewhat complicated) by using this more general formulation. As we discuss below, either formulation can be rationalised in an optimal contracting framework.*

8 *In order for fluctuations in* w *to be completely hedgable (with default-free contracts) we need to assume that* w *is costlessly observable and verifiable. For example,* w *might represent a firm's exposure to gold price risk because the firm holds 100 bricks of gold. In this case, the exposure can be hedged if market participants can verify that the firm actually owns the bricks. For a discussion of how credit risks could interfere with hedging transactions, see footnotes 19, 28 and 31. The additional assumption that hedging does not affect the expected future level of* w *would follow from risk neutrality on the part of investors. It is straightforward to extend our analysis to the case where systematic risk is priced in equilibrium.*

9 *Concavity of the profit function is clearly a necessary condition for* any *model in which hedging raises value.*

10 *The first-order condition (4) and the implicit function theorem together imply that* I^**, satisfies*

$$\frac{dI^*}{dw} = \frac{-C_{ee}}{f_{II} - C_{ee}}$$

at $I = I^*$. *We assume that the second-order conditions with respect to investment are satisfied, so that the denominator of this expression is always negative.*

11 *See, for example, Fazzari, Hubbard and Petersen (1988) and Hoshi, Kashyap and Scharfstein (1991).*

12 *One way to rationalise this assumption would be to suppose that the assets in place consist of physical capital that has some value in liquidation, whereas the new investment is in intangible assets (eg, R&D, market share, etc) that have no value in liquidation.*

13 *This analysis assumes that there exists an optimally chosen* D *such that* $1 - G(D) - cg(D) > 0$ *and that investors' zero-profit constraint (9) is satisfied. Otherwise, there would be no solution to the problem in (8), and no investment would take place.*

14 *The same restriction on the hazard rate also implies that* $C_{ee} > 0$. *This can be seen by twice differentiating equation (13), and then by noting that equation (9) implicitly defines* $D = D(\epsilon)$.

15 *In the section on non-linear hedging strategies we consider alternative, non-linear hedging strategies that involve instruments such as options.*

16 *To see what (14) implies for actual futures positions and prices, define* x_0 *as the current futures price and* q_1 *as the future spot price of the variable in question. The variable* ϵ *then corresponds to* $\epsilon = (q_1/x_0)$ *and a hedging position of* h *corresponds to selling* $h(w_0/x_0)$ *futures contracts.*

17 *Assuming that the mean of* ϵ *is one implies, as before, that the expected level of wealth is unaffected by the amount of hedging.*

18 *If* x *and* y *are normally distributed, and* $a(\ )$ *and* $b(\ )$ *are differentiable functions, then* $\mathrm{cov}(a(x),b(y)) = E_x[a_x]E_y[b_y]\mathrm{cov}(x,y)$. *See Rubinstein (1976) for a proof. Note that if we were to assume that* ϵ *is lognormally distributed (with the same mean and variance as above), we would arrive at results very similar to those given throughout the chapter.*

19. *Note that while* $h^* < 0$ *or* $h^* > 1$ *may (according to equation (20)) be optimal for the firm, such positions may implicitly leave the firm with negative first-period resources in some states. As a consequence, the capital market may no longer charge default-free prices for futures contracts, because these contracts can now involve credit risk. For example, a firm with initial wealth consisting of nothing but 100 gold bricks may not be able to buy more* on net, *because it has no non-gold collateral. (That firm would have no resources to pay for the additional purchases if the price of gold were to fall to zero.) Similarly, a firm that sells futures contracts for more than the equivalent of 100 gold bricks might be unable to make good on its position when gold prices rise sufficiently. This entire credit risk issue disappears, however, if we are willing to assume that the investment function satisfies the Inada conditions, ie, that the marginal product of investment is infinite at* $I = 0$. *In this case the optimal hedge ratio in equation (20) endogenously ensures that firm resources (and hence investment) are positive in all states.*

20 *We thank Tim Luehrman for suggesting this case to us.*

21 *In this particular case, there is no default risk associated with the futures position that implements the desired hedge ratio. The futures position will only incur large losses in those states where assets in place are extremely valuable. In such states the funds that can be raised against assets in place ensure that the firm will make good on its future position.*

22 *Conversations with Don Lessard were especially helpful in motivating the work in this section. See Adler and Dumas (1983) for an overview of the traditional arguments for hedging exchange rate risk.*

23 *Note that our earlier formulation in the previous section can be interpreted as a degenerate case of equation (22), with* $\beta = 0$ *and* I^H *fixed at zero – ie, no investment in one of the two countries.*

24 *In this formulation, the external borrowing facility is also denominated in the home currency. In terms of the CSV model developed in the section on hedging in an optimum contractual model, this amounts to assuming that the payoff* x *on the pre-existing asset is home currency denominated. Thus, we are suppressing the issues relating to changing financing opportunities raised in the section on changing financing opportunities.*

25 *Effectively, this assumes that the foreign currency price of non-tradeable goods is not affected by exchange rate changes.*

26 *This will be correct provided that this domestic currency is constant.*

27 *Note that with* $\bar{\epsilon} = 1$, *the expected future spot rate is equal to the forward rate.*

28 *It is also important to check whether the candidate solution that emerges from (26) and (27) involves negative wealth in any states. If so, then an additional, non-negativity constraint on internal wealth,* $w \geq 0, \forall\epsilon$, *might also be imposed in the maximisation problem, in order to address the concerns about credit risk raised in footnote 19.*

29 *To see this, note that with non-stochastic production technology.* $F_I = P_w$, *which by (28) is a constant.*

30 *By put-call parity, one can achieve an equivalent hedge by using only the put (or call) option together with a different quantity of futures, or by using options alone.*

31 *If the oil production is literally certain to be 100 million barrels, then forward contracts do not involve credit risk, and would allow complete hedging. However, if, more realistically, production quantities are uncertain or subject to moral hazard problems, forward contracts* will *involve some credit risk, and therefore represent an imperfect hedging vehicle.*

32 *Adler (1992) also considers the implications of product market competition for hedging policy.*

33 *The quote is from "Shareholders Applaud Risk Management",* Corporate Finance, *June/July 1992.*

34 *This reasoning is certainly consistent with Fazzari, Hubbard and Petersen (1988) who found that investment was least sensitive to cashflow for high-dividend firms.*

35 *Nance, Smith and Smithson also find that smaller firms are less likely to hedge. This fact is generally inconsistent with our model if one believes that smaller firms are more likely to be liquidity constrained due to greater informational asymmetries. However, the tendency toward greater information asymmetries may be offset by relationships with certain capital providers, such as banks. Also, if there are fixed costs of setting up a hedging programme, the gains from hedging for small firms may not be enough to justify the cost.*

BIBLIOGRAPHY

Adler, M., 1992, "Exchange Rate Planning for the International Trading Firm", Working paper, Columbia University.

Adler, M., and B. Dumas, 1983, "International Portfolio Choice and Corporation Finance: A Synthesis", *Journal of Finance* 38, pp. 925–84.

Block, S. B., and T. J. Gallagher, 1986, "The Use of Interest Rate Futures and Options by Corporate Financial Managers", *Financial Management* 15, pp. 73–8.

Brealey, R. A., and S. C. Myers, 1991, *Principles of Corporate Finance* (New York: McGraw-Hill).

Breeden, D., and S. Viswanathan, 1990, "Why do Firms Hedge? An Asymmetric Information Model", Working paper, Duke University.

Bulow, J., J. Geanakoplos and P. Klemperer, 1985, "Multi-Market Oligopoly: Strategic Substitutes and Complements", *Journal of Political Economy* 93, pp. 488–511.

DeMarzo, P., and D. Duffie, 1992, "Corporate Incentives for Hedging and Hedge Accounting", working paper, Northwestern University.

Diamond, D., 1984, "Financial Intermediation and Delegated Monitoring", *Review of Economic Studies* 51, pp. 393–414.

Fazzari, S. M., R. G. Hubbard and B. C. Petersen, 1988, "Financing Constraints and Corporate Investment", *Brooking Papers on Economic Activity* 2, pp. 141–206.

Froot, K. A., D. S. Scharfstein and J. C. Stein, 1989, "LDC Debt: Foregiveness Indexation, and Investment Incentives", *Journal of Finance* 44, pp. 1,335–50.

Gale, D., and M. Hellwig, 1985, "Incentive-Compatible Debt Contracts 1: The One-Period Problem", *Review of Economic Studies* 52, pp. 647–64.

Gertler, M., and R. G. Hubbard, 1988, "Financial Factors in Business Fluctuations", in *Financial Market Volatility* (Kansas City: Federal Reserve Bank of Kansas City).

Hoshi, T., A. Kashyap and D. Scharfstein, 1991, "Corporate Structure, Liquidity, and Investment: Evidence from Japanese Industrial Groups", *Quarterly Journal on Economics* 56, pp. 33–60.

Hoshi, T., D. Scharfstein and K. Singleton, 1993, "Japanese Corporate Investment and Bank of Japan Guidance of Commercial Bank Lending", in K. Singleton (ed), *Japanese Monetary Policy* (Chicago: University of Chicago and NBER).

Jensen, M. C., and W. H. Meckling, 1976, "Theory of the Firm: Managerial Behavior, Agency Costs and Ownership Structure", *Journal of Financial Economics* 3, pp. 305–60.

Kashyap, A. K., O. A. Lamont and J. C. Stein, 1993, "Credit Conditions and the Cyclical Behavior of Inventories", Working paper, MIT.

Lessard, D., 1990, "Global Competition and Corporate Finance in the 1990s", *Journal of Applied Corporate Finance* 1, pp. 59–72.

Lewent, J. C., and A. J. Kearney, 1990, "Identifying, Measuring, and Hedging Currency Risk at Merck", *Journal of Applied Corporate Finance* 1, pp. 19–28.

Luehrman, T. A., 1990, "Jaguar plc", 1984, Harvard Business School Case No. N9-290-005.

Myers, S. C., 1977, "Determinants of Corporate Borrowing", *Journal of Financial Economics* 5, pp. 147–75.

Myers, S. C., and N. Majluf, 1984, "Corporate Financing and Investment Decisions When Firms Have Information that Investors Do Not Have", *Journal of Financial Economics* 3, pp. 187–221.

Nance, D. R., C. W. Smith and C. W. Smithson, 1993, "On the Determinants of Corporate Hedging", *Journal of Finance* 48, pp. 267–84.

Rawls, S. Waite, W. and C. W. Smithson, 1990, "Strategic Risk Management", *Journal of Applied Corporate Finance* 1, pp. 6–18.

Rubinstein, M., 1976, "The Valuation of Uncertain Income Streams and the Pricing of Options", *Bell Journal of Economics* 7, pp. 407–26.

Smith, C. W., C. W. Smithson, and D. Sykes Wilford, 1990, *Strategic Risk Management* (Institutional Investor Series in Finance) (New York: Harper and Row).

Smith, C. W., and R. Stulz, 1985, "The Determinants of Firms' Hedging Policies", *Journal of Financial and Quantitative Analysis* 20, pp. 391–405; reprinted as Chapter 6 of the present volume.

Stulz, R., 1984, "Optimal Hedging Policies", *Journal of Financial and Quantitative Analysis* 19, pp. 127–40.

Stulz, R., 1990, "Managerial Discretion and Optimal Financing Policies", *Journal of Financial Economics* 26, pp. 3–27.

Titman, S., and R. Wessels, 1988, "The Determinants of Capital Structure Choice", *Journal of Finance* 43, pp. 1–19.

Townsend, R. M., 1979, "Optimal Contracts and Competitive Markets with Costly State Verification", *Journal of Economic Theory* 21, pp. 265–93.

Wall, L. D., and J. Pringle, 1989, "Alternative Explanations of Interest Rate Swaps: An Empirical Analysis", *Financial Management* 18, pp. 59–73.

8

Rethinking Risk Management*

René M. Stulz

The Ohio State University

This chapter explores an apparent conflict between the theory and current practice of corporate risk management. Academic theory suggests that some companies facing large exposures to interest rates, exchange rates or commodity prices can increase their market value by using derivative securities to reduce their exposure. The primary emphasis of the theory is on the role of derivatives in reducing the variability of corporate cashflows and, in so doing, reducing various costs associated with financial distress.

The actual corporate use of derivatives, however, does not seem to correspond closely to the theory. For one thing, large companies make far greater use of derivatives than small firms, even though small firms have more volatile cashflows, more restricted access to capital, and thus presumably more reason to buy protection against financial trouble. Perhaps even more puzzling is that many companies appear to be using risk management to pursue goals other than reducing variance.

Does this mean that the prevailing academic theory of risk management is wrong, and that "variance-minimisation" is not a useful goal for companies using derivatives? Or, is the current corporate practice of risk management misguided and in urgent need of reform? In this chapter I answer "no" to both questions, while at the same time suggesting there may be room for improvement in the theory as well as the practice of risk management.

The chapter begins by reviewing some evidence that has accumulated about the current practice of corporate risk management. Part of this evidence takes the form of recent "anecdotes", or cases, involving large derivatives losses. Most of the evidence, however, consists of corporate responses to surveys. What the stories suggest, and the surveys seem to confirm, is the popularity of a practice known as "selective" as opposed to "full-cover" hedging. That is, while few companies regularly use derivatives to take a "naked" speculative position on FX rates or commodity prices, most corporate derivatives users appear to allow their views of future interest rates, exchange rates, and commodity prices to influence their hedge ratios.

Such a practice seems inconsistent with modern risk management theory, or at least the theory that has been presented thus far. But there is a plausible defense of selective hedging - one that would justify the practice without violating the efficient markets tenet at the centre of modern financial theory. In this chapter I attempt to explain more of the corporate behaviour we observe by pushing the theory of risk management beyond the variance-minimisation model that prevails in most academic circles. Some companies, I argue below, may have a comparative advantage in bearing certain financial risks (while other companies mistakenly think and act as if they do). I accordingly propose a somewhat different goal for corporate risk management - namely, the *elimination of costly lower-tail outcomes* - that is designed to reduce the expected costs of financial trouble while preserving a company's ability to exploit any comparative advantage in risk-bearing it may have. (In the jargon of

**Originally published in the* Journal of Applied Corporate Finance *9(3) (1996), pp.8-24. The author is grateful for extensive editorial assistance from Don Chew, and for comments by Steve Figlewski, Andrew Karolyi, Robert Whaley and participants at a seminar at McKinsey, at the Annual Meeting of the International Association of Financial Engineers and at the French Finance Association.*

finance specialists, the fundamental aim of corporate risk management can be viewed as the purchase of "well-out-of-the-money put options" that eliminate the downside while preserving as much of the upside as can be justified by the principle of comparative advantage.)

Such a modified theory of risk management implies that some companies should hedge all financial risks, other firms should worry about only certain kinds of risks, and still others should not worry about risks at all. But, as I also argue below, when making decisions as to whether or not to hedge, management should keep in mind that risk management can be used to change both a company's capital structure and its ownership structure. By reducing the probability of financial trouble, risk management has the potential both to increase debt capacity and to facilitate larger equity stakes for management.

This chapter also argues that common measures of risk such as variance and value at risk (VAR) are not useful for most risk management applications by non-financial companies, nor are they consistent with the objective of risk management presented here. In place of both VAR and the variance of cashflows I suggest a method for measuring corporate exposures that, besides having a foundation in modern finance theory, should be relatively easy to use.

I conclude with a discussion of the internal "management" of risk management. If corporate risk management is focused not on minimising variance, but rather on eliminating downside risk while extending the corporate quest for comparative advantage into financial markets, then much more attention must be devoted to the evaluation and control of corporate risk management activities. The closing section of this chapter offers some suggestions for evaluating the performance of risk managers whose "view-taking" is an accepted part of the firm's risk management strategy.

Risk management in practice

In one of their series of papers on Metallgesellschaft, Chris Culp and Merton Miller make an observation that may seem startling to students of modern finance: "We need hardly remind readers that most value-maximising firms do not hedge."[1] But is this true? And, if so, how would we know?

Culp and Miller refer to survey evidence - in particular, to a Wharton–Chase study that sent questionnaires to 1,999 companies inquiring about their risk management practices.[2] Of the 530 firms that responded to the survey, only about a third answered "yes" when asked if they ever used futures, forwards, options or swaps. One clear finding that emerges from this survey is that large companies make greater use of derivatives than smaller firms. Whereas 65% of companies with a market value greater than US$250 million reported using derivatives, only 13% of the firms with market values of US$50 million or less claimed to use them.

What are the derivatives used to accomplish? The only uses reported by more than half of the corporate users are to hedge contractual commitments and to hedge anticipated transactions expected to take place within 12 months. About two-thirds of the companies responded that they never use derivatives to reduce funding costs (or earn "treasury profits") by arbitraging the markets or by taking a view. Roughly the same proportion of firms also said they never use derivatives to hedge their balance sheets, their foreign dividends or their economic or competitive exposures.

The Wharton–Chase study was updated in 1995, and its results were published in 1996 as the Wharton–CIBC Wood Gundy study. The results of the 1995 survey confirm those of its predecessor, but with one striking new finding: over a third of all derivative users said they sometimes "actively take positions" that reflect their market views of interest rate and exchange rates.

This finding was anticipated in a survey of Fortune 500 companies conducted by Walter Dolde in 1992 and published in this journal in the following year.[3] Of the 244 companies that responded to Dolde's survey, 85% reported having used swaps, forwards, futures or options. As in the Wharton surveys, larger companies reported greater use of derivatives than smaller firms. And, as Dolde notes, such a finding confirms the experience of risk management practitioners that the corporate use of derivatives requires a considerable upfront investment in personnel, training and computer hardware and software - an investment that could discourage small firms.

But, as we observed earlier, there are also reasons why the demand for risk management products should actually be greater for small firms than for large - notably the greater probability of default caused by unhedged exposures and the greater concentration of equity ownership in smaller companies. And Dolde's survey provides an interesting piece of evidence in support of this argument. When companies were asked to estimate what percentages of their exposures they chose to hedge, many respondents said that it depended on whether they had a view of future market movements. *Almost 90% of the derivatives users in Dolde's survey said they sometimes took a view.* And, when the companies employed such views in their hedging decisions, the smaller companies reported hedging significantly greater percentages of their FX and interest rate exposures than the larger companies.

Put another way, the larger companies were more inclined to "self-insure" their FX or interest rate risks. For example, if they expected FX rates to move in a way that would increase firm value, they might hedge only 10%–20% (or maybe none) of their currency exposure. But if they expected rates to move in a way that would reduce value, they might hedge 100% of the exposure.

Like the Wharton surveys, the Dolde survey also found that the focus of risk management was mostly on transaction exposures and near-term exposures. Nevertheless, Dolde also reported "a distinct evolutionary pattern" in which many firms "progress from targeting individual transactions to more systematic measures of ongoing competitive exposures".[4]

The bottom line from the surveys, then, is that corporations do not systematically hedge their exposures, the extent to which they hedge depends on their views of future price movements, the focus of hedging is primarily on near-term transactions, and the use of derivatives is greater for large firms than small firms. Many of the widely-reported derivative problems of recent years are fully consistent with this survey evidence, and closer inspection of such cases provides additional insight into common risk management practices. We briefly recount two cases in which companies lost large amounts of money as a result of risk management programmes.

METALLGESELLSCHAFT

Although the case of Metallgesellschaft continues to be surrounded by controversy, there is general agreement about the facts of the case. By the end of 1993, MGRM, the US oil marketing subsidiary of Metallgesellschaft, contracted to sell 154 million barrels of oil through fixed-price contracts ranging over a period of 10 years. These fixed-price contracts created a huge exposure to oil price increases that MGRM decided to hedge. However, it did not do so in a straightforward way. Rather than hedging its future outflows with offsetting positions of matching maturities, MGRM chose to take "stacked" positions in short-term contracts, both futures and swaps, and then roll the entire "stack" forward as the contracts expired.

MGRM's choice of short-term contracts can be explained in part by the lack of longer-term hedging vehicles. For example, liquid markets for oil futures do not go out much beyond 12 months. But it also appears that MGRM took a far larger position in oil futures than would have been consistent with a variance-minimising strategy. For example, one study estimated that the minimum-variance hedge position for MGRM would have required the forward purchase of only 86 million barrels of oil, or about 55% of the 154 million barrels in short-maturity contracts that MGRM actually entered into.[5]

Does this mean that MGRM really took a position that was long some 58 million barrels of oil? Not necessarily. As Culp and Miller demonstrate, had MGRM adhered to its professed strategy and been able to obtain funding for whatever futures losses it incurred over the entire 10-year period, its position would have been largely hedged.[6]

But even if MGRM's net exposure to oil prices was effectively hedged over the long term, it is also clear that MGRM's traders had not designed their hedge with the aim of minimising the variance of their net position in oil during the life of the contracts. The traders presumably took the position they did because they thought they could benefit from their specialised information about supply and demand – and, more specifically, from a persistent feature of oil futures known as "backwardation", or the long-run tendency of spot prices to be higher than futures prices. So, although MGRM was effectively hedged against changes in spot oil prices, it nevertheless had what amounted to a long position in "the basis". Most of this long position in the basis represented a bet that the convenience yields on crude oil – that is, the premiums of near-term futures over long-dated futures – would remain positive as they had over most of the past decade.

When spot prices fell dramatically in 1993, MGRM lost on its futures positions and gained on its cash positions – that is, on the present value of its delivery contracts. But because the futures positions were marked to market while the delivery contracts were not, MGRM's financial statements showed large losses. Compounding this problem of large "paper losses", the backwardation of oil prices also disappeared, thus adding real losses to the paper ones. And, in response to the reports of mounting losses, MG's management chose to liquidate the hedge. This action, as Culp and Miller point out, had the unfortunate consequence of "turning paper losses into realised losses" and "leaving MGRM exposed to rising prices on its remaining fixed-price contracts".[7]

DAIMLER-BENZ

In 1995 Daimler-Benz reported first-half losses of DM1.56 billion, the largest in the company's 109-year history. In its public statements, management attributed the losses to exchange rate losses caused by the weakening dollar. One subsidiary of Daimler-Benz, Daimler-Benz Aerospace, had an order book of DM20 billion, of which 80% was fixed in dollars. Because the dollar fell by 14% during this period, Daimler-Benz had to take a provision for losses of DM1.2 billion to cover future losses.

Why did Daimler-Benz fail to hedge its expected dollar receivables? The company said that it chose not to hedge because the forecasts it received were too diverse, ranging as they did from DM1.2 to DM1.7 per dollar. Analysts, however, attributed Daimler-Benz's decision to remain unhedged to its view that the dollar would stay above DM1.55.[8]

These two brief case studies reinforce the conclusion drawn from the survey evidence. In both of these cases, management's view of future price movements was an important determinant of how (or whether) risk was managed. Risk management did not mean minimising risk by putting on a minimum-variance hedge. Rather, it meant choosing to bear certain risks based on a number of different considerations, including the belief that a particular position would allow the firm to earn abnormal returns.

Is such a practice consistent with the modern theory of risk management? To answer that question, we first need to review the theory.

The perspective of modern finance

The two pillars of modern finance theory are the concepts of efficient markets and diversification. Stated as briefly as possible, market efficiency means that markets don't leave money on the table. Information that is freely accessible is incorporated in prices with sufficient speed and accuracy that one cannot profit by trading on it.

Despite the spread of the doctrine of efficient markets, the world remains full of corporate executives who are convinced of their own ability to predict future interest rates, exchange rates and commodity prices. As evidence of the strength and breadth of this conviction, many companies during the late 1980s and early 1990s set up their corporate treasuries as "profit centres" in their own right – a practice that, if the survey evidence can be trusted, has been largely abandoned in recent years by most industrial firms. And the practice has been abandoned with good reason: behind most large derivative losses – in cases ranging from Orange County and Baring Brothers to Procter & Gamble and BancOne – there appear to have been more or less conscious decisions to bear significant exposures to market risks with the hope of earning abnormal returns.

The lesson of market efficiency for corporate risk managers is that the attempt to earn higher returns in most financial markets generally means bearing large (and unfamiliar) risks. In highly liquid markets such as those for interest rate and FX futures – and in the case of heavily traded commodities like oil and gold as well – industrial companies are unlikely to have a comparative advantage in bearing these risks. And so, for most industrial corporations, setting up the corporate treasury to trade derivatives for profit is a value-destroying proposition. (As I will also argue later, however, market efficiency does not rule out the possibility that management's information may be better than the market's in special cases.)

But if the concept of market efficiency should discourage corporations from *creating* corporate exposures to financial market risks, the companion concept of diversification should also discourage some companies from *hedging* financial exposures incurred through their normal business operations. To explain why, however, requires a brief digression on the corporate cost of capital.

Finance theory says that the stock market, in setting the values of companies, effectively assigns minimum required rates of return on capital that vary directly with the companies' levels of risk. In general, the greater a company's risk, the higher the rate of return it must earn to produce superior returns for its shareholders. But a company's required rate of return, also known as its cost of capital, is said to depend only on its non-diversifiable (or "systematic") risk, not on its total risk. In slightly different words, a company's cost of capital depends on the strength of the firm's tendency to move with the broad market (in statistical terms, its "covariance") rather than its overall volatility (or "variance").

In general, most of a company's interest rate, currency and commodity price exposures will not increase the risk of a well-diversified portfolio. Thus, most corporate financial exposures represent "non-systematic" or "diversifiable" risks that shareholders can eliminate by holding diversified portfolios. And because shareholders have such an inexpensive risk management tool at their disposal, companies that reduce their earnings volatility by managing their financial risks will not be rewarded by investors with lower required rates of return (or, alternatively, with higher P/E ratios for given levels of cashflow or earnings). As one example, investors with portfolios that include stocks of oil companies are not likely to place higher multiples on the earnings of petrochemical firms just because the latter smooth their earnings by hedging against oil price increases.

For this reason, having the corporation devote resources to reducing FX or commodity price risks makes sense only if the cashflow variability arising from such risks has the potential to impose "real" costs on the corporation. The academic finance literature has identified three major costs associated with higher variability: (1) higher expected bankruptcy costs (and, more generally, costs of financial distress); (2) higher expected payments to corporate "stakeholders" (including higher rates of return required by owners of closely held firms); and (3) higher expected tax payments. The potential gains from risk management come from its ability to reduce each of these three costs – and I review each in turn below.[9]

RISK MANAGEMENT CAN REDUCE BANKRUPTCY COSTS

Although well-diversified shareholders may not be concerned about the cashflow variability caused by swings in FX rates or commodity prices, they will become concerned if such variability materially raises the probability of financial distress. In the extreme case, a company with significant amounts of debt could experience a sharp downturn in operating cashflow – caused in part by an unhedged exposure – and be forced to file for bankruptcy.

What are the costs of bankruptcy? Most obvious are the payments to lawyers and court costs. But, in addition to these "direct" costs of administration and reorganisation, there are some potentially larger "indirect" costs. Companies that wind up face considerable interference from the bankruptcy court with their investment and operating decisions. And such interference has the potential to cause significant reductions in the ongoing operating value of the firm.

If a company's shareholders view bankruptcy as a real possibility – and to the extent that the process of reorganisation itself is expected to reduce the firm's operating value – the expected present value of these costs will be reflected in a company's *current* market value. A risk management programme that costlessly eliminates the risk of bankruptcy effectively reduces these costs to zero and, in so doing, increases the value of the firm.

The effects of risk management on bankruptcy costs and firm value are illustrated in Figure 1. In the case shown in the figure, hedging is assumed to reduce the variability of cashflow and firm value to the degree that default is no longer possible. By eliminating the possibility of bankruptcy, risk management increases the value of the firm's equity by an amount roughly equal to bankruptcy costs (Bc) multiplied by the probability of bankruptcy

1. Debt, equity, and firm value with bankruptcy costs

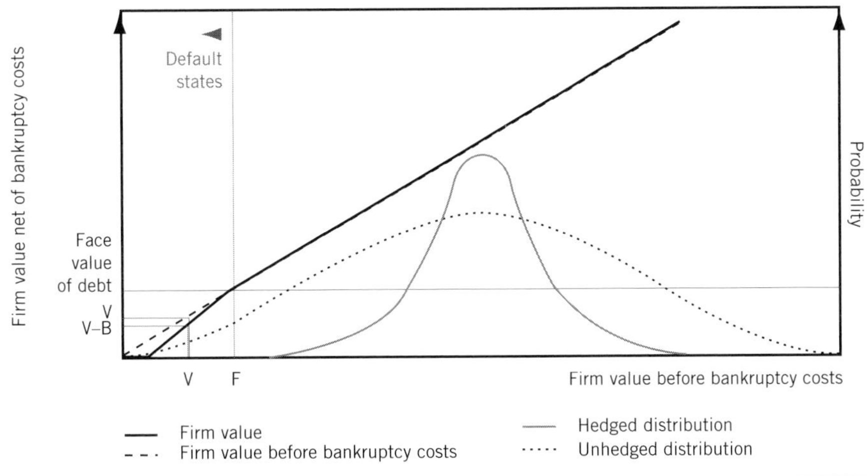

if the firm remains unhedged (pBU). For example, let's assume that the market value of the firm's equity is US$100 million, bankruptcy costs are expected to run US$25 million (or 25% of current firm value), and the probability of bankruptcy in the absence of hedging is 10%. In this case, risk management can be seen as increasing the current value of the firm's equity by US$2.5 million (10% × US$25 million), or 2.5%. (Keep in mind that this is the contribution of risk management to firm value *when the company is healthy*; in the event that cashflow and value should decline sharply from current levels, the value added by risk management increases in absolute dollars, and even more on a percentage-of-value basis.)

This argument extends to distress costs in general. For instance, as a company becomes weaker financially, it becomes more difficult for it to raise funds. At some point, the cost of outside funding - if available at all - may become so great that management chooses to pass up profitable investments. This "underinvestment problem" experienced by companies when facing the prospect of default (or, in some cases, just a downturn in earnings[10]) represents an important cost of financial distress. And, to the extent that risk management succeeds in reducing the perceived *probability* of financial distress and the costs associated with underinvestment, it will increase the current market value of the firm.

RISK MANAGEMENT CAN REDUCE PAYMENTS TO "STAKEHOLDERS" (AND REQUIRED RETURNS TO OWNERS OF CLOSELY HELD FIRMS)[11]

Although the shareholders of large public companies can often manage most financial risks more efficiently than the companies themselves, the case may be different for the owners - or owner-managers - of private or closely held companies. Because such owners tend to have a large proportion of their wealth tied up in the firm, their required rates of return are likely to reflect all important sources of risk, those that can be "diversified away" by outside investors as well as those that cannot. In such circumstances, hedging financial exposures can be thought of as adding value by reducing the owners' risks and hence their required rates of return on investment.

And it's not just the owners of closely held companies that value the protection from risk management. In public companies with dispersed ownership, non-investor groups such as managers, employees, customers and suppliers with a large stake in the success of the firm typically cannot diversify away large financial exposures. If there is a chance that their "firm-specific" investments could be lost because of financial distress, they are likely to require added compensation for the greater risk. Employees will demand higher wages (or reduce their loyalty or perhaps their work effort) at a company where the probability of layoff is greater. Managers with alternative opportunities will demand higher salaries (or maybe an equity stake in the company) to run firms where the risks of insolvency and financial embarrassment are significant. Suppliers will be more reluctant to enter into long-term contracts, and trade creditors will charge more and be less flexible, with companies whose prospects are more uncertain. And customers concerned about the company's ability to fulfil warranty obligations or service their products in the future may be reluctant to buy those products.

To the extent that risk management can protect the investments of each of these corporate stakeholders, the company can improve the terms on which it contracts with them and so increase firm value. And, as I discuss later in more detail, hedging can also facilitate larger equity stakes for managers of public companies by limiting "uncontrollables" and thus the "scope" of their bets.

RISK MANAGEMENT CAN REDUCE TAXES

The potential tax benefits of risk management derive from the interaction of risk management's ability to reduce the volatility of reported income and the progressivity (or, more precisely, the "convexity") of most of the world's tax codes. In the US, as in most countries, a company's effective tax rate rises along with increases in pre-tax income. Increasing marginal tax rates, limits on the use of tax-loss carry-forwards and the alternative minimum tax all work together to impose higher effective rates of taxation on higher levels of reported income and to provide lower percentage tax rebates for ever larger losses.

Because of the convexity of the tax code, there are benefits to "managing" taxable income so that as much of it as possible falls within an optimal range - that is, neither too high nor too low. By reducing fluctuations in taxable income, risk management can lead to lower tax payments by ensuring that, over a complete business cycle, the largest possible proportion of corporate income falls within this optimal range of tax rates.

Risk management and comparative advantage in risk-taking

Up to this point we have seen that companies should not expect to make money consistently by taking financial positions based on information that is publicly available. But what about information that is not publicly available? After all, many companies in the course of their normal operating activities acquire specialised information about certain financial markets. Could not such information give them a comparative advantage over their shareholders in taking some types of risk?

Let's look at a hypothetical example. Consider company X that produces consumer durables using large amounts of copper as a major input. In the process of ensuring that it has the appropriate amount of copper on hand, it gathers useful information about the copper market. It knows its own demand for copper, of course, but it also learns a lot about the supply. In such a case, the firm will almost certainly allow that specialised information to play some role in its risk management strategy.

For example, let's assume that company X's management has determined that, when it has no view about future copper prices, it will hedge 50% of the next year's expected copper purchases to protect itself against the possibility of financial distress. But, now let's say that the firm's purchasing agents persuade top management that the price of copper is far more likely to rise than fall in the coming year. In this case, the firm's risk manager might choose to take a long position in copper futures that would hedge as much as 100% of its anticipated purchases for the year instead of the customary 50%. Conversely, if management becomes convinced that copper prices are likely to drop sharply (with almost no possibility of a major increase), it might choose to hedge as little as 20% of its exposure.[12]

Should the management of company X refrain from exploiting its specialised knowledge in this fashion, and instead adhere to its 50% hedging target? Or should it, in certain circumstances, allow its market view to influence its hedge ratio?

Although there are clearly risks to selective hedging of this kind - in particular, the risk that the firm's information may not in fact be better than the market's - it seems quite plausible that companies could have such informational advantages. Companies that repurchase their own shares based on the belief that their current value fails to reflect the firm's prospects seem to be vindicated more often than not. And though it's true that management may be able to predict the firm's future earnings with more confidence than the price of one of its major inputs, the information companies acquire about certain financial markets may still prove a reasonably reliable source of gain in risk management decisions.

THE IMPORTANCE OF UNDERSTANDING COMPARATIVE ADVANTAGE

What this example fails to suggest, however, is that the same operating activity in one company may not necessarily provide a comparative advantage in risk-bearing for another firm. As suggested above, the major risk associated with "selective" hedging is that the firm's information may not in fact be better than the market's. For this reason, it is important for management to understand the source of its comparative advantages.

To illustrate this point, take the case of a foreign currency trading operation in a large commercial bank. A foreign currency trading room can make a lot of money from taking positions, provided, of course, that exchange rates move in the anticipated direction. But, in an efficient market, as we have seen, banks can reliably make money from position-taking of this sort only if they have access to information before most other firms. In the case of FX, this is likely to happen only if the bank's trading operation is very large - large enough that its deal flow is likely to reflect general shifts in demand for foreign currencies.

Most FX dealers, however, have no comparative advantage in gathering information about changes in the value of foreign currencies. For such firms, management of currency risk means ensuring that their exposures are short-lived. The most reliable way to minimise exposures for most currency traders is to enlarge their customer base. With a sufficient number of large, highly active customers, a trading operation has the following advantage: if one of its traders agrees to buy yen from one customer, the firm can resell them quickly to another customer and pocket the bid–ask spread.

In an article entitled "An Analysis of Trading Profits: How Trading Rooms Really Make Money", Alberic Braas and Charles Bralver present evidence suggesting that most FX trading profits come from market-making, not position-taking.[13] Moreover, as the authors of this article point out, a trading operation that does not understand its comparative advantage in trading currencies is likely not only to fail to generate consistent profit, but to endanger its existing comparative advantage. If the source of the profits of the trading room is really the customer base of the bank and not the predictive power of its traders, then the bank must invest in maintaining and building its customer base. A trading room that mistakenly believes the source of its profits to be position-taking will take large positions that, on average, will neither make money nor lose money. More troubling, though, is that the resulting variability of its trading income is likely to unsettle its customers and weaken its customer base. Making matters worse, it may choose a compensation system for its traders that rewards profitable position-taking instead of valuable coordination of trading and sales activities. A top management that fails to understand its comparative advantage may waste its time looking for star traders while neglecting the development of marketing strategies and services.

How can management determine when it should take risks and when it should not? The best approach is to implement a *risk-taking audit*. This would involve a comprehensive review of the risks to which the company is exposed, both through its financial instruments and liability structure and through its normal operations. Such an audit should attempt to answer questions such as the following: Which of its major risks has the firm proved capable of "self-insuring" over a complete business cycle? If the firm chooses to hedge "selectively", or leaves exposures completely unhedged, what is the source of the firm's comparative advantage in taking these positions? Which risk management activities have consistently added value without introducing another source of volatility?

Once a firm has decided that it has a comparative advantage in taking certain financial risks, it must then determine the role of risk management in exploiting this advantage. As I argue below, risk management may paradoxically enable the firm to take *more* of these risks than it would in the absence of risk management. To illustrate this point, let's return to our example of company X and assume that it has valuable information about the copper market which enables it to earn consistently superior profits trading copper. Even in this situation, such trading profits are by no means a sure thing; there is always the possibility that the firm will experience significant losses. Purchasing far-out-of-the-money calls on copper in such a case could actually serve to increase the firm's ability to take speculative positions in copper. But, as I argue in the next section, a company's ability to withstand large trading losses without endangering its operating activities depends not only on its risk management policy, but also on its capital structure and general financial health.

The link between risk management, risk-taking and capital structure

In discussing earlier the benefits of risk management, I suggested that companies should manage risk in a way that makes financial distress highly unlikely and, in so doing, preserves the financing flexibility necessary to carry out their investment strategies. Given this primary objective for risk management, one would not expect companies with little or no debt financing - and, hence, a low probability of financial trouble - to benefit from hedging.

In this sense, risk management can be viewed as a direct substitute for equity capital. That is, the more the firm hedges its financial exposures, the less equity it requires to support its business. Or, to put it another way, the use of risk management to reduce exposures effectively increases a company's debt capacity.

2. Optimal hedging for firms AAA, BBB, S&L

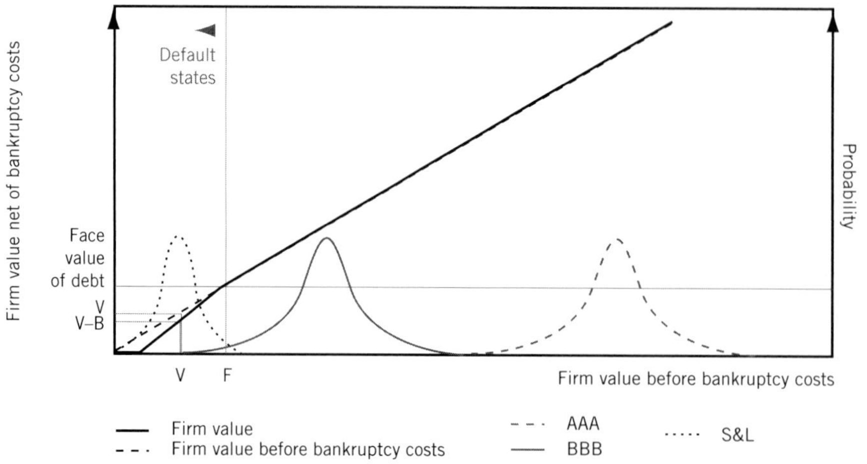

Moreover, to the extent that one views risk management as a substitute for equity capital - or, alternatively, as a technique that allows management to substitute debt for equity - then it pays companies to practise risk management only to the extent that equity capital is more expensive than debt. As this formulation of the issue suggests, a company's decisions to hedge financial risks - or to bear part of such risks through selective hedging - should be made jointly with the corporate capital structure decision.

To illustrate this interdependence between risk management and capital structure, consider the three kinds of companies shown in Figure 2. At the right-hand side of the figure is company AAA, so named because it has little debt and a very high debt rating. The probability of default is essentially zero; thus the left or lower tail of AAA's distribution of potential outcomes never reaches the range where low value begins to impose financial distress costs on the firm. Based on the theory of risk management just presented, there is no reason for this company to hedge its financial exposures; the company's shareholders can do the same job more cost-effectively. And, should investment opportunities arise, AAA will likely be able to raise funds on an economic basis, even if its cashflows should decline temporarily.

Should such a company take bets on financial markets? The answer could be yes, provided that management has specialised information that would give it a comparative advantage in a certain market. In AAA's case, a bet that turns out badly will not affect the company's ability to carry out its strategic plan.

But now let's consider the company in the middle of Figure 2, BBB. Like the company shown earlier in Figure 1, this firm has a lower credit rating and there is a significant probability that it could face distress. What should BBB do? As shown in Figure 1, this firm should probably eliminate the probability of encountering financial distress through risk management. In this case, even if management feels that there are occasional opportunities to profit from market inefficiencies, hedging exposures is likely to be the best policy. In company BBB's case, the cost of having a bet turn sour can be substantial, since this would almost certainly imply default. Consequently, one would not expect the management of such a firm to let its views affect the hedge ratio.

Finally, let's consider a firm that is in distress - which we'll call "S&L". What should it do? Reducing risk once the firm is in distress is not in the interest of shareholders. If the firm stays in distress and eventually defaults, shareholders will end up with near-worthless shares. In these circumstances, a management intent on maximising shareholder value will not only accept bets that present themselves, but will *seek out* new ones. Such managers will take bets even if they believe markets are efficient because introducing new sources of volatility raises the probability of the "upper-tail" outcomes that are capable of rescuing the firm from financial distress.

BACK TO THE CAPITAL STRUCTURE DECISION

As we saw in the case of company AAA, firms that have a lot of equity capital can make bets without worrying about whether doing so will bring about financial distress. One would therefore not expect these firms to hedge aggressively, particularly if risk management is costly and shareholders are better off without it.

The major issue that such companies must address, however, is whether they have too much capital - or, too much equity capital. In other words, although risk management may not be useful to them *given their current leverage ratios*, they might be better off using risk management and increasing leverage. Debt financing, of course, has a tax advantage over equity financing. But, in addition to its ability to reduce corporate taxes, increasing leverage also has the potential to strengthen management incentives to improve efficiency and add value. For one thing, the substitution of debt for equity leads managers to pay out excess capital - an action that could be a major source of value added in industries with overcapacity and few promising investment opportunities. Perhaps even more important, however, is that the substitution of debt for equity also allows for greater concentration of equity ownership, including a significant ownership stake for managers.

In sum, the question of what is the right corporate risk management decision for a company begs the question of not only its optimal capital structure, but its optimal *ownership* structure as well. As suggested above, hedging could help some companies to increase shareholder value by enabling them to raise leverage - say, by buying back their shares - and increase management's percentage ownership. For other companies, however, leaving exposures unhedged or hedging "selectively" while maintaining more equity may turn out to be the value-maximising strategy.

Corporate risk-taking and management incentives

Management incentives may have a lot to do with why some firms take bets and others do not. As suggested, some companies that leave exposures unhedged or take bets on financial markets may have a comparative advantage in so doing; and, for those companies, such risk-taking may be a value-increasing strategy. Other companies, however, may choose to take financial risks without having a comparative advantage, particularly if such risk-taking somehow serves the interests of those managers who choose to expose their firms to the risks.

We have little convincing empirical evidence on the extent of risk-taking by companies, whether public or private. But there is one notable exception: a study by Peter Tufano of the hedging behaviour of 48 publicly traded North American gold mining companies that was published in the September 1996 issue of the *Journal of Finance*.[14] The gold mining industry is ideal for studying hedging behaviour in the sense that gold mining companies tend to be single-industry firms with one very large price exposure and a wide range of hedging vehicles, from forward sales to exchange-traded gold futures and options, to gold swaps and bullion loans.

The purpose of Tufano's study was to examine the ability of various corporate risk management theories to explain any significant pattern of differences in the percentage of their gold price exposures that the companies choose to hedge. Somewhat surprisingly, there was considerable variation in the hedging behaviour of these 48 firms. One company, Homestake Mining, chose not only to hedge none of its exposure, but to publicise its policy while condemning what it called "gold price management". At the other extreme were companies like American Barrick that hedged as much as 85% of their anticipated production over the next three years. And whereas about one in six of these firms chose to hedge none of its exposure and sold *all* of its output at spot prices, another one in six firms hedged 40% or more of its gold price exposure.

The bottom line of Tufano's study was that the only important systematic determinant of the 48 corporate hedging decisions was managerial ownership of shares and, more generally, the nature of the managerial compensation contract. In general, the greater management's direct percentage share ownership, the larger the percentage of its gold price exposure a firm hedged. By contrast, little hedging took place in gold mining firms where management owns a small stake. Moreover, managerial compensation contracts that emphasise options or option-like features were also associated with significantly less hedging.

As Tufano acknowledged in his study, this pattern of findings could have been predicted from arguments that Clifford Smith and I presented in a theoretical paper in 1985.[15] Our argument was essentially as follows: as we saw in the case of closely held companies, managers with a significant fraction of their own wealth tied up in their own firms are likely to consider all sources of risk when setting their required rates of return. And this could help explain the tendency of firms with heavy managerial equity ownership to hedge more of their gold price exposures. In such cases, the volatility of gold prices translates fairly directly into volatility of managers' wealth, and manager-owners concerned about such volatility may rationally choose to manage their exposures. (How, or whether, such hedging serves the interests of the companies' outside shareholders is another issue, one that I return to shortly.)

The propensity of managers with lots of stock options but little equity ownership to leave their gold price exposures unhedged is also easy to understand. As shown in Figure 3, the one-sided payoff from stock options effectively rewards management for taking bets and so increasing volatility. In this example, the reduction in volatility from hedging makes management's options worthless (that is, the example assumes these are well-out-of-the-money options). But if the firm does not hedge, there is some probability that a large increase in gold prices will cause the options to pay off.

What if we make the more realistic assumption that the options are *at the money* instead of far out of the money? In this case, options would still have the power to influence hedging behaviour because management gains more from increases in firm value than it loses from reductions in firm value. As we saw in the case of the S&L presented earlier, this "asymmetric" payoff structure of options increases management's willingness to take bets.[16]

But if these differences in hedging behaviour reflect differences in managerial incentives, what do they tell us about the effect of risk management on shareholder value? Without directly addressing the issue, Tufano implies that neither of the two polar risk management strategies – hedging none of their gold exposure vs hedging 40% or more – seems designed to increase shareholder value, while both appear to serve managers' interests. But can we therefore conclude from this study that neither of these approaches benefits shareholders?

Let's start with the case of the companies that, like Homestake Mining, choose to hedge none of their gold price exposure. As we saw earlier, companies for which financial distress is unlikely have no good reason to hedge (assuming they see no value in changing their current capital structure.) At the same time, in a market as heavily traded as gold, management is also not likely to possess a comparative advantage in predicting gold prices. And, lacking either a motive for hedging or superior information about future gold prices, management has no reason to alter the company's natural exposure to gold prices. In further defence of such a policy, one could also argue that such a gold price exposure will have diversification benefits for investors seeking protection against inflation and political risks.

3. Impact of options in managerial compensation contracts

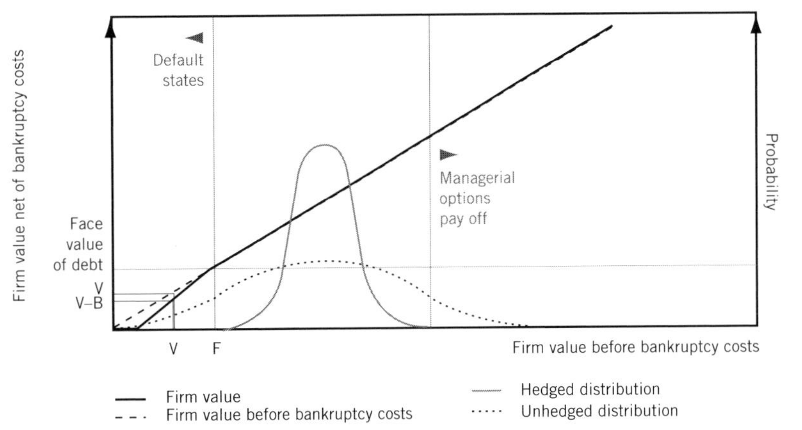

On the other hand, as Smith and I pointed out, because stock options have considerably more upside than downside risk, such incentive packages could result in a misalignment of managers' and shareholders' interests. That is, stock options could be giving managers a one-sided preference for risk-taking that is not fully shared by the companies' stockholders; and, if so, a better policy would be to balance managers' upside potential by giving them a share of the downside risk.

But what about the opposite decision to hedge a significant portion of gold price exposures? Was that likely to have increased shareholder value? As Tufano's study suggests, the managers of the hedging firms tend to hold larger equity stakes. And, as we saw earlier, if such managers have a large fraction of their wealth tied up in their firms, they will demand higher levels of compensation to work in firms with such price exposures. *Given that the firm has chosen to concentrate equity ownership*, hedging may well be a value-adding strategy. That is, if significant equity ownership for managers is expected to add value by strengthening incentives to improve operating performance, the role of hedging is to make these incentives even stronger by removing the "noise" introduced by a major performance variable – the gold price – that is beyond management's control. For this reason, the combination of concentrated ownership, the less "noisy" performance measure produced by hedging and the possibility of higher financial leverage[17] has the potential to add significant value. As this reasoning suggests, risk management can be used to facilitate an organisational structure that resembles that of an LBO.[18]

To put the same thought another way, it is the risk management policy that allows companies with large financial exposures to have significant managerial stock ownership. For, without the hedging policy, a major price exposure would cause the scope of management's bet to be too diffuse, and "uncontrollables" would dilute the desired incentive benefits of more concentrated ownership.

Although Tufano's study is finally incapable of answering the question "Did risk management add value for shareholders?", the study nevertheless has an important message for corporate policy. It says that, to the extent that risk-taking within the corporation is decentralised, it is important to understand the incentives of those who make the decisions to take or lay off risks.

Organisations have lots of people doing a good job, and so simply doing a good job may not be enough to get promoted. And, if one views corporate promotions as the outcome of "tournaments" (as does one strand of the academic literature), there are tremendous incentives to stand out. One way to stand out is by volunteering to take big risks. In most areas of a corporation, it is generally impossible to take risks where the payoffs are large enough to be noticeable if things go well. But the treasury area may still be an exception. When organised as a profit centre, the corporate treasury was certainly a place where an enterprising executive could take such risks and succeed. To the extent that such possibilities for risk-taking still exist within some corporate treasuries, top management must be very careful in establishing the appropriate incentives for its risk managers. I return to this subject in the final section of the chapter.

4. World market portfolio return September 1985 to December 1995

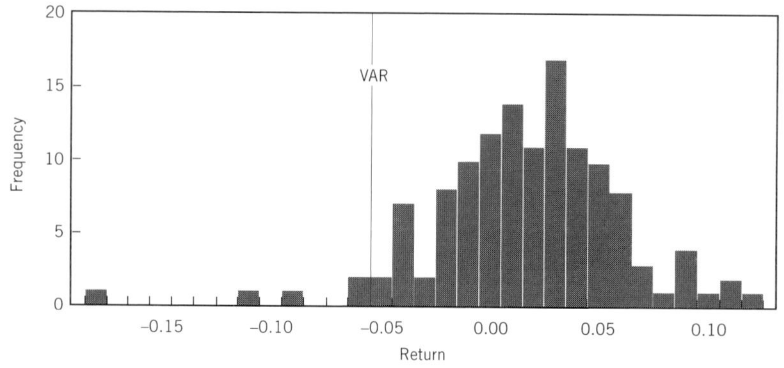

Measuring risk (or improving on VAR)

As I mentioned at the outset, the academic literature has focused on volatility reduction as the primary objective of risk management, and on variance as the principal measure of risk. But such a focus on variance, as we have seen, is inconsistent both with most corporate practice and with the theory of risk management presented in this chapter. Rather than aiming to reduce variance, most corporate risk management programmes appear designed just to avoid "lower-tail outcomes" while preserving upside potential. Indeed, as I suggested earlier, some companies will hedge certain downside risks precisely in order to be able to increase their leverage ratios or to enlarge other financial exposures in ways designed to exploit their comparative advantage in risk-taking.

Many commercial banks and other financial institutions now attempt to quantify the probability of lower-tail outcomes by using a measure known as "value at risk", or VAR. To illustrate the general principle underlying VAR, let's assume you are an investor who holds a stock portfolio that is fully diversified across all the major world markets. To calculate your VAR you'll need the kind of information that is presented graphically in Figure 4, which is a histogram showing the distribution of monthly returns on the Morgan Stanley Capital International world market portfolio from September 1985 to December 1995 inclusive.

How risky is that portfolio? One measure is the standard deviation of the portfolio's monthly returns. Over that roughly 10-year period the average monthly return was 1.23%, with a standard deviation of 4.3%. This tells you that, about two-thirds of the time, your actual return would have fallen within a range extending from a loss of 3.1% to a gain of 5.5%.

But what if one of your major concerns is the size of your monthly losses if things turn out badly, and you thus want to know more about the bottom third of the distribution of outcomes? Let's say, for example, that you want to know the maximum extent of your losses in 95 cases out of 100 – that is, within a 95% "confidence interval". In that case, you would calculate the VAR evaluated at the 5% level, which turns out to be a loss of 5.9%. This VAR, represented by the vertical line in the middle of Figure 4, is obtained by taking the monthly average return of 1.23% and subtracting from it 1.65 times the standard deviation of 4.3%. And, if you wanted to know the dollar value of your maximum expected losses, you would simply multiply 5.9% times the dollar value of your holdings. That number is your monthly VAR at the 95% confidence level.

Although the VAR is now used by some industrial firms to evaluate the risks of their derivatives portfolios, the measure was originally designed by J. P. Morgan to help financial institutions monitor the exposures created by their trading activities. In fact, for financial institutions that trade in liquid markets, a *daily* VAR is likely to be even more useful for monitoring trading operations than the monthly VAR illustrated above. Use of a daily VAR would tell an institution that it could expect, in 95 cases out of 100, to lose no more than X% of its value before unwinding its positions.

The special appeal of VAR is its ability to compress the expected distribution of bad outcomes into a single number. But how does one apply such a measure to the corporate risk management we have been discussing? Despite its advantages for certain uses, VAR cannot really be used to execute the risk management goal presented in this chapter – namely, the elimination of lower-tail outcomes to avoid financial distress. The fact that there is a 95% probability that a company's loss on a given day, or in a given month, will not exceed a certain amount called VAR is not useful information when management's concern is whether firm value will fall below some critical value *over an extended period of time*. The question management would like to be able to answer is this: if we define financial distress as a situation where we cannot raise funds with a rating of BBB, or where our cashflows or the value of equity fall below some target, what is the probability of distress over, say, the next three years? VAR by itself cannot answer this question – nor can traditional measures of volatility.

It is relatively simple to calculate VAR for a financial institution's portfolio over a horizon of a day or a week. It is much less clear how one would compute the VAR associated with, say, an airline's ongoing operating exposure to oil prices. In evaluating their major risks, most non-financial companies will want to know how much volatility in their cashflows or firm value an exposure can be expected to cause over periods of at least a year, and often considerably longer. Unfortunately, there are at least two major difficulties in extending the VAR over longer time horizons that may not be surmountable.

First, remember that a daily VAR at the 99th percentile is one that is expected to occur on one day out of 100. The relative precision of such a prediction makes it possible to conduct empirical checks of the validity of the model. With the large number of daily observations, one can readily observe the frequency with which the loss is equal or greater than VAR *using reasonably current data*. But, if we attempt to move from a daily to, say, a one-year VAR at the same 99th percentile, it becomes very difficult to calculate such a model, much less subject it to empirical testing. Since an annual VAR at the 99th percentile means that the loss can be expected to take place in only one year in every 100, one presumably requires numerous 100-year periods to establish the validity of such a model.

The second problem in extending the time horizon of VAR is its reliance on the normal distribution. When one is especially concerned about "tail" probabilities – the probabilities of the worst and best outcomes – the assumption made about the statistical distribution of the gains and losses is important. Research on stock prices and on default probabilities across different classes of debt suggests that the tail probabilities are generally larger than is implied by the normal distribution. A simple way to understand this is as follows. If stock returns were really normally distributed, as many pricing models assume, market declines in excess of 10% in a day would be extremely rare – say, once in a million years. The fact that such declines happen more often than this is proof that the normal distribution does not describe the probability of lower-tail events correctly.

Although this is not an important failing for most applications in corporate finance, including the valuation of most securities, it can be critical in the context of risk management. For example, if changes in the value of derivatives portfolios or default probabilities have "fatter tails" than those implied by a normal distribution, management could end up significantly understating the probability of distress.

AN ALTERNATIVE TO VAR: USING CASHFLOW SIMULATIONS TO ESTIMATE DEFAULT PROBABILITIES

Moreover, even if we could calculate a one-year VAR for the value of the firm and be reasonably confident that the distribution was normal, the relevant risk measure for hedging purposes would not be the VAR computed at the one-year horizon. A VAR computed at the one-year horizon at the 99th percentile answers the question: What is the maximum loss in firm value that I can expect in 99 years out of 100? But when a company hedges an exposure, its primary concern is the likelihood of distress *during the year*, which depends on the value of the cumulative loss throughout the year. Thus, it must be concerned about the path of firm value during a period of time rather than the distribution of firm value at the end of the period.

Given this focus on cumulative changes in firm value during a period of time, perhaps the most practical approach to assessing a company's probability of financial distress is to conduct sensitivity analysis on the expected distribution of cashflows. Using Monte Carlo simulation techniques, for example, one could project the company's cashflows over a 10-year horizon in a way that is designed to reflect the combined effect of (and any interactions among) all the firm's major risk exposures on its default probability. The probability of distress over that period would be measured by the fraction of simulated distributions that falls below a certain threshold level of cumulative cashflow. Such a technique could also be used to estimate the expected effect of various hedging strategies on the probability of distress.[19]

One of the advantages of using simulation techniques in this context is their ability to incorporate any special properties (or "non-normalities") of the cashflows. As we saw earlier, the VAR approach assumes that the gains and losses from risky positions are "serially independent", which means that if your firm experiences a loss today, the chance of experiencing another loss tomorrow is unaffected. But this assumption is likely to be wrong when applied to the operating cashflow of a non-financial firm: if cashflow is poor today, it is more likely to be poor tomorrow. Simulation has the ability to build this "serial dependence" of cashflows into an analysis of the probability of financial distress.

Managing risk-taking

As we have seen, a hedging strategy that focuses on the probability of distress can be consistent with an increase in risk-taking. With such a strategy, the primary goal of risk management is to eliminate lower-tail outcomes. Using risk management in this way, it is possible for a company to increase its volatility while also limiting the probability of a bad outcome that would create financial distress. One example of such a strategy would be to lever up the firm while at the same time buying way-out-of-the-money put options that pay off if the firm does poorly. Focusing on lower-tail outcomes is also fully consistent with managing longer-term economic or competitive exposures, as opposed to the near-term transaction exposures that most corporate risk management seems designed to hedge.

But how would the firm decide whether the expected payoff from taking certain financial bets is adequate compensation for not only the risk of losses, but also the expected costs of financial distress? And, once management decides that it is a value-increasing proposition to undertake certain bets, how would the firm evaluate the success of its risk-taking efforts?

To evaluate if the bet is worth taking, let's start by supposing that we are willing to put an explicit cost on the increase in the probability of distress resulting from betting on certain markets. In that case, the trade-off for evaluating a bet for the company becomes fairly simple: the expected profit from the bet must exceed the increase in the probability of distress multiplied by the expected cost of distress.[20] Thus, a bet that has a positive expected value and no effect on the probability of distress is one that the firm should take. But a bet with positive expected profit that significantly increases the probability of financial distress may not appear profitable if the costs of a bad outcome are too large. In such cases, it makes sense for the firm to think about using risk management to reduce the probability of distress. By hedging, management may be able to achieve a reduction in cashflow variability that is large enough that an adverse outcome of the bet will not create financial distress.

Given that management has decided that the bet is worth taking, how does it evaluate the outcome of the strategy? Consider first the case of our firm AAA discussed earlier. Recall that this firm is not concerned about lower-tail outcomes and thus has no reason to hedge. When evaluating the outcome of the bet in this case, the appropriate benchmark is the expected gain *adjusted for risk*. It is not enough that the bet ends up earning more than the risk-free rate or even more than the firm's cost of capital. To add value for the company's shareholders the bet must earn a return that is higher than investors' expected return on other investments of comparable risk.

For example, there is considerable evidence that holding currencies of high-interest rate countries earns returns that, on average, exceed the risk-free rate. This excess return most likely represents "normal" compensation for bearing some kind of risk – say, the higher inflation and interest-rate volatility associated with high interest rate countries. And because such a strategy is thus *expected* to earn excess returns, it would not make sense to reward a corporate treasury for earning excess returns in this way. The treasury takes risks when it pursues that strategy, and the firm's shareholders expect to be compensated for these risks. Thus, it is only the amount by which the treasury exceeds the expected return – or the "abnormal return" – that represents *economic profit* for the corporation.

So, the abnormal or excess return should be the measure for evaluating bets by company AAA. But now let's turn to the case of company BBB, where the expected increase in volatility from the bet is also expected to raise the probability of costly lower-tail outcomes. In such a case, as we saw earlier, management should probably hedge to reduce the probability of financial trouble to acceptable levels. At the same time, however, top management should also consider subjecting its bets to an even higher standard of profitability to compensate shareholders for any associated increase in expected financial distress costs.

How much higher should it be? One method would be to assume that, instead of hedging, the firm raises additional equity capital to support the expected increase in volatility associated with the bet. In that case, the bet would be expected to produce the same risk-adjusted return on capital as the bet taken by company AAA, but on a larger amount of imputed "risk" capital.[21]

In sum, when devising a compensation scheme for those managers entrusted with making the firm's bets, it is critical to structure their incentive payments so that they are encouraged to take only those bets that are expected to increase shareholder wealth. Managers should not be compensated for earning average returns when taking larger than average risks. They should be compensated only for earning more than what their shareholders could earn on their own when bearing the same amount of risk.

This approach does not completely eliminate the problem discussed earlier caused by incentives for individuals to stand out in large organisations by taking risks. But traditional compensation schemes only reinforce this problem. If a risk-taker simply receives a bonus for making gains, he has incentives to take random bets because he gets a fraction of his gains while the firm bears the losses. Evaluating managers' performance against a risk-adjusted benchmark can help discourage risk-taking that is not justified by comparative advantage by making it more difficult for the risk-taker to make money by taking random bets.

Conclusion

This chapter presents a theory of risk management that attempts to go beyond the "variance-minimisation" model that dominates most academic discussions of corporate risk management. I argue that the primary goal of risk management is to eliminate the probability of costly lower-tail outcomes – those that would cause financial distress or make a company unable to carry out its investment strategy. (In this sense, risk management can be viewed as the purchase of well-out-of-the-money put options designed to limit downside risk.) Moreover, by eliminating downside risk and reducing the expected costs of financial trouble, risk management can also help move companies toward their optimal capital and ownership structure. For, besides increasing corporate debt capacity, the reduction of downside risk could also encourage larger equity stakes for managers by shielding their investments from "uncontrollables".

This chapter also departs from standard finance theory in suggesting that some companies may have a comparative advantage in bearing certain financial market risks – an advantage that derives from information it acquires through its normal business activities. Although such specialised information may occasionally lead some companies to take speculative positions in commodities or currencies, it is more likely to encourage selective hedging, a practice in which the risk manager's view of future price movements influences the percentage of the exposure that is hedged. This kind of hedging, while certainly containing potential for abuse, may also represent a value-adding form of risk-taking for many companies.

But, to the extent that such view-taking becomes an accepted part of a company's risk management programme, it is important to evaluate managers' bets on a risk-adjusted basis and relative to the market. If managers want to behave like money managers, they should be evaluated like money managers.

1 *Culp and Miller (1995), p. 122. For the central idea of this chapter, I am indebted to Culp and Miller's discussion of Holbrook Working's "carrying-charge" theory of commodity hedging. It is essentially Working's notion – and Culp and Miller's elaboration of it – that I attempt in this chapter to generalise into a broader theory of risk management based on comparative advantage in risk-bearing.*

2 *The Wharton School and The Chase Manhattan Bank, NA (February 1994),* Survey of Derivative Usage Among US Non-Financial Firms.

3 *Dolde (1993), pp. 33–41.*

4 *Dolde (1993), p. 39.*

5 *Mello and Parsons (1995).*

6 *More precisely, Culp and Miller's analysis shows that, ignoring any complications arising from basis risk and the daily mark-to-market requirement for futures, over the 10-year period each rolled-over futures contract would have eventually corresponded to an equivalent quantity of oil delivered to customers.*

7 *See Culp and Miller (1995), 7(4), p. 63.*

8 *See* Risk *magazine, October 1995, p. 11.*

9 *For a discussion of the benefits of corporate hedging, see Smith and Stulz.*

10 *This argument is made in Froot, Scharfstein and Stein (1993).*

11 *The discussion in this section and the next draws heavily on Smith and Stulz (1985), cited in footnote 9.*

12 *For a good example of this kind of selective hedging policy, see the comments by John Van Roden, Chief Financial Officer of Lukens, Inc., in his 1995 article "Bank of America Roundtable on Corporate Risk Management". As a stainless steel producer, one of the company's principal inputs is nickel; and Lukens' policy is to allow its view of nickel prices to influence how much of its nickel exposure it hedges. By contrast, although it may have views of interest rates or FX exposures, such views play no role in hedging those exposures.*

13 *See Braas, and Bralver (1990).*

14 *Tufano (1996).*

15 *Smith and Stulz (1985).*

16 *Additional empirical support for the importance of the relation between the option component of managerial compensation contracts and corporate risk-taking was provided in a recent study of S&Ls that changed their organisational form from mutual ownership to stock ownership. The study finds that those "converted" S&Ls, where management has options, choose to increase their one-year gaps and, hence, their*

exposure to interest rates. The study also shows that the greater the percentage of their interest rate exposure on S&L hedges, the larger the credit risk it takes on. The authors of the study interpret this finding to argue, as I do here, that risk management allows firms to increase their exposures to some risks by reducing other risks and thus limiting total firm risk. See Schrandt and Unal (1996).

17 *Although Tufano's study does not find that firms that hedge have systematically higher leverage ratios, it does find that companies that hedge less have higher cash balances.*

18 *For a discussion of the role of hedging in creating an LBO-like structure, see my 1990 study "Managerial Discretion and Optimal Financing Policies",* Journal of Financial Economics, *pp. 3–26.*

19 *For an illustration of the use of Monte Carlo analysis in risk management, see Stulz and Williamson, "Identifying and Quantifying Exposures".*

20 *One possible approach to quantifying the* expected *costs of financial distress involves the concept of American "binary options" and the associated option pricing models. An example of a binary option is one that would pay a fixed amount, say, US$10, if the stock price of IBM falls below US$40. Unlike standard American put options, which when exercised pay an amount equal to (the strike price of) US$40 minus the actual price, the holder of a binary option receives either US$10 or nothing, and exercises when the stock price crosses the US$40 barrier. Such options can be priced using modified option pricing models.*

The connection between binary options and risk management is this: the present value of a binary option is a function of two major variables: the probability that firm value will fall below a certain level (in this case, US$40) and the payoff in the event of such a drop in value (US$10). By substituting for the US$10 payoff its own estimate of how much additional *value the firm is likely to lose* once its value falls to a certain level and gets into financial trouble, *management can then estimate the expected present value of such costs using a binary option pricing model. This is the number that could be set against the expected profit from the firm's bet in order to evaluate whether to go ahead with the bet.*

21 *The amount of implicit "risk capital" (as opposed to the actual cash capital) backing an activity can be calculated as a function of the expected volatility (as measured by the standard deviation) of the activity's cashflow returns. For the distinction between risk capital and cash capital, and a method for calculating risk capital, see Merton and Perold (1993). For one company's application of a similar method for calculating risk capital, see Zaik* et al. *(1996). For a theoretical model of capital budgeting that takes into account firm-specific risks, see K. Froot and J. Stein, "Risk Management, Capital Budgeting, and Capital Structure Policy for Financial Institutions: An Integrated Approach", Working Paper 96-030, Harvard Business School Division of Research.*

BIBLIOGRAPHY

Braas, A., and C. Bralver, 1990, "How Trading Rooms Really Make Money?", *Journal of Applied Corporate Finance*, 2(4).

Culp, C. L. and M. Miller, 1995, "Hedging in the Theory of Corporate Finance: A Reply to Our Critics", *Journal of Applied Corporate Finance*, 8(1); reprinted as Chapter 14 of the present volume.

Dolde, W., 1993, "The Trajectory of Corporate Financial Risk Management", *Journal of Applied Corporate Finance*, 6, (Autumn), pp. 33–41.

Froot, K., D. Scharfstein and J. Stein, 1993, "Risk Management: Coordinating Corporate Investment and Financing Policies", *Journal of Finance*, 48, pp. 1629–58; reprinted as Chapter 7 of the present volume.

Mello, A., and J. E. Parsons, 1995, "Maturity Structure of a Hedge Matters: Lessons from the Metallgesellschaft Debacle", *Journal of Applied Corporate Finance*, 8(1), pp. 106–20; reprinted as Chapter 12 of the present volume.

Merton, R. C., and A. Perold, 1993, "Theory of Risk Capital for Financial Firms", *Journal of Applied Corporate Finance*, 6(3).

Schrandt, C. M. and H. Unal, 1996, "Coordinated Risk Management: On and Off-balance Sheet Hedging and Thrift Conversion", working paper, The Wharton School, University of Pennsylvania.

Smith, C. W., and R. Stulz, 1985, "The Determinants of Firms' Hedging Policies", *Journal of Financial and Quantitative Analysis*, 20, pp. 391–405; reprinted as Chapter 6 of the present volume.

Stultz, R., 1990, "Managerial Discretion and Optimal Financing Policies", *Journal of Financial Economics*, pp. 3–26.

Stulz, R., and R. Williamson, "Identifying and Quantifying Exposures", in *Financial Risk and the Corporate Treasury* (London: Risk Publications).

Tufano, P., 1996, "Who Manages Risk? An Empirical Examination of the Risk Management Practices of the Gold Mining Industry", *Journal of Finance*, (September).

Van Roden, J., 1995, "Bank of America Roundtable on Corporate Risk Management", *Journal of Applied Corporate Finance*, 8(3).

Zaik, E. *et al*, 1996, "RAROC at Bank of America: From Theory to Practice", *Journal of Applied Corporate Finance*, 9(2).

THE MGRM CONTROVERSY – HEDGING OBJECTIVES DO MATTER

9

Metallgesellschaft and the Economics of Synthetic Storage*

Christopher L. Culp and Merton H. Miller

The University of Chicago

MG Refining & Marketing, Inc (MGRM), a US subsidiary of the German industrial conglomerate Metallgesellschaft AG (MG AG), is a contender for the world's record in derivatives-related losses - US$1.3 billion by press accounts at year-end 1993. Unlike many of its rivals for that record, however, MGRM was not using derivatives as part of a treasury function, with a view to enhancing the return on an investment portfolio or to lowering the firm's interest expense.

MGRM's derivatives were part and parcel of its *marketing* programme, under which it offered long-term customers firm price guarantees for up to ten years on gasoline, heating oil and diesel fuel purchased from MGRM. The firm hedged its resulting exposure to spot price increases to a considerable extent with futures contracts. Because futures contracts must be marked to market daily, cash drains must be incurred to meet variation margin payments when futures prices fall. After several consecutive months of falling prices in the autumn of 1993, MGRM's German parent reacted to the substantial margin calls by liquidating the hedge.

The top management of the parent corporation has yet to make clear why it chose to unwind the futures leg of the hedge while the fixed-price contracts were still in force. That MGRM had no way of financing the margin payments, except on distress terms, cannot be the explanation. Even if MGRM had been locked out of public capital markets, it hardly needed to go "hat-in-hand" to strangers unfamiliar with its strategy. Over 100 of the world's leading banks were *already* creditors to MG AG; and Deutsche Bank, one of the world's largest financial institutions, was both a major creditor *and* a major stockholder of MGRM's parent. If new sources of outside credit had to be tapped, the programme should have been "self-financing" because the flow contracts increased in expected value as oil prices fell. Other ways of staunching the cash drains on the futures, while still remaining hedged, were also available had the firm really been facing a binding cash constraint.

Perhaps the supervisory board of the parent believed that MGRM was not hedging, but "speculating" on oil prices. The team the supervisory board called in to liquidate the futures positions, after all, had resolved an earlier oil derivatives fiasco for Deutsche Bank - the notorious Klöckner speculative episode of some six years before.[1] Possibly the supervisory board of the parent misinterpreted the appeals by its MGRM subsidiary for more cash as "doubling-up" or, at the least, as the telltale sign of a business failure in the making. Or perhaps the supervisory board had other corporate motives of its own for ending the programme.[2]

Whatever the reason, the decision to liquidate the futures leg proved unfortunate on several counts, turning "paper losses" into realised losses, sending a distress signal to MGRM's over-the-counter (OTC) derivatives counterparties, and leaving MGRM exposed to rising prices on its remaining fixed-price contracts.

**Originally published in the* Journal of Applied Corporate Finance *7(4) (1995), pp. 62-76. For comments on earlier drafts (under various titles), the authors owe thanks to Malcolm Basing, Halsey Bullen, Don Chew, George Constantinides, Kent Daniel, Dean Furbush, Ken French, Steve Hanke, Steve Kaplan, Randy Kroszner, Bill Margrabe, Mark Mitchell, Todd Petzel, Richard Roll, José Scheinkman, Charles Smithson and to a number of industry and derivatives specialists, many of whom prefer to remain anonymous (even those who agree with us!). Special thanks are due to Barbara Kavanagh for helpful discussions on credit risk and funding risk.*

In this chapter we explore in more detail the economics of MGRM's delivery/hedging programme, a strategy aptly dubbed "synthetic storage".[3] But despite the frequent references throughout to MGRM, this chapter is not a case study in the usual sense. Too many essential facts about the programme and its liquidation have still not been made public and perhaps never will be, given that one of the key lawsuits in the case has been sent to private arbitration.[4] Our focus here will be mainly on the economic logic underlying a synthetic storage programme like MGRM's. In particular, we show such a strategy is neither inherently unprofitable nor fatally flawed, *provided* top management understands the programme and the long-term funding commitments necessary to make it work.

Did MGRM's marketing/hedging programme make economic sense?

MG'S MARKETING PROGRAMME

MG AG is a 112-year-old enterprise owned largely by institutional investors, including Deutsche Bank AG, Dresdner Bank AG, Daimler-Benz, Allianz and the Kuwait Investment Authority. At the end of 1992, MG AG had 251 subsidiaries with activities ranging over trade, engineering and financial services. Its subsidiary responsible for US petroleum marketing was MGRM.

In December 1991, MGRM recruited from Louis Dreyfus Energy Corporation Arthur Benson and his management team, whose key marketing strategy was to offer long-term customers firm price guarantees for five, and in some cases up to ten, years on gasoline, heating oil and diesel fuel purchased from MGRM. So successful, apparently, were these marketing efforts that by September 1993 MGRM had sold forward the equivalent of over 150 million barrels of petroleum products in its flagship, long-term "flow delivery" contracts.[5] In conjunction with those forward short positions, MGRM entered long into futures and OTC derivatives, such as commodity swaps.

MGRM's derivatives positions protected the firm and its creditors against the *principal* risk the programme faced - that is, the risk that rising spot prices would erode the gross profit margins on its fixed-price forward sales. Price protection *per se*, however, need not be presumed the primary motivation for the hedging. The combined delivery/hedging strategy was intended to maximise the expected profits from marketing and storing oil products, a field in which MGRM possessed special expertise and superior information, without having to gamble on directional movements in spot prices, an activity in which MGRM had no such comparative advantage.[6]

The bulk of MGRM's futures positions were on the New York Mercantile Exchange (Nymex) in the most liquid contracts of between one and three months to maturity based on New York harbour regular unleaded gasoline, New York harbour No. 2 heating oil and West Texas Intermediate (WTI) grade light, sweet crude oil.[7,8] Liquidity was an important consideration in MGRM's overall strategy, because it lowered the cost of managing its positions to meet seasonal changes in the demand and supply of heating oil and gasoline.[9]

Most of MGRM's fixed-price contracts also contained an "option" clause allowing counterparties to terminate their contracts early if market prices surged above the fixed price at which MGRM was selling the oil product. Why MGRM included these sell-back options in the first place will become clearer later. But because contingent liabilities of that kind can raise the spectre of "runs" on a supplier, MGRM sought to reassure its customers by contractually agreeing to remain fully hedged[10] - a policy it was prepared to follow for the separate reasons already noted.

HEDGING LONG-DATED OBLIGATIONS WITH SHORT-DATED FUTURES[11]

Borrowing short and lending long is an oft-cited recipe for financial disaster. But for MGRM, unlike, say, the S&Ls of the 1980s, or the more recent episode in Orange County, California - an episode purportedly surpassing even MGRM in losses incurred - maturity mismatch was not the real culprit.

Counter-intuitive as it may seem, a firm *can* use short-dated futures to hedge its long-term delivery commitments against spot oil price increases simply by purchasing a "stack" of short-dated futures equivalent to its remaining delivery obligations. Note, in this connection, that we are not here saying (nor have we ever said) that such a stacked hedge is a *perfect* hedge, whatever that may mean.[12] The strategy involves risks other than the principal one of market price risk, and those additional risks will be considered in due course later.

The mechanics of a stacked hedging strategy are straightforward. On the first delivery date, the firm buys in the spot market for delivery, offsets all its maturing futures contracts, and re-establishes a long position in the new front-month (ie, one-month) futures contract -

this time, though, with its long futures positions reduced by the amount delivered on its flow contracts. On the next settlement date, the hedger again decreases the size of its futures position by the amount delivered and rolls the rest forward to the next maturing one-month futures contract. And so on, month by month.[13,14]

A three-period example

To convince yourself that such a stacked hedging strategy can protect a firm's gross profit margin, consider the following three-period example in which a firm enters fixed-price flow contracts to sell 1,000X barrels of oil monthly for US$20/barrel.[15] Suppose prices happen to rise over time as follows:

$$S_0 = \$17 \qquad S_1 = \$18 \qquad S_2 = \$19 \qquad S_3 = \$20$$

where S_t denotes the spot price at time t. Given those prices, we can approximate the time t prices of the futures contract in the stack by invoking the familiar "cost of carry" formula:[16]

$$F_{t,t+1} = S_t[1 + b_{t,t+1}] = S_t[1 + r_{t,t+1} + z_{t,t+1} - d_{t,t+1}]$$

where the one-period "basis", $b_{t,t+1}$, includes the interest cost of physical storage $r_{t,t+1}$, the physical cost of storage $z_{t,t+1}$, the "convenience yield" of having physical inventories on hand $d_{t,t+1}$, and all assumed known at the start of period t and all expressed as a fraction of the time t spot price.

Suppose further that the current one-period interest rate, storage cost and convenience yield are

$$r_{0,1} = 0.005 \qquad z_{0,1} = 0.01 \qquad d_{0,1} = 0.015$$

and that those values happen to change over time as follows:

$$r_{1,2} = 0.008 \quad r_{2,3} = 0.01$$
$$z_{1,2} = 0.015 \quad z_{2,3} = 0.02$$
$$d_{1,2} = d_{2,3} = 0.007$$

Given these values for the above variables and the assumed path for spot prices, the one-period futures prices and bases will evolve as follows:

$$F_{0,1} = \$17.00 \quad F_{1,2} = \$18.29 \quad F_{2,3} = \$19.44$$
$$b_{0,1} = 0.0 \quad b_{1,2} = 0.016 \quad b_{2,3} = 0.023$$

When the basis is positive and thus the current futures price is higher than the current spot price, the market is said to be in "contango" for that period. Although not typical of oil markets, we are assuming in this example, to make the role of storage costs stand out most sharply, that the market moves unexpectedly into contango at time 1 and stays there.

Table 1 shows the cashflow and income statements over the three periods for a firm selling 1000X barrels of oil each period for US$20/barrel. The firm holds initially three futures maturing at month one, then rolls into two contracts maturing at month two, and finally into one contract maturing at month three.

Table 1. Hedging long-dated obligations with short-dated futures

	Cash flows (US$)			Income (US$)		
	(1)	(2)	(3)	(4)	(5)	(6)
Month	Spot[a]	Futures[b]	Net cashflow	Gross flow contract income[c]	Net cost of carry[d]	Net income
1	2,000X	3,000X	5,000X	3,000X	0X	3,000X
2	1,000X	1,420X	2,420X	3,000X	(580X)	2,420X
3	0X	560X	560X	3,000X	(440X)	2,560X
Total	3,000X	4,980X	7,980X	9,000X	(1,020X)	7,980X

[a] $1{,}000X \times (20 - S_t)$
[b] (No. of contracts) $\times X \times 1{,}000 \times (F_{t,t} - F_{t-1,t})$
[c] $1{,}000X \times (20 - S_0)$
[d] (No. of contracts) $\times X \times 1{,}000 \times (S_{t-1} - F_{t-1,t})$

In month one, for example, the firm delivers 1,000X barrels at US$20/barrel on its flow contract, obtaining that oil by buying in the spot market at US$18/barrel. Its spot cashflow (column (1)) thus is US$2,000X. At the same time, the firm offsets the three futures it had previously initiated in month zero at a price of US$17.00/barrel, re-establishing at US$18.29/ barrel two new long positions maturing in month two. Because spot and futures prices must be equal at maturity, its month one futures cashflow (column (2)) is US$3,000X = 3X × 1,000 × [18–17].

Column (4) shows the gross margin on the flow contract. Because the firm hedged when the spot price was US$17/barrel, it "locks in" a gross margin per period of US$3,000X. The net cost of carry (Column (5)) reflects the storage costs the firm effectively pays each month when it rolls over its stack of futures. At the end of month one, for example, the firm offsets its three futures at US$18/barrel and re-establishes a position of two futures at US$18.29/ barrel. Its implicit storage cost for the second month thus is US$580X = 2X × 1,000 × [18–18.29]. The *net* margin for the hedger (Column (6)) is thus its gross margin from the fixed-price deliveries less the implicit cost of storing oil using futures.

Note also that while the hedger's monthly net margin over the entire period need not equal its monthly net cashflow, the firm's *total* net margin equals the *total* net cashflow, regardless of spot price movements. In this sense, the firm's net worth is indeed fully hedged against spot price risk.

THE BENEFITS AND COSTS OF SYNTHETIC STORAGE

Our example above has been constructed deliberately with the basis positive and rising. In oil markets, however, unlike most commodity markets, the basis is typically *negative*; that is, the spot price is greater than the futures price because the convenience yield often exceeds the cost of physical storage plus the interest cost of storage. In the case of crude oil, for example, the front-month basis, defined as $F_{t,t+1} - S_t / S_t$, averaged -0.0082 over the period May 1983 to September 1994; and for heating oil, the proportional basis averaged -0.0096 from January 1980 to September 1994.[17]

The negative basis, usually referred to as "backwardation", occurs when the current demand for oil is high relative to current supply. Because firms may need physical oil on hand to avoid inventory stock-outs, spot prices rise above futures prices to reward firms for "lending" their inventory to the current spot market, as it were.[18] When the market is in backwardation, a stacked hedger remains hedged against spot price changes, but its net margin is *higher* than the gross margin to reflect the negative net cost of carry. The firm is still paying the cost of storage, of course, but the presence of those costs is masked by the high convenience yield.

The stacked hedging strategy of synthetic oil storage does differ from actual physical storage in some important respects, however. In the physical storage strategy, the firm pays its own marginal costs of storage and receives its own marginal convenience yield. By contrast, under the synthetic storage strategy, the firm pays the marginal storage cost net of the convenience yield for the marginal physical storer. A firm expecting its own marginal cost of storage to be higher than the marginal cost of storage in the futures price would thus be better off *ex ante* hedging with futures rather than physical storage. By the same token, fully-integrated producing firms with lower marginal costs of storage - such as Exxon with tank farms around the world - typically find it more efficient to store physically rather than synthetically.

WERE "ROLLOVER COSTS" A BASIC FLAW IN THE STRATEGY?

Critics have argued that "the crushing impact of [MGRM's] monthly rollover costs"[19] made MGRM's hedging method a "basically flawed trading strategy".[20] The rollover cost is the difference between the price of the maturing futures contract and the price at which the new futures position is established times the size of the stack. As long as the rollovers are in front-month contracts and occur near the maturity date, the price of the expiring futures contract is essentially the spot price because the two must converge at maturity. The rollover cost is thus just the basis expressed as a lump-sum dollar value. In our previous illustration, for example, the time 1 rollover cost per contract would be $F_{1,1} - F_{1,2} = S_1 - F_{1,2} =$ US$18 – US$18.29, or a cost of US$0.29. (Adjusted for the size of the stack, this total rollover cost of US$580X appears in Column (5) of Table 1 in the row corresponding to month two.)

Because the front-month rollover cost per contract is simply the basis in another form, expected rollover costs are quite literally the marginal expected implicit costs of interest and physical storage less the convenience yield built into futures prices. As noted earlier, the one-month net cost of storage and interest *averaged* less than zero over the last ten years. Even so, some critics believe the decision to liquidate MGRM's futures hedge was justified because those costs were becoming excessive in the autumn of 1993.[21] And indeed, by historical standards, the rollover costs then may well have been perceived as unusually high. For crude oil, the November 1993 mid-month rollover cost was US$0.33/barrel compared to a mean over the entire sample of -US$0.2091/barrel, placing that month in the 86th percentile of the historical sample. For heating oil, the corresponding values were US$0.0021/gallon, -US$.0076/gallon and the 56th percentile; and for gasoline, US$.0187/gallon, -US$.0082/gallon and the 89th percentile.[22] (See Appendix 2.)

We remind readers, however, that the liquidation of the hedge, though relieving MGRM of the net costs of oil storage, exposed it instead to spot price risk on its still-outstanding flow contracts. And spot price risk is huge relative to basis risk. In a regression of front-month futures prices ($F_{t,t+1}$) on the contemporaneous spot price S_t, the value of R^2 will measure the fraction of the variance in futures prices explained by the variation in spot prices. For crude oil (May 1983 to February 1994), the R^2 was 0.99, for heating oil (January 1980 to September 1994) the value was 0.96, and for gasoline (December 1984 to September 1994) the value was 0.95. Or, to put it the other way around, no more than 1–5% of the historical variation in futures prices can be traced to variations over time in the basis.[23]

Not only do variations in the basis thus account for little of the intertemporal variation in futures prices, but we also know that the lump-sum dollar basis (ie, the rollover cost) varies inversely with spot prices. For WTI crude, heating oil and gasoline, the simple correlation coefficients of each basis with spot prices were -0.359, -0.091 and -0.453, respectively, for the sample periods noted above. If, therefore, the supervisory board's decision to liquidate the hedge in mid-December 1993 was done to avoid rollover costs, that decision turned out to be doubly-cursed when crude and heating oil prices rose *and* rollover costs fell in early 1994 – triply-cursed, in fact, because the futures positions were unwound in mid-December 1993 *after* the December rollovers had already occurred.

Finally, critics of MGRM rarely seem to recognise that rollover costs by themselves tell us nothing about the profitability of a *combined* delivery/hedging strategy. A combined delivery/hedging programme of the kind MGRM was following must not be judged by the storage or related costs it happens to incur *over any short interval of time*. What counts, rather, is the programme's profit potential over the long haul or, as finance specialists might prefer to put it, its expected net present value. How to compute the requisite net present value for a *hedged* delivery programme is far from obvious, but we sketch out the method for doing so in the next section; the mathematical details are published elsewhere.[24]

THE MARKETING/HEDGING DECISION AS A CAPITAL BUDGETING PROBLEM

Calculating the net present value of a combined delivery/hedging programme would be simplicity itself, of course, in a futures market with a complete set of contracts covering every maturity for which the flow commitments had been made. As long as the fixed price for deliveries in period T exceeds the current T-period futures price, the locked-in *net* profit on the period T delivery is precisely the difference between the two prices. By going long X T-period futures contracts for each 1,000X barrels of period T delivery commitments, MGRM would both have hedged the delivery commitments *and* reduced basis or rollover risk (but, by the same token, also giving up any rollover gains). The set of futures contracts actually available, however, is *not* rich enough to support such a strategy – a pure "strip", as it is called in the trade. Nymex has no liquid contracts for crude beyond 18 months to maturity and a year to maturity in heating oil.[25]

Though futures contracts are not available for all maturities, their prices can be approximated by repeated application of the cost of carry formula. In particular, the presumptive basis for a T-period futures contract would be the *expected* value of the storage and interest cost net of convenience yield over T periods. If the cash receipt on a period-T fixed-price delivery discounted at that expected basis exceeds the current price of oil, the programme has a positive *expected* net present value.[26] Stated more formally, a firm will enter into a hedged N-period fixed-price delivery programme to sell one unit of oil each period if the programme has a positive expected NPV at time $t = 0$ – that is, if

$$E_t(NPV_t) = \sum_{j=t+1}^{N} \frac{K_j}{1+E_t(b_{t,j})} - (N-t) \times S_t > 0 \qquad (1)$$

where K_j is the fixed price of a time j delivery, S_t is the time-t spot price, and $E_t(b_{t,j})$ is the basis expected to prevail from time t to j evaluated with information available at time t.

Although different hedging strategies may have different values for the $E_t(b_{t,j})$ terms in equation (1), we show elsewhere that under plausible assumptions about equilibrium futures pricing, MGRM's strategy must have the same *expected* NPV at time 0 as a pure strip.[27] *Realised* outcomes may differ from their expectations, however. Some strategies may thus have higher or lower net profits *ex post*, depending on how the bases happen to evolve over time relative to initial conditional expectations.

That the expected NPV might be positive for MGRM does not mean, of course, that the expected NPV is necessarily negative for MGRM's customers. MGRM's customers, almost by definition, have very high marginal storage costs and place a high value on security of delivery.[28] Those customers might have opted for synthetic storage themselves, of course, but as episodic "do-it-yourself" users of derivatives have come to recognise, risk management professionals have a considerable comparative advantage in those matters.

THE ECONOMIC FUNCTION OF THE SELL-BACK OPTIONS

The expected value of the programme can be re-calculated each period to reflect the arrival of new information. In the example above, we assumed that the market moved at time 1 unexpectedly into contango, which would change the discount rates used in expected NPV calculations *after* time 0. Using the value of $b_{1,2}$ realised at time 0 for $E_1(b_{1,2})$, 0.016, and assuming $E_1(b_{1,3}) = 0.032 = 2 \times 0.016$, the expected NPV of the programme *conditional* on information available at time 1 is

$$E_1(NPV_1) = \left[\left(\frac{20}{1.016} + \frac{20}{1.032}\right) - 18 \times 2\right] \times 1{,}000X = \$3{,}065X$$

The conditional expected NPV at time 2 using the still-higher one-period basis prevailing then is US$550X. Despite the two unexpected increases in the basis, the conditional expected NPV of the programme is positive at the beginning of all three periods.

Now suppose instead that spot prices beyond period 0 were to increase more rapidly than before, say, as

$$S_0 = \$17 \quad S_1 = \$19 \quad S_2 = \$21 \quad S_3 = \$23$$

The initial expected NPV of the programme would still be positive (US$9,000X), and hence a rational corporation would again accept the policy at time 0. The conditional expected NPV is also positive at time 1 (US$1,065X). But now the conditional expected NPV of the programme would be negative at time 2 (-US$1,550X). A firm committed to the combined delivery/hedging programme at time 0, though still technically hedged, would then seem to be profiting handsomely on the stack of futures but "losing money" on the flow contracts. If the firm could possibly end the programme by "buying out its customers" for *less* than it expects to pay for servicing them, it would.

Bilaterally-negotiated contracts cannot be unwound at zero cost, however, especially on favourable terms. Getting out of such contracts means negotiating their unwinding with customers on a case-by-case basis. The Master Agreements of the International Swaps and Derivatives Association (ISDA), for example, allow counterparties to choose a method of calculating "close-out settlement values" in the event OTC derivatives terminate early. In the absence of an "event of termination or default", the unwinding counterparty must obtain the consent of the other party and negotiate the terms of the unwind, not always an easy or inexpensive task.[29,30]

As a substitute for negotiated unwinds under a master agreement, MGRM chose to add the early exercise options to its flow contracts. These options take effect when the front-month futures price rises above the fixed delivery price in the flow contract. On exercising their options, customers receive a pre-specified monetary payment equal to one-half the difference between the front-month futures price and the fixed price in the flow contract times the total volume remaining on the flow contract. The sell-back options thus not only specify in advance the method of calculating a "close-out price", but also eliminate the need for negotiating the close-out itself.

Although customers might wish to exercise their sell-back options if they expect spot prices in the future to fall, they might well wish to do so even if they regarded a surge in spot prices as permanent. Remember that they must compare the immediate cash payment on exercise with the *present value* of expected future differences between spot prices and the delivery prices over the remaining life of the contract. And if the customers, unlike MGRM, are neither hedged nor otherwise well-diversified corporations, their discount rates must reflect the risk of changing spot prices as well as their own time-value of money. In any event, the likelihood that customers will exercise their buy-back options at some time in the life of their contracts cannot be ignored in appraising MGRM's synthetic storage programme. Computing the exact present value to MGRM of those embedded "reverse options" is a task of great technical difficulty, but whether the exercise rights rested with MGRM or its customers, the value of those options would clearly be substantial in a world in which spot prices are highly volatile. By the same token, the presence of the options substantially reduces the effective tenor of the flow delivery contracts.[31]

THE EXPECTED NET PRESENT VALUE WHEN PRICES FALL

When prices fall, a repeat of the previous calculations holding the expected bases constant would find the conditional expected net present value for MGRM actually rising, suggesting that a company in MGRM's position should be even more anxious to continue the programme. This may seem paradoxical, of course, because of cash drains on the futures stack and management's possible reaction to them. Those cash drains, however, are essentially *sunk costs* at this point and, as such, should have no effect on current decisions about whether to *continue* the programme. And because the firm is still hedged, those costs are not even sunk irrevocably but will eventually be recovered by the fixed-price deliveries over time.

Calculating the conditional expected NPV for MGRM when prices fall *and* the bases change is more difficult, because the effects are at least partially offsetting. To separate the effects, suppose first the term structure undergoes a uniform, parallel downward shift as spot prices fall. The discount rate in equation (1) would be unaffected, and the expected net present value would rise one-for-one with the fall in the spot price. When prices fall, however, prices of short-term futures typically will fall by more than deferred prices, giving rise to the "horizontal tornadoes" or "diving boards" about which oil derivatives specialists never cease to prattle. But precisely because these effects are concentrated at the short end, their impact on the conditional expected NPV is limited. They show up essentially as a temporary rise in *expected* rollover costs, thus reducing the gross present value of *near-term* deliveries. If the basis were assumed to remain at its high throughout the life of the contracts, the discounting effect would eventually overwhelm the spot-price effect for deliveries as well. But more reasonable estimates of the expected bases for deferred deliveries, calculated from historical market norms, would leave the expected NPV for the deferred deliveries and the programme as a whole positive.[32]

CUSTOMER INCENTIVES AND CREDIT RISK

Though MGRM would have no obvious incentive to terminate its flow contracts early when prices fall, its *customers* might. The sell-back options, however, specify no termination rights in the event of price *declines*. Customers could unwind their contracts after a price decline only by buying their way out; but they would have no positive incentive to do so unless MGRM offered to settle for less than the present value of the customers' purchase obligations. And indeed, that appears exactly what MGRM did in January 1994 when a new management awakened only belatedly to its naked price exposure following the futures liquidation. Despite the positive gross present value of the flow contracts to MGRM, it offered customers the right to terminate their contracts *with no close-out payment to MGRM* – "leaving money on the table", as they say on Wall Street.[33] How much money new management effectively burned in this fashion was still unknown at the time of this writing, but the cancelled contracts could have been for as much as 60 million barrels.[34]

Although some customers not released from their contracts might well have had incentives to "walk away" when prices fell, we remain unconvinced that customer credit risk could justify the draconian relief strategy of liquidating the futures hedge. Even in the face of price declines in 1993, no customer defaults have been documented. MGRM had stipulated in its flow contracts that none of its smaller customers could rely on MGRM for more than 20% – usually only 5–10% – of their annual required input purchases. Because MGRM was the only firm selling long-dated fixed-price delivery contracts, this ensured that at least 80% of the input

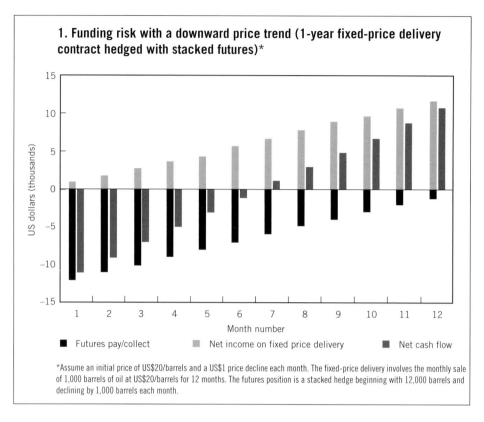

1. Funding risk with a downward price trend (1-year fixed-price delivery contract hedged with stacked futures)*

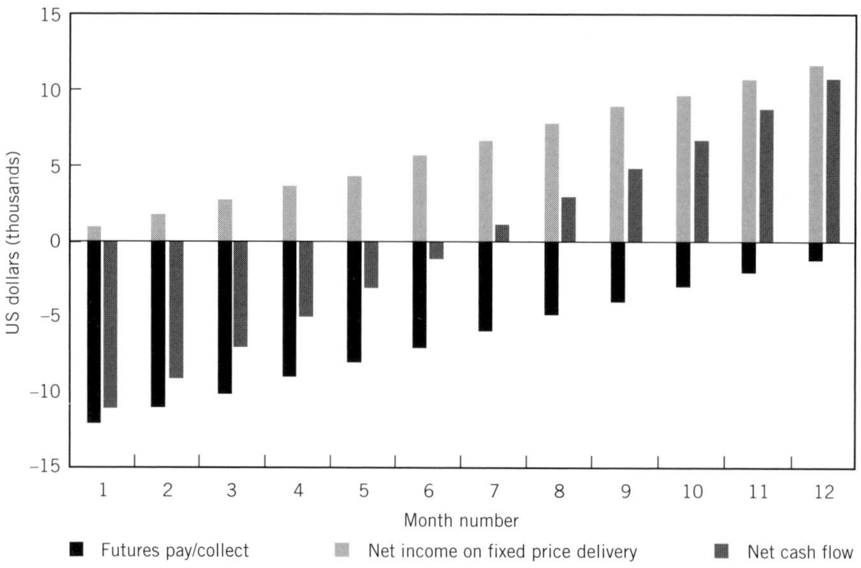

*Assume an initial price of US$20/barrels and a US$1 price decline each month. The fixed-price delivery involves the monthly sale of 1,000 barrels of oil at US$20/barrels for 12 months. The futures position is a stacked hedge beginning with 12,000 barrels and declining by 1,000 barrels each month.

purchases by those firms were being made at *variable* prices. Many of these smaller firms, moreover, were selling oil products at retail prices – far slower to adjust to market conditions than their wholesale input purchase prices.[35] Consequently, the smaller customers would be losing money on and thus might want to exit their flow contracts precisely when they are *making* money from the more than 80% of variable inputs purchased at the lower spot price. Nor should it be assumed in assessing the credit risks in MGRM's strategy that MGRM's customers were all of the "mom and pop" variety. MGRM's customer base also included large firms, Chrysler Corp, Browning-Ferris Industries Corp and Thornton Oil Corp among them.

SHOULD MGRM HAVE USED LONG-DATED FUTURES?

Exactly as in the short-dated stacked hedging strategy, MGRM could have held an amount of futures always equal to its remaining delivery obligations, but this time in contract months with deferred maturity dates. As before, MGRM would have to roll over its hedge every month. This time, however, the current position would be rolled into the new *deferred* contract. This strategy, like MGRM's, would have protected the firm against the risk of rising spot prices.[36]

But the long-dated futures strategy was not obviously a superior alternative for a programme as large as MGRM's. Volume and open interest are lower for longer-dated commodity futures contracts, so longer-dated futures would have had substantially higher transaction costs. Lower relative liquidity would also have made it difficult and much costlier for MGRM to switch its hedge between heating oil, gasoline and crude as seasonal conditions dictated. A long-dated stack would also still have to be rolled each month, often a costly and challenging task in a relatively illiquid contract.

Because long-dated futures prices are imperfectly correlated with front-month prices, moreover, using long-dated futures would have exposed MGRM to basis risk on its customer sell-back options – that is, when the customers exercised their options, the long-dated contract price might not have risen as much as the front-month price on which the options were written. Of course, one might imagine that MGRM might then have based the settlement value of the sell-back options on the deferred futures contract, but that would be to miss the point of those options. As with other options, the sell-back options are most valuable when prices are more volatile. In one sense, the spot price itself would have been the ideal asset on which to write the sell-back options, if indeed the concept of the "spot price" were better defined. Given the complexities of delivery grades, geography, liquidity and the like, however, using the front-month futures contract here, as elsewhere in commodity markets, is the best approach to defining the "spot commodity".

Was funding risk to blame?

"Funding risk," or liquidity risk, has been defined as "[t]he inability to meet cashflow obligations at an acceptable price as they become due..."[37] Funding risk is a natural suspect for MGRM's problems because futures hedging programmes can require substantial infusions of cash to meet variation margin calls when prices are falling. In 1993, oil and oil product prices fell precipitously after OPEC failed to reach agreements on its production quotas, and substantial margin payments were due from MGRM to Nymex.

THE FUNDING RISK OF A MARKETING PROGRAMME HEDGED WITH FUTURES

In Figure 1 we illustrate the funding risk that a stacked hedger faces when prices fall in a 12-month example (with a zero basis for simplicity). Assume the price of oil falls steadily from US$20/barrel by US$1 every month, and that margin calls are monthly. The cashflows are for a single flow contract to sell 1,000 barrels of WTI crude each month at US$20/barrel, and for a futures hedge of 12 contracts in the first month declining by one contract each subsequent month.

Note first that stacking creates a cashflow asymmetry over time between futures pays and collects and the net income on the fixed-price contract. Each US$1 oil price decrease (increase) between settlement dates triggers a pay (collect) on the futures position that is $12 - t + 1$ times larger than the net inflow (outflow) on the 12-month fixed-price contract, where t is the settlement month number. Thus, the cash requirements are largest in the early part of the programme when the stack is large and reverse later as deliveries occur.

Although Figure 1 is designed to depict the funding risk of stacked futures, it is important to keep in mind that cashflows of the same order of magnitude would be required on *any* futures strategy in which the entire remaining delivery commitment is hedged. The only difference is the less than perfect correlation between futures prices of all maturities. Because short-dated futures are more volatile than long-dated futures, the cash inflows and outflows on a short-dated stack may be larger than those on a long-dated stack, but only marginally so.

The large cash infusions the stacked hedging programme would require if prices fell can hardly have come as a surprise to the original management team at MGRM. You don't have to be a rocket scientist, after all, to prepare something like Figure 1. Given those likely cash drains, the team at MGRM would presumably not have maintained or expanded its programme in the summer and autumn of 1993 unless it thought it had firm assurances from its parent and bank creditors that a secure line of credit was there on which to draw. As things turned out, MGRM had no such firm commitment, though the reasons why are still in dispute (and in litigation).

HOW MIGHT THE CASH NEEDS HAVE BEEN FINANCED AT THE TIME?

The evidence suggests that funding risk alone was not responsible for the untimely end of MGRM's futures hedge; alternatives *were* available. That MGRM had no access to external financing, except on ruinous, distress terms, cannot be taken seriously. Even if MGRM had been locked out of public capital markets, it hardly needed to go "hat-in-hand" to strangers unfamiliar with its strategy. Over 100 of the world's leading banks were *already* creditors to MG AG; and Deutsche Bank and Dresdner Bank, two of the world's largest financial institutions, were both major creditors *and* major stockholders of MGRM's parent. And those very same creditors did agree, after all, on January 15, 1994, to a US$1.9 billion capital infusion to MG AG, raising the perplexing question of why that step was taken to cover the liquidation of the hedge rather than to continue financing it.[38]

If the expected net present value of the programme was positive and substantial, moreover, the programme as a whole should have been viewed as an asset by *any* would-be lenders.[39] Indeed, because the intrinsic asset value of the combined programme was locked-in, the programme was "self-financing" in the sense that the accreting gains on the flow contracts as oil prices fell should, in principle, have provided the economic equivalent of at least partial collateral to finance margin calls on the futures leg. Press accounts indicate that several banking institutions, including Chemical Bank and JP Morgan, made just such an offer to MGRM but were rebuffed by the new management team.[40] The puzzle thus remains as to why alternative sources of financing could not have been arranged.

Several authorities with whom we have discussed the possibility of collateralising the margin loan have expressed concerns that the flow contracts alone might not have been usable as collateral because of the inability to "perfect a lien" on forward contracts. If the contracts could not serve directly as collateral, an obvious alternative for firms like MGRM (assuming existing debt covenants allowed it) would be to sell the programme as a whole, as was done when the Development Finance Corp of New Zealand failed;[41] or, to spin off the *combined* delivery/hedging programme into a new subsidiary, as is routinely done with accounts receivable subsidiaries or issuers of "securitised products".[42] The stock of the new subsidiary could then be posted as collateral for the loan, with the additional covenant that the subsidiary remain hedged at all times.[43]

If the new affiliate remained hedged, it could continue to service its obligations to the bank no matter how much prices rose. Both firms would benefit from this arrangement; the new subsidiary obtains the funding it needs to continue its hedging/delivery programme, thus earning the gross profit locked-in by hedging, and the bank earns interest on its loan.

Note in this connection that under these circumstances, the bank has no need to insist on a variance-minimising hedge. The function of the variance-minimising hedge is usually taken to be reducing a firm's reliance on the capital market for external financing by lowering the variance of the firm's cashflows. But what sense does a variance-minimising hedge at the new subsidiary make for a bank that is *supplying* (at a price) the external financing the variance-minimising hedge is intended to reduce?

MGRM might also have been able to staunch the cash drains on its futures positions if prices fell further by purchasing futures puts. Such an emergency strategy was in fact suggested by Benson and his team to the new MGRM management but was rejected. To the new team, still concerned about MGRM's cash drain on its futures position, Benson's suggestion must have seemed a classic "hair of the dog" remedy – in which a badly hung-over drunk proposes to start off the day with a double shot of whisky.[44]

MANAGING FUNDING RISK *EX ANTE*

Admittedly, arrangements like those above can be difficult to negotiate quickly and under duress, even when not embittered by managerial feuds and finger-pointing. Firms hoping to initiate potentially cash-intensive combined delivery/hedging programmes like MGRM's might be well advised, therefore, to do an unsecured borrowing *up front* (in presumably calmer waters) equal to the initial face value of its total futures position – a so-called "pure synthetic" strategy. Rather than depositing only the required minimum initial margin with a futures exchange clearinghouse, such firms could give this *total amount* to the clearinghouse in T-bills thus ensuring that no further cash outlays would be required over the life of the hedge, regardless of price movements.[45] It can be argued, of course, that no lender could have assurance that the unsecured loan would in fact be used to purchase T-bills and posted as margin. But this potential agency problem could be solved by requiring the borrower to keep the funds on deposit at the lender bank. The lender bank would then pay all variation margin calls of the borrower by drawing down its margin-equivalent deposit account.[46]

The real culprit

The forced liquidation of MGRM's futures highlights an ill-defined, catch-all risk category dubbed "operational risk" by the Group of Thirty's Global Derivatives Study Group.[47] In the Group's open-ended definition, operational risk is associated with systems failures, natural disasters, or personnel problems. But operational risk also covers unapproved speculative activities by subordinates not detected by the senior management and board until serious losses have occurred.[48] In referring to MGRM, for example, the General Accounting Office (GAO) states that "poor operations controls were reportedly responsible for allowing losses at this firm to grow to such levels".[49]

A FAILURE OF UNDERSTANDING?

MGRM faced operational risk, to be sure, but the opposite of that assumed by the GAO and many others: the supervisory board may not have understood that MGRM was hedging and not speculating. As noted earlier, the team the supervisory board called in to liquidate the futures positions had also been used to resolve the Klöckner speculative episode for Deutsche Bank.[50] The supervisory board may have interpreted MGRM's appeals for more cash as "doubling-up" or, at the least, as the all-too-typical symptom of an imminent business failure. Or perhaps the supervisory board, in light of the power struggles then going on within MG AG,[51] may have deliberately chosen not to understand MGRM's programme.

In any case, unwinding MGRM's futures positions, though widely applauded in some parts of the press then and now, proved unfortunate on several counts.[52] By the time MGRM began to unwind its positions in mid-December, the price of oil had fallen to its low of roughly US$14/barrel. The precipitous liquidation of MGRM's futures hedge thus turned "paper losses" on that leg into realised losses and left MGRM exposed to rising spot prices on its still-outstanding flow delivery contracts. And indeed, as noted earlier, when the new management awakened to its naked price exposure following the liquidation, it began negotiating unwinds of its flow contracts without demanding *any* compensation for its positive expected future cashflows.

In fairness to MG AG, however, ending a combined delivery/hedging programme is never costless. As noted earlier, unwinding bilateral contracts may require concessions from the party initiating the unwind. The supervisory board increased the cost of ending the programme both by giving *full* concessions to its counterparties and by not following the common practice of unwinding both legs of a hedged transaction as close to simultaneously as possible.

If MGRM had not unwound its futures, the positive daily pays received when prices recovered in 1994 would have given it a substantial positive cash inflow. MGRM's forced liquidation, moreover, sent a signal to MGRM's OTC derivatives counterparties that its credit standing might be in jeopardy, thereby increasing calls for collateral to keep its OTC positions open and making it virtually impossible to establish new OTC positions. (See Appendix 1.)

ACCOUNTING AND DISCLOSURE

Operational risk can also arise from the accounting and auditing process.[53] Under German accounting rules, assets normally are valued at the lower of historical cost or market value, "Locom". The US Generally Accepted Accounting Principles (GAAP), by contrast, allow for "hedge accounting" if a specific hedge transaction can be linked to a specific obligation.[54] Hedge accounting under GAAP then allows the firm to account for the hedge transaction in the same manner as the underlying transaction using either mark-to-market or deferral accounting.

The more conservative German accounting rules thus tend to exaggerate economic losses in hedge operations. In the typical hedge transaction, the profitable leg of the hedge will be valued at cost, thus deferring the gain, while the losing leg of the trade is accounted for at its lower market value, thus recording the loss. By contrast, GAAP would allow both transactions to be deferred or both marked-to-market. Accounting losses under German accounting rules can thus exceed those losses under GAAP for a legitimate hedge transaction.

Whether this difference in accounting treatments was significant in MGRM's case is difficult for outsiders to judge. We do know that Arthur Andersen & Co had audited MG Corp and its affiliates until September 30, 1993 and showed a US$61 million *profit* under US GAAP before special reserves for MGRM.[55] By contrast, MG's German auditor Klynveld Peat Marwick Goerdeler Deutsche Treuhand Gesellschaft (KPMG) showed an accounting loss of US$291 million for the same period for MGRM under German accounting rules, though press accounts suggest that these losses may have been deliberately inflated to discredit the previous management.[56] The discrepancy in the two audits may well have had an unfortunate consequence for MGRM if the accounting loss under German accounting conventions had been perceived as a *real* loss on the combined delivery/hedging programme.

That the almost universally cited figure of US$1.3 billion for MGRM's loss on oil derivatives might contain "big bath" write-offs seemed likely to us from the publicly available information on the company's positions. But the US$1.3 billion figure for *gross* cash losses has since been confirmed in an auditors' report commissioned in 1994 by the shareholders of MG AG.[57] The auditors put the *net* loss at US$1.0 billion, but only because they grossly underestimate the appreciation in the value of the flow contracts as prices fell. We have estimated the real 1993 net loss in the combined delivery/hedging programme to be about US$200 million.[58]

Conclusion

Why did MGRM's synthetic storage programme come to such grief? Was it fatally flawed – an accident waiting to happen? Or was it killed off prematurely? Although we lean to the latter view, we recognise that the deeper issue of the long-run viability of synthetic storage programmes like MGRM's cannot yet be settled definitively. The identification problem is insuperable: many contending theories, but only a single observation! We can only hope that other firms, in the petroleum industry or elsewhere, adopt programmes similar to MGRM's. If indeed any are willing to follow MGRM's pioneering path, perhaps our account here may at least help show them where they are most likely to run into trouble along the way.

To avoid being ambushed, top managers and directors of those firms need not become derivatives experts – as some legislators and regulators at the moment seem to be urging – but they must understand the essential logic behind their firms' marketing and hedging strategies and the long-term commitments needed to make the programmes work. Otherwise, their firms may encounter not the classical gambler's ruin problem – they will be hedging and not gambling, after all – but an insidious new phenomenon of the derivatives age: an economically sound hedging programme may be liquidated prematurely because highly visible rollover costs and temporary cash drains may be construed by top management as gambling losses. Perhaps we might call this new phenomenon "hedger's ruin".

Appendix 1

OVER-THE-COUNTER DERIVATIVES

MGRM negotiated OTC derivatives contracts largely maturing in three months or less to mimic its futures stack. The OTC positions thus were for all practical purposes indistinguishable from futures – setting credit risk aside. But the OTC products subjected MGRM to some risks that the futures did not, and the premature liquidation of MGRM's hedge transformed these risks into reality. OTC derivatives do not utilise margin explicitly and usually do not involve cashflows other than those occurring on settlement dates. Adverse price movements thus do not *always* precipitate cashflows between OTC derivatives counterparties. But sometimes they do.

Cash flow needs could have arisen on OTC derivatives if MGRM's perceived credit risk changed. "Credit enhancements" are often demanded by counterparties to reduce their credit exposure to institutions with increased default potential. The three most common forms of credit enhancements accepted by dealers are cash collateral, securities collateral and third-party guarantees of performance. Of the dealers using collateral surveyed by the Group of Thirty, over 70% vary the amount of collateral depending on their exposure to the counterparty. Specifically, at least 55% of those dealers demand additional collateral if their counterparty receives a credit downgrade.[59]

For short-dated OTC contracts, counterparties would use collateral much as exchanges use margin. OTC dealers would simply require advance posting of collateral before rolling into a new OTC contract. MGRM would thus have faced potential funding needs on its OTC contracts if it or its parent experienced a perceived credit deterioration. When the supervisory board of MG began liquidating the futures hedge in full public view, it became apparent that the flow contracts were being "unhedged". This prompted calls for collateral from OTC counterparties and impaired MGRM's ability to roll over the short-dated OTC contracts.

MGRM might have avoided concentrating its OTC hedge in longer-dated OTC derivatives because they can be difficult to liquidate. Master agreements governing most OTC derivatives usually do not allow firms in MGRM's position simply to decide to terminate. On the contrary, adverse credit events give the *non*-defaulting counterparties the right to terminate the swap early but do *not* usually give that right to the defaulting counterparty.[60] If, therefore, MGRM's counterparties chose to demand collateral in accordance with negotiated master agreements rather than terminate the contracts, MGRM would either have had to post the collateral, default on the contracts, sell them to another party, or negotiate close outs with the original counterparties – all expensive choices.

Long-term OTC derivatives subject their users to counterparty credit risk. On 10-year commodity swaps, *any* corporation is likely to be perceived as a potential credit risk, making costly credit enhancements or collateral requirements possible. Perhaps more importantly, few OTC derivatives dealers would enter into such a long-dated commodity swap without in turn also hedging that risk.

Dealers virtually always either hedge their exposures directly or enter into offsetting transactions when negotiating a transaction. If a dealer hedges its exposure from entering 10-year commodity swaps, it loads the cost of hedging that contract into the price of the transaction paid by its counterparty. Because a dealer would have to use a strategy such as stacking and rolling, it would in turn presumably pass along those costs (and perhaps add a risk premium) to MGRM. As a large corporation already involved in derivatives, there is no reason to believe MGRM's cost of hedging directly with futures would have been higher than those of an OTC dealer.

Appendix 2

DATA

We obtained daily settlement prices for futures contracts of all maturities on Nymex light, sweet crude oil, New York harbour regular unleaded gasoline and No. 2 New York harbour heating oil from the Futures Industry Institute (FII) in Washington DC. Spot data were also obtained from FII for crude oil and heating oil but were unavailable for gasoline.

A monthly time series of front-month futures prices was constructed for each commodity based on an assumed rollover date. For light, sweet crude, rollovers are assumed to occur on the 15th of the month or on the first business day preceding the 15th when the 15th is not a business day. For heating oil and gasoline, the front-month contract is rolled over on the last business day of the month.

We define the relation between spot and futures prices in the text in two ways. When we refer to the "basis", we define it as a fraction of the spot price, or

$$b_{t,t+1} = F_{t,t+1} - S_t/S_t$$

measured on the first business day *following* an assumed rollover. The December 1993 heating oil basis, for example, is measured on December 1, 1993, corresponding to the rollover initiated on November 30, 1993.

Because spot prices were unavailable for gasoline, we define the gasoline basis as $F_{t,t+1} - F_{t,t}/F_{t,t}$, or the proportional difference between the one-month futures price and the maturing futures contract price. Spot and futures prices must converge at futures maturity, so this is a reasonable approximation to the actual gasoline spot-futures basis.

Our second measure for the relation between spot and futures prices is the "lump-sum basis", defined as $F_{t,t+1} - S_t$. Like the proportional basis, we measure the lump-sum basis on the first business day following a rollover.

We define "rollover costs" as the difference between the maturing futures contract price and the price of a new one-month futures contract one day hence ($F_{t,t+1} - F_{t,t}$). Because we measure rollover costs near the expiration date of the maturing futures contract, the convergence of spot and futures prices at maturity ensures that the lump-sum basis is closely related to per contract rollover costs. We make the simplifying assumption that rollovers are non-synchronous, so the rollover cost is the difference in the price of the futures contract being offset on the rollover date and the price of the new contract into which the firm rolls *on the next business day*. Rollover costs are thus assumed realised when the new front-month contract price is sampled. As with the basis, the observation for the December 1993 rollover is thus dated December 1, 1993.

In the absence of spot data for gasoline, we assume the lump-sum basis and per contract rollover costs are the same.

1. *See Gilpin (1994).*

2 *For an account of the internal politics behind the liquidation decision, see Eckhardt and Knipp (1994). We thank our colleague Rudi Schadt for his help in translating this very revealing article. See also* Heinz Schimmelbusch v. Ronaldo Schmitz, Deutsche Bank AG and Metallgesellschaft AG, *Civ. Act. No. 94-134662, Supreme Court of the State of New York (December 16, 1994).*

3 *MGRM also engaged in "synthetic refining" by going long crude oil and short refined oil product futures (or vice versa) – in industry parlance, trading the "crack spread." (See Merton, 1995. To keep the story uncluttered, however, we will focus here mainly on MGRM's long-term flow contract and synthetic storage programme.*

4 *Press accounts and statements from the new management of MG AG, possibly self-serving, have raised questions about the role MGRM's "offtake agreements" with Castle Energy might have played in the decision to liquidate MGRM's futures hedge. Because the public record on this matter is far from complete, however, we shall here and throughout be treating MGRM's combined delivery/hedging programme as independent of the Castle Energy programme.*

5 W. Arthur Benson v. Metallgesellschaft Corp et al, *Civ Act No. JFM-94-484, USDCD Md. (1994) p. 5.*

6 *MGRM's programme is squarely in the tradition of Holbrook Working rather than in the these-days more familiar context of "variance-minimising hedging". Stated differently, MGRM might be considered as effectively "risk-neutral" with little concern for the expected costs of bankruptcy given the financing commitments it believed it had from its parent and deep-pocketed shareholder/creditors. Much of the discussion of hedging in the finance and trade literatures is thus applicable only peripherally to our analysis of MGRM.*

7 *Under Nymex rules, MGRM had been granted a "hedging exemption", allowing it to hold total futures*

positions of 55 million barrels (25 million barrels of WTI crude, 15 million barrels of gasoline and 15 million barrels of heating oil). Nymex rules also limit substantially the amount held in the front or delivery month contract. For simplicity of exposition, however, we assume throughout that the entire position was in the front-month futures contract even though, as will become clearer later, this assumption exaggerates some of the costs of managing the programme.

8 *The major portion of MGRM's hedge was actually in "over-the-counter" (OTC) derivatives, including commodity swaps and forwards. If it hedged a total of 150 million barrels, its OTC position would have been on the order of 95 million barrels. These OTC positions, rarely more than three months to maturity, were functionally equivalent to the futures MGRM held, so that, for simplicity, we proceed as if MGRM's entire hedge was in futures. MGRM's OTC position is discussed in Appendix 1.*

9 *For an account of how futures may be used in seasonal inventory management, see Working (1953) and Working (1962).*

10 *Just how to interpret that contractual obligation to remain hedged is precisely the issue in one prominent and highly contentious court case. See* Thornton Oil Corp v. MG Refining and Marketing, Inc *Civ. Act. No. 94-CI-01653, Jefferson Circuit Court Div. Five, Ky (March 29, 1994).*

11 *Portions of this section are based on Culp and Miller (1994).*

12 *The only perfect hedge can be found in a Japanese garden, as accountants often quip. Certainly the so-called "variance-minimising hedge", which would presumably involve a smaller stack, does not meet the test of perfection in this context for a variety of reasons. The key coefficients underlying the "optimal" hedge ratio can only be estimated from past data subject to considerable error. A hedge designed solely to minimise the variance of net cashflows in the face of price changes, moreover, need not be maximising expected returns to the firm. Important managerial and control motivations for corporate hedging also exist that are not always well-captured by a variance-minimising approach.*

13 *Because futures contracts, unlike forward contracts, are marked to market daily, normal market practice is to reduce the size of a hedge by "tailing". (See, for example, Kawaller, 1994, and the references therein.) We ignore this adjustment in our examples for simplicity.*

14 *Note that while the policy is dynamic in the sense that the number of contracts in the stack changes over time, the policy is not appropriately described as "dynamic hedging". Unlike true dynamic hedging, the synthetic storage stack adjusts not to changes in* prices, *but only to the quantities actually delivered. MGRM, it is true, might well have increased its expected long-run profits by dynamic hedging - increasing the stack as prices rise, and decreasing it as prices fall. But there are no free lunches. Catastrophic losses can result if prices gap unexpectedly and adversely while the futures portfolio is being rebalanced - as dynamic hedgers in a variety of contexts have learned to their sorrow over the years.*

15 *Crude oil is used in the examples because prices and the quantities for crude are denominated in more tractable units than heating oil and gasoline.*

16 *For a succinct explanation of the cost of carry formula, see Miller (1991).*

17 *Past results, of course, are no guarantee of future performance - a phrase familiar enough from mutual fund prospectuses - but ample theoretical grounds exist for believing that the numbers above are not just sample-dependent flukes.* See *Litzenberger and Rabinowitz (1994).*

18 *See Williams (1986) and the references therein.*

19 *M. J. Hutchinson (1994), "The Metallgesellschaft Affair: Risk Management in the Real World", Memorandum (October 10), p. 3. Hutchinson was a member of the management team that took over in December 1993 and unwound MGRM's futures positions.*

20 *W. Falloon (1994).*

21 *See, for example, Hutchinson (1994) and Falloon (1994).*

22 *Some critics of MGRM have argued that MGRM's position in the oil market was so large by November that its very presence kept the market in contango, presumably because prices were bid up by other traders on the contracts into which they knew MGRM had to roll each month and bid down on the contracts MGRM was offsetting. Assuming MGRM held as many futures contracts as Nymex allowed firms with a hedge exemption, MGRM would have held 25,000 WTI crude futures, 15,000 gasoline futures and 15,000 heating oil futures. Those amounts would have constituted 6.32%, 11.06% and 7.88% of the total Nymex open interest in December 1993 in those products - hardly numbers to suggest MGRM was driving the market. Note also that crude oil, at least, remained in contango as late as March, long after MGRM's futures liquidation.*

23 *No evidence of which we are aware supports the notion that a structural change in market conditions occurred in 1993. Although realised rollover costs were high, the coefficients of determination of futures prices regressed on spot prices in 1993 are virtually the same as those for the full sample.*

24 *See Culp and Miller (1995b).*

25 *WTI crude futures are also listed for maturities of 21, 24, 30 and 36 months to maturity, but those contracts are relatively illiquid.*

26 *For a detailed proof, see Culp and Miller (1995), "The Net Present Value of Hedged Commodity Contracts".*

27 *Culp and Miller (1995), "The Net Present Value of Hedged Commodity Contracts".*

28 *The Chrysler Corp, for example, had a policy of putting five gallons of gasoline into every completed car coming off its assembly lines. Failure to have gasoline on-hand could mean shutting down the whole assembly line.*

29 *For a discussion of the costs of unwinding, see Culp and Kavanagh (1994).*

30 *See the ISDA Master Agreements (1992), ∬5–6 (events which trigger terminations of the Agreements), ∬7 (restrictions on transfers) and ∬6(e)(i)–(ii) (method of payment for close-out netting after a default or early termination). The ISDA Master Agreements are not the only master agreements, but they are the most widely used for common OTC derivatives contracts.*

31 *The uncertainty about the true tenor of the flow contracts will also seriously complicate the calculation of the size of the appropriate tail. See our earlier reference to tailing.*

32 *An upward-sloping term structure, moreover, implies a market expectation of rising spot prices and, hence, a declining basis. See, for example, Fama and French (1987).*

33 *"Plaintiff W. Arthur Benson's Reply to Defendants MG Corp. and MGR&M's Memorandum in Opposition to Plaintiff's Motion for Permission to Depose MG Corp's Former General Counsel",* W. Arthur Benson v. Metallgesellschaft Corp et al, *(1994), p. 3.*

34 *See Culp and Miller (1995a), "Auditing the MG Shareholders' Audit", mimeo., The University of Chicago, Graduate School of Business (March).*

35 *Note that the sluggishness of retail price adjustment works in the opposite way when wholesale prices rise. As retail prices rise more slowly, MGRM's customers might well welcome the immediate cash payment from MGRM in return for terminating their long-term flow contracts.*

36 *MGRM also might have employed several variations of this strategy, such as combining it with a strip for listed contract months – that is, matching futures maturities to flow contract deliveries for the listed futures contracts and stacking in the most deferred futures contract to hedge deliveries beyond that maturity. For a flow contract with 5 or 10 years to maturity, however, this strip and stack would be closer to a long-dated stack than a strip for most of the contract's tenor.*

37 *Office of the Comptroller of the Currency, 1993, "Risk Management of Financial Derivatives",* Banking Circular no. 277 *(October 27).*

38 *Some believe that the liquidation of MGRM's programme was inevitable once press reports of liquidity problems at MGRM appeared in early December 1993. It is hard to believe, however, that a reassuring statement from Deutsche Bank at that point would not have quieted those concerns.*

39 *If lenders perceived, however, that MGRM itself as a company had a negative present value (as some have suggested because of the offtake agreements with Castle Energy mentioned earlier), even secured lending might have been problematic.*

40 *See Eckhardt and Knipp (1994) and* Heinz Schimmelbusch v. Ronaldo Schmitz. *The precise details of those offers, however, have not been made clear.*

41 *See Culp and Kavanagh (1994).*

42 *For an example, see Kavanagh, Boemio and Edwards, Jr, (1992).*

43 *If existing covenants preclude splitting off the delivery/hedging programme, the funds would have to be provided by an equity infusion or additional subordinated debt. When MG AG was restructured in January 1994, additional equity and subordinated debt were indeed added.*

44 *For an account of the new team's views on liquidation strategy, see Gilpin (1994).*

45 *Not the least of the advantages in the notion of a pure synthetic strategy is its putting to rest, once and for all, the widely-held view that the "maturity mismatch" in a long-term delivery programme hedged with short-term futures must inevitably give rise to financial distress when prices fall.*

46 *Either form of the pure synthetic strategy would allow the firm to earn interest on its margin or margin-equivalent deposit. Thus, despite the seemingly large numbers of the* principal *values involved, the total* interest *cost would only be the net difference in interest paid on the loan and the interest earned. If prices fall, of course, the amount of funds on deposit earning interest will fall below the principal on the loan. In this sense, when prices fall there is an additional interest cost to the firm over and above the interest cost built into the basis, but the opposite is also true when prices rise.*

47 *Global Derivatives Study Group (1993),* Derivatives: Practices and Principles *(Washington, DC: The Group of Thirty), July.*

48 *See Global Derivatives Study Group (1993), pp. 50–1.*

49 *General Accounting Office (1994),* Financial Derivatives: Actions Needed to Protect the Financial System, *GAO/GGD-94-133, May, p. 4.*

50 *See Gilpin (1994).*

51 *See Eckhardt and Knipp (1994).*

52 *Contrary to many press accounts, the unwinding was* not *undertaken in response to the removal of MGRM's hedging exemption by Nymex. In fact, the hedging exemption expired at the end of December 1993, by which time the liquidation of MGRM's hedge was well under way.*

53 *For another account of how MGRM's problems trace in part to accounting and disclosure rules, see Edwards (1994).*

54 *This is called a "micro hedge". If a hedge transaction cannot be associated with a specific balance sheet entry, it does not necessarily receive hedge accounting treatment under GAAP. See, for example, Francis (1990).*

55 *See* Benson v. Metallgesellschaft Corp et al *(1994).*

56 *See Eckhardt and Knipp (1994).*

57 *Coopers & Lybrand Treuarbeit Deutsche Revision and Wollert-Elmendorff Treuhand, 1995,* Report No. 4011742 RE: The Special Audit in Accordance with Paragraph 142 Section 1 AktG of Metallgesellschaft Aktiengesellschaft Frankfurt am Main, *February.*

58 *See Culp and Miller (1995a).*

59 *Group of Thirty Global Derivatives Study Group (1994),* Appendix III: Survey of Industry Practice, *in* Derivatives: Practices and Principles, *Washington, DC, The Group of Thirty, March.*

60 *See Culp and Kavanagh (1994).*

BIBLIOGRAPHY

Culp, C. L., B. T. Kavanagh, R. Boemio and G. A. Edwards, Jr., 1992, "Asset-Backed Commercial Paper Programs", *Federal Reserve Bulletin*, 78(2), pp. 107–18.

Culp, C. L., and B. T. Kavanagh, 1994, "Methods of Unwinding Over-the-Counter Derivatives Contracts in Failed Depository Institutions: Federal Banking Law Restrictions on Regulators", *Futures International Law Letter* 14(3–4) (May/June), pp. 1–19.

Culp, C. L., and M. H. Miller, 1994, "Hedging a Flow of Commodity Deliveries with Futures: Lessons from Metallgesellschaft", *Derivatives Quarterly*, 1(1).

Culp, C. L. and M. H. Miller, 1995a, "Auditing the MG Shareholders' Audit", mimeo, The University of Chicago, Graduate School of Business (March).

Culp, C. L., and M. H. Miller, 1995b, "The Net Present Value of Hedged Commodity Contracts", mimeo, The University of Chicago, Graduate School of Business.

Eckhardt, J., and T. Knipp, 1994, "Das Protokoll einer Vermeidbaren Krise", *Handelsblatt* (November 4), pp. 28–9.

Edwards, F. R., 1994, "Systemic Risk in OTC Derivatives Markets: Much Ado About Not Too Much", presented before the conference on Coping with Financial Fragility: A Global Perspective, Maastricht, (September), 7-9, pp. 28–9.

Falloon, W., 1994, "The Market Responds", *Risk* 7(10).

Fama, E. F., and K. R. French, 1987, "Commodity Futures Prices: Some Evidence on Forecast Power, Premiums, and the Theory of Storage", *Journal of Business*, 60 (January).

Francis, J., 1990, "Accounting for Futures Contracts and the Effect on Earnings Variability", *The Accounting Review* 65(4).

Gilpin, K., 1994 "Trying to Rescue a Soured Oil Bet", *New York Times* (March 9), D1.

Kavanagh, B., T. R. Boemio and G. A. Edwards, Jr, (1992), "Asset-Backed Commercial Paper Programs", *Federal Reserve Bulletin* 78(2), February, pp. 107–18.

Kawaller, I. G.,, 1994, "Comparing Eurodollar Strips to Interest Rate Swaps", *Journal of Derivatives* 2(1), pp. 67–79.

Litzenberger R. H. and Nir Rabinowitz, 1994, "Backwardation in Oil Futures Markets: Theory and Empirical Evidence", Working paper, The Wharton School.

Merton, R. C., 1995, "Financial Innovation and the Management and Regulation of Financial Institutions", *Journal of Banking and Finance*, 19(1).

Miller, M. H., 1991, "Equilibrium Relations Between Cash and Futures Markets", in *Financial Innovations and Market Volatility* (Cambridge, Blackwell)

Williams, J., 1986, *The Economic Function of Futures Markets* (Cambridge: Cambridge University).

Working, H, 1953, "Futures Trading and Hedging", *American Economic Review* (June) pp. 314–43; reprinted as Chapter 3 of the present volume.

Working, H, 1962, "New Concepts Concerning Futures Markets and Prices", *American Economic Review* (June) pp. 432–59; reprinted as Chapter 4 of the present volume.

10

Auditing the Auditors*

Christopher L. Culp and Merton H. Miller
The University of Chicago

Anyone wondering how a company could run up more than US$1 billion of losses on oil derivatives while remaining hedged will be disappointed by the recently released auditors' report on Metallgesellschaft Refining & Marketing (MGRM). The report, commissioned last year by the shareholders of MGRM's parent Metallgesellschaft AG (MG AG), was prepared by auditors C & L Treuarbeit Deutsche Revision and Wollert-Elmendorff Industrie Treuhand.[1]

The auditors deserve thanks for providing, at long last, some justification for the oft-cited figure for MGRM's losses of US$1.3 billion. But that figure turns out simply to be a tabulation of the cash payments on *one* leg of a hedge. To establish the *net* profit or loss to shareholders from MGRM's oil programmes during 1993, the gains on the other and offsetting leg of the hedge must also be considered. And in that task, which requires more than just arithmetic, we believe the auditors are wide of the mark.

Because MGRM's marketing/hedging activities were many and complex, a quick overview of its two primary programmes and their vocabulary is essential, before turning to detailed calculations of net profits and losses. Under its flagship "firm-fixed" programme, MGRM agreed to sell oil at fixed prices and fixed quantities monthly for as much as five to 10 years in the future. In its smaller "firm-flexible" programme MGRM agreed to sell oil products still at a fixed price, but according to a delivery schedule determined by the customers. The customers also agreed to take delivery at the fixed price on any contracted oil purchases not made by the end of the firm-flexible contract tenors.

To avoid speculating on the future direction of oil prices MGRM hedged its firm-fixed and firm-flexible contracts using mainly short-dated futures and short-dated commodity swaps functionally equivalent to futures. The futures and swaps were held in amounts corresponding to MGRM's entire remaining delivery obligations. When the hedging contracts matured, MGRM rolled forward the whole stack, minus current period deliveries, into new futures and swap contracts of one to three months maturity.

MGRM's stack and roll hedging policy was certainly not a "minimum variance" strategy of the kind many academics view as the only legitimate type of "hedge" – any futures contracts held beyond that minimum-variance level being condemned as "speculation". Nevertheless, it did successfully insulate the firm-fixed contracts from rising spot prices.[2] But when prices fell, as they did in 1993, cash payments had to be made for variation margin calls on the losing futures leg or to meet collateral requirements on the futures-equivalent swaps. And when prices of near-term futures contracts fell by more than the prices for deferred deliveries (giving rise to a "contango" market), the strategy also imposed "rollover costs" on the firm. In December 1993, the MG AG supervisory board, after a year of falling prices (and hence of large cash variation margin payments) and several months of contango, ordered the liquidation of substantial portions of MGRM's futures hedge. A major purpose of the auditors' report was to establish how much MG AG actually lost on its ill-fated oil programme.

Financial loss estimates

The auditors estimate MGRM's total losses from June 1, 1992, to December 31, 1993, as US$1.277 billion gross, US$1.06 billion net. Their loss estimates (page 43, §3.4.1) are broken down as in Table 1.

Originally published in Risk *magazine 8(4) (1995), pp. 36–9.*

Table 1. Auditors' loss estimates

	US$ million
Loss in capital	1,277
Interest expense based on loss of capital	13
Losses from physical deliveries	3
Negative market value of firm-flexible contracts	12
Positive market value of firm-fixed contracts	−245
Total net loss	**1,060**

The auditors' US$1.277 billion estimate for *gross* losses is higher than estimates we made in autumn 1994 based on the incomplete data then publicly available. To simplify the calculations, we had assumed that all of MGRM's 150 million barrels of forward contract commitments were hedged solely with one-month futures and, for want of a precise breakdown by product, that those futures were all in crude oil.[3] From January to December 1993, one-month crude oil futures fell by US$4.34 a barrel. MGRM's recorded losses from *price declines alone* in 1993 would thus have been US$650 million at most by our count. If the auditors' tabulation of a US$1.277 billion cash loss is indeed correct, either the weighted-average prices on the other contracts actually held must have fallen by more than the crude oil we took as representative, or the auditors are including more cash drains than those traceable to spot price declines alone.

Some of those additional cash drains are the rollover costs incurred when prices on short-term futures and futures-equivalent contracts fell by more than those of longer-term contracts in the last quarter of 1993. Calculating those rollover costs from published data on futures prices at the relevant rollover dates, we had put the total for the entire year at about US$250 million – comparable to the auditors' own estimate of US$260 million (20% of their total gross loss estimate of US$1.277 billion) – bringing our total gross loss up to US$900 million, but still some US$400 million below the auditors' figure.

An alternative calculation

If we seem not to be contrite about so large a discrepancy, remember that both their US$1.277 billion and our US$900 million refer only to *gross* losses on the futures leg. What matters to the shareholders, however, are the *net* losses after allowing for gains on the other leg. After netting both legs, we put MGRM's net losses for 1993 at something of the order of US$200 million, or only one-fifth of the auditors' net loss estimate of US$1.06 billion. Why is the auditors' estimate so different from ours?

The explanation lies in the subtractions the auditors made – or, more accurately, failed to make – in going from their gross loss (US$1.277 billion) to their net loss (US$1.06 billion). Note, in particular, the US$245 million for "positive market value of firm-fixed contracts" in the table. Why that particular figure? What does it mean and how did the auditors compute it? Does it represent the *initial* values of the firm-fixed contracts? Or the *year-end* value? Or is it the *increase* in the value of those contracts as prices fell? Here, alas, the auditors are far from clear. And without access to the company books and to the precise valuation formulas the auditors used, outsiders have no way of verifying their calculations. Rather than guess where the auditors' numbers may have come from, therefore, we will present our own estimate of MGRM's net loss.

Assumptions

To estimate MGRM's 1993 net loss, we make the following generally conservative simplifying assumptions:

- ❑ MGRM sold forward 150 million barrels of oil at the *beginning* of 1993 instead of expanding its programme in successive steps to that amount by December.
- ❑ The entire amount sold forward was in the firm-fixed programme.
- ❑ All of MGRM's contracts had tenors of 10 years.
- ❑ The entire forward sale was hedged with one-month futures.
- ❑ Month-end figures can be used for estimating spot price changes.
- ❑ And all deliveries and hedging were in WTI crude oil.

Our net loss estimate

At the core of MGRM's programme is its gross profit locked in by hedging. Because MGRM hedged its *spot price risk* with futures, its profit margin for each physical delivery was locked in when the hedge was initiated as the difference between the fixed selling price in the contracts, K, and the spot price at the time the hedge was initiated, S_0, multiplied by the amount delivered. The total gross profit – the sum of the net cashflows on the combined programme over time – is thus *independent of the realisation of random spot prices over time*. The auditors do not disclose the Ks in MGRM's programme, but hints in the text suggest that the profit margin of US$3/barrel we assumed for ease of calculation is not far off. The December 31, 1992, spot price was US$19.785/barrel, implying a K of US$22.785/barrel under our assumptions.

Because MGRM began its programme in 1993, we assume that the capital value of the expected *net* profits on the firm-fixed contracts was entered in MGRM's books as an asset at the beginning of 1993. That value would be the total gross profit from the programme locked in by hedging less the *expected* rollover costs, based on information available when the programme was initiated.[4] We put initial expected rollover costs at zero, which is actually conservative given the mild backwardation (the opposite of contango) normally found in the crude market and present in early 1993. MGRM became hedged at the initial spot price of US$19.785/barrel, so the net economic value of its firm-fixed programme at the beginning of 1993 (treated as a "receivable") must have been

$$\text{US\$3/barrel} \times (1.25 \text{ million barrels}) \times (120 \text{ months}) = \text{US\$450 million}$$

Note that this amount represents a discounted net present value. The discount rate, including interest costs, is subsumed in expected rollover costs.[5]

To complete our estimate of the net loss for 1993, we must first subtract the *unexpected, realised* 1993 rollover cost, which we put earlier at US$250 million. Then we must adjust the initial value of the programme, evaluated assuming zero expected rollover costs, for any change in *expected future* rollover costs over the remaining life of the programme. That is, if new information received in 1993 raised the conditional expected future rollover costs for 1994 and beyond, that increase must be counted as a loss in 1993.

Estimating the change in expected future rollover costs would have been easy if the relationship between futures prices of different maturities – the so-called "commodity price term structure" – had remained constant while prices were falling in 1993. Expected future rollover costs would then have been the same as those expected when the programme was initiated. But the term structure did *not* stay flat. Prices at the short end fell by more than deferred prices – an instance of the "horizontal tornadoes" or "diving-board effect" to which oil derivatives specialists so often refer. How to factor the exact shape of the term structure into estimates of future rollover costs is by no means obvious, however.

We believe a reasonable and conservative approach in the light of all the available information about oil markets is to take the WTI crude oil 18-month term structure observed on December 1, 1993, as an estimate of expected rollover costs *for the next 18 months*. Beyond 18 months, we take the term structure as horizontal, implying that rollover costs beyond 18 months are expected to be zero. We can defend not using observed term structure values because the relatively low transaction volume in those contracts substantially increases the standard errors of forecasts based on observed values – standard errors that are notoriously wide even in forecasting interest rates from the much more liquid Treasury yield curve. Using the long-run average slope of the term structure is thus likely to be a better estimate for deferred rollover costs than the costs implied by the entire observed term structure. By assuming that the term structure flattens out after 18 months, moreover, we are actually being conservative, because the long-run average slope of the term structure is negative. Taking the above mixture of short-run and long-run values, we calculate the expected cumulative 18-month rollover cost to be US$2.465/barrel, making the expected rollover cost for the remaining life of the programme under our assumptions US$370 million.

Putting all the pieces together, then – and remembering that, thanks to the hedge, the pure spot price change (net of rollover costs) raises the capital value of the flow contracts by exactly as much as the cash loss on the futures – we calculate the net 1993 loss for MGRM as the *initial* capital asset value of the programme less unexpected rollover costs and the change in conditional expected rollover costs, or

$$\text{US\$450 million} - \text{US\$250 million} - \text{US\$370 million} = -\text{US\$170 million}$$

Thus, even after ruling out any future rollover gains from backwardation, we estimate MGRM's 1993 net loss at roughly US$170 million – still just a fifth of the auditors' estimate.

Losing even US$170 million is hardly pleasant, but that figure does not indicate that the whole programme was a mistake and should never have been started.[6] It is simply the cumulative loss to the end of 1993 – that is, after one year of operation. Those losses would be correspondingly reduced were we to recompute the cumulative losses on a programme continued to the end of 1994, by which time the term structure would have flattened substantially. In fact, if the term structure had become completely horizontal by mid-1994 and was expected to stay that way, the cumulative 1994 year-end of the programme would show an unexpected rollover *gain* on the stacked hedge *and* an increase in the capital asset value of the programme atttributable to the decline in conditional expected future rollover costs.

The distinction between *realised* and *expected* rollover costs is crucial for understanding the point we made in our November 1993 letter to *Risk* magazine that "once a firm chooses the stacked, short-term futures strategy, the issues of 'curve risk' and of term structure 'horizontal tornadoes' ... are irrelevant".[7] Only the relative prices of the contracts *actually being rolled* – not the full observed term structure – determine *realised* rollover costs for a hedger using a short-dated futures stack. The shape at later months might affect estimates of *expected* rollover costs, but only for those who believe that the observed term structure at any point in time is not only a reliable but actually the *only* reliable estimate of expected future bases on short-maturity futures. Otherwise, the observed term structure is in fact largely irrelevant.

What if MGRM had sold its programme?

Rather than keep its hedging/delivery programme intact after December 1993, MGRM might have realised the year-end capital asset value of its flow contracts in a lump sum by selling it to another firm.[8] Selling the programme at the year-end would have allowed MGRM to offset against the futures losses the effective increase in its gross profit margin from the 1993 spot price declines. MGRM had locked in an assumed gross profit margin of US$3/barrel beginning in 1993, when the spot price was US$19.785/barrel, but a purchaser of MGRM's combined hedging/delivery programme would lock in a gross margin at the lower December 1993 spot price of US$14.21/barrel. With an assumed K of US$22.785/barrel, the purchaser would thus have a gross margin of US$8.575/barrel, and in principle MGRM could charge a purchaser for that increase in capital value. It could not, however, charge a purchaser for the expected future rollover costs of the programme, so MGRM's receipts on the sale of its combined programme to an appropriate purchaser would be:

$$\text{US\$8.575/barrel} \times (1.25 \text{ million barrels/month}) \times (108 \text{ months}) - \text{US\$370 million}$$
$$= \text{US\$788 million}$$

MGRM's 1993 total gross profit after selling the programme would thus be its 1993 realised gross profits on deliveries already made less realised costs *plus* the proceeds from the sale of its programme. Assuming MGRM sold 15 million barrels in 1993, its 1993 gross profits from deliveries would have been US$45 million. The realised costs would have been the 1993 realised rollover cost *plus* the cash loss on the futures position due to spot price declines, which together represent the total loss on the futures leg. Because spot WTI crude prices fell by US$4.825/barrel from January 4 to December 30, 1993, the spot price loss on the futures position in 1993 was US$776 million. MGRM's net economic loss in 1993 would thus have been

$$\text{US\$45 million} - \text{US\$250 million} - \text{US\$776 million} + \text{US\$788 million}$$
$$= -\text{US\$193 million}$$

Had MGRM sold its programme, therefore, its net 1993 loss would have been virtually the same as if the programme had continued, which is hardly surprising. But the sale would at least have ended the cash drain with which MG AG's supervisory board had become so obsessed.

On the other hand, if prospective buyers of MGRM's programme expected future rollover costs to be greater than US$370 million, MGRM would have done better to continue the programme. Either way, we can be sure that the *worst possible* solution as of December 1993 was to eliminate the hedge and cancel the flow contracts without adequate compensation.

How much did MGRM leave on the table?

That MG AG in effect blundered into this worst case for a substantial fraction of its programme is now a matter of record in the auditors' report. The supervisory board ordered a substantial unwinding of the futures positions, and subsequently began cancelling many of its forward contracts with no payment required from customers.

How much money MGRM threw away in the process cannot be estimated with exactitude. The US$788 million it might have received from the sale of its programme was clearly foregone, but had MG's new management demanded payment from its customers for cancelling its contracts it might not have received that much. The US$788 million, after all, assumes that the purchaser of the delivery contracts is hedged. If MGRM's customers were neither hedged nor otherwise well-diversified corporations, they would presumably have been willing to pay an amount equal only to the present value of expected future differences between spot prices and the fixed delivery price. Customers' discount rates would reflect the risks of changing spot prices plus their own time value of money - figures that are virtually impossible for outsiders to guess. But in any event, if customers were willing to pay less than could have been received from a sale of the combined programme to another firm, MGRM clearly should have sold them rather than repurchased them.

The auditors defend MG's decision to cancel over 40 million barrels of MGRM's contracts without compensation in early 1994 by arguing that MGRM's new management kept the profitable firm-fixed contracts and cancelled only the firm-flexible contracts it believed were unprofitable. But were those contracts really losers?

The auditors view the firm-flexible programme from MGRM's perspective as a combination of short American call options and long European put options. The calls reflect customers' right to purchase oil at any time for a fixed price, and the puts reflect MGRM's right to sell any *unpurchased* oil back to customers at the end of the contracts. The auditors first estimate the value of the customers' position by applying some unspecified method of valuing an American call option with a strike price equal to the contract delivery price and with assumed estimates of volatility over the next six years of 15%, 30% and 45%. For MGRM's put, they presumably use a put option pricing model evaluated at the same strike price and volatilities. Subtracting MGRM's put value from the customer call value yields −US$37 million when volatility is 45%, −US$12 million at 30%, and +US$18 million at 15%. The auditors take the middle value for volatility; hence their figure of −US$12 million for the value of the firm-flexible contracts.

Treating MGRM's firm-flexible contracts as simultaneously a short American call and long European put, however, neglects a critical aspect of the firm-flexible programme: the value of MGRM's option to sell at the fixed price any unpurchased oil to its customers when the contracts mature depends on the amount of oil customers bought before maturity. That makes the task of valuing the options far more difficult than the auditors seem to have realised. Rather than presenting the tedious mathematics here, a detailed analysis of how to value the firm-flexible contracts directly has been published elsewhere.[9] But it is straightforward to show that - contrary to the auditors' assertions - MGRM was not cancelling worthless contracts in early 1994.

MGRM followed a hedging policy of holding futures and swaps equal in amount to total remaining oil deliveries - often called a "one-for-one" hedge. The same one-for-one hedging policy would also have made the gross profit on MGRM's firm-flexible contracts independent of spot price realisations, thus locking in the initial gross profit margin.[10] As with the firm-flexible contracts, the net margin would simply have been the gross margin locked in initially less the rollover costs of hedging.

We assumed earlier the firm-fixed programme had a gross margin of about US$3/barrel. The gross margin on the firm-flexible programme must presumably have been at least that high or even higher to reflect the premium MGRM collected for writing a sort of call option to customers. If anything, then, our earlier estimate of a US$170 million net 1993 economic loss, which assumed that all 150 million barrels were in the firm-fixed contracts, may have been *too large*.

But what of the auditors' claim that MGRM's cancellation of the firm-flexible contracts with no payment required was justified? Based on our earlier estimates and method, selling the firm-flexible programme to another firm prepared to hedge it should have allowed MGRM to realise roughly US$300 million. Perhaps the auditors got the figure of −US$12 million by estimating the value of the *unhedged* contracts, given the liquidation of the futures hedge before the audit period ended. Even so, valuing the contracts unhedged still ignores MGRM's ability to sell the programme to another firm, which could in turn re-hedge the programme.

That customers might not have been willing to pay as much as another firm to get out of their contracts is indeed entirely plausible, for reasons explained earlier. But public information suggests customers were willing to pay *something*. On December 22, 1993, one of MGRM's biggest firm-flexible customers reportedly paid MGRM US$2 million to terminate its firm-flexible contracts on 2.1 million barrels of oil. The new management accepted the offer. Two months later, when most of the remaining firm-flexible contracts were cancelled with no compensation required from customers, MG refunded the US$2 million.[11]

Without knowing customer discount rates, we cannot judge whether the US$2 million was a reasonable estimate of that customer's actual present value, much less what other customers would have paid. But the homogeneity of MGRM's customer base makes it likely that if one was willing to pay, others would. MGRM could thus have continued the programme, sold it to another firm, or unwound the contracts with the original customers - all for a positive price - and presumably would have chosen the alternative that maximised, not minimised, its profits. The auditors' contention that the new management was justified in its firm-flexible contract cancellations must be regarded as completely unsupported, both in the auditors' report and by our own reckoning.

Conclusion

If the auditors had hoped their report would quiet the controversies that have been raging over MG's oil derivatives programme, they have failed. Their lengthy report raises as many questions about the report itself as it answers about MG. We have focused here on just two of the more questionable analyses and conclusions that relate most directly to our own previous work: their estimate of the net economic loss on MGRM's oil programme in 1993; and the value they assign to the firm-flexible contracts. The shareholders can only hope that answers to the remaining questions come out in court, where all testimony is under oath and must be backed up with verifiable evidence and precise calculations.

1 *All references to the shareholders' audit, including page and section references, are based on the English translation: C & L Treuarbeit Deutsche Revision and Wollert-Elmendorff Industrie Treuhand, Report No. 4011742 RE: "The Special Audit in Accordance with Paragraph 142 Section 1 AkrG of Metallgesellschaft Aktiengesellschaft Frankfurt am Main" (February 6, 1995). We are grateful to José Scheinkman for helpful comments, but the usual disclaimers apply.*

2 *See Culp and Miller (1995a) and (1994b).*

3 *See Culp and Miller (1995a).*

4 *For simplicity, we ignore throughout the embedded options in MGRM's contracts. See the discussion in Culp and Miller (1995a).*

5 *See equation (1) in Culp and Miller (1995a).*

6 *For a given set of* Ks *the initial viability of the programme - on which we as outsiders can take no position - can be found by using the net present value criterion we present in Culp and Miller (1995a).*

7 *Culp and Miller (1994a), p. 18.*

8 *See our discussion in Culp and Miller (1995a).*

9 *Culp and Miller (1995b).*

10 *MGRM deliberately eschewed a policy of dynamic or delta hedging. We explain why that decision was consistent with its business objectives in Culp and Miller (1995c).*

11 *See Ma (1995), ∫4.4.3. We thank an anonymous shareholder for forwarding a copy of the manuscript to us.*

BIBLIOGRAPHY

Culp, C. L., and M. H. Miller, 1994a, "Slaughter those Sacred Cows", *Risk* November, p. 18.

Culp, C. L., and M. H. Miller, 1994b, "Hedging a Flow of Commodity Derivatives with Futures: Lessons from Metallgesellschaft", *Derivatives Quarterly* 1(1), pp. 7-15.

Culp, C. L., and M. H. Miller, 1995a, "Metallgesellschaft and the Economics of Synthetic Storage", *Journal of Applied Corporate Finance* 7(4), pp. 62-76; reprinted as Chapter 9 of the present volume.

Culp, C. L., and M. H. Miller, 1995b, "The Net Present Value of Hedged Commodity Deliveries", Working paper.

Culp, C. L., and M. H. Miller, 1995c, "Hedging in the Theory of Corporate Finance: A Reply to Our Critics", *Journal of Applied Corporate Finance* 8(1), pp. 121-7; reprinted as Chapter 14 of the present volume.

Ma, C. W., 1995, "Rebuttal to the Special Audit Report", manuscript sent to MG AG shareholders, March 7.

11

Simulating Supply*

Nicolas P. Bollen and Robert E. Whaley
University of Utah; Duke University

Much has been written about the controversy surrounding the financial crisis at MG Refining & Marketing (MGRM), a US subsidiary of Germany's Metallgesellschaft AG. MGRM's positions in petroleum derivatives generated losses reportedly topping US$1 billion in late 1993. These losses, and the aftermath within the company, generated enormous public controversy, including several rounds of academic debate regarding MGRM's use of derivatives. Were the positions in derivatives a speculative gamble, or part of a viable programme to sell petroleum products forward at fixed prices and hedge using nearby futures contracts?

In 1991, MGRM developed a series of contracts for long-term customers whereby MGRM committed to deliver petroleum products at fixed prices over a period of up to 10 years. These contracts were highly successful: by December 1993, the company had sold forward approximately 160 million barrels of petroleum. To hedge these commitments, MGRM purchased short-dated futures contracts and over-the-counter (OTC) derivatives with total underlying volume equal to the total commitments, a so-called one-to-one stacked hedge. When the futures approached maturity, they were "rolled" into new positions by selling the maturing futures and purchasing a new set of nearby futures. The unusual steady decline in petroleum prices in autumn 1993 led to severe "roll" losses, and triggered a series of articles that argued both for and against MGRM's use of derivatives and the overall viability of the company's combined marketing and hedging strategy.

Using various analyses, critics of MGRM generally concluded that the company took long futures/OTC derivatives positions far in excess of a variance-minimising hedge (Pirrong, 1997, and Mello and Parsons, 1995). The "hedge", therefore, contained a huge bet that oil prices would rise. Since oil prices fell in 1993, the one-to-one hedge lost more money than a variance-minimising hedge would have, simply because the hedge ratio was larger than it should have been.

Supporters of MGRM counter that the combined marketing and hedging strategy was almost certain to produce a profit if left in place (Culp and Miller, 1995a). The decision to close out the derivative positions was a case of mistaking a funding problem for an all-out bankruptcy. Further, the variance-minimising hedge championed by MGRM's critics is not always optimal. Some companies have a comparative advantage in bearing certain financial risks, and should be willing to capitalise on it (Stulz, 1996). In the case of MGRM, the company was clearly banking on a relatively stable phenomenon in petroleum futures contracts in which the "roll" generates positive profits much of the time (Edwards and Canter, 1995).

This chapter contributes to the debate by analysing the portfolio of supply contracts sold by MGRM as of December 1993. We first describe the nature of the long-term, fixed-supply contracts sold by the company. Next, historical petroleum price data are used to simulate the cashflows resulting from the supply contracts and various hedging strategies. We find that the simulated strategy always produces a positive profit when completed, but there is a 33% probability of hitting a cash position of -US$1 billion along the way. We then calculate what MGRM's cash position would have been at the end of March 1997 had the programme been fully funded and left in place. We find that the programme would have earned in excess of US$1.1 billion, covering even the most pessimistic accounts of the losses sustained from MGRM's programme.[1] We close with some concluding remarks.

Originally published in Risk *magazine 11(9) (1998), pp. 143–7.*

Metallgesellschaft's supply contracts

Table 1 contains a summary of MGRM's portfolio of long-term supply contracts as of December 1993.[2] As the Table shows, MGRM had sold long-term supply contracts on a total volume of around 6.7 billion gallons of petroleum products. Around 57% of the total committed volume was heating oil and the rest was unleaded gasoline. Around 63% of the total volume was committed under "firm-fixed" contracts with fixed delivery schedules and the rest was committed under "45-day" contracts with flexible delivery schedules.

Under the terms of the firm-fixed supply contracts, MGRM agreed to provide unleaded gasoline or heating oil at a fixed monthly rate over a fixed term at a fixed price. Around 88.5% of the firm-fixed contracts had a term of 10 years at contract inception, 11.2% had five years and 0.3% had two years. Table 1 reports the weighted (by contract volume) average fixed price of the contracts by underlying product and by contract maturity. The average fixed price for the two-year firm-fixed contracts on unleaded gasoline, for example, is US$0.6501 a gallon.

Around 62% of the total volume of the firm-fixed contracts had "exit letters" that provided immediate cash settlement when the spot month futures price reached a pre-defined "exit price". The cash settlement amount equals half the difference between the exit price and the fixed price times the remaining volume of the contract. For the contracts with exit letters, Table 1 includes the weighted (by contract volume) average exit price. The five-year firm-fixed contracts with exit letters on unleaded gasoline, for example, had an average exit price of US$0.6414.

Under the terms of the 45-day supply contracts, as with the firm-fixed contracts, MGRM agreed to provide unleaded gasoline or heating oil in fixed total volume over a fixed term at a fixed price agreed upon today. The 45-day contracts differ in that the contract holder chooses the amount and timing of contract deliveries. Any undelivered portion of the total volume will be delivered at the end of the contract's term. About 82.6% of the 45-day contracts had a term of 10 years at contract inception, and 17.4% had five years. The weighted (by contract volume) average fixed prices of the four types of 45-day contracts are also provided in Table 1. The average fixed price of the five-year contracts on heating oil, for example, is US$0.6223.

Hedging supply contracts

MGRM chose to hedge its long-term supply commitments by buying nearby futures contracts (or, alternatively, OTC forward or swap contracts) with underlying volume equal to the contracted delivery volume, a so-called "one-to-one stacked hedge" – "one-to-one" because the underlying futures volume equals the committed volume and "stacked" because only the nearby futures are used. As the futures contracts neared expiry, they were

Table 1. Summary of MGRM's long-term fixed-supply contracts: December 1993

Term of contract in years	Type of contract	Millions of gallons outstanding	Weighted average fixed price (US$)	Weighted average exit price (US$)
Heating oil				
2	Firm-fixed	15.18	0.6012	
5	Firm-fixed	222.36	0.5925	
5	Firm-fixed	54.17	0.5815	0.6239
10	Firm-fixed	1,054.13	0.5890	
10	Firm-fixed	1,592.35	0.5728	0.6286
5	45-day	322.73	0.6223	
10	45-day	542.70	0.6207	
	Subtotal	**3,803.63**		
Unleaded gasoline				
2	Firm-fixed	5.78	0.6501	
5	Firm-fixed	31.09	0.6339	
5	Firm-fixed	12.69	0.6209	0.6414
10	Firm-fixed	292.79	0.5886	
10	Firm-fixed	942.48	0.5924	0.6270
5	45-day	107.19	0.6409	
10	45-day	1,504.91	0.6199	
	Subtotal	**2,896.94**		
	Total	**6,700.57**		

"rolled", ie, the contracts were sold and new near-month contracts were bought. As deliveries were made on the long-term supply contracts, the futures position was commensurately reduced.

Ideally, MGRM or any other supplier could trade in derivatives with maturity equal to the contracted delivery of the underlying asset. MGRM's commitments stretched out up to 10 years, however, whereas futures contracts on petroleum are only actively traded out a few months. The unusual steady decline of petroleum prices in autumn 1993 led to large losses on the futures contracts that were only partially offset by cash gains on the delivery specified in the supply contracts. Critics maintain that MGRM overhedged, and was in fact speculating on oil prices.

Most of MGRM's critics support a minimum-variance hedging strategy that seeks to take positions in exchange-traded or OTC derivatives to minimise exposure to risk. The standard argument for a firm to minimise cashflow variance is that it reduces the probability of bankruptcy and associated costs of financial distress. Should a firm such as MGRM employ a minimum-variance hedge? There are at least two reasons why not. First, supply contracts expose the provider to the downside risk that prices will rise, but also the upside "risk" that prices will fall. A minimum-variance hedge reduces both sources of "risk". But an option-like payout structure could minimise the downside risk while preserving the upside potential of the strategy. The exit letter, for example, limits the supplier's losses when prices rise by prematurely terminating the contract. Second, a one-to-one stacked hedge can generate relatively stable profits by exploiting the historical tendency for futures prices to rise as they approach maturity. The choice of hedging strategy involves a risk-return trade-off that should be considered when comparing alternative trading strategies. In the rest of this section, we describe two simple hedging strategies and compare their performance using simulation.

FIXED HEDGE RATIOS

A fixed hedge, such as MGRM's, involves buying derivatives with underlying volume equal to a fixed percentage of the committed volume. MGRM's reason for using the one-to-one stacked hedge was presumably to guard against spikes in the price of heating oil and unleaded gasoline. In the event of a price spike, MGRM would have a sufficient number of futures contracts to match contracted deliveries or to cover early liquidation payouts. Since these payouts were calculated as half the remaining volume times the liquidation premium, a hedge ratio of 0.5 might seem appropriate. Recall, though, that early liquidations occur when spot prices rise above the exit price – a hedge of greater than 0.5 would generate extra revenue for MGRM since its long futures position would be larger. In addition, MGRM's implementation of the "stack-and-roll" strategy was intended to capture profits from relatively stable backwardation in the unleaded gasoline and heating oil futures prices.

MATURITY-SPECIFIC HEDGE RATIOS

A "tailed" hedge hedges only the present value (not the full value) of a known future commitment to deliver at a fixed price. Assuming monthly deliveries over a full 10-year contract term and a 5% annualised interest rate, tailing the hedge requires only 79% of the number of futures contracts required under a one-to-one hedge. With monthly deliveries over a full five-year contract term, tailing the hedge requires about 88% of the number of contracts of a one-to-one hedge. And with monthly deliveries over a two-year contract term, tailing the hedge requires about 95% of the number of contracts of a one-to-one hedge. Note that tailing the hedge implies that for a given supply contract, the appropriate hedge ratio grows over time as the contract nears maturity, and is effectively equivalent to the one-to-one hedge for short-dated commitments. Tailing the hedge is widely regarded as a necessary part of variance-minimisation, and is used in this chapter as the main alternative to the fixed hedge ratio strategies.

ASSESSING HEDGE PERFORMANCE BY SIMULATION

With details of MGRM's supply contracts and descriptions of alternative hedging strategies in hand, we are now in position to answer the question: was the one-to-one stacked hedge a reasonable strategy? Our goal is to conduct risk analysis of MGRM's supply programme as the company might have done on November 15, 1991, directly prior to implementation of the strategy. To proceed, we first estimate parameters of models of spot and futures prices. Next, we use the models to generate random price paths and to simulate profits from the supply programme with alternative hedging strategies. The simulated profit distributions of the strategies will allow us to evaluate their risk-return trade-offs and to determine whether the one-to-one stacked hedge was reasonable.

MODEL ESTIMATION

Our first task is to estimate parameters of models of spot and futures prices. The data are monthly observations of unleaded gasoline and heating oil futures contracts traded on the New York Mercantile Exchange (Nymex) from December 1985 to November 1991, a total of 72 observations. The upper half of Figure 1 shows a plot of the spot price data. We use the nearby futures as the spot price and the second nearby as the hedging instrument.

The model of spot prices we estimate specifies mean-reversion in expected price changes and correlation between heating oil and gasoline prices:[3]

$$\ln\left(\frac{S_{i,t}}{S_{i,t-1}}\right) = \alpha_i(\beta_i - S_{i,t-1}) + \varepsilon_{i,t} \qquad i = 1,2$$

$$(\varepsilon_{1,t},\varepsilon_{2,t}) \sim \text{BVN}\,(0,\sigma_1^2,0,\sigma_2^2,\rho) \tag{1}$$

where BVN denotes the bivariate normal function. Mean reversion appears to be an important feature in the oil prices shown in Figure 1. For example, oil prices spiked temporarily in autumn 1990 as a result of the Gulf War. The correlation between heating oil and gasoline prices, also apparent in Figure 1, results from the common dependence on crude oil. The specification of model (1) also ensures positive prices.

To estimate the historical features of futures prices, we first define the basis as

$$b_{i,t} = \ln\left(\frac{F_{i,t}}{S_{i,t}}\right) \tag{2}$$

The basis implied by the spot and futures prices in our data set are plotted in the lower half of Figure 1. We estimate parameters of the following model for the basis for unleaded gasoline and heating oil:

$$b_{i,t} = \alpha_i b_{i,t-1} + \beta_i S_{i,t-1} + \varepsilon_{i,t} \qquad i = 1,2$$

$$(\varepsilon_{1,t},\varepsilon_{2,t}) \sim \text{BVN}(0,\sigma_1^2,0,\sigma_2^2,\rho) \tag{3}$$

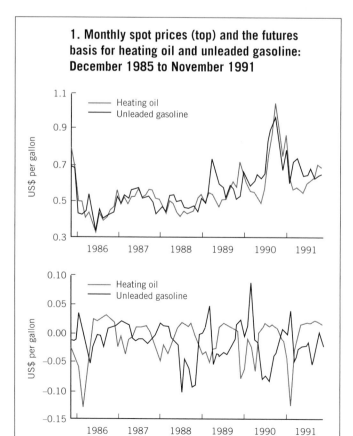

1. Monthly spot prices (top) and the futures basis for heating oil and unleaded gasoline: December 1985 to November 1991

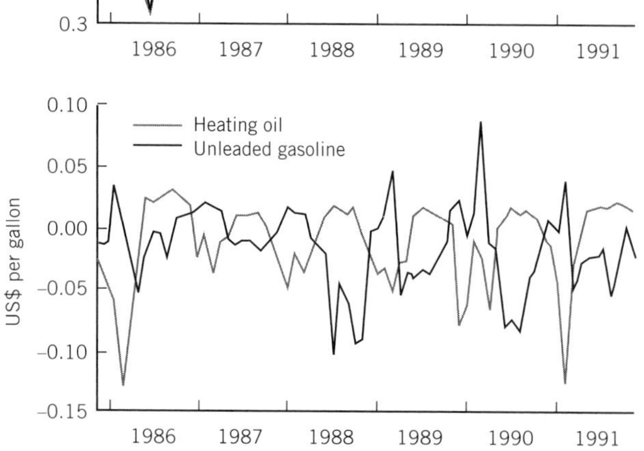

This model allows for serial correlation in the level of the basis, a feature that stands out in Figure 1, and a dependence on the underlying spot price. The relation of the basis to the spot price may arise from the inverse relation between convenience yield and the level of inventory. When inventories are low, the spot price is high since the commodity is scarce, and the convenience yield from holding the commodity is also high, hence the basis is low. So we should expect a minus sign on b in equation (3). Correlation between shocks to the basis of gasoline and heating oil is motivated by the asynchronous demand cycles of the petroleum products and their impact on inventories and convenience yield.

Parameters of the models, presented in Table 2, are estimated using maximum likelihood. For both models, all parameters are significant at all usual levels using heteroscedasticity-consistent standard errors. Note that for the spot price dynamics, the correlation between gasoline and heating oil is about 0.7. For the basis dynamics, the correlation is about -0.4, consistent with asynchronous convenience yields for gasoline and heating oil.

SIMULATION PROCEDURE

For a single simulation, a series of random spot and futures prices is generated consistent with mean-reverting spot price dynamics and the model of basis dynamics estimated above. For a given randomly generated pair of spot price and basis, the simulated futures price is constructed as

$$F_t = S_t e^{b_t} \quad (4)$$

For each simulation, the initial spot and futures prices are set equal to their values on November 15, 1991, approximately one month prior to the implementation of the MGRM supply contract programme, to replicate the market conditions that existed at the time. The fixed prices of the contracts were set at US\$0.08 above the prevailing spot price on November 15, 1991 to reflect the "margin" built into each supply contract. For those contracts that included an exit provision, the exit price of the contract was set at US\$0.1354 above the spot for heating oil and US\$0.1144 above for unleaded gasoline. The exit price consists of the US\$0.08 margin plus a weighted average of the premiums of the exit prices above the fixed prices shown in Table 1.

The terminal profits from each simulation run are recorded when all contracts have been completely honoured. To illustrate, consider the simulated profits from a hedged, 10-year, firm-fixed commitment. In the first month, the monthly deliverable quantity of either unleaded gasoline or heating oil is delivered at the fixed price for a gain (loss) equal to the difference between the fixed price and the prevailing spot price times the delivered amount. At the same time, the futures position realises a gain (loss) equal to the size of the hedge position times the nearby futures price change. The gain (loss) on the sale of the oil product is then added to the gain (loss) on the futures position, and then the sum is carried forward for 119 months to account for the time value of money. In addition, for those supply contracts with an exit letter, the simulated spot price is used to determine whether the exit provision is triggered. If the spot price exceeds the exit price, the cashflow generated from the exit clause is calculated as half the difference between the fixed price and the exit price times the remaining volume of the contract. The contract is then terminated. The procedure is repeated for months two to 120, with the number of gallons in the futures hedge being reduced each month by the monthly deliverable quantity. In each simulation run, the terminal profits of competing hedging strategies are calculated.

The simulation is performed 5,000 times to cover the full gamut of possible price paths. For each simulation, we analyse the performance of fixed hedge ratios between zero and 1.0, in increments of 0.05, as well as a tailed strategy using a 5% interest rate.

Table 2. Parameter estimates of models of spot price and futures basis dynamics for heating oil and unleaded gasoline

Parameter	Estimate	Std error	t-statistic
Panel A: Spot price dynamics			
α_{Oil}	0.342	0.111	3.065
β_{Oil}	0.539	0.038	14.368
σ_{Oil}	0.110	0.010	11.176
α_{Gas}	0.391	0.104	3.745
β_{Gas}	0.560	0.035	15.989
σ_{Gas}	0.116	0.013	9.017
ρ	0.705	0.079	8.899
Panel B: Basis dynamics			
α_{Oil}	0.663	0.089	7.473
β_{Oil}	–0.009	0.005	–1.803
σ_{Oil}	0.025	0.003	7.694
α_{Gas}	0.424	0.146	2.906
β_{Gas}	–0.015	0.008	–1.846
σ_{Gas}	0.029	0.003	9.248
ρ	–0.358	0.104	–3.436

Table 3. Summary statistics of simulated payouts from MGRM's supply contracts and a range of hedging strategies (US\$ million)

Ratio	Mean	Std dev	Min	Max	% > 0	% ≤ 0
0.00	1,348.60	365.56	382.47	2,567.13	100.00	0.00
0.05	1,481.37	348.35	570.46	2,547.17	100.00	0.00
0.10	1,614.15	342.14	722.85	2,597.81	100.00	0.00
0.15	1,746.92	347.52	756.76	2,754.94	100.00	0.00
0.20	1,879.70	363.99	790.67	2,977.78	100.00	0.00
0.25	2,012.47	390.13	824.58	3,298.50	100.00	0.00
0.30	2,145.24	424.17	858.50	3,619.23	100.00	0.00
0.35	2,278.02	464.36	870.03	3,939.95	100.00	0.00
0.40	2,410.79	509.26	759.75	4,260.67	100.00	0.00
0.45	2,543.57	557.73	649.46	4,581.39	100.00	0.08
0.50	2,676.34	608.92	539.18	4,902.12	100.00	0.58
0.55	2,809.12	662.20	428.89	5,222.84	100.00	1.60
0.60	2,941.89	717.09	318.61	5,543.56	100.00	3.22
0.65	3,074.67	773.27	208.33	5,864.28	100.00	5.82
0.70	3,207.44	830.46	98.04	6,185.00	100.00	9.58
0.75	3,340.22	888.47	–12.24	6,505.73	99.98	14.12
0.80	3,472.99	947.16	–122.53	6,826.45	99.98	18.46
0.85	3,605.76	1,006.39	–232.81	7,147.17	99.98	22.48
0.90	3,738.54	1,066.09	–343.10	7,467.89	99.96	25.94
0.95	3,871.31	1,126.18	–453.38	7,788.62	99.96	29.54
1.00	4,004.09	1,186.59	–563.66	8,109.34	99.92	33.36
Tailed	3,303.34	807.29	315.73	6,253.29	100.00	4.16

The last two columns show the percentage of simulations resulting in a positive terminal profit and the percentage of simulations leading to a cash deficit above US\$1 billion at some point during the simulation.

SUMMARY STATISTICS

Table 3 lists some summary statistics for the simulations categorised by the hedging strategy. For each hedging strategy, we calculated the minimum and maximum terminal profit levels over the 5,000 simulations. We also recorded the average terminal profit level, the standard deviation, the percentage of the simulations resulting in a positive terminal profit and the percentage of the simulations that witnessed a cash balance of less than -US\$1 billion at some point during the simulation.

Table 4. Cash balance probabilities over a range of time horizons and catastrophe levels for three hedging strategies: no hedge, a one-to-one hedge and a 5% tailed hedge

	No hedge			One-to-one hedge			Tailed hedge		
Month	≤ $0	≤ -$500m	≤ -$1bn	≤ $0	≤ -$500m	≤ -$1bn	≤ $0	≤ -$500m	≤ -$1bn
1	7.72	0.00	0.00	62.64	19.38	1.26	62.52	3.92	0.00
2	10.96	0.00	0.00	66.10	30.94	5.82	65.48	11.20	0.10
3	14.08	0.00	0.00	67.26	35.80	8.82	66.76	15.56	0.26
4	13.82	0.00	0.00	66.68	36.04	10.48	65.62	17.42	0.34
5	12.64	0.00	0.00	65.96	36.02	11.86	65.08	16.96	0.38
6	11.76	0.00	0.00	62.76	35.68	11.50	61.30	17.44	0.70
7	11.42	0.00	0.00	61.58	34.48	11.84	59.84	16.44	0.76
8	10.82	0.00	0.00	60.92	33.12	10.92	58.96	15.30	0.84
9	10.34	0.00	0.00	57.54	31.86	10.36	54.98	14.40	0.86
10	9.62	0.00	0.00	54.24	29.58	10.14	51.08	13.42	0.80
11	9.34	0.00	0.00	52.08	26.76	10.06	48.88	12.72	0.78
12	8.54	0.00	0.00	50.38	25.50	8.58	46.64	10.88	0.76
24	1.10	0.00	0.00	21.86	8.58	2.40	16.32	2.38	0.18
36	0.04	0.00	0.00	7.54	2.28	0.42	3.86	0.32	0.00
48	0.00	0.00	0.00	2.66	0.64	0.12	0.82	0.06	0.00
60	0.00	0.00	0.00	0.96	0.28	0.06	0.24	0.04	0.00
72	0.00	0.00	0.00	0.52	0.10	0.02	0.06	0.00	0.00
84	0.00	0.00	0.00	0.24	0.08	0.00	0.02	0.00	0.00
96	0.00	0.00	0.00	0.12	0.04	0.00	0.02	0.00	0.00
108	0.00	0.00	0.00	0.10	0.02	0.00	0.00	0.00	0.00
120	0.00	0.00	0.00	0.08	0.02	0.00	0.00	0.00	0.00

The hedge ratio has a dramatic impact on the minimum terminal profit level. For the case of zero hedging, the minimum is about US$382 million. As the hedge ratio increases to 0.35, the minimum profit level increases, then begins to decline. For hedge ratios between 0.00 and 0.70, none of the 5,000 simulations results in a negative terminal profit. For hedge ratios above 0.70, the maximum loss increases in magnitude with the hedge ratio. The negative outcomes are quite rare, however, as all hedging strategies record a positive terminal profit over 99.9% of the time.[4] This result indicates that the combined marketing and hedging programme is almost always profitable if funded to maturity.[5]

The hedge ratio also has a dramatic impact on the maximum terminal profit level. The maximum profit without hedging is about US$2.6 billion. The maximum profit rises with the hedge ratio and reaches a maximum of more than US$8.1 billion for the one-to-one hedge ratio. The average profit also increases with the hedge ratio, from US$1.3 billion without hedging to US$4 billion with a hedge ratio of 1.0. This results from the "roll" profits referred to earlier. The increase in average profits is generally accompanied by an increase in the standard deviation of profits. The minimum variance hedge is 0.10. The variation in profitability for higher hedge ratios, however, may be desirable if the variation is on the upside, a point we will return to shortly.

Perhaps the most interesting result from Table 3 is the last column, the percentage of simulations resulting in a cash position of less than -US$1 billion at some point during the simulation. Hedge ratios of up to 0.4 result in a "catastrophe probability" of 0%. For higher hedge ratios, the probability increases significantly. Indeed, for a hedge ratio of 1.0, the probability of a catastrophe is about 33%. This result indicates that the cash problems at MGRM could have been anticipated.

How did MGRM's strategy compare with the tailed hedge? The tailed hedge is a lower risk strategy with lower expected returns, as can be seen by comparing the last two lines of Table 3. The tailed hedge also has a higher minimum profit level, a lower maximum profit level and a lower catastrophe probability of about 4%. To assess the risk-return trade-off between the two strategies, it is necessary to consider the shape of their distributions, as discussed below. But first, we explore the catastrophe levels in greater detail.

Table 4 lists the percentage of the 5,000 simulations for which the cash balance was at or below three levels (zero, -US$500 million and -US$1 billion) over time for three hedging strategies (no hedge, one-to-one hedge and a 5% tailed hedge). For the case of no hedging, the probability of achieving a negative cash balance reaches a maximum of 14% in month three, declines to about 9% in month 12 and falls to zero shortly thereafter. The probability of achieving a balance of -US$500 million or worse is zero. For both of the other strategies, the probability of achieving a negative cash balance is much higher early on, reaching a maximum of about 67% in month three. However, for both of the other strategies, the probability declines rapidly so that, by the end of the programme, there is virtually a 100% probability of breaking even. The probability of achieving a balance of -US$500 million or worse reaches a maximum of 36% in month four for the one-to-one hedge and 17.4% in month six for the tailed hedge. Further, the probability of achieving a balance of -US$1 billion or worse reaches a maximum of about 12% in months five to seven for the one-to-one hedge and about 1% for the tailed hedge in month nine. These results indicate that the worst-case outcomes occur in the first year of the programme. In addition, the probability of breaking even approaches 100% rather quickly for all hedging strategies considered.

HISTOGRAMS OF SIMULATED PROFITS

Comparison of the risk-return trade-offs of alternative hedging strategies hinges on the shape of the simulated distributions. If variation of outcomes occurs on the upside, then variation is desirable. Figure 2 is a histogram of the simulated payouts for the supply contracts with a one-to-one hedge and a tailed hedge. With the one-to-one hedge, the probability distribution is "flattened", with a dramatic increase in the probability of extremely good outcomes. There is also a slightly higher probability of an extremely bad outcome but its effect pales by comparison. Figure 2 illustrates clearly why variance-minimisation is not always an appropriate hedging objective.

Projected cash balance

The remaining question surrounding the MGRM hedging controversy is "What would have happened if the original hedging strategy had been left in place?" We answer this question by simulating the monthly net cashflows of MGRM's fixed-supply contract assuming a one-to-one stacked hedge. Using the actual history of petroleum prices from December 16, 1993 to March 1997, we calculate what the balance would have been at the end of March 1997 if the stacked hedge were left in place.

MECHANICS OF THE NET CASHFLOW CALCULATION

The fixed supply contract positions shown in Table 1 form the basis of our analysis. MGRM is assumed to have these positions in place as of December 31, 1993. Along with the fixed-supply contracts, MGRM is assumed to be long 3.8 billion gallons of the nearby heating oil futures contract and 2.9 billion gallons of the nearby unleaded gasoline futures contract.

The deliveries on the fixed-supply contracts as well as the rolls of the futures contract positions are assumed to occur on the fifteenth day of each month. Each month, the net cashflow for each hedged supply contract position is calculated. To illustrate, consider the net cashflow calculations for the two-year firm-fixed heating oil contracts on their first delivery date, January 17, 1994. On January 17, the two-year firm-fixed contracts had 15,183,970 gallons outstanding. Since the contracts had rateable monthly deliveries over two years, the amount assumed to be delivered on January 17 is 15,183,970/24 or 632,665 gallons. The average fixed price for these two-year contracts was US$0.6012 a gallon and the price of heating oil on January 17 was US$0.5267 a gallon. Hence, the two-year fixed supply contracts on heating oil produced a cashflow of 632,665 × (US$0.6012 - US$0.5267) = US$47,134. The remaining contract volume is then reduced by 632,665 gallons.

To hedge the futures contracts, a one-to-one stacked hedge is used. To hedge the 15,183,970 gallons of two-year firm-fixed contracts outstanding, 15,183,970 gallons of the nearby heating oil futures were assumed to be bought on December 16, 1993 and sold on January 17, 1994. The nearby futures contract in this case was

2. Simulated payouts from MGRM's supply contracts with a one-to-one stacked hedge and a 5% tailed hedge

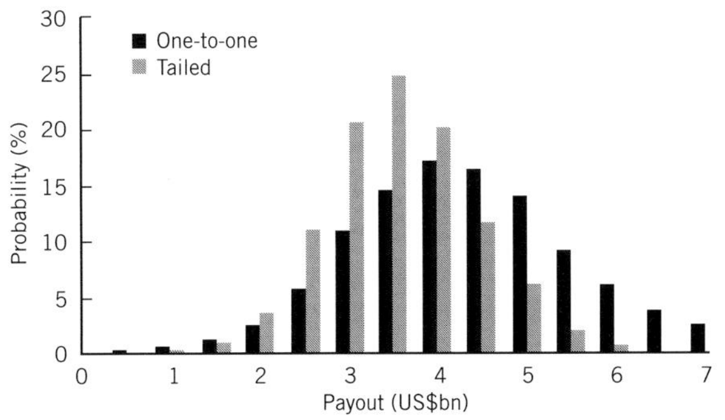

Table 5. Simulated cashflows from MGRM's supply contracts and a one-to-one stacked hedge: January 1994 to March 1997 (US$ million)

Delivery	Firm-fixed hedge	45-day hedge	Exit cashflow	45-day cashflow	Total
Heating oil					
55.99	569.28	133.88	–35.45	–1.73	721.97
Unleaded gasoline					
13.03	231.33	197.12	–14.23	–1.53	425.72
Both products					
69.02	800.60	331.00	–49.68	–3.27	1,147.68

the February 1994 contract. Its price on December 16, 1993 was US$0.4549 a gallon and its price on January 17, 1994 was US$0.5267. Consequently, the long futures hedge on the two-year firm-fixed heating oil contracts produced a gain of 15,183,970 × (US$0.5267 – US$0.4549) or US$1,090,209. The net cashflow for the two-year firm-fixed heating oil contracts was therefore US$1,137,343.

SIMULATION RESULTS

A summary of the net cashflows is provided in Table 5. The results indicate that had the long-term fixed supply contracts and their one-to-one stack-and-roll futures hedge programme been left in place, the aggregate net cashflow would have been US$1.1 billion, covering even the most pessimistic of MGRM's reported losses in 1993. Though this evidence may be discounted by some as resulting from a lucky string of price changes since 1993, it nonetheless answers a question in the minds of those that have followed the Metallgesellschaft controversy.

Conclusions

This chapter contributes to the debate surrounding the financial crisis at MGRM by analysing the portfolio of supply contracts sold by the firm in 1993. Using historical data on spot and futures prices of heating oil and unleaded gasoline, we simulate the terminal future value of cashflows from the contracts and a variety of hedging strategies, assuming that each strategy is funded, as necessary, until all the committed product is delivered. We find that though MGRM's combined supply and hedging programme is almost always profitable after all contracts are honoured, there is a significant probability that the firm's cash balance drops below -US$1 billion at some point. Further, the worst-case outcomes are most likely to occur in the first year of the programme. These results indicate that the program is indeed a "cash cow", but that, to be milked, a substantial capital commitment may be necessary early on. Further, we show that variance-minimisation is not always an optimal goal. MGRM's hedging strategy has more variance than a tailed hedge, but the variation seems to exist on the upside. In sum, our results suggest that the short-term losses at MGRM were a predictable intermediate outcome of a viable marketing/hedging strategy.

1 *An analysis of the actual losses sustained by MGRM is performed in Culp and Miller (1995b).*

2 *We are grateful to Siegfried Holdapp for providing us with MGRM's contract information.*

3 *We estimated parameters of several simpler models of spot and futures price dynamics using maximum likelihood. The simpler models were easily rejected in favour of the models described in the chapter using likelihood ratio statistics. Details are available from the authors.*

4 *For very low hedge ratios, however, a significant number of the simulations are not profitable. With a zero hedge, for example, about 30% of the simulations lose money.*

5 *For a more detailed explanation of this phenomenon, see Culp and Miller (1995a).*

BIBLIOGRAPHY

Culp, C., and M. Miller, 1995a, "Metallgesellschaft and the Economics of Synthetic Storage", *Journal of Applied Corporate Finance* 7(4), pp. 62–76; reprinted as Chapter 9 of the present volume.

Culp, C., and M. Miller, 1995b, "Auditing the Auditors", *Risk* April, pp. 36–9; reprinted as Chapter 10 of the present volume.

Edwards, F., and M. Canter, 1995, "The Collapse of Metallgesellschaft: Unhedgeable Risks, Poor Hedging Strategy, or Just Bad Luck?", *Journal of Future Markets* 15(3), pp. 211-64; reprinted as Chapter 13 of the present volume.

Mello, A., and J. Parsons, 1995, "The Maturity Structure of a Hedge Matters: Lessons from the Metallgesellschaft Debacle", *Journal of Applied Corporate Finance* 8(1), pp. 106–20; reprinted as Chapter 12 of the present volume.

Pirrong, C., 1997, "Metallgesellschaft: A Prudent Hedger Ruined, or a Wildcatter on Nymex?", *Journal of Futures Markets* 17(5), pp. 543–78; reprinted as Chapter 17 of the present volume.

Stulz, R., 1996, "Rethinking Risk Management", *Journal of Applied Corporate Finance* 9(3), pp. 8–24; reprinted as Chapter 8 of the present volume.

12

Maturity Structure of a Hedge Matters: Lessons from the Metallgesellschaft Debacle*

Antonio S. Mello and John E. Parsons

University of Wisconsin at Madison; Charles River Associates

At the start of 1994 Metallgesellschaft AG, the 14th largest corporation in Germany, stood on the brink of bankruptcy as a result of more than US$1 billion in losses from trading in oil futures. The futures trades were part of a sophisticated strategy ostensibly conceived by its New York subsidiary to hedge against dangerous swings in the price of oil and oil-related products. How could a set of transactions that purportedly "locked in" profits, making the firm safer, in fact lead the firm to bankruptcy? Understanding the mistakes made by Metallgesellschaft is critical if other firms are to avoid a similar fate without forsaking the significant benefits available from a correctly planned hedging strategy.

The parent corporation Metallgesellschaft AG is a large conglomerate with interests in a wide variety of metal, mining, and engineering businesses, including 15 major subsidiaries. Total sales in 1993 topped DM26 billion (US$16 billion) on assets of DM17.8 billion (US$10 billion) and with total employment of 43,292. Metallgesellschaft is closely held with over 65% of its stock owned by seven institutional investors, including the Emir of Kuwait, Dresdner Bank, Deutsche Bank, Allianz, Daimler-Benz, the Australian Mutual Provident Society and MIM Holdings Ltd of Australia. Some of these are also important creditors to the firm.

Metallgesellschaft's US subsidiary (MG Corp) was reorganised in 1986 with equity capital of US$50 million and net sales of US$1.7 billion from trading in US government bonds, foreign currency, emerging market instruments, and various commodities. The US subsidiary's oil business, organized under MG Refining & Marketing (MGRM), grew significantly between 1989 and 1993. In 1989 the company obtained a 49% stake in Castle Energy, a US oil exploration company, whose transformation into a refiner MGRM helped finance. MGRM contracted with Castle Energy to purchase their output of refined products - approximately 46 million barrels per year - at guaranteed margins for up to 10 years, and assembled a large network of infrastructure necessary for the storage and transport of oil products. During 1992 and 1993, MGRM succeeded in signing a large number of long-term contracts for delivery of gasoline, heating oil, and jet fuel oil to independent retailers. By late 1993 MGRM had become an important supplier. In addition MGRM ran large trades in energy-related derivatives. Its portfolio included a wide variety of over-the-counter (OTC) forwards, swaps, and puts, and it did large amounts of trading in futures contracts on crude oil, heating oil, and gasoline on a number of exchanges and markets.

MGRM as a financial intermediary

MGRM had no competitive advantage in its cost of supply. It did not own significant amounts of oil in the ground and the refineries run by Castle were old and inefficient. Instead, MGRM's business plan laid out a marketing strategy based on long-term pricing.[1]

*Originally published in the Journal of Applied Corporate Finance 8(1) (1995), pp. 106-20.

MGRM's management believed that independent retailers required protection against temporarily high spot prices for their supplies. According to MGRM, spot price movements quickly impacted the wholesale price of refined oil products but not the retail price. While retailers attached to large integrated oil companies were able to ride out the temporary squeezes on margins, independent retailers often faced a severe liquidity crunch. And while retailers could buy products under contracts protecting them against these temporary price surges, MGRM believed these contract price terms were unnecessarily high given the recent history of spot prices.

This was the central premise of MGRM's strategy. MGRM believed it possible to arbitrage between the spot oil market and the long-term contract market. This arbitrage required skilled use of the futures markets in oil products, and this was to be MGRM's stock in trade.

MGRM developed several novel contract programmes. First, MGRM offered a "firm-fixed" programme, under which the customer would agree to a fixed monthly delivery of oil products at a set price. By September of 1993, MGRM was obligated for a total of 102 million barrels under this type of contract. About 95.5 million barrels were covered by contracts running for 10 years, with most of the remainder covered by contracts running for five years.[2]

A second programme, called "firm-flexible" contracts, included a set price and a specified total volume of deliveries over the life of the contract, but gave the customer extensive rights to set the delivery schedule - up to a maximum of 20% of its needs in any year - and with 45 days' notice. By September of 1993, MGRM was obligated for a total of 52 million barrels under this type of contract. About 47.5 million barrels were covered by contracts running for 10 years and 10.5 million barrels were covered by contracts running for five years.

MGRM also ran a third programme of "guaranteed margin" contracts, under which it agreed to make deliveries at a price that would assure the independent operator a fixed margin relative to the retail price offered by its geographical competitors. The contract could be extended annually for a defined period and at MGRM's discretion. By September of 1993, MGRM was obligated for a total of 54 million barrels under this type of contract, although MGRM's renewal option meant that these volumes were not firm obligations. It is the first two programmes involving 154 million barrels of obligations for periods up to 10 years that constituted MGRM's designated short position in oil.

Although the contracts appear to deliver price protection in a straightforward manner, in fact the advantage to MGRM's customers was more roundabout. A familiar problem with long-term fixed-price contracts is that the protection offered on one side of the contract creates its own financial squeeze on the other side; that is, when the contract is deep in the money for the seller, the buyer may in fact be forced into default or at least a renegotiation of the terms. To minimise this danger, MGRM limited the annual volume supplied under contract to no more than 20% of the customer's needs. Of course, this also minimised the degree to which MGRM's contract would resolve the squeeze on a retailer during a period of high spot prices.

In order to both minimise the default risk in times of low spot prices and meet the customer's liquidity needs in times of high spot prices, MGRM included in its contracts a cash-out option. In times of high spot prices, customers could call for cash settlement on the full volume of outstanding deliveries over the life of the contract, thus receiving a cash infusion exactly when they were otherwise liquidity constrained. Under the *firm-fixed* contracts the customer would receive *one-half* the difference between the current nearby futures price and the contract price, multiplied by the entire remaining quantity of deliveries. Under the *firm-flexible* contracts the customer would receive the full difference between the second-nearest futures price and the contract price, multiplied by the portion of deliveries called.[3]

Through its pricing terms and these options, MGRM had assumed a good deal of its customers' oil price risk. To hedge this risk MGRM used a strategy known as the rolling stack. At the peril of some oversimplification, the strategy worked as follows. MGRM opened a long position in futures stacked in the near month contract. Each month MGRM would roll the stack over into the next near month contract, gradually decreasing the size of the position. Under this plan the total long position in the stack would always match the short position remaining due under the supply contracts. As of September 1993, the stack consisted of some 55 million barrels in futures on crude oil, heating oil, and gasoline, primarily in the near or next month contract, and a portfolio of similarly short-dated OTC swap contracts bringing the total hedge to the full 154 million barrels of delivery obligated under the supply contracts. MGRM thus had a hedge ratio of one-to-one.[4]

Table 1. Cashflow deficit created by a maturity mismatched hedge

Month (A)	Near month futures price (US$/barrel) (B)	Next month futures price (US$/barrel) (C)	Supply contracts: Deliveries (million barrels) (D)	Supply contracts: Net receipts (US$ million) (E)	Futures stack: Size of stack (million barrels) (F)	Futures stack: Monthly settlement (US$ million) (G)	Net position: Net cashflow (US$ million) (H)	Net position: Accumulated net cashflow (US$ million) (I)
March	20.16	20.30	0.00	0.0	154.0	0.0	0.0	0.0
April	20.22	20.42	1.28	1.0	152.7	(12.3)	(11.3)	(11.3)
May	19.51	19.83	1.28	1.9	151.4	(139.0)	(137.1)	(148.4)
June	18.58	18.90	1.28	3.1	150.2	(189.3)	(186.2)	(334.6)
July	17.67	17.92	1.28	4.3	148.9	(184.7)	(180.4)	(515.0)
August	17.86	18.30	1.28	4.0	147.6	(8.9)	(4.9)	(519.9)
September	16.86	17.24	1.28	5.3	146.3	(212.5)	(207.2)	(727.1)
October	18.27	18.38	1.28	3.5	145.0	150.7	154.2	(572.9)
November	16.76	17.06	1.28	5.4	143.7	(234.9)	(229.5)	(802.4)
December	14.41	14.80	1.28	8.5	142.5	(380.9)	(372.4)	(1,174.8)

(B) As the maturity of the near month futures price approaches, this price becomes a proxy for the prevailing spot price. This is the price it will cost to supply monthly delivery requirements and the price at which the stack of futures will be closed out.
(C) This is the price at which the stack of futures contracts will be rolled over into the next month.
(D) Monthly deliveries equal the total initial position divided by 120 months, 154 million barrels/120 months.
(E) Monthly profit on the supply contract equals the difference between the contract delivery price – constant at US$21/barrel – and the prevailing settlement price on the near month futures contract shown in column (B), multiplied by the volume of deliveries shown in column (D): $E = [21 - B]*D$.
(F) The initial long position is 154 million barrels. It declines monthly by the volume of deliveries under the supply contract.
(G) Settlement on the futures position equals the price on the near month futures contract shown in column (B) less the price prevailing the month before when the position was opened and shown in column (C), multiplied by the number of contracts held at the start of the month shown in column F: $G = [B_t - C_{t-1}]*F_{t-1}$.
(H) Net cashflow is the sum of profits on the deliveries under the supply contract and settlement of the futures contracts: $H = E + G$.
(G) Accumulated net cashflow is the sum of all the net cashflow for prior months: $I_t = I_{t-1} + H_t$.

Mismatched maturity in the hedge

The distinctive characteristic of this strategy is that MGRM was running a hedge with a maturity structure that did not match that of its delivery contracts. This had two critical consequences. First, it significantly *increased* the variance of the firm's cashflow at the outset of the strategy, making it vulnerable to an enormous liquidity crisis - exactly the opposite of what one would expect from a well designed hedging strategy. Second, it exposed the firm to an excessive amount of basis risk - variations in the value of the short-dated futures positions not compensated by equal and opposite variations in the value of the long-dated delivery obligations - so that the rolling stack had not actually succeeded in locking-in the value of the delivery contracts. We illustrate these two problems in turn.

CASHFLOW TROUBLE WITH A SHORT-DATED HEDGE

A rolling stack of short-dated futures initially increases the variance of cashflow because movements in the price of oil within the month create losses or gains on the entire stack of contracts - losses or gains that must be settled by the end of the month - while compensating gains or losses on deliveries are realised only gradually over the remaining 10 years of the delivery contract. We illustrate this danger with an example in Table 1.

To see the effect of an oil price decrease on current cashflow, look at May, the second month of the contract. A US$0.71/barrel drop in the price of oil from US$20.22 to US$19.51/barrel creates realised losses of US$139 million on the more than 152 million barrels of futures contracts outstanding going into the month, while only raising realised gains on the month's deliveries of oil by US$900,000, a 154-to-1 ratio of losses to gains.[6] In November and December, the eighth and ninth months of the contracts, the consecutive oil price drops create realised losses on the futures portfolio of US$235 and US$381 million, respectively, while raising realised gains on the monthly deliveries by only US$2 and US$3.1 million. The cashflow deficit grows monthly, so that at the end of the year it is just over US$1.17 billion.[7]

The danger of this type of cashflow problem is all too often overlooked. Recommendations for designing a good hedge too often focus exclusively on reducing variance in the total value of the firm's projects and underplay the consequences that different hedges have for variability and timing of cashflow. But often the firm's very reason for hedging is to assure a positive cashflow so that it can fund upcoming investments without turning to external sources for additional financing.[8] The strategic motivation for hedging should determine the choice of tactics, the choice of hedging instruments, but this simple fact is too often overlooked.[9] Even if a rolling stack of short-dated futures could help to lock in the total value of the long-term delivery contracts, the fact that it increases the initial variability of the firm's cashflow so significantly can make it a worse than useless hedging strategy.

Metallgesellschaft clearly needed to pay attention to cashflow. MGRM's parent corporation was facing a long-term liquidity crisis of its own and could not afford to finance cash shortfalls at its subsidiary. A series of expansions in the late 1980s and early 1990s had cost the company dearly and had not yet paid off as expected. Between 1989 and 1992, the company's fixed assets rose from DM2.124 billion to DM6.617 billion. During the same period, its reported return on capital fell from 13.1% to 6.7%, and its actual return had probably fallen further still. MG's accumulated cashflow deficit between 1988 and 1993 ran to DM5.65 billion and was financed with a DM4.44 billion increase in net debt and three equity issues yielding DM1.21 billion. The US subsidiary had also been forced to raise capital through a public sale of stock in Castle Energy. By 1993 the parent corporation was forced to turn to asset sales as a tool for continued financing of its central lines of business. Employment fell between 1992 and 1993 from 62,547 to 43,292. The company had already cut its dividend and was considering omitting the next dividend entirely. In light of these circumstances, the parent corporation had recently announced that its subsidiaries were to be independent profit centres and could not expect to be easily financed by the parent company.

MGRM's foray into the oil trading business emerges, then, as a singularly bad fit for the parent corporation in its current circumstances. Just when the parent corporation was faced with low cashflow and a weak balance sheet, its US subsidiary embarked on a business plan that involved functioning as a financial intermediary to independent oil retailers. MGRM's strategy was based upon its readiness to assume the oil price risk that independent operators would otherwise be forced to bear, but MG itself could not afford to shoulder the risk. MGRM might have tried to offload this risk in a number of ways - for example, by selling the contracts and taking its profit in the form of an origination fee. Or it might have managed the risk using a hedge that was the mirror image of its short obligation.[10] By choosing a hedge of short-dated futures contracts, however, MGRM actually exacerbated the problem, increasing the total risk of a large negative cashflow in the near term.

When cashflows matter, the rolling stack may be worse than no hedge at all, as we now illustrate. To evaluate the full effects of the rolling stack hedge under a wide variety of possible spot price paths, not just the extremely unfavourable one occurring in 1993, we constructed a simulation model of MGRM's financial condition for the life of the delivery contracts.

The inputs to the model are displayed in Table 2 along with the results. MGRM is assumed to have a contract obligation to deliver 150 million barrels of oil products over a period of 10 years, or 1.25 million barrels a month. The contract delivery price is US$20/barrel, and MGRM has a cost of making delivery equal to US$2/barrel, yielding a net price of US$18/barrel MGRM buys oil at the prevailing spot price, which starts at US$17/barrel and which for any horizon is expected to be US$17/barrel, but which may vary from month to month with an annual variance of 12%. The rate of interest is 7%. Under these assumptions, the contract for long-term delivery of oil has a value of US$10 million.

The contract is, however, very risky. For example, should the price of oil rise to US$21, then MGRM would have a monthly cashflow deficit of US$3.25 million.

Our assumption about the cost paid by MGRM if it has a sudden cash shortfall requiring external financing is also detailed in Table 2. The cost increases with the amount of financing required. Because of this cost, a constant low-risk cashflow is more beneficial to MGRM than the risky cashflow. Running our simulation model with this cost incorporated, we find that the value to MGRM of the unhedged contract declines to US$9.86 million. The cost of external financing reduces the value of the contract by US$0.74 million.

When a rolling stack with a one-to-one hedge ratio is included in our simulation model, the results are striking. The costs of external financing *increase* dramatically, to US$4.75 million, so that the value of the contract hedged with a rolling stack is actually less than the value of the contract unhedged!

Table 2. *Ex-ante* valuation of contracts unhedged and hedged with a running stack*

Inputs to simulation model:	
Duration of contract	10 years
Total delivery obligation	150 million barrels
Monthly delivery	1.25 million barrels
Fixed contract delivery price	US$20/barrel
Cost of delivery	US$2/barrel
Initial spot price of oil	US$17/barrel
Annual interest rate	7%
Annual convenience yield less cost of storage	7%
Cost of external financing:	
US$1 million/month	0 basis points
US$10 million/month	0.2 basis points
US$50 million/month	2.2 basis points
Results:	
Present value of contract	US$63.6 million
Cost of financing, unhedged	US$ 4.4 million
Net value of contract, unhedged	US$59.2 million
Cost of financing, rolling stack	US$28.5 million
Net value of contract, rolling stack	US$35.1 million

*Value estimates are derived using a standard contingent claims model to price commodity-related assets and related hedges: see M. Brennan and E. Schwartz (1985), "Evaluating Natural Resource Investments", *Journal of Business* 58, pp. 135–57.

It was exactly a liquidity crisis like the one described in Table 1 that precipitated Metallgesellschaft's brush with bankruptcy. MGRM had been losing money on its futures position throughout 1993. The consequences had already been felt within the US subsidiary by the end of the summer as the firm's credit lines were used up and, for example, traders in the emerging markets group were unable to find counterparties for some of their swap transactions. When the oil price fell yet more precipitously at the end of the year, the company did not have sufficient cash to continue rolling over its stack of oil futures contracts as planned and could not meet a large number of its other obligations until it received an emergency line of credit from its bankers.

Losses eventually totalled nearly US$1.3 billion. By January the firm was close to declaring bankruptcy and its future was not clear. MG eventually negotiated a US$1.9 billion bailout from its bankers in tandem with a plan to shed assets such as its auto parts manufacturing business, its tin mining operations, its recently acquired heating equipment, stainless steel, and boiler making lines, and others. MG was also forced to scale back a number of its central businesses, cutting employment in these businesses by more than 7,500 and reducing planned capital outlays by one-half, to a level below depreciation. The company has also since withdrawn from its lead position in the construction of a new copper smelter in Indonesia.

In short, the cumulative effect of the original trading losses and the firm's bankruptcy has been severe. The price of a share fell by half, from a high of DM427 (US$246) in November 1993, prior to news of the oil trading losses, to DM216 (US$125) in February 1994, after the rescue plan was organised.

WAS THE FIRM VALUE-HEDGED?

MGRM's management tried to downplay the significance of the liquidity crisis, arguing that it was *merely* a liquidity crisis and that the cash losses on the stack of futures were matched by an increase in the value of the supply contracts: the drop in oil prices that created losses on the stack of futures would mean a lower cost of meeting future delivery requirements under the long-term supply contracts. Summed over the life of the contract, the extra profits earned on future deliveries would exactly match the initial losses on the stack of futures. So although the firm faced a short-run liquidity crisis like the one illustrated in Table 1, the value of its total assets, they claimed, had not actually declined and so the firm was solvent.[11] MG's financial crisis, however, was more than just a liquidity crisis. The losses on its future contracts were real; it is simply not true that these losses were matched by an equivalent increase in the value of the supply contracts.

MGRM hedged its long-run delivery commitments with an equal number of futures contracts. While this one-to-one hedge portfolio appears sensible, it was not. This brings us to the second problem with a hedge portfolio of mismatched maturity structure: basis risk. One barrel of oil for delivery in one month is simply not equal in present value to one barrel of oil for delivery in 10 years, and the value of the two differently dated obligations do not move in lock step. In general, spot prices are more variable than futures prices, and a one dollar fall in the current spot price of oil implies a smaller change in the expected price of oil any time in the future. As a result, it is unlikely that a drop in the current price of oil creates gains on the delivery contracts that match in present value terms the losses incurred on the stack of short-dated futures.[12]

To illustrate the effect that this has on MGRM's net position, we have provided in Table 3 some reasonable estimates for the present value factors relating a US$1 movement in the prevailing spot price of oil with the change in expected value of forward contracts for oil at different dates. While a US$1 increase in the spot price of oil would increase the expected value of a 6-month forward contract by US$0.941, it would increase the expected value of a 5-year forward obligation by only US$0.520 or approximately one-half. A 10-year forward obligation would increase by only US$0.266. These estimates make clear that there may

Table 3. Relationship between the changing oil price and the value of forward delivery commitments

Time forward to delivery	First derivative of present value with respect to spot price	Time forward to delivery	First derivative of present value with respect to spot price
1 month	0.991	5 years	0.520
6 months	0.941	6 years	0.454
12 months	0.884	7 years	0.398
2 years	0.776	8 years	0.348
3 years	0.678	9 years	0.304
4 years	0.594	10 years	0.266

Based on data in R. Gibson and E. Schwartz (1990), "Stochastic Convenience Yield and the Pricing of Oil Contingent Claims", *Journal of Finance* 45, pp. 959–76.

Table 4. Unrealised gains on the delivery contracts based on monthly price changes in 1993

Month	Outstanding delivery obligation (million barrels)	Monthly price change (US$/barrel)	Present value factor for remaining deliveries	Total change in contract value (US$ million)
March	154.0	0.00	0.56	0.00
April	152.7	0.06	0.56	(5.11)
May	151.4	(0.71)	0.56	60.24
June	150.2	(0.93)	0.56	78.59
July	148.9	(0.91)	0.57	76.57
August	147.6	0.19	0.57	(15.92)
September	146.3	(1.00)	0.57	83.43
October	145.0	1.41	0.57	(117.12)
November	143.7	(1.51)	0.58	124.87
December	142.5	(2.35)	0.58	193.45
Total				478.99

be variation in the spot price that changes the value of the stack of short-dated futures without a comparable offsetting movement in the expected value of the long-dated delivery contracts.[13]

In Table 4 we calculate how the value of the outstanding contracts may have changed as the spot price fell during 1993: calculations are based on the factor estimates given in Table 3. In May, with 151.4 million barrels of oil to be delivered over a little less than 10 years, and with a US$0.71 drop in the price of oil, the present value of the outstanding delivery obligation increases by 56% of the changed cost of supply – that is, by US$60.24 million, an amount far less than the US$139 million loss on the futures portfolio in the same month. The cumulative increase in the value of the delivery contracts during 1993 was US$479 million, less than one-half the losses on the futures portfolio.

A comparison of the monthly losses on the futures portfolio in 1993 against the monthly realised and unrealised income on the delivery contracts is shown in Figure 1. The cumulative loss for 1993, net of unrealised increases in the value of the delivery contracts, is more than US$695 million.

The situation described in these tables is a generous picture of what actually befell MGRM. Oil prices dropped in late 1993 due to conflicts within OPEC that temporarily added supplies onto the market. The expectation of the long-term spot price 3, 4 and 5 years out was largely unchanged so that the losses on the stack of futures were actually matched by little if any change in the capitalised value of the supply contracts.

Because of basis risk, if one is committed to using a stack of short-dated futures contracts, then it is necessary to use a hedge ratio much smaller than MGRM's one-to-one hedge. A comparison of the minimum variance hedge against the one-to-one hedge run by MGRM over the 10 years of the programme is presented in Table 5. Two alternative minimum variance hedge calculations are shown, corresponding to alternative assumptions about the underlying delivery contracts being hedged. Using the present value factors shown in Table 3, the minimum variance hedge ratio (A) for a 10-year monthly annuity of oil deliveries is about 0.56; and, so, to cover 154 million barrels in delivery over 10 years would initially require a stack of only about 86 million barrels.

Revising the minimum variance hedge ratio to incorporate the effect of the cash-out options is technically quite difficult, but we have made an illustrative calculation based on the assumption that the contracts were all to be cashed out at the end of the third year, the horizon assumed by MGRM's management. This calculation yields the second minimum variance hedge

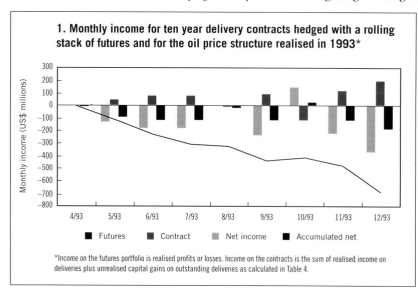

1. Monthly income for ten year delivery contracts hedged with a rolling stack of futures and for the oil price structure realised in 1993*

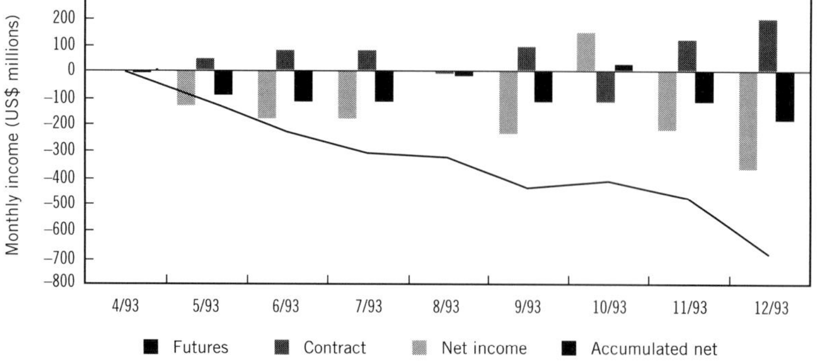

*Income on the futures portfolio is realised profits or losses. Income on the contracts is the sum of realised income on deliveries plus unrealised capital gains on outstanding deliveries as calculated in Table 4.

ratio, ratio (B), in which the firm's optimal stack is still only 87.3 million barrels at the outset.[14]

There are additional reasons to believe that the long-term contracts had not increased in value as much as the stack of futures had lost value. The risk of default by some of the independent operators was great and naturally increasing as the price of oil fell. In valuing the supply contracts it is necessary to take into account the high probability of default or renegotiation in the shadow of possible future defaults. Renegotiation is a very common event for fixed-price delivery contracts, as distinguished from the sort of financial forward contracts financial economists are used to valuing and as opposed to the futures contracts used to hedge the supply obligation.

MGRM's management was aware of the danger that fixed-price terms designed to benefit the retailers on one side of spot price movements could hurt those same retailers on the other side, and it had placed limits on the quantity of oil products provided to each retailer under the contract specifically to minimise the danger of just this sort of default or renegotiation problem. But however intelligently the programme was designed, some significant risk of renegotiation or non-performance remained, and it is essential to factor this in when estimating the true value of MGRM's short exposure.[15] This extra default risk on the supply contracts means that a drop in oil prices does not create a one-to-one increase in the value of the contracts to match the drop in the value of the futures.

MGRM's choice of maturity structure for its hedge produced enormous deadweight costs on the firm. These costs could have been avoided with a smaller hedge ratio or using a hedge with a better matched maturity structure. But is the issue here really the right hedge for the delivery contracts? In fact, analysing the stack of futures as a hedge has been a little misleading as we shall now see.

Hedging or speculation

If our preceding analysis is correct, it leaves us with some puzzling questions. Why did management choose a hedge with a mismatched maturity structure? And why did management run such a large stack? The answers are revealing of the depth of the problems at MGRM, and they give us some insight to the questions raised above about the valuation of the delivery contracts themselves.

Far from being simply a hedge meant to lock in profits generated by the long-term delivery contracts, the rolling stack itself was intended by MGRM management to be a source of profits. The company's business plan reads:

> As is well documented in standard textbooks, a hedge is said to be perfect when the gain (or loss) in the cash market is totally offset by the loss (or gain) in the futures market. However, it is important to recognise that if a hedge programme is carefully designed to "lock in" a favourable basis between spot and futures prices at the most advantageous time, hedging can generate trading profits which can substantially enhance the operating margin. Our proposed risk management programme, discussed below, not only protects the pump profit margins with a minimum amount of risk from the spot market, but also offers us an opportunity for extraordinary upside profit with no additional risk. (2, p. 2)

Locking in return was clearly only one part of MGRM's motivation for buying the futures contracts. The second part was speculation. Management believed that prices on a wide variety of oil-related derivatives often deviated from fundamentals and that profits could be made with the right trades. MGRM's management had identified a long list of mispricings, and a large part of their time was spent analysing market data in order to quickly recognise others as they might arise. Far from being simply a subordinate element of MGRM's general business strategy, we believe that MGRM's overall position in oil-related derivatives was driven more by its own belief that these financial instruments were mispriced than by a need for hedging its underlying activity in the cash markets – the tail wagging the dog, so to speak.

Table 5. A comparison of the one-for-one hedge with the minimum variance hedge under alternative assumptions

Year	One-for-one hedge (million barrels)	Minimum variance hedge of a 10-year annuity of forward deliveries (million barrels)	Hedge ratio A	Minimum variance hedge assuming option exercise at year 3 (million barrels)	Hedge ratio B
0	154.0	85.5	0.56	87.3	0.57
1	138.6	81.2	0.59	83.1	0.60
2	123.2	76.2	0.62	78.2	0.63
3	107.8	70.5	0.65	72.2	0.67
4	92.4	64.0	0.69		
5	77.0	56.5	0.73		
6	61.6	48.0	0.78		
7	46.2	38.3	0.83		
8	30.8	27.1	0.88		
9	15.4	14.4	0.94		
10	0.0	0.0	1.00		

In evaluating a portfolio of futures contracts as a hedge, one should generally assume that the prevailing price structure is "fair", so that the contracts themselves have zero net present value. The benefit of the contracts should not be in the value they yield directly to the company, but in whether they succeed in locking in the value of the company's underlying business. One hedge is better than another, not because the particular instruments used are priced more favourably, but because the instruments provide a better lock on profits being earned elsewhere.

MGRM did not make the key assumption of fair market prices in choosing its hedge. As the previous quote indicates, MGRM's management believed that a good hedge can create value because the prevailing market prices are not fair. The prevailing prices for long-dated oil instruments, they believed, were too high relative to the prevailing pattern of prices for short-dated oil. According to their estimates, the second component of the business as described above, the speculation on the basis, had a positive value. Moreover, MGRM chose not to hedge the delivery contracts with long-dated instruments precisely because management felt that the prevailing price structure for those instruments was too high: ie, the first component of the business as described above, the delivery contracts cum long-dated hedge, had a negative net present value.

In sum, MGRM's management wanted to sell the long-dated instruments and buy the short-dated ones. Thinking of the short-dated contracts as MGRM's hedge of its delivery contracts has the situation turned on its head. In fact, it was the favourable returns MGRM imagined to be available on short-dated futures that gave a value to a business of signing up customers for long-term delivery contracts. The following passage from its business plan illustrates how this way of thinking worked at MGRM:

> *Even if we do not have a 10-year forward product in place,* we still should take advantage of the pricing inefficiency between the spot crude market and the crude oil reserves market. Using the data from the previous section, when the spot crude oil prices rose to $44, the 18-month forward was only at $28, and the reserves were valued at $6.25. With this kind of price scenario, we should look into buying crude oil reserves and selling crude oil swaps. (1, p. 7, emphasis added)

BACKWARDATION AND PROFITING FROM THE ROLL

What was the source of the favourable returns on short-dated oil futures? The rolling stack was a bet placed by MGRM management on the persistent backwardation that arises in the oil market. Buying a near month futures contract when the market is in backwardation means buying at a price low relative to the prevailing spot. Assuming that the prevailing spot price remains constant, then as the contract matures and the futures price increases to the spot the position makes a profit.

MGRM's front-to-back hedging strategy was designed to reap this anticipated "roll return". It is because MGRM viewed this anticipated monthly return as an extra profit, unrelated to the need to hedge its delivery commitments, that it was not reluctant to run an excessively large stack. MGRM planned to maximise the return from backwardation by timing the placement of its hedges in different months and commodities. During the winter months, approximately November to March, the futures price for heating oil is generally below the spot price and the market exhibits backwardation, moving closer to a cost-of-carry relationship during the summer months. The opposite seasonal pattern arises for gasoline. MGRM believed it could make extra profit by exploiting the cyclical nature of the backwardation:

> It is during these off-seasons or weak periods that we have to secure this negative refinery economics. With the existence of the energy futures market, we can create a "paper refinery" which can produce oil products from $1.25 to $1.50 per barrel cheaper than a standard US$800 million oil company refinery, by taking advantage of the *inefficiencies* created in the illiquid distant contract months in the futures market. (2, pp. 2–3, emphasis added)
>
> This profit is made possible as the 12-month spreads are established at the most advantageous level (ie, taking advantage of the narrow backwardation when the gasoline market is weak) and continuously rolling forward to capture the market inefficiency whenever it occurs. (2, p. 19)

It needs to be emphasised at this point that there may be good reasons why markets for oil products move into backwardation and of course why they do so in a cyclical fashion. If the seasonal swing in gasoline and heating oil prices is an equilibrium reflective of the underlying fundamentals of supply and demand in the heating oil and gasoline markets, then it offers no special profit opportunities and no reason to run a front-to-back hedging strategy. The same is true for backwardation in oil in general.[16]

Although MGRM's management never did any appropriate estimations of the size of the basis risk, MGRM's management implicitly believed that the amount of backwardation was often too much to be accounted for by fundamentals and that a strategy of purchasing the near-month futures contract and rolling them over in each market during its period of backwardation would produce a profit on average. They based this belief on a simple simulation of the returns to a strategy of purchasing a one-month oil futures contract and rolling it over. Using the recent historical data, they found, the strategy would have made money.[17]

But such data has very little to do with identifying a good hedge and everything to do with identifying a good speculative investment strategy. The two are not at all the same thing! The fact that this strategy is open to any and all investors only serves to reinforce the point that it is an essentially speculative bet, not an argument for a hedging strategy being driven by MGRM's business in supplying the long-term market. In fact, a good number of Wall Street houses market their own commodity investment vehicles using return data on just such a strategy run over the same period of time.[18]

The profitability of the rolling stack of near month contracts was central to MGRM's entire set of profit calculations. Had the long-term contracts been evaluated based upon a hedge with a longer maturity structure, their profitability would have disappeared. This fact helps to highlight the extent to which MGRM's very choice of business line was essentially a bet on the basis.

A rolling stack of near month futures can be run for either hedging or for speculative purposes. Unravelling these two distinct motives is the key to drawing the right lessons from MG's financial crisis. We do not wish to argue with the speculative motive for rolling oil futures - although the mere fact that the strategy was good in the past is for us a rather weak argument. We are not taking a stand that this speculative investment was a bad one for any investor. MGRM's management took a position that the prevailing price structure in oil was not an equilibrium structure. There is clearly room for disagreement. Differences of opinion make a horse-race and there will always be some investors willing to take either side of such a bet.

But while there is room for one to argue that a rolling stack of short-dated contracts is a good speculative investment, we think it is important to make a clear distinction between a good speculative investment and a sound hedge. The short-dated contracts were not a sound hedge. In a very important sense they were not meant to be. The very fact that MGRM's management believed the short-dated stack was a good speculative investment undermines the argument that it was a good hedge. A speculative investment is a risky undertaking. But the hedge is supposed to reduce the corporation's risk. MG cannot be both hedging and speculating in the oil futures business. As MGRM added to its stack of near-month futures it was not trying to decrease its risk, contract by contract; it was trying to multiply its bet on backwardation, it was increasing the corporation's capital at risk, a different matter entirely.

MGRM's strategy document makes clear that the mechanical rolling stack described earlier is a stark oversimplification of MGRM's trading in the futures markets. MGRM planned from the beginning to shift its position among contract months for a given commodity as well as from commodity to commodity - gasoline to heating oil to crude - according to management's own beliefs about where profits were to be had. It was MGRM's readiness to speculate on a variety of perceived mispricings in oil derivatives that explains the many variations in their positions. MGRM's management had identified a long list of mispricings, and a large part of their time was spent analysing market data in order to quickly recognise others as they might arise. MGRM was to operate as any other speculator in the financial markets, buying low and selling high.

How would management know which prices were "low" and which were "high"? MGRM developed what amounted to a traditional technician's trading system. For a first approximation, they modelled the historical experience in each of the markets and operated on the standard assumption that the price patterns of the past would mechanically extend into the future. Then, for improved profit performance they developed some mathematical signals to anticipate the peaks of cyclical price movements:

> If we can take advantage of the market weakness in establishing the hedges, we should also make use of the strength of the market in taking off the hedges. For example, the maximum values for the inter-month spread are, respectively, 19.36, 21.84, 25.35 and 21.58 cents per gallon in 1986, 1987, 1988 and 1989. Therefore, instead of taking off the hedges ratably, it may be possible to take off the hedges at a much higher level, thus improving the profit margins... By liquidating the spreads at their peak or close to the peak, we are capturing the positive refinery economics in lifting our hedges without giving back any of the profit margin that a normal refinery would lose during its off-season low-demand period. Therefore, we need some reliable exit indicators to suggest an optimal time to take off the hedges. (2, p. 19)

The exit indicators chosen are embarrassingly old fashioned: they are the standard computational techniques for identifying a local maximum in a function and therefore rely heavily upon very questionable assumptions about the smoothly cyclical structure of commodity futures prices. In addition to modifying its basic running stack, MGRM's management conducted a number of so-called "arbitrages" otherwise completely unrelated to its basic delivery contracts. Members of the management team claimed that at least US$25 million a month were made exploiting such transient arbitrage opportunities in addition to the longer-term mispricings that formed the core of MGRM's speculative strategy.

Once one investigates MGRM's actual transactions in futures and takes note of management's very clearly articulated belief that there were speculative profits to be had, the decision of the creditors to bring the operation under control is thrown into a different light. A speculation with one's own money is one thing, a speculation with the creditors' several billion dollars is another thing entirely. And while a speculation may properly be put on to the balance sheet of an appropriately capitalised investment house, the very same speculation does real damage on the balance sheet of an industrial corporation, especially one with a weak balance sheet. Adding a speculative financial investment to the balance sheet is the simplest, most obvious example of what is politely known as "the risk shifting game". Creditors quite wisely make great efforts to prevent such actions by the management.[19]

Conclusion

The case of Metallgesellschaft provides a wide array of lessons for businesses interested in properly hedging their exposure to various risks.

Taking MGRM's decision to provide long-term contracts for granted and focusing instead on the design of the hedge used to manage the risk of the business, one can use the Metallgesellschaft case to elucidate the importance of maturity structure in hedging as in every other product line of finance. A hedge with a mismatched maturity structure can create enormous funding risks. The case of Metallgesellschaft only reinforces the recommendations of the Group of Thirty that a corporation's position needs to be stress tested and evaluated against worst case scenarios. It is folly to put in place a seemingly innocuous hedge without careful regard for the possibly temporary but nevertheless large amount of financing it may require in the event of unfavourable price movements. If, as is often the case, the original reason for hedging is to avoid funding problems arising in the course of the firm's normal operations, then cashflow patterns ought to be the starting point and not an afterthought in the choice of hedging instruments. The maturity structure of a hedge is also central to the degree to which the firm's value is actually hedged; a mismatch in maturity structure means that the firm has assumed important risks.

The Metallgesellschaft case also illuminates the fine line that sometimes exists between hedging and speculating. The lingo of the derivatives industry and its relative novelty has allowed a number of speculative activities to be passed off as "risk management". MGRM's losses in late 1993 made this pretence no longer possible, and Metallgesellschaft's shareholders and creditors took the necessary remedial actions to limit the sorry consequences. MGRM's use of a one-for-one hedge of near month futures looks superficially to be a straightforward purchase of insurance against capital gains and losses on its delivery contracts. In reality, the entire line of business was a bet on the basis, a bet on the roll return earned by the futures contracts in a backwardated market. Adding this bet on to the balance sheet of a major industrial corporation was a disastrous mistake. Recognising the bets implicit in a variety of hedging strategies requires careful attention. As the Metallgesellschaft case illustrates, the stakes can be high.

Reply to Culp and Miller

MGRM's strategy has received support in a recent paper by Christopher Culp and Merton Miller, "Metallgesellschaft and the Economics of Synthetic Storage", which appeared in the *Journal of Applied Corporate Finance* (Winter 1995) and is reproduced as Chapter 9 of this volume. Since our analysis of Metallgesellschaft's debacle differs significantly from theirs, we sketch here the main points of agreement and differences between the two chapters. The areas of agreement are much greater than might be supposed, given the large degree of public controversy surrounding the case.

First, there is agreement that using a rolling stack to hedge a flow of deliveries may produce temporarily large negative cashflows. The warnings of the Group of Thirty regarding potential funding risks and the need for thorough stress tests of any derivative strategy should be kept in mind when considering the rolling stack. There is also agreement that the cashflow losses in the case of Metallgesellschaft were quite large. Culp and Miller estimate US$650 million from price declines and another US$250 million due to rollover costs, for a total cashflow loss on the futures leg of the transaction of US$900 million. In our Table 1 we estimated US$1.17 billion. The special auditors calculated losses on the futures and OTC swaps portfolios at US$413 million by the end of September 1993 and at over US$1.276 billion by the end of December. MGRM's original management had estimated losses on the rolling stack of US$434 million to September, prior to the spectacular price drop in November and December. The differences among all of these estimates is small relative to the range in which all of the estimates lie and given the assumptions buried in each of the calculations. US$900 million is a large cashflow deficit to finance in a single calendar year.

Second, there is agreement that the rolling stack with a one-to-one hedge ratio leaves a firm exposed to basis risk. This shows up in Culp and Miller's Table 1 as an increase in the net cost of carry (the rollover costs) and therefore a divergence between the anticipated contract income and the realised cashflow or income. Culp and Miller break the firm's risks down into two components, spot price risk and rollover risk, and they emphasise that the rolling stack fully hedges the firm against the spot price risk. We, on the other hand, emphasize that in hedging the firm fully against spot price risk, the rolling stack leaves the firm very exposed to rollover risk.

There also appears to be growing agreement that this basis risk was large for MGRM. Elsewhere Culp and Miller recently estimated that oil price movements in 1993 increased rollover costs by US$620 million – an increase of US$250 million in realised rollover costs in 1993 and of US$370 million in expected future rollover costs.[20] This US$620 million figure is very close to our own estimate of a US$695 million net loss on MGRM's contract and futures positions.[21]

Both the firm's exposure to funding risk and its exposure to basis risk are a result of its choice of a hedge with a mismatched maturity structure. In another paper we have used Culp and Miller's own illustrative example of "synthetic storage" and shown that a firm that had hedged using a maturity matched strip of futures instead of a stack would have been exposed to less variation in the timing of its cashflows, and would have completely hedged the basis risk.[22] The contrast between the strip and the stack makes clear that it was MGRM's use of a stack of short-dated futures contracts to hedge a set of long-dated delivery obligations that opened the door to the losses incurred in 1993.

Although both sides seem to agree that MGRM was exposed to significant funding and basis risk, there is disagreement about whether these risks undermined the business plan from the start. Naturally this disagreement carries over to a different assessment about how the parent corporation responded when these risks became apparent at the end of 1993. We believe that the business plan and hedging strategy were essentially and significantly flawed. Culp and Miller, on the other hand, believe the delivery contracts were valuable and that the funding risk and basis risk mentioned above were worth the bet. Correspondingly, we believe it was appropriate to try and close down as much of MGRM's activities as possible in December 1993, even at certain costs, while Culp and Miller believe it was still valuable and closing it down merely dissipated this value. Since we have already made our case, we turn to a few particulars of this dispute.

We think Culp and Miller play down the funding risk too much and lean far too much on the idea that MG's creditors and shareholders should have readily coughed up extra cash. Culp and Miller have argued that MG *could not* have really faced a liquidity constraint, except as Deutsche Bank and others foolishly chose not to continue financing the oil business. But we have documented in fact that Metallgesellschaft faced a liquidity crunch *prior* to MGRM's huge losses at the end of 1993, and that it took a variety of actions consistent with this fact both before the futures trading crisis and afterwards: for example, it was forced both times to sell other assets in order to improve liquidity. Speaking of Deutsche Bank as if it had unlimited pockets is simply not facing up to the real-world constraints that had already been evidenced. We believe that cashflow mattered for Metallgesellscaft and MGRM management should have paid attention to funding risks in its choice of maturity structure of its hedge or, alternatively, in its decision to pursue the entire strategy of operating as a financial intermediary.

Culp and Miller believe that MG's pre-existing relationships with many banks should have made it possible to survive a brief liquidity crisis had the company remained behind the basic strategy. We note, on the other hand, that a plethora of creditors, each with a different stake in the firm and different circumstances of its own, can in some cases ensure deadlock should the firm have to negotiate additional financing or a restructuring of debt. It is management's job to design a hedge precisely to avoid the dangers inherent in such a process.

Culp and Miller believe that the funding risks at hand were obvious, that "you don't have to be a rocket scientist" to see the possible cash drains. But if one assumes away the possibility that management made a mistake – as this argument does – then one can never learn from the mistakes management actually makes. We think that the possible cashflow drains were ignored, rocket scientists or not. We have seen nothing in the documentary record at MGRM to suggest that they had done any "worst case" simulation. On the contrary, only after experiencing large losses partway through 1993 did they consider the use of put options to place a floor on the possible cash losses from their hedging. The opportunity of using puts had always been available but had never been considered until *after* enormous losses had been incurred. As Culp and Miller themselves note, there were a large variety of alternative corporate and financial structures that could have been used, including spinning off a subsidiary with the delivery contracts and the hedge: many of these might have been viable had they been pursued *before* the firm faced its liquidity crisis. That they were only entertained in the midst of a crisis highlights the failure of forethought at MGRM.

Our own review of MGRM's strategy documents and other materials suggests that they were fixated on the historical record of regular profits from their proposed strategy: they made the classic mistake of devising a technical trading strategy based on past data without testing it out of sample. And they made another classic mistake of not "stress testing" their derivative trading strategy. MGRM's business plan includes a few scenario analyses of projected profits, but the worst outcomes displayed are "minimum profit" scenarios and do not reveal the possibility of any cash drain.

A good illustration of how easy it is to underestimate the problem of possibly negative cashflow is Culp and Miller's own suggestion for a pure synthetic strategy, a suggestion made with no number attached. Under this strategy MGRM deposits with the clearinghouse collateral in the form of T-bills equal to the initial face value of its total futures position, "thus ensuring that no further cash outlays would be required over the life of the hedge, regardless of price movements". Just how much in T-bills would have been required given MGRM's position? Assuming no basis risk, we estimate more than US$3 billion, a hefty sum indeed! A calculation recognising possible losses due to basis risk would raise the number higher still. Culp and Miller say that the notion of a pure synthetic strategy puts to rest once and for all the view that maturity mismatch gave rise to financial distress. We think, on the contrary, that the US$3 billion figure illustrates perfectly the significance of the maturity mismatch problem: when that number is compared against the rest of the parent corporation's balance sheet, the idea that MGRM would have received funding becomes dubious to say the least.

A final point of difference we have with Culp and Miller is our claim that MGRM was actively speculating in oil derivatives. Although Culp and Miller downplay this possibility, we think their representation of MGRM's strategy as "synthetic storage" makes *our* point. The firm was not hedging any real storage activity. Rather it was constructing storage using the financial markets, betting that the prevailing cost of long-term deliveries relative to the implicit cost of storage reflected in the history of short-term oil futures prices. We have already pointed out above that this strategy is essentially a speculation on the basis risk. There seems to be agreement on the formal mathematical facts describing MGRM's strategy but some difference in how we each judge these facts.

We claim, moreover, that a careful examination of MGRM's actual business plan as well as the history of its trading activities and most especially the exaggerated size of its stack all lead one to the conclusion the MGRM's management was speculating. It was MGRM's management who justified the rolling stack using calculations of the historic profit an arbitrary investor would have made rolling over a one-month crude oil futures contract: these calculations did not include any careful analysis of the net present value of synthetic storage. The calculations in the business plan regarding synthetic storage are riddled with assumptions about mispriced contracts and the opportunity available to profit by buying in at highs and selling at lows. Nowhere in the business plan does MGRM's management do any accounting for basis risk and the appropriate discount to charge for it. Not only was MGRM's strategy speculative, but it exhibited all the features of classically mistaken speculations. MGRM's decision to run a "front-to-back" strategy is just the oil market equivalent of riding the yield curve in the bond market, with all the dangerous consequences that entails.

1 Business Plan for MG Refining and Marketing, Inc, December 1, 1991 to May 31, 1992.

2 *A comprehensive overview of MGRM's programmes and positions is available in the report of the special auditor requested by the extraordinary shareholders meeting of February 24, 1994,* Bericht über die Sonderprüfung nach 142 Abs. 1 AktG bei der Metallgesellschaft Aktiengesellschaft, gemäß Beschluß der außerordentlichen Hauptversammlung am 24 Februar 1994, *by C&L Treuarbeit and Wollert-Elmendorff, January 20, 1995.*

3 *Attention to the customer's particular circumstances is key in valuing these options. To see why, notice that under the terms of the* firm-fixed *contracts the customer would forgo half the amount by which the contract was in the money. Therefore the customer has a significant disincentive to exercising the option except as their own liquidity needs outweigh the capital loss involved. The actual duration of MGRM's forward obligation is therefore highly variable and, due to its dependence on the customer's circumstances, difficult to anticipate. Note, moreover, that the duration may be either shorter or* longer *than that of an annuity since under the flexible contracts the customer had the right to delay taking deliveries until it believed spot prices put its option in the money.*

In mid-1993 MGRM succeeded in renegotiating the terms of the option in a little more than half of the firm-fixed *contracts so that cash settlement would occur automatically once the near-month futures price reached a certain level. The customers received a concession on the delivery price in exchange for losing this option.*

4 *The full details of MGRM's trading were more complicated than this simple characterization. For example, since some customers could alter the delivery schedule and since the options in the supply contracts allowed the buyer to advance maturity of the contract it was envisioned that the quantity of futures contracts rolled over might change to match the changing quantity of short positions retired. Moreover, MGRM maintained a long position in a variety of contract months, not only the near-month contract, and had flexibility to alter the exact maturity structure of its stack. Finally, MGRM shifted its position among different oil products independently of the products shorted under the delivery contracts. For full details of the actual positions see the special auditor's report previously cited and court documents in* W. Arthur Benson v. Metallgesellschaft Corp et al, *Civ. Act. No. JFM-94-484, US District Court for the District of Maryland, 1994. Also relevant is MGRM's own* Policy and Procedures Manual, *1992, although its trades were not always faithful to these guidelines.*

5 *The example is a simplified version of what happened to MGRM since we have assumed that all of the contracts were signed in March of 1993 and that the rolling stack consists entirely of near month crude oil futures contracts. The actual losses as reported by the special auditors differ modestly in timing.*

6 *Of course it is not just the monthly variation in the spot price that determines MGRM's losses on its futures stack. What matters is the monthly realisation of the spot price relative to the futures price at which the position was opened, ie, how the entire term structure of oil prices moves from month to month. In 1993 this movement was characterised both by a marked fall in the spot price and a persistent contango. It is the combination that yields the exact cashflow consequences for MGRM.*

7 *The realised losses on the rolling stack detailed in Table 1 do not include the cash contributions necessary to meet margin calls and so significantly understate the cashflow deficit created by a rolling stack.*

8 *See Froot, Scharfstein and J. Stein (1993).*

9 *We have made this point elsewhere in Mello, Parsons and Triantis.*

10 *Constructing a mirror image hedge of a forward contract can be difficult. The mark-to-market feature of futures makes it difficult to use them to exactly match the maturity of a forward delivery obligation even when, as in the case of a strip, the nominal maturity is the same. Because settlement of the futures occurs continuously, cashflows resulting from price movements are paid out earlier than under a forward obligation with nominally identical maturity. In any case, due to the long maturity of MGRM's forward commitments an appropriate strip of exchange-traded futures was not feasible. MGRM could have used the OTC market to construct an instrument with appropriate maturity. The OTC market makes it possible to custom design an instrument to mirror the maturity structure of the delivery obligations inclusive of the options.*

11 *MG's liquidity crisis was never* merely *a liquidity crisis. Even if the firm were solvent and merely needed a cash infusion, a liquidity crisis itself can create real costs. MG had a large number of bankers, and while this may seem advantageous, the question of who shall provide the extra financing and with what seniority relative to the preexisting debt obligations opens up a Pandora's box of manoeuvring and negotiation, all of which may impose deadweight losses on the firm. And while one may be critical of the bankers for engaging in such conduct, one should also be critical of the management for not anticipating these kinds of problems in its design of the hedge. It is no use complaining about the costs that arise in*

going to the market for external funds when the very purpose of the hedge should be to avoid this necessity in the first place!

12 *For data on oil see Gibson and Schwartz (1990 and 1991), and also Edwards and Canter (1995). For data on other commodities see Fama and French (1988).*

13 *The present value factors shown in Table 3 provide only a rough order of magnitude for the relation being estimated. The values shown were derived at a particular historical period and are only the local change in value for a small change in price. A detailed calculation is beyond the scope of this chapter.*

14 *These two simple hedge ratio calculations have been made for ease of exposition. The proper ratio incorporating the options can be calculated using the appropriate differential equations as shown in Gibson and Schwartz (1990). In recognising the cashout option it is important to remember that customers holding the firm-fixed contracts would forgo half of the profit on the contract should they call. MGRM's exposure, therefore, to the volume called is only one-half the nominal volume and it should hold maximally a one-to-two ratio of futures to deliveries to cover this exposure.*

15 *MGRM's accountants, Arthur Andersen, had always recognised the possibility of defaults, adding to reserves against this possibility. After the adverse price movements in 1993 KPMG suggested that this reserve might need to be increased. See "Draft Report on Handelsbilanz II Financial Statements", KPMG, January 14, 1994.*

16 *For an equilibrium model producing persistent backwardation, see Litzenberger and Rabinowitz (1994), "Backwardation in Oil Futures Markets: Theory and Empirical Evidence", Working paper, Wharton School, University of Pennsylvania. Of course, if futures prices are backwardated according to the predictions of this model, then a strategy of buying the futures contract does not yield a positive net present value when properly discounted to recognise its risk.*

17 *See especially the paper "MG Refining and Marketing Inc: Hedging Strategies Revisited" in* W. Arthur Benson v. Metallgesellschaft Corp et al, *Civ. Act. No. JFM-94-484, US District Court for the District of Maryland, 1994.*

18 *See, for example,* The JPMCI – A Commodity Benchmark, *JP Morgan, September 20, 1994.*

19 *The agency problems to which we are referring here arise both between the shareholders and the creditors and between the subsidiary management and the shareholders. A good introduction to the problems of shareholder-creditor relations in general and the risk shifting game in particular is given in Brealey and Myers (1991),* Principles of Corporate Finance, *Chapter 18, 4th edn (New York: McGraw Hill).*

20 *Culp and Miller (1995).*

21 *Curiously, in their paper that appeared in the* Journal of Applied Corporate Finance, *Culp and Miller give the impression that basis risk is a relatively minor issue, referencing their own estimates of the high correlation between spot and front month futures prices. Despite the impression raised that these correlation figures are high, in fact, they are consistent with the data we referenced and used to construct Table 3, 4 and 5. For example, Culp and Miller focus on the basis risk within one month and find* R^2 *values of 0.99 for crude oil, 0.96 for heating oil, and 0.95 for gasoline, while the factor we used to relate a US$1 change in the prevailing spot price to the change in the expected value of a one-month forward delivery obligation was 0.991, relatively close. And as the time to maturity of the forward obligation increases, the effect of imperfect correlation within any single month is compounded, yielding the other factors shown in Table 3 of our paper. The one month correlation data in Culp and Miller's paper therefore appear perfectly consistent with our estimates of US$650 million net loss due to basis risk. This fact seems to be borne out by Culp and Miller's own later estimate of the total change in rollover costs, which appeared in their* Risk *magazine article.*

22 *Mello and Parsons (1995), "Hedging a Flow of Commodity Deliveries with Futures: Problems with a Rolling Stack", in* Derivatives Quarterly, *Fall.*

BIBLIOGRAPHY

Culp, C. L., and M. Miller, 1995, "Auditing the MG Shareholders' Audit", *Risk*, v. 8, n. 4 (April); reprinted as Chapter 10 of the present volume.

Edwards, F., and M. Canter, 1995, "The Collapse of Metallgesellschaft: Unhedgeable Risks, Poor Hedging Strategy, or Just Bad Luck?", *The Journal of Futures Markets*, 15(3); reprinted as Chapter 13 in the present volume.

Fama E., and K. French, 1988, "Business Cycles and the Behavior of Metals Prices", *Journal of Finance* 43, pp. 1075–94.

Froot, K. A., D. S. Scharfstein and J. C. Stein, 1993, "Risk Management: Coordinating Corporate Investment and Financing Policies", *Journal of Finance* 48(5), pp. 1629–58; reprinted as Chapter 7 of the present volume.

Gibson, R., and E. S. Schwartz, 1990, "Stochastic Convenience Yield and the Pricing of Oil Contingent Claims", *Journal of Finance* 45, pp. 959–76.

Gibson, R., and E. S. Schwartz, 1991, "Valuation of Long Term Oil-Linked Assets", in *Stochastic Models and Option Values*, D. Lund and B. Kendal, eds (Amsterdam: North-Holland), pp. 73–101.

Litzenberger, R., and N. Rabinowitz, 1994, "Backwardation in Oil Futures Markets: Theory and Empirical Evidence", Working paper, Wharton School, University of Pennsylvania.

Mello, A., and J. Parsons, 1995, "Hedging a Flow of Commodity Deliveries with Futures: Problems with a Rolling Stack", *Derivatives Quarterly* (Fall).

Mello, A., J. Parsons and A. Triantis, "An Integrated Model of Multinational Flexibility and Financial Hedging", forthcoming in the *Journal of International Economics*.

13

The Collapse of Metallgesellschaft: Unhedgeable Risks, Poor Hedging Strategy, or Just Bad Luck?*

Franklin R. Edwards and Michael S. Canter

Columbia University

In late 1993 and early 1994 MG Corporation, the US subsidiary of Germany's 14th largest industrial firm, Metallgesellschaft AG (MG AG), reported staggering losses on its positions in energy futures and swaps. Only a massive US$1.9 billion rescue operation by 150 German and international banks kept Metallgesellschaft AG from going into bankruptcy, an event that could have had far-reaching consequences for MG's creditors, suppliers and 58,000 employees.

During 1993 MG's US oil trading subsidiary, MG Refining and Marketing (MGRM), established very large derivatives positions in energy futures and swaps (equivalent to about 160 million barrels of oil), from which it would profit handsomely if energy prices were to rise. But instead of rising, energy prices (crude oil, heating oil and gasoline) fell sharply during the latter part of 1993, causing MGRM to incur unrealised losses and margin calls on these derivatives positions in excess of US$900 million.

Initial press reports indicated that MG's predicament was the result of massive speculation in energy futures and off-exchange over-the-counter (OTC) energy swaps by MGRM. Some members of Metallgesellschaft AG's supervisory board also characterised MGRM's oil trading activities as "a game of roulette". And when MG's supervisory board installed new management at MGRM near the end of 1993, the new management team declared that "speculative oil deals ... had plunged Metallgesellschaft into the crisis."[1]

Not all press reports, however, have held to this view. Some have suggested that MGRM's derivatives activities were in fact part of a complex oil marketing and hedging strategy that it was pursuing. In particular, MGRM reportedly was using its derivatives positions to hedge price exposure on forward-supply contracts that committed it to supply approximately 160 million barrels of gasoline and heating oil to end-users over the next 10 years at fixed prices. The fixed supply prices in these contracts, negotiated at the time that the contracts were established, were typically three to five dollars a barrel higher than prevailing spot prices when the contracts were negotiated (and were MGRM's profit margins or mark-ups).[2]

The forward-delivery contracts also contained a "cash-out" option for MGRM's counterparties. If energy prices were to rise above the contractually fixed price, MGRM's counterparties could choose to sell the remainder of its forward obligations back to MGRM for a cash payment of one-half the difference between the prevailing near-month futures price and the contractually fixed supply price times the total volume remaining on the contract.

**Originally published in the* Journal of Applied Corporate Finance *8(1) (1995), pp. 86–105, as an abbreviated version of an article in the* Journal of Futures Markets *15(3) May 1995. For a complete set of citations, references and figures, see the latter article.*

Most of the forward-delivery contracts were negotiated during the summer of 1993, when energy prices were low and falling. Energy end-users apparently saw an attractive opportunity to lock in low energy prices, and MGRM apparently saw an equally attractive opportunity to develop long-term profitable customer relationships that it could build on in pursuing its long-run strategy of developing a fully-integrated oil business in the US.[3] MGRM's counterparties in these forward contracts were retail gasoline suppliers, large manufacturing firms and some government entities. Although many of the end-users were small, some were substantial firms: Chrysler Corp, Browning-Ferris Industries Corp and Comcar Industries (which uses 60 million gallons of diesel fuel a year).

In 1989, as part of its efforts to develop a fully-integrated oil business in the US, MGRM also acquired a 49% interest in Castle Energy, a US oil exploration company, which it then helped to become an oil refiner. In order to assure a supply of energy products in the future, MGRM agreed to purchase Castle's entire output of refined products (estimated to be about 126,000 barrels a day) at guaranteed margins for up to 10 years into the future. In addition, MGRM set about to develop an infrastructure to support the storage and transportation of various oil products.

MGRM's fixed-price forward-delivery contracts exposed it to the risk of rising energy prices. If energy prices were to rise in the future, it could find itself in the unprofitable position of having to supply energy products to customers at prices below prevailing spot prices. More important, if prices rose high enough and remained high, the profit margins in the contracts would be eroded and MGRM could end up taking substantial losses for years to come.

MGRM hedged this price risk with energy futures and OTC swaps. Not to have hedged would have put MGRM (and therefore MG) in the position of making a substantial bet that energy prices would either fall or at least not rise in the future. Had MGRM been able to hedge its price risk successfully, it stood to make substantial profits. By locking in an average contractual mark-up of US$4 a barrel on its forward energy sales over 10 years, it would have earned profits of approximately US$640 million.

The controversy surrounding MG's fate is whether MGRM's hedging strategy was in fact ever capable of locking in these profits. Critics contend that its hedging strategy was fatally flawed, and exposed the firm to unacceptable risks. The objective in this chapter is to examine the risks that MGRM was taking and to clarify the risk trade-offs that it was making. In addition, the chapter provides as many facts as are available so that readers can judge for themselves whether MGRM's hedging strategy exposed the firm to an unreasonable risk.

A complicating factor in evaluating a hedger's risk exposure is that all hedgers take some risk. As every student of futures markets knows, hedgers are "speculators on the basis", trading a greater price risk for a lesser basis risk.[4] To determine whether a particular hedger's strategy is sound, the risk assumed by the firm must be evaluated in the context of the firm's objectives. The objective of MGRM's hedging strategy was to protect the profit margins in its forward-delivery contracts by insulating them from increases in energy prices. The overall strategic objective of MG, however, was to develop a fully integrated oil business in the US. MGRM's role in this strategy was to market and supply petroleum products to end-users, which it did through its forward-delivery programme. The soundness of MGRM's hedging strategy, therefore, should be judged against both its specific hedging objective as well as the firm's overall strategic objective.

MGRM's short-dated stack hedging strategy

MGRM hedged the risk of rising energy prices with both short-dated energy futures contracts and OTC swaps. It acquired long futures positions on the New York Mercantile Exchange (Nymex), and entered into OTC energy swaps entitling it to receive payments based upon floating energy prices while making fixed payments. MGRM's counterparties in these swaps were large OTC swap dealers such as banks. By the fourth quarter of 1993, MGRM held long futures positions on the Nymex equivalent to 55 million barrels of gasoline, heating oil and crude oil (55,000 contracts), and had swap positions of 100 to 110 million barrels – substantial positions by any measure. MGRM's total derivatives position was virtually identical to its forward-supply commitments: 160 million barrels. Thus, MGRM hedged its forward-supply commitments "barrel for barrel" (or with a hedge ratio of one).[5]

An important aspect of MGRM's hedging strategy was that its derivatives positions were concentrated (or "stacked") in short-dated futures and swaps that had to be "rolled forward" continuously to maintain the position.[6] In general, its futures and swap positions were in contracts with maturities of at most a few months from the current date. It therefore had to roll these contracts forward periodically (probably monthly) to maintain its hedge. As MGRM rolled its derivatives positions forward each month, it reduced the size of its derivatives positions by the amount of the product delivered to customers that month, maintaining a one-to-one hedge.

This "stack and roll" strategy can be profitable when markets are in *backwardation* – that is, loosely speaking, when spot prices are higher than futures prices. But when markets are in *contango* – futures prices are higher than spot prices – the strategy will result in losses. In a backwardation market, a strategy of continually rolling short-dated positions forward yields "rollover gains" because oil for immediate delivery ("nearby" oil) gets a higher price than does, say, three-month oil ("deferred-month" oil). In a contango market, however, MGRM would incur rollover losses; it would be forced to purchase deferred-month futures at higher prices than the prices it could sell these contracts for as they neared expiration. Thus, the success of MGRM's "stack and roll" strategy partially depended on whether energy markets were going to be in contango or backwardation.

What went wrong?

MGRM's problems surfaced in late 1993 when energy spot prices tumbled. As a result, it experienced large unrealised losses on its stacked long futures and swap positions and incurred huge margin calls.[7] MGRM's problems were compounded by the fact that energy futures markets went into a contango price relationship for almost the entire year of 1993, causing it to incur substantial costs each time it rolled its derivatives positions forward.

If energy prices had risen rather than fallen, MGRM would not have had a problem. It would have had unrealised gains on its derivatives positions and positive margin flows (or cash in-flows). Although it would also have had unrealised losses on its forward-delivery obligations, no one would have cared. But energy prices did fall, from around US$19 a barrel of crude oil in June of 1993 to less than US$15 a barrel in December 1993, causing MGRM to have to come up with enormous amounts of money to fund margin calls. In December 1993, at the height of what to many seemed like a liquidity crisis, MG's supervisory board fired MGRM's management and brought in new management, which quickly made the decision to liquidate the bulk of MGRM's derivatives and forward-delivery positions.

Was MGRM's short-dated, stack, hedging strategy fatally flawed? Critics assert that this strategy exposed it to three significant and related risks: *rollover risk, funding risk and credit risk*. It was exposed to rollover risk because of uncertainty about whether it would sustain gains or losses when rolling its derivatives positions forward. Critics also believe that MGRM was exposed to funding risk because of the mark-to-market conventions that applied to its short-dated derivatives positions. Finally, they claim that MGRM was exposed to credit risk because its forward-delivery counterparties might default on their long-dated obligations to purchase oil at fixed prices. Each of these risks is examined in the sections of the chapter that follow.

Physical storage as an alternative hedging strategy

To better understand MGRM's rationale for choosing to hedge with short-dated derivatives, it is instructive to examine why it did not hedge by physical storage.[8] MGRM clearly could have hedged the price risk on its forward-delivery contracts by purchasing and storing the amount of physical oil (or other energy products) needed to meet its forward-supply commitments, thereby locking in today's energy prices. This strategy, however, while assuring that MGRM would have the oil it needed in the future, would have locked in a *loss* rather than a profit.

Physical storage is not costless. Funds must be committed to the immediate purchase of oil ("financing" costs), and there are "storage" costs – storage tanks, insurance and so forth. In MGRM's case, these costs would have exceeded the profit margins built into its forward-supply contracts, so that it would have ended up losing money on its forward-delivery contracts. In fact, if total storage costs were to exceed 7.33 cents per barrel per month, a strategy of physical storage would have resulted in a net loss for MGRM. The actual cost of physical storage is considerably higher.[9] Thus, while a strategy of physical storage could have successfully eliminated MGRM's price risk, it also would have eliminated the profits on its forward sales.[10]

By using short-dated derivatives, or a "synthetic" storage strategy, MGRM believed that it could successfully hedge its price risk while having to pay what was in effect a lower cost of storage.[11] More specifically, it believed that, because energy futures markets are often in

Table 1. Summary of rollover gains and losses using three-day rollover rule* April 1983 to December 1992

		Crude oil	Heating oil	Gasoline
Summary statistics (Apr 1983 to Dec 1992)**	Mean rollover	0.25	0.32	0.45
	Mean of all rollover gains	0.48	1.10	0.86
	Mean of all rollover losses	–0.24	–0.33	–0.51
	Cumulative rollover gain	29.63	37.69	43.58
	Frequency of a rollover gain	67%	45%	70%
Frequency of a rollover gain	Jan	67%	89%	50%
	Feb	78%	78%	13%
	Mar	67%	100%	38%
	Apr	80%	100%	75%
	May	40%	70%	88%
	Jun	50%	10%	88%
	Jul	70%	0%	88%
	Aug	60%	0%	100%
	Sep	80%	0%	88%
	Oct	70%	0%	88%
	Nov	80%	50%	75%
	Dec	70%	60%	56%
Cumulative rollover gains by month**	Jan	3.70	13.20	0.02
	Feb	3.80	10.68	–2.75
	Mar	1.99	9.77	–3.18
	Apr	2.09	8.41	5.95
	May	2.03	1.71	5.59
	Jun	2.24	–1.46	6.17
	Jul	1.82	–3.76	5.63
	Aug	0.71	–3.89	6.88
	Sep	3.17	–3.74	7.00
	Oct	2.39	–3.29	8.94
	Nov	2.66	–1.02	3.10
	Dec	3.03	11.09	0.23
Cumulative rollover gains by year**	1983	1.14	–0.60	
	1984	–0.55	6.18	–0.25
	1985	9.50	6.75	11.75
	1986	1.53	5.32	3.36
	1987	3.64	0.70	0.17
	1988	1.42	2.83	8.58
	1989	7.96	12.15	6.35
	1990	1.15	2.33	7.47
	1991	4.23	3.97	7.56
	1992	–0.39	–1.94	–1.41

*All rollovers are calculated using a three-day rollover rule: on the third day prior to the last day of trading we sell the near-month contract and buy the contract month which is the second closest to delivery. The rollover gain or loss is calculated as the near-month price minus the second-month price. Data for gasoline begins in December 1984. We have also calculated these statistics after excluding the extreme observations in late 1989. The results do not change appreciably, except for heating oil, where the mean rollover becomes 0.20 and the mean of all rollover gains becomes 0.85.
**All rollover gains, losses, and means are reported in US$/barrel. Heating oil and gasoline are traded on a US$/gallon basis. There are 42 gallons per barrel.
Data source: Knight-Ridder Futures Markets Database

"backwardation", when it rolled its short-dated derivatives positions forward through time it would receive a "convenience yield" that would offset or reduce the implicit costs of storing oil. The success of MGRM's hedging strategy, therefore, depended on the belief that it would profit from rolling forward its short-dated derivatives positions.

MGRM's belief that rollovers would be profitable

Some idea of what MGRM believed its rollover gain was likely to be can be obtained from data on historical price relationships in energy markets. To estimate likely rollover gains and losses, however, two assumptions must be made about exactly how MGRM went about rolling its positions forward.[12] First, we assumed that each month MGRM purchased the futures contract with the second closest delivery date (hereafter referred to as the "second-month" futures), requiring delivery in approximately one month from the purchase date. Second, we assumed that four days prior to the end of trading on these contracts (or three days prior to the last day of trading on the contracts), MGRM sold these contracts and again purchased second-month futures contracts.[13] This rolling-forward trading strategy is referred

1. Crude oil monthly rollover gains and losses*
April 1983 to September 1994

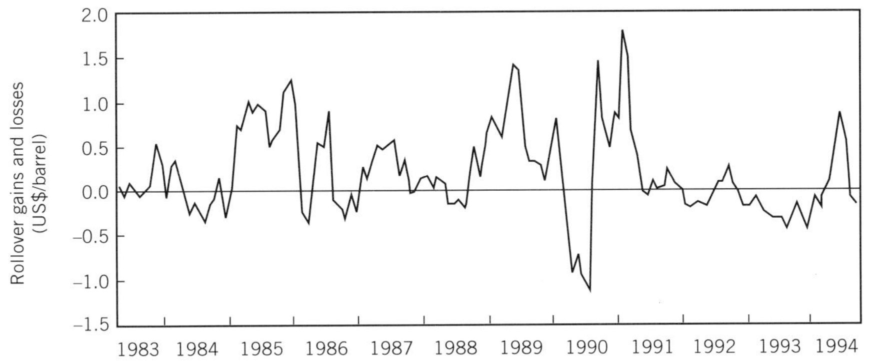

*Data source: Knight-Ridder.

to as the "three-day rollover rule". The rollover gains and losses that result from this rule are calculated as the near-month futures price minus the second-month futures price on the third day prior to the last day of trading.[14] (Other rollover rules were also analysed with similar results.)[15] Closing (or settlement) prices are used for all calculations.

Table 1 shows how MGRM would have fared using the three-day rollover rule during the nearly 11-year period from April 1983 to December 1992.[16] These results are based on daily data for crude oil, heating oil and gasoline, using closing (or settlement) prices. Several results in Table 1 are noteworthy. First, energy markets show a high *frequency of backwardation*, or a high frequency of rollover gains. For example, in the case of crude oil futures, on about 67% of the rollover dates the price of the second-month futures contract was below the price of the "spot" futures contract (or the contract closest to delivery). Thus, in crude oil futures MGRM would have made a positive return, or had a rollover gain, on two thirds of its rollovers. The corresponding figures for heating oil and gasoline futures are 45% and 70%, respectively. (Monthly rollover gains and losses are shown in Figure 1 for crude oil.)[17]

Second, dividing all rollover dates into two categories based on whether the market was in contango or backwardation on that date, the *average monthly rollover gain far exceeds the average monthly rollover loss*. The average monthly rollover losses and gains in crude oil, heating oil and gasoline are, respectively, -US$0.24/barrel versus US$0.48/barrel; -US$0.33/barrel versus US$1.10/barrel; and -US$0.51/barrel versus US$0.86/barrel. Given these disparities in the magnitude of average rollover gains and losses, rollovers would have produced a net loss only if the frequency of contango in these markets were to far exceed the frequency of backwardation, which, as we have seen, is not the case.

In markets prone to backwardation, as are energy futures markets, it is not surprising to find that average price backwardation exceeds average price contango. The amount of contango is limited by arbitrage to the "full cost-of-carry" (cash-and-carry arbitrage). In contrast, when markets are in backwardation, there is no arbitrage-limiting boundary to restrict the amount of backwardation.[18] This asymmetrical characteristic can be seen in Figure 1, which plots monthly rollover gains and losses for crude oil from 1983 to 1994.

Finally, aggregating all rollover gains and losses produces a *net average monthly rollover gain* for all three energy futures: US$0.25/barrel for crude oil; US$0.32/barrel for heating oil; and US$0.45/barrel for gasoline (see Table 1). Thus, if past price relationships in energy futures markets are a good predictor of future price relationships, MGRM could have expected to make a profit by rolling its short-dated derivatives position forward through time. Stated another way, the price characteristics of energy futures markets appear to reward a "synthetic" storage hedging strategy by permitting hedgers in effect to avoid the full costs (or any cost) of storage.

The intuition behind this result is that energy markets are characterised by frequent, seasonal shortages of the physical commodity, and at these times there is a substantial "convenience yield" embedded in futures prices. For commercial reasons, energy-supplying firms are willing to hold the physical commodity even though expected spot prices are considerably below current spot prices, providing an opportunity for others to purchase forward oil at prices that do not reflect storage costs for physical product.

These results need to be qualified in two ways. First, in reality MGRM need not have been so inflexible about when it rolled its positions forward. It could, for example, have rolled on days when particularly favourable price relationships existed, in which case our findings would understate the potential benefits to MGRM in holding short-dated futures and rolling these forward through time. On the other hand, our analysis implicitly assumes that MGRM would have been able to execute at the observed prices, which may not always have been possible.

The seasonality of price relationships in energy markets is also evident. Table 1 provides data on "rollover frequencies" for each calendar month and on "cumulative" rollover gains or losses by both calendar month and year. In general, heating oil is in backwardation and exhibits rollover gains from December to March; gasoline is in backwardation and exhibits rollover gains from April to November. Further, backwardation in heating oil and gasoline markets coincides with the approach of the end of the heating oil and gasoline "high-demand" seasons, when energy suppliers are reducing their inventories in anticipation of falling demand. Backwardation appears to be a general characteristic of crude oil futures.

Table 2. Rollover gains and losses using a three-day rollover rule and changes in spot prices 1993*

	Rollover date	Rollover gain or loss	Changes in spot prices
Crude oil	Jan 15, 1993	–0.16	–0.54
	Feb 17, 1993	–0.03	0.46
	Mar 17, 1993	–0.13	0.84
	Apr 16, 1993	–0.24	–0.03
	May 17, 1993	–0.32	–0.63
	Jun 17, 1993	–0.30	–0.81
	Jul 16, 1993	–0.28	–1.49
	Aug 17, 1993	–0.43	0.71
	Sep 17, 1993	–0.30	–0.85
	Oct 15, 1993	–0.11	1.20
	Nov 17, 1993	–0.38	–1.23
	Dec 16, 1993	–0.42	–2.81
	Total	–3.10	–5.18
Heating oil	Jan 26, 1993	–0.12	–1.09
	Feb 23, 1993	–0.03	0.85
	Mar 26, 1993	0.44	0.17
	Apr 27, 1993	0.01	–0.97
	May 25, 1993	–0.11	–0.46
	Jun 25, 1993	–0.24	–0.83
	Jul 27, 1993	–0.33	–0.27
	Aug 26, 1993	–0.42	0.51
	Sep 27, 1993	–0.43	0.09
	Oct 26, 1993	–0.30	–0.38
	Nov 23, 1993	–0.30	–0.77
	Dec 27, 1993	–0.03	–2.52
	Total	–1.86	–5.67
Gasoline	Jan 26, 1993	–0.58	0.20
	Feb 23, 1993	–1.71	–0.14
	Mar 26, 1993	–0.43	1.86
	Apr 27, 1993	–0.26	0.17
	May 25, 1993	–0.07	–0.21
	Jun 25, 1993	–0.16	–1.64
	Jul 27, 1993	–0.23	–0.87
	Aug 26, 1993	0.32	0.17
	Sep 27, 1993	–0.34	–2.00
	Oct 26, 1993	–0.09	–0.07
	Nov 23, 1993	–0.50	–1.62
	Dec 27, 1993	–0.81	–3.21
	Total	–4.87	–7.34

*All rollovers are calculated using a three-day rollover rule: on the third day prior to the last day of trading we sell the near-month contract and buy the contract which is the second closest to delivery. The rollover gain or loss is the near-month price minus the second-month price. To proxy for changes in spot prices we use changes in near-month futures prices. Spot price changes are from one rollover date to the next. All prices are reported in US$/barrel. Total figures may differ from the sum of the monthly figures because of rounding.
Data source: Knight-Ridder Futures Markets Database

Given this seasonality, it is possible that MGRM could have further increased its net rollover gain by moving its futures and swap positions from one commodity to another depending on the time of year and the expected backwardation in the respective markets.[19] Though such a strategy would have entailed more (cross-hedging) basis risk, the high correlations among the different energy prices suggest that this added risk would not have been large.[20]

Thus, at least on the basis of past price relationships, it does not seem unreasonable for MGRM to have expected that over a long period of time (such as 10 years) its hedging strategy would have produced a net rollover gain.

Did MGRM have a rollover risk?

A key issue is whether MGRM was exposed to a significant rollover risk. If markets were to experience an unusually long period of contango, MGRM could have been exposed to significant rollover losses; it would consistently have been forced to buy high and sell low in rolling its positions forward. We estimate that had a typical contango market occurred at the beginning of MGRM's hedging programme and lasted for a period of only one year and two months, its entire profit mark-up could have been wiped out.[21]

Some idea of the likelihood of MGRM's experiencing rollover losses for extensive periods of time can be gleaned from past data on the volatility of the "second-month" basis.[22] The standard deviations of the daily second-month basis for the 1983–1992 period for heating oil and gasoline are, respectively, US$0.89/barrel and US$0.85/barrel.[23] Thus, given a mean rollover gain in the range of US$0.25 to US$0.45/barrel per month, the possibility of rollover losses occurring is not insignificant.

It is revealing, however, to compare this rollover risk to the price risk that MGRM had on its forward-supply commitments. MGRM's price risk depended on the expected volatility of spot prices for heating oil and gasoline over the 10-year contractual period. Using data from the 1983–92 period, the respective standard deviations of daily heating oil and gasoline prices were US$5.96 and US$5.17/barrel.[24] Thus, if the respective basis and price standard deviations are used to measure

2. Crude oil monthly rollover gains and losses in 1993–1994 versus maximum roll gains and losses prior to 1993*

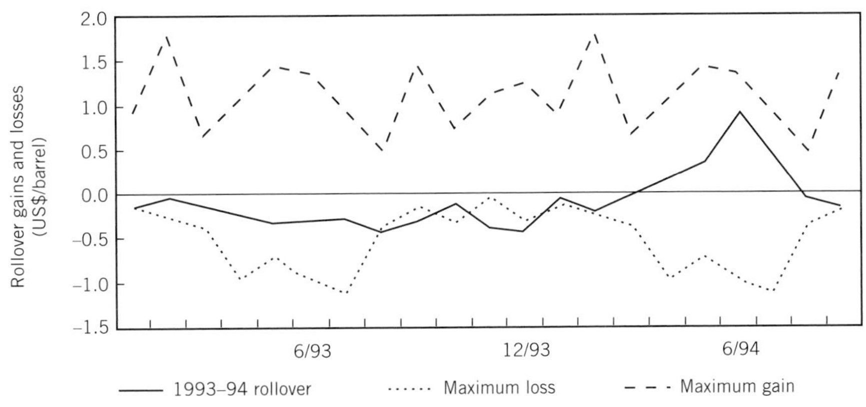

*Data source: Knight-Ridder.

MGRM's respective risk exposures, its short-dated hedging strategy exposed it to rollover risk on the order of 15% of its price risk.

Despite these statistics, 1993 turned out to be a disaster for MGRM. In 1993 crude oil was in contango every month, heating oil was in contango every month except March and April, and gasoline was in contango every month except August. Thus, virtually every time that MGRM rolled its positions forward, it sustained losses. If it is assumed that MGRM had positions on for the entire year and had to roll these forward every month, its cumulative roll *losses* for the year would have been US$1.86/barrel for heating oil, US$4.87/barrel for gasoline, and US$3.10/barrel for crude oil. (See Table 2.) Had MGRM sustained roll losses of this magnitude for very long, its profit margins of US$3 to US$5 would have been quickly eroded.

How predictable were the contango markets that occurred in 1993? The monthly rollover gain and loss frequencies reported in Table 1 suggest that the probability of a string of contango months occurring in the particular months in which they occurred in 1993 is extremely small - in fact, close to zero.[25] Nevertheless, there have been unusual strings of contango months in the past. In particular, for the 12-month period from May 1991 until May 1992, heating oil was in contango 10 out of 12 months; from July 1986 until June 1987, gasoline was in contango 9 out of 12 months; and from January 1992 until December 1992, crude oil was in contango 8 out of 12 months. Thus, the string of contango months in 1993, though unusual, was not without some precedent.

Alternatively, 1993 can be compared to a "worst-case" scenario constructed with past data. Figure 2 plots the rollover losses for crude oil that occurred in each month during 1993 against the *maximum* (or "worst-case") rollover losses (or contango) that occurred in the past in *each* of the calendar months (using data from the period April 1983, to December 1992).[26] In other words, the *maximum* calendar-month rollover losses consist of the worst January rollover loss that occurred in any of the previous 10 years, the worst February rollover loss in any previous year, and so forth, for every calendar month. As shown in Figure 2, the monthly rollover losses that occurred in 1993 were generally quite similar, though with some exceptions, to the maximum rollover losses that occurred in earlier years.

Critics also contend that MGRM's rollover strategy was fatally flawed because of the size of its derivatives positions. They argue, first, that its derivatives positions were large enough to move the market from backwardation into contango; and second, that MGRM's counterparties (or traders) were in a position to extract from MGRM a monopoly price when it rolled positions forward, forcing it to sell at a lower price and buy at a higher price because of their market power *vis-à-vis* MGRM.

MGRM's positions, however, were not large relative to total open interest. Its total futures positions constituted only about 6.7% of total open interest, and its combined futures and swaps positions constituted about 20% of total open interest.[27] In addition, it seems unlikely that traders would have had monopoly power relative to MGRM. There are no significant barriers to entry into trading futures on an exchange, and in OTC swap markets there are a large number of potential counterparties. MGRM could have moved positions from one energy market to another, and from exchange to off-exchange positions, and could have rolled positions forward on many different dates.

In summary, past data provides reasonable support for MGRM's presumption that it could expect to earn a net rollover gain. But in relying on past data to predict future rollover gains, MGRM was implicitly making two critical assumptions: that the structure of energy futures markets would not change significantly in the future (that history would repeat itself), and that a history of only 10 years is long enough to provide accurate long-term forecasts of rollover returns. While such assumptions may seem "heroic" to many observers, there is some reason to believe that periodic price backwardation is a permanent feature of energy markets. Seasonal spikes in demand coupled with a shortage of storage facilities appear to assure that backwardation will continue to exist. On the other hand, institutional speculators in commodity markets (such as commodity pools), which have been growing rapidly in recent years, may in the future compete away the positive roll returns on which MGRM's strategy depended.[28]

Finally, although hedgers commonly assume a stable market structure in formulating their hedging policies,[29] a characteristic that may distinguish MGRM from other hedgers is that its strategy required an assumption that the market structure would be stable for a very long period of time. Further, even with a stable market structure, MGRM could only be assured of a net rollover gain if it were able to continue its hedging programme for a long period of time. In the short run almost any outcome was a possibility, as MGRM's experience in 1993 clearly revealed. In addition, the "early cash-out" options in MGRM's forward-delivery contracts could have caused it to end its hedging strategy unexpectedly.[30] In particular, had its customers exercised their options subsequent to a period during which MGRM incurred rollover losses, it would have had to end its hedging programme before being able to offset these losses with rollover gains. Finally, to reap the expected long-term rollover gains, MGRM implicitly assumed that it could fund whatever rollover losses it sustained in the short run. The soundness of MGRM's short-dated hedging strategy, therefore, must be judged on the basis of the reasonableness of these assumptions.

Rollover risk: lessons from other commodities

To get some idea of the reliability of using past price data to predict future rollover returns, we examine two commodity futures with longer price histories than energy futures: soybeans and copper. These commodity futures are similar to energy futures in that they also exhibit periods of recurring contango and backwardation price relationships. Daily data for soybean and copper futures are available for the 30-year period 1965 to 1994, permitting an analysis of three separate 10-year periods.

Tables 3 and 4 provide, for each of these periods, various statistics for soybean and copper futures on the frequency of contango and backwardation price relationships as well as summary statistics on the size of rollover gains and losses (similar statistics were provided earlier in Table 1 for crude oil, heating oil and gasoline futures).[31] In the first period, 1965 to 1974, both soybeans and copper were in backwardation much of the time (44% and 62%, respectively) so that the average rollover gains were 5.52 cents per bushel and 1.47 cents per pound.[32] During the second period (1975–84), however, rollover returns for soybeans and copper were quite different. Rather than rollover gains, both soybeans and copper experienced rollover losses on average. Further, the frequency of backwardation dropped precipitously, to 23% for soybeans and 3% for copper. In the third period (1985–94), rollover gains and losses were again quite different than they were in the second period. Thus, these data suggest that in commodity futures markets it would not be surprising to find that average rollover returns during any 10-year period would not be a good predictor of average rollover returns during any successive 10-year period.

A striking parallel to what happened to MGRM in 1992 and 1993 also can be seen in the soybeans and copper data. During the last year of the first time period (1974) and the first year of the second time period (1975), rollover returns for soybeans and copper turned sharply negative, similar to what happened to rollover returns for energy futures in 1992 and 1993. If one were standing in 1974 or 1975, would one have concluded that rollover returns for soybeans and copper would soon revert to being positive, or that they would remain negative for an indefinite period of time? As it turned out, rollover returns remained negative for most of the next 10 years, finally reverting to being positive in 1986 and 1987. Thus, in 1975 a bet that rollover returns would soon turn positive again would have gone sadly awry.

Table 3. Summary of rollover gains and losses using three-day rollover rule for soybeans and copper 1965 to 1994*

Soybeans		1965–74	1975–84	1985–94
Summary statistics for soybeans (1965–94)	Mean rollover	5.52	-4.56	-0.50
	Mean of all rollover gains	16.74	10.14	9.59
	Mean of all rollover losses	-3.50	-8.91	-6.86
	Cumulative rollover gain	386.12	-319.00	-34.75
	Frequency of a rollover gain	44%	23%	36%
Frequency of a rollover gain for soybeans	Jan	20%	0%	10%
	Mar	20%	0%	0%
	May	10%	30%	50%
	Jul	80%	70%	70%
	Aug	90%	50%	60%
	Sep	70%	10%	60%
	Nov	20%	0%	0%
Cumulative rollover gains by month for soybeans	Jan	-21.25	-110.00	-58.00
	Mar	-0.88	-107.50	-57.75
	May	25.13	-13.75	-15.75
	Jul	161.25	26.25	62.25
	Aug	197.75	47.00	92.75
	Sep	53.13	-44.50	2.50
	Nov	-29.01	-116.50	-60.75
Copper		**1965–74**	**1975–84**	**1985–94**
Summary statistics for copper (1965–94)	Mean rollover	1.47	-0.94	1.65
	Mean of all rollover gains	2.64	1.15	3.87
	Mean of all rollover losses	-0.48	-1.03	-0.53
	Cumulative rollover gain	88.03	-56.60	97.60
	Frequency of a rollover gain	62%	3%	49%
Frequency of a rollover gain for copper	Jan	70%	10%	40%
	Mar	70%	0%	60%
	May	80%	0%	50%
	Jul	50%	0%	30%
	Sep	60%	0%	60%
	Dec	40%	10%	56%
Cumulative rollover gains by month for copper	Jan	12.80	-16.30	16.25
	Mar	25.02	-8.70	22.80
	May	16.51	-9.15	13.20
	Jul	9.85	-8.55	3.40
	Sep	15.40	-14.10	33.30
	Dec	8.45	0.20	8.65

*All rollovers are calculated using a three-day rollover rule: on the third day prior to the last day of trading we sell the near-month contract and buy the contract month which is the second closest to delivery. The rollover gain or loss is calculated as the near-month price minus the second-month price. For soybeans all rollover gains, losses, and means are reported in cents per bushel, for copper they are reported in cents per pound. Our data ends in September 1994.
Data source: Knight-Ridder

Table 4. Cumulative rollover gains by year for soybeans and copper*

Year	Soybeans	Copper
1965	31.14	21.67
1966	42.37	5.85
1967	16.24	3.66
1968	9.25	13.50
1969	18.12	10.60
1970	-17.62	8.05
1971	-14.50	-1.30
1972	23.87	-2.80
1973	297.75	19.80
1974	-20.50	9.00
1975	-9.25	-3.50
1976	-29.00	-1.90
1977	54.25	-2.90
1978	-1.75	-4.20
1979	-58.50	-2.05
1980	-94.75	-16.35
1981	-69.25	-9.45
1982	-27.75	-6.50
1983	-63.50	-5.35
1984	-19.50	-4.40
1985	-2.25	-3.30
1986	56.75	-2.60
1987	12.00	5.45
1988	-53.25	46.40
1989	29.25	16.05
1990	-61.75	29.25
1991	-29.00	7.35
1992	-12.25	-2.10
1993	3.25	-2.55
1994	22.50	3.65

*All rollovers are calculated using a three-day rollover rule: on the third day prior to the last day of trading we sell the near-month contract and buy the contract month which is the second closest to delivery. The rollover gain or loss is calculated as the near-month price minus the second-month price. For soybeans all rollover gains, losses, and means are reported in cents per bushel, for copper they are reported in cents per pound. Our data ends in September 1994.
Data source: Knight-Ridder

There are several possible explanations for the unreliability of past price data in predicting future rollover returns. First, a period of 10 years may simply not be long enough to identify the true (structural) price relationship, or to infer long-run equilibrium rollover returns. Second, markets and structural price relationships can change from one period to the next, as fundamental economic events occur. If this happens, equilibrium rollover returns can be quite different in different time periods. Finally, because the distribution of rollover returns in commodity futures tends to be characterised by relatively high variances (relative to mean rollover returns), relying solely on past mean rollover returns for any finite period of time can result in large prediction errors. MGRM's hedging strategy, which depended on positive rollover returns, was vulnerable to any one (or to all) of these possibilities.

MG's alleged funding problem

A combination of falling energy prices and a contango market caused MGRM to have to fund sizeable cash outflows in 1993. Between June and December in 1993 crude oil prices declined by nearly US$6/barrel, forcing MGRM to post nearly US$900 million to maintain its hedge positions. In response, MG's supervisory board replaced MG's top management and liquidated MGRM's derivatives and forward-supply contracts positions, ending MG's foray into the US oil market.

MG's funding needs in 1993 can be decomposed into two components: funds to finance margin calls (or unrealised losses) on its derivatives positions due to declines in energy prices and funds to finance rollover losses due to contango markets (discussed above). Falling energy prices and contango markets, of course, may not be unrelated phenomena: falling energy prices are usually an indication that there are no product shortages, and in the absence of such shortages contango price relationships are normal. The bulk of MGRM's funding needs in 1993 arose, however, from having to meet margin calls due to price declines and not from rollover losses (see Table 2).

It is not obvious why MGRM would have had a problem funding these margin calls. Consider, for example, the following hypothetical situation. Suppose that MGRM's hedge was such that falling energy prices, although resulting in unrealised losses on its derivatives positions, also resulted in equal and offsetting unrealised *gains* on its fixed-price, forward-supply contracts. Since MGRM's forward-supply contracts locked in a fixed sale price for future deliveries, these contracts could be expected to increase in value as energy prices fell because MGRM's expected cost of supplying oil in the future also would fall, making the contracts more profitable. Given equal and offsetting gains and losses on its derivatives and forward-delivery contracts, it is not clear why MGRM would have had a funding problem. Arguably, it should have been able to borrow against the collateral of its now more valuable forward-delivery contracts.

There are two potential "economic" explanations for why MGRM may have encountered difficulty in using its forward-delivery contracts as collateral to fully fund its margin outflows.[33] First, it may not in fact have had equal and offsetting unrealised gains on its forward-delivery contracts. In that event it would have had to increase its general debt obligations to obtain the necessary funding, and its creditors may have balked if MG was already heavily indebted. Second, MGRM's forward-delivery contracts may have lacked the necessary "transparency" for creditors to lend against them, or at least for creditors to lend an amount necessary to cover its margin needs. In particular, it may have been difficult for MG's creditors to evaluate the counterparty credit risk embedded in MGRM's forward-delivery contracts.

THE FUNDING RISKS IMPLICIT IN MGRM'S HEDGING STRATEGY

MGRM's hedging strategy had two features that, as it turned out, may have had important funding implications. First, it used a one-to-one hedge instead of a "minimum-variance" hedge.[34] Second, it did not take into consideration the mismatch that existed in the timing of its expected cashflows (or, it did not "tail" its hedge).

MGRM's one-to-one hedging strategy

MGRM's strategy of using a one-to-one hedge could have caused a potential funding problem because it did not result in equal and offsetting unrealised gains in its forward-delivery contracts when energy prices fell. Alternatively stated, when energy prices fell, the value of MGRM's forward contracts did not increase by as much as the value of its derivatives positions would have declined, creating an imbalance in unrealised gains and losses.

MGRM's one-to-one hedge strategy had this consequence for two reasons. First, for this strategy to produce equal and offsetting changes in the value of MGRM's forward-delivery contracts, there would have to be a one-to-one price relationship between "forward" and spot energy prices, which is not the case in energy markets. More specifically, changes in the value of its forward-delivery contracts depended on changes in *forward* energy prices, while changes in the value of its short-dated derivatives positions depended on changes in *spot* energy prices. Because MGRM's forward-supply contracts called for it to deliver energy products over many years in the future, changes in the value of these contracts should have reflected expectations about what spot prices were likely to be at the various times when MGRM was expected to make deliveries. A reasonable procedure for valuing these forward-delivery contracts would thus have been to use forward prices as

Table 5. Price volatilities of different contract months and volatilities of intertemporal bases* 1990 to 1992

Contract maturity	Heating oil futures standard deviation	Gasoline futures standard deviation
One month	4.91	4.03
Two months	4.91	3.53
Three months	4.70	3.19
Six months	3.36	3.23
Nine months	2.48	3.19

Intertemporal basis	Heating oil intertemporal bases standard deviation	Gasoline intertemporal bases standard deviation
One-month – two-month	0.84	1.01
One-month – three-month	1.39	1.68
One-month – six-month	2.69	2.48
One-month – nine-month	3.07	2.44

*All volatilities are calculated using daily closing futures prices on the New York Mercantile Exchange. The volatilities are calculated using price levels. To create continuous time series for the different contract months all contracts are rolled into the next month three days prior to the last trading day of the near-month contract.
Data source: Knight-Ridder Futures Markets Database

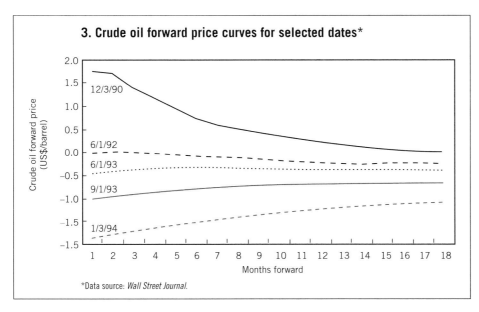

3. Crude oil forward price curves for selected dates*

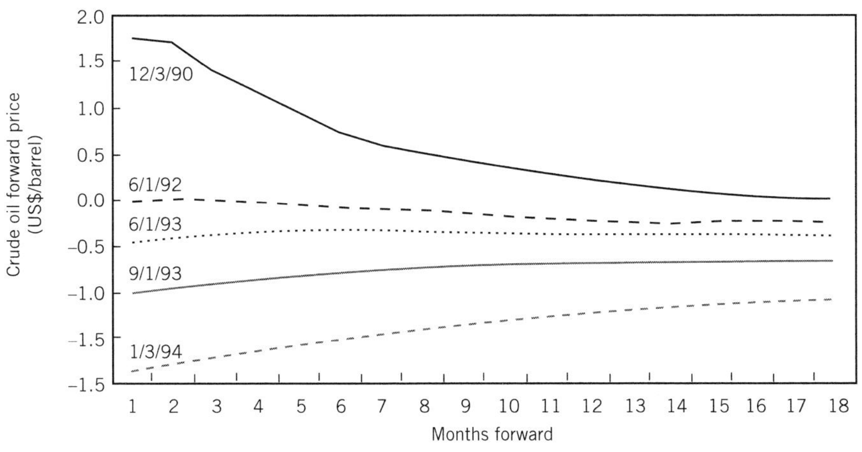

*Data source: *Wall Street Journal.*

predictors of future spot prices. In contrast, MGRM's derivatives positions were short-dated and their value depended solely on current spot prices. Thus, since the valuation of MGRM's derivatives and forward-delivery contracts depended on different prices, a one-to-one hedge strategy would result in equal and offsetting unrealised gains and losses on its forward and derivatives positions only if there were also a one-to-one relationship between spot and forward prices.

There is good reason to believe that a one-to-one relationship between spot and forward prices does not exist in energy markets. Theoretically, we would expect a US$1 change in spot prices to cause a less than US$1 change in forward prices. Changes in contemporary demand and supply conditions, which cause changes in current spot prices, can be expected to have less of an effect on prices five or 10 years from now, and therefore to generate smaller changes in forward prices than spot prices.

The evidence confirms this intuition. As shown in Table 5, the volatility of more distant futures prices is considerably less than the volatility of spot energy prices.[35] (See also Figure 3, which plots forward price curves for selected dates using available energy futures prices.)[36] It is clear that the volatility of forward prices is considerably less than that of spot prices, and that the price volatility of distant-month futures declines sharply even over a period as short as a year.[37]

A reasonable estimate of the price relationship between spot and forward energy prices over a 10-year period is 0.50; that is, a US$1 increase (decrease) in the current spot price will on average result in only a US$0.50 increase (decrease) in forward prices over a 10-year period. (See the regression estimates reported in Table 6.)[38] Given this estimate, when spot energy prices fell in 1993, MGRM's one-to-one hedge ratio would have resulted in an increase in the value of its forward-delivery contracts that was only half as large as the unrealised loss that it sustained on its short-dated derivatives contracts.

The second reason that MGRM's one-to-one hedging strategy would not have resulted in equal and offsetting gains on its forward-supply contracts is that it did not account for the mismatch that existed in the timing of the expected cashflows on its forward-supply contracts and its hedge positions. Even assuming a one-to-one relationship between spot and forward prices, the later realisation of the cashflows on MGRM's forward-delivery contracts would have resulted in a smaller change in the net present value of these contracts than on its derivatives contracts for *a given change in price*. In contrast to MGRM's short-dated derivatives, most of the cashflows (or revenues) from its forward-supply contracts would not have occurred until many years later. Conse-

Table 6. Regression estimates of relationship between spot and forward prices* 1990 to 1992

	Heating oil futures		Gasoline futures	
Time to expiration	**β**	**R^2**	**β**	**R^2**
Two-month futures	0.735	0.84	0.740	0.80
Three-month futures	0.625	0.79	0.650	0.75
Six-month futures	0.513	0.80	0.562	0.76
Nine-month futures	0.492	0.79	0.520	0.72

*$\Delta F(t,T) = \alpha + \beta\, \Delta F(t,t+1) + e$, where F(t,T) is the futures price at time t for delivery at time T. Δ signifies the daily change in price. Separate regressions are run for the cases where $T = t + 2$, $t + 3$, $t + 6$, $t + 9$. Thus for $t + 2$, changes in two-month futures prices are regressed on changes in near-month futures prices, for $t + 3$ changes in three-month futures prices are regressed on changes in near-month futures prices, etc. To create continuous time series for the different contract months all contracts are rolled into the next contract month three days prior to the last day of trading of the near-month contract. The β coefficients reported in the table are the regression coefficients and represent the minimum-variance hedge ratio that should be used to hedge a forward obligation in month T. All of the regression coefficients reported below are statistically significant at the one percent level. A Durbin–Watson test showed little serial correlation in the error terms in all cases. We obtained similar estimates after excluding Gulf War observations.

quently, to produce equal and offsetting unrealised gains and losses, MGRM would have had to adjust (or "tail") its hedge in order to put the expected cashflows from its forward-delivery contracts on an equivalent footing to the cashflows generated by its derivatives positions.[39] The use of a one-to-one hedge ratio did not accomplish this.

Taking both the likely price relationship between spot and forward energy prices and the "tailing" factor into consideration (and for the moment ignoring the options embedded in the forward-delivery contracts), it is estimated that MGRM would have needed a derivatives position of less than half of the position that it actually held in order to equate changes in the net present value of its forward-supply contracts to changes in the net present value of its derivatives positions.[40] More specifically, it would have needed a derivatives position of about 61 million barrels to hedge forward commitments of 160 million barrels. (See our article in the *Journal of Futures Markets*.)

Had MGRM used this smaller hedge position, its funding situation in 1993 when energy prices fell would have been significantly altered. First, with a derivatives position less than half as large as it actually held, its *net* unrealised losses (on both its forward-delivery contracts and derivatives positions) would have been virtually zero. Second, its margin calls would have been less than half of what they were. Finally, while not exclusively a funding problem, had MGRM held a smaller short-dated derivatives position in 1993, its rollover losses also would have been reduced substantially. Of course, if prices had risen instead of falling as they did in 1993, and had markets remained in backwardation, MGRM's one-to-one hedge would have worked out beautifully, producing substantial cash (or margin) inflows and large rollover profits.

The customer cash-out option

An argument has been made that MGRM, nevertheless, needed a one-to-one hedge ratio because of the customer "cash-out" options embedded in its forward-supply contracts. Specifically, in the event of an increase in spot energy prices, its customers had an option to "cash-out", or to liquidate their forward obligations to purchase oil and receive a cash payment from MGRM based on the future value of these contracts to customers.[41]

Two aspects of these contracts are noteworthy. First, the cash payment depends on near-month (or spot) energy prices, and not on forward energy prices (or expected spot prices). Second, MGRM and the customer shared equally in the customer's prospective gains due to higher energy prices. Thus, these options would be in-the-money for a customer only if the cash-out payment were greater than the net present value of the remaining forward-deliveries on the contract. This could occur, for example, if near-month futures prices rose much faster than forward prices. Alternatively, even if the forward-delivery contracts were not in-the-money for MGRM's customers (or even though the net present value of the forward contracts exceeded the option's value), they may nevertheless have exercised their cash-out options if they needed liquidity.

In either case, MGRM had to be prepared to make such up-front, lump-sum payments. Notwithstanding this possibility, it still did not need a one-to-one hedge. Suppose, for example, that a US$10/barrel increase occurred in spot energy prices within a year of MGRM writing the forward-delivery contracts, and that for whatever reason all of its customers opted to exercise their early cash-out options. What futures position would MGRM have needed to generate gains sufficient to cover its option payouts? Clearly, it would not have needed a one-to-one hedge because the maximum that customers could receive was 50% of the gain from the US$10 increase in spot prices. In the more general case, where the probability of exercise is less than one, a hedge ratio of 0.5 would more than cover MGRM's potential option payments. Thus, the customer "cash-out" options embedded in MGRM's forward-delivery contracts did not require use of a one-to-one hedging strategy.

For all of the reasons discussed above, MGRM's one-to-one hedge exposed the firm to funding risk that it could have avoided had it used a "minimum-variance" hedge ratio. In particular, a derivatives position about half as large as the one it actually used would have substantially reduced its funding needs in 1993 while at the same time providing reasonable protection against unpredictable fluctuations in energy prices. Further, had MGRM held a smaller short-dated derivatives position in 1993, its rollover losses would have been less.

Why, then, a one-to-one hedge ratio?

It is not known why MGRM chose to use a one-to-one hedge, but the following is a feasible rationale. To see the logic of using a one-to-one hedge, suppose that MGRM had been able to hedge with a "strip" (or a series) of forward contracts, where the contractual amounts and the expiration dates exactly matched the dates and the amounts of MGRM's forward-delivery obligations. In this case it is clear that a one-to-one hedge would have locked in all future delivery prices, and as such would have locked in the profit margins on MGRM's forward-delivery contracts. This hedging strategy also would not have been exposed to rollover risk and possibly not to funding risk as well (assuming an absence of "settling-up" provisions in the forward contracts).

The point of this "strip hedge" example is to show that ultimately MGRM would have needed a one-to-one hedge against all of its forward-supply obligations to insulate itself completely from rising energy prices. Thus, had it used a hedge ratio of less than one, it would have had to increase this ratio to one as the dates of its forward-delivery commitments drew near - or to adjust its hedge "dynamically" over time. Such adjustments could have imposed significant costs on MGRM had energy prices risen, and this may have deterred it from using a hedge ratio of less than one. (For an example of such dynamic hedging costs, see our *Journal of Futures Markets* article cited earlier.)

Thus, in choosing a one-to-one hedging strategy, MGRM consciously made a risk trade-off: in exchange for better protection against rising energy prices, it exposed itself to both greater funding risk and to greater rollover risk. Presumably, it had reasons to believe that the latter risks were less significant than were the potential consequences of rising energy prices.

NON-TRANSPARENCY AND CREDIT RISK

A second potential funding obstacle for MGRM was that its forward-delivery contracts may have lacked the transparency necessary for creditors to be willing to accept them as collateral. In particular, the enhanced value of its forward-delivery contracts due to falling energy prices was dependent on the willingness and the ability of its counterparties to meet their future obligations. Critics argue that MGRM was exposed to substantial non-performance risk because of the long-duration of its forward-supply contracts. Further, as energy prices fell, this risk could be expected to increase because of the growing disparity between the contractually-fixed sales prices and prevailing spot prices. Thus, without concrete information about the characteristics of MGRM's counterparties, its creditors might have been reluctant to lend against the collateral of its forward-delivery contracts.

It is well-known that the probability of a firm defaulting rises with time - or that "cumulative" default rates rise with time. Studies of bond defaults by Moody's suggest the probability of an issuer defaulting by the 10th year after issuance is much larger than the probability of its defaulting during the first year. For a B-rated issuer, for example, the probability of default during the first year is 8.31%, but rises to an impressive 39.96% by the 10th year.[42]

MGRM apparently recognised this default risk and sought to mitigate it by contracting to supply only a fraction of a customer's energy needs. If energy prices fell, customers would still be able to purchase most of the product they needed at the lower market prices. Further, when energy prices are falling, end-users typically have higher-than-normal profits for some time because retail prices commonly lag wholesale prices in energy markets.

Whatever the validity of these arguments, the key issues are whether MGRM's non-performance exposure was such that it could have reasonably predicted its losses arising from non-performance, and, if so, whether its profit mark-ups were sufficiently high to cover the expected credit losses. Well-diversified credit risks are insurable risks. The fundamental question, therefore, is whether MGRM charged a "self-insurance" risk premium that was high enough to cover its expected credit losses.

Given the available information, it is difficult to answer either of these questions. For example, without knowing how many customers MGRM had, or what businesses its customers were in, it is not possible to determine whether MGRM was sufficiently diversified. Further, without information about the balance sheets and income statements of MGRM's customers, it is impossible to attach a likelihood of default to them as a group. Until such information becomes available, therefore, there is no way of judging MGRM's credit exposure. Nevertheless, if MGRM's creditors did not have the necessary information to evaluate the nature and size of MGRM's credit exposure, they may have been reluctant to lend against the collateral of its forward-delivery contracts.

Did MGRM really have a funding problem?

Numerous press reports suggested that MGRM's hedging strategy unravelled because of a "liquidity" problem, an inability to raise the necessary funds to meet its margin calls. But this view is questionable. While MGRM's need to raise substantial funds clearly resulted in a complete reassessment of its strategy, it seems highly unlikely that MG's supervisory board would have jettisoned an otherwise sound strategy simply because of a short-term liquidity need. This view is based upon two considerations: the particular ownership structure of MG, and the fact that MG did not avail itself of funding that *was* available to it.

MG's ownership structure makes it highly unlikely that a simple liquidity problem would cause its owners to abandon an otherwise sound and profitable long-run investment strategy. MG is a classic German firm; ownership is concentrated in the hands of a few large owners with easy access to credit. Seven institutional investors hold just over 65% of the its stock. Deutsche Bank and Dresdner Bank, Germany's largest and second largest commercial banks, together directly own 33.82% of the stock. This does not include MG stock that these banks hold (or control) through mutual funds or as a custodian. Thus, the ownership and control of MG rests squarely in the hands of Germany's two largest banks: Deutsche Bank and Dresdner Bank. Not surprisingly, the Chairman of MG's supervisory board also is a prominent member of the Management board of Deutsche Bank.

MG's ownership and debt structure also makes it unlikely that its problem was that of a "liquidity-constrained" firm. If its owners – some of which are among the largest financial institutions in the world – viewed its business and hedging strategies as sound, they clearly had the "deep-pockets" to finance it through short-run reversals. Further, potential conflicts between the equity and debt holders were greatly mitigated by the ownership and debt structure of MG. Deutsche Bank and Dresdner Bank are both major stockholders and creditors of MG.

Finally, the non-transparency of MGRM's forward-delivery contracts should not have been a critical factor for a closely-held firm such as MG. While such non-transparency may be a severe obstacle to raising external funds, MG's owners were in a position to obtain complete information without compromising the propriety of the firm's operations.

There is also evidence that in late 1993 funding was in fact available to MG. First, it had an unrestricted DM 1.5 billion Euro-credit line with 48 banks that it chose not to draw on. This credit line, arranged in May 1992, by Dresdner Bank, was never used. Second, on December 7, 1993, Chemical Bank (and possibly other banks) reportedly approached MGRM about the possibility of providing financing on the basis of securitising its forward-supply contracts. The precise terms offered by these banks, of course, are unknown. But the fact that MG did not avail itself of these financing opportunities suggests that its supervisory board believed that the real problems lay elsewhere.

Conclusions

Our view is that MG's fate was decided not by its inability to deal with a short-term liquidity need but by a sharp disagreement between its supervisory board and its "old" management about the fundamental soundness of MGRM's forward-delivery programme. MGRM's losses in 1993 undoubtedly caused MG's supervisory board to change its assessment of the potential risks involved in its forward-delivery programme. This reassessment probably focused on two basic risks: rollover risk and credit risk. The unusual contango price relationships that occurred in energy markets in 1993 made clear that sustained rollover losses were not only theoretically possible but could in fact occur. In addition, the sharp fall in energy prices in 1993 brought into sharper relief the potential non-performance risk that MGRM had on its forward-delivery contracts. Thus, although there is no way of knowing exactly what motivated MG's supervisory board's actions to end MGRM's forward-delivery programme, it appears that it acted on the belief that MGRM's strategy was fatally flawed – that its exposure to either or both rollover risk and credit risk did not justify the expected returns on its forward-delivery programme.[43]

This chapter has examined both of these risks, and has provided statistical information where possible for readers to judge for themselves whether MGRM's judgments with respect to these risks were flawed. With respect to rollover risk, the reasonableness of MGRM's judgment that this risk was neither excessive nor unmanageable comes down to the reasonableness of its assumption that the last 10 years of price history in energy markets can be relied on to make predictions about what price relationships will be for the indefinite future. With respect to credit risk, the issue is whether MGRM correctly evaluated its exposure and priced this risk accordingly. While MGRM's credit risk was not insignificant, we have no information which suggests that its exposure in this regard was excessive.

A central controversy surrounding the MG case is whether MG's supervisory board took the right action when it ordered the liquidation of MGRM's positions in December 1993.

This action implicitly reflects two key decisions that the board had to make: *whether* to abandon MGRM's programme; and, if it decided to abandon the programme, *when* to liquidate MGRM's positions. With respect to its decision to abandon MGRM's programme entirely, the reasonableness of this decision is not clear cut. In particular, in December 1993, there was no way to be certain that the price structure in energy markets had not already changed or would not change in the future, imposing higher rollover costs on MGRM. With respect to the board's decision about when to liquidate MGRM's derivatives position, this decision clearly seems ill-timed, at least in retrospect. When the bulk of the liquidation occurred, between December 20 and December 31, 1993, energy prices were at their lowest in many years, resulting in substantial losses on MGRM's derivatives positions when they were sold. In addition, in order to eliminate exposure on its forward-supply contracts due to rising prices, MGRM liquidated many of these contracts as well, apparently waiving cancellation penalties on the contracts, thereby giving up potential unrealised gains that could have offset its derivatives losses.

Had MG's supervisory board not ordered the liquidation until sometime later, the situation would be far different today. From December 17, 1993, when the new management took control, to August 8, 1994, crude oil prices increased from US$13.91 to US$19.42 a barrel, heating oil prices increased from US$18.51 to US$20.94 a barrel, and gasoline prices increased from US$16.88 to US$24.54 a barrel. Given these price increases, MGRM would have had a massive inflow of margin funds on its derivatives positions. Nevertheless, it must also be recognised that if energy prices had continued to fall, say to US$10 a barrel, rather than rising, MGRM would have sustained even greater losses than it did.[44] It is not clear, therefore, how much weight should be given to retrospective criticisms in judging the timing of the supervisory board's decision to liquidate MGRM's positions.

Regardless of whether MG's supervisory board's decision to abandon MGRM's hedging strategy was the correct one, it is clear that at some point a lack of understanding at the supervisory board level played an important role in MGRM's fate. In particular, on November 19, 1993, the supervisory board decided to extend the contract of its then Management board Chairman, Heinz Schimmelbusch, for another five years. But just four weeks later, the same supervisory board fired Schimmelbusch. Why the sudden turnaround? Did the board not understand MGRM's hedging strategy prior to December 1993? And if it did not, should it have? Alternatively, did the board initially assess the risks that MGRM was taking and find them acceptable, but later change its collective mind and decide that these risks were unacceptable? Still another possibility is that the board simply did not understand MGRM's strategy and panicked in the face of huge margin calls.

Edwards and Canter versus Culp and Miller: what are the critical differences?

To clarify the debate surrounding the MG case, it may be useful to contrast our views with those expressed by Christopher Culp and Merton Miller in Chapter 9 of this volume. First, we agree with Culp and Miller that it is possible to hedge long-dated obligations with short-dated futures (or derivatives), but we believe that this strategy entails more risk than Culp and Miller appear to acknowledge. Hedging long-dated obligations with short-dated derivatives involves a potentially significant "rollover risk" because of the difficulty of predicting the term structure of forward energy prices over long periods of time. Culp and Miller, in contrast, argue that all that counts "is the programme's profit potential over the long haul or, as finance specialists might prefer to put it, its expected net present value". They minimise the importance of rollover risk, noting that "the one-month net cost of storage and interest *averaged* less than zero over the last 10 years." Thus, Culp and Miller have greater faith than we in the efficacy of using past price relationships to predict future forward price relationships (or to predict future rollover returns). Although hardly definitive, we provide evidence from other commodity markets (soybeans and copper) that reliance on past price relationships to infer future "rollover returns" can be quite dangerous.

Second, we believe that a sound hedging strategy should not require the hedger to "stay in the game" until its long-run strategy pays off. A hedger should be able to unwind its positions at any time without sustaining substantial (or life-threatening) losses. Culp and Miller, by their use of the terms "gambler's ruin" and "hedger's ruin", suggest that MGRM should have been allowed to continue to operate until the long-run profit potential of its combined delivery/hedging programme was realised. In particular, they appear to argue that MGRM should have been allowed to stay in the game long enough to realise the anticipated rollover gains. In our view such a strategy would have entailed a significant bet that contango markets would not prevail over any significant period of time in the future. In any case, as MGRM's experience in 1993 clearly shows, MGRM's hedging programme turned out to be quite vulnerable to early exit. Further, because of the early cash-out options in MGRM's forward-delivery contracts, it should not have come as a surprise to MGRM that it might have to unwind its hedged delivery programme much sooner than the lengthy contractual periods stated in its forward-delivery contracts (such as 10 years).

Third, in contrast to Culp and Miller, we do not believe that MGRM's hedge was "self-financing": that the value of its forward-delivery contracts increased in value by the same amount as its short-dated derivatives contracts decreased in value as energy prices declined. The difference here with Culp and Miller turns primarily on our different methods for calculating the net present value of MGRM's combined delivery and hedging programme. We argue that, in valuing MGRM's positions at a given moment in time (say "t"), it makes sense to use the information contained in the term structure of forward energy prices at time t. Specifically, our methodology uses forward energy prices and current interest rates at time t to calculate net present values at time t. In contrast, Culp and Miller use an "expected basis" as the critical discount factor in their net present value formula, where this "expected basis" is not obtained from the term structure at time t. Rather, they use as their expected basis an average basis obtained from historical data. We are dubious about a procedure which uses such an average (or constant) basis to determine net present values at different times. In addition, neither our procedure for calculating net present values nor theirs takes into consideration the uncertain term (maturity) of MGRM's forward-delivery contracts due both to the early cash-out options and to the "firm-flexible" provisions included in some of these contracts.[45]

Fourth, while we agree with Culp and Miller that MGRM's "funding problem" was probably not the critical factor in bringing down the firm, we argue that this is true because of MG's ownership structure, rather than because MGRM's hedged delivery programme was self-financing. Both Culp and Miller and we contend that because MG was owned and controlled by "deep-pocket" investors - some of the largest financial institutions in the world, it should have had access to sufficient funding. Nevertheless, it is difficult to draw definitive conclusions about this issue because neither Culp and Miller nor we have all of the facts with respect to MG's funding situation.

Fifth, given our method of calculating the net present value of MGRM's hedged delivery programme, we argue that MGRM could have substantially reduced its funding needs as well as its rollover losses by using a minimum-variance hedging strategy instead of a one-to-one hedge. But we show that in doing so MGRM would have exposed itself to potential dynamic hedging costs. In addition, we agree that if funding were no obstacle, as Culp and Miller believe, the case for MGRM using a minimum-variance hedging strategy is considerably weaker.

Finally, although we are uncertain about exactly what Culp and Miller's overall view of MGRM's hedged delivery programme is, they seem to "lean to" the view that its programme was "economically sound" but was "killed off prematurely" by the "unfortunate" and "precipitous liquidation of MGRM's futures hedge" in December 1993. With respect to this liquidation decision, we are more agnostic than they. Succinctly stated, we believe that MGRM's rollover and credit exposures at that time were such that a reasonable case could have been made for the unwinding of its positions. However, we agree with Culp and Miller that "too many essential facts about [MGRM's] programme and its liquidation have still not been made public" for us to evaluate definitively the correctness of MG's liquidation decision.

1 *See* W. Arthur Benson v. Metallgesellschaft Corp et al, Civ Act No. JFM-94-484, Supplemental Memorandum of W. Arthur Benson Relative to Judicial Estoppel.

2 *See affidavit of* W. Arthur Benson v. Metallgesellschaft Corp et al, Civ Act No. JFM-94-484, USDCD Md. *(October 13, 1994). MGRM's mark-ups were the same regardless of the length of the contracts. Critics have argued that higher mark-ups should have been used for longer-term contracts, perhaps because of increasing credit risk. See* Special Audit Report of MG AG *prepared by C&L Treuarbeit Deutsche Revision and Wollert-Elmendorff, Frankfurt, Germany (January 20, 1995).*

3 *Alternatively, it has been contended that MGRM entered into these contracts in order to book unrealised profits against the futures losses it had at that time. See* Special Audit Report *(1995).*

4 *The "basis" is the difference between the price of the instrument that is being used to hedge (in the case of*

MGRM, near-month futures and swaps) and the price of the instrument or commitment that is being hedged (forward sales in the case of MGRM.) "Basis risk" is the volatility of the basis. All hedgers, by definition, choose to assume basis risk as a trade-off for eliminating the price risk they would have if they did not hedge, presumably because the basis risk is less than the price risk. See Edwards and Ma (1992).

5 *See Exhibit C in affidavit of Benson (1994). This exhibit shows that as of October 1, 1993, MGRM had sold forward approximately 93 million barrels of heating oil and 67 million barrels of gasoline, and that it had hedged these commitments by buying futures and swaps in the approximate amount of 39 million barrels of heating oil, 16 million of gas-oil, 58 million of gasoline and 47 million of crude.*

6 *A "stack" hedge refers to a futures position being "stacked" or concentrated in a particular delivery month (or months) rather than being spread over many delivery months. In MGRM's case, it placed the entire 160 million barrel hedge in short-dated delivery months, rather than spreading this amount over many, longer-dated, delivery months. "Rolling over" this stacked position refers to the process of rolling it forward: selling contract months which will soon expire and purchasing (or replacing these contracts with) deferred-month contracts. Common reasons for using short-dated stack hedges are that liquidity is much better in near-month contracts, that longer-dated derivatives may not be available on reasonable terms, and that hedgers hold certain expectations about how the term structure of forward prices will change in the future. In a recent article, MGRM's short-dated, stack, hedging strategy is referred to as a "textbook" hedging strategy. See Culp and Miller (1994).*

7 *Futures contracts are marked-to-market daily by exchanges, and traders are required to post with the exchange any losses they incur. While swap contracts usually are not formally marked-to-market, it is not uncommon for counterparties in swap agreements to call for additional collateral from losing counterparties as losses mount. In addition, swap contracts entail cashflows on settlement dates. Thus, in terms of cashflows, short-dated OTC swaps are very similar to futures contracts.*

8 *Physical storage is defined simply as purchasing and storing oil, and not physical storage in conjunction with "reverse cash-and-carry" arbitrage to take advantage of backwardation. The latter would involve continually making and taking delivery of oil.*

9 *The statistics in Table 1 suggest that carrying costs would be in the order of US$0.24/barrel per month. Further, a study of energy markets reported that storage space for oil above ground is limited and entails an "extremely high cost per unit value". See Litzenberger and Rabinowitz (1993).*

10 *A strategy of physical storage would also have exposed MGRM to some risk. First, there would have been some "funding risk" because of uncertainty about future carrying costs (such as interest rates). Second, because of the customer "cash-out" options in MGRM's forward-delivery contracts, MGRM was exposed to "market risk". Had customers exercised their options, MGRM would have had to sell a large volume of physical oil at short notice to produce the cash needed to meet its cash-out obligations.*

11 *Culp and Miller refer to MGRM's hedging programme as "synthetic storage" in Culp and Miller (1995).*

12 *No information is available on exactly how MGRM conducted its rollovers.*

13 *The last day of trading for heating oil and gasoline is the last business day of the month preceding the delivery month; for crude oil it is the third business day prior to the 25th calendar day of the month preceding the delivery month.*

14 *Alternatively, roll gains (losses) can be calculated as the change in the second-month futures price minus the change in the spot price over the same period. This methodology yielded nearly identical results during the 1983–92 period.*

15 *Specifically, we analysed (1) a 10-day rollover rule using a near-month stack and (2) a three-day rule using a stack in six-month futures. The results of this analysis appear in the original* Journal of Futures Markets *article and can be obtained from the authors.*

16 *The period from April 1983 to December 1992 was chosen because trading in crude oil futures did not begin until 1983. Also, gasoline futures did not start trading until December 1984. The period of analysis ends in December 1992, in order to make the results comparable with what happened to MGRM in 1993. Data is from the Knight-Ridder futures markets database.*

17 *Similar graphs for heating oil and gasoline can be obtained from the authors.*

18 *The ability to do reverse cash-and-carry arbitrage is limited because a shortage of the physical commodity makes it difficult and costly to borrow the physical commodity in order to short it. For a discussion of arbitrage bounds when there are restrictions on short-selling, see Lien (1986).*

19 *MGRM apparently did this. See affidavit of Benson (1994).*

20 *The simple correlation coefficients for daily changes in near-month futures prices are: 0.84 between crude oil and gasoline, and 0.88 between crude oil and heating oil.*

21 *See Appendix 1.B of our* Journal of Futures Markets *article. This calculation assumes an average contractual mark-up of US$4, a constant interest rate of 6%, and an average monthly rollover cost of US$0.24 – the average monthly rollover loss in crude oil during the 1983–92 period when crude oil was in contango. (See Table 1.) In addition, it assumes that MGRM rolled forward its entire position every month.*

22 *The daily "second-month" basis is calculated by subtracting daily "nearby" closing futures prices from daily closing "second-month" futures prices.*

23 *Daily settlement prices are used for over 2,400 trading days, from April 1983 to September 1994. In calculating* daily *basis volatilities, a random rollover date is implicitly assumed. The standard deviations of* *the "second-month" basis are calculated using only the roll dates generated by the three-day rollover rule. These are US$1.25/barrel for heating oil, and US$0.89 for gasoline, which are higher than the volatilities calculated assuming a random rollover date.*

24 *Near-month futures prices are used as proxies for spot prices because data on spot prices are notoriously bad.*

25 *This assumes that monthly rollover gains and losses are independent of one another. If this were not true, the probability of MGRM's experiencing a string of contango months would be higher.*

26 *Similar graphs for heating oil and gasoline can be obtained from the authors.*

27 *Taking only MGRM's futures positions, MGRM constituted about 6.7%* (55,000/(160,000 + 200,000 + 450,000)) *of the combined highest total open interest of gasoline, heating oil and crude oil during December 1993. If MGRM's swap positions are also included (because its swap counterparties would have been hedging with futures), these combined positions would have constituted about 20%* (160,000/810,000) *of total open interest in December 1993.*

28 *An example of a recent institutional investment product aimed directly at taking advantage of the well-known price backwardation in energy futures markets is Goldman Sachs' "commodity index". Petroleum products have a heavy weight in this index, and a substantial portion of the "advertised" return on this index is predicated on the continued existence of price backwardation in energy futures markets.*

29 *For example, when hedgers rely on regression analysis to choose both the commodities to hedge with and the hedge ratio to use, they are relying on historical data being a good predictor of future price relationships. See Edwards and Ma (1992), Chapters 5 and 6.*

30 *According to the* Special Audit Report *(1995), MGRM believed that the average life of a typical forward-delivery contract that included the cash-out option was between 2.5 and 3 years.*

31 *Similarly to the earlier procedure for energy futures, a three-day rollover rule is used to calculate rollover gains and losses. The last day of trading in the soybean futures contract is seven days prior to the last business day of the delivery month. The last day of trading in copper futures is the third-to-last business day of the month. Rollovers occur in the main contract months for each of the commodities: January, March, May, July, August, September and November for soybeans; and, January, March, May, July, September and December for copper.*

32 *In order to compare these rollover gains with the earlier findings for energy futures, they can be restated as average percentage returns by dividing the average rollover gains by the respective average prices during the period. Thus, in the 1965–74 period, the average rollover returns were 1.48% and 2.4% for soybeans and copper while for crude oil, heating oil and gasoline the average rollover returns during the 1983–92 period were, respectively, 1.12%, 1.24% and 1.80%.*

33 *"Economic" obstacles should be distinguished from "legal" obstacles. It is possible, for example, that there may have been some difficulty in creditors perfecting legal title to MGRM's forward-delivery contracts in the event of a default by MG.*

34 *A "minimum-variance" hedge attempts to minimise the variance in the firm's per-unit hedged revenues due to changes in price levels.*

35 *Distant futures prices are used as proxies for forward energy prices.*

36 *Reliable price data for futures contracts more distant than nine months are not available. There is little trading in many distant months, so that settlement prices are often not realistic prices. They may, for example, be "interpolated" prices.*

37 *The volatility of nine-month futures is from 50 to 65% of the volatility of spot futures prices.*

38 *The forward price curves plotted in Figure 3 also suggest that forward prices quickly flatten out, so that price volatility for more distant forward prices may not be much different than that reflected in nine-month futures prices. Our presumption, therefore, is that the price relationship reflected in the regression of spot prices on nine-month futures (shown in Table 6) would hold for more distant forward prices as well.*

39 *Adjusting the hedge ratio for differences in the timing of cashflows is known as "tailing" the hedge. It is well-known that failure to tail the hedge "...could force the premature liquidation and seriously disrupt a well-considered hedging or trading strategy." I. G. Kawaller and T. W. Koch (1988), "Managing Cash Flow Risk in Stock Index Futures: The Tail Hedge",* Journal of Portfolio Management *14, p. 41. See also Figlewski, Landskroner and Silber (1991).*

40 *There are other ways to derive the appropriate hedge ratio. Gibson and Schwartz, 1990, use a two-factor contingent claims pricing model to estimate hedge ratios for oil deliverable in the future. They find, for example, a hedge ratio of about 0.5 would be appropriate for hedging oil deliverable in five years and a ratio of about 0.25 would be appropriate for oil deliverable in 10 years. See Gibson and Schwartz (1990). The authors wish to thank John Parsons for bringing this paper to their attention.*

41 *There were no customer options that could be triggered by a decline in energy prices.*

42 *Fons (1994).*

43 *MG's supervisory board's rejection in December of alternative actions that could have protected MGRM against further margin outflows also is evidence that it did not believe that MGRM's forward-delivery strategy was fundamentally sound. For example, MGRM could have protected itself against further margin outflows due to price declines by purchasing put options on energy products, which were available in December 1993. This strategy would have neutralised further margin outflows on MGRM's long futures*

and swap positions and may have been able to lock in the net gains that MGRM had as of that time. In addition, the characterisation of MGRM's hedging strategy as "a game of roulette" by members of MG's supervisory board certainly suggests that the board believed that MGRM's strategy was fatally flawed.

44 *Culp and Miller, in Chapter 9, argue that MG should not have liquidated in December, 1993 because at that time the term structure of oil prices was upward sloping (contango). However, it should be noted that the term structure was also upward-sloping for virtually all of 1993, during which time spot oil prices fell sharply.*

45 *Approximately one third of MGRM's forward-delivery contracts gave customers the right to request that deliveries be deferred until the last day of the contract. Thus, the timing of futures cashflows from these contracts was highly uncertain. See* Special Audit Report (*1995*).

BIBLIOGRAPHY

Culp, C. L., and M. H. Miller, 1994, "Hedging a Flow of Commodity Deliveries with Futures: Lessons from Metallgesellschaft", *Derivatives Quarterly* 1(1).

Culp, C. L., and M. H. Miller, 1995, "Metallgesellschaft and The Economics of Synthetic Storage", *Journal of Applied Corporate Finance*, 7(4); reprinted as Chapter 9 of the present volume.

Edwards, F. R., and C. W. Ma, 1992, *Futures & Options* (New York: McGraw-Hill).

Figlewski, S., Y. Landskroner, and W. Silber, 1991, "Tailing the Hedge: Why and How", *The Journal of Futures Markets*, 11, pp. 200–12.

Fons, J. S., 1994, "Using Default Rates to Model the Term Structure of Credit Risk", *Financial Analysts Journal,* pp. 25–32.

Gibson, R., and E. S. Schwartz, 1990, "Stochastic Convenience Yield and the Pricing of Oil contingent Claims", *The Journal of Finance*, 45, pp. 959–76.

Kawaller, I, G., and T. W. Koch, 1988, "Managing Cash Flow Risk in Stock Index Futures: The Tail Hedge", *Journal of Portfolio Management*, 14.

Lien, Da-Hsiang D., 1986, "Asymmetric Arbitrage in Futures Markets: An Empirical Study", *The Journal of Futures Markets*, 6.

Litzenberger, R. H., and N. Rabinowitz, 1993, "Backwardation in Oil Futures Markets: Theory and Empirical Evidence", Rodney L. White Center for Financial Research, Wharton School of the University of Pennsylvania.

14

Hedging in the Theory of Corporate Finance: A Reply to Our Critics*

Christopher L. Culp and Merton H. Miller

The University of Chicago

On first reading the comments on our Metallgesellschaft papers[1] by Antonio Mello and John Parsons (hereafter "M&P"),[2] we had the eerie feeling that perhaps they were confusing our MGRM with another company of the same name. Surely M&P must have realised that for *our* MGRM, their standard finance models of corporate hedging were not appropriate. The standard models, focusing as they do on reducing costs of financial distress, *might* have been appropriate if our MGRM had been a stand-alone firm with independent, outside creditors. But it wasn't.

MG Refining and Marketing, Inc (MGRM) was one subsidiary of a large German conglomerate, MG AG, in which Deutsche Bank, one of the world's biggest banks, was not only the leading creditor but, thanks to multiple cross-holdings with other stockholder firms like Allianz and Daimler Benz, also the controlling shareholder. True, the parent MG AG did undergo a major financial restructuring in January 1994, following a year of losses by MGRM and other subsidiaries, but some believe that this presumed near brush with "bankruptcy" was deliberately precipitated to provide cover for a change in management.

Rather than apply the standard finance model of hedging to a firm we saw as just the lengthened shadow of Deutsche Bank, we turned instead to the "carrying-charge hedging" model proposed long ago by Holbrook Working after years of studying the hedging policies of commercial grain merchants such as Cargill.[3] Although we gave citations in our paper to Working's analysis and its applicability to MGRM, M&P appear not to have bothered to check out those references. We begin here, therefore, by reproducing the relevant passages from the writings of Holbrook Working and by showing how Working's theory of hedging explains MGRM's strategy.

The motivation for MGRM's hedge

Holbrook Working categorises standard finance models of hedging (including what is now called variance-minimising hedging) as "pure risk-avoidance hedging".[4] Firms may hedge their value to reduce the expected costs of financial distress.[5] Or firms may hedge to reduce the variability of their net cashflows.[6] In either case, the hedging reflects some "concavity" in the firm's profit or value function that makes a value-maximising corporation behave *as if* it were a risk-averse investor solving a traditional portfolio selection problem rather than a capital budgeting problem.

CARRYING-CHARGE HEDGING

Pure risk-avoidance hedging is only one of several types of real-world hedging that Working identifies. MGRM's strategy represents what he would call "carrying-charge hedging" and what we called "synthetic storage". Working explains:

> Whereas the traditional concept [of hedging] implies that hedging is merely a collateral operation that … would influence the stockholding only through making it a less risky

**Originally published in the* Journal of Applied Corporate Finance *8(1) (1995), pp. 121–7. The authors acknowledge with thanks helpful discussions with Todd Petzel and José Scheinkman.*

business, the main effect of carrying-charge hedging is to transform the operation from one that seeks profit by anticipating changes in price level to one that seeks profit from anticipating changes in price relations.[7]

Carrying-charge hedging, in other words, may be undertaken by value-maximising corporations to exploit their superior information about price *relations*, like the basis, while remaining "market neutral" with respect to spot prices. MGRM, like other carrying-charge hedgers, was essentially in the business of "trading the basis" without exposing itself to spot price risk.

Pure risk-avoidance hedging typically assumes that firms enter into forward contracting *and then* decide how to manage the risk of the position. Working's contribution was to recognise that the cash transaction and the hedge were two parts of a joint decision-making process. When information is asymmetric, he explains that

> Hedging is not necessarily done for the sake of reducing risks. The role of risk-avoidance in most commercial hedging has been greatly overemphasised in most economic discussions. Most hedging is done largely, and may be done wholly, because the information on which the merchant or processor acts leads logically to hedging .... To put it briefly, we may say that hedging in commodity futures involves the *purchase or sale of futures in conjunction with another commitment, usually in the expectation of a favourable change in the relation between spot and futures prices.*[8] (Emphasis his.)

Absent superior information, value-maximising firms may not only avoid the hedging, but may well shun the underlying activity itself.[9]

That carrying-charge hedging may be undertaken by value-maximising firms principally if not wholly to exploit a perceived informational advantage does *not* mean that carrying-charge hedging is "speculation". Working also argues that risks are, in fact, reduced by carrying-charge hedging, even though its primary motivation need not be risk reduction:

> Hedging we found not to be primarily a sort of insurance, nor usually undertaken in the expectation that spot and futures prices would rise or fall equally. It is a form of arbitrage, undertaken most commonly in expectation of a favourable change in the relation between spot and futures prices. *The fact that risks are less with hedging than without is often a secondary consideration.*[10] (Emphasis added.)

Because a value-maximising firm engaged in synthetic storage exchanges its natural exposure to the absolute price level for a net exposure to *relative prices*, synthetic storage almost always reduces the variance of the value of the firm. Had MGRM undertaken its long-term marketing programme *unhedged*, the volatility of its net income would have been proportional to the volatility of *spot* prices. Hedged, the volatility of MGRM's net income was proportional instead to the volatility of the bases reflected in the futures contracts MGRM held (ie, contracts with one, two and three months to maturity). As we have shown, the volatility of spot prices is huge relative to the volatility of the bases in those contracts.[11] Hence, MGRM chose to exploit its informational advantage by hedging rather than simply taking a position in the underlying commodity.

That MGRM saw itself as a carrying-charge hedger in the Working tradition is clear in this excerpt from MG AG's 1991/92 *Annual Report*, on which the supervisory board members of MG AG placed their signatures:

> While the futures markets provide hedging vehicles that reflect the realities of the crude oil markets, petroleum products remain a different story. Regional supply-demand differences can introduce major basis risk .... A solid presence in the physical markets and the resulting awareness of local refinery economics enable the MG Energy Group to turn that difficulty into an advantage.[12]

Like Working, MGRM even referred to its hedging objective as a type of basis arbitrage:

> At any given point in time, certain parts of the commodity market may be over-valued or under-valued relative to that commodity's own forward price curve, to other commodities, or to other markets .... That, in turn, provides attractive opportunities from an arbitrage standpoint.[13]

WHAT ABOUT EXPECTED BANKRUPTCY COSTS?

MGRM's strategy of carrying-charge hedging rather than standard finance risk-avoidance hedging makes perfect sense under the assumption that *basis risk* exposed MGRM to no real threat of bankruptcy, whereas naked spot price exposure might well have.[14] M&P seem to believe that MGRM should have been much more concerned with bankruptcy, even in its core business of basis trading. Addressing bankruptcy concerns by reducing the size of the programme as M&P and others have recommended can be a mixed blessing, however. As explained in Edwards and Ma, "Hedgers ... may be willing to assume more risk in order to assume greater profits. Eliminating all ... risk often means eliminating all profit, a condition that most businesses cannot tolerate for long".[15]

M&P's obsession with bankruptcy in this case rests heavily on their interpretation of the events of December 1993 in which the cashflow strains of MGRM's hedge supposedly did in the programme. But the turn of events *ex post* does not establish whether MGRM was correct in seeing itself as an effectively risk-neutral corporation *ex ante* – particularly so in this case, because of the still unresolved doubts over whether that liquidity crisis was real or contrived.

As a stand-alone firm, MGRM and its outside creditors might well have been concerned with the costs of bankruptcy or depleted cash for investment expenditures, especially after the large margin calls of late 1993. But MGRM was *not* a stand-alone firm. Deutsche Bank was not only the principal *inside* creditor and principal shareholder of MG AG, but thanks to its cross-holdings, it was also effectively the *controlling* shareholder. With Deutsche Bank thus standing *in loco parentis*, as it were, what sense does it make to assume that MGRM could be brought to ruin by the cash requirements of a *hedged* programme? And does anyone seriously think that Nymex would have allowed MGRM to take positions as large as 55,000 contracts without an assurance that Deutsche Bank stood behind the firm? Or that swap dealers would have negotiated nearly 100 million additional barrels of contracts without requiring enormous collateral? As one swap dealer commented, "[T]here was a feeling in the market that [MGRM] was the Bundesbank: the Bundesbank would bail out Deutsche Bank, which stood behind MG. The ultimate risk was the country".[16,17]

Surely no controversy would have arisen about Deutsche Bank's ability to finance MGRM's programme without flinching had the programme been for 15 million barrels rather than 150 million barrels. The issue thus comes down to how big a commitment is "too big" for a Deutsche Bank; and, if there was such a maximum that Deutsche Bank was prepared to back, why the supervisory board of MG AG had not communicated it as policy earlier.

As a further irony, Thornton Oil Corp sued MG when the new management's boasts of having narrowly averted bankruptcy first surfaced.[18] Even though its delivery contracts were "out-of-the-money", Thornton wanted its contracts to continue and demanded assurances from MG to that effect. The issue had not arisen earlier because the customers had been contractually assured that MGRM would remain hedged, with Deutsche Bank believed to be standing behind the agreements through thick or thin.[19]

WHY A ONE-FOR-ONE HEDGE?

Because synthetic storage or carrying-charge hedging differs from pure risk-avoidance hedging, so naturally does the "optimal" hedging strategy. For a carrying-charge hedger, that optimal strategy is "one-for-one" (subject, of course, to any tailing).[20] M&P's frequent stigmatising as "speculation" any futures held in excess of the much smaller "optimal" hedge implied by their analysis is thus just a verbal trick.[21]

A firm entering into a carrying-charge hedge does so because of superior information it has on *relative* prices (ie, the basis), not on *absolute* spot prices. M&P believe this amounts to saying that futures are "mispriced". Not so. Futures prices reflect the equilibrium expected basis conditional on information possessed by the *marginal* market participant. That MGRM's conditioning information might be different from that of the marginal participant does not imply a mispricing, though it does offer a sufficient rationale for carrying-charge hedging.

MGRM's simple one-for-one hedging strategy had a further important *organisational* advantage for the shareholders of its German parent MG AG: it could easily be monitored at the end of every trading day.[22] By comparing the amount of futures and swaps to the underlying customer contracts, MG AG's management board could safely leave the details of the hedging programme to MGRM without fear that someone might be covertly betting the ranch on price moves in Leeson/Barings fashion.

What was the initial net present value of the programme?

Our quarrel with M&P is more than just the semantic issue of what constitutes "hedging" and what constitutes "speculation". By using inappropriate assumptions in their models, M&P have also been led to misestimate – by a *huge* amount – the true value of MGRM's combined hedging/delivery programme.

M&P's Table 2 summarises what they call *"ex ante"* estimates of the value of MGRM's customer contracts, both hedged and unhedged. Using an estimate of US$3/barrel for the initial gross profit margin, they put the gross present value of the contracts at US$63.6 million for 150 million barrels of customer contract sales. Their estimates of net value are US$59.2 million for the unhedged contracts and US$35.1 million for the hedged programme.

M&P's simulated estimates of gross and net present values can only be described as weird. They assume, among other things, a US$2/barrel "cost of delivery". Actually, the prices in MGRM's contracts were FOB, making M&P's deduction of a US$2/barrel delivery cost totally absurd. But, we suppose, once M&P had made up their minds that the programme was worthless, what was another two or three hundred million dollars?

M&P's adjustment from the gross present value of the programme unhedged to the net present value of the programme hedged is equally strange. The costs of financing the hedge are driven almost entirely by M&P's assumption that external financing costs rise exponentially as prices fall. But the issue of whether *any* external financing really was required is what the shouting is all about. And it is still very much a matter of dispute, currently being fought out in courtrooms around the world. Had Deutsche Bank stepped up to the plate in December the way MGRM's original management expected it to and the way it actually did two months later in the MG AG restructuring, no "external" financing would have been needed. In sum, rather than present a well-reasoned estimate of the value of the programme, M&P simply *assume* the answer they wanted.

The correct approach for computing the initial value of MGRM's programme was presented and illustrated in our earlier article (chapter 9), but we gave no precise calculations.[23] The numbers appear, however, in our recent article in *Risk* magazine (chapter 10).[24] We assume there that MGRM sold forward 150 million barrels of oil in its flow contracts at a US$3/barrel gross margin. We take the *expected* basis as zero, which is actually a conservative assumption for early 1993 given the backwardation in the market at the time (as well as historically). Our estimate of the initial discounted expected net present value at the inception of MGRM's programme was at least US$450 million – an amount US$414.9 million higher than M&P's!

What was the 1993 net economic loss?

In addition to their estimates of initial gross and net present values, M&P attempt to estimate MGRM's gross and net *losses* in 1993. They put the gross losses on MGRM's hedge in their Table 1 at about US$1.174 billion. To get to their net loss estimate, they subtract the *change* in the value of MGRM's customer contracts in 1993 from their gross loss estimate. Using "present value factors" based on a paper by Gibson and Schwartz,[25] which M&P present in their Table 3, they estimate in Table 4 the gain on the customer contracts as about US$479 million in 1993. (Curiously, M&P seem to sense no "cognitive dissonance" between their estimate that the contracts *gained* in value by nearly half a billion dollars in 1993, but were worth only US$59 million to start with. Can it be that one of the co-authors did Table 2 and the other Table 4?) Subtracting that US$479 million from the US$1.174 billion gross loss gives them a net loss of US$695 million for MGRM that year.

Gibson and Schwartz, on whom M&P rely so heavily, freely concede that their present value factors for oil delivered in the future turned out to be extremely low, surprisingly so even to them. Their model implies that prices of oil derivatives are determined at the margin by risk-averse investors who demand a premium over and above the riskless rate for bearing convenience yield (ie, basis) risk.[26] Their reasoning is reminiscent of Keynes' classic discussion of the returns to speculators and hedgers.[27] Keynes believed that commodity futures risk premiums were positive and large, but his view commands little support.[28] Although Gibson and Schwartz assume the presence of a risk premium in oil, they recognise that it can be estimated only subject to substantial measurement error.[29] For that reason, they warn that their present value factors "must be interpreted with caution" – advice, alas, M&P ignored.[30]

Our valuation model, in contrast with Gibson and Schwartz (hence, also M&P), but in accordance with most discussions of commodity pricing these days, assumes that equilibrium prices for oil derivatives are determined by buyers and sellers who are effectively risk-neutral.

We have presented our own method of calculating MGRM's 1993 net economic loss elsewhere and need not repeat the calculations in detail here.[31] Suffice it to say that when we put all the separate pieces together – and remembering that, thanks to the hedge, the pure spot price change (net of rollover costs) raises the capital value of the flow contracts by exactly as much as the cash loss on the futures – we calculate the net 1993 loss for MGRM as the *initial* capital asset value of the programme less unexpected 1993 rollover costs and less the change in conditional expected rollover costs during the year, or

$$\text{US\$450 million} - \text{US\$250 million} - \text{US\$370 million} = -\text{US\$170 million}$$

Thus, even after ruling out any future rollover gains from backwardation, we estimate MGRM's 1993 net loss at roughly US$170 million, or just a fourth of M&P's US$695 million net loss estimate.

Losing even US$170 million is hardly pleasant, needless to say, but that figure by itself does not indicate that the programme should have been ended in 1993. The US$170 million is simply the cumulative loss through the year 1993 – that is, after one year of operation. Those losses would be correspondingly reduced were we to recompute the cumulative losses on a programme continued through the end of 1994, by which time the flattening of the term structure would have dramatically reduced realised and conditional expected future rollover costs. In fact, by April 1995, had the programme been continued it would have shown a substantial *net profit*.

WHAT WERE THE ALTERNATIVES IN DECEMBER 1993?

M&P argue that "[t]he lingo of the derivatives industry and its relative novelty has allowed a number of speculative activities to be passed off as 'risk management.' MGRM's losses in late 1993 made this pretense no longer possible, and Metallgesellschaft's shareholders and creditors took the necessary remedial actions to limit the sorry consequences." But to invoke past losses as a justification for ending the programme is to be taken in by the sunk cost fallacy. Regardless of how big past losses may have been, the test for *continuing* a programme is the same as for *initiating* it: is the conditional expected net present value positive? After the spot price decline of US$5.575/barrel in 1993, which widened the gross margin in the customer contracts to more than US$8/barrel, the net present value at that point was surely positive.

Even if management wanted to end its participation in the programme, the 1993 increase in the capital value of the customer contracts could, in principle at least, have been realised by selling the programme to another firm. MGRM could not, of course, recover past losses simply by selling the programme at market prices (any more than an investor can recover *past* losses by selling a stock), but at least selling the programme would have staunched the cash drains with which MG AG's supervisory board had become so obsessed.[32] Whether to continue the programme or sell it can be shown to depend almost entirely on whether prospective buyers' expectation of future rollover costs were less than MGRM's.[33]

MGRM also had a third alternative. Rather than continuing the programme intact or selling the programme as a whole, the company could have attempted to scale down the programme by simultaneously reducing the hedge and unwinding its customer contracts at the best possible prices. And after a US$5.575/barrel decline in spot prices in 1993, the "best possible price" for unwinds should have been substantial.[34] What MG AG's supervisory board actually did in December 1993 was none of the above. They liquidated much of MGRM's futures hedge and cancelled valuable customer contracts *with no compensation required*.[35] As we have explained elsewhere, this decision cost shareholders dearly.[36]

Postscript on Edwards and Canter

We apologise to Messrs Edwards and Canter (E&C) for neglecting their paper and concentrating exclusively on M&P.[37] E&C bring little to the party that has not already been covered by us – several times, actually – except their computation of "variance-minimising" hedge ratios. We ignored variance-minimising hedge ratios because, as explained earlier, they are irrelevant for MGRM. Anyway, E&C did not even calculate them correctly.[38] E&C do allow explicitly for "tailing", but we had ignored this adjustment only for simplicity of exposition.[39]

E&C also remind us that MGRM's programme would have suffered even greater losses than the US$170 million we estimated for 1993 had the market gone further into contango. We certainly have no quarrel with that, but E&C might have mentioned that the market did *not* slip further into contango in 1994. Quite the contrary. Nor do we disagree with their computations of rollover costs for beans and copper, although we are not sure what point E&C were trying to make with them. That virtually all markets for storable, non-petroleum commodities are normally in contango is well known, after all. Perhaps they were simply cautioning firms proposing to offer MGRM-style long-term, fixed-price contracts in beans or copper to be sure and set their initial gross margins higher than might be appropriate for a chronically backwardated market like crude oil.

1 *Culp and Miller (1995a).* See also *Culp and Miller (1994) and Culp and Miller (April 1995b), the latter reprinted as chapter 10.*

2 *Mello and Parsons (1995a), reprinted as chapter 12.* See also *Mello and Parsons (1995b).*

3 *Working's contributions may perhaps have been overlooked in the corporate finance literature because he was addressing them essentially to an audience of agricultural economists. His contributions, however, include early formulations of the cost of carry model for futures prices and the "efficient markets hypothesis".* See *Working (1948, 1949a and 1949b). Working's analysis of hedging on the Chicago futures exchanges is highlighted in the papers contained in Peck (1977).*

4 *Working (1962). Unless otherwise noted, all page references to Working's articles are from Peck (1977).*

5 See, for example, *Clifford, Smithson and Wilford (1989).*

6 See, for example, *Froot, Scharfstein and Stein (1993), reprinted as chapter 7.*

7 *Working (1962), p. 249.*

8 *Working (1953), reprinted as chapter 3, quoted from Peck (1977), pp. 148–9.*

9 *We need hardly remind readers that most value-maximising firms do not, in fact, hedge. Chase Manhattan Bank and The Wharton School recently surveyed 1,999 non-financial US firms randomly selected from CompuStat tapes. Of the 530 firms responding, only 35% answered "yes" when asked if their firms buy or sell futures, forwards, options, or swaps.* See *Smithson (1995), p.159.*

10 *Working (1953), p. 163.*

11 See *Culp and Miller (1995a), p. 67. No more than 1 to 5% of the historical variation in front-month futures prices can be traced to variations over time in the basis.*

12 *Metallgesellschaft AG* Annual Report, *1991/92, p.40.*

13 *"MGRM: Hedging Strategies Revisited", Exhibit E in* W. Arthur Benson v. Metallgesellschaft Corp et al, *Civ Act. No JFM-94-484. USC.D. Md. (October 3, 1994), E13.*

14 *Looking at the problem in this way is equivalent to seeing MGRM as "locally" risk-neutral. Positive bankruptcy costs, for example, might have led MGRM to hedge its spot price risk, but once hedged it behaved as an essentially risk-neutral basis trader.* See *Culp and Miller (1995a), footnote 6.*

15 *Edwards and Ma (1992), p. 141.*

16 *Quoted in Shirreff (1994), pp. 42–3.*

17 *Remember also that Deutsche Bank had earlier announced to all – in MG AG's 1992–93 company newsletter, no less – that it had increased MG's five-year credit line to DM1.5 billion, a credit line intended, among other things, to serve as "a permanently available reserve of liquidity".* See *"DM1.5 Billion Credit Line Granted to MG",* MG UPDATE: Company News from Around the World *(2/92). MG officials now claim that the credit line was intended only as a back-up provision for the Commercial Paper Program. But as even MG AG's Special Auditors note, no such restriction was mentioned in the documentation for the credit facility.* See *MG AG's Special Audit: 3.3.3.5.*

18 See Thornton Oil Corp v. MG Refining and Marketing, Inc, *Civ. Act. No 94CI101653, Circuit Court of Jefferson County, KY, 1994.*

19 *Three related cases involve counter-claims by several customers against MGRM that it has not provided adequate assurances of its ability to honour its long-term customer contracts – assurances that were apparently sufficient* ex ante. See *Counterclaim,* MG Refining and Marketing, Inc v. Knight Enterprises, Inc. v. MG Refining and Marketing, Inc, et al, *Civ. Act. No 94-2512, USDCSDNY, April 4, 1994; Counterclaim,* MG Refining and Marketing, Inc v. R.L. Jordan Oil Company, Inc, *Civ. Act. No 94-7804, USDCSDNY, October 27, 1994; Counterclaim,* MG Refining and Marketing, Inc v. A.T. Williams Oil Company v. MG Refining and Marketing, Inc, et al, *Civ. Act. No 94-7862, USDCSDNY, October 31, 1994.*

20 *Technically, the objective function is to maximise expected net present value subject to remaining market-neutral.*

21 *In this version of their paper, M&P now admit that MGRM* was *hedged against spot price risk, but they dismiss the hedging strategy as "rolling the dice" on the basis. That is like saying a market-neutral swap dealer is rolling the dice on credit risk.*

22 *The Group of Thirty has endorsed the notion of transparent exposure monitoring, though not necessarily daily.* See *Global Derivatives Study Group (1993).*

23 See *Culp and Miller (1995a), equation (1). Strictly speaking,* S_t *in equation (1) is part of the summand, and the entire summand should be multiplied by* $(1 + E_t(w_{t,j}))$*, the interest-adjusted basis. We omitted that term for simplicity, because our concern there was with sufficient conditions for profitability under worst-case assumptions (ie, contango). Including this term only increases the number of situations for which the sufficiency test is satisfied.*

24 *Culp and Miller (April 1995b).*

25 *Gibson and Schwartz (1990).*

26 *Gibson and Schwartz rely on a general methodology developed by Brennan and Schwartz (1979).*

27 *Keynes (1950), pp. iii–v.*

28 See, for example, *Telser (1958) and Dusak (1973).*

29 See also *Fama and French (1987).*

30 *Gibson and Schwartz (1990), pp. 972–3.*

31 See *Culp and Miller (1995b).*

32 *By purchasing puts, MGRM could have both limited its cash outlays and bought itself time to decide on the appropriate means for ending the programme.*

33 See *Culp and Miller (1995b).*

34 *That customers might have been willing to pay less than another firm buying the whole programme cannot be ruled out. Customers presumably would use a higher discount rate than MGRM or an outside bank in valuing the contracts. Once MGRM's troubles became public, moreover, customers would have possessed an unusual amount of leverage over MGRM in negotiating the prices for bilateral unwinds or transferring the contracts to another firm.*

35 *That MG's cancelled contracts had* some *value is confirmed on the public record. On December 22, 1993, one of MGRM's biggest firm-flexible customers reportedly paid MGRM US$2 million to terminate its firm-flexible contracts. New management accepted the offer. Two months later when most of the remaining firm-flexible contracts were cancelled with no compensation required from customers, MG refunded the US$2 million it had been paid earlier.* See *Ma (1995), 4.4.3.*

36 *Culp and Miller (1995b).*

37 *Edwards and Canter (1995a), reprinted as chapter 13.* See also *Edwards and Canter (1995b).*

38 *For an equally irrelevant but econometrically superior estimation method,* see *Pirrong (1995).*

39 See *Culp and Miller (1995a), footnote 13.*

BIBLIOGRAPHY

Brennan, M. J., and E. S. Schwartz, 1979, "A Continuous Time Approach to the Pricing of Bonds", *Journal of Banking and Finance* 3.

Clifford, W., Jr, C. W. Smithson and D. S. Wilford, 1989, "Financial Engineering: Why Hedge?" *Intermarket* 6(7)

Culp, C. L., and M. H. Miller, 1994, "Hedging a Flow of Commodity Deliveries with Futures: Lessons from Metallgesellschaft", *Derivatives Quarterly* 1(1), pp. 7–15.

Culp, C. L., and M. H. Miller, 1995a, "Metallgesellschaft and the Economics of Synthetic Storage", *Journal of Applied Corporate Finance* 7(4), pp. 62–76; reprinted as Chapter 9 of the present volume.

Culp, C. L., and M. H. Miller, 1995b, "Auditing the Auditors", *Risk* 8(4), pp. 36–9; reprinted as Chapter 10 of the present volume.

Dusak, K., 1973, "Futures Trading and Investor Returns: An Investigation of Commodity Market Risk Premiums", *Journal of Political Economy* 87(6).

Edwards, F. R., and M. S. Canter, 1995a, "The Collapse of Metallgesellschaft: Unhedgeable Risks, Poor Hedging Strategy, or Just Bad Luck?" *Journal of Applied Corporate Finance* 8(1), pp. 86–105; reprinted as Chapter 13 of the present volume.

Edwards, F. R., and M. S. Canter, 1995b, "The Collapse of Metallgesellschaft: Poor Hedging Strategy or Just Bad Luck?" *Journal of Futures Markets* 15(3).

Edwards, F. R., and C. W. Ma, 1992, *Futures and Options* (New York: McGraw-Hill, Inc).

Fama, E. F., and K. R. French, 1987, "Commodity Futures Prices: Some Evidence on Forecast Power, Premiums, and the Theory of Storage", *Journal of Business* 60(1).

Froot, K. A., D. S. Scharfstein and J. C. Stein, 1993, "Risk Management: Coordinating Corporate Investment and Financing Policies", *Journal of Finance* 48(5), pp. 1629–58; reprinted as Chapter 7 of the present volume.

Gibson, R., and E. S. Schwartz, 1990, "Stochastic Convenience Yield and the Pricing of Oil Contingent Claims", *Journal of Finance* 45(3).

Global Derivatives Study Group, 1993, *Derivatives: Practices and Principles* (Washington, DC: The Group of Thirty).

Keynes, J. M., 1950, *The Theory of Money: Volume II, The Applied Theory of Money*, VI, 29 (London: Macmillan).

Ma, C. W., 1995, "Rebuttal to the Special Audit Report", manuscript sent to MG AG shareholders, March 7.

Mello, A. S., and J. E. Parsons, 1995a, "Hedging a Flow of Commodity Deliveries with Futures: Problems with a Rolling Stack", *Derivatives Quarterly* 1(4).

Mello, A. S., and J. E. Parsons, 1995b, "Maturity Structure of a Hedge Matters: Lessons from the Metallgesellschaft Debacle", *Journal of Applied Corporate Finance* 8(1), pp. 106–20; reprinted as Chapter 12 of the present volume.

Peck, A. E., ed., 1977, *Readings in Futures Markets Book I: Selected Writings of Holbrook Working* (Chicago: Board of Trade of the City of Chicago).

Pirrong, S. C., 1997, "Metallgesellschaft: A Prudent Hedger Ruined, or a Wildcatter on Nymex?", *Journal of Futures Markets* 17(5), pp. 543–78; reprinted as Chapter 17 of the present volume.

Shirreff, D., 1994, "In the Line of Fire", *Euromoney*, pp. 42–3.

Smithson, C. W., 1995, "The Wharton/Chase Derivatives Survey", in *Managing Financial Risk: 1995 Yearbook* (Princeton, NJ: The Chase Manhattan Bank), p.159.

Telser, L., 1958, "Futures Trading and the Storage of Cotton and Wheat", *Journal of Political Economy* 66.

Working, H., 1948, "Theory of the Inverse Carrying Charge in Futures Markets", *Journal of Farm Economics* 30.

Working, H., 1949, "The Investigation of Economic Expectations", *American Economic Review.*

Working, H., 1949, "The Theory of Price of Storage", *American Economic Review* December.

Working, H., 1953, "Futures Trading and Hedging", *American Economic Review* June; reprinted as Chapter 3 of the present volume.

Working, H., 1962, "Concepts Concerning Futures Markets and Prices", *American Economic Review* June, pp. 248–53.

THE MATHEMATICS OF HEDGING LONG-DATED OBLIGATIONS WITH SHORT-DATED FUTURES

15

Analytics Underlying the Metallgesellschaft Hedge: Short-Term Futures in a Multiperiod Environment*

Jimmy E. Hilliard

University of Georgia

In a widely publicised case involving the use of derivatives, Metallgesellschaft Refining & Marketing (MGRM) apparently attempted to hedge long-term flow commitments for oil by sequentially stacking short-dated (nearby) futures contracts (Culp and Miller, 1994) with each stack settled after one period. According to the *Wall Street Journal*, MGRM controlled derivative positions equivalent to 160 million barrels of oil, roughly 80 times the daily output of Kuwait! The hedge reportedly consisted of over-the-counter contracts and futures positions in unleaded gasoline, No. 2 Heating Oil and West Texas Intermediate Crude. Since MGRM was effectively long in futures, they suffered tremendous losses when oil prices fell. When margin calls were not met, MGRM was forced to liquidate these positions. Later, spot prices rose so that MGRM was whipsawed - first they lost on their huge long position in futures and then they lost on spot purchases as prices rose. According to Culp and Miller (1994), they reported a US$1.33 billion loss in 1993. Sensational stories and lawsuits followed with the removal of senior MG officers by the supervisory board. At issue was whether MGRM's increasing long position in futures were hedging bona-fide contractual flows or whether they were a "bet" on prices taken to recoup past losses (*Economist*, 1995). While Culp and Miller (1994) tend to support the hedging programme of MGRM, Mello and Parsons (1995) focus on the mistakes made by Metallgesellschaft and point out issues regarding basis risk, the maturity structure of the hedge, credit requirements, and a possible speculative motive on the part of Metallgesellschaft. Edwards and Canter (1995) are more agnostic in their views of the MG liquidation decision. They state, however, that a reasonable case could be made for unwinding the hedge based on MGRM's rollover and credit exposure.

This chapter takes no position on the controversy. Instead, it develops the analytics underlying the hedging of long-term flow commitments with short-term futures contracts. Central to this analysis is the notion of a stacked hedge. The idea is as follows: a firm with say, one unit supply commitments repeatedly takes long positions in contracts with one period until settlement. In the first period, long positions are taken in n nearby contracts. In period two, long positions are taken in n nearby contracts, etc, until only one contract is required in the final period. Absent interest rates, cost-of-carry and basis risk, this procedure can be shown to "lock-in" the current spot price on all future production. The procedure fixes price at the futures level if rates and cost-of-carry are non-zero. The flow commitment is assumed to be non-stochastic.

Originally published in the Review of Quantitative Finance and Accounting, *12(3) (1999), pp. 195–219. The author acknowledges the helpful comments of Ekkehart Boehmer, Don Chance, Christopher Culp, Jim Moser, Don Rich, Adam Schwartz, Richard Stehle, and participants in seminars at Humboldt University (Berlin), the International Association of Financial Engineers, The University of Miami, the University of Georgia, the University of Central Florida and the European Financial Management Meeting.*

The contributions of the chapter include the determination of minimum variance hedging paths for multiperiod flow portfolios and the evaluation of both period-by-period and end-of-horizon volatilities under various hedging schemes. The analysis allows for basis risk, non-zero cost-of-carry, and spot price diffusion processes that have negative, zero, or positive market price of risk (MPR). Commodity flows are assumed to be deterministic. The results are developed in the context of an efficient market and standard equilibrium pricing models. The chapter extends the results of Culp and Miller (1994, 1995) in several ways. It develops sufficient conditions for an optimal hedging path, and considers the effects of basis risk and the market price of risk in the context of a standard diffusion equation. Earlier papers with some of the features of this chapter are those by Baesel and Grant (1982), Grant (1984) and McCabe and Frankle (1983). These papers examine a form of the stacked hedge, albeit not in the context of capital market theory and specification via diffusion equations. The additional specifications made in this chapter allow more insight into the phenomena and generate a rich set of implications.

The model for stacked hedges

The notation is as follows: There is an n-period horizon with non-stochastic flows m_i, at times t_i, $i = 1,2,\ldots,n$. For convenience, let $t_o = 0$ and $t_i = i \cdot \Delta$ where Δ is time between flow events. Spot prices are denoted by $P(t)$ and futures (forward) prices by $F(t,T)$, where t is today and T is the settlement date.[1] Since the hedging setup depends only on prices at t_i and t_{i+1}, the notation is typically simplified by the convention that $P_i \equiv P(t_i)$, $F_i \equiv F(t_i,t_i + \Delta)$ and $F(t_i + \Delta, t_i + \Delta) \equiv F_{i,i}$ where F_i is the price of the contract at initiation and $F_{i,i}$ is the price at settlement. The change in futures price is denoted by $\Delta F_i \equiv F_{i,i} - F_i$ and the change in spot price by $\Delta P_i \equiv P_{i+1} - P_i$. The basis is defined as $B_i = F_i - P_i$ and basis change relative to the settlement date as $\Delta B_i = \Delta F_i - \Delta P_i$. Basis risk is the volatility (standard deviation) of ΔB_i. Note that there is no basis risk when the futures price converges to the spot price, ie, when $F_{i,i} = P_{i+1}$ since in this case $\Delta B_i = (P_{i+1} - F_i) - P_{i+1} - P_i) = P_i - F_i$ is known at time t_i and is therefore non-stochastic. The notation is summarised in a time line format in Table 1.

A hedging strategy is established at the beginning of each period. The strategy is restricted to one-period contracts. At the end of the period, futures positions are reversed and cash from both spot and futures is deposited into risk-free accounts and held until termination of the multiperiod hedge. The problem is to find the hedging path x_i, $i = 0,1,\ldots,n - 1$ with the property that $Var(V_0)$ is minimised, where

$$V_0 = \sum_{i=1}^{n} \exp(r\Delta \cdot (n - i)) \cdot (m_i P_i + x_{i-1} \Delta F_{i-1}) \qquad (1)$$

V_0 is thus the future value of net cashflows at time n under the continuously compounded reinvestment rate r. The flow m_i is positive when assets must be sold and negative when assets must be bought. Minimising the variance of V_0 is more complex than it appears since the hedge ratio, x_k, may depend on both past and futures hedge parameters. The next section establishes sufficient conditions under which x_k will depend on neither past nor futures hedge ratios.

General results

This section establishes four basic results about the hedging path without requiring strong assumptions about the stochastic processes governing prices. A condition on variances and covariances is required for result two; result three requires additionally the law of one price, and result four adds the requirement of an independent increment process.

Table 1. Time line and definitions

Definition	Period 1	Period 2	Period 3	... Period n	
Time	t_o	t_1	t_2	t_{n-1}	t_n
Spot price	P_o	P_1	P_2	P_{n-1}	P_n
Futures price	$F_o \rightarrow F_{0,0}$	$F_1 \rightarrow F_{1,1}$	$F_2 \rightarrow F_{2,2}$	$F_{n-1} \rightarrow F_{n-1,n-1}$	
Hedge ratio	X_o	X_1	X_2	X_{n-1}	
Flow		M_1	M_2	M_{n-1}	M_n

The time between periods is delta. Futures price at the beginning of the interval is F_i and the ending price is F_{ii}. Settlement price = spot price if there is no basis risk, ie, $F_{ii} = P_{i+1}$.

Consider the expression at time k for hedged cashflows forthcoming from period k + 1 to period n. The expression is

$$V_k = \sum_{i=k+1}^{n} \exp(r\Delta \cdot (n-i)) \cdot (m_i P_i + x_{i-1} \Delta F_{i-1}) \tag{2}$$

It is important to establish sufficient conditions for x_i, $i \geq k$, to be independent of all earlier hedges. When the ratios are path independent, the backwards solution technique can be used to develop the optimal hedging path. For example, this suggests that state variables (prices) at step $n-1$ be independent of previous ratios, x_j, $j \leq n-2$ so that the one-period problem can be solved at time $n-1$. If prices at $n-2$ are likewise independent of ratios at earlier times the two-period problem can be solved, and similarly, all previous ratios can in theory be obtained in a recursive manner. Essentially, this is the dynamic programming algorithm that requires, among other conditions, that the optimal policy at state k be independent of earlier policies.

Result 1. The minimum variance policy path x_i, $i = k, k+1, \ldots, n-1$ is independent of earlier policies $x_0, x_1, \ldots, x_{k-1}$ if the hedger is a price taker and if net proceeds at earlier settlement dates are invested in assets uncorrelated with spot and futures commodity prices.

The rationale is straightforward. The conditional distribution of prices at time k will not be affected by the previous hedging path if the hedger is a price taker. Furthermore, net hedging proceeds must be invested in uncorrelated assets, else accumulated cash, depending on past hedge ratios, may be correlated with future cashflows which are to be hedged. In the model developed here, cash at each settlement period is invested in a risk-free asset. Thus, in all but the most pathological cases, the backwards solution technique may be used to obtain the optimal hedging path.

Next, it is useful to have a result regarding minimum variance ratios and the state variables. Hedge ratios are said to be state independent and therefore non-stochastic if they are not a function of spot or futures prices. They will typically be constant or at most a function of the parameters of these processes (when there is basis risk). Essentially, state independence ensures that all current and future hedge ratios can be calculated at the beginning of the time horizon (time zero). If hedge ratios are not state independent, analytic solutions will typically be intractable and depend on the numerical evaluation of a tree (bivariate if there is basis risk) similar to the methodology used in option pricing.

Consider the first order condition for minimum variance hedge ratios. The solution for the hedge ratio x_k^* is of the form:

$$x_k^* = -\text{Cov}(A + B^*, B) / \text{Var}(B) \equiv y_k + \theta_k \tag{3}$$

where

$$y_k = \text{Cov}(A, B) / \text{Var}(B)$$

$$\theta_k = \text{Cov}(B^*, B) / \text{Var}(B)$$

$$A = \sum_{i=k+1}^{n} m_i P_i \exp((r \cdot \Delta(n-i))$$

$$B^* = \sum_{i=k+1}^{n-1} x_i^* \Delta F_i \exp((r \cdot \Delta \cdot (n-i-1))$$

and

$$B = \Delta F_k \exp(r\Delta \cdot (n-k-1))$$

In component form, equation (3) is written (let $r = 0$ for conciseness in this expression):

$$x_k^* = -\text{Cov}\left(\sum_{i=k+1}^{n} m_i P_i + \sum_{i=k+1}^{n-1} x_i^* \Delta F_i, \Delta F_k \right) / \text{Var}(\Delta F_k) \tag{4}$$

1. Multiperiod hedge ratios – basic results

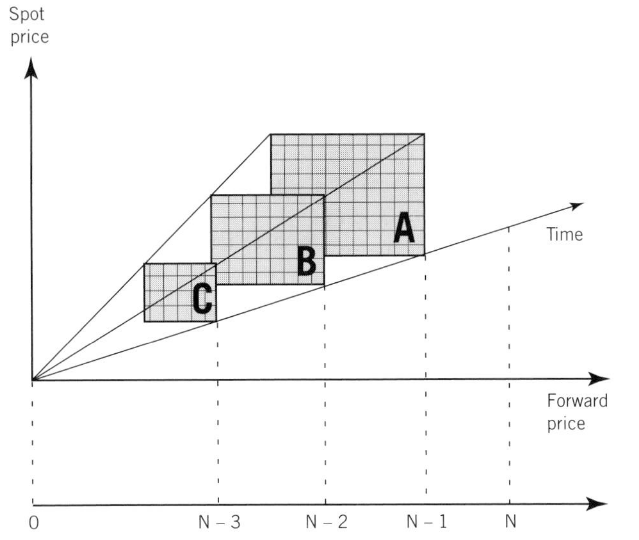

Result 1. Backward solutions – hedge ratios may be selected for grid A, then B, then C, etc.
Result 2. Constant hedge ratios – hedge ratios on grid A are constant, as are those on grid B and all other grids.
Result 3. Myopic hedge ratios – hedge ratios on grid C do not depend on those on grids A and B. All ratios are calculated independently of those on other grids.

Equation (4) highlights the fact that analytic calculation of x_k^* is difficult unless hedge ratios x_i^* are state independent, ie, unless they are independent of random variables.

The result required is:

Result 2. Hedge ratios are state independent and therefore non-stochastic if the conditions in Result 1 hold and if

β_{ik} is non-stochastic, $k = 0,1,\ldots,n-1$, $i = k+1,\ldots,n$

and

α_{ik} is non-stochastic, $k = 0,1,\ldots,n-2$, $i = k+1,\ldots,n-1$

where

$$\beta_{ik} = \mathrm{Cov}(P_i, \Delta F_k) \,/\, \mathrm{Var}(\Delta F_k)$$

and

$$\alpha_{ik} = \mathrm{Cov}(\Delta F_i, \Delta F_k) \,/\, \mathrm{Var}(\Delta F_k)$$

This result is easily shown by iteration, beginning with $k = n-1$, giving the state independent solution:

$$x_k^* = -\sum_{i=k+1}^{n} m_i \beta_{ik} \exp(-r\Delta(i-k-1)) - \sum_{i=k+1}^{n-1} x_i^* \exp(-r\Delta(i-k))\alpha_{ik} \tag{5}$$

so that present and future hedge ratios can be computed by iteration at time zero.

It is also convenient to have a result on hedging "myopia". The hedge is myopic if it is path independent and if, in addition, the optimal hedge ratio x_k^* does not depend on future optimal hedge ratios, x_i^*, $i \geq k+1$. The result follows from equation (5).

Result 3. The hedge is myopic if Result 2 holds, and if, in addition, the increments ΔF are independent.

Independent increments imply that $\alpha_{ik} = 0$ (equivalently, $\mathrm{Cov}(B,B^*) = 0$) so that the second set of terms in equation (5) vanishes.

Results 1, 2, and 3 address backward solutions, constant hedge ratios across the state space, and myopia. Figure 1 is a graphic description of the basic implications. The next result uses minimum variance hedge ratios to develop the expression for future cashflows when price convergence and the cost-of-carry relation holds. In frictionless markets, this is equivalent to the no-basis risk condition.

Result 4. Let r be the continuously compounded reinvestment rate and let the cost-of-carry model of the form $F_i = P_i \exp(b\Delta)$ hold at the beginning of period i and let $F_{i,i} = P_{i+1}$ at the settlement date. Then the hedge ratio

$$x_k^* = -\sum_{j=k}^{n-1} m_{j+1} \exp((b-r)\cdot(j-k)\Delta), \quad k = 0,1,\ldots,n-1$$

gives risk-free cashflows at the end of period n. The compounded value of these flows is

$$V_0^* = \sum_{j=0}^{n-1} m_{j+1} F_0 \exp(b\cdot j\Delta)\cdot \exp(r\cdot(n-1-j)\Delta)$$

The expression for x_k^* follows from evaluating equation (5) using the assumed conditions and the relation (which also follows from the assumptions)

$$P_i = \sum_{i=k}^{i-1} \Delta F_j \exp(b\Delta(i-j-1)) + P_k \exp(b\Delta(i-k)), \quad i \geq k+2 \tag{6}$$

The compounded value of the cashflows V_0 is obtained by using the minimum variance hedge ratios in equation (1).

Result 4 has fundamental implications. Importantly, period-n accumulated wealth is risk-free when convenience yield is non-stochastic and there is otherwise no basis risk. In this case wealth depends only on the present futures price F_0. In fact, the second expression in Result 4 is the expected value of all future cashflows compounded until period n (assuming the market price of risk is zero). For example, if the market price of risk of the commodity is zero, F_0 is the expected value of P_1, $F_0\exp(b\Delta)$ the expected value of P_2,..., and $F_0\exp(b(n-1)\Delta)$ the expected value of P_n. In summary, under the above assumptions and a stacked hedge, all future output is sold for the currently expected value of future output. The next part of the chapter examines models of spot and futures prices that generate basis risk and allow for a non-zero market price of risk.

Price generating processes

It is necessary to assume specific price processes to compute variances when the futures price is not perfectly correlated with the spot price, ie, when there is basis risk. The price generating process assumed is the usual geometric Brownian motion with parameters b, λ, and σ. The diffusion is written

$$dP = P(b + \lambda\sigma)dt + P\sigma\, dZ \tag{7}$$

where b is the cost-of-carry, λ is the market price of risk, and σ is the instantaneous volatility. In the typical case, $b = r - d + u$, where r is the instantaneous risk-free rate, d is dividend or convenience yield and u is storage cost expressed in proportion form. The market price of risk times volatility ($\lambda\sigma$) is the risk premium required from holding the underlying spot asset. This linear form for required return, $\mu = b + \lambda\sigma$ is a feature of most equilibrium models of pricing, including, eg, the CAPM and APT. Under the Cox, Ingersoll and Ross (1985) equilibrium formulation, the risk premium is the negative of the asset's rate of return with the rate of change of marginal utility of wealth. Although the price of risk may depend on both time and the underlying variable, it is assumed to be constant is the following sections. Another version of this model, more realistic but requiring an additional state variable, has been posited and tested by Gibson and Schwartz (1989) and (1990). Consistent with the theory of storage that posits an inverse relationship between the level of inventories and net convenience yield, they posit a stochastic net convenience yield with mean reverting properties. Similarly, evidence of mean reversion in commodity prices is found by Bessembinder *et al* (1995). The evidence of mean reversion in financial assets is found to be weak, however. In general, multiperiod hedges with short-term contracts are subject to unhedged risk if convenience yield is stochastic. Specifically, "term structure" shifts in futures prices will lead to uncertain levels of accumulated wealth under multiperiod hedges with short-term futures.

The solution of equation (7) for price at time t, given time t_0, is

$$P_t = P_0 \exp((b + \lambda\sigma - 0.5\sigma^2)t + \sigma Z(t)) \tag{8}$$

where Z(t) is a Wiener–Levy process with mean zero and variance t. Under the standard cost-of-carry model the futures price is

$$F(t,T) = P_t \cdot \exp(b(T-t)) \tag{9}$$

and the expression for the change in futures price over the interval t_i to $t_i + \Delta$ is

$$\Delta F_i = F_{i,i} - F_i = P_{i+1} - P_i\exp(b\Delta) \tag{10}$$

The model has the following notable properties: first, conditional on information at time t_i, the variance of ΔF_i equals that of P_{i+1} and thus that of ΔP_i. Second, there is a deterministic change in the basis unless $b = 0$. If the cost-of-carry is positive (negative), the futures price is above (below) the spot price and the futures price changes more (less) than the spot price, albeit in a predictable fashion. Futures above (below) spot prices is a condition referred to in the literature as contango (backwardation). Fluctuations in spot prices can be perfectly hedged in all of the above cases.

A MODEL FOR BASIS AND HEDGING RISK

In this section, a model of futures prices is developed which provides for basis risk. The model is most appropriate when the spot asset is not perfectly correlated with the asset underlying the futures contract and when prices may not converge. The model is of the form:

$$F(t,T) = P_t \exp(b(T - t)) \cdot Q(t,T) \tag{11}$$

where Q is a lognormal diffusion with volatility parameter η and mean one. For the interval $t_i < t < t_{i+1}$, the expression for futures price is:

$$F(t,t_{i+1}) = P_t \cdot \exp(b(t_{i+1} - t)) \cdot \exp((-.5\eta^2)(t - t_i) + \eta Z_2(t - t_i)) \tag{12}$$

The rationale for this model is as follows: Z_2 is the Wiener–Levy process that introduces hedging risk, and η is its volatility. The second term in equation (12) has expected value one with volatility growing in the usual square root proportion to elapsed time. The cost-of-carry part of the expression changes in a deterministic manner and hedging risk adds fluctuations to the path. The increasing volatility over the interval is not central to the model since volatility is evaluated only at the end-points of the interval.[2] When volatility is zero, the model reduces to the usual cost-of-carry model. Finally, the model in equation (11) preserves the lognormal distribution of futures prices, ie, equation (11) can be rewritten as

$$\log_e(F(t,t_{i+1}) / P_t) = b(t_i - t) + \log_e(Q) \tag{13}$$

where $\log_e(Q)$ is normal. The diffusion of F on the interval is

$$dF/F = \lambda\sigma\, dt + \sigma\, dt + \sigma\, dZ + \eta\, dZ_2 = \lambda\sigma\, dt + \sqrt{(\sigma^2 + \eta^2)}\, dZ^* \tag{13a}$$

which has instantaneous drift $\lambda\sigma$ and volatility $\sqrt{(\sigma^2 + \eta^2)}$.

The difference in futures prices, ΔF_i, follows directly from equation (12) and is given by

$$\Delta F_i = P_i \exp(b\Delta)(\exp(\lambda\sigma\Delta - 0.5\sigma^2\Delta + \sigma Z(t_{i+1} - t_i) - .5\eta^2\Delta + \eta Z(t_{i+1} - t_i)) - 1) \tag{14}$$

Notice that terms like $Z(t_{i+1} - t_i)$ have independent increments with variance Δ. The time epoch must be preserved on the random terms since time-displaced covariances must be computed in determining hedge volatility.

Minimum variance hedge ratios

Optimal hedge ratios are developed in this section based on the diffusion processes given in equations (8) and (14). First, we establish that optimal hedge ratios, viewed at all times (including t_0), are state independent and therefore non-stochastic.

The formulas for the conditional covariances necessary to compute hedges ratios are developed in the Appendix. The covariances and variances needed here, conditional on information at time k, are:

$$\mathrm{Cov}(P_i, \Delta F_k) = P_k^2 \exp((b + \lambda\sigma)(i - k + 1)\Delta) \cdot (\exp(\sigma^2\Delta) - 1),\ i > k \tag{15}$$

$$\mathrm{Cov}(\Delta F_i, \Delta F_k) = P_k^2 \exp((b\Delta + (b + \lambda\sigma) \cdot (i - k + 1)\Delta)) \times (\exp(\lambda\sigma\Delta + \sigma^2\Delta) - \exp(\sigma^2\Delta) - \exp(\lambda\sigma\Delta) + 1) \tag{16}$$

$$\mathrm{Var}(\Delta F_k) = P_k^2 \exp(2(b + \lambda\sigma)\Delta) \cdot (\exp(\sigma^2\Delta + \eta^2\Delta) - 1) \tag{17}$$

$$\mathrm{Var}(P_k) = P_k^2 \exp(2(b + \lambda\sigma)\Delta) \cdot (\exp(\sigma^2\Delta) - 1) \tag{18}$$

$$\mathrm{Cov}(P_i, \Delta F_k) / \mathrm{Var}(\Delta F_k) = \gamma \exp((b + \lambda\sigma)(i - k - 1)\Delta) \quad (19)$$

$$\mathrm{Cov}(\Delta F_i, \Delta F_k) / \mathrm{Var}(\Delta F_k) = \omega \exp((b + \lambda\sigma)(i - k)\Delta) \quad (20)$$

where

$$\gamma = (\exp(\sigma^2\Delta - 1)) / (\exp(\sigma^2\Delta + \eta^2\Delta) - 1) \quad (21)$$

and

$$\omega = (\exp(\lambda\sigma\Delta + \sigma^2\Delta) - \exp(\sigma^2\Delta) - \exp(\lambda\sigma\Delta) + 1) / (\exp(\sigma^2\Delta + \eta^2\Delta) - 1)\exp(\lambda\sigma\Delta) \quad (22)$$

From equation (3), optimal hedge ratios depend on the ratio of covariances to variances developed in equations (19) and (20) as well as constant factors related to flow, cost-of-carry and the risk-free rate. But notice that for the model posited, these ratios are independent of random variables P and ΔF. In fact, all optimal hedging ratios can be developed at time zero due to this independence on the level of random variables. Applying these results and the relation $\mathrm{Cov}(aX,bY) = ab\mathrm{Cov}(X,Y)$ for a, b deterministic and X,Y random gives the following results for optimal hedge ratios for $k = 0,1,2,\ldots,n-1$:

$$x_k^* = y_k + \theta_k \quad (23)$$

$$y_k = -\gamma(m_{k+1} + m_{k+2}\exp((b + \lambda\sigma - r)\Delta) + \ldots + m_n \exp((b+\lambda\sigma - r)(n - k - 1)\Delta)) \quad (24)$$

$$\theta_k = -\omega(x_{k+1}^* \exp((b + \lambda\sigma - r)\Delta) + \ldots + x_{k-1}^* \exp((b + \lambda\sigma - r)(n - k - 1)\Delta)) \quad (25)$$

Note that the optimal hedge ratio at time t_k depends on all future hedge ratios, x_{k+i}^*, if $\theta_k \neq 0$. However, a sufficient condition for $\theta_k \neq 0$ is $\omega = 0$, and from equation (22), $\omega = 0$ when $\lambda = 0$. In short, a sufficient condition for hedge ratios to be myopic is that the market price of risk of the commodity is zero. Stronger assumptions for myopia are (1) a risk-neutral world, or (2) basis risk is zero. In any case, the myopic solution y_k is approximately optimal since, by equation (21), ω approaches zero as the hedging interval approaches zero. But, more importantly, note that the formula for x^* is recursive so that x_{n-1}^* can be computed first, then $x_{n-2}^* \ldots x_0^*$. Expressed as a function of flows, m, the minimum variance hedge ratio can also be expressed as

$$x_k^* = -\gamma(m_{k+1} + \exp(a)\cdot(1 - w)m_{k+2} + \ldots + \exp(a(n - k - 1)\cdot(1 - w)^{n-k-1} m_n)) \quad (26)$$

where $k = 0,1,\ldots,n-1$ and $a \equiv (b + \lambda\sigma - r)\Delta$. This formulation shows that, in effect, all ratios can be computed at time zero since all future ratios are known for the stochastic processes posited here. They can be computed independently of spot and futures prices. Therefore, lack of myopia is not a significant computational disadvantage for standard diffusions used to describe capital market prices.

The results are more intuitive than they may appear. The expression for gamma (γ) for small intervals, Δ, reduces to $\sigma^2/(\sigma^2 + \eta^2)$, the ratio of spot volatility to total volatility. Gamma has the effect of attenuating the magnitude of the optimal hedge ratio. In fact, for relatively large basis risk ($\eta \gg \sigma$), the optimal hedge ratio approaches zero. Note also that equation (26) is identical to that of Result 2 (which assumes no basis risk) when $\gamma = 1$ and $\omega = 0$. Furthermore, if there is no basis risk, zero interest rates and zero cost-of-carry, the optimal ratio at t_k is the negative of future output $(\Sigma_{i=k+1}^{n} m_i)$. This is the standard result found in other analyses of stacked hedges (eg, Culp and Miller, 1995).

Expected values, volatility and hedge properties

The computational formulas and properties of an optimally hedged portfolio are developed next. This section addresses expected values, end-of-period volatility, hedging and basis risk, hedging and the market price of risk, and single period volatilities.

EXPECTED VALUES

The expected value at time zero of cashflows at the end of the planning horizon is:

$$E(V_0) = E\left(\sum_{i=1}^{n} \exp(r\Delta(n-i))\cdot\left(m_i P_i + x_{i-1}^* \Delta F_{i-1}\right)\right) \quad (27)$$

but basic calculations give

$$E(P_i) = P_0 \exp((b + \lambda\sigma)i\Delta) \tag{28}$$

and

$$E(\Delta F_i) = P_0 \exp((b + \lambda\sigma)i\Delta) \cdot (\exp(\lambda\sigma\Delta) - 1) \tag{29}$$

The first term in equation (27) is the unhedged expected value of output when prices have an expected growth rate per period of $\mu \equiv (b + \lambda\sigma)$. Expected futures price change is positive (negative) as λ is positive (negative). When the market price of risk is zero, or under risk neutral assumptions, the expected value of futures price change is zero, and in any event the futures price change is zero to second order because of the term $\exp(\lambda\sigma\Delta) - 1$ in equation (29).

VARIANCES

The variance equation, while not difficult to derive, is algebraically cumbersome. To compute the variance of hedged cashflows, matrix notation is utilised as follows:

$$\underline{\alpha}' = (m_1 \exp((n-1)r\Delta) m_2 \exp((n-2)r\Delta) \ldots m_n)$$

$$\underline{\beta}' = (X_0^* \exp((n-1)r\Delta) X_1^* \exp((n-2)r\Delta) \ldots X_{n-1}^*)$$

$$\underline{P}' = (P_1\ P_2 \ldots P_n)$$

and

$$\underline{\Delta F}' = (\Delta F_0\ \Delta F_1 \ldots \Delta F_{n-1})$$

With these definitions, the cashflows compounded to the end of the horizon can be written:

$$V_0 = \underline{\alpha}'\ \underline{P} + \underline{\beta}'\ \underline{\Delta F} \tag{30}$$

with variance

$$\mathrm{Var}(V_0) = \underline{\alpha}'\,\Omega_P\,\underline{\alpha} + \underline{\beta}'\,\Omega_F\,\underline{\beta}' + 2\underline{\beta}'\,\Omega_{FP}\,\underline{\alpha} \tag{31}$$

where Ω_P is the covariance matrix of $\underline{P}$, Ω_F the covariance matrix of $\underline{\Delta F}$, and Ω_{FP} the matrix of pairwise covariances between $\underline{\Delta F}$ and $\underline{P}$. When there is no basis risk, $\underline{\beta}'\Omega_{FP}\underline{\alpha} = -\underline{\beta}'\Omega_F\underline{\beta}' = \underline{\alpha}'\Omega_P\underline{\alpha}$ and in this case $\mathrm{Var}(V_0)$ is zero.

2. Hedging and basis risk

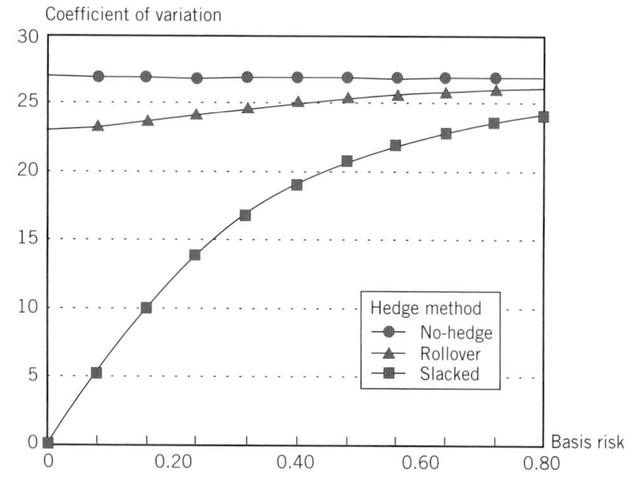

Basis risk is the ratio of basis variance to the sum of basis and spot variance. The coefficient of variation is the ratio of portfolio volatility to risk-neutralised expected cashflows at the end of the horizon. The cost of carry is 2.5% and the assumed rate of reinvestment is 6% pa. The planning horizon is 10 years. The market price of risk is zero.

HEDGING AND BASIS RISK

Figure 2 compares the stacked, rollover, and no-hedge strategy when there is basis risk. The vertical axis is the coefficient of variation (CV) of period-n cashflows. Specifically,

$$CV = \mathrm{Std}(V_0) / |E(V_0)| \tag{32}$$

and the horizontal axis is the per cent of basis risk, ie $\gamma \cong \sigma_\epsilon^2 / (\sigma_\epsilon^2 + \sigma_\eta^2) \times 100$ and $(1 - \gamma) = \sigma_\eta^2 / (\sigma_\epsilon^2 + \sigma_\eta^2) \times 100$, where the approximation form is used for γ. Figure 2 shows the stacked hedge being superior to both the no-hedge and rollover strategy by the CV criterion. And in fact, the CV is very near zero for small levels of basis risk, rising monotonically as basis risk increases. The rollover hedge does not perform very well by this criterion since it essentially replaces spot price variability with futures price variability.

HEDGING AND THE MARKET PRICE OF RISK

When the market price of risk is positive, a long hedger can remove risk and, at the same time, lower the expected cost of purchasing flows. Of course the converse follows for a negative price of risk (expected cost is higher). To demonstrate this, suppose the producer contracts to furnish one unit of a commodity for K dollars. If the producer does not hedge, the profit at the end of one period is $K - P_1$ with expected value

$$\pi_n = K - E(P_1) = K - P_0 \exp((b + \lambda\sigma)\Delta) \tag{33}$$

If the commodity price is locked in by a long hedge, then the profit is $K - F(0,\Delta)$, with expected value

$$\pi_h = K - F(0,\Delta) = K - P_0 \exp(b\Delta) \tag{34}$$

using the cost-of-carry model for the futures price. For positive (negative) market price of risk, the hedge strategy has higher (lower) expected profit. In either case, the hedge strategy has lower volatility. Figure 3 demonstrates the concept for positive cost-of-carry and positive market price of risk. Figure 3 uses the notation $F(t,T) = \hat{E}(P_T)$ to emphasise the fact that the futures price is the risk-neutralised expectation of the future spot price. The expected costs for long and short hedgers are also given in Table 2 for positive and negative market price of risk.

3. Expected costs and the long hedge

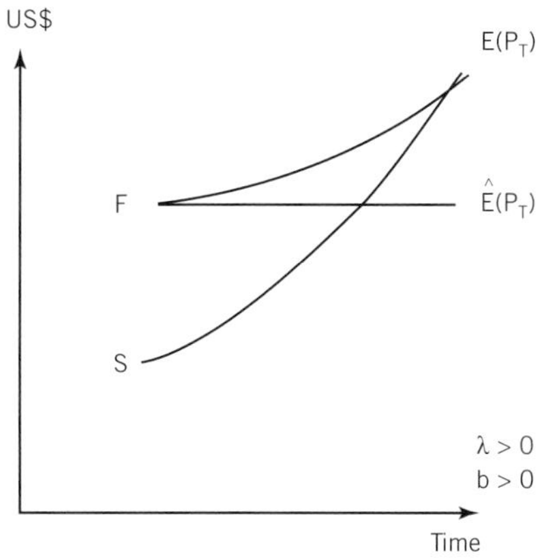

When the cost-of-carry is positive, the forward price exceeds the spot price. In this case the long hedge has expected profit so that net expected portfolio cost, F, is less than expected commodity cost. The hedge cost equals the risk-neutral expected value of future commodity cost. This hedge reduces both volatility and expected cost.

In some cases the hedge produces higher expected profits and lowers risk. But the hedge does not produce a "free lunch" in the context of a well-diversified portfolio. Specifically, note the cashflow in the no-hedge case is $K - P_1$, where P_1 is a random variable with positive market price of risk. But minus $P_1(-P_1)$ has a negative market price of risk. Therefore, it reduces the systematic risk of the diversified portfolio. However, the outflow for the hedger is fixed and provides no benefit to the well-diversified portfolio. For firms not well diversified, the use of the hedge can provide significant benefits when this diversification cannot be performed as efficiently by shareholders.

PER PERIOD VOLATILITY OF HEDGES

The stacked hedge has minimum variance, given the planning horizon. However, volatility can be exacerbated during intermediate periods. In fact, the volatility of the stacked hedge will exceed that of the rollover and no-hedge strategies in early periods. This results from the fact that each period "loads up" on all future flows over the planning horizon. Thus the ratio will be largest in the first period, monotonically declining thereafter.

The per period volatility model follows directly from the equation for cash flows. Let C_i be the net cash flow in period i. Then, $Vo = \Sigma_{i=1}^{n} C_i \exp(r(n - i)\Delta)$, where

$$C_i = m_i P_i + x_i^* \Delta F_{i-1} \tag{35}$$

with variance

$$Var(C_i) = m_i^2\, Var(P_i) + (X_i^*)^2\, Var(\Delta F_{i-1}) + 2m_i X_i^*\, Cov(P_i, \Delta F_{i-1}) \tag{36}$$

an expression easily evaluated with equations (16), (17), and (18). Because these are per

Table 2. Hedging and the market price of risk

	Market price positive	Market price negative
Buyer (long hedge)	Expected portfolio cost less than expected commodity cost	Expected portfolio cost more than expected commodity cost
Seller (short hedge)	Expected portfolio revenues less than expected commodity price	Expected portfolio revenues more than expected commodity price

The hedge portfolio always has less volatility. It is also optimal in terms of expected price for the buyer (seller) when the market price of risk is positive (negative).

period measures, all parameters are computed conditional on information available at the beginning of the period. The hedge ratio, X_i^*, is opposite in sign to flows, m_i. In the early part of the hedge, X_i^* is much greater than m_i and a large unhedged position is created. For example, the period-one variance of a ten-period stacked hedge of unit output when there is no basis risk is

$$\mathrm{Var}(C_1) = \mathrm{Var}(P_1) + (10)^2\,\mathrm{Var}(\Delta F_0) - 20\,\mathrm{Cov}(P_1, \Delta F_0) = 91\,\mathrm{Var}(P_1) \qquad (37)$$

This increases volatility in the first period, as measured by the standard deviation, by a multiple of 9.539, or about 854%.

Applications

A number of examples are given to demonstrate the application of the stacked, rollover and no-hedge strategies. The first several strategies show the results when there is no basis risk. After that, several analyses of basis risk and period-by-period volatility are demonstrated.

Table 3 summarises the results of a simple hedge where there is no basis risk, no carrying cost, zero interest rates and zero market price of risk. A firm must purchase two million units of output ("oil") at the end of each of the next 10 years. The spot price of the oil is US$18 per barrel and the futures price (by the cost-of-carry model) is also US$18. The stacked hedge "locks in" the futures price for total purchases. Specifically, note that the hedge ratio for the stacked hedge is, respectively, 20 million units, 18 million units,…, and 2 million units for periods one to nine. At each period, the hedge ratio is the sum of future production (see equation (24)). Prices change to US$16 per barrel at the (end) beginning of period (one) two. The firm loses US$2 × 20 million, or US$40 million, from the period one hedge and spends US$16 × 2 million in the spot market for a net outlay of US$72 million. In all remaining periods, prices remain at US$16 per barrel so that the net cash outflow is US$32 million per period. The total cash outflow at the end of 10 years is US$360 million. The effect is to precisely lock in the futures price. That is, 2 × 10 million = 20 million barrels must be purchased at the one-period futures price of US$18. Locking in the futures price means that the total outlay should be US$18 × 20 million = US$360 million. But this exact result has been achieved by the stacked hedge. Under a perfect hedging scheme, dubbed the "standard", one might expect a perfect outflow of US$36 million per period. If the market is sufficiently liquid, this could have been achieved by a "strip" of 2 million hedges maturing in consecutive years. Note that the rollover hedge of 2 million units per period in the nearby contract provides protection for the first period only. In this example, this lack of protection is an advantage since prices fell. Best of all, for the scenario posited, was a no-hedge strategy.

Table 4 is identical to Table 3 except for the spot price scenario. In Table 4, the spot price is initially US$18 but it rises to US$20 dollars and stays there until the end of the horizon. In

Table 3. Hedging inputs in an initially declining market with zero interest rates and no carrying costs: stacked, rollover and unhedged (spot) portfolios

			Hedge ratio		Net cash (US$)			
End of period	Spot price (US$)	Forward price (USS)	Rollover	Stacked	Spot	Rollover	Stacked	Standard
0	18	18	2	20				
1	16	16	2	18	–32	–36	–72	–36
2	16	16	2	16	–32	–32	–32	–36
3	16	16	2	14	–32	–32	–32	–36
4	16	16	2	12	–32	–32	–32	–36
5	16	16	2	10	–32	–32	–32	–36
6	16	16	2	8	–32	–32	–32	–36
7	16	16	2	6	–32	–32	–32	–36
8	16	16	2	4	–32	–32	–32	–36
9	16	16	2	2	–32	–32	–32	–36
10	16	16			–32	–32	–32	–36
Totals			20	110	–320	–324	–360	–360

Two million units of input are purchased each year. The cost-of-carry is assumed to be zero and the reinvestment rate of intermediate cashflows is zero. Net cash is the cash outlay in the current period for each portfolio assumption. "Standard" is the perfect hedge result, ie, it is the cashflow that would be expected if each period's price is as expected at the beginning of time period one. Total cash outflow under standard is beginning spot × total purchases = –US$18 × 20 million = –US$360 million. The stacked hedge achieves the same total outlay although there is variability in net cashflows from period to period.

this case the stacked hedge nets US$2 × 20 million at the period one settlement, exactly offsetting the spot outlay of US$20 × 2 million. The aggregate cashflow is locked in as before, at US$360 million, while the no-hedge strategy suffers by comparison with an outflow of US$400 million. Table 5 is included to show the effectiveness of the stacked hedge when spot prices fluctuate and when the reinvestment rate of cashflows is 6%. As in the previous example, the stacked hedge gives the same compounded cash outflow as the standard hedge, US$478.62 million.

Table 6 introduces a carrying cost of 2.5%. Otherwise, it is the same as Table 5. This table demonstrates the "no free lunch" rule expected in efficient capital markets. Specifically, the hedger does not avoid carrying costs since these are included in futures prices. The stacked hedge still gives the same result as the Standard (think of a strip with a liquid market) but the total cash outflow is US$543.838 million, (*vis-à-vis* US$468 million in Table 5) reflecting the carrying costs assumed in this example.

An example with non-zero market price of risk and basis risk is presented in Table 7. In this example, $\sigma_\epsilon = 0.15$, $\sigma_\eta = 0.05$, cost-of-carry is 2.5% and the reinvestment rate is 6%. Two units are purchased per period so long positions are taken in futures contracts. The price of risk is negative in panel A. One is tempted to conclude here that a free lunch exists. Notice that for every level of basis risk, measured by σ_η, the expected cashflow is greater for

Table 4. Hedging inputs in an initially rising market with zero interest rates and no carrying costs: stacked, rollover and unhedged (spot) portfolios

End of period	Spot price (US$)	Forward price (USS)	Hedge ratio: Rollover	Hedge ratio: Stacked	Net cash (US$): Spot	Net cash (US$): Rollover	Net cash (US$): Stacked	Net cash (US$): Standard
0	18	18	2	20				
1	20	20	2	18	–40	–36	0	–36
2	20	20	2	16	–40	–40	–40	–36
3	20	20	2	14	–40	–40	–40	–36
4	20	20	2	12	–40	–40	–40	–36
5	20	20	2	10	–40	–40	–40	–36
6	20	20	2	8	–40	–40	–40	–36
7	20	20	2	6	–40	–40	–40	–36
8	20	20	2	4	–40	–40	–40	–36
9	20	20	2	2	–40	–40	–40	–36
10	20	20			–40	–40	–40	–36
Totals			20	110	–400	–396	–360	–360

Two million units of input are purchased each year. The cost-of-carry is assumed to be zero and the reinvestment rate of intermediate cashflows is zero. Net cash is the cash outlay in the current period for each portfolio assumption. "Standard" is the perfect hedge result, ie, it is the cashflow that would be expected if each period's price is as expected at the beginning of time period one. Total cash outflow under Standard is beginning spot × total purchases = –US$20 × 18 million = –US$360 million. The stacked hedge achieves the same total outlay although there is variability in net cashflows from period to period.

Table 5. Hedging inputs in a market with fluctuating prices and no carrying costs: stacked, rollover and unhedged (spot) portfolios

End of period	Spot price (US$)	Forward price (US$)	Hedge ratio: Rollover	Hedge ratio: Stacked	Net cash FV (10): Spot	Net cash FV (10): Rollover	Net cash FV (10): Stacked	Net cash FV (10): Standard
0	18	18	2					
1	17	17	2	15.4953	–58.3442	–61.7762	–84.9343	–61.7762
2	16	16	2	14.3298	–51.7144	–54.9465	–74.8724	–58.1787
3	17	17	2	13.0923	–51.7467	–48.7028	–31.8208	–54.7906
4	18	18	2	11.7782	–51.5999	–48.7332	–34.7179	–51.5999
5	19	19	2	10.3828	–51.2946	–48.5949	–37.2793	–48.5949
6	20	20	2	8.9012	–50.8500	–48.3075	–39.5344	–45.765
7	21	21	2	7.3279	–50.2831	–47.8887	–41.5100	–43.0998
8	20	20	2	5.6574	–45.0999	–47.3549	–51.4785	–40.5899
9	20	20	2	3.8835	–42.4735	–42.4735	–42.4735	–38.2261
10	20	20		2	–40	–40	–40	–36
Totals			20	92.8484	–493.41	–488.78	–478.62	–478.62

Two million units of input are purchased each year. The cost-of-carry is assumed to be zero and the reinvestment rate of intermediate cashflows is 6%. Net cash FV(10) is the future value at period 10 of the cash outlay in the current period. "Standard" is the perfect hedge result, ie, it is the cashflow that would be expected if each period's price is as expected at the beginning of time period one. Total cash outflow under Standard is the sum of each periods purchases × expected risk neutralised spot prices compounded until period 10 = –US$478.62 million. The stacked hedge achieves the same total outlay although there is variability in net cashflows from period to period.

Table 6. Hedging inputs in a market with fluctuating prices and positive carrying costs: stacked, rollover and unhedged (spot) portfolios

End of period	Spot price (US$)	Forward price (US$)	Hedge ratio		Net cash FV (10)			
			Rollover	Stacked	Spot	Rollover	Stacked	Standard
0	18	18.4557	2	17.1720				
1	17	17.4304	2	15.7124	–58.3442	–63.3401	–101.239	–63.3401
2	16	16.4050	2	14.2009	–51.7144	–56.3375	–88.0346	–61.1616
3	17	17.43045	2	12.6355	–51.7467	–49.9357	–38.8878	–59.0579
4	18	18.4557	2	11.0143	–51.5999	–49.9669	–41.2832	–57.0267
5	19	19.4810	2	9.3354	–51.2946	–49.8251	–43.2017	–55.0653
6	20	20.5063	2	7.5966	–50.8500	–49.5304	–44.6905	–53.1713
7	21	21.5316	2	5.7960	–50.2831	–49.1010	–45.7930	–51.3425
8	20	20.5063	2	3.9312	–45.0999	–48.5537	–55.1089	–49.5766
9	20	20.5063	2	2	–42.4735	–43.5487	–44.5869	–47.8714
10	20	20.5063		0	–40	–41.0126	–41.0126	–46.2249
Totals			20	99.3943	–493.4063	–501.1517	–543.8382	–543.8383

Two million units of input are purchased each year. The cost-of-carry is assumed to be 2.5% p.a. and the reinvestment rate of intermediate cashflows is 6%. Net cash FV(10) is the future value at period 10 of the cash outlay in the current period. "Standard" is the perfect hedge result, ie, it is the cashflow that would be expected if each period's price is as expected at the beginning of time period one. Total cash outflow under Standard is the sum of each periods purchases × expected risk-neutralised spot prices compounded until period 10 = –US$543.838 million. The stacked hedge achieves the same total outlay although there is variability in net cashflows from period to period.

Table 7. Effect of market price of risk on results

Basis risk (Eta)	Stacked hedge		Rollover hedge		No hedge	
	E(FV)	STD	E(FV)	STD	E(FV)	STD
Panel A: $\lambda = -0.2$						
0.0	–302.132	0.0	–267.25	0.230653	–259.351	0.268021
0.03	–300.328	0.058069	–266.943	0.232263	–259.351	0.268021
0.06	–295.718	0.108874	–266.148	0.236359	–259.351	0.268021
0.09	–289.955	0.148926	–265.135	0.241446	–259.351	0.268021
0.12	–284.372	0.178577	–264.133	0.246343	–259.351	0.268021
0.15	–279.589	0.199946	–263.256	0.250518	–259.351	0.268021
0.18	–275.728	0.215299	–262.536	0.253876	–259.351	0.268021
0.21	–272.687	0.22644	–261.961	0.256512	–259.351	0.268021
0.24	–270.31	0.234655	–261.507	0.258571	–259.351	0.268021
0.27	–268.446	0.240824	–261.147	0.260182	–259.351	0.268021
0.3	–266.973	0.245541	–260.861	0.261454	–259.351	0.268021
Panel B: $\lambda = 0$						
0.0	–302.132	0.0	–302.132	0.273454	–302.132	0.323148
0.03	–302.132	0.063731	–302.132	0.275554	–302.132	0.323148
0.06	–302.132	0.120689	–302.132	0.280914	–302.132	0.323148
0.09	–302.132	0.167193	–302.132	0.287599	–302.132	0.323148
0.12	–302.132	0.203003	–302.132	0.29407	–302.132	0.323148
0.15	–302.132	0.229782	–302.132	0.299612	–302.132	0.323148
0.18	–302.132	0.249639	–302.132	0.304089	–302.132	0.323148
0.21	–302.132	0.264426	–302.132	0.307617	–302.132	0.323148
0.24	–302.132	0.275557	–302.132	0.310379	–302.132	0.323148
0.27	–302.132	0.284053	–302.132	0.312546	–302.132	0.323148
0.3	–302.132	0.290635	–302.132	0.314259	–302.132	0.323148
Panel B: $\lambda = 0.2$						
0.0	–302.132	0.0	–344.095	0.326038	–354.575	0.392342
0.03	–304.004	0.070437	–344.504	0.3288	–354.575	0.392342
0.06	–308.905	0.134686	–345.558	0.335861	–354.575	0.392342
0.09	–315.277	0.188909	–346.901	0.344701	–354.575	0.392342
0.12	–321.731	0.232216	–348.231	0.353291	–354.575	0.392342
0.15	–327.493	0.265709	–349.395	0.360677	–354.575	0.392342
0.18	–332.311	0.291259	–350.35	0.366662	–354.575	0.392342
0.21	–336.215	0.310724	–351.113	0.371391	–354.575	0.392342
0.24	–339.336	0.325644	–351.716	0.3751	–354.575	0.392342
0.27	–341.829	0.337195	–352.193	0.378016	–354.575	0.392342
0.3	–343.826	0.346244	–352.573	0.380324	–354.575	0.392342

E(FV) is expected end of horizon flow and STD is their volatility. Spot volatility is 15%, basis volatility 5%, the cost-of-carry is 2.5% and the reinvestment rate is 6%. Two units per period of inflow are to be hedged. Initial spot price is US$18 per unit.

Table 8. Volatility of cashflow by periods

		Hedge ratio			Cash flow volatility		
End of period	Flow (units)	No hedge	Stacked hedge	Rollover hedge	No hedge	Stacked hedge	Rollover hedge
0		0	17.172	2	0.321153	2.436268	0
1	–2	0	15.7124	2	0.321153	2.201894	0
2	–2	0	14.2009	2	0.321153	1.959171	0
3	–2	0	12.6354	2	0.321153	1.707803	0
4	–2	0	11.0143	2	0.321153	1.447482	0
5	–2	0	9.33536	2	0.321153	1.177888	0
6	–2	0	7.59665	2	0.321153	0.89869	0
7	–2	0	5.796	2	0.321153	0.609548	0
8	–2	0	3.93121	2	0.321153	0.310107	0
9	–2	0	2	2	0.321153	2.23E–08	0
10	2						

The cost-of-carry is 2.5% and the risk–free rate is 6%. Spot volatility is 15% pa and basis volatility is 5%. The market price of risk is 0.25. The volatility is normalised by P_0, initial price.

the stacked hedge. In addition, the standard deviation is also less for every level of basis risk. However, presumably the risk in these cashflows were valuable in diversifying the marginal utility of wealth (or the marginal utility of aggregate consumption under a more general model, see Cox *et al*, 1985). That is, the negative market price of risk λ means that these cashflows are useful for diversification purposes. However, the firm-specific portfolio may not be well diversified so that, to the firm, this is indeed a useful hedging strategy. When the market price of risk is zero, panel B, all expected cashflows are equal but the stacked hedge has the smallest standard deviation. In panel C, with positive market price of risk, the stacked hedge has a reduced cashflow since one must pay to hedge this risk away, or, put differently, there is an expected loss on the hedging positions. As before, the stacked hedge results in the smallest volatility.

Table 8 is an example of the per period volatility in a typical case. In this example, 2 million units are purchased each period. The cost-of-carry is 2.5%, reinvestment rate is 6%, spot volatility is 15% and basis volatility is 5%. The market price of risk is 0.25. The volatility is normalised by the initial price. The large differences in hedge ratios in early periods cause striking differences in per period volatility. The first period volatility is zero for the rollover hedge, 0.321153 for no-hedge and 2.436268 for the stacked hedge, almost eight times the volatility of the no-hedge strategy. Volatility of the no-hedge and rollover hedge remains constant over period and the stacked hedge declines to zero at the last period (since it is equivalent to the rollover hedge at that point).

The phenomena just noted, together with stochastic convenience yield, was apparently the major mathematical cause of the failure of the MGRM hedge. When oil prices fell, they suffered tremendous losses on their long positions (reported to be about 160 million barrels of oil (*Wall Street Journal*, 1995)), which were subsequently liquidated. Later, they suffered opportunity losses as spot prices rose. Had MGRM maintained a stacked hedge, the eventual outcome would have been an approximately (approximate because of stochastic convenience yield) risk-free stock of cash at the end of the planning horizon (reportedly about 10 years).

Summary

Fundamental results for constructing risk-free hedges with short-term futures contracts are developed. The stacked hedge insures risk free cashflows at the end of a planning horizon under very weak assumptions. Under a geometric Brownian model of prices, the stacked hedge is also shown to have variance minimising properties. The downside of the stacked hedge is that it introduces huge early period volatility.

The analysis demonstrates other features of efficient capital markets. For example, hedgers do not escape storage costs by hedging as these costs are impounded in futures and forward prices as noted by Culp and Miller (1995). There is also no free lunch in the risk-return trade-off which accrues from hedging in the context of participants with a well diversified portfolio. However, for firms who are price takers with largely firm-specific investments, hedging can be of value when the firm can diversify more efficiently than shareholders. That is, the firm with a long hedge might benefit both from lowered volatility and higher expected return when the market price of risk is positive.

Appendix

This appendix provides the calculations necessary to obtain the expected values and covariances of spot prices and futures price change. The results follow directly from statistical definitions and use the independent increments property of Wiener–Levy processes. Both conditional and unconditional covariances are developed. In general, the conditional parameters are used to compute hedge parameters while the unconditional parameters are used to compute the subjective hedging variance at the inception of the hedge.

RANDOM VARIABLES

$$P_i = P_k \exp((b + \lambda\sigma - .5\sigma^2)(i - k)\Delta + \sigma Z(t_i - t_k)) \tag{A1}$$

$$\Delta F_k = P_k \exp(b\Delta)(\exp(\lambda\sigma\Delta - .5\sigma^2\Delta + \sigma Z(t_{k+1} - t_k) + \eta Z_2(t_{k+1} - t_k) - .5\eta^2\Delta) - 1) \tag{A2}$$

Expected values, $i > k$

$$\begin{aligned} E(P_i) &= P_k E(\exp((b + \lambda\sigma - .5\sigma^2)(i - k)\Delta + \sigma Z(t_i - t_k))) \\ &= P_k \exp((b + \lambda\sigma)(i - k)\Delta) \end{aligned} \tag{A3}$$

$$\begin{aligned} E(\Delta F_k) &= P_k E(\exp(b\Delta) \cdot \exp(\lambda\sigma\Delta - .5\sigma^2\Delta + \sigma Z(t_{k+1} - t_k) + \eta Z_2(t_{k+1} - t_k) - .5\eta^2\Delta) - 1) \\ &= P_k \exp(b\Delta)(\exp(\lambda\sigma\Delta) - 1) \end{aligned} \tag{A4}$$

Conditional covariances, $i > k$

Cov(ΔF_k,P_i)

First, compute the joint expectations at time t_k. Define A and B as,

$$A \equiv \exp(b\Delta) \cdot \exp(\lambda\sigma\Delta - .5\sigma^2\Delta + \sigma Z(t_{k+1} - t_k) + \eta Z_2(t_{k+1} - t_k) - .5\eta^2\Delta) \tag{A5}$$

and

$$B \equiv \exp((b + \lambda\sigma - .5\sigma^2)(i - k)\Delta + \sigma Z(t_i - t_k)) \tag{A6}$$

so that

$$E(\Delta F_k, P_i) = P_k^2 \exp(b\Delta)\, E(A \cdot B - B) \tag{A7}$$

To evaluate $A \cdot B$, note that $Z(t_i - t_k) = Z(t_i - t_{k+1}) + Z(t_{k+1} - t_k)$ so that

$$\mathrm{Var}(Z(t_i - t_k) + Z(t_{k+1} - t_k)) = \mathrm{Var}\,(Z(t_i - t_{k+1}) + 2Z(t_{k+1} - t_k)) \tag{A8}$$

and, by independent increments,

$$\mathrm{Var}(Z(t_i - t_k) + Z(t_{k+1} - t_k)) = (i - k - 1 + 4)\Delta = (i - k + 3)\Delta \tag{A9}$$

This gives

$$E(A \cdot B) = \exp((\lambda\sigma\Delta(i - k + 1) + b(i - k)\Delta + \sigma^2\Delta) \tag{A10}$$

and

$$E(B) = \exp((b + \lambda\sigma)(i - k)\Delta) \tag{A11}$$

Using these equations and expectations computed in (A3) and (A4) gives the final result:

$$\mathrm{Cov}(\Delta F_k, P_i) = P_k^2(\exp((b + \lambda\sigma)(i - k + 1)\Delta) \cdot (\exp(\sigma^2\Delta) - 1) \tag{A12}$$

Cov(ΔF_k, ΔF_i)

The covariance of ΔF_k and ΔF_i may be non-zero due to the joint dependence on the underlying spot price. Conditioning on time k and proceeding as before, let

$$D \equiv \exp(\lambda\sigma\Delta - .5\sigma^2\Delta + \sigma Z(t_{k+1} - t_k) + \eta Z_2(t_{k+1} - t_k) - .5\eta^2\Delta) \quad (A13)$$

$$F \equiv \exp(\lambda\sigma\Delta - .5\sigma^2\Delta + \sigma Z(t_{i+1} - t_i) + \eta Z_2(t_{i+1} - t_i) - .5\eta^2\Delta) \quad (A14)$$

so that, using the definitions in (A1) and (A2)

$$\begin{aligned} E(\Delta F_k \Delta F_i) &= P_k \exp(2b\Delta) \cdot E(P_i D \cdot F - P_i \cdot A - P_i \cdot F + P_i) \\ &= P_k^2 (\exp(2b\Delta + (b + \lambda\sigma)(i - k)\Delta) \cdot (\exp(2\lambda\sigma\Delta + \sigma^2\Delta) \\ &\quad - \exp(\lambda\sigma\Delta + \sigma^2\Delta) - \exp(\lambda\sigma\Delta) + 1) \end{aligned} \quad (A15)$$

Subtracting expected values gives the final result:

$$\begin{aligned} Cov(\Delta F_k, \Delta F_i) = P_k^2(\exp(b\Delta + (b + \lambda\sigma)(i - k + 1)\Delta)) \cdot (\exp(\lambda\sigma\Delta + \sigma^2\Delta) \\ - \exp(\sigma^2\Delta) - \exp(\lambda\sigma\Delta) + 1) \end{aligned} \quad (A16)$$

Notice this will be zero if λ, the market price of risk is zero.

Var(ΔF_k)

Since ΔF_k is lognormal with drift parameter $b + \lambda\sigma$ and variance parameter $\sigma^2 + \eta^2$, it follows immediately from equation (A2) that the variance can be written

$$Var(\Delta F_k) = P_k^2 \exp(2(b + \lambda\sigma)\Delta) \cdot (\exp(\sigma^2\Delta + \eta^2\Delta) - 1) \quad (A17)$$

UNCONDITIONAL COVARIANCES (TIME ZERO)

Cov(ΔF_k,P_i), i > k

First, express P_i in terms of P_k so that

$$E(\Delta F_k P_i) = E(P_k^2) \exp(b\Delta) E(D \cdot G - G) \quad (A18)$$

since P_k is independent of D and G. The expression for D is given in equation (A12) and

$$G \equiv \exp((b+\lambda\sigma - .5\sigma^2)(i - k)\Delta + \sigma Z(t_i - t_k) \quad (A19)$$

Evaluating equation (A17) and subtracting means gives

$$\begin{aligned} Cov(\Delta F_k, P_i) = \exp(b\Delta + (b + \lambda\sigma)(i - k)\Delta) \cdot (E(P_k^2) (\exp(\lambda\sigma\Delta + \sigma^2\Delta) - 1) \\ \cdot E^2(P_k) (\exp(\lambda\sigma\Delta) - 1)) \end{aligned} \quad (A20)$$

for i > k.

Cov(ΔF_k,P_i), i ≤ k

In this case, the D and G terms in equation (A17) are also independent so that the final result simplifies to

$$Cov(\Delta F_k, P_i) = \exp(b\Delta + (b + \lambda\sigma)(k - i)\Delta) \cdot Var(P_i) (\exp(\lambda\sigma\Delta) - 1) \quad (A21)$$

for i ≤ k.

Cov(ΔF_k,F_i), k ≠ i

Using the same approach as before and for i > k, a little algebra gives

$$E(\Delta F_k, F_i) = E(P_k^2)\exp(2b\Delta + (b + \lambda\sigma)(i - k)\Delta) \cdot (\exp(2\lambda\sigma\Delta + \sigma^2\Delta) - \exp(\lambda\sigma\Delta + \sigma^2\Delta) - \exp(\lambda\sigma\Delta) + 1) \tag{A22}$$

The result, after subtracting means is

$$\mathrm{Cov}(\Delta F_k \Delta F_i) = E(\Delta F_k, \Delta F_i) - E^2(P_k)\exp(2b\Delta + (b + \lambda\sigma)(i - k)\Delta) \cdot (\exp(\lambda\sigma\Delta) - 1)^2 \tag{A23}$$

When $i = k$, the variance is

$$\mathrm{Var}(\Delta F_k) = P_0^2\exp(2b\Delta + 2(b + \lambda\sigma)k\Delta) \cdot (\exp(\sigma^2 k\Delta)(\exp(\lambda\sigma\Delta + \sigma^2\Delta + \eta^2\Delta) - 2\exp(\lambda\sigma\Delta) + 1) - (\exp(\lambda\sigma\Delta) - 1)^2) \tag{A24}$$

Cov(P_k,P_i)

The covariance is easily computed from the definition of P and is given by

$$\mathrm{Cov}(P_k, P_i) = P_0^2\exp((b + \lambda\sigma)(k + i)\Delta) \cdot (\exp(\sigma^2 k\Delta) - 1) \tag{A25}$$

for $i \geq k$.

1 *The terms forward and futures are sometimes used interchangeably since the price behaviour of these contracts is identical under non-stochastic interest rates as assumed in this chapter.*

2 *Several other points should be noted. At time $t = t_i$, the model is identical to the cost-of-carry model. It is possible to add a constant, say K_i, which defines the displacement of the futures price from that implied by the cost-of-carry model at the beginning of the interval. This makes no difference in the hedging formulation since the constant vanishes when ΔF_i is computed.*

BIBLIOGRAPHY

Baesel, J., and D. Grant, 1982, "Optimal Sequential Futures Trading", *Journal of Financial and Quantitative Analysis* 17(5), pp. 683–95.

Bessembinder, H., J. Coughenour, P. Seguin and M. Smoller, 1995, "Mean Reversion in Asset Prices: Evidence from the Futures Term Structure", *The Journal of Finance* 50(1), pp. 361–75.

Cox, J. C., J. E. Ingersoll and S. Ross, 1985 "An Intertemporal General Model of Asset Prices", *Econometrica* 53(2), pp. 363–84.

Culp, C. L., and M. Miller, 1994, "Hedging a Flow of Commodities with Futures: Lessons from Metallgesellschaft", *Derivatives Quarterly*, pp. 7–15.

Culp, C. L., and M. Miller, 1995, "Metallgesellschaft and the Economics of Synthetic Storage", *Journal of Applied Corporate Finance* 7(4); reprinted as Chapter 9 of the present volume.

Edwards, F., and M. Canter, 1995, "The Collapse of Metallgesellschaft: Unhedgeable Risks, Poor Hedging, or Just Bad Luck", *Journal of Futures Markets* 15(3), pp. 211–64; reprinted as Chapter 13 of the present volume.

"Germany's Corporate Whodunnit", *The Economist* 71, February 4, 1995.

Gibson, R., and E. Schwartz, 1989, "Valuation of Long Term Oil-Linked Assets", Anderson Graduate School of Management, UCLA, Working paper, pp. 6–89.

Gibson, R., and E. Schwartz, 1990, "Stochastic Convenience Yield and the Pricing of Oil Contingent Claims", *Journal of Finance* 45(3), pp. 959–76.

Grant, D., 1984, "Rolling The Hedge Forward: An Extension", *Financial Management* 13, pp. 26–8.

Mello, A. S., and J. E. Parsons, 1995, "Maturity structure of a Hedge Matters: Lessons Learned from the Metallgesellschaft Debacle", *Journal of Applied Corporate Finance*; reprinted as Chapter 12 of the present volume.

McCabe, G. M., and C. T. Frankle, 1983, "The Effectiveness of Rolling the Hedge Forward in the Treasury Bill Futures Market", *Financial Management* 12(2), pp. 21–9.

Wall Street Journal, January 27, 1995.

Hedging Long-Maturity Commodity Commitments with Short-Dated Futures Contracts*

Michael J. Brennan and Nicholas I. Crew
University of California, Los Angeles; Analysis Group/Economics

The Metallgesellschaft incident of December 1993 has led to interest in the related issues of the extent to which long-dated commitments to deliver (or receive) a fixed amount of a commodity can be hedged by rolling over a series of short-term futures contracts, and how this can best be accomplished.[1] In this chapter we analyse the hedging problem in terms that are familiar to economists, and consider the ability of different models of futures prices to yield trading strategies in short-dated futures contracts that provide effective hedges for long-term commitments.

In a series of papers, Culp and Miller (1994, 1995) analyse this problem with special reference to Metallgesellschaft and present numerical examples that suggest that a perfect hedge is possible. As we shall show, their analysis rests on the implicit assumption that the convenience yield on the underlying commodity is deterministic, an assumption that is in conflict with the data. They argue correctly that the funding required to meet the variation margin on the hedge is an inappropriate measure of the interim success of the strategy, but their analysis, and that of Edwards and Canter (1995), is presented in terms of "rollover gains", a concept which is foreign to economists and which, we shall argue, does not correspond to the economic concept of gain or profit. In the first section we show how the final profit on a commitment matched by a "stack-and-roll" hedge is related to the sum of the "rollover gains" over the life of the commitment, but show that the rollover gain in any single period bears no relation to the economic profit earned in that period.

The difficulty in measuring the interim success of a hedging programme is that in general there exists no market price for the underlying commitment that is being hedged. It is therefore necessary to have a *model* of how the price is determined, both in order to determine the appropriate hedge strategy, and to measure the current position at a point in time prior to the maturity of the commitment.[2] Such models of futures or forward prices[3] have been developed by Brennan (1987)[4] and Gibson and Schwartz (1990).[5] These models and the hedging strategies implied by them are presented in the second section.

In the third section we describe the data that we use in our empirical evaluations of hedging effectiveness. In the fourth section we evaluate the hedge strategies derived from the models of futures prices, by examining their ability to provide trading strategies in short-dated futures contracts to hedge forward commitments in oil, with maturities corresponding to those of extant long-dated traded futures contracts. We choose these particular commitments to hedge because the availability of the long-dated futures price allows us to calculate the present value of the commitment each period, which permits us to measure the periodic

**Originally published in M. A. H. Dempster and S. R. Pliska,* Mathematics of Derivative Securities *(1997), pp. 165–87. Reprinted with the permission of Cambridge University Press. The authors would like to thank seminar participants at the 1995 INQUIRE-Europe Meetings, the University of Tilburg, Seoul National University and the Conference in Honor of Fischer Black at UCLA. They are happy to acknowledge that this paper received the 1995 First Prize at the INQUIRE-Europe Meetings.*

hedging errors under the strategies. Of course, we would prefer to be able to assess directly the ability of the strategies to hedge much longer-term commitments;[6] while we are not able to do this, our results for commitments of maturities up to 24 months should provide useful indications of the efficacy of these strategies, since the evidence is that the futures price curve is essentially flat for longer maturities. For comparison, we also analyse the stack-and-roll hedge proposed by Culp and Miller (1994, 1995), and a minimum variance hedge suggested by Edwards and Canter (1995). We find that hedge strategies that take account of stochastic variation in the convenience yield lead to monthly hedging errors with a standard deviation which is only about 25% of that obtained from the simpler stack-and-roll strategy.

Rollover gains and the profits on a hedged commitment

Consider a firm that makes a forward commitment to deliver one unit of a commodity, say a barrel of oil, at time T, in return for a payment of US\$K at that time. The present value of the profit of entering into this commitment at $t = 0$ is $Ke^{-rT} - PV_0(P_T)$, where r is the interest rate, P_T is the spot price at time T and $PV_t(P_T)$ denotes the present value at time T of the (uncertain) future amount P_T to be received at time T. If this commitment is held to maturity, uncertainty about P_T means that the total profit realised from entering into and meeting the commitment will be uncertain. This uncertainty could in principle be eliminated by entering into a futures contract of maturity T. However, in practice, there is no market for long-term futures contracts. One suggested solution is to roll over a series of long positions in a short maturity futures contract which, without loss of generality, we shall take as the nearby futures contract: such a hedging strategy is often referred to as a "stack-and-roll" strategy.

To analyse the profit under a stack-and-roll strategy it will be convenient initially to assume that the interest rate is zero. Let $F_{t,\tau}$ denote the futures price at time t for delivery at time $t + \tau$. Then π_t, the profit that is realised at time t from holding the commitment from time $t - 1$, matched by an offsetting long position of n one-period futures contracts, is equal to the change in the value of the futures position less the change in the present value of the delivery commitment:

$$\pi_t = -[PV_t(P_T) - PV_{t-1}(P_T)] + n[F_{t,0} - F_{t-1,1}] \qquad (1)$$

The cumulative profit from entering into the commitment and hedging it in this fashion till maturity is obtained by summing equation (1) over $t = 1,\ldots,T$, and adding the expression for the profit realised when the contract is entered into, $Ke^{-rT} - PV_0(P_T)$. Recognising that $F_{T,0} = PV_T(P_T) = P_T$, the cumulative profit, Π, when the hedge ratio, n, is set equal to unity, may be written as

$$\Pi = K - F_{0,1} + \sum_{t=1}^{T-1}(F_{t,0} - F_{t,1}) \qquad (2)$$

The quantity $(F_{t,0} - F_{t,1})$ is referred to by Culp and Miller (1994, 1995) and Edwards and Canter (1995) as the "rollover gain"; thus the cumulative profit is the difference between the contract price K and the one-period forward price, $F_{0,1}$, plus the cumulative rollover gains realised over the life of the strategy. The intuition behind the expression is that if it were possible to enter a futures contract at time 0 at a price $F_{0,1}$ and hold the contract until maturity at time T when its price would be equal to the spot price, the realised profit would simply be $K - F_{0,1}$, the gains on the future contract exactly offsetting changes in the price of the underlying commodity. The stack-and-roll strategy does this, except for the price "gaps" that arise when one contract is closed out and another is entered into; it is these price gaps that give rise to the rollover gains or losses.

Equation (2) is no more than an accounting identity, and although it is tempting to identify the amount of the rollover gain realised in a period as the part of the final aggregate profit that is realised in that period, such an identification is wrong. Note first that the rollover gain does not appear in expression (1) for the economic profit realised in the period ending at time t; hence the rollover gain is not the same as the economic profit. In fact, economic gains and losses in futures markets can arise only from *changes* in the prices of the same futures contract, and not from *differences* between the prices of *different* futures contracts at a point in time which is what the "rollover gain" is.

Thus far we have assumed that the interest rate is zero. To allow for a non-zero interest rate, r, it is necessary to "tail" the hedge by adjusting the number of futures contracts, so that n, the number of one-period futures contracts entered into at time T is equal to $e^{-r(T-t-1)}$.[7] Thus with a tailed stack-and-roll hedge, the second term in equation (1) is multiplied by $e^{-r(T-t)}$, and the aggregate realised profit will still be given by equation (2).

It is apparent that the profit from a tailed stack-and-roll hedge will be riskless only if the rollover gains are certain when the contract is entered into. This requires that the basis between the price of the one-period futures contract and the maturing contract be predictable. Figure 1 shows the end of month rollover gains for the two-month Nymex light oil futures contract[8] between 1983 and 1994. It is apparent that the rollover gains are highly volatile and, while the mean is positive, it is only US$0.14 per barrel per month, and the standard deviation is US$0.34. Moreover, since the serial correlation of the rollover gains is 0.76, it would be rash to suppose that the rollover risk could be diversified away over time for a long-term commitment. Figure 2 shows the corresponding rollover gains for a three-month contract.[9] The mean of the monthly gains is now US$0.27, and the standard deviation is US$0.65, while the serial correlation is 0.79. As these figures show, there is considerable uncertainty about future rollover gains, and therefore about the final realised profit from a stack-and-roll hedging strategy.

Equation (1), adjusted for the tailing of the hedge by setting n equal to $e^{-r(T-t-1)}$, implies that the periodic *economic profit* will be riskless only if the change in the future value of the amount to be delivered under the contract (ie the change in the implicit futures or forward price for delivery at time T) is equal to the change in the price of the contract. This requires that the implied futures price curve shift up and down in a parallel fashion.[10] Figure 3 plots the futures price curves for the ends of alternate years from 1983 to 1994. It is apparent that the assumption of parallel shifts is not a good one, even within the limited maturity range of traded futures contracts: in some periods the term structure of futures prices slopes up, while in others it slopes down. In the following section we will consider two models of the behaviour of futures prices that allow for non-parallel shifts in the term structure of futures prices, and derive the hedging strategies that correspond to them.

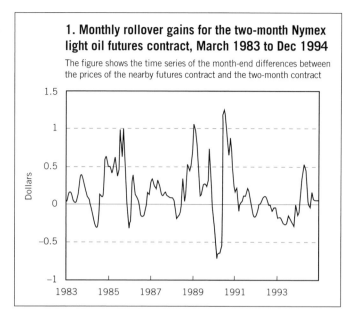

1. Monthly rollover gains for the two-month Nymex light oil futures contract, March 1983 to Dec 1994

The figure shows the time series of the month-end differences between the prices of the nearby futures contract and the two-month contract

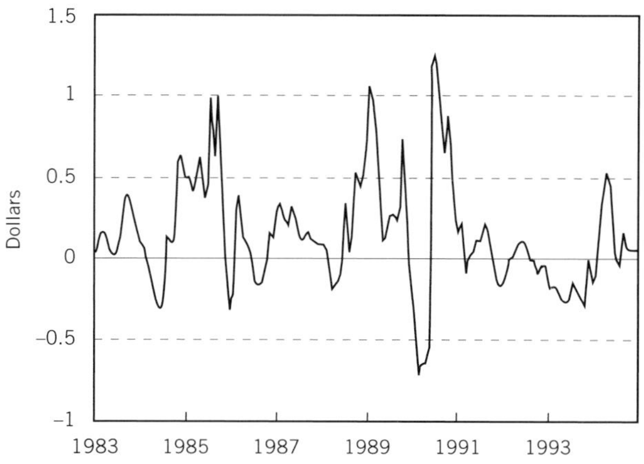

2. Monthly rollover gains for the three-month Nymex light oil futures contract, March 1983 to Dec 1994

The figure shows the time series of the month-end differences between the prices of the nearby futures contract and the three-month contract

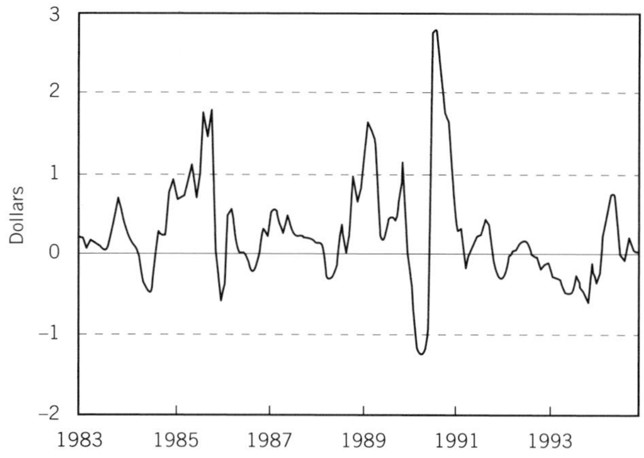

3. Term structure of oil futures prices. Nymex light oil contract, end of alternate years 1983 to 1994

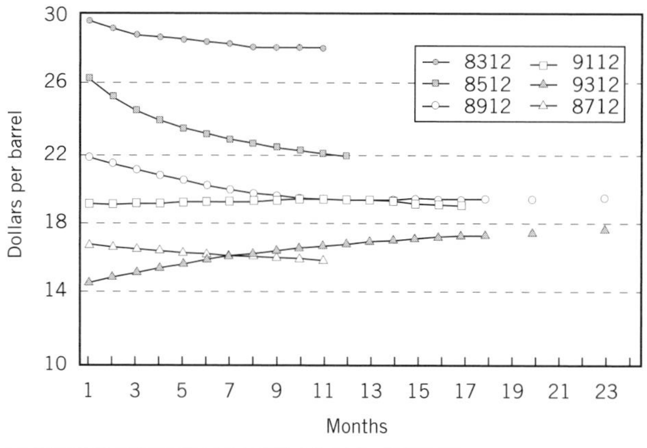

Futures prices and hedging with stochastic convenience yields

The convenience yield of a commodity is defined as the flow of services that accrues from possession a physical inventory but not to the owner of a contract for future delivery. The marginal convenience yield includes both the reduction in costs of acquiring inventory, and the value of being able to profit from temporary local (or grade specific) shortages of the commodity through ownership of an additional unit of inventory. The profit may arise either from local price variations, or from the ability to maintain a production process despite local shortages of a raw material. The convenience services yielded by an inventory depend upon the identity of the individual storing it; however, competition between potential storers will ensure that in equilibrium the marginal convenience yield net of storage costs will be equalised across all storers. Then, assuming that there exists a positive inventory of the commodity, the relation between spot and futures prices will reflect this marginal net convenience yield in a manner which we will now develop.[11]

It will be helpful to make explicit the dependence of the futures price on the current spot price. Therefore, let $F(P,t,\tau)$ denote the futures price at time T for delivery at $t+\tau$, when the current spot price is P, and let $PVC(t,\tau)$ denote the present value of the marginal net convenience yield over the interval $t,\ldots,t+\tau$. Then the relation between the futures price, the current spot price and the convenience yield may be written as

$$F(P,t,\tau)e^{-rt} = P - PVC(t,\tau) \tag{3}$$

The left hand side of equation (3) is the present value of a forward purchase commitment: this is equal to the current spot price less the value of the convenience services that would be available to a storer having physical possession of a marginal unit of the commodity up to the maturity of the forward commitment.

It follows from equation (3) that the rollover gain from a tailed stack-and-roll strategy is given by

$$e^{-r(T-t)}[F(P,t,0) - F(P,t,1)] = e^{-r(T-t)}\, PVC(t,1) \tag{4}$$

Therefore, unless the convenience yield is deterministic so that $PVC(t,1)$ is known, the rollover gain will be uncertain. Thus, except in this special and unlikely case in which the futures price curve shifts only in a parallel fashion, a stack-and-roll strategy does not provide a perfect hedge.

In order to model the behaviour of the structure of futures prices implied by equation (3) it is necessary to model the behaviour of the marginal convenience yield. The (marginal net) convenience yield depends on the level of inventories; the higher the current level of inventories, the less will merchants and manufacturers be willing to pay to have an additional unit on hand. Since spot prices are also likely to be associated with the level of inventories, a natural simplifying assumption is that the instantaneous rate of convenience yield is a function of the spot price, $C(P)$, where P is the spot price. The simplest assumption is that the convenience yield is proportional to the spot price.

THE CONSTANT (PROPORTIONAL) CONVENIENCE YIELD MODEL

If the convenience yield is proportional to the current spot price: $C(P) = cP$, then it is not difficult to show[12] that the term structure of futures prices is given by

$$F(P,t,\tau) = Pe^{(r-c)\tau} \tag{5}$$

and the present value at time T of the uncertain future amount $P_{t+\tau}$ to be received at $t+\tau$ is

$$PV_t(P_{t+\tau}) = e^{-r\tau}\, F(P,t,\tau) = Pe^{-c\tau} \tag{6}$$

The only source of uncertainty in this setting is the spot price P. The derivative of the present value of a commitment to deliver one barrel of oil in T periods with respect to the spot price is e^{-cT}, and the derivative of a τ period futures price with respect to P is $e^{(r-c)\tau}$. Therefore to hedge the T period delivery commitment it is necessary to take a long position in $n = e^{-[r\tau + c(T-\tau)]}$ futures contracts.

However, as the results of Brennan (1991) show, the constant proportional convenience yield model is too simple to be descriptive of the behaviour of futures prices for most commodities. Therefore, we turn to a more realistic model.

THE BRENNAN AUTONOMOUS CONVENIENCE YIELD MODEL

Brennan (1987, 1991) assumes that C, the instantaneous net marginal rate of convenience yield measured in dollars per unit of inventory per period, follows the simple mean-reverting process:

$$dC = \alpha(m - C)dt + \eta dz_C \tag{7}$$

where $\alpha > 0$ is the speed of adjustment, m is the long run mean rate of convenience yield, and dz_C is the increment to a standard Gauss–Wiener process. This assumption about the behaviour of the convenience yield is motivated by the consideration that if the convenience yield is high because inventories are low, storage firms will tend[13] to have an incentive to increase their investment in inventories which, in turn, will tend to reduce the convenience yield. The commodity spot price is assumed to follow the exogenously given stochastic process:

$$\frac{dP}{P} = \mu dt + \sigma(P,C)dz_P \tag{8}$$

where dz_P is the increment to a Gauss–Wiener process and $dz_P dz_C = \rho dt$, and μ, the expected rate of price change, may be stochastic.

Under these assumptions, the futures price will depend upon the current instantaneous rate of convenience yield, as well as the current spot price, so we write it as $F(P,C,\tau)$. It is shown in the Appendix that the futures price under the Brennan model is given by

$$F(P,C,\tau) = (P - PVC(C,\tau))e^{r\tau} \tag{9}$$

where

$$PVC(C,\tau) = \frac{m^*}{r}(1 - e^{-r\tau}) - \frac{m^* - C}{\alpha + r}(1 - e^{-(\alpha+r)\tau}) \tag{10}$$

and $m^* \equiv m - \lambda^*/\alpha$, where λ^* is a risk adjustment parameter, so that m^* is the risk-adjusted mean rate of convenience yield.

Consider now the problem of hedging a commitment to deliver one barrel of oil at a date T periods in the future. The present value of the commitment may be written as

$$PV_0(P_T) = F(P,C,T)e^{-rT} = P - PVC(C,T) \tag{11}$$

Using equations (10) and (11), the derivatives of the present value of the commitment with respect to P and C are

$$\frac{dPV}{dP} = 1$$
$$\frac{dPV}{dC} = \frac{-1}{\alpha + r}(1 - e^{-(\alpha+r)T}) \tag{12}$$

while, using equations (9) and (10), the derivatives of the price of a futures contract with maturity, τ, are

$$\frac{dF}{dP} = e^{r\tau}$$
$$\frac{dF}{dC} = \frac{-1}{\alpha + r}(e^{r\tau} - e^{-\alpha\tau}) \tag{13}$$

In order to hedge a commitment of maturity T it is necessary to hold a portfolio of futures contracts with the same sensitivities to P and C. Using equations (12) and (13), the hedge portfolio consists of n_1 and n_2 contracts of maturities τ_1 and τ_2 respectively where n_1 and n_2 are the solutions to

$$n_1 e^{r\tau_1} + n_2 e^{r\tau_2} = 1$$
$$n_1 e^{-\alpha\tau_1} + n_2 e^{-\alpha\tau_2} = e^{-(\alpha+r)T} \tag{14}$$

THE GIBSON-SCHWARTZ MODEL

Gibson and Schwartz (1990) follow Brennan in assuming a mean-reverting process for the instantaneous convenience yield; however, they define the instantaneous convenience yield in terms of dollars per dollar of inventory per period. This implies that $C(P)$ is written as δP, where δ follows the mean-reverting process:

$$d\delta = k(m_\delta - \delta)dt + \xi dz_\delta \tag{15}$$

with $dz_\delta dz_P = \rho dt$. Arbitrage arguments similar to those developed above imply that the forward or futures price, $F(P,t,\tau)$ can be written as[14]

$$F(P,\delta,\tau) = P\exp\left\{-\frac{\delta(1 - e^{-k\tau})}{k} + A\tau + \frac{1}{2}v^2\tau\right\} \tag{16}$$

where

$$v^2 = \left(\sigma_P^2 + \frac{\xi^2}{k^2} + 2\frac{\rho\sigma_P\xi}{k}\right)\tau + \frac{\xi^2(1 - e^{-2k\tau})}{2k^3} + 2\frac{\xi(\sigma_P\rho - \frac{\xi}{k})(1 - e^{-k\tau})}{k^2} \tag{17}$$

and

$$A(\tau) = (r - \tfrac{1}{2}\sigma_P^2 - \tilde{m})\tau + \frac{\tilde{m}(1 - e^{-k\tau})}{k} \tag{18}$$

$$\tilde{m} = m_\delta - \frac{\lambda_\delta\xi}{k} \tag{19}$$

The hedge portfolio for a commitment of maturity T is found by equating the derivatives of the present value of the commitment with respect to the spot price P and the convenience yield rate, δ, to the corresponding derivatives of the value of the hedge portfolio. Using equations (11) and (16), this yields the following equations for the numbers of futures contracts of maturities τ_1 and τ_2:

$$n_1F(P, \delta, \tau_1) + n_2F(P, \delta, \tau_2) = e^{-rT}(P, \delta, T)$$

$$n_1(1 - e^{-k\tau_1})F(P, \delta, \tau_1) + n_2(1 - e^{-k\tau_2})F(P, \delta, \tau_2) = (1 - e^{-k\tau_1})e^{-kT}F(P, \delta, T)e^{-rT} \tag{20}$$

The solutions to equations (14) and (20) determine the composition of the portfolio of futures contracts of maturities τ_1 and τ_2 which will hedge a fixed commitment of maturity T, when futures prices are described by the Brennan, and the Gibson–Schwartz, models of the convenience yield, respectively. Note that to determine the hedge portfolio weights in the Brennan model it is necessary to estimate only the single, speed of adjustment parameter, α. For the Gibson–Schwartz model it is necessary to estimate the speed of adjustment parameter, δ, and forward price of the commitment being hedged, $F(P,\delta,T)$.[15] This is estimated from equation (16) using the current estimated value of δ and an estimate of the risk-adjusted mean of the convenience yield process, m. In the section on empirical results we shall describe the estimation of the speed of adjustment parameters for the two models and the mean parameter, m, for the Gibson–Schwartz model, and investigate the effectiveness of their implied hedges empirically.

Data

The data that were used to evaluate the hedging strategies were end of month settlement prices on futures contracts for light crude oil quoted on Nymex for the period March 1983 to December 1994.[16] We label the contracts as "nearby", "two-month", "three-month", etc, these designations corresponding roughly to the remaining time to maturity of the contracts. Table 1 reports the average of the number of days to maturity for each of the contracts as of the end of each month of the sample period. Note that the longer maturity contracts only became available towards the end of our sample period, and even then were not available each

Table 1. Summary statistics on Nymex light oil futures contracts from March 1983 to December 1994

Nominal contract maturity (months)	Average number of days to maturity	Month of first price observation	Number of monthly observations
Nearby	20.5	1983.3	134
2	51.0	1983.3	134
3	81.4	1983.3	134
6	172.7	1983.3	134
9	262.0	1983.11	134
12	355.2	1983.11	94
15	446.6	1984.10	73
18	537.9	1989.9	55
21	629.5	1990.11	17
24	720.7	1990.11	15

month; as a result, the number of observations for the 21- and 24-month contracts is only 17 and 15. Continuously compounded interest rates for monthly maturities of one to 12 months were taken from the Fama Treasury Bill files for the end of each month of the sample period; the rates for intermediate maturities were linearly interpolated according to the number of days. Interest rates for maturities beyond 12 months were estimated by assuming that the yield curve was flat beyond 12 months.

For each month from April 1985 to December 1994, α, the speed of adjustment parameter of the Brennan convenience yield model, was estimated as follows. The value of the instantaneous convenience yield, c, for each of the prior months was approximated from the prices of the two nearby futures contracts by assuming that the rate of convenience yield was constant over this interval.[17] From this time series of instantaneous convenience yields, α, the speed of adjustment parameter of the stochastic process (7), was estimated using the exact discrete model corresponding to (7). Note that the number of time series observations used to estimate α increases each month as one more historical observation becomes available; the smallest number of observations is 25 in April 1985.

4. Time series of speed of adjustment estimates

The figure shows estimated values of α, the speed of adjustment parameter for the Brennan model, and δ, the speed of adjustment parameter for the Gibson–Schwartz model. The estimates are derived from monthly convenience yield estimates from March 1983 up to date, using the exact discrete form corresponding to the diffusion process

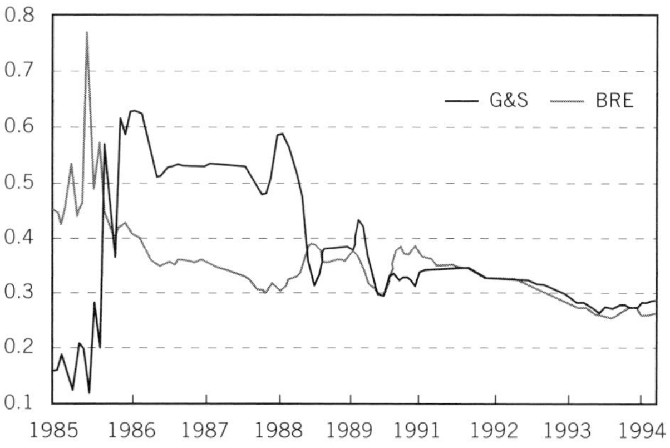

Similarly, for each month from March 1985 to December 1994, k, the speed of adjustment parameter of the Gibson-Schwartz model, was estimated over the previous months, using estimates of the instantaneous convenience yield constructed under the assumption that δ was constant till the maturity of the second nearest futures contract.[18] Again, the number of time series observations used to estimate δ increases from a minimum of 24 in March 1985. The time series of estimates of α and δ are plotted in Figure 4. The estimates show considerable volatility in the early part of the sample period, reflecting in part the small number of observations used in estimation. By 1989 the estimates of the parameters for both models settle down in the neighbourhood of 0.3 which corresponds to a half-life of 2.3 months for deviations of the convenience yield from its long-run mean.

It is also necessary to estimate m to implement the hedge for the Gibson-Schwartz model. This was done for each month by finding the value that minimised the sum of the squared price prediction errors for the three to six month contracts using equations (16) to (18).

Empirical results

The hedge properties of four basic strategies were evaluated using the oil futures price data. These strategies are the Brennan, the Gibson-Schwartz, the stack-and-roll, and the Edwards-Canter minimum variance strategy. Two variants of the Brennan and Gibson-Schwartz strategies were implemented: the first using two- and three-month futures to construct the hedge portfolio, and the second using two- and six-month futures.[19] Two variants of the stack-and-roll and Edwards-Canter hedges were implemented: the simple version and the tailed version. These latter hedges were all implemented using the two-month futures contract. The hedges were designed to hedge fixed commitments with maturities ranging from six to 24 months, and the present values of these commitments were computed each month using the observed futures prices and interest rates for these maturities. All the hedges were revised monthly and the monthly hedge errors were calculated as described below.

Specifically, for each month t, for each liability maturity τ, the hedging error under each of the policies was computed as follows. First, the present value of the liability under the commitment at the beginning of the month was computed by discounting the futures price for the corresponding maturity:

$$L_{t-1,T} = e^{-r_{t-1,T}T} F_{t-1,T} \tag{21}$$

where $r_{t,T}$ is the continuously compounded T period interest rate at the beginning of month t, $F_{t,T}$ is the T period futures price at the beginning of the month, and $L_{t,T}$ is the value of the liability. The change in the present value of the liability over the month is defined by $\Delta L_{t,T} \equiv L_{t,T-1} - L_{t-1,T}$. Suppose that the hedge consists of n_1 and n_2 futures contracts of maturi-

5a. Cumulative hedge errors: 12-month hedge

The figure shows the cumulated monthly errors in dollars from hedging a fixed maturity 12-month commitment using stack-and-roll (S&R) and Edwards–Canter (E&C) hedges

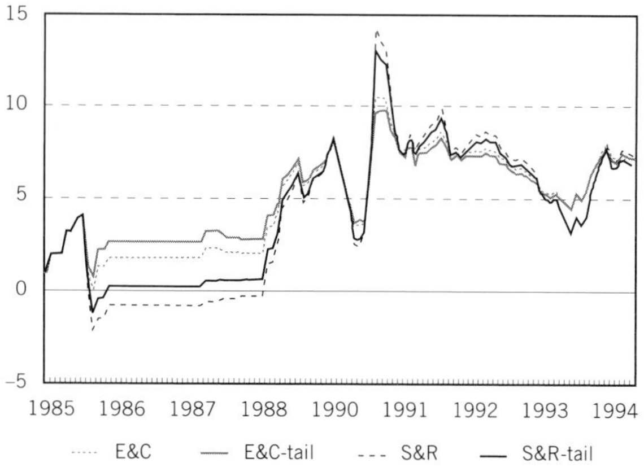

5b. Cumulative hedge errors: 12-month hedge

The figure shows the cumulated monthly errors in dollars from hedging a fixed maturity 12-month commitment using Brennan (BRE) and Gibson–Schwartz (G&S) hedges

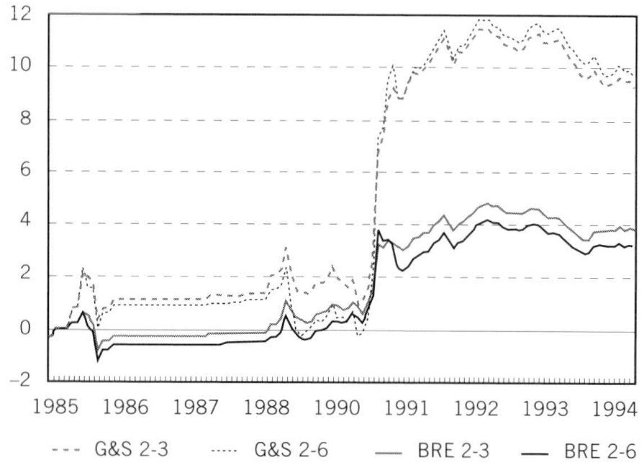

5c. Cumulative hedge errors: 12-month hedge

The figure shows the cumulated monthly errors in dollars from hedging a fixed maturity 12-month commitment using stack-and-roll (S&R) and Gibson–Schwartz (G&S) hedges

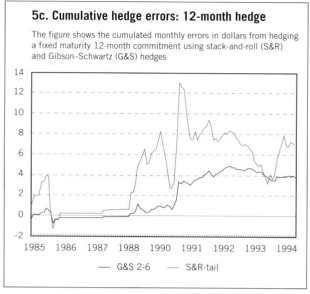

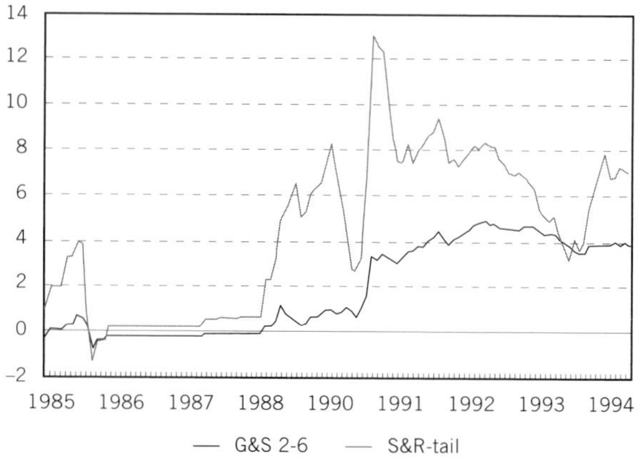

5d. Cumulative hedge errors: 18-month hedge

The figure shows the cumulated monthly errors in dollars from hedging a fixed maturity 18-month commitment using stack-and-roll (S&R) and Edwards–Canter (E&C) hedges

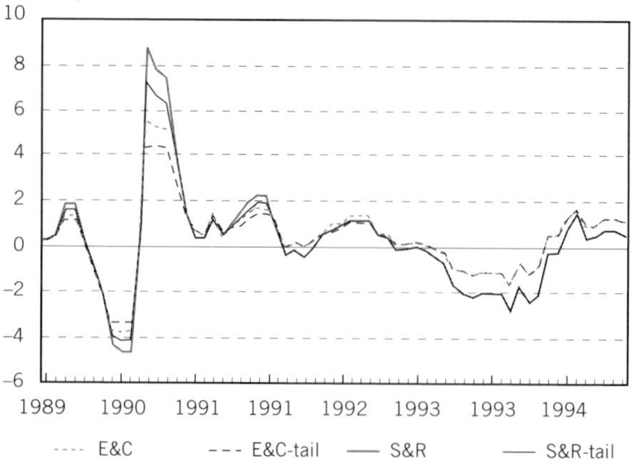

ties τ_1 and τ_2. Then the change in the hedger's wealth over the month, from hedging a T period liability, $\Delta W_{t,T}$ is given by

$$\Delta W_{t,T} = -\Delta L_{t,T} + n_1 \Delta F_1 + n_2 \Delta F_2 \tag{22}$$

where ΔF_s is the change in the τ_s period futures price during month t. Finally, the hedging error, $E_{t,T}$, is defined as the difference between the change in wealth and the riskless return on the present value of the liability:

$$E_{t,T} = \Delta W_{t,T} - (e^{r_{t-1,1}} - 1)\, L_{t-1,T} \tag{23}$$

For the Brennan and Gibson-Schwartz models, n_1 and n_2 were calculated from equations (14) and (20) respectively. For the simple stack-and-roll strategy, $n_1 = 1$, $n_2 = 0$, while for the tailed stack-and-roll strategy $n_1 = e^{-rT}$. For the Edwards–Canter strategy, $n_1 = \beta$, where β is the coefficient from the regression of the change in the six-month futures price on the change in the nearby futures price estimated over all prior months; for the tailed version the coefficient is multiplied by e^{-rT}.[20]

The means and standard deviations of the monthly hedging errors, measured in dollars per barrel of oil committed, for the various strategies are reported in Table 2 for commitment maturities of 6–24 months at three-month intervals. In reviewing this table it is important to remember that these are the errors from hedging the same *fixed maturity* commitment each month.

5e. Cumulative hedge errors: 18-month hedge

The figure shows the cumulated monthly errors in dollars from hedging a fixed maturity 18-month commitment using Brennan (BRE) and Gibson–Schwartz (G&S) hedges

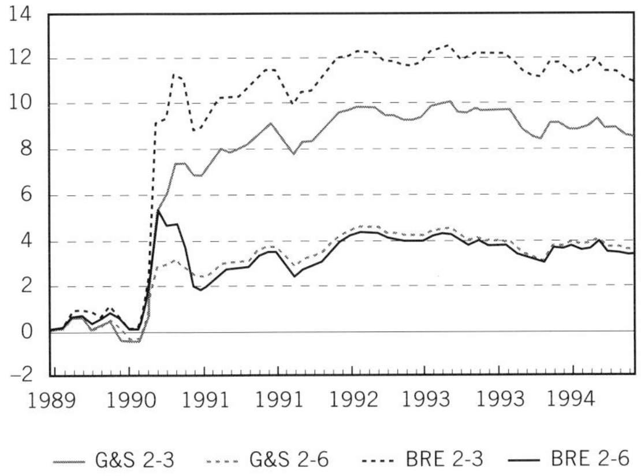

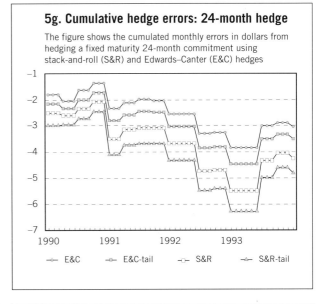

5g. Cumulative hedge errors: 24-month hedge

The figure shows the cumulated monthly errors in dollars from hedging a fixed maturity 24-month commitment using stack-and-roll (S&R) and Edwards–Canter (E&C) hedges

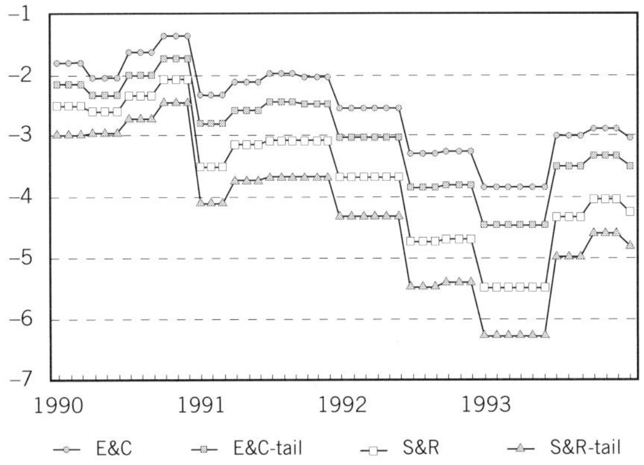

5f. Cumulative hedge errors: 18-month hedge

The figure shows the cumulated monthly errors in dollars from hedging a fixed maturity 18-month commitment using stack-and-roll (S&R) and Gibson–Schwartz (G&S) hedges

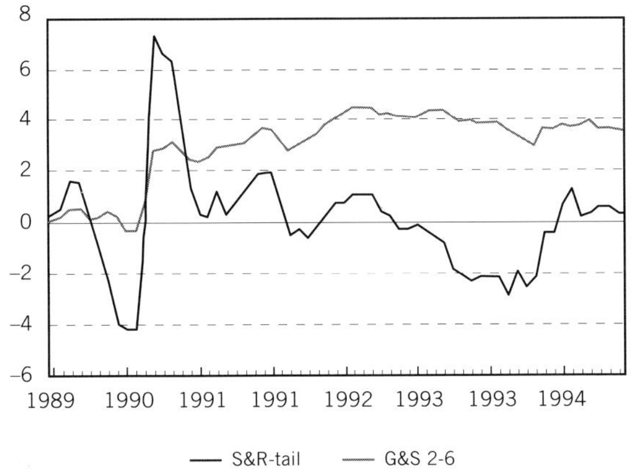

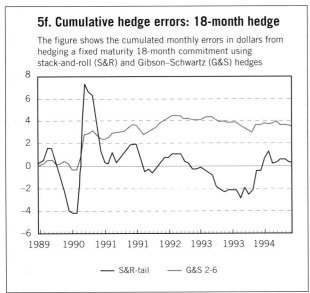

5h. Cumulative hedge errors: 24-month hedge

The figure shows the cumulated monthly errors in dollars from hedging a fixed maturity 24-month commitment using Brennan (BRE) and Gibson–Schwartz (G&S) hedges

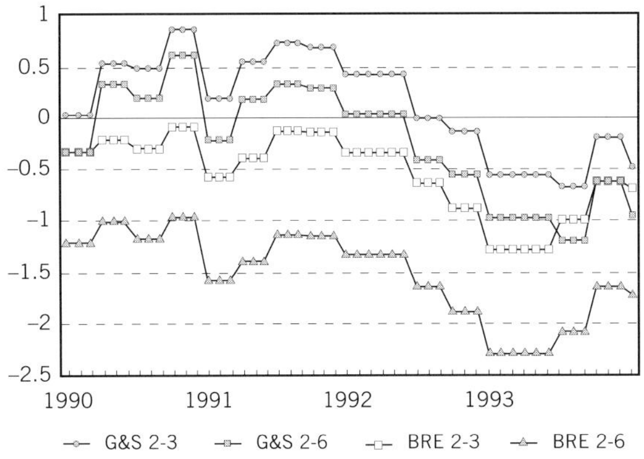

5i. Cumulative hedge errors: 24-month hedge

The figure shows the cumulated monthly errors in dollars from hedging a fixed maturity 24-month commitment using stack-and-roll (S&R) and Gibson–Schwartz (G&S) hedges

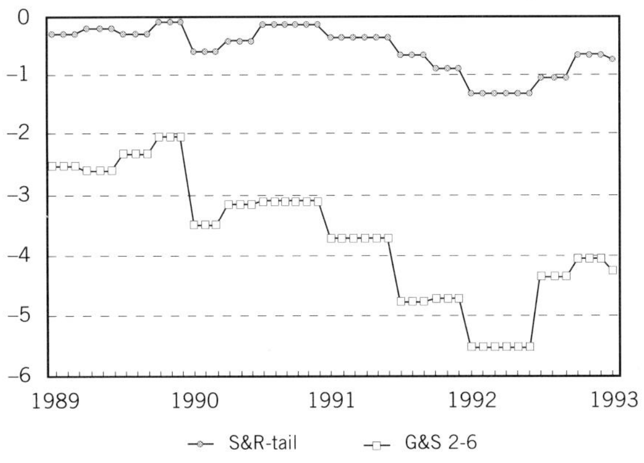

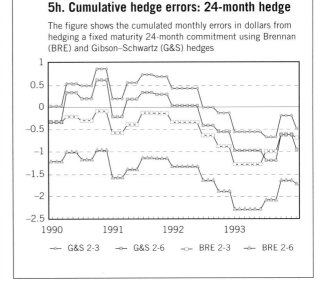

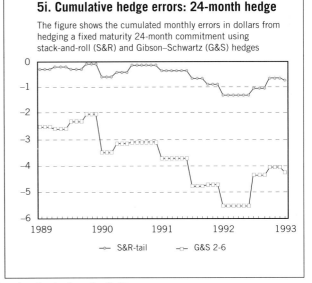

First we observe that out to 18 months the standard deviation of the hedge errors increases monotonically with the maturity of the commitment; there is a discrete drop in the standard deviations beyond 18 months but this reflects the fact that the 21- and 24-month contracts have been available (and therefore the hedge errors could be calculated) only since December 1990, and even since then these contracts are not traded every month, so that the numbers of observations for these maturities are only 17 and 15, as compared with 54 for the 18-month maturity. Overall, for all maturities, the worst performing strategy is the simple stack-and-roll strategy, followed by the tailed version of the strategy. The next worst strategies are generally the Edward–Canter "minimum variance" strategies. The best performing strategy throughout is the Gibson-Schwartz strategy executed in the two- and six-month futures contracts, and the second best is the Brennan strategy in the same contracts. The Gibson-Schwartz strategy has a standard deviation of US$0.40 per month for the 18-month maturity, compared with US$1.66 for the simple stack-and-roll. Overall, it appears that substantial gains in hedging efficiency can be achieved by taking account of the variability in the convenience yield.

Ironically, the ranking in terms of the mean errors for the 18-month maturity is almost

Table 2a. Mean hedging errors

This Table reports the means of the monthly errors in hedging a forward commitment of one barrel of oil deliverable at a fixed future maturity, under different strategies, over the period May 1985 to December 1994 or subperiods for which futures price data where available.

	6 month	9 month	12 month	15 month	18 month	21 month	24 month
S&R	0.06	0.10	0.08	0.05	0.01	–0.26	–0.32
$S\&R_{tailed}$	0.06	0.09	0.08	0.04	0.01	–0.23	–0.28
E&C	0.05	0.09	0.09	0.04	0.02	–0.18	–0.23
$E\&C_{tailed}$	0.05	0.08	0.09	0.04	0.02	–0.16	–0.20
BRE_{2and3}	0.02	0.06	0.11	0.17	0.21	–0.02	–0.06
BRE_{2and6}	n.a.	0.02	0.04	0.08	0.06	–0.09	–0.12
$G\&S_{2and3}$	0.04	0.07	0.11	0.13	0.16	–.003	–0.03
$G\&S_{2and6}$	n.a.	0.02	0.05	0.08	0.07	–0.04	–0.05
No. of observations	116	116	85	67	54	17	15

S&R: stack-and-roll strategy
E&C: minimum variance hedge of Edwards–Canter (tailed strategies adjust the hedge for the time value of money).
BRE_{2and3}(BRE_{2and6}): strategy derived from Brennan model of futures prices implemented using two- and three-month (two- and six-month) maturity futures contracts.
$G\&S_{2and3}$($G\&S_{2and6}$): strategy derived from Gibson–Schwartz model of futures prices implemented using two- and three-month (two- and six-month) maturity futures contracts.

Table 2b. Standard deviation of monthly hedging errors

This Table reports the standard deviations of the monthly errors in hedging a forward commitment of one barrel of oil deliverable at a fixed future maturity, under different strategies, over the period May 1985 to December 1994 or subperiods for which futures price data where available.

	6 month	9 month	12 month	15 month	18 month	21 month	24 month
S&R	0.70	0.99	1.30	1.44	1.66	0.92	0.99
$S\&R_{tailed}$	0.64	0.90	1.16	1.27	1.43	0.81	0.86
E&C	0.44	0.65	0.89	0.97	1.14	0.66	0.71
$E\&C_{tailed}$	0.43	0.60	0.79	0.85	0.97	0.58	0.62
BRE_{2and3}	0.31	0.54	0.77	0.90	1.08	0.38	0.41
BRE_{2and6}	n.a.	0.19	0.38	0.51	0.67	0.36	0.41
$G\&S_{2and3}$	0.29	0.46	0.61	0.64	0.69	0.33	0.35
$G\&S_{2and6}$	n.a.	0.17	0.29	0.34	0.40	0.23	0.26
No. of observations	116	116	85	67	54	17	15

See note to Table 2a.

exactly reverse the ranking in terms of standard deviations! However, we are not inclined to accept these results at face value, but rather attribute to chance the fact that, for example, the mean error of the stack-and-roll hedge during this period was US$0.01. Figures 5a–f show the performance of the different hedge strategies by aggregating over time the monthly hedging errors for selected strategies. The first three figures relate to the 12-month commitment hedge for which there are 85 monthly observations. The flat parts of the figures correspond to periods when there was no 12-month future outstanding to allow calculation of a hedge error. Figure 5a shows that the stack-and-roll and Edwards–Canter hedges performed similarly whether tailed or not, but that the hedge errors quickly cumulated to US$5–10 per barrel. Figure 5b shows the Brennan and Gibson–Schwartz hedges. When implemented in the two- and three-month futures they perform badly. The reason for this is that the sensitivity of these futures prices to changes in the convenience yield is not very different; as a result it is necessary to take large offsetting positions in the two maturities to hedge out the convenience yield sensitivity, and this increases the importance of model specification and estimation errors.[21] By comparison, the two- and six-month hedge performs very well except in the second half of 1990 when the cumulative error of Gibson–Schwartz (two, six months) increases by about US$2.50. However, this was the time of the Iraqi invasion of Kuwait, an extremely turbulent period in oil markets as shown in Figure 7. The spot price more than doubled from US$17.05 in June to US$39.50 in September. Figure 5c compares the tailed stack-and-roll hedge with the Gibson–Schwartz (two, six months) on the same scale, and shows the substantial gains in effectiveness made possible by the Gibson–Schwartz strategy.

Figures 5d–f repeat a similar analysis for hedging an 18-month commitment. Again, the stack-and-roll and Edwards–Canter hedges perform similarly, and the Brennan and Gibson–Schwartz (two, six month) hedges are also similar, and perform well except during the period of extreme price turbulence in 1990. Figures 5g–h relate to a hedge for a

24-month commitment. Here there are only 15 monthly price changes to be hedged, so that the results cannot be regarded as in any way definitive. However, we note that the cumulative error of the Gibson-Schwartz (two-, six-month) hedge is less than US$1.00, which is about one quarter that of the tailed stack-and-roll hedge.

Figures 6a and 6b show the hedge portfolios for the Edwards-Canter, Brennan and Gibson-Schwartz (two-, six-month) strategies for a 12-month commitment. The Edwards-Canter strategy takes a long position of about 0.7 barrels in the two-month maturity; the volatility of the hedge in the first few months reflects the small number of observations used to estimate the hedge ratio. Note that the stack-and-roll hedge (before tailing) takes a long position in one barrel per barrel of commitment. The Brennan, and Gibson-Schwartz, strategies take very similar positions - roughly 1.3 barrels long in the six-month maturity and 0.2 barrels short in the two-month maturity. There is relatively little variation in the hedge position over time (once the initial volatility due to estimation error is passed), despite the wide variation we have noted in the level and slope of the futures pricing curves.

6a. Hedge ratios for the Edwards–Canter 12-month hedge

The figure shows the estimated number of two-month futures contracts to be held long to hedge a 12-month fixed maturity commitment using the Edwards–Canter tailed hedge

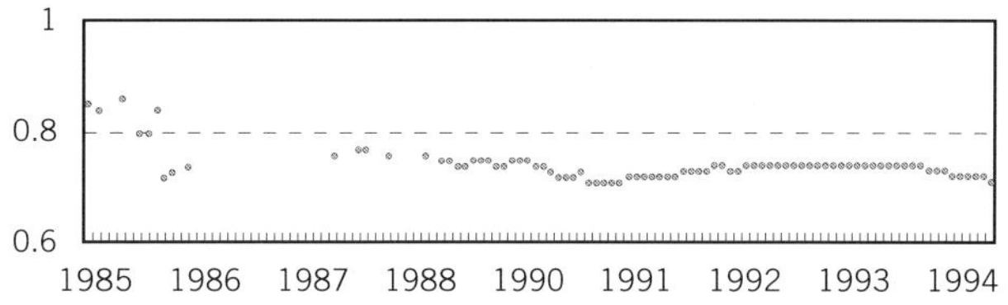

6b. Hedge ratios for the Brennan and Gibson–Schwartz 12-month hedge

The figure shows the estimated number of two- and six-month futures contracts to be held long to hedge a 12-month fixed maturity commitment using the Brennan (BRE) and Gibson–Schwartz (G&S) models

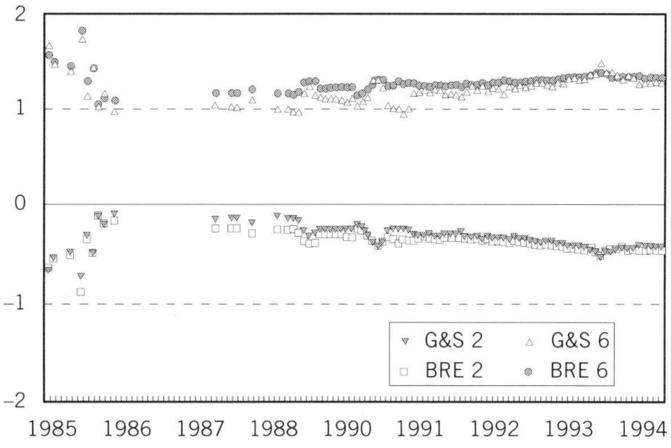

7. Spot and futures prices of oil, second half of 1990

The figure shows the spot and futures prices of Nymex light oil contract, month ends June to December 1990

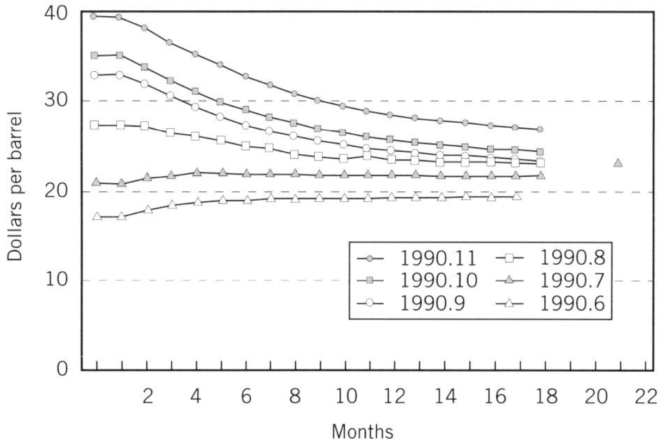

Conclusion

In this chapter we have developed two new models for constructing hedges for long-term commodity commitments using short-term futures contracts, and have compared their performance with that of the simpler stack-and-roll and minimum variance hedges, using monthly data on the prices of light crude oil. We find that the models of Brennan and of Gibson-Schwartz perform significantly better than the two simpler models, the Gibson-Schwartz model reducing the standard deviation of the hedge error by about 75% relative to the stack-and-roll strategy.

Our analysis suffers from two limitations, one empirical and one theoretical. On the empirical side, we have had to limit the maturity of the commitments whose hedges were analysed to the maturity of the longest available futures contract. Clearly it would be desirable to test the effectiveness of the strategies in hedging longer-term commitments if data on the prices of the these could be obtained on a periodic basis. A significant limitation of our theoretical models is the assumption that interest rates are deterministic. For longer time horizons, uncertainty about future interest rates becomes important for the hedge strategies, and therefore it would be desirable to extend the Brennan and Gibson-Schwartz models to allow for stochastic interest rates. We leave this for subsequent work.

Appendix

Applying Itô's Lemma to the futures price, $F(P,C,\tau)$,

$$dF = \left[-F_\tau + \tfrac{1}{2}F_{PP}\sigma^2P^2 + F_{PC}\rho\sigma\eta + \tfrac{1}{2}F_{CC}\eta^2\right]dt + F_P dP + F_C dC \qquad \text{(A1)}$$

Consider a storage firm that invests one dollar in an inventory of the commodity, hedging its investment by shorting $(PF_P)^{-1}$ futures contracts. The return on this hedged investment, including the convenience yield is

$$P^{-1}\left[C - F_P^{-1}\left[-F_\tau + \tfrac{1}{2}F_{PP}\sigma^2P^2 + F_{PC}\rho\sigma\eta + \tfrac{1}{2}F_{CC}\eta^2 + F_C\alpha(m - C)\right]\right]dt - (PF_P)^{-1}F_C\eta dz_C \tag{A2}$$

The investment is not riskless because of the influence of the stochastic convenience yield on the futures price. We assume that the risk premium associated with any asset which is perfectly (positively) correlated with the stochastic change in the convenience yield is proportional to the standard deviation of the return on the asset. Then the equilibrium expected return on the above portfolio may be written as $r - (PF_P)^{-1}F_C\lambda_\eta$, where λ is a constant of proportionality. Equating this to the drift term in equation (A2) and rearranging, we obtain the following partial differential equation for the futures price:

$$\tfrac{1}{2}F_{PP}\sigma^2P^2 + F_{PC}\rho\sigma\eta + \tfrac{1}{2}F_{CC}\eta^2 + F_P(rP - C) + F_C(\alpha(m - C) - \lambda\eta) - F_\tau - 0 \tag{A3}$$

The solution to this equation may be written as

$$F(P,C,\tau) = (P - PVC(C,\tau))e^{r\tau} \tag{A4}$$

where

$$PVC(C,\tau) = \frac{m^*}{r}(1 - e^{-r\tau}) - \frac{m^* - C}{\alpha + r}(1 - e^{(\alpha+r)\tau}) \tag{A5}$$

and $m^* \equiv \frac{\lambda^*}{\alpha}$.

1 *See Culp and Miller (1994, 1995), Edwards and Canter (1995), Mello and Parsons (1995), Neuberger (1995) and Ross (1995).*

2 *Strictly speaking, prior to the period in which the commitment corresponds to the longest available futures contract.*

3 *In this chapter we assume that the interest rates are non-stochastic so that the futures and forward prices are the same. See Cox, Ingersoll and Ross (1981).*

4 *Later published as Brennan (1991).*

5 *Garbade (1993) presents a model which is a special case of Brennan (1991).*

6 *The commitments undertaken by Metallgesellschaft had maturities of 5–10 years.*

7 *More precisely, to account for daily settlement, the number of contracts should be adjusted daily to* e^{-ry}, *where* y *is the exact number of years to maturity of the commitment from the following day. The formula in the test implicitly assumes that settling up takes place only at the maturity of each futures contract; that is, it treats the futures as short-dated forwards.*

8 *The rollover gain is defined as the difference between the price of the nearby futures contract and the next shortest contract, and corresponds to the gains from a strategy of going long in the second nearby contract and rolling over at the end of every month.*

9 *Defined as the one-month futures price less the three-month futures price.*

10 *The reader will note the analogy with the assumption of parallel shifts in the yield curve that underlies the derivation of the duration model of bond price hedging. Indeed, the stack-and-roll policy has much in common with a duration matched bond price hedge in Treasury Bill futures.*

11 *Previous authors who have discussed the convenience yield include Kaldor (1939), Working (1948, 1949), Brennan (1985), Telser (1958), and Fama and French (1987).*

12 *See Brennan and Schwartz (1985).*

13 *Only tend to because the investment decisions of storage firms will depend upon the expected rate of change in the commodity price as well as upon the convenience yield.*

14 *Jamshidian and Fein (1990) appear to have been the first to develop a closed form expression for the futures price in this model.*

15 *Recall that we wish to evaluate a technique for hedging that does not rely on observation of the commitment value (though our evaluation of the technique does).*

16 *On November 30, 1990, there was a limit move in futures prices that affected all but the nearby contract. Therefore we substituted the prices for November 29.*

17 *This is similar to the procedure followed by Gibson and Schwartz (1990). Note that with a constant convenience yield,* C*, the futures price is given by* $F(P,C,\tau) = Pe^{r\tau} + C/r\ (1 - e^{r\tau})$. *Subtracting two adjacent futures prices yields an estimate of* C.

18 *Under the Gibson–Schwartz model the expression for the futures price when the convenience yield is constant is* $F(P,t,\tau) = Pe^{(r-\delta)\tau}$. *The ratio of the two nearby futures prices yields a simple estimate of* δ.

19 *By a* τ *month contract we mean the contract which is* τ*th closest to maturity: this will have a maturity which does not exceed* τ *months. See Table 1.*

20 *The reason that we use the six-month contract to calculate* β *is that we wish to assess the effectiveness of the hedge for a commitment whose market value cannot be observed.*

21 *For example, to hedge a 12-month liability the average position for the Gibson–Schwartz two- and three-month strategy would be a short position of 2.3 contracts in the two-month maturity and long 3.2 contracts in the three-month maturity. The corresponding hedging using two- and six-month contracts would be only short 0.3 two-month contracts and long 1.2 six-month contracts.*

BIBLIOGRAPHY

Brennan, M. J., 1987, "The Cost of Convenience and the Pricing of Commodity Contingent Claims", Working paper, Columbia Futures Center.

Brennan, M. J., 1991, "The Price of Convenience and the Valuation of Commodity Contingent Claims", in *Stochastic Models and Option Values*, D. Lund and B. Oksendal, eds (North Holland).

Brennan, M. J., and E. S. Schwartz, 1985, "Evaluating Natural Resource Investments", *Journal of Business* 58, pp. 133–55.

Cox, J. C., J. E. Ingersoll and S. A. Ross, 1981, "The Relation Between Forward Prices and Futures Prices", *Journal of Financial Economics* 9, pp. 321–46.

Culp, C. L., and M. H. Miller, 1994, "Hedging a Flow of Commodity Deliveries with Futures: Lessons from Metallgesellschaft", *Derivatives Quarterly* 1, pp. 7–15.

Culp, C. L., and M. H. Miller, 1995, "Metallgesellschaft and the Economics of Synthetic Storage", *Journal of Applied Corporate Finance* 7, pp. 62–76; reprinted as Chapter 9 of the present volume.

Edwards, F., and M. Canter, 1995, "The Collapse of Metallgesellschaft: Unhedgeable Risks, Poor Hedging Strategy, or Just Bad Luck?", *Journal of Futures Markets*; reprinted as Chapter 13 of the present volume.

Fama E. F., and K. R. French, 1987, "Commodity Futures Prices: Some Evidence on Forecast Power, Premiums and the Theory of Storage", *Journal of Business* 60, pp. 55–74.

Garbade, K. D., 1993, "A Two-Factor, Arbitrage-Free, Model of Fluctuations in Crude Oil Futures Prices", *Journal of Derivatives* 1, pp. 86–97.

Gibson, R., and E. S. Schwartz, 1990, "Stochastic Convenience Yield and the Pricing of Oil Contingent Claims", *Journal of Finance* 45, pp. 959–76.

Jamshidian, F., and M. Fein, 1990, "Closed-Form Solutions for Oil Futures and European Options in the Gibson–Schwartz Model: A Note", Working paper, Merrill Lynch Capital Markets.

Kaldor, N., 1939, "Speculation and Economic Stability", *Review of Economic Studies* 7, pp. 1–27.

Mello, A. A., and J. E. Parsons, 1995, "Maturity Structure of a Hedge Matters: Lessons from the Metallgesellschaft Debacle", *Journal of Applied Corporate Finance* 8, pp. 106–20; reprinted as Chapter 12 of the present volume.

Neuberger, A., 1995, "How Well Can You Hedge Long Term Exposures with Multiple Short-Term Futures Contracts?", Unpublished manuscript, London Business School.

Ross, S. A., 1995, "Hedging Long Run Commitments: Exercises in Incomplete Market Pricing", *preliminary draft*; reprinted as Chapter 19 of the present volume.

Telser, L. G., 1958, "Futures Trading and the Storage of Cotton and Wheat", *Journal of Political Economy* 66, pp. 233–44.

Working, H., 1948, "Theory of the Inverse Carrying Charge in Futures Markets", *Journal of Farm Economics* 30, pp. 1–28.

Working, H., 1949, "The Theory of the Price of Storage", *American Economic Review* 39, pp. 1,254–62.

17

Metallgesellschaft: A Prudent Hedger Ruined, or a Wildcatter on Nymex?*

Stephen Craig Pirrong

Washington University

The travails of the firm Metallgesellschaft (MG) have received much attention in both academic circles and the financial press. The battle lines on the issue are clearly drawn. On one side, critics of MG (including Mello and Parsons, 1995) claim that the firm's energy market trading was rashly speculative, and as a result of adverse movements in oil prices, the firm suffered real mark-to-market losses of as much as one billion dollars. On the other side, defenders of the firm – notably Culp and Miller (1994) – claim that the firm employed a prudent and potentially very lucrative strategy of hedging long-term energy delivery obligations with short-term futures and swaps. In this view, MG's bankers mistook a mere liquidity problem resulting from margin calls on futures positions for a full-blown insolvency crisis, unwisely unwound the firm's hedge position and prematurely terminated some of its long-term delivery contracts.

Which view is correct ultimately depends upon the dynamics of energy prices and how these dynamics affect optimal hedge ratios. MG implemented a barrel-for-barrel hedge. That is, it bought one barrel of short-term energy futures or swaps for each barrel of oil it was committed to deliver, regardless of whether it was obligated to deliver in six months or 10 years. There are strong reasons to believe *a priori* that this hedging strategy forced the firm to bear more risk than necessary. However, Culp and Miller defend the one-for-one hedge, claiming that MG employed an innovative synthetic storage (or carrying charge hedging) strategy that increased firm value while protecting MG against spot price increases over the 10-year life of the programme. They recognise that this strategy forced the firm to bear basis risk, but claim that this basis risk was small relative to the risk inherent in the firm's fixed-price contracts.

A definitive resolution of this debate cannot be achieved through *a priori* argument; the data must be the ultimate arbiter. This chapter undertakes a thorough analysis of the dynamics of crude oil futures prices to determine the riskiness of the barrel-for-barrel strategy relative to alternative strategies available to the firm. This analysis of variance-minimising hedge ratios is more thorough and employs more sophisticated econometric techniques than previous studies by Mello and Parsons (1995) and Edwards and Canter (1995). It thus allows a more complete critique of the prudence of the barrel-for-barrel strategy.

The empirical results are starkly revealing. Given the behaviour of crude oil prices, the variance-minimising hedge ratio during 1993 was far less than one. Indeed, for delivery obligations with maturities as short as 15 months, the variance-minimising hedge ratio was around 0.5, implying that MG's barrel-for-barrel hedge actually increased the firm's exposure to oil price risk. Even under very conservative assumptions the data imply that MG's exposure to energy price risk was greater with a barrel-for-barrel futures and swap hedge than it would have been if the firm had not hedged its long-term delivery commitments at all! Consideration of options embedded in the firm's cash market contracts does not alter the fundamental result. Moreover, the prospect of earning gains every time it rolled over its futures positions did not justify taking this additional risk. Thus, it is impossible to view the firm's strategy as a prudent exercise in risk management.

**This paper was first published in the* Journal of Futures Markets *17(5) (1997), pp. 543–78, and is reprinted by permission of John Wiley & Sons, Inc.*

The empirical results imply that the combined futures–long-term contract position exposed the company to severe losses in the event of a steepening of the term structure of energy prices. This indeed occurred in 1993. Simulation estimates of the profitability of the barrel-for-barrel strategy during this period imply that the firm lost approximately US$800 million on a mark-to-market basis. These estimates, which correspond closely to accounting estimates of MG's losses, contradict the claim that the firm's losses were a mirage caused by misleading accounting standards that failed to reflect mark-to-market gains on its deferred delivery contracts.

MG's energy market activities

The details of MG's energy market activities have been the subject of much coverage, so a short overview will suffice here. In 1991, an MG subsidiary – MG Refining and Marketing (MGRM) – entered the business of supplying American heating oil and gasoline retailers. To do so, it offered these retailers unprecedented five- and 10-year fixed-price contracts. These contracts were of two types. The firm-fixed contracts specified delivery schedules. The firm-flexible contracts allowed buyers to choose the delivery schedule with certain restrictions. Under the firm-flexible contracts, buyers were allowed to defer or accelerate purchases but were required to buy all quantities deferred by the end of the contract. Thus, these contracts permitted buyers to choose the timing of deliveries but not their quantity. These contracts also allowed the buyers to terminate at will. At termination of the firm-fixed contracts, the buyers received a payment of one-half of the difference between the prevailing spot price of West Texas Intermediate light crude oil and the fixed price in the contract, multiplied by the quantity remaining under the contract. Under the firm-flexible contracts, the buyers received the full difference between the two-month futures price and the contract price.

By September 1993, MG had entered contracts obligating it to deliver 102 million barrels of refined products under firm-fixed contracts. The tenor on 94% of these contracts was 10 years; the remainder had a five-year tenor. MG was obligated to deliver 47.5 million barrels of products under 10-year firm-flexible contracts and 10.5 million under five-year firm-flexible deals. Approximately one-third of these obligations were entered into during September 1993. In addition, MG entered into an arrangement to purchase refined products from Castle Energy Corp, a small US refiner. MG agreed to supply the refinery with most of the 100,000 barrels a day of crude oil it required and agreed to purchase the refinery's daily output of 40,000 barrels a day of gasoline and 35,000 barrels a day of heating oil and other distillates.

To protect itself against increases in energy prices, MG purchased crude oil and gasoline futures contracts and entered into OTC energy swaps. Rather than matching the expiration dates of the futures contracts with the dates of its delivery obligations to Castle and its customers, MG bought primarily near-month (ie, next-to-expire) crude oil and gasoline contracts. In the terminology of the futures trade, this is referred to as a stacked hedge, because all hedging positions are stacked on a single contract month rather than spread over several contract months. MG's OTC swaps were also of relatively short maturity. The expirations of these contracts were predominately less than or equal to three months. MG purchased one 1,000 barrel futures contract or its swap equivalent for each 1,000 barrels of the firm's short position regardless of the expiration date of the short position. That is, the firm hedged barrel-for-barrel, and thus by mid- to late 1993 had bought 160 million barrels of futures and swaps to cover its 160 million barrel cash market position.

The determination of hedge ratios to create a synthetic forward position

The riskiness of a barrel-for-barrel hedging strategy depends crucially upon the dynamics of energy prices. To see why, consider a firm that desires to minimise the variance of the payoff on a deferred forward delivery obligation (the short position) in crude oil. This focus on variance minimisation is not intended to imply that only variance-minimising hedges were appropriate for MG. Instead, variance minimisation serves as a benchmark against which to measure actual trading strategies; by comparing actual hedge ratios to variance-minimising ratios, it is possible to quantify (a) the speculative component of a trading strategy, and (b) the risk of the actual trading strategy.

The fixed price in the forward obligation to be hedged is f. MG was short a bundle of many forward positions, but because the analysis is identical for each forward contract in the bundle, for simplicity the analysis focuses upon hedging a single element of the bundle;

repeating the following analysis for each element produces the appropriate hedge ratio for MG's entire swap position.

Assume that the firm is constrained to employ a single hedging instrument – the next-to-expire crude oil futures contract (the nearby contract).[1] The deferred obligation expires at time T. The firm can adjust the number of nearby contracts it buys at M equally spaced times between time t_0 (the present) and T. That is, the firm can hedge dynamically. Each interval is $\Delta t = (T - t_0)/M$ in length. Because the nearby crude contracts expire monthly, each interval is less than or equal to one month in duration. As M grows arbitrarily large, the firm effectively employs a continuously adjusted dynamic hedging strategy. Through this strategy, the firm attempts to replicate the payoffs to a forward position, thereby creating a synthetic forward contract.

The change in the price of a unit of the deferred over a time interval ending at t equals $\Delta F_{t,T} \equiv F_{t,T} - F_{t-\Delta t,T}$, where $F_{t,T}$ is the forward price at t for delivery at T. Because the payoff to the deferred delivery obligation occurs at time T and because MG is short, the change in the present value of the deferred obligation is $v_{t,T} \equiv -e^{-r(T-t)}\,\Delta F_{t,T}$.[2] The change in the price of the nearby contract over the same time interval equals $\Delta S_t \equiv S_t - S_{t\Delta t}$. Because futures contracts are marked-to-market, the hedger realises this gain or loss when it occurs. At $t - \Delta t$ the firm buys $\beta_{t,T}$ units of the nearby contract to hedge each unit of its deferred obligation over the interval $[t - \Delta t, t]$. By T, the firm's realised profit or loss equals

$$\Pi_T = \sum_{i=1}^{M} e^{r(T-t_0-i\Delta t)}\left[\beta_{t_0+i\Delta t,T}\,\Delta S_{t_0+i\Delta t} - \Delta v_{t_0+i\Delta t,T}\right] - F_{t_0,T}$$

The firm's objective at t_0 is to minimise $E_{t_0}(\Pi_T - E_{t_0}\Pi_T)^2$.[3]

Determination of the variance-minimising hedge strategy for each t requires the solution of an extremely complex dynamic programming problem that allows the hedge ratio at t to depend upon expected hedge ratios for $t' > t$ (Chan, 1992; Duffie and Jackson, 1991; and Lien and Luo, 1994). If mean price changes are non-zero, even in relatively simple cases involving time-varying spot and forward price dynamics, solution of this dynamic programming problem is not practical even for M on the order of two or three. It is therefore necessary to approximate the optimal dynamic variance-minimising hedging solution by a sequence of myopic hedge ratios which minimise the variance of the one-period hedge gain or loss; that is, the $\beta_{t,T}$ that minimises $E_{t-\Delta t}[\beta_{t,T}\Delta S_t - \Delta v_{t,T} - E_{t-\Delta t}\Pi_t]^2$ for $t = t_0 + i\Delta t$, $i = 1,\ldots,M$, where $\Pi_t = \beta_{t,T}\Delta S_t - \Delta v_{t,T}$. This is the approach taken in other studies of hedging with time-varying parameters, such as Kroner and Sultan (1991).

In the present case, the use of a series of single-period variance-minimising hedges to approximate dynamically optimised hedges probably involves little cost in terms of accuracy. The Appendix shows that myopic hedge ratios are equal to those produced as the solution to the dynamic programming problem if S_t and $F_{t,T}$ are martingales (see also Duffie and Jackson, 1991), and in the subsection "Exploratory data analysis" on page 235 it is shown that one cannot reject the hypothesis that past price changes do not explain current price changes for either nearby and deferred futures, which justifies the use of myopic hedge ratios even in a dynamic hedging problem.

It is well known that the optimal $\beta_{t,T}$ for one-period-ahead hedging is given by

$$\beta_{t,T} = -\frac{\operatorname{cov}(\Delta S_t, \Delta v_{t,T})}{\operatorname{var}(\Delta S_t)} = \frac{e^{-r(T-t)}\operatorname{cov}(\Delta F_{t,T}, \Delta S_t)}{\operatorname{var}(\Delta S_t)} \tag{1}$$

This can be rewritten as

$$\beta_{t,T} = e^{-r(T-t)}\frac{\sigma(\Delta F_{t,T})}{\sigma(\Delta S_t)}\operatorname{corr}(\Delta F_{t,T}, \Delta S_t) \tag{2}$$

where $\sigma(\Delta F_{t,T})$ is the standard deviation in interval in the change in the price of the deferred obligation i, $\sigma(\Delta S_t)$ is the standard deviation of the change in the nearby price and $\operatorname{corr}(\Delta F_{t,T}, \Delta S_t)$ is the correlation between the change in the nearby price and the change in the deferred price.[4]

These correlations and variances may change over time for a variety of reasons. First, it is plausible *a priori* that oil prices are stationary (Dixit and Pindyck, 1994). Stationarity causes the volatility of the deferred to rise as time passes. Second, the theory of storage implies that the variances and correlations should depend upon the spread between spot and deferred prices (net of interest and storage costs). When supplies are short, the market is in backwardation. An increase in the severity of backwardation causes an increase in both spot and deferred volatilities, a decrease in the ratio of deferred volatility to spot volatility and a decline in the correlation between spot and deferred prices (Ng and Pirrong, 1994). Because backwardation is a random variable, this implies that hedge ratios should change randomly as well. Third, shocks to the oil market (due to OPEC policy changes, for example) can cause changes in the relevant variances and correlations and, thus, in hedge ratios. Given these three factors, variance-minimising hedging requires a methodology for quantifying how the relevant correlation and variances change. There are a variety of means to address this problem. This next section describes a Garch-based methodology because it can take each of these factors into account.[5]

BACKWARDATION-ADJUSTED GARCH

Backwardation-adjusted Garch (BAG) is a two-stage technique that adjusts variances and covariances to reflect the three factors noted in the prior section. See Ng and Pirrong (1994) for a detailed presentation of this technique. In the first stage, to model the mean return of the nearby and the deferred one regresses the change in the nearby (deferred) price against lagged changes in nearby and deferred prices and the lagged level of backwardation. This latter variable is defined as

$$z_{t-1} = \{\ln[F_{t-1,T} - w(T-t+1)] - \ln S_{t-1}\}/(T-t+1) - r$$

In words, it is the percentage difference between the actual futures price and the full-carry price calculated from the spot price, the cost of storage, w, and the interest rate.[6] The residual from the spot equation is ε_t, and the residual from the futures equation is η_t. In the second stage, one uses the residuals from the mean equations to estimate jointly a modified Garch model of the conditional variances and covariances of the nearby and deferred return. In addition to the traditional Garch terms, this model includes the squared lagged backwardation as an explanatory variable. This allows variances and covariances to depend upon the degree of backwardation in the market. This model is estimated with the use of quasi-maximum likelihood. Formally, the equations for the conditional variance of the deferred return, $h_{F,t}$, and the conditional variance of the nearby return, $h_{S,t}$, are

$$h_{S,t} = \omega_S + \delta_1 h_{S,t-1} + \delta_2 \varepsilon_{t-1}^2 + \delta_3 z_{t-1}^2 \qquad (3)$$

$$h_{F,t} = \omega_F + \phi_1 h_{F,t-1} + \phi_2 \eta_{t-1}^2 + \sigma_3 z_{t-1}^2 \qquad (4)$$

The inclusion of the z_{t-1}^2 terms allows the degree of backwardation to affect volatility. The conditional spot-forward covariance is

$$\sigma_{S,F,t} = \rho\sqrt{h_{S,t}h_{F,t}} + \theta z_{t-1}^2 \qquad (5)$$

A Garch model that does not include a backwardation term can also be employed to determine hedge ratios:

$$h_{S,t} = \omega_S + \delta_1 h_{S,t-1} + \delta_2 \varepsilon_{t-1}^2 \qquad (3')$$

$$h_{F,t} = \omega_F + \phi_1 h_{F,t-1} + \phi_2 \eta_{t-1}^2 \qquad (4')$$

$$\sigma_{S,F,t} = \omega_{S,F} + \mu_1 \sigma_{S,F,t-1} + \mu_2 \varepsilon_{t-1}\eta_{t-1} \qquad (5')$$

This model does not allow the variance-covariance matrix of spot and futures returns to depend upon backwardation, but it does allow the covariance between spot and futures residual returns at t to depend upon the lagged covariance and the product of the lagged residuals.

In each model, hedge ratios are given by

$$\beta_{t,T} = e^{-r(T-t)} \frac{F_{t,T}}{S_t} \frac{\sigma_{S,F,t}}{h_{S,t}}$$

SUMMARY AND IMPLICATIONS

The BAG model allows the estimation of time-varying variance-minimising hedge ratios that reflect how fundamental supply-and-demand conditions affect the dynamics of energy prices. On *a priori* grounds there are strong reasons to believe that hedge ratios should be far less than one, especially for distant-deferred obligations.

Culp and Miller (1995a) object to the variance-minimising framework for a variety of reasons. First, they claim that estimates of variance-minimising hedge ratios are imperfect because data are "subject to considerable error". This is true, but estimates of hedge ratios that are conditional upon data, and consistent with an understanding of the fundamental dynamics of commodity prices, are better than naïve estimates of hedge ratios that are conditional upon no data at all and inconsistent with theoretical understanding.

Second, Culp and Miller argue that a variance-minimising hedge does not necessarily maximise firm value. This is correct. Variance-minimising strategies are not the only legitimate hedges. Instead, the variance-minimising hedge should be used as a benchmark to evaluate the relative importance of the hedging and speculative components present in most derivative trading strategies. Firms trade higher variance for higher expected returns. Anderson and Danthine (1981) demonstrate that in addition to variance, the optimal hedge ratio also depends upon a firm's estimate of the drift in the futures price. Similarly, Working (1962) notes that most hedgers do not strive to minimise risk but also take positions on expected movements in the basis due to their possession of private information. That is, most hedges involve a speculative component when firms underhedge or overhedge (relative to the variance-minimising hedge ratio) to exploit perceived differences between futures prices and their expectations of future spot prices or future basis movements. Perhaps MG's managers possessed information that led them to expect a rise in spot oil prices or widening of the basis, and this led them to choose a barrel-for-barrel hedge. Such a justification for their strategy is completely different from risk avoidance, however. Deviations between the barrel-for-barrel ratio and the variance-minimising ratio therefore measure the importance of the speculative component of MG's strategy. Because it will be shown that these deviations are large, it may be concluded that MG's strategy was largely speculative.[7]

Variance-minimising hedging in the crude oil market

This section analyses data from the crude oil futures market for the period March 20, 1989, to June 20, 1994, to determine whether MG overhedged. Oil futures began trading in 1983; the analysis is based on data starting in 1989 because there are gaps in the trading of the 13- to 15-month maturity contracts prior to March 1989. Moreover, since the Gulf War period (August 2, 1990–February 28, 1991) is plausibly structurally different from the preceding and succeeding periods, the model is also estimated using post-Gulf War data only. This sample spans the period 1/3/91 to 20/6/94.

MG's cash market commitments extended 10 years into the future. As a result, it would be desirable to analyse the relationships between nearby futures prices and the prices of crude oil for all delivery periods between two months and 10 years into the future. Unfortunately, there are no continuous time series of reliable data on forward or futures prices of maturities longer than 15 months. Even this somewhat limited analysis provides valuable information. As will be seen, the data exhibit a monotonically decreasing relationship between the variance-minimising hedge ratio and the maturity of the forward obligation being hedged. This implies that the 14- or 15-month hedge ratio is a conservative estimate of the two-year or 10-year hedge ratio. The results, based on an analysis of the 15-month and earlier hedge ratios are, therefore, conservative.

EXPLORATORY DATA ANALYSIS

Recall that single-period (myopic) hedge ratios are appropriate for a dynamic hedge when nearby and deferred futures prices are martingales. The data provide strong evidence that oil futures prices are martingales. Regressions of the spot price change versus 10 lagged spot price changes, 10 lagged 15-month futures price changes, the difference between the nearby and 15-month deferred futures prices and a constant have very low R^2s, and one cannot reject the null that all coefficients in this regression equal 0. The p value in this test equals 0.41. Similarly, in regressions of the 15-month deferred futures price change versus 10 lagged nearby futures price changes, 10 lagged 15-month futures price changes, the nearby 15-month price difference and a constant one cannot reject the null that all coefficients are jointly 0; the p value equals 0.64. Comparable results are obtained for different deferred

Table 1. Daily crude oil futures return variances 21/3/89–20/6/94

Maturity	Variance
1	6.09E–4
2	4.59E–4
3	3.72E–4
4	3.25E–4
5	2.95E–4
6	2.73E–4
7	2.54E–4
8	2.40E–4
9	2.27E–4
10	2.19E–4
11	2.13E–4
12	2.07E–4
13	2.03E–4
14	1.96E–4
15	1.92E–4

Table 2. Daily crude oil futures return variances 1/3/91–20/6/94

Maturity	Variance
1	2.22E–4
2	1.95E–4
3	1.67E–4
4	1.47E–4
5	1.32E–4
6	1.21E–4
7	1.10E–4
8	1.03E–4
9	9.88E–5
10	9.51E–5
11	9.23E–5
12	8.92E–5
13	8.68E–5
14	8.50E–5
15	8.30E–5

Table 3. Correlations between nearby crude oil futures return and deferred crude oil futures returns 21/3/89–20/6/94

Maturity	Correlation
2	0.947
3	0.934
4	0.925
5	0.913
6	0.899
7	0.885
8	0.870
9	0.855
10	0.841
11	0.826
12	0.794
13	0.796
14	0.759
15	0.749

Table 4. Correlations between nearby crude oil futures return and deferred crude oil futures returns 1/3/91–20/6/94

Maturity	Correlation
2	0.989
3	0.978
4	0.967
5	0.954
6	0.941
7	0.922
8	0.909
9	0.896
10	0.885
11	0.875
12	0.864
13	0.854
14	0.845
15	0.836

month futures price changes. Moreover, the bicorrelation test developed by Hsieh (1989) also fails to reject the hypothesis that expected price changes at t, conditional on all earlier price changes, equal 0 for nearby and deferred futures prices. No individual test statistic is significant for the first 15 lags, and the Q-statistic testing the hypothesis that the first 15 bicorrelations are jointly zero equals 14.30 for the nearby futures price change. The p value on this test equals 0.5. Thus, one cannot reject the hypothesis that the expected price change of the next expiring oil futures contract (conditional on past price changes) equals zero. Similar results are obtained for longer maturities. This implies that single-period hedge ratios are appropriate.

A preliminary analysis of the data also strongly suggests that a one-for-one hedge is not variance-minimising. Tables 1 and 2 present futures return variances in the complete and post-Gulf War samples, respectively. Variances decrease monotonically with time to expiration, consistent with oil price stationarity. This would tend to induce a variance-minimising hedger to choose a hedge ratio of less than one. Tables 3 and 4 present correlations between the one-month oil futures return and returns on contracts with maturities greater than one month. The correlations are monotonically decreasing with expiration and are far below one for maturities of 10 months or more. Combined with the effect of tailing, these preliminary results strongly suggest that a barrel-for-barrel hedge is far larger than necessary to minimise variance.

BAG HEDGE RATIOS

The BAG analysis provides very strong evidence that variance-minimising crude oil hedge ratios are substantially less than one. To carry out this analysis, the model described earlier in the subsection on backwardation-adjusted Garch is first estimated with the use of returns on one and 10- to 15-month crude oil futures contracts for the 20/3/89–20/6/94 period. The resulting parameter estimates from the 20/3/89–20/6/94 sample demonstrate that the variances of spot and deferred returns and the covariance between these returns depend upon z_{t-1}^2 in a statistically significant way. Table 5 reports these estimates for the 11- and 15-month maturities. (Results for other maturities are similar, so are omitted.) Moreover, as theory predicts, the spread has a more pronounced effect on spot returns than forward returns. Furthermore, as expected, the covariance between nearby and deferred returns falls as z_{t-1}^2 increases. Post-Gulf War results (not reported) are somewhat different. In this case, the coefficients on z_{t-1}^2 are of the right sign but are not significant in either the variance equations or the covariance equation.

Table 5. Backwardation-adjusted Garch estimates (T-statistics in parentheses) 21/3/89–20/6/94

	Maturity			
	11 months		15 months	
ω_s	1.0E–6	(0.3460)	1.0E–6	(0.659)
δ_1	0.9168	(83.80)	0.9176	(76.81)
δ_2	0.0724	(6.99)	0.0726	(6.29)
δ_3	9.4E–5	(2.45)	5.6E–5	(2.01)
ω_F	1.0E–6	(0.217)	1.0E–6	(0.364)
ϕ_1	0.9125	(73.94)	0.9155	(68.11)
ϕ_2	0.0750	(6.78)	0.0745	(3.99)
ϕ_3	5.0E–5	(2.79)	3.2E–5	(2.55)
ρ	0.8343	(53.66)	0.801	(41.23)
θ	–2.8E–5	(–1.53)	–1.16E–4	(–2.48)
Θ	0.1760	(12.09)	0.1944	(9.26)
Log L	8329		8186	

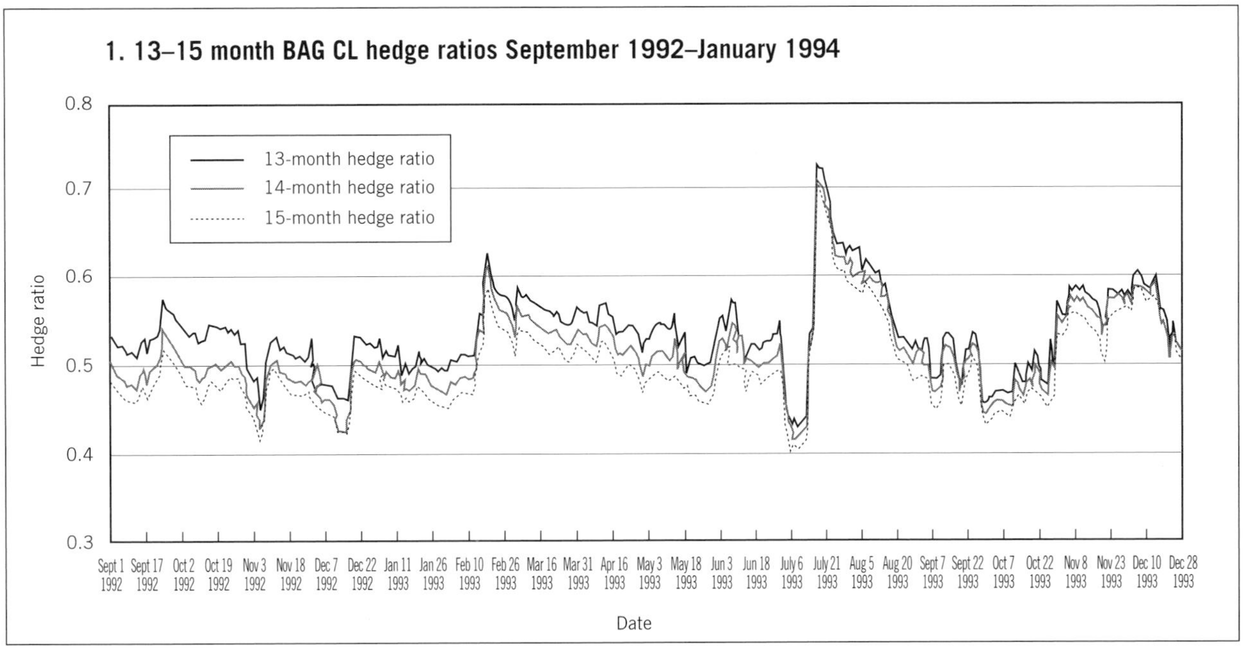

To calculate hedge ratios with the BAG model, parameter values are updated by re-estimating the model on a weekly basis. Thus, for hedge ratios for the seven-day period commencing 1/9/92, parameters estimated over the 21/3/89–31/8/92 period are used. For hedge ratios for the seven-day period commencing 8/9/92, parameters estimated on a 21/3/89–7/9/92 sample are used, and so on. This ensures that hedge ratio estimates are based on information available to MG when it was making its decisions. Using these parameters, the fitted value of the spot return variance and the spot-deferred return covariances are calculated to determine variance-minimising hedge ratios.

Figure 1 illustrates the variance-minimising hedge ratios for the 13- to 15-month maturities over the late 1992–early 1994 period, during which MG's hedging strategy was in place. For the September 1992–June 1993 period, variance-minimising hedge ratios were typically less than 0.5 for these longer times to expiration. For the June–December 1993 period, hedge ratios ranged between 0.5 and 0.6. Thus, the barrel-for-barrel hedge was not variance-increasing for these maturities but was still considerably overhedged. Figure 2 illustrates the variance-minimising hedge ratios estimated from the post-Gulf War subsample. Although the hedge ratios are somewhat higher than those depicted in Figure 1, they are still consistently smaller than one. In sum, these results provide strong evidence that the barrel-for-barrel strategy did not substantially reduce MG's risk.

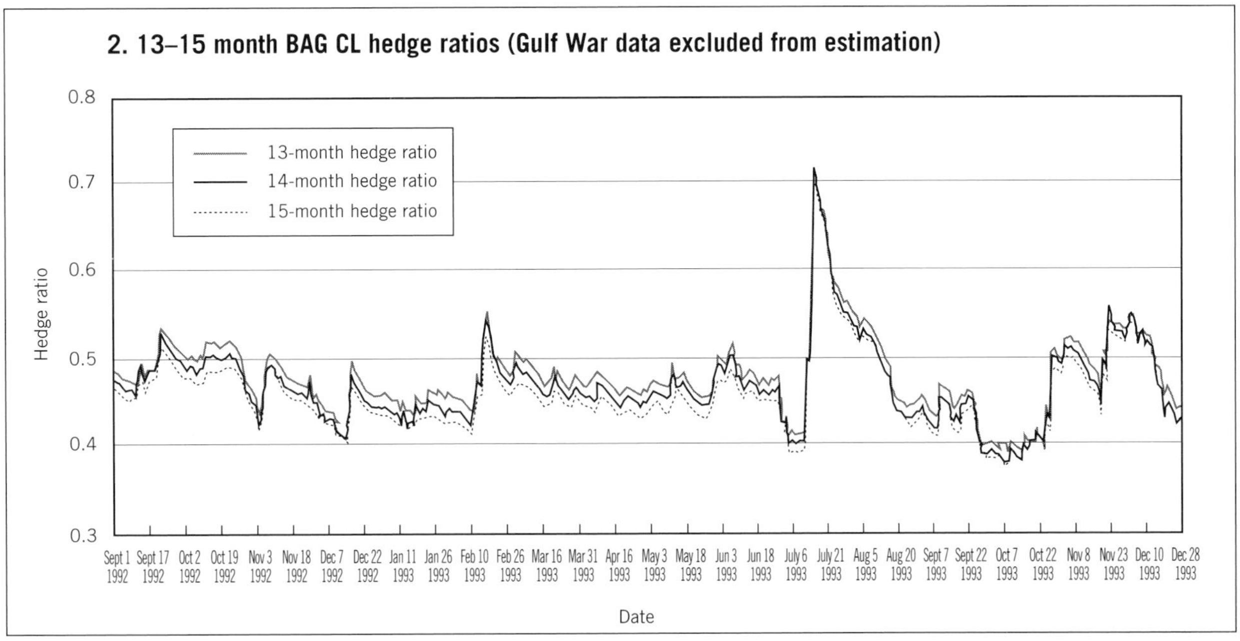

3. Ratio of hedged variance to minimised variance (Gulf War period excluded from estimation)

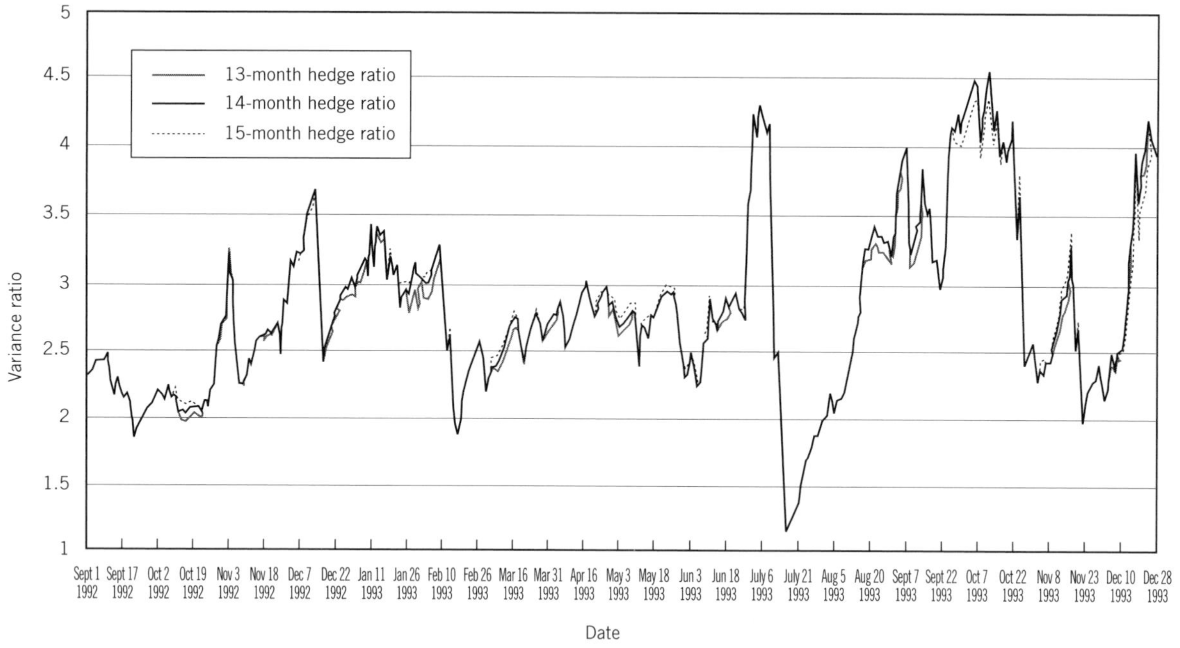

These inflated hedge ratios increased the variance of MG's position. To estimate the effects of overhedging on this variance, the fitted variances for the spot and deferred futures returns are used to calculate the variance of the returns on MG's positions in the 13- to 15-month maturities. Formally, this variance is equal to

$$h_t = (1 - \beta_{t,T})^2 S_t^2 h_{S,t} + (1 - R^2_{F,t}) F^2_{t,T} e^{-2r(T-t)} h_{F,t}$$

where $R^2_{F,t} = \sigma^2_{S,F,t} / h_{S,t} h_{F,t}$ is the squared correlation between the spot and futures returns. Figure 3 depicts

$$h_t / \left[(1 - R^2_{F,t}) e^{-2r(T-t)} F^2_{t,T} h_{F,t}\right] = 1 + (1 - \beta_{t,T})^2 S_t^2 h_{S,t} / \left[(1 - R^2) e^{-2r(T-t)} F^2_{t,T} h_{F,t}\right]$$

for the September 1992–December 1993 period, where the hedge ratios and squared correlations are calculated based on the estimates from the samples that exclude the Gulf War. That is, this figure depicts the ratio between the variance of the barrel-for-barrel hedge and that of the variance-minimising hedge for the 13- to 15-month maturities. The ratio ranges from 1.19 to 4.50. Thus, even for these relatively short maturities (recall that MG was hedging obligations dated out to 120 months) MG bore between 19 and 350% more risk than was necessary.

The variance of MG's position was not only larger than that of the variance-minimised position – at times it was larger than the variance of the unhedged forward contracts. Figure 4 depicts the ratio of the variance of the hedged, barrel-for-barrel position to the variance of the unhedged forward contracts for the 13-, 14- and 15-month maturities. Even with the use of the more conservative post-Gulf War sample estimates, the variance of the MG position was typically between 0.6 and 0.8 times the variance of the unhedged position for the 13- to 15-month maturities. At times – especially during the autumn of 1993 – the variance of the barrel-for-barrel position was larger than the variance of the unhedged forward contracts for 13- to 15-month delivery dates.

Although these results from the 13- to 15-month maturities clearly indicate that a barrel-for-barrel hedge was far riskier than alternatives available to the firm, they do not provide a complete picture of just how risky the strategy was. Theory strongly suggests that the 15-month variance-minimising hedge ratios should be higher than hedge ratios for more distant delivery obligations. Indeed, hedge ratios should decrease monotonically with maturity because of tailing, the stationarity of oil prices and the declining substitutability between spot oil and more distant deferred oil.

4. Ratio of hedged variance to unhedged variance (Gulf War period excluded from estimation)

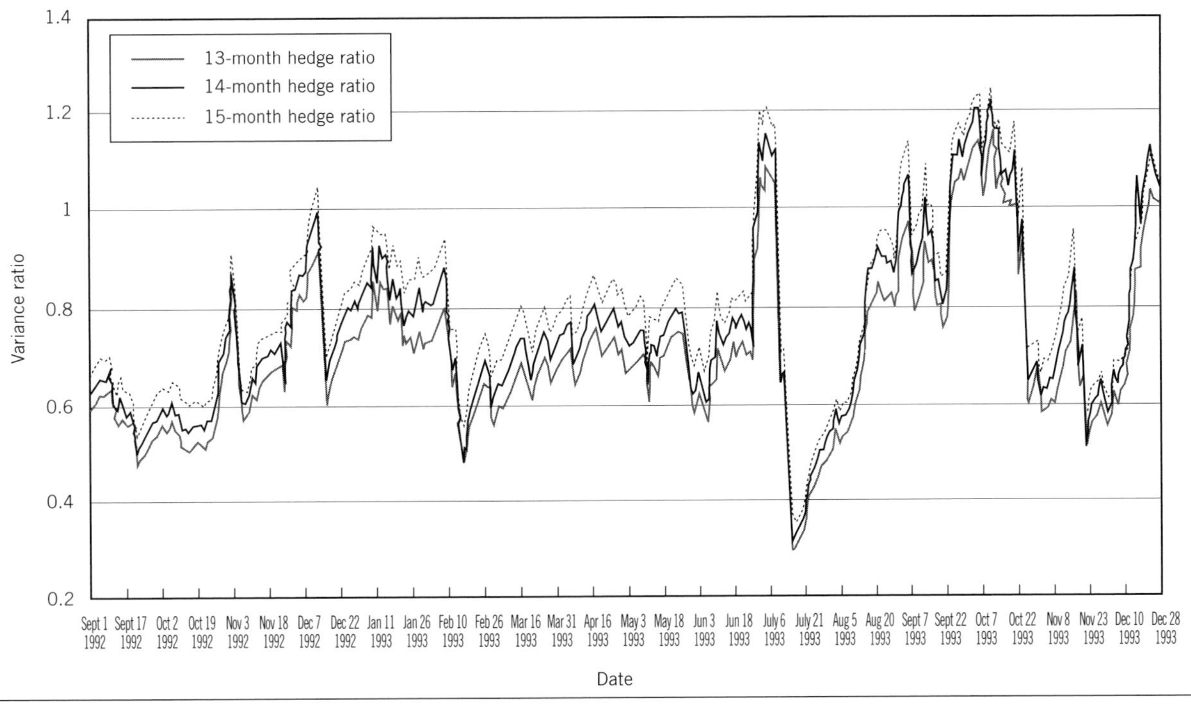

The latter two effects cannot be estimated because of the limitations of the data. *Taking only the tailing effect into account,* however, it is possible to show that even when the hedged-to-unhedged variance ratio was less than one for the 15-month contracts, MG's entire hedged position was riskier than its unhedged contracts. If we make the conservative assumptions that (1) MG discounted all cashflows at a 6% rate, and (2) the covariance between spot oil returns and the forward price returns for maturities beyond 15 months equalled the spot 15-month covariance, it is possible to estimate the variance ratio for the aggregate position. Specifically, under conservative assumptions, it is possible to calculate a *downward-biased* measure of the ratio between the variance of MG's entire position and the variance of its forward contract portfolio alone.

It is necessary to know the variance-covariance matrix of all 120 forward price changes to calculate this ratio. This is computationally impossible in the BAG model, but, by assuming that all forward price changes are perfectly correlated, one can construct an *upward-biased* measure of the variance of the unhedged position:

$$V_U = \sum_{i=1}^{120} \text{var}(e^{-ri\delta}\Delta F_{t,t+i\delta}) + 2\sum_{i=1}^{120}\sum_{j\neq 1} \left[\text{var}(e^{-rj\delta}\Delta F_{t,t+j\delta})\ \text{var}(e^{-ri\delta}\Delta F_{t,t+i\delta})\right]^{0.5}$$

where δ is one month (ie, 1/12th year).This estimate is biased upward because correlations between different forward prices are in fact less than one. Also, assume that $(\Delta F_{t,t+i\delta}) = \text{var}(\Delta F_{t,t+15\delta})$ for $j > 15$. This contributes additional upward bias because stationarity causes variances to decline as j increases.

Under the same conservative assumptions, a *downward-biased* measure of the difference between the variance of MG's total position (including long futures and short forwards) and V_U equals

$$V_H = (120)^2\ \text{var}(\Delta S_t) - (2)(120)\sum_{i=1}^{120} e^{-ri\delta}\ \text{cov}(\Delta S_t,\ \Delta F_{t,t+i\delta})$$

where for $i \geq 15$, $\text{cov}(\Delta S_t,\ \Delta F_{t,t+i\delta}) = \text{var}(\Delta S_t)\ \beta_{t,t+15\delta}$. This creates a downward-biased measure of the variance difference because it assumes that covariances between spot price changes and forward price changes for more than 15 months to delivery do not decline with time to expiration as theory suggests.

A downward-biased estimate of the ratio of the hedged position variance to the unhedged variance equals $1 + (V_H/V_U)$. *Despite the downward bias of this measure (which may be extreme), the ratio exceeds one for all but eight days in 1993. Indeed, at times this ratio is in excess of 2.5; on October 12, 1993, the variance of the hedged position was at least 160% larger than the variance of the unhedged position. On average, during 1993 the variance of the hedged position was at least 60% greater than the variance of the unhedged position.* Ironically, the variance ratio rose precipitously around the same time as MG dramatically increased its position in September 1993. In effect, the firm was increasing the size of an increasingly risky position. Thus, the BAG hedge ratio estimates provide extremely strong evidence that the MG strategy increased, rather than reduced, the firm's risk.

In sum, the data provide no support for a barrel-for-barrel hedging strategy as a prudent means to synthesise a distant-deferred forward position. The most favourable hedge ratio estimates (from the post-Gulf War BAG model) imply that the barrel-for-barrel strategy was at least two to four times riskier than the variance-minimised position. Moreover, extremely conservative estimates imply that the barrel-for-barrel strategy substantially increased the riskiness of MG's position for virtually all of 1993. A severely downwards-biased estimate implies that MG's hedged position was almost always riskier – and sometimes substantially so – than its position in the delivery contracts alone. *Thus, all of the evidence strongly demonstrates that rather than serving to protect the firm against oil price movements, MG's futures trades actually increased the risk for the firm.*[8]

It should also be recognised that in addition to forcing MG to bear more variance than necessary, the barrel-for-barrel strategy also resulted in substantial kurtosis. The Garch models all demonstrate that the distribution of oil returns is very fat-tailed. The point estimates of Θ in these models fall around 0.2. Because this parameter estimates the inverse of the number of degrees of freedom of the joint distribution of spot and futures returns, this implies that crude oil returns follow a t distribution with only five degrees of freedom. Thus, the excessive spot crude oil futures position (excessive relative to the variance-minimising position) also imposed substantially more kurtosis on the firm than was necessary. Risk-averse parties with consistent preferences dislike both variance and kurtosis (Ingersoll, 1987). Therefore, the barrel-for-barrel hedge was even more costly for the firm than the excess variance alone would imply.

It is important to emphasise that the riskiness of the strategy is not primarily attributable to stacking all positions on the nearby contract. The maximum variance reduction at any t equals 1 minus the squared correlation between spot and forward returns at that t. Setting the squared correlation at t equal to $\sigma^2_{S,F,t}/h_{S,t}h_{F,t}$ (using the daily projected values from the BAG and Garch models) demonstrates that a stacked hedge with a variance-minimising hedge ratio would have reduced variance for 13- to 15-month forward positions by between 70% and 80% throughout 1993. Although including deferred futures contacts and longer-term swaps in the hedge could have reduced risk further, it is certainly possible that the additional transactions costs attributable to the lower liquidity of these contracts would have outweighed the benefits of the additional risk reduction.[9] Thus, it was not the stacking *per se* that presented problems. Instead, it was the overhedging of the stack that grossly inflated the risk of MG's position.

The main effect of MG's futures strategy was to transform the nature of the risk it faced. Without futures, MG was vulnerable to a rise in the level of oil prices. With a futures position that was larger than the variance-minimising position stacked on the nearby contract, MG was vulnerable to a steepening of the term structure of crude oil prices. The firm's position hedged against some risks (a parallel shift in the term structure) but raised its exposure to others (a steepening of this structure). Thus, the strategy embedded both speculative and hedging components: it speculated on the basis between nearby and deferred oil prices, while hedging against spot oil price changes.

Even a cursory visual analysis of the basis between nearby and deferred prices illustrates the potential dangers of this strategy. Figure 5 plots the difference (ie, basis) between the spot and 15-month crude futures prices for the March 1989–June 1994 period. Note that the basis is quite volatile. Moreover, with the Gulf War period excluded (the huge spike in the basis resulting from the war goes off the graph, which makes it impossible to evaluate basis variability as in more normal periods), it is clear that substantial basis risk was inherent in a barrel-for-barrel strategy. The graph shows that the spot price fell relative to the 15-month futures price in mid-1989, late 1989 to mid-1990, late 1991 and late 1992 by amounts approximately equal to or larger than the amount by which the basis fell during the period MG's strategy was in place. Thus, the behaviour of the spot–15-month basis illustrates the pitfalls inherent in a barrel-for-barrel strategy.

5. Spot–15-month CL basis

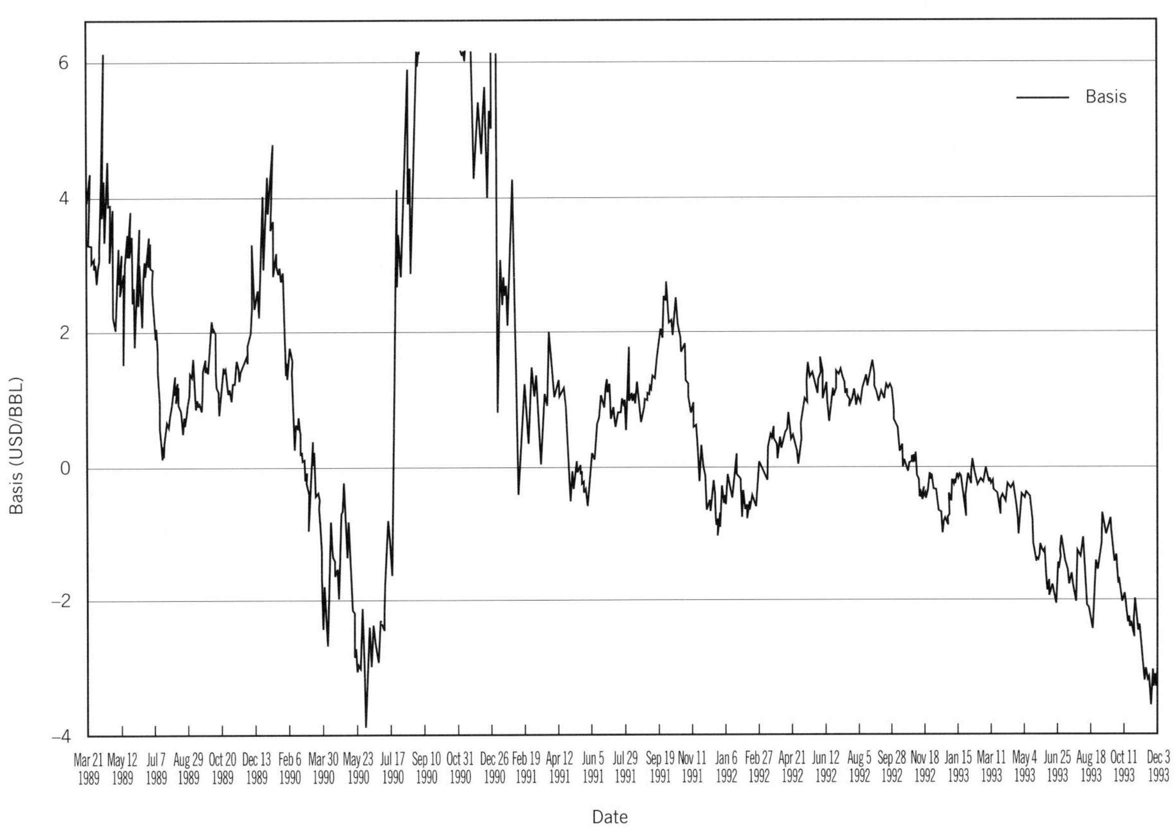

Culp and Miller (1995a, 1995b, 1995c, 1995d) characterise MG's strategy in virtually identical terms, but they apparently fail to appreciate just how risky this basis speculation was.[10] Although Culp and Miller recognise the possibility for term structure shifts (which they refer to as "covariance risk"), they do not quantify the risks these shifts actually create for a firm with a barrel-for-barrel stacked hedge. They claim (1995d) that the basis risk inherent in MG's strategy was so small that it exposed MGRM to no real threat of bankruptcy whereas naked spot price exposure may well have. They justify this assertion by noting that the correlation between spot and nearby futures prices is high. This is not the relevant correlation, however. Instead, the correlations between the nearby futures price and deferred forward prices determine basis risk. All of the empirical results contained herein demonstrate conclusively that this correlation is small enough to make basis risk considerable. *Indeed, the evidence implies that this basis risk was substantially greater than the risk of the short forward contracts alone!*

Overhedging also exacerbated the pressures on MG's liquidity. Whereas its cash market contracts did not impose substantial demands on MG's cashflows, its futures contracts were marked-to-market daily. As a result, the firm needed cash to finance margin calls as the nearby futures price fell in late 1993. It was the inability to finance these margin flows that forced the firm to seek assistance from its bankers. The liquidity strains resulting from overhedging could have impaired the efficient operation of the firm. In the presence of information asymmetries, a fall in liquidity can force a firm to forgo positive NPV projects (Froot, Scharfstein and Stein, 1994). Therefore, overhedging was undesirable not only because it exacerbated MG's solvency risk; the liquidity risk inherent in overhedging made it even less desirable for the firm to use a barrel-for-barrel strategy. Put differently, whereas the objective function in Frost *et al*'s equation (11) and the hedge ratios explicitly consider only solvency, expanding the analysis to include liquidity considerations strengthens the conclusion that barrel-for-barrel hedging was inappropriate.

The barrel-for-barrel strategy was undesirable even if one accepts Culp and Miller's claim that Deutsche Bank and other MG creditors mistook a liquidity crisis for a solvency crisis, and thus intervened unwisely by forcing the firm to scale back its oil market activities. Barrel-for-barrel hedging increased the likelihood of such a mistaken intervention because it increased MG's liquidity needs. Thus, regardless of whether one examines liquidity or solvency considerations, barrel-for-barrel hedging was ill-advised.

The results presented in this section provide compelling evidence that MG's strategy was highly speculative. It is the most reliable evidence pertaining to this question presented to date. Mello and Parsons (1995) calculate hedge ratios based on the model estimates of Gibson and Schwartz (1991). Their evidence is somewhat suspect because (as the authors admit) the estimates imply an implausibly high risk premium in oil futures prices. It is also somewhat dated as the Gibson–Schwartz sample period ends four years prior to the beginning of MG's involvement in the oil market. Edwards and Canter (1995) use a simple regression analysis to calculate hedge ratios. This methodology does not take into account the stochastic nature of volatility and covariances in the energy market. Moreover, it does not take into account how backwardation affects variance-minimising hedge ratios. Thus, the results presented here are based on a more flexible and complete analysis of oil price dynamics than utilised in previous studies of MG.

Unless one is willing to argue that MG's managers possessed appreciable information advantages regarding future basis movements, it is difficult to conclude that the barrel-for-barrel strategy was prudent. An analysis of the *ex post* performance of the hedge casts considerable doubt upon the prescience of MG's managers. The next section addresses this issue in detail.

The magnitude of losses attributable to barrel-for-barrel hedging

To determine the gains or losses attributable to barrel-for-barrel hedging, the payoffs to this strategy are estimated with the use of some assumptions about size of the cash and futures positions and the behaviour of the term structure for maturities greater than 15 months. The parameters necessary to calculate gains/losses – namely, the size and maturity of the cash position – are set equal to the public descriptions of MG's activities. However, because the exact details of MG's strategy are not known, the simulation results are merely illustrative. It is important to remember that the exact details of MG's cash market, futures market or swap positions at each relevant date are not known. Moreover, these simulations do not take into account the option features of the MG cash market contracts. Given these caveats, the simulation results do suggest that a barrel-for-barrel strategy on a 10-year, 160 million barrel position could have led to economic losses of upwards of US$800 million over the January 2, 1993–January 3, 1994 period.

Simulated profits/losses are calculated as follows. It is assumed that as of 2/1/93 MG was obligated to deliver 107 million barrels/120 = 893,333 = Q_1^* barrels of crude oil each month from 2/1/93 to 1/9/2002. To reflect the increase in MG's contractual obligations in September 1993, it is assumed that, as of 15/9/93, MG was obligated to deliver (160 million – 7.14 million barrels)/120 = 1,273,777 = Q_2^* barrels of crude oil in each of the next 120 months; the reduction of 7.14 million barrels reflects deliveries from February to September 1993. It is assumed that MG held one barrel in the nearby futures contract for each barrel in cash contract delivery commitments. That is, as of 2/1/93, it is assumed that MG was long 107 million barrels of the February contract, and on 15/9/93 it was long 152,853,333 - million barrels of the October contract. On the first business day of each month, this position is reduced by Q_i^* barrels to reflect the expiration of a delivery commitment, where $i = 1$ before 15/9/93, and $i = 2$ afterwards.

On each business day, the gain/loss on the nearby futures position is determined by multiplying the change in the nearby price by the size of the nearby futures position. Moreover, on the first business day of each month the gains on the expiring delivery commitment are calculated as follows. The per-barrel gain/loss on the first business day is set equal to – 1 times the difference between the price of the nearby contract and the price of that month's contract as of 2/1/93. For example, on February 1, 1993, the per barrel gain/loss is set equal to – 1 times the difference between the March 1993 futures price on that date and the March 1993 futures price as of 2/1/93. This difference is then multiplied by Q_i^*.

For each business day in the estimation period, the gains/losses on the long nearby futures position and any expiring delivery commitment are added to determine a daily gain/loss. In addition, interest on the cumulative gain/loss carried over from the previous business day is calculated with the use of the three-month Treasury-bill rate. Given that MG's financing cost was larger than the Treasury-bill rate, this is a conservative assumption. For each business day, t, in the sample period, the gain/loss on the nearby position, the gain/loss on any expiring delivery commitment and the net interest expense at t are then

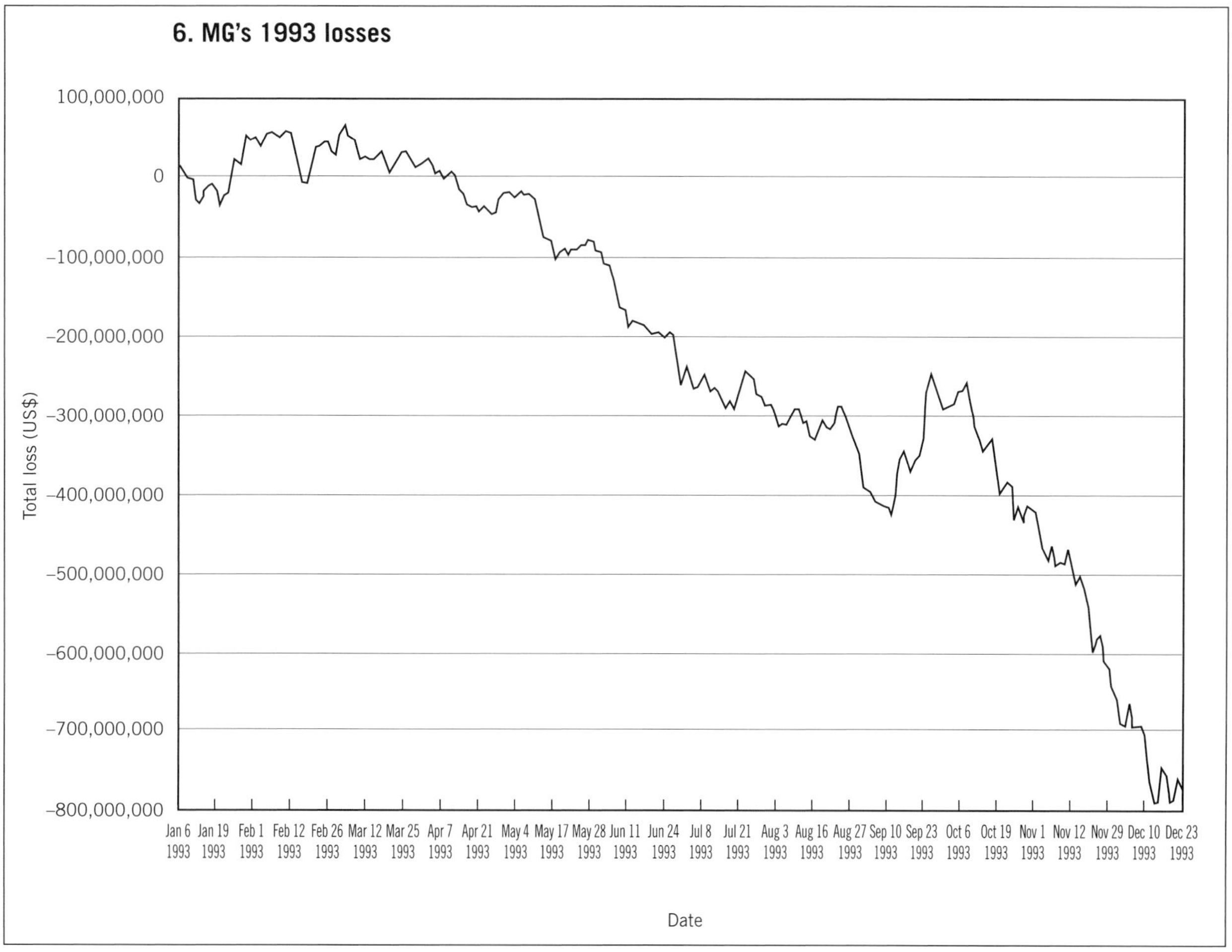

added to the cumulative gain/loss carried over from t – 1 to determine the cumulative gain/loss at t.

This process is repeated daily until 3/1/94. On that day, the unexpired delivery commitments are valued as follows. It is assumed that as of 2/1/93 the forward prices for delivery commitments for all months from March 1994 and beyond are equal to the April 1994 futures price on 2/1/93. That is, as of 2/1/93, the term structure of crude oil prices beyond 15 months is assumed flat. Call this price, $F_{2/1/93,15}$. Similarly, as of 15/9/93 the term structure beyond 15 months is flat, with a price, $F_{15/9/93,15}$. For each month, the difference is calculated between the price of the futures contract expiring closest to (but after) March 1994 and $0.67F_{2/1/93,15} + 0.33F_{15/9/93,15}$. The averaging reflects that MG entered into one-third of its contracts in September, 1993. This difference is then discounted back to 3/1/94 by the appropriate Treasury rate and multiplied by Q_2^*. For example, for the July 1, 1994, delivery commitment, the difference is calculated between the August 1994 futures price and $0.67F_{2/1/93,15} + 0.33F_{15/9/93,15}$, this difference is discounted back to 3/1/94 with the use of the six-month Treasury-bill rate, and this discounted price difference is multiplied by Q_2^*.

To value as of 3/1/94 the forward commitments dated after May 1995, it is assumed that the forward prices for these delivery dates equal the June 1995 futures price. That is, it is assumed that the term structure of crude oil prices for delivery more than 15 months hence is flat as of 3/1/94. Call this price, $F_{3/1/94,15}$. The change in the forward price on these delivery commitments over the 2/1/93–3/1/94 period is set equal to $0.67F_{2/1/93,15} + 0.33F_{15/9/93,15}$. For each delivery date this difference is discounted back to 3/1/94 by the appropriate Treasury rate and multiplied by Q_2^*. For instance, the price difference for the 2/1/96 delivery commitment is discounted with the use of the yield on the two-year Treasury note.

The marked-to-market values of these forward commitments on 3/1/94 are added to the cumulative gain/loss on the nearby futures and the gains/losses on the 1/2/93–1/12/93 delivery commitments to calculate the cumulative gain/loss on the entire MG position over the 2/1/93–3/1/94 period. Because all outstanding forward commitments are marked-to-market, the resulting total is an estimate of the economic gain/loss of a barrel-for-barrel strategy.

This methodology implies that the losses on a barrel-for-barrel strategy over the period 2/1/93 to 3/1/94 were equal to approximately US$800 million. This is due to a loss of US$1,090 million on crude oil futures and expired delivery commitments and a gain of about US$290 million on unexpired delivery commitments. If MG had used variance-minimising hedge ratios rather than a barrel-for-barrel futures position throughout the period, their losses would have fallen by almost 78%, to only US$181 million. To derive this estimate, variance-minimising hedge ratios are based on the post-Gulf War BAG estimates. Ratios for maturities in excess of 15 months are set equal to the 15-month hedge ratio multiplied by the relevant tailing factor. For example, on each day the 24-month hedge ratio is set equal to the 15-month hedge ratio multiplied by the discount factor relevant between month 15 and month 24. Because this almost certainly leads to upward-biased estimates of variance-minimising hedge ratios for delivery commitments 16 months and more into the future, the loss estimate of US$181 million is biased upwards as well.

Figure 6 illustrates how these losses grew over the course of 1993. Prices actually moved in MG's favour in the first five months of 1993 and the firm profited accordingly. In June and in subsequent months, however, the term structure steepened appreciably; MG's ballooning losses during this period reflect these price movements.

It is interesting to note that these losses are comparable to those presented in a audit by the German accounting firms C&L Treuarbeit Deutsche Revision and Wollert-Elmendorff Industrie Treuhand. Based on an analysis of MGRM's accounting data, these firms report a gross loss on the futures and forward positions of US$1.277 billion, and a gain of US$245 million on the unexpired delivery commitments, for a net loss of US$1.06 billion. (The residual is attributable to losses on firm-flexible contracts not considered in this study.)

It should also be noted that if liquidity shortages imposed costs upon the firm or made mistaken intervention by creditors more likely (as posited by Culp and Miller) the marked-to-market losses do not reveal the full scope of MG's problems. The roughly US$1.1 billion loss on the futures position (net of gains on expired delivery commitments) represents the immediate demand on MG's cashflows. If the firm had used a variance-minimising hedge ratio (that is, if it minimised solvency risk), its cash outflows under the hedging programme would have equalled only US$.471 billion - about 57% less than the loss actually realised. Thus, if liquidity strains reduce firm value, the US$800 million marked-to-market loss understates the costs of barrel-for-barrel hedging because the firm also incurred costs attributable to the extra liquidity drains attributable to overhedging.

The large losses quantified here underscore the speculative nature of MG's strategy and cast doubt on the prescience of its managers. Although even the most well informed market participants lose money at times, the magnitude of the losses realised in 1993 strongly suggests that MG's management did not possess so acute an ability to forecast basis movements to justify the immense risks inherent in their strategy.

The effects of embedded options on hedge ratios

The preceding analysis calculates hedge ratios under the assumption that MG's forward contracts did not embed any options. Recall, however, that the firm-fixed supply contracts did permit the buyers to terminate their contracts and, upon said termination, receive one-half of the difference between the prevailing spot price (measured by the nearby futures price) and the fixed price established in the contract times the volume remaining under the contract. Formally, if a customer were to exercise this option at time t, he or she would receive $0.5Q(S_t - f)$, where f is the fixed price under the contract, Q is the volume remaining under the contract and (as before) S_t is the spot price. Upon exercise, the customer would terminate his right to receive refined products at the fixed price for the remaining life of the contract.

Culp and Miller claim that this feature of the MG contracts made it even more desirable to use nearby futures contracts to hedge the energy price risk inherent in the supply contracts. They state that "MRGM could liquidate an equivalent amount of futures positions to cover the required cash outlay. Because both the hedge and the early exercise option relied upon the front-month futures contract, the price in MGRM's hedge was the same as that governing early termination options. MGRM therefore faced no covariance risk ... from the risk of early exercise."

In reality, the effect of the embedded option is much more complicated; it could have either exacerbated or mitigated the overhedging problem. In essence, it is necessary to account for the fact that oil price changes also affect the value of the forward contracts that customers would forfeit when exercising the option. When this factor is taken into account, the values of the early-out option and the position necessary to hedge it both depend upon the entire term structure of oil prices.

From MG's perspective, the firm-fixed contracts were equivalent to a portfolio consisting of a receive fixed-pay floating energy swap and a short position in a call option on this swap. There are N delivery months remaining on the swap, and MG must deliver Q/N units of petroleum products on each delivery date. Call Z_t the value or the swap to MG at time t. That is:

$$Z_t = \sum_{i=1}^{N} e^{-ri\delta} \frac{Q}{N} (f - F_{t,t+i\delta})$$

As before, $F_{t,t+i\delta}$ gives the forward price for delivery at $t + i\delta$ as of t, and δ equals 1 month (ie, 1/12 of a year). The value of the swap to MG's customers (ie, its counterparties) is $-Z_t$.

If the customer exercises the option embedded in the MG contracts, he or she receives

$$0.5(S_t - f)Q - (-Z_t) = 0.5(S_t - f)Q + Z_i \equiv A_t$$

The $-(-Z_t)$ term enters the expression because, upon exercising the option, the customer gives up his swap position, which is worth $-Z_t$ to him.

Define $q(A_t,T,t)$, the value of the option to terminate the contract and receive a payment of $0.5(S_t - f)Q$ as a function of A_t, the ending date on the contract and the current date. This option is a call on the portfolio A_t, with a strike price of 0. Then, the value of MG's position at time t is

$$\Pi = Z_t - q(A_t,T,t) \tag{6}$$

To determine how many nearby futures contracts to purchase to hedge this obligation, first recognise that

$$\frac{\partial \Pi}{\partial F_{t,t+i\delta}} = \frac{\partial Z_t}{\partial F_{t,t+i\delta}} \left[1 - \frac{\partial q(A_t,T,t)}{\partial A_t}\right] = -e^{-ri\delta} \frac{Q}{N} \left[1 - \frac{\partial q(A_t,T,t)}{\partial A_t}\right] \equiv \Delta_F(t,t+i\delta) > -\frac{Q}{N}$$

The inequality follows because the option increases in value as A_t increases (ie $\partial q/\partial A_t > 0$). Moreover,

$$\frac{\partial \Pi}{\partial S_t} = -\frac{\partial q(A_t,T,t)}{\partial A_t}\frac{\partial A_t}{\partial S_t} = -0.5Q \frac{\partial q(A_t,T,t)}{\partial A_t} \equiv \Delta_S < 0$$

If only the nearby contract is used to hedge, the total number of nearby contracts to buy to hedge the entire swap and embedded option is

$$H_T \equiv -\sum_{i=1}^{N} \left[e^{ri\delta}\Delta_F(t,t+i\delta)\beta_{t,t+i\delta}\right] - \Delta_S = \sum_{i=1}^{N} \frac{Q}{N}\left[\beta_{t,t+i\delta}\left(1 - \frac{\partial q}{\partial A_t}\right) + 0.5\frac{\partial q}{\partial A_t}\right]$$

This may be either larger or smaller than the total number of nearby contracts required to hedge the swap alone, depending on whether the average hedge ratio (absent the option) is less than or greater than 0.5. Recall that a position is variance-increasing if it is more than twice as large as the total variance-minimising hedge. The barrel-for-barrel strategy is thus risk-increasing in the absence of the embedded option if

$$\sum_{i=1}^{N} \frac{Q}{N} \beta_{t,t+i\delta} < 0.5Q$$

If this expression holds, rewriting H_T implies

$$H_T = \left(1 - \frac{\partial q}{\partial A_t}\right)\sum_{i=1}^{N}\frac{Q}{N}\beta_{t,t+i\delta} + \frac{\partial q}{\partial A_t}0.5Q < \left(1 - \frac{\partial q}{\partial A_t}\right)0.5Q + \frac{\partial q}{\partial A_t}0.5Q = 0.5Q$$

Therefore, if the barrel-for-barrel position increases variance in the absence of the embedded option, it increases the variance if the contract includes the option as well. The option feature mitigates the overhedging somewhat, but not enough to turn the barrel-for-barrel strategy into a true hedge.

In sum, the analysis of this section demonstrates that the options embedded explicitly in MG's firm-fixed contracts cannot reverse, and may strengthen, the conclusions drawn in the previous sections. Because the empirical results presented earlier demonstrate that buying nearby contracts barrel-for-barrel resulted in substantial overhedging in the absence of these options, the option analysis strengthens the conclusion that MG's strategy almost certainly increased the variance of the firm's payoffs.

The options embedded in the firm-flexible contracts are more difficult to analyse than those in the firm-fixed deals. The 15-month hedge ratios estimated earlier are likely to provide an upper bound on the hedge ratios for delivery commitments two years and beyond even in the presence of this option, however. The drop in oil prices (combined with the mean-reversion in oil prices) during the life of the programme gave buyers a strong incentive to defer, rather than accelerate, deliveries. Because more distant deliveries require smaller hedge ratios, this bias towards deferral suggests that the no-option hedge ratios overestimate the with-option hedge ratios for firm-flexible contracts as well.

Rollover profits and the prudence of the barrel-for-barrel hedge

It has been argued that MG's policy allowed the firm to profit from the backwardation typical in energy markets by rolling over its futures at a profit. That is, when the market is in backwardation, at the expiration date of each contract the firm could expect to sell the expiring future at a price that exceeded that at which it purchased the next-to-expire contract. Arthur Benson, the main architect of MG's strategy, apparently relied upon such reasoning (Benson affidavit, 1994). Edwards and Canter (1995, p. 224) state that "it does not seem unreasonable for MGRM to have expected that over a long period of time (such as 10 years) its hedging strategy would have produced a net rollover gain". Edwards and Canter, however, recognise that there were appreciable risks in such a strategy.

An analysis of this argument reveals that the expected gain from rolling over nearby futures for K periods in a market that is in backwardation is equal to the current difference between the spot price of oil and the K-period forward price. If each successive nearby futures price is expected to exceed the next expiring futures price for K consecutive months, the sum of these differences equals the difference between the current spot price and the K-month futures price. As a result, in a driftless futures market, the expected cost of oil incurred in a rollover strategy ending in month K equals the current forward price of oil for delivery in month K. This strategy is riskier than the variance-minimised replication of the K-month forward contract, however, so it is dominated by that strategy.

These points are readily grasped by expressing the firm's cost of acquiring oil to satisfy its contractual obligation (denoted by C) to deliver oil in K months as follows:

$$C = S_K - \sum_{i=1}^{K}[F_{i,i} - F_{i-1,i}] = S_K + F_{0,1} - F_{K,K} + \sum_{i=1}^{K-1}[F_{i,i+1} - F_{i,i}]$$

Here $F_{i,j}$ is the forward price of oil in month i for delivery in month j, and S_K is the spot price of oil in month K. For simplicity, this expression assumes that the interest rate equals 0, which simplifies the notation but has no effect on the results. In this expression, the total cost equals the spot price of oil in month K, S_K, minus the total realised rollover gains on futures contracts. The summation term is the total rollover gain, where in month i the rollover gain is defined as the deferred price minus the expiring price, $F_{i,i+1} - F_{i,i}$. With driftless futures prices, this expression implies that $E_0(C) = E_0(S_K) = F_{0,K}$. Also note that the convergence of spot and futures implies $S_K = F_{K,K}$. Therefore,

$$E_0(C) = E_0\left\{F_{0,1} - \sum_{i=1}^{K-1}[F_{i,i+1} - F_{i,i}]\right\} = F_{0,K}$$

Because $F_{0,1}$ equals the price of acquiring oil one month after the initiation of the strategy, this expression states that the one-month forward price net of the rollover gains expected over K months equals the K-period forward price of oil. In essence, the expected rollover gains reduce the expected cost of acquiring oil for delivery in K months below the current spot price of oil. But, in a market in backwardation, the K-month forward price is also below the current spot price by the same amount. That is, the expected total rollover gain equals the amount of backwardation over K months. The barrel-for-barrel rollover strategy is riskier than the variance-minimising replication of the K-period forward price, however. Thus, there were less risky ways for MG to exploit the backwardation in the market than a barrel-for-barrel rollover every month.

Summary and conclusions

A thorough analysis of the behaviour of oil prices demonstrates clearly that MGRM's strategy of purchasing one barrel of spot crude oil to hedge the sale of crude oil months into the future was almost certainly risk-increasing, rather than risk-reducing. The reasons for this are clear. First, the stationarity of oil prices implies that volatilities decline systematically with time to expiration. Second, the correlation between spot and deferred prices is imperfect, and this correlation also declines systematically as time to expiration of the deferred increases. A variance-minimising hedger should reduce hedge ratios far below one in response to these factors. MG did not.

Empirical estimates provide extremely compelling evidence that, owing to this overhedging, MG's position of long futures and short forwards was substantially riskier than its short position in forward contracts alone. Therefore, this strategy subjected the firm to the risk of real economic loss, not just accounting loss. The firm was vulnerable to a steepening of the oil price term structure, an event that occurred soon after it implemented its strategy. A simulation of the economic losses a firm employing such a strategy would have incurred produces figures that are comparable to the magnitude of the losses publicly recognised by MG. Thus, the data provide compelling evidence that MG's strategy imposed substantial risk upon the firm *ex ante* and that the *ex post* losses were substantial.

This is not to say that all firms should employ variance-minimising hedges when trading derivatives: informed speculation is a common part of any risk-management strategy. The relevant question is whether MG possessed the information advantage required to justify its immense speculative position. There is substantial reason to doubt that any firm, let alone a relative newcomer to the energy markets like MG, has a large enough informational advantage to justify the immense risks of what was arguably the largest time spread ever undertaken in commodity markets. The losses incurred in the last half of 1993 certainly cast significant doubt on the firm's ability to predict the movements of oil prices. Given the huge losses incurred in late 1993, a Bayesian estimating the probability distribution of MG's information advantage would almost certainly place little weight on the possibility that the firm was well informed and great weight on the possibility that it did not possess superior information, regardless of the charitability of his priors concerning the prescience of MG's managers.

Appendix

If the futures prices are martingales, then $E_{t_0}[\Pi_T - E_{t_0}\Pi_T]^2 = E_{t_0}\Pi_T^2$. Consider the determination of the first hedge ratio ($\beta_{t_0+\Delta t,T}$) in dynamic hedge that accounts for possible dependencies between hedge ratios at any time t and hedge ratios at subsequent times $t' > t$. The relevant first-order condition is

$$\frac{dE_{t_0}\Pi_T^2}{d\beta_{t_0+\Delta t}} = 0 = 2E_{t_0}\left\{\beta_{t_0+\Delta t}\,\Delta S^2_{t_0+\Delta t} - \Delta S_{t_0+\Delta t}\,\Delta v_{t_0+\Delta t,T} + \Delta S_{t_0+\Delta t}\sum_{i=2}^{M}\left[\beta_{t_0+i\Delta t,T}\,\Delta S_{t_0+i\Delta t} - \Delta v_{t_0+i,\Delta t,T}\right]\right\}$$

The first two terms in this expression are present in a single-period variance-minimising hedge ratio. The product of the first period spot price change and the sum of gains and losses in subsequent periods reflects the possible intertemporal dependencies among hedge ratios. Consider a representative term:

$$E_{t_0}\left[\Delta S_{t_0+\Delta t}\,\beta_{t_0+i\Delta t,T}\,\Delta S_{t_0+i\Delta t}\right]$$

The hedge ratio at $t_0 + i\Delta t$ may depend upon previous realisations of ΔS_t and $\Delta v_{t,T}$. However, by the law of iterated expectations

$$E_{t_0}\left[\Delta S_{t_0+\Delta t}\,\beta_{t_0+i\Delta t,T}\,\Delta S_{t_0+i\Delta t}\right] = E_{t_0}\{\Delta S_{t_0+\Delta t}\,\beta_{t_0+i\Delta t,T}\left[E_{t_0+(i-1)\Delta t}(\Delta S_{t_0+i\Delta t})\right]\}$$

where the inner expectation is conditional on all price changes up to $t_0 + (i - 1)\Delta t$. Because S_t is a martingale by assumption, this inner expectation is 0, the entire expression equals 0. Therefore, this expression disappears from the first-order condition, as do all other terms included in the summation. Consequently, the hedge ratio produced as the solution to the dynamic programming problem collapses to the single-period hedge ratio. It is possible to demonstrate that this result obtains for $t > t_0$ as well.

1 *In general, it is not optimal to rely upon only a single hedging instrument. If there are multiple sources of risk in oil prices (eg, the term structure shifts up and down* and *twists) then a firm can enjoy better hedging effectiveness if it uses several hedging instruments. The approaches described below can be used to determine multiple-instrument hedge ratios. The very fact that MG employed only the nearby contract strongly suggests that they were not interested in hedging alone, but were also speculating on movements in the term structure.*

2 *For simplicity, the analysis assumes that interest rates are non-stochastic, and the term structure of interest rates is flat. This expression holds because the value of the forward contract equals* $e^{-r(T-t)}(f - F_{t,T})$. *If interest rates are stochastic, futures prices and forward prices may differ owing to the effect of marking to market on the timing of cashflows. Cox, Ingersoll, and Ross (1981) demonstrate that this effect is important only to the extent that changes in interest rates and futures prices are correlated. Because the correlations between crude oil returns and percentage changes in interest rates are extremely small, this consideration is ignored hereafter. Specifically, over the July 1987–June 1994 period, the correlation between the percentage change in the three-month T-Bill rate and the percentage change in the spot oil price is 0.01; the correlations between the percentage change in the percentage changes in the six- and 12-month T-Bill rates and the percentage changes in futures prices with six and 12 months to expiration, respectively, are less than 0.005.*

3 *For simplicity, it is assumed that the firm's hedging horizon corresponds to the maturity of the delivery obligation. This is not necessary. It is possible to choose a hedging horizon that is less than this maturity. Under the martingale assumption employed below, however, the firm optimally employs a myopic hedge ratio that is independent of the hedging horizon.*

4 *The discount factor multiplying the correlation/standard deviation term reflects the fact that cashflows on the forward contracts are not received until the delivery date. Adjusting for this deferral of cashflows by reducing the hedge ratio by the discount factor is called* tailing the hedge. *This consideration is relevant only to the extent that (a) the hedge position is large enough to permit a match between the size of the tailed hedge and an integer number of futures contracts, and (b) the time to delivery is long enough to make the effect of discounting appreciable. Both cases are certainly relevant in the MG case. Therefore, MG could have and should have tailed its hedges to reflect cashflow timing mismatches between forwards and futures.*

5 *Earlier drafts of this chapter included hedge-ratio estimates based on alternative methodologies, including backwardation adjusted regression, and factor models. These methods are cruder in crucial aspects than the Garch, so these results are not reported here. The relevant results are available on request.*

6 *One cannot observe the actual value of* w. *It is estimated in the following way. Arbitrage precludes* $z_t > 0$; *that is, prices cannot be above full-carry. Therefore, the value of the smallest* w *is found such that* $z_t < 0$ *for all maturities and all days. This value is used as the estimate of* w.

7 *Edwards and Canter (1995) suggest that a hedge ratio of less than one was appropriate on variance-minimisation grounds, but claim that MG had a defensible rationale for its barrel-for-barrel strategy. In brief, they attribute MG's strategy to the firm's beliefs that oil prices would rise over the life of the hedge. This is essentially a speculative rationale like that advanced in theory by Anderson and Danthine.*

8 *It should also be noted that the hedge ratios estimated herein for maturities less than 15 months are almost certainly conservative estimates of the hedge ratios for maturities extending from 16 months to 10 years. First, holding variances and covariances constant, tailing the hedge causes hedge ratios to fall with time to maturity. Second, in the 10- to 15-month maturity range, both the correlation between the spot and deferred futures and the ratio between the deferred futures variance and the spot variance decline as maturity increases. This is consistent with the stationarity of oil prices and the fact that more distant contracts are progressively poorer substitutes for spot oil. If this trend continues as maturities are extended beyond 15 months, this would also induce a fall in hedge ratios.*

9 *Mello and Parsons (1995) suggest matching the maturity dates of the hedge instrument to the dates of the delivery obligations. It should be noted that the* R^2 *for the entire position is not linearly related to the* R^2*s of the individual contracts, because hedging errors for different maturities are correlated. This correlation is almost certainly positive for all combinations of maturities. Moreover, to calculate the percentage variance reduction, it is also necessary to know the variance of the unhedged position in all 120 forward contracts. Determination of the correlation structure of hedging errors and the variance of the unhedged position requires knowledge of the entire* 121×121 *variance-covariance matrix of spot and forward price changes. This is computationally impossible in the Garch model. It is possible to calculate an* upward-biased *measure of percentage variance reduction by making some assumptions about the covariance structure as when calculating the variance ratio in the third section. During 1993, this measure ranged between 0.65 and 0.98, with a mean of 0.87.*

10 *To provide some perspective on the size of the speculative component, the hedge ratio estimates imply that roughly 55% of the 160 million barrel futures and swap position was speculative. The resulting 88 million barrel figure is 88 times the speculative position limit for crude oil.*

BIBLIOGRAPHY

Anderson, R., and J. Danthine, 1981, "Cross-Hedging", *Journal of Political Economics* 89, pp. 1182-96.

Benson, A., 1994, "Affidavit of W. Arthur Benson v. Metallgesellschaft Corp (and Others)", USDC of Maryland, Civil Action JFM-94-484.

Chan, A., 1992, "Optimal Dynamic Hedging Strategies with Financial Futures Contracts Using Nonlinear Conditional Heteroskedasticity Models", unpublished doctoral dissertation, Michigan Business School.

Cox, J., J. Ingersoll and S. Ross, 1981, "The Relationship between Forward Prices and Futures Prices", *Journal of Financial Economics* 9, pp. 321-46.

Culp, C., and M. Miller, 1994, "Hedging a Flow of Commodity Deliveries with Futures: Lessons from Metallgesellschaft", *Derivatives Quarterly* 1, pp. 7-15.

Culp, C., and M. Miller, 1995a, "Metallgesellschaft and the Economics of Synthetic Storage", *Journal of Applied Corporate Finance* 7, 62-76; reprinted as Chapter 9 of the present volume.

Culp, C., and M. Miller, 1995b, "Auditing the Auditors", *Risk* 8(4), pp. 36-40; reprinted as Chapter 10 of the present volume.

Culp, C., and M. Miller, 1995c, "Letter to the Editor", *Risk* 8(6), p. 8.

Culp, C., and M. Miller, 1995d, "Hedging in the Theory of Corporate Finance: A Reply to Our Critics", *Journal of Applied Corporate Finance* 8, pp. 121-7; reprinted as Chapter 14 of the present volume.

Dixit, A., and R. Pindyck, 1994, *Investment under Uncertainty* (Princeton, NJ: Princeton University Press).

Duffie, D., and Jackson, M., 1991, "Optimal Hedging and Equilibrium in a Dynamic Futures Market", *Journal Economic Dynamics and Control* 14, pp. 21-33.

Edwards, F., and M. Canter, 1995, "The Collapse of Metallgesellschaft: Unhedgeable Risks, Poor Hedging Strategy, or Just Bad Luck?" *Journal of Futures Markets* 15, pp. 211-64; reprinted as Chapter 13 of the present volume.

Froot, K., D. Scharfstein and J. Stein, 1994, "Risk Management: Coordinating Corporate Investment and Financing Policies", *Journal of Finance* 48, pp. 1629-58; reprinted as Chapter 7 of the present volume.

Gibson, R., and E. Schwartz, 1991, "Stochastic Convenience Yield and the Pricing of Oil Contingent Claims", *Journal of Finance* 45, pp. 959-76.

Hsieh, D., 1989, "Testing for Nonlinear Dependence in Daily Foreign Exchange Rates", *Journal of Business* 62, pp. 339-68.

Ingersoll, J., 1987, *Theory of Financial Decision Making* (Totowa, NJ: Rowman & Littlefield).

Kroner, K., and J. Sultan, 1991, "Foreign Currency Futures and Time Varying Hedge Ratios", *Pacific-Basin Capital Market Research* 2.

Lien, D., and X. Luo, 1994, "Multiperiod Hedging in the Presence of Conditional Heteroskedasticity", *Journal of Futures Markets* 14, pp. 927-55.

Mello, A., and J. Parsons, 1995, "The Maturity Structure of a Hedge Matters: Lessons from the Metallgesellschaft Debacle", *Journal of Applied Corporate Finance* 8, pp. 106-20; reprinted as Chapter 12 of the present volume.

Ng, V., and C. Pirrong, 1994, "Fundamentals and Volatility: Storage, Spreads, and the Dynamics of Metals Prices", *Journal of Business* 67, pp. 203-30.

Working, H., 1962, "New Concepts Concerning Futures Markets and Prices", *American Economic Review* 52, pp. 248-53.

18

Hedging Long-Term Exposures with Multiple Short-Term Futures Contracts*

Anthony Neuberger

London Business School

This chapter analyses the problem facing an agent who has a long-term commodity supply commitment, and who wishes to hedge that commitment using short maturity commodity futures contracts. As time evolves, the agent has to roll the hedge as old futures contracts mature and new futures contracts are listed. This gives rise to hedge errors. The optimal hedging strategy is characterised in a world where contracts of several different maturities coexist. The strategy is independent both of the agent's risk aversion and, under certain conditions, of beliefs about expected returns from holding futures contracts. The methodology is compared with approaches based on dynamic models of the term structure. It is tested on data from the oil futures market.

How well can a long-term exposure to commodity prices be hedged using traded commodity futures? Futures contracts provide an excellent tool for risk management. They are highly leveraged, they have low transaction costs, and counter-party risk is small. They are traded on markets that are generally transparent and closely regulated. But most contracts, and in particular the most liquid contracts, tend to be of short maturity. The investor who wishes to hedge a long-term exposure has to keep rolling the hedge into longer-dated contracts. If the prices of the contracts at the time of the rollover do not conform exactly to the particular model being used, errors will arise when positions in one contract are closed out and positions in another are opened up. Rollover risk becomes an important source of hedging error. A model which is used for the design of long-term hedging strategies needs to capture the cross-sectional features of futures prices.

The model presented in this chapter starts out from an assumption about the relationship between the price of the longest-dated contract in the market and the contemporaneous prices of shorter-dated contracts. The parameters of the model are estimated from cross-sectional rather than time series regressions. In this way the model directly reflects the risks attendant on rolling over contracts. It turns out that, for the particular problem addressed here, it is then unnecessary to make any explicit assumptions about the dynamics of prices.

The basic setup posits an agent who has written a long-term fixed price supply contract for a commodity. The agent is assumed to have access to a futures market where contracts of different maturities are traded, but where the longest maturity matures before the commitment falls due. The desire for hedging comes because the agent is risk averse, and wishes to maximise expected utility. The model shows how an optimal hedge can be constructed.

**Originally published in the* Review of Financial Studies *12(3) (1998), reproduced with the permission of the Society for Financial Studies and Oxford University Press. The author is grateful for valuable help and comments from Wayne Ferson, Adam Apter, Dick Brealey, Michael Brennan, Mark Britten-Jones, Mark Grinblatt, Stephen Hall, Julian Franks, Michael Rockinger, an anonymous referee and also from participants at the 1995 European Finance Association meeting, the 1996 Western Finance Association and the 1996 Corporate Risk Management Conference at UCLA. He is also grateful to Rajiv Guha for substantial research assistance. Address correspondence to the author at London Business School, Sussex Place, London NW1 4SA, UK.*

The equating of optimal hedging with utility maximisation may seem rather restrictive, particularly in the light of the growing literature on why firms hedge (see Smith and Stulz, 1985; Bessembinder, 1991; and Froot, Scharfstein and Stein, 1993; see also Mello and Parsons, 1995, in the specific context of commodity price hedging). Other motives for corporate hedging – such as minimising the variance of cashflows, taxable income or accounting earnings, or avoidance of financial distress – may all be important, and will in general lead to somewhat different hedging strategies. Yet even in these cases the characteristics of an economic value hedge, such as considered here, are important. To the extent that an asset or liability can be hedged, it can also be valued. The hedging strategy creates a synthetic long-term forward price; knowledge of that price is useful in many different contexts.

Previous research on the use of futures for hedging (notably Ederington, 1979; McCabe and Franckle, 1983; Baesel and Grant, 1982; and Grant, 1984) restricts itself to a world in which just one futures contract trades at a time. But in most futures markets, many different maturities trade simultaneously. It seems plausible that hedging could be greatly improved by using several maturities simultaneously. We show that this is indeed the case.

More recent work in this area has built on Gibson and Schwartz (1990) and Brennan (1991). In particular, Gibson and Schwartz model the term structure of commodity prices by assuming that the spot price and the convenience yield from holding the physical commodity follow a joint diffusion process of specified form. By imposing no arbitrage conditions they obtain a partial differential equation which all contingent claims must satisfy. Provided that the set of hedging instruments is at least as large as the number of state variables (two in this case) any other contingent claim can be valued exactly and hedged perfectly.

This approach is powerful since it embeds the hedging problem in the much wider problem of creating a consistent framework for pricing and hedging all contingent claims. But it does have certain drawbacks. First, the model assumes that all futures are fairly priced relative to each other, and hence implicitly assumes away rollover risk. Second, since any two futures provide a perfect hedge, the model cannot suggest which particular maturities should be used if there are more than two.

Ross (1995) has a model of commodity prices which admits of many factors. He recognises that in principle it would be possible to hedge all the factors, and hence hedge any long-term commitment perfectly, if there were enough contracts with different maturities and if all the parameters of the model were known. He points out the difficulty in estimating the model with sufficient precision to design perfect hedging strategies, and argues that in practice it is not possible to hedge away all risk. He therefore models the problem in an incomplete market setting by restricting the number of maturities traded to be less than the number of factors; in particular he concentrates on strategies which use just one maturity at a time.

In our model, incompleteness is built in from the outset. The state variables are the prices of traded futures contracts. Futures contracts have a finite life. The price at which a contract first trades is a stochastic function of the prices of other contracts. This opening price provides new information that cannot be hedged using existing securities. The key assumption of the model is that the expected value of the opening price is a linear function of the prices of the other contracts. We impose no other restrictions on the dynamics of futures prices.

This chapter is laid out as follows: in the first section the basic model is set out, and solved for the special case where futures prices follow a martingale. The second section relaxes the martingale assumption and asks whether agents' willingness to write long-term supply commitments is affected by their beliefs about the behaviour of futures prices. In the third section the model is tested using oil futures data. The final section concludes.

The basic model

THE SETUP

For convenience, the underlying commodity will be referred to as oil, but the approach applies to commodities generally. The problem to be examined is this: an agent contracts to sell one barrel of oil in T months time[1] at a price of K and chooses to hedge her exposure in the traded oil futures market. What is her optimal trading strategy? How well can she hedge?

The model is set in continuous time. Time is measured in months. The supply contract is written at time 0 and matures at time T. At the beginning of each month a new futures contract starts trading. It matures exactly $N(< T)$ months later. So at any time during the month there are exactly N futures contracts trading; as one matures a new one is introduced.[2] $F(t,n)$ is the price at time t of the futures contract which matures at time n, where n is an integer. This price exists for all integers n in the range $[t, t + N]$. $\mathbf{F}_t$ denotes the $N \times 1$ vector of futures prices traded at time t, and F_i is the ith element of the vector with F_1 being the price of the longest maturity trading and F_N the price of the near-month contract.

The sequence of events at the turn of the month is as follows. The new N-month contract opens. The futures prices at other maturities may adjust, and the agent may trade. Then all positions in the near-term contract are closed out at the spot price. Thus, at the very start of a month, when t is an integer, there are instantaneously $N + 1$ contracts trading - the maturing contract, the just-opened long-dated contract, and $N - 1$ continuing contracts. By convention, the vector of futures prices $\mathbf{F}_t$ at the start of the month consists of the spot and the $N - 1$ continuing contracts. The following assumptions are made:

[A1] There are no market frictions. There are no transaction costs, taxes, spreads or market impacts from trades carried out by the agent. Contracts are cash settled immediately on a continuous basis; no other margins are required. Contracts are infinitely divisible.

[A2] There is no risk of default. Both parties to the forward oil supply contract will certainly honour their commitments, as will the parties to futures market transactions.

[A3] The agent can borrow or lend without limit at the riskless rate of interest.

Since the focus of this chapter is on commodity price risk, interest rate risk is ignored. Without further loss of generality[3] we assume:

[A4] The riskless interest rate is zero.

A futures position at time t is represented by the $N \times 1$ vector $\Delta = \{\delta_1, \ldots, \delta_N\}$. The agent's cash position at time t is X_t; X_0 is zero. At time T the agent buys oil on the spot market, delivers it to the customer and receives K. The spot price equals the price of the futures contract which matures at that time, $F(T,T)$. The agent's terminal wealth W is $K + X_T - F(T,T)$.

The effect of these assumptions is that the agent is free to choose a hedge strategy represented by a vector process Δ_t. The change in the agent's cash position at time t is the product of the futures position and the change in futures prices:

$$dX = \Delta'.d\mathbf{F}$$
$$\text{so} \quad X_T = \int_{t=0}^{T} \Delta_t'.d\mathbf{F}_t \tag{1}$$

If $N \geq T$ all risk can be removed by holding one contract of the T-maturing futures. This would lock in a cost of $F(0,T)$ and so ensure terminal wealth of $W = K - F(0,T)$. But in general $T > N$ and it is impossible to construct a perfect hedge. The last two assumptions concern the behaviour of futures prices:

[A5] Futures prices follow a martingale.

[A6] At the beginning of a month, when t is an integer, a new N-month contract is listed. The price at which it is expected to open, given the prices of the other contracts, is:

$$\begin{aligned} E[F(t,t+N)|\mathbf{F}_t] &= \alpha + \sum_{i=1}^{N} \beta_i F(t,t+N-i) \\ &= \alpha + \beta'.\mathbf{F}_t \end{aligned} \tag{2}$$

where β is a constant $N \times 1$ vector, and α is a constant. The innovation is represented by ε_t, so $\varepsilon_t \equiv F(t,t+N) - E[F(t,t+N)|\mathbf{F}_t]$.

The martingale assumption [A5] will be relaxed in the second section. Assumption [A6] is critical to the model. It says that the price at which a new contract trades, given the prices of all other traded contracts, is a linear function of the prices of those traded contracts plus a noise term. The implications of this assumption, its consistency with other models of commodity prices and its empirical validity will be tested against oil futures prices in the third section. We will refer to equation (2) as the *forecasting equation*.

THE OPTIMAL HEDGE

We show that there exists a unique hedging strategy, independent of the agent's utility function, which dominates all others in the sense of second order stochastic dominance. The derivation of the optimal hedge is in two steps. We show first that the expected cost of delivery is a linear function of the current term structure of futures prices. The second step is to prove that the optimal hedge is the one which most closely hedges changes in the expected cost of delivery.

All proofs are in Appendix A.

LEMMA 1. *The expected cost of delivery is a linear function of current futures prices:*

$$E[F(T,T)|\mathbf{F}_t] = \alpha^{(n)} + \beta^{(n)}.\mathbf{F}_t \tag{3}$$

where n *is the largest integer* $\leq T - t$, *and* $\alpha^{(n)}$ *and* $\beta^{(n)}$ *are functions of the original* α *and* β, *as set out in Appendix A.*

Call the right-hand side of equation (3) Y_t. Assumption [A6] extrapolates from the current set of N futures contracts to give a price for the next futures contract to be listed. The equation can be applied repeatedly to extend the term structure a further month. Y_t can then be interpreted as an estimate of the price at which a contract maturing at time T would trade if it were listed at time t. With this interpretation, Lemma 1 says that the expected future spot price is equal to the extrapolated futures price.

Consider the behaviour of Y at the turn of the month. t is an integer, and Y is a function of the futures contracts which mature at times t to $t + N - 1$. An instant later, at time t_+, Y is a function of the contracts which mature at $t + 1$ to $t + N$. In general this will mean that Y will jump. Since Y is a linear function of traded prices, it can be hedged perfectly intra-month through a static hedging strategy. It cannot be hedged over the month end because that jump reflects the difference between the price at which the long-dated contract trades and its expected price given the contemporaneous prices of the other contracts. This is economically plausible. The agent adjusts Y_t, the expectation at time t of the spot price at maturity, because of the arrival of new information. The information is the surprise in the long-dated futures price.

LEMMA 2. *At the turn of the month when* t *is an integer and a new contract is listed, the extrapolated futures price,* Y_t, *jumps, and the size of the jump is given by*

$$Y_{t^+} - Y_t = \beta_1^{(T-t-1)}\varepsilon_t \tag{4}$$

The characterisation of the optimal hedge follows immediately:

PROPOSITION 1. *The optimal hedge is to set*

$$\Delta_t = \beta^{(n)} \tag{5}$$

where n is the largest integer $\leq (T - t)$.

The agent's terminal wealth is given by

$$W = K - Y_0 - e \quad \text{where} \quad e \equiv \sum_{n=1}^{T-N} \beta_1^{(T-n-1)}\,\varepsilon_n$$

If the innovation in the forecasting equation has constant variance σ^2 *then the error term has variance*

$$\sigma^2 \sum_{n=1}^{T-N} (\beta_1^{(T-n-1)})^2 \tag{7}$$

The optimal hedge can be implemented as follows:

- ❑ first regress $F(t, t + N)$, the price of the new long-dated futures contract, on $\mathbf{F}_t$, the vector of current prices, to estimate β,
- ❑ then use the recursive relationships set out in Appendix A to compute $\beta^{(n)}$.

The hedge creates a synthetic long-term forward oil contract with an expected delivery cost equal to the expected future spot price. The hedge is not perfect. The error is a weighted sum of the surprises in the prices at which the new long-dated contracts come on stream. Any other hedging strategy has these same hedge errors plus an additional contribution from imperfectly hedged changes in futures prices. The hedging strategy is optimal for any risk averse agent. We will refer to this optimal strategy as the *linear hedging strategy*.

Further intuition about the optimal hedge can be obtained by recognising that it involves hedging the expected future spot price at T. Now by the law of iterated expectations this can be written as:

$$E[F(T,T)|\mathbf{F}_0] = E[E[\ldots E[F(T,T)|\mathbf{F}_{T-N}]\ldots|\mathbf{F}_1]|\mathbf{F}_0]$$

Note that the expectations are all linear in the relevant futures prices. Going back in time, use the martingale assumption [A5] to replace the end-month price by the beginning-month price. Use assumption [A6] to replace the price of a contract which has just come on stream by a linear combination of contracts which have been trading for months. Since the expectation is linear, hedge ratios are state independent, and the terminal pay-off to the strategy is independent of the dynamics of the state variables.

SIMPLE EXTENSIONS TO THE MODEL

No account has been taken of the time value of money. If short term interest rates are not zero but are equal to some known function of time $r(t)$ the results go through largely unaltered. The only difference is that it is necessary to "tail" the hedge[4] to account for the time value of money from when cashflows arise on the hedge until time T. Stochastic interest rates pose more of a problem, but provided that rates do not jump and rate changes are uncorrelated with oil price changes, the model remains intact.

To see this, let B_t denote the price at time t of a discount bond which matures at time T. Suppose that the agent invests any cash and does any borrowing by holding or shorting the discount bond. Reinterpret X_t as the face value of the agent's holding of the discount bond at time t. Then the dynamics of X are no longer given by equation (5) but by

$$dX_t = \frac{\Delta_t'.d\mathbf{F}_t}{B_{t+\mathbf{dt}}} \tag{8}$$

If the bond price is not stochastic, or if it follows a Brownian diffusion with bond price changes which are locally uncorrelated with changes in the vector of futures prices, the results in Proposition 1 go through unaltered apart from the need to "tail" the hedge. The optimal hedging strategy is now to set

$$\Delta_t = B_t\beta^{(n)} \tag{9}$$

where n is the largest integer $\leq (T - t)$.

Terminal wealth under this strategy remains as in Proposition 1. The extension of the model to take account of correlation between interest rate changes and changes in the oil would be a much more substantial affair, and is not considered in this chapter. We have examined the hedging problem when the commitment has the form of a "bullet" - to supply a quantum at some fixed future time. Given a "flow" commitment, where the commodity is to be supplied at a certain rate between two points in time, the optimal hedge is just the sum of the hedges for the individual deliveries. More complex commitments, for example where the customer can choose when the commodity is supplied, are not linear in prices, and their treatment is beyond the scope of this chapter.

Speculation and hedging

We have assumed that futures prices follow a martingale. This is restrictive. It means that there is no speculative motive for trading futures, only a hedging motive. How robust are our results to this assumption? We have shown that the optimal hedge can be obtained by regressing changes in the expected cost of delivery on changes in actual futures prices. Does this still hold if futures prices do not follow a martingale?

If futures prices have a predictable drift component, the optimal strategy will depend on the agent's preferences. We set the problem in an expected utility framework. To avoid complex dependence on wealth levels, constant absolute risk aversion is assumed. In place of the martingale assumption [A5], assume:

[A5′] The agent's objective is to maximise:

$$E\left[-\frac{1}{\lambda}e^{-\lambda\tilde{W}}\right] \tag{10}$$

where λ is a risk aversion coefficient and W is the agent's terminal wealth.

It is worth noting that the linear hedging strategy ($\Delta_t = \beta^{(n)}$) still leads to the agent locking in a price of Y_0 with a hedge error of e whether or not futures prices follow a martingale process. What changes is that it is no longer necessarily the optimal strategy. So we can still implement the strategy and compute the corresponding hedge error even if futures prices have predictable drift components. Since the strategy is feasible it places a lower bound on the expected utility of the optimal hedge.

If there are predictable drift components, they can be exploited whether the agent has a long-term supply commitment to hedge or not. Call the optimal strategy in the absence of a supply commitment the *speculative strategy*, Δ^S. The corresponding expected utility of terminal wealth G^S will be a function of the cash holding X, the current level of prices $\mathbf{F}_t$ and time t. When taking on the supply commitment the optimal strategy changes. In addition to a speculative motive for trading there is also a hedging motive. The optimal strategy is $\Delta^S + \Delta^H$. The following proposition shows that, unless the long-term supply commitment provides a natural hedge against the risks of speculative trading, the incremental trading generated by the supply commitment, Δ^H, is independent of the drift.

PROPOSITION 2. *If shocks to* G^S, *the expected utility of wealth from speculative trading, which occur when a new contract is listed, are independent of the innovation* ε_t, *then:*
(1) the optimal trading strategy is the sum of two strategies: a speculative strategy which the agent would follow if there were no forward commitment to hedge, and a hedging strategy which is the same as in the martingale case.
(2) the break-even price at which the agent could write the long-term contract and maintain the same expected utility is

$$Y_0 + \frac{1}{\lambda}\,\mathrm{Log}\,E\left[e^{\lambda e}\middle|\mathbf{F}_0\right] \tag{11}$$

If the hedge error is normally distributed this can be written as

$$Y_0 + \tfrac{1}{2}\lambda\,\mathrm{Var}\left[e\right] \tag{12}$$

(3) if the change in expected utility and the surprise in prices are generally positively (negatively) correlated the break-even price is lower (higher).

While it is possible to conceive of beliefs which would induce a correlation between ε_t and contemporaneous changes in G^S, these beliefs tend to be rather elaborate. In the absence of correlation, the break-even price is the extrapolated futures price for the appropriate maturity plus a risk premium which depends on the agent's risk aversion and on the variance of the hedge error. The break-even price does not reflect the agent's beliefs about the drift in futures prices. This is because the agent is free to speculate on the drift by trading in short dated contracts without having to write long-term contracts.

Empirical evidence

We test the model using the crude oil futures contract traded on the New York Mercantile Exchange (Nymex). Our data cover the period 1 July 1986–31 December 1994. The contract is the most actively traded crude oil contract in the world with daily volume in 1994 averaging over 100,000 contracts per day, and open interest amounting to over 400,000 contracts. The contract is for physical delivery of 1000 barrels of crude, and is based on West Texas Intermediate (WTI) grade. Contracts for the next eighteen consecutive months are traded, together with four long contracts which start out with maturities of 21, 24, 30 and 36 months. Trading is by open outcry during the day, and electronically when the floor is closed.

Up to 1989, the longest maturity contracts were 12 months, but there was very little activity in some of the longer-dated contracts. The data set includes daily settlement prices for contracts maturing in each of the next nine months and for some longer contracts. 90% of trading volume in the data set is in contracts with four months or less to maturity; less than 3% is in contracts with more than nine months remaining. Although activity in the longer-dated contracts increases over time, volume in the longer-dated contracts remains relatively low (even in the last two years of the data set only 3% of contracts traded had a maturity beyond one year).

The nature of the data set imposes limitations on the types of test it is possible to perform. The ideal would be to estimate the model, use it for hedging a series of long-term contracts, and compute statistics showing the performance of the hedge. Yet if "long-term" commitments means commitments extending over several years, it would require several decades of data to obtain a sufficient number of independent observations. With the available data set we carry out a number of separate studies which together cast light on the validity and utility of the model.

The central assumption of the extrapolation model is the linearity of the forecasting equation. One concern is that non-linearity, amplified by extrapolation, might make the model unreliable. To explore this, we examine the performance of the extrapolation model in a world where the linearity assumption is known to be false. In particular, we use two of the dynamic models of the term structure of futures prices discussed by Schwartz (1997) and show that the extrapolation model is well-behaved.

Next, we test the model's performance in hedging a three year contract using contracts with up to eight months to maturity, and also how well it hedges an eight-month contract using contracts of up to three months. In both cases, the extrapolation model is compared with the Gibson–Schwartz (1990) two factor model ("the GS model") which is used as a benchmark. The reason for looking at both the three-year and the eight-month horizon is that the former setting is probably more typical of the way in which the model would actually be applied while tests on the eight-month horizon have more statistical power.

In the final set of tests we examine the validity of the assumptions of the extrapolation model, estimate the model parameters and assess the quality of the hedging strategy.

ROBUSTNESS OF THE MODEL TO NON-LINEARITY

We examine how the extrapolation model is affected by non-linearity. We assume that the world corresponds exactly to some dynamic term structure model where the forecasting equation is non-linear, and evaluate how well the extrapolation model performs. The advantage of this approach is that it isolates the issue of non-linearity from problems such as parameter uncertainty which are considered separately.

Assume then that the world corresponds exactly to the GS model, where there are two state variables (the spot price and the instantaneous convenience yield) which follow a joint diffusion process. The price of a futures contract can be expressed as a function of the state variables, and any long-dated commitment can be hedged perfectly using just two futures contracts. The forecasting equation is exact: the price at which a new contract opens is a function of the prices of any two other traded contracts. But the key assumption of the extrapolation model is violated since the function is non-linear.[5] The question we explore is whether, using realistic parameters (those estimated by Schwartz, 1997, Table VI, column 2) for the GS model, it is still possible to make effective use of the extrapolation model. In particular, how well can one hedge a five year commitment using just two futures contracts with no more than nine months to maturity, rolling the position every two months?

The joint distribution of the five-, seven- and nine-month futures prices is given by the model, so β_1 and β_2 can be estimated by regressing the nine-month on the five- and seven-month prices. The hedge ratios $\beta_1^{(60)}$ and $\beta_2^{(60)}$ can be computed, and the hedged portfolio is:

$$F(t,t+60) - \beta_1^{(60)} F(t,t+9) - \beta_2^{(60)} F(t,t+7)$$

The unconditional volatility of the hedged portfolio is then calculated using the GS model.[6]

The results are summarised in Table 1 (scenario 1). The annualised volatility of the five year price is 25.9%. The volatility of the hedged portfolio is 0.82%. The linear approximation does not prevent the hedge from removing almost all the risk.

The extrapolation model gives the optimal hedge as short 2.89 of the seven-month, and long 3.93 of the nine-month contract, so the hedge is net long approximately 1 barrel of oil. But the quality of the hedge is not driven just by the net exposure to the oil market. A simple hedge consisting of one nine-month contract would have a much higher volatility of 9.1%.

Table 1. Volatility of hedged portfolios in a Gibson–Schwartz world

	Two-factor model				Three-factor model	
Scenario:	**1**	**2**	**3**	**4**	**5**	**6**
Volatility of five-year contract						
Unhedged	25.88%	18.27%	14.95%	11.67%	14.31%	11.66%
One-to-one hedge	9.14%	11.32%	11.35%	6.91%	11.24%	7.58%
Two-contract hedge	0.82%	1.02%	1.58%	0.64%	2.12%	1.51%
Three-contract hedge	0.08%	0.13%	0.24%	0.07%	1.88%	0.89%
Volatility of 10-year contract						
Unhedged	25.88%	18.27%	14.94%	11.66%	14.44%	11.80%
One-to-one hedge	8.85%	11.74%	9.95%	6.17%	9.08%	6.73%
Two-contract hedge	1.24%	1.30%	1.84%	0.71%	3.08%	2.26%
Three-contract hedge	0.08%	0.13%	0.24%	0.07%	2.62%	1.71%

Hedged portfolios are constructed using the extrapolation method. Their volatility is then calculated in a Gibson–Schwartz world. The six scenarios use the parameter estimates made by Schwartz (1997, Tables 6 and 9), and are derived from oil market data. The first four scenarios are based on Schwartz's two-factor model; the last two on his three-factor model. The first four scenarios differ in the period over which the estimates are made (1985–95, 1990–95, 1990–95 and 1993–96, respectively) and the data used (one and two use futures up to nine months, three also uses a 17-month contract while four uses swap data). Scenarios five and six use the same data sets as scenarios three and four respectively. In the one-to-one hedge the long-dated contract is hedged by one nine-month contract. The two-contract hedge uses seven- and nine-month contracts, while the three-contract hedge uses five-, seven- and nine-month contracts.

The quality of the hedge is improved if more contract maturities are used. Using three contracts, of five, seven and nine months, the volatility of the hedged portfolio falls to 0.08%.

Schwartz (1997) estimates the GS model using four different data sets, and gets substantially different parameter values. As can be seen from Table 1, the volatility of the hedged and unhedged portfolios do vary, but for each set of estimates the same conclusions are apparent: the extrapolation method does succeed in removing the great bulk of the risk of a long-term commitment, the model's success does not derive mainly from hedging changes in the level of oil prices but comes also from hedging changes in the convenience yield, and a three-contract hedge comfortably improves on a two-contract hedge. The lower panel shows very similar results for the hedging of a 10 year commitment.

Schwartz (1997) also considers a three-factor term structure model, which incorporates stochastic interest rates as well as a stochastic spot price and convenience yield. Using his parameter estimates (Schwartz, 1997, Table 9) we follow exactly the same procedure as before. The results are set out in the last two columns of Table 1. Again, the extrapolation model performs rather well, though somewhat less well than in the two-factor model case.

In Appendix B, we provide some theoretical insight into the divergence between the extrapolation model and the GS model, and show that the extrapolation model is likely to work best when the convenience yield is not too volatile, and shocks to the convenience yield die away quickly.

We have shown that in a world where the key assumption of the extrapolation model is violated, the model gives an effective hedging strategy. This is encouraging evidence for the robustness of the extrapolation model, but says nothing about its merits relative to alternative models.

REPLICATING A THREE-YEAR FUTURES CONTRACT

We use the extrapolation model and the GS model to hedge a three-year commitment using futures contracts with no more than eight months to maturity. At month t the parameters of each model are estimated using prices up till that month. Using the model and the current price of the contracts to be used for hedging, the three-year futures price is estimated. We postulate an agent who sells one barrel of oil forward, for delivery at time $t + 36$, at the model price, who then hedges it using short-dated futures contracts (up to eight months) as the model dictates. Eight months from the date the commitment is due, at month $t + 28$, the final delivery price is locked in using an eight-month contract, and the profit or loss determined. If the model works perfectly, the profit will be zero.

The exercise is repeated each month. With the passage of time the volume of past data increases, and the model can be estimated with increasing precision. With the data set beginning in July 1986, the exercise starts in December 1988, using 18 months of data for model estimation. First delivery follows three years later, in December 1991.

Table 2. Hedging a three-year commitment

	Hedge error			
	Root mean square (US$/barrel)	Std dev. (US$/barrel)	Turnover (contracts)	Extreme cash position (US$/barrel)
Extrapolation methods				
6, 7, 8 months	1.44	1.43	488	3.68 to –2.72
4, 6, 8 months	1.07	1.06	60	4.20 to –2.26
6, 8 months	1.16	1.16	48	4.12 to –1.50
Gibson–Schwartz model				
6, 8 months	2.53	1.46	75	5.28 to –1.53
One-to-one hedge				
8 months	3.75	2.54	15	6.90 to –2.26
No hedge	3.35	3.32	0	0.00

(Hedge contract maturities are immediately after they have been rolled forward)

The table shows the performance of different strategies for hedging a three-year commitment using futures contracts of up to eight months. The hedge is run monthly from December 1988 for 45 months. For each strategy both the root mean square hedge error and the standard deviation of the hedge error are reported. Turnover is total number of futures contracts taken out (long or short) per contract hedged, averaged over the 45 months. The cash position is defined as the net cumulative margin paid on the futures position; for each hedge the maximum and minimum cash position is computed and the numbers are averaged over the 45 months. With both the one-to-one hedge and the no hedge the long-term commitment is concluded at the price of the eight-month future; for the other models the contract is written at model price. The one-to-one hedge consists of a single eight-month contract which is rolled every two months.

The exercise is repeated each month, with the last commitment made in August 1992, when there are six years of data to estimate the model. Thus the hedging exercise is repeated a total of 45 times. The results are set out in Table 2.

Three different variants of the extrapolation method are considered. The first uses the three longest available contracts, with the position being rolled every month, so at the beginning of each month the hedge consists of contracts with six, seven and eight months to maturity. The root mean square hedge error averages US$1.44/barrel over the period. The strategy requires a lot of trading – on average 488 contracts are traded per contract hedged.

The second strategy uses alternate months' futures contracts and is rebalanced every two months. It performs rather better. The error is US$1.07/barrel, and it only requires an average of 60 futures contracts to be traded per contract hedged. The reduction in trading volume is partly due to the lower frequency with which the hedge is rebalanced, and partly due to the smaller size of positions held at any time. The third strategy uses just two contracts, and is rebalanced bi-monthly. It performs only slightly worse than a three-contract hedge, and turnover is slightly reduced.

The GS hedge is implemented using contracts which initially have six and eight months to maturity and is rolled every two months. The parameters are estimated using a Kalman filter as described in Schwartz (1997). On the basis of the estimated model parameters and the prices of the two contracts used for hedging at the beginning of each two-month period, the theoretical hedge ratios are computed. The ratios vary slightly over the two-month period as the slope of the term structure changes. In practice the changes are small and the effect on the hedging strategy is negligible, so the hedge is implemented as a static hedge within each period. The root mean square error of the GS hedge is US$2.53/barrel. This is much higher than for the extrapolation hedges. The turnover is marginally higher than the bi-monthly extrapolation hedge.

To provide some basis of comparison, we also look at the risk from following a simple one-to-one hedging strategy, where a single eight-month contract is held for two months and then rolled forward; we also show what happens if the commitment is not hedged at all. For the one-to-one hedge and the no hedge strategies, there is no model price for the three-year commitment, so the hedge profit is computed on the assumption that the contract is written at the eight-month futures price. This may overstate the hedge error since the eight-month price may not be an unbiased estimator of the three-year price. For these two strategies the standard deviation may be a better measure of hedging error than the root mean square.

The hedge errors are plotted in Figure 1. The top chart shows the results for the extrapolation hedges, while the lower chart shows the other strategies. The two charts are drawn to the same scale and show the hedging error (measured in US$/barrel) for a particular hedging strategy plotted against the month in which the hedge was started. The magnitude of

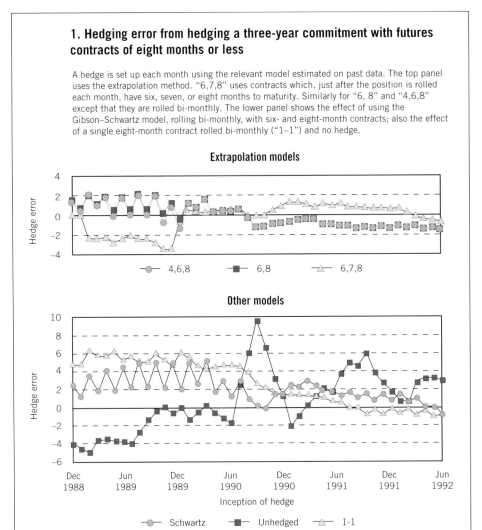

1. Hedging error from hedging a three-year commitment with futures contracts of eight months or less

A hedge is set up each month using the relevant model estimated on past data. The top panel uses the extrapolation method. "6,7,8" uses contracts which, just after the position is rolled each month, have six, seven, or eight months to maturity. Similarly for "6, 8" and "4,6,8" except that they are rolled bi-monthly. The lower panel shows the effect of using the Gibson–Schwartz model, rolling bi-monthly, with six- and eight-month contracts; also the effect of a single eight-month contract rolled bi-monthly ("1–1") and no hedge.

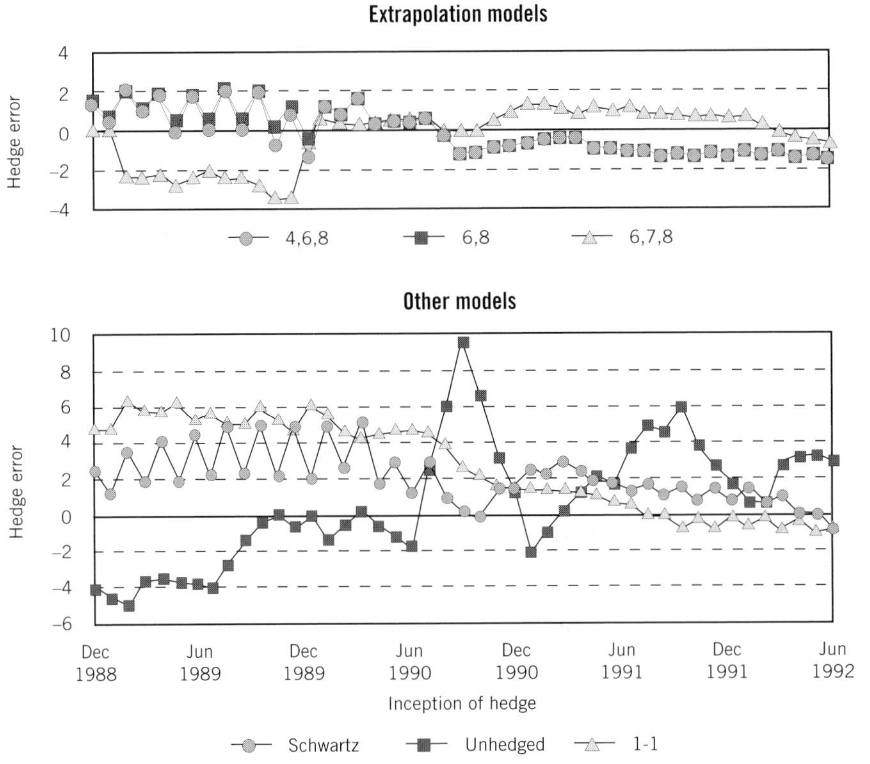

the errors tends to decline over the period. In the case of the GS and extrapolation models, this could be explained by the improvement in parameter estimation which comes as more data are used to estimate the model, but it does not account for the improvement in the performance of the one-to-one hedge where no parameters are estimated. Part of the improvement is likely to be due to the easier hedging environment in the second half of the period when the shape of the term structure was less volatile.

Some of the plots show a sawtooth pattern in the early part of the period. This is due to bi-monthly rebalancing. In any one month, a hedge that originated an even number of months ago might be long the eight-month contract and short the six-month. A similar hedge that originated a month earlier or later would be long the seven-month contract and short the five-month. Normally the hedge gain or loss would be very similar for these two positions. However, with the turmoil in the oil market in 1990–91, there were large swings in prices which led to differences of up to US$1/barrel between similar hedge portfolios in some months.

The cashflows that arise during the life of a hedge are of some interest. Table 2 shows the average across all the 45 months of the largest positive and negative cash balances on each strategy. Apart from the no-hedging strategy where there are no interim cashflows, it is movement in the level of oil prices rather than choice of hedging strategy that is the most important determinant of the size of interim cashflows.

The conclusions we can draw from this exercise are suggestive, but not conclusive. The 45 different profit figures for each hedge are not independent estimates of the error since the hedging periods overlap. The agent is actively managing each hedge over a period of 28 months, so the 45 data points do not even constitute two non-overlapping periods. Furthermore, the Gulf War comes in the middle of the period and has considerable impact on the oil market. However, the results do provide evidence, which we confirm below, that the extrapolation model does reduce risk substantially, and appears to do better in this regard than the GS model.

Table 3. Hedging performance of Gibson–Schwartz and extrapolation models

	Extrapolation model		Gibson–Schwartz model		
Contracts used:	1, 2, 3	2, 3	1, 3	2, 3	Unhedged
Root mean square error in hedging an eight-month future (cents/barrel/month):					
12/88–12/94	28.14	27.34 (0.6403)	53.15 (0.0000)	31.91 (0.1605)	117.97 (0.0000)
3/91–12/94	9.35	10.13 (0.3397)	23.48 (0.0000)	16.20 (0.0000)	69.74 (0.0000)

The root mean square error is computed by measuring the change in the price of an eight-month contract, hedged by contracts which initially have one to three months till maturity, over the following month.

Numbers in parentheses are p-values for the hypothesis that the hedging strategy is no worse than the extrapolation hedge using one-, two- and three-month contracts; they are computed following the procedure in Granger and Newbold (1986, p. 279).

HEDGING AN EIGHT-MONTH FUTURES CONTRACT

To enhance the power of the tests we look at hedging an eight-month rather than a three-year commitment. Not only are there then more non-overlapping periods, but the market at eight months is sufficiently liquid that changes in the value of the hedge and of the underlying commitment can be compared on a monthly basis.

At the start of each month, the parameters of each model are estimated using all prior data. The hedge for an eight-month contract is constructed using futures with three months or less remaining. The position is held for a month and the hedge error measured. The procedure is repeated in subsequent months and the root mean square hedge error computed. The results are shown in Table 3.

For all methods the hedging error is very much larger in the early part of the period. In part this results from having less data earlier from which to estimate the parameter values, but in the main it is due to the great turbulence around the period of the Gulf War. So we report results both for the period as a whole, and also for the period from March 1991. The ranking of the methods is similar whichever period we look at. Both Gibson–Schwartz and the extrapolation method reduce risk compared with not hedging, the extrapolation method being more effective than Gibson–Schwartz. The difference between the two is statistically highly significant in the period excluding the Gulf War.

There is no great benefit in using a third contract in the extrapolation method. The ranking of the two- and three-contract hedges changes depending on the period chosen, and the difference are not statistically significant in either period. Perhaps this is not surprising since the position taken in the one-month contract when it is used is very small.[7] In using Gibson–Schwartz, it is much better to use two- and three-month contracts for hedging than one and three-month contracts; using the one-month contract picks up short term volatility which is not reflected in the eight-month price.

It might be argued that the relatively poor performance of the GS model is due to problems in estimating the parameters or in implementing the hedge. The hedge ratios in the GS model depend only on the futures prices, which are in our data set, and the mean reversion rate of the convenience yield, κ. Even if the value of κ is chosen to minimise the hedging error, the hypothesis that the (2,3) GS model provides a better hedge than the extrapolation model is rejected at the 1% level in the post Gulf War period.

To test whether the performance of the GS hedge could be attributed to the use of a static rather than a dynamic hedge as the model strictly implies, the hedge returns were re-estimated as follows. At the beginning and end of each month the theoretical price of the eight-month future is estimated from the prices of the contracts used for hedging it. If the model is correct, and the hedge balanced dynamically, the change in the value of the hedge equals the change in the theoretical price of the eight-month contract over the month. It turns out that the hedge returns as measured in this way are virtually identical to the static hedge returns (there is a correlation of 0.997 between the two measures), and there is virtually no impact on the size of hedge errors.

The three-factor model described in Schwartz (1997) can also be used to hedge an eight-month contract with one-, two- and three-month contracts, but the results are very poor. The absolute value of the hedge ratios required to hedge all three factors are so large (typical values are +11, -27 and +18 contracts respectively for every eight-month contract hedged) that the performance is no better than not hedging at all.

Table 4. Estimation of the forecasting equation

Period	1986–94	1986–94	1986–94	1986–90	1990–94	1986–94
No. of observations	102	102	102	51	51	51
R^2	99.997%	99.996%	99.996%	99.997%	99.995%	99.968%
α	0.42	1.14	0.02	–0.47	12.46	0.10
β_1	2.078 (0.103)	2.116 (0.082)	1.839 (0.016)	2.054 (0.153)	2.015 (0.099)	——
β_2	–1.232 (0.215)	–1.353 (0.150)	–0.840 (0.016)	–1.222 (0.280)	–1.236 (0.172)	1.979 (0.089)
β_3	0.035 (0.96)	0.237 (0.069)	——	0.169 (0.129)	0.215 (0.076)	——
β_4	0.331 (0.204)	——	——	——	——	–1.216 (0.143)
β_5	–0.395 (0.179)	——	——	——	——	——
β_6	0.229 (0.105)	——	——	——	——	0.232 (0.057)
β_7	–0.047 (0.036)	——	——	——	——	——
β_8	0.001 (0.009)	——	——	——	——	——
Standard error (¢/barrel)	1.57	1.58	1.67	1.72	1.37	4.75

The forecasting equation is: $F(n,n+8) = \alpha + \sum_{i=1}^{8} \beta_i F(n,n+8-i) + \tilde{\varepsilon}_n$

Standard errors in parentheses.

IMPLEMENTING THE MODEL FOR LONG-TERM COMMITMENTS

We now test the assumptions of the extrapolation model (notably assumption [A6]), estimate the forecasting equations for different hedging instruments, and compute hedge ratios for different maturities. We also estimate the size of hedging error, taking account of errors in estimating the model parameters.

Assuming that the longest-dated liquid contract suitable for hedging is the eight-month contract, the first step is to estimate the forecasting equation:

$$F(t,t+8) = \alpha + \sum_{i=1}^{8} \beta_i F(t,t+8-i) + \varepsilon_t \tag{13}$$

Given the very weak evidence for stationarity in oil prices, it might seem problematic using ordinary least squares (OLS) for estimation. Augmented Dickey–Fuller tests for a unit root were generally inconclusive. For the longer dated futures contracts we were unable to reject the existence of a unit root even at the 10% level; for the shorter contracts we could reject unit roots. But OLS is still efficient and consistent if the series form a co-integrating system (see Engle and Granger, 1987). Using Johansen's method (Johansen, 1991) there is strong evidence of co-integration; the null that the series were not co-integrated was rejected at the 1% level.

The forecasting equation is estimated using OLS. The results are set out in Table 4. The very high correlation coefficients in the regressions are unsurprising. While oil prices are volatile the shape of the term structure at any point in time is quite smooth. Virtually all the model's power in predicting the price of the new long-dated contract comes from the prices of the two or three longest-dated contracts trading. We therefore set β_4 to β_8 equal to zero, and take the forecasting equation in our base case to be as in the third column of Table 4. The error in forecasting the price of the new contract is under 1.60¢/barrel.

We found no evidence of parameter instability, seasonality or non-linearity. The fifth and sixth columns of Table 4 estimate the regression over the two halves of the period separately. A Chow test was carried out to test the hypothesis that the true parameters are identical in the two halves. With an F-statistic of 1.84, the null cannot be rejected at conventional significance levels. We tested for seasonality by including monthly dummies in the regressions. Using a Wald test, the hypothesis that all the coefficients were zero could not be rejected even at the 20% significance level. We tested for non-linear terms by regressing the eight-month price on both the five- to seven-month prices and on their squared values; we were again unable to reject the null at the 20% level.

The hedge error in the model was shown in Proposition 1 to be the weighted sum of the prediction errors. The time series behaviour of the error is therefore important. Returning to the base case (as in the third column of Table 4) the Durbin–Watson statistic is 2.22. Using a Lagrange multiplier test, there is no evidence of serial correlation in the residuals (chi-square of 1.55, with a p-statistic of 21%).

We have already seen (in the section on replicating a three-year futures contract) that the extrapolation model seems to work well when rebalanced every two months, so the last column of Table 4 shows the regression of the eight-month price on the sixth, fourth and second month. The equation was estimated using data from alternate months. The fit,

Table 5.

Panel A: The optimal hedging strategy with monthly rebalancing

Maturity (in months)	**8**	**9**	**12**	**24**	**48**	**72**
Hedge composition:						
Eighth month	1	2.12 (0.08)	4.70 (0.43)	7.65 (1.29)	7.26 (2.23)	6.52 (2.97)
Seventh month	0	–1.35 (0.15)	–4.65 (0.76)	–8.50 (1.90)	–8.13 (2.78)	–7.30 (3.52)
Sixth month	0	0.24 (0.07)	0.94 (0.35)	1.80 (0.74)	1.73 (0.83)	1.55 (0.91)
Total (gross)	1	3.71 (0.30)	10.29 (1.53)	17.95 (3.83)	17.12 (5.73)	15.38 (7.31)
Total (net)	1	1.00 (0.00)	0.99 (0.01)	0.95 (0.07)	0.86 (0.20)	0.77 (0.30)
Hedge Error (US$/barrel)	0	0.02	0.09	0.40	0.84	1.18

Panel B: The optimal hedging strategy with bi-monthly rebalancing

Maturity (in months)	**8**	**9**	**12**	**24**	**48**	**72**
Hedge composition:						
Eighth month	1	1.98 (0.09)	2.70 (0.21)	3.66 (0.66)	2.92 (0.94)	2.27 (1.08)
Sixth month	0	–1.22 (0.14)	–2.18 (0.33)	–3.62 (0.91)	–2.92 (1.09)	–2.27 (1.18)
Fourth month	0	0.23 (0.06)	0.46 (0.13)	0.85 (0.33)	0.69 (0.33)	0.54 (0.32)
Total (gross)	1	3.43 (0.29)	5.34 (0.67)	8.13 (1.86)	6.53 (2.33)	5.08 (2.56)
Total (net)	1	1.00 (0.00)	0.99 (0.01)	0.89 (0.07)	0.69 (0.17)	0.54 (0.22)
Hedge Error (US$/barrel)	0	0.05	0.11	0.44	0.83	1.08

Panel C: Risk of unhedged portfolio

(US$/barrel)	0	1.16	2.20	4.02	6.35	8.29

The table shows the composition of the optimal hedge according to the maturity of the supply commitment. In panel A, the hedge is rolled over each month into futures contracts with six, seven and eight months to expiry. The forecasting equation used is that estimated in column 3 of Table 4. In panel B, the hedge is rolled over every two months into futures contracts with four, six and eight months to expiry. The forecasting equation used is that estimated in column 7 of Table 4. Figures in parentheses are standard errors; the standard errors are computed by approximating the quantities by linear functions of the regression parameters, and using the covariance matrix from the regression equation. The hedge error in the bottom line of Panels A and B includes the error in estimating the coefficients of the forecasting equation.

unsurprisingly, is somewhat less good than the earlier regressions as demonstrated by the slightly lower R^2 and the higher standard error. But this is offset by the fact that the hedge does not have to be rolled so frequently. There was no evidence of parameter instability, seasonality, non-linearity or serial correlation in the residuals.

Using the extrapolation methodology we compute the optimal hedge for different horizons in the base case. The results are set out in the top panel of Table 5. To interpret the table, consider the last column in the top panel. If the agent has contracted to supply one barrel of oil in six years time and seeks to hedge using futures contracts with up to eight months to maturity, the optimal strategy is to go long 6.52 barrels of the eight-month, short 7.30 barrels of the seven-month and long 1.55 barrels of the five-month. This implies a gross position of 15.38 barrels and a net long position of 0.77 barrels. The agent would need to revise the position monthly as the maturity of each futures contract shortens, and as the maturity of the supply commitment reduces.

The optimal hedge involves very large long and short positions - to hedge an exposure of one barrel more than a year away requires a gross position in excess of 10 barrels in the futures market. Although the hedge looks stable - the optimal hedge is very similar for any T in excess of two years - maintaining it requires considerable trading. As the eight-month contract becomes a seven-month contract the agent must turn a long position into a short, and similarly for the other contracts. The volume of trading each month equals the size of the gross position.

Although the optimal hedge looks highly leveraged, the principal determinant of hedge returns is movements in the level of the oil price; at 72 months for example the correlation between the return on the optimal hedge and on a single eight-month contract is 0.939. So the net exposure is a useful statistic to look at. As can be seen from Table 5 the net position, which starts at one barrel, remains close to unity for many months. This results from the fact that the estimated coefficients of the forecasting equation sum almost exactly to unity. It is consistent with models in which the price of oil is non-stationary.

Standard errors of the hedge ratios are shown in the Table.[8] The hedge error, as recorded in the bottom row, reflects both the rollover errors at the turn of the month as set out in Proposition 1, and the error in estimating the parameters of the model.

The collinearity of futures prices manifests itself in large standard errors in the estimated hedge ratios. The standard errors on the net hedge position are much smaller than on the gross. The standard errors increase steeply with the time horizon, though the net hedge position is still different from zero at conventional significance levels at 72 months. The hedge error increases with the time horizon, going from US$0.40/barrel at 24 months to US$1.18/barrel at 72 months.

The strategy of rebalancing the portfolio alternate months obviously has attractions in terms of containing transaction costs. So panel B of Table 5 shows the implications of restricting both the estimation of the forecasting equation and the hedging strategy to contracts which mature on alternate months. The bi-monthly strategy is highly correlated with the monthly strategy of Panel A; in hedging a 72-month commitment for example the correlation between the two is 0.993 (this compares with a correlation of 0.939 with a strategy of holding a single contract). The strategies differ in the size of the hedge. The bi-monthly hedge is net long 0.54 contracts at 72 months as against 0.77 contracts for the monthly hedge. But this appears to be the result of estimation differences rather than substance. The differences are well within the standard errors. Further, the bi-monthly hedge was estimated using half the months in the sample; a bi-monthly hedge estimated on the other months yields an estimate of the net position which is slightly higher than the monthly hedge.

The amount of trading required is much reduced by hedging bi-monthly; at 72 months the bi-monthly hedge requires trading only five contracts every two months against 15 contracts per month for the monthly hedge. A small part of this six-fold reduction in turnover comes from the lower net position held. The major gain comes from the smaller gross position required to hedge changes in the shape of the term structure, and the fact that positions are held for two months rather than one; together these factors reduce turnover roughly four-fold.

It is interesting to compare the standard errors of the two strategies. Some caution is needed inasmuch as each set of standard errors is computed on the basis that the model used is correctly specified. But taking the numbers at face value, it appears that rebalancing every two months does not reduce hedging efficiency to any appreciable extent, except possibly for very short horizons. This conclusion is supported by the high correlation between the two sets of hedging returns.

To put the hedging errors into context, Panel C of Table 5 shows the error if the agent does not hedge at all[9] (until eight months before maturity when the position is hedged perfectly with a futures contract). The extrapolation method reduces the risk of an unhedged 72-month contract by 85% (with the hedge error dropping from US$8.29 to US$1.18/barrel); the gains are proportionately still larger at shorter maturities.

We now investigate whether the model can be applied using just the most liquid contracts, those with up to three months to maturity. The forecasting equation, where the three-month contract is expressed as a linear function of the three shorter contracts, is misspecified. The Durbin–Watson statistic is 1.53 and there is strong evidence of serial correlation in the residuals (using a Lagrange multiplier test, the chi-square is 6.06, with a p-statistic of 1.4%). There is also evidence of a time trend. But most significantly from the viewpoint of the model, there is evidence of non-linearity. The price of the three-month contract depends on the squared difference between the first and second month prices. Table 6 shows the forecasting equation with these additional terms. It also shows that the violations of our assumptions, which were not observed in the previous regression using the eight-month contract, do not result from the unusual conditions in the oil market around the time of the Gulf War in 1990–91, but are clearly significant in the rest of the data.

The existence of a time trend, and in particular any uncertainty in measuring the magnitude of the trend,

Table 6. Forecasting equation using near-month contracts

	Full sample	Excluding Oct. 1990 to Jan. 1991
No. of observations	102	97
α	0.379** (0.071)	0.189** (0.040)
β_1	1.736** (0.068)	1.854** (0.069)
β_2	–0.802** (0.089)	–0.975** (0.108)
β_3	0.043 (0.029)	0.109* (0.042)
γ	0.111** (0.032)	0.150* (0.058)
δ	0.00070 (0.00037)	0.00046** (0.00017)
ρ	0.528** (0.101)	0.194* (0.095)
Standard error	0.0486	0.0362
Adjusted R^2	0.99979	0.99974
Durbin–Watson	2.09	1.54

* significant at 5% level;
** significant at 1% level.

The equation estimated is

$$F(t,t+3) = \alpha + \beta_1 F(t,t+2) + \beta_2 F(t,t+1) + \beta_3 F(t,t) + \gamma[F(t,t+2) - F(t,t+1)]^2 + \delta t + \varepsilon_t$$

where the error term itself follows an AR(1) process:

$$\varepsilon_t = \rho\varepsilon_{t-1} + \eta_t$$

Standard errors in parentheses.

will create additional uncertainty in the expected price at which long-term commitments can be locked in, but the extrapolation method remains optimal. The existence of positive autocorrelation in the error specification will make the aggregate hedging error under the extrapolation method larger than it would be otherwise. If the nature of the serial correlation can be correctly identified, it should be possible to correct the error estimate to take account of it. Non-linearity in the forecasting equation is more problematic since it suggests that the optimal hedge should vary according to the level of prices. That would require a major extension to the model that is beyond the scope of this chapter. Of course the extrapolation method can still be used with very short-dated contracts; and, despite its theoretical problems, it may give - as we have seen in the section on hedging an eight-month futures contract - quite good results in practice. But we cannot claim that it is optimal, and it would be unwise to put any reliance on estimates of hedging errors, analogous to those in Table 5, which are made from within the model.

The extrapolation model appears to be well specified for oil futures contracts at around eight months maturity. We have looked at two rival specifications, both involving three hedging contracts, one of which requires rebalancing alternate months. Both strategies remove the bulk of the price risk in a long-term commitment, with the bi-monthly strategy having an advantage in terms of lower transaction volume. The model fits less well at the very short end of the term structure.

Conclusions

Futures exchanges offer a range of contracts of different maturities that are designed to manage risk. An agent wishing to use futures contracts to hedge a long maturity exposure has a difficult problem in deciding how best to do it. This chapter has set out a robust and simple way of addressing the problem.

The empirical results suggest that one could expect to remove around 85% of the risk (as measured by the standard deviation of the hedge error) of a six-year oil supply commitment by hedging with medium maturity futures contracts (up to eight months). This is after allowing for errors in the estimation of the parameters of the model. We also used the extrapolation model to hedge an eight-month contract using contracts with three months or less to maturity. Despite evidence that the assumptions of the model are violated for these maturities, it substantially out-performs the Gibson–Schwartz model.

The robustness of the model derives from the paucity of assumptions made about the processes driving the term structure of commodity prices. No assumptions are made about the number of state variables, about the processes they follow, or about the way risk is priced. The key assumption is that the expected price at which the new long-dated contract starts trading is a linear function of the prices of existing contracts. While strictly inconsistent with some models of the term structure of commodity prices, evidence was presented suggesting that it can still give good results in practice.

An attractive feature of the model is the close relation between parameter estimation and the computation of hedge ratios. The model parameters are estimated by cross-sectional regression of prices of contracts of different maturities. The regression coefficients are chosen to minimise the difference between the actual and expected opening price of the new long-dated contract. Since it is these differences which, aggregated every time the hedge is rolled, constitute the error in the hedge, parameter estimation and hedging strategy are closely linked. This contrasts with the more traditional approach where the parameters are estimated by fitting the entire process. The model is then used to compute the optimal hedge ratio. The more direct approach is less vulnerable to problems arising from model misspecification.

In applying the model one would wish to choose suitable hedging instruments, taking account of the depth and liquidity of the market and the size of transaction costs. In this chapter we have started to explore alternative formulations, using different sets of contracts for hedging and different rebalancing frequency. The model assumes that the forecasting equation is correctly specified, so our results have been suggestive rather than definitive. It would be useful to set the model in a framework where different formulations could be compared. It would also be interesting to extend the empirical work in this chapter to look at markets on other assets.

Appendix A

PROOF OF LEMMA 1

The proof of the Lemma is by induction:

1) *Lemma 1 holds for* $t = T$:

$$E[F(T,T)|\mathbf{F}_T] = F(T,T)$$

so set

$$\alpha^{(0)} = 0;\ \beta_k^{(0)} = \begin{cases} 1 & \text{if } k = N \\ 0 & \text{otherwise} \end{cases} \tag{A1}$$

2) *If Lemma 1 holds for* $t = T - n$ *for some integer* n, *it holds for* $t = T - n - \eta$ *for any* $0 < \eta < 1$:

$$\begin{aligned} E[F(T,T)|\Omega_{T-n-\eta}] &= E[E[F(T,T)|\mathbf{F}_{T-n}]|\mathbf{F}_{T-n-\eta}] \\ &= E[\alpha^{(n)} + \beta^{(n)\prime}.\mathbf{F}_{T-n}|\mathbf{F}_{T-n-\eta}] \\ &= \alpha^{(n)} + \beta^{(n)\prime}.\mathbf{F}_{T-n-\eta} \end{aligned} \tag{A2}$$

The first line is the law of iterated expectations; the second is true by hypothesis; the third follows because of the martingale assumption.

3) *If Lemma 1 holds for* $t = T - n_+$ *(that is just after the shortest future matures and a new contract is listed) it holds for* $t = T - n$:

$$\begin{aligned} E[F(T,T)|\Omega_{T-n}] &= E[E[F(T,T)|\mathbf{F}_{T-n+}]|\mathbf{F}_{T-n}] \\ &= E[\alpha^{(n-1)} + \beta^{(n-1)\prime}.\mathbf{F}_{T-n+}|\mathbf{F}_{T-n}] \\ &= \alpha^{(n-1)} + \sum_{k=2}^{N} \beta_k^{(n-1)} F(T-n,\ T-n+N+1-k) \\ &\quad + \beta_1^{(n-1)}\left(\alpha + \sum_{k=1}^{N} \beta_k F(T-n,\ T-n+N-k)\right) \end{aligned} \tag{A3}$$

The first line is the law of iterated expectations, and the second is true by hypothesis. The third uses assumption [A6] to replace $F(T - n_+, T - n + N)$ by its expectation at time $T - n$. Assembling terms the proposition holds with

$$\alpha^{(n)} = \alpha^{(n-1)} + \beta_1^{(n-1)}\alpha$$

$$\beta_k^{(n)} = \begin{cases} \beta_{k+1}^{(n-1)} + \beta_1^{(n-1)}\beta_k & \text{if } k < N \\ \beta_1^{(n-1)}\beta_k & \text{if } k = N \end{cases} \tag{A4}$$

PROOF OF LEMMA 2

The change in Y at the turn of the month is caused by the difference between the expected opening price of the new N-month contract and its actual price. Since the weight of the contract in S_n is just $\beta_1^{(T-n-1)}$, Lemma 2 follows immediately.

PROOF OF PROPOSITION 1

If the agent follows some strategy Δ_t, her terminal wealth will be

$$\begin{aligned} W &= K - Y_T + \int_{t=0}^{T} \Delta_t'.d\mathbf{F}_t \\ &= K - Y_0 + \int_{t=0}^{T} \{\Delta_t'.d\mathbf{F}_t - dY_t\} \end{aligned} \tag{A5}$$

But from Lemmas 1 and 2:

$$\int_{t=0}^{T} dY_t = \int_{t=0}^{T} \beta^{(n)'}.d\mathbf{F}_t + \sum_{n=1}^{T-N} \beta_1^{(t-n-1)}\tilde{\varepsilon}_n \tag{A6}$$

so the agent's terminal wealth can be written as

$$W = K - Y_0 + \int_{t=0}^{T} \{\Delta_t - \beta^{(n)'}\}d\mathbf{F}_t - \sum_{n=1}^{T-N} \beta_1^{(t-n-1)}\tilde{\varepsilon}_n \tag{A7}$$

The integral and summation are both sums of independent mean zero random variables. The best the hedge can do is to set the integral equal to zero - hence the proposition. Any alternative strategy adds noise, and hence is dominated in the sense of second degree stochastic dominance.

PROOF OF PROPOSITION 2

Define $G^S(\mathbf{F},X,t)$ as the expected utility of terminal wealth of an agent with no commitments who has cash X at time t when the term structure of futures prices is $\mathbf{F}$, and who follows an optimal hedging strategy. Let that strategy be Δ^S.

It follows immediately that

$$G^S(\mathbf{F},X,t) = -\frac{1}{\lambda} e^{-\lambda X} f(\mathbf{F},t)$$

where $f(\mathbf{F},T) = 1$

$$G^S(\mathbf{F},X,t) = E\left[G^S(\mathbf{F} + d\mathbf{F}, X + \Delta^{S'}.d\mathbf{F}, t + dt)\middle|\mathbf{F}_t = \mathbf{F}, X_t = X\right] \tag{A8}$$

$$\Delta^S = \underset{\Delta}{\text{ArgMax}}\; E\left[G^S(\mathbf{F} + d\mathbf{F}, X + \Delta'.d\mathbf{F}, t + dt)\middle|\mathbf{F}_t = \mathbf{F}, X_t = X\right]$$

The first equation reflects the agent's exponential utility function; the second says that if the agent follows her chosen strategy, expected utility is a martingale, and the third equation says that the chosen strategy is optimal.

Now define the function

$$G^H(\mathbf{F},t) \equiv e^{\lambda(Y_t - K)}\, E\left[\exp\left(\lambda \sum_{n=n^*}^{T-N} \beta_1^{(n)'}\, \varepsilon_n\right)\middle|\mathbf{F}_t = \mathbf{F}\right] \tag{A9}$$

The significance of G^H is as follows: if futures prices follow a martingale then the expected utility of terminal wealth of an agent who has committed to supply 1 barrel of oil at time T and price K is $-G^H/\lambda$. The optimal hedging strategy in such a case is given by

$$\Delta^H = \beta^{(n)} \tag{A10}$$

To prove Proposition 2 we need to show that the expected utility function of an agent with a supply commitment when futures prices are not martingales is

$$G^* \equiv G^S G^H \tag{A11}$$

and the optimal hedging strategy is

$$\Delta^* \equiv \Delta^S + \Delta^H \tag{A12}$$

G^* satisfies the boundary condition

$$G^*(\mathbf{F},X,T) = G^S(\mathbf{F},X,T)\, G^H(\mathbf{F},T) = -\frac{1}{\lambda} e^{\lambda(F(T,T) - K - X)} \tag{A13}$$

Note that

$$G^H + dG^H = \exp\{\lambda\,\Delta^{H\prime}.d\mathbf{F}\}\,G^H(\mathbf{F},t) \qquad \text{(A14)}$$

except when t is an integer, and that when t is an integer $E[dG^H \mid F_t] = 0$.

Under trading strategy ΔG^* evolves as follows during the month (t non-integer):

$$G^*(\mathbf{F} + d\mathbf{F}, X + \Delta'.d\mathbf{F}, t + dt) = G^S(\mathbf{F} + d\mathbf{F}, X + (\Delta - \Delta^H)'.d\mathbf{F}, t + dt)\,G^H(\mathbf{F},t) \qquad \text{(A15)}$$

From this, two things follow immediately: first, the optimal trading strategy is Δ^*, second, under this strategy G^* is a martingale.

All we now need to prove the first part of the proposition is to show that at the turn of the month, when t is an integer, G^* is a martingale. But we know that G^S and G^H, are both martingale over the month end, so G^* will also be martingale provided that:

$$E\left[dG^S dG^H \middle| \mathbf{F}_t\right] = 0 \qquad \text{(A16)}$$

This proves the first part of the proposition.

For breakeven $G^*(\mathbf{F},X,0) = G^S(\mathbf{F},X,0)$, so $G^H(\mathbf{F},0) = 1$. The second part of the proposition then follows from equation (A8).

Appendix B

RELATIONSHIP BETWEEN THE EXTRAPOLATION MODEL AND DYNAMIC TERM-STRUCTURE MODELS

In a k-factor dynamic term-structure model there are k factors which follow a joint diffusion process. Using the standard no arbitrage arguments and specifying the form of the price of risk, one can in general express any derivative claim as a function (implicit or explicit) of the state variables. So in particular, there is a *pricing function* which relates the price of a futures contract to its maturity and to the value of the state vector **S**. Suppose that $N \geq k$, so that there are at least as many futures contracts trading at any one time as there are factors. Then the value of the state vector (which may not be directly observable) can be inferred exactly from prices of the traded contracts (which can be observed directly) by inverting the pricing function, under quite weak conditions.[10] The price of any other contingent claim can also be expressed in terms of the prices of traded contracts. In particular, the opening price of a contract is a function of the prices of the other contracts that are trading. For any integer t:

$$F(t, t + N) = h(\mathbf{F}_t) \qquad \text{(B1)}$$

where $h(\cdot)$ is some function which depends on the model. Comparing this with assumption [A6] shows two major differences. Equation (B1) holds exactly while [A6] has a noise term, and [A6] is linear in $\mathbf{F}_t$ while equation (B1) may not be. Now, the linearity assumption [A6] holds exactly (with zero error) if the pricing function can be written as a sum of no more than N multiplicatively separable functions of the state vector and time to maturity, in the following way:

$$F(t,n) = \alpha(n - t) + \sum_{i=1}^{N} f_i(\mathbf{S})\,g_i(n - t) \qquad \text{(B2)}$$

where $\alpha(\cdot)$ and the $g_i(\cdot)$ are functions of the time to maturity, and the $f_i(\cdot)$ are functions of the state variables.

To see that this is true, find the α, $\beta = \{\beta_j \mid j = 1,\ldots,n\}$ which solve the equation set

$$g_i(N) = \sum_{j=1}^{N} \beta_j g_i(N - j) \qquad \text{for } i = 1,\ldots,N$$

$$\alpha = \alpha(N) - \sum_{j=1}^{N} \beta_j\,\alpha(N - j) \qquad \text{(B3)}$$

(if F can be expressed as the sum of fewer than N multiplicative terms, the solution will not be unique and there will be an infinite set of hedging strategies) then it follows immediately that

$$F(t,t+N) = \alpha + \sum_{i=1}^{N} \beta_i F(t,t+N-i) \qquad \text{(B4)}$$

Equation (B2) may not hold exactly for the model of interest for any finite value of N. Reasoning informally, we may conjecture that the more closely the approximation holds, the better the extrapolation model will perform. To explore the implications of approximating the pricing function in this way, consider the GS model. The futures price is a function of S, the spot price and d, the convenience yield:

$$F(t,n) = Se^{A(n-t)-B(n-t)d} \qquad \text{(B5)}$$

where A(.) and B(.) are functions of time to maturity and depend on the parameters of the diffusion process and the price of risk. Using a Taylor's series expansion:

$$F(t,n) = \sum_{i=0}^{\infty} f_i(\mathbf{S})\, g_i(n-t)$$

where

$$f_i(\mathbf{S}) \equiv S\frac{(\bar{d}-d)^i}{i!} \qquad \text{(B6)}$$

$$g_i(n-t) \equiv e^{A(n-t)-B(n-t)\bar{d}}\, B(n-t)^i$$

and

$$\bar{d} \equiv E[d]$$

2. Effectiveness of the extrapolation method in a Gibson–Schwartz world

The extrapolation method is used to compute the optimal hedge for a five-year contract in a Gibson–Schwartz world. Either two or three hedging contracts with nine months or less to expiration are used. The graph shows the instantaneous volatility of the hedged portfolio as a function of Φ, $= \sigma_2^2/k^3$ where σ_2 is the volatility of the convenience yield and κ is its rate of mean reversion. The different observations correspond to the scenarios 1–4 in Table 1. The conjecture is that the lower the value of Φ, the closer the model is to linearity and the better the extrapolation method works.

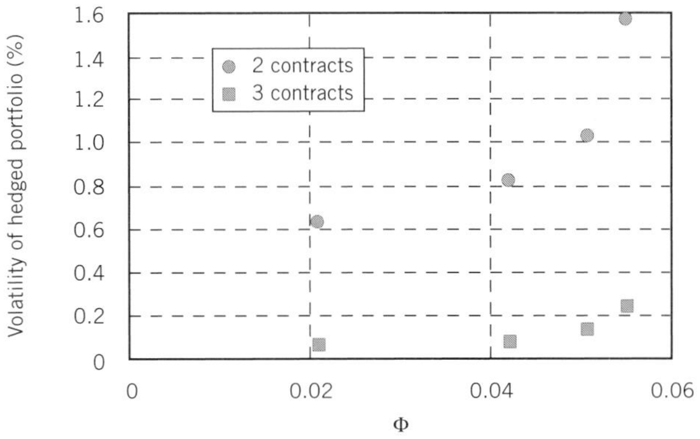

This has the form of equation (B2) with N = ∞. To measure the impact of ignoring higher order terms, note that the ratio of successive terms in the series is

$$\frac{f_i(\mathbf{S})g_i(n-t)}{f_{i-1}(\mathbf{S})g_{i-1}(n-t)} = \frac{(\bar{d}-d)}{i} B(n-t) \qquad \text{(B7)}$$

The unconditional variance of the convenience yield, d, is $\sigma_2^2/2\kappa$ where σ_2 is the volatility of the convenience yield and κ is the rate at which its mean reverts. $B(\tau)$ is equal to $(1-e^{-\kappa\tau})/\kappa$, which increases from 0 to $1/\kappa$ as τ goes from 0 to infinity. So the variance of the right hand side of equation (B7) is of order σ_2^2/κ^3, a ratio we denote by ϕ. We conjecture that the approximation of the infinite series by just N terms will be better the smaller is ϕ. The extrapolation model will work best when the convenience yield is not too volatile and any shocks die out quickly.

To test the conjecture that the quality of the hedge depends on ϕ we make use of the fact that Schwartz (1997) gives four different sets of estimates for the model parameters based on different sample periods and using different contract maturities. The statistic ϕ varies from 0.021 to 0.055, with a value of 0.042 in the base case. There is a reasonable correlation between the level of ϕ and the volatility of the hedged portfolio, as shown in Figure 2.

1 *The extension to flow contracts, where the agent contracts to deliver a certain flow of oil over a period, is done in the section "Simple extensions to the model".*

2 *It is convenient to assume that the date in the month when new contracts are introduced is the same as the date on which contracts mature, but nothing in the model hangs on this.*

3 *The extension to non-zero interest rates is covered in the section "Simple extensions to the model".*

4 *Tailing reduces the hedge ratios by a factor of* $-\mathbf{exp}\int_t^T r(u)du$.

5 *From equation (18) in Schwartz (1997), the forecasting equation takes the form:*

$$F(t,t+N) = kF(t,t+m)^{-\theta}\, F(t,t+n)^{1+\theta}$$

where k *and* θ *depend only on* N, m *and* n *and the model parameters.*

6 *The volatility of the hedged portfolio in general varies with the level of the convenience yield. The figures in Table 1 are root mean variances, where the variances are averaged across realisations of the convenience yield.*

7 *The holding of the one-month contract typically accounts for under 10% of the gross number of contracts held in the hedge portfolio.*

8 *The hedge ratios are functions of the coefficients of the forecasting equation. The standard errors are computed by approximating these functions by their first order Taylor series expansions around their estimated value.*

9 *The error is computed as:*

$$\sqrt{\sigma^2 \sum_{n=1}^{T-n} (\beta_1^{(T-n-1)})^2 + \sum_{n=1}^{T-N} (\beta^{(T-n-1)}.\mathrm{Cov}(d\mathbf{F}.d\mathbf{F}').\beta^{(T-n-1)})}$$

The first part is the unhedgable error in the extrapolated price that occurs when the hedge is rolled over, while the second is the variance of the change in the extrapolated futures price over the course of each month. The actual covariance matrix is used as an estimate of the true one. Implicitly the methodology assumes that changes in the futures price vector are serially independent, and their covariance is constant. Estimates made using the bi-monthly model coincide with the estimates in Table 5, which use the monthly model, to within 15%.

10 *For the pricing function to be invertible, the mapping of the state vector into the price space has to be one-to-one.*

BIBLIOGRAPHY

Baesel, J., and D. Grant, 1982, "Optimal Sequential Futures Trading", *Journal of Financial and Quantitative Analysis* 17, pp. 683–95.

Bessembinder, H., 1991, "Forward Contracts and Firm Value", *Journal of Financial and Quantitative Analysis*, 26, pp. 519–72.

Brennan, M. J., 1991, "The Price of Convenience and the Valuation of Commodity Contingent Claims" in D. Lund and B. Oksendal (eds.), *Stochastic Models and Option Values* (Elsevier Science Publishers).

Ederington, L. H., 1979, "The Hedging Performance of the New Futures Markets", *Journal of Finance* 34, pp. 157–70; reprinted as Chapter 2 of the present volume.

Engle, R., and C. Granger, 1987, "Co-integration and Error Correction: Representation, Estimation and Testing", *Econometrica* 55, pp.251–76.

Froot, K. A., D. S. Scharfstein and J. C. Stein, 1993, "Risk Management: Coordinating Corporate Investment and Risk Management Policies", *Journal of Finance* 48, pp. 1,629–58; reprinted as Chapter 7 of the present volume.

Gibson, R., and E. S. Schwartz, 1990, "Stochastic Convenience Yield and the Pricing of Oil Contingent Claims", *Journal of Finance* 45, pp. 959–76.

Grant D., 1984, "Rolling the Hedge Forward: an Extension", *Financial Management* 13, pp. 26–8.

Granger C. W. J., and P. Newbold, 1986, *Forecasting Economic Time Series,* second edn (New York: Academic Press).

Howard C.T., and L.J. D'Antonio, 1991, "Multiperiod Hedging Using Futures: a Risk Minimisation Approach in the Presence of Autocorrelation", *Journal of Futures Markets* 11, pp. 697–710.

Johansen, S., 1991, "Estimation and Hypothesis Testing of Co-integration Vectors in Gaussian Vector Autoregressive Models", *Econometrica* 59, pp. 1,551–80.

McCabe, G. M., and C. T. Franckle, 1983, "The Effectiveness of Rolling the Hedge Forward in the Treasury Bill Futures Market", *Financial Management* 12, pp. 21–9.

Mello, A., and J. Parsons, 1995, "Maturity Structure of a Hedge Matters: Lessons from the Metallgesellschaft Debacle", *Journal of Applied Corporate Finance* 8, pp. 106–20; reprinted as Chapter 12 of the present volume.

Ross S., 1995, "Hedging Long Run Commitments: Exercises in Incomplete Market Pricing", Working paper, Yale School of Management; reprinted as Chapter 19 of the present volume.

Schwartz, E. S., 1997, "Presidential Address: The Stochastic Behavior of Commodity Prices: Implications for Valuation and Hedging", *Journal of Finance* 52, pp. 923–73; reprinted as Chapter 20 of the present volume.

Smith, C. W., and R. M. Stulz, 1985, "The Determinants of Firms' Hedging Policies", *Journal of Financial and Quantitative Analysis* 20, pp. 391–405; reprinted as Chapter 6 of the present volume.

19

Hedging Long-Run Commitments: Exercises in Incomplete Market Pricing*

Stephen A. Ross

MIT

Futures markets rarely extend beyond a few years, but whether this formal incompleteness is economically relevant depends on whether short-term markets are adequate substitutes for the missing long-run ones. In a Markov state world, it is sufficient that the existing markets span the state variables, but, as a practical matter, the portfolios that span the states may involve arbitrarily large long and short positions that depend on errors in model estimation. We show that a class of simple policies exists that hedge the future delivery of a commodity and that these policies are robust to errors and optimal in the sense that beating them requires more information. These strategies are extensions of the familiar policies of "tailing the hedge", and they are compared both theoretically and empirically with the policy of rolling a fixed futures position examined in connection with the trading problems of Metallgesellschaft.

Introduction

Whether markets are incomplete or not seems to have passed from an issue of science to one of religion. It is a truism that markets are not complete in the obvious sense that there exist contingencies that have no clearly associated markets, but, it is not always immediately clear how meaningful this is for either pricing or efficiency. Some contingencies may have no markets but may be so trivial as to be insurable in the sense that their associated events are small and independent of the rest of the economy. Others may be replicable while not directly traded. However, whether replicable or not, one dimension along which markets are clearly incomplete is that of time. Most traded derivatives markets - futures and options - extend only a few years at most in time and, even when they are formally quoted further out, there is generally little or no liquidity in the far contracts.

Yet it is becoming increasingly common in the world of derivatives to be faced with long-run commitments while liquid markets only provide trading opportunities over shorter-run horizons. This was brought to the fore by the recent problems encountered by the German firm Metallgesellschaft, which had sold commitments to deliver oil products out as far as 10 years in the future while the current futures and derivatives markets offer liquidity only out about one year. This implies that rolling over short contracts - perhaps in combination with holding physicals - is the only available hedge. It is well known that if there are enough such markets to span changes in the information set, then markets can be completed by sequential trading. It is also well known that there are both practical and theoretical limitations that often make such approaches difficult to implement.

In a series of papers, Culp and Miller (1994a, 1994b), Mello and Parsons (1994, 1995), Edwards and Canter (1995), Brennan and Crew (1995) and Neuberger (1995) have analysed the Metallgesellschaft approach to hedging the contracts they sold. Metallgesellschaft had

Originally published in Economic Notes (1997), Banca Monte dei Paschi di Siena SpA, Italy. The author is grateful to Ken French, John Cox, Jon Ingersoll and Richard Roll for their helpful comments, to Mike Selman of Metallgesellschaft Corp for supplying the data and for helpful discussions, and to the participants in seminars at Northeastern University, the Wharton School, Warwick Business School UCLA and the Isaac Newton Institute at Cambridge. All errors are the author's responsibility.

sold contracts which – in their simplest form – called for the delivery of a constant monthly quantity of oil product at a prespecified constant price. To hedge these commitments, Metallgesellschaft constructed what Culp and Miller call a "stacked hedge". A stacked hedge is one in which short (one-month) futures contracts are established for the entire quantity that is deliverable over the life of the contract. In the following month, when the contracts mature, delivery is taken on just enough physical to satisfy the current delivery requirement and the remaining contracts are rolled over to the next month.

Culp and Miller display a number of features of this hedge and argue that it is a desirable way to insulate Metallgesellschaft from the movements of the market price. The other authors, who may be thought of collectively as critics of this position, offer alternative analyses. Our work differs from that of both Culp and Miller and their critics in that we employ the continuous martingale diffusion methodology to develop a general formula for the gains and losses from an arbitrary hedging strategy. We then use this result to prove the robustness of some simple exponential strategies, after having first shown that more complex exact hedging strategies are highly sensitive to potential measurement errors. We examine the Culp and Miller positions in this chapter as an example of the general problem of constructing robust hedges against positions that extend beyond the lives of marketed contracts and of the more general theory that we develop.

The first section sets up the basic futures structure for valuing contracts that extend beyond the limit of the traded contracts. The focus of the analysis is the simplest problem, that of hedging a fixed future delivery commitment. The next section extends the analysis to a model with multiple state variables – we argue that model misspecification and estimation problems render perfect hedges unattainable. The third section introduces and analyses the concept of a robust hedging strategy. The following section takes a careful look at some particular examples, including the stacked hedge and combinations of commitments. Finally a brief empirical analysis of the oil market is provided and a bootstrap procedure introduced to examine the performance of the hedges in the previous section; the concluding remarks follow.

The basic set-up

FUTURES CONTRACTS

Consider the following simple problem. A commitment has been made to deliver one unit of a commodity at a time T in the future. There exists a spot market for the commodity and futures markets that extend out to $t < T$. How should one go about hedging the commitment?

If the commodity is an asset – such as gold – then one simple approach is to hold the physical itself. In effect the physical is like a long-lived future contract. By purchasing it the holder is assured of having it at the future date less the insurance and storage costs plus any dividend equivalents it might generate in the period. For an asset like gold for which costs and dividends are essentially zero, the futures price would be driven by arbitrage to be the current spot price amortised up at the riskless term structure. Indeed the gold forward curve is often used as a surrogate forward interest curve.

At the other end of the spectrum would be a commodity such as wheat, which is so expensive to store that it is not so much an asset as it is a consumption good. Holding the physical over some period T that extends out years would be inefficient at best and infeasible at worst. For such a commodity, price is determined on an annual basis by the harvest cycle and, short of investing in the farm production process itself, there is probably no way to effect a hedge using current futures.

A commodity like oil is somewhere between gold and an agricultural commodity. Storage and transport costs are sufficiently high (and storage capacities sufficiently limited) that local – both geographical and in time – supply and demand conditions determine spot prices, but there is certainly some capacity for long-run storage. In the oil market, for example, the estimated cost of storage is currently about US\$0.25 per barrel per month on a base price of about US\$15 per barrel, or about 20% per year. In such cases we expect the future price to be linked to the current price, but weakly and declining with time. The expected shortfall between the change in the spot price of such a commodity and an appropriate (risk-adjusted) asset return is referred to as the convenience yield. This refers to the opportunity cost which the holder pays for the convenience of possessing the commodity.

For concreteness, assume that the spot price of the commodity follows an Itô process

$$dS = \mu(\cdot)dt + \sigma(\cdot)dz$$

where the drift, μ, and speed, σ, are arbitrary non-anticipating functions, and z is a Wiener process. Notice that the dynamics specified for the spot price are not the dynamics for a holder of the physical commodity. With storage costs, wastage and insurance, the actual change in value will be dS-Costs. As a practical matter, whether it is sensible to hold the physical depends on the costs of doing so.

It is in the specification of the drift and the volatility that the linkage between the present and the future is established. We will assume that the drift is mean-reverting and for the present we can leave the volatility arbitrary;

$$dS = k(\theta - S)dt + \sigma(\cdot)dz$$

where θ is the long-run level to which the spot price reverts and k is the speed of adjustment. By assuming a process for the spot price we are implicitly saying that it is the result of a complex equilibrium that takes account of storage and transport costs as well as demand, production and future supply considerations.

Since the commodity is not an asset in the same sense that a stock is an asset, ie, since the change in its value is not a rate of return, the usual rules of derivative asset pricing do not apply. Of course, a contingent contract whose payoff is the value of the spot commodity at date T is an asset. Similarly, if the asset pays no dividends over $[0,T]$ and can be costlessly stored (custodied), then the current value of the asset would just be the asset spot price, S. But, since the asset cannot be stored and held over the period except at high cost, it is not an asset in the typical sense and the usual risk-neutral hedging argument does not apply. In particular, we cannot value a contract derivative to the asset by taking the expected discounted terminal value subject to the martingale measure where $\mu = r$, the risk-free rate of interest. (Doing so would, of course, just result in a current value of S.)

However, we can price any derivative security by taking the discounted expectation under the martingale measure retaining the actual drift of the spot price. This produces the following result for the value of a long dated contract paying $S(T)$ at time T.

THEOREM 1 *Assuming that the stochastic process for the spot price is mean-reverting in the martingale measure or, equivalently, that there is no significant risk adjustment for the commodity price, the current value,* $P(S,T)$, *of an asset paying* $S(T)$ *at time* T *is given by*

$$P(S,T) = e^{-rT}\{Se^{-kT} + \theta(1 - e^{-kT})\}$$

PROOF From the basic no arbitrage theorem of finance (see Ross, 1976, 1978; Cox and Ross, 1976; or Harrison and Kreps, 1979), we know that there exists a martingale or risk-neutral measure, $E(\cdot)$, such that

$$P(S,T) = E\{e^{-\int r dt}\, S(T)\}$$

where the expectation is taken over the stochastic interest rate path and the stochastic commodity price.[1] For simplicity we assume that interest rates are uncorrelated with the commodity price and write the discount factor as e^{-rT}.[2] Hence

$$P(S,T) = e^{-rT}\{S(T)\}$$

Under the assumption of the theorem that there is no systematic risk correction for the commodity or, equivalently, if we are directly modelling its movement in the martingale measure, then we can compute the value by simply taking the expectation. To compute this expectation, let

$$m(t) \equiv E(S(t)\,|\,S,0)$$

Differentiating, we have

$$\begin{aligned} m(t + dt) &= E(S(t + dt)\,|\,S,0) \\ &= E(S(t) + dS_t\,|\,S,0) \\ &= m(t) + k(\theta - m(t))dt \end{aligned}$$

or

$$dm/dt = k(\theta - m)$$

which has the solution

$$m(T) = Se^{-kT} + \theta(1 - e^{-kT})$$

Hence

$$\begin{aligned} P(S,T) &= E\{e^{-\int rdt}\, S(T) \,|\, S,0\} \\ &= e^{-rT}\{Se^{-kT} + \theta(1 - e^{-kT})\} \end{aligned}$$

Despite its simplicity, this is an important result; for one thing it flips on its head the textbook intuition derived from option pricing theory. For this simple problem, the volatility is irrelevant and only the drift matters. We can use this result to find the delta of the optimal hedge

$$\delta \equiv \partial P / \partial S = e^{-(r+k)T} < 1$$

Notice that discounting together with mean-reversion implies that the optimal hedge involves holding less than a one-for-one position in the commodity. Continuing to assume that interest rates are uncorrelated with the commodity price, we have the following result.

THEOREM 2 *The associated futures price is the asset price without amortisation*

$$F(S,T) = Se^{-kT} + \theta(1 - e^{-kT})$$

PROOF The futures price is that price which makes the futures contract valueless. Under the assumption of no correlation with interest rates, Cox, Ingersoll and Ross (1978) show that this is the same as the forward price. But, the forward price is simply that price which, when discounted to the present equals the value of the asset.

Notice that for an asset, such as gold, q is zero and $k = -r$, resulting in $P(S,T) = S$ and $F(S,T) = Se^{rT}$.

If a T-period forward contract were available it would be held one for one as a perfect hedge. By contrast, a T-period futures contract would also be a perfect hedge, but it would be held e^{-rT} for one. The reason for this difference is that, as time moves on, the change in the value of the futures contract is the change in the futures price, which, in turn, reflects the change in the undiscounted expected future spot price. By contrast, the change in the value of the forward contract is not the change in the forward price, rather it is the change in the discounted expected future spot price which coincides with the change in the current value of the commitment.

Of course, inflationary expectations will generally impact both the value of the commodity and the level of interest rates. The mean-reversion model can also be interpreted as describing the real movement of the deflated commodity price. A simple approach to modelling this phenomenon is to adjust the long-run equilibrium value q to rise at an exponential rate. This is formally equivalent to modelling the real price as mean-reverting.

LEMMA A *If* π *denotes the anticipated inflation rate and if the real price,* $q = e^{-pt}S$, *follows the mean-reverting process*

$$dq = k^*(\theta^* - q)\,dt + \sigma^*(\cdot)\,dz$$

then the nominal spot price, S, *follows the process*

$$dS = k(\theta e^{\pi t} - S)\,dt + \sigma(\cdot)\,dz$$

where

$$\sigma = e^{\pi t}\sigma^*$$
$$k = k^* - \pi$$

and

$$\theta = k^*\,\theta^*/(k^* - \pi)$$

PROOF Differentiating, we have

$$\begin{aligned} dS &= d(e^{\pi t}q) \\ &= \pi S dt + e^{\pi t}[k^*(\theta^* - q)dt + \sigma^*(\cdot)dz] \\ &= k(\theta e^{\pi t} - S)dt + s(\cdot)dz \end{aligned}$$

Notice that the coefficient of mean-reversion is now in real terms, and that the long-run equilibrium is also adjusted. With this modification, applying Theorem 1 to the real price, the value of the contract is given by

$$\begin{aligned} P(S,T) &= e^{-rT}e^{\pi T}[Se^{-k^*T} + \theta^*(1 - e^{-k^*T})] \\ &= e^{-rT}[Se^{-kT} + \theta^*(e^{\pi T} - e^{-k^*T})] \end{aligned}$$

Adapting Theorem 2, the current futures price for a contract paying off at time t will be given by

$$F(S,T) = [Se^{-kT} + \theta^*(e^{\pi T} - e^{-kT})]$$

where we have altered the formula to allow for a time-dependent drift of π in the commodity price. Notice that as $t \to \infty$, $F(S,t) \to \theta^* e^{\pi t}$.

With or without an inflation adjustment, not only does the futures price differ from that for the future on an asset, but so, too, does the volatility of the futures price. If the commodity were an asset (with no payouts), then the futures price would be the current spot price amortised up at the discount rate

$$e^{rT}S$$

Clearly this is more volatile than the current spot price, although, since it is an expectation of the future spot price, we expect it to be less volatile than the realised future spot price. When S is not an asset price, this latter result will still hold, but since we have broken the arbitrage-enforced intertemporal link between spot prices we can no longer expect the futures price to be more volatile than the current spot price. Taking the Itô differential of the futures price, we see that

$$dF = e^{-kT}\sigma(\cdot)dz$$

Hence the volatility of the futures contract diminishes exponentially in time with the coefficient of mean-reversion. If there is no mean-reversion ($k = 0$), then the futures contract has the same volatility as the spot. Notice that, as expected, the futures price is driftless in the martingale measure

$$E\{dF\} = 0$$

The basis, $b(t)$, is defined as the difference between the futures contract price and the current spot price, S. If the forward curve is falling then the market is in backwardation and the basis is negative. A rising curve describes a market in contango with a positive basis. Ignoring the inflation adjustment for the moment, and applying our formula for the futures price we have the following result.

THEOREM 3 *The basis*

$$b(t) = (e^{-kt} - 1)(S - \theta)$$

The slope of the basis at the current time, 0, *is given by*

$$\begin{aligned} b_t = db/dt\,|_0 &= k(\theta - S) \\ &= E\{dS\}/dt \end{aligned}$$

PROOF Applying Theorem 2, we have

$$\begin{aligned} b(t) &= F(S,t) - S \\ &= \{Se^{-kt} + \theta(1 - e^{-kt})\} - S \\ &= (e^{-kt} - 1)(S - \theta) \end{aligned}$$

and taking the derivative at the origin produces the second result.

Thus, the market will be in backwardation if the current spot price is above the long-run equilibrium value, θ, and in contango if it is below that equilibrium value.[3]

The stochastic process for the spot price must respect the bounds imposed by the costs of holding the commodity. If the costs are negligible then the familiar arbitrage between the physical and the futures applies. In general, the market contango is limited by the interest and storage costs of the commodity:

$$b(t) \leq (e^{rt} - 1) + C(t)$$

If the commodity is in elastic supply, then backwardation is limited as well by the ability to borrow physicals, ie, acquire them forward, and sell them spot. Indeed, backwardation is a clear sign of a commodity that has an inelastic spot market; only some external convenience yield can justify storage when futures purchase is cheaper.

If we now wished to hedge the long-term commitment using the short futures, we could hold a delta hedge futures contract position,

$$\begin{aligned}\text{delta hedge} &= e^{-rT} e^{-kT}/e^{-kt} \\ &= e^{-rT - k(T-t)}\end{aligned}$$

and adjust the hedge over time by rolling these contracts at or before their maturity. With the inflation-adjusted model the delta hedge is unchanged, but, using Lemma A, the adjustment of k means that the sensitivity of the value of the commitment to changes in the current spot price can also be written as

$$e^{-(r+k)T} = e^{-(r+k^*)T}$$

where $r = r - \pi$, the real rate of interest.

Interestingly, the delta hedge is independent of the spot price and the long-run equilibrium value, θ. It is also independent of the process for the volatility, which could depend on a variety of state variables.

How well does this hedge strategy perform? – ie, if we roll over these contracts, constantly maintaining the delta hedge, what will be the value of the position at time T and how will this compare with the value of the contract at that time, $S(T)$? Under the maintained premise that the delta hedge is always in place and that the process is as we have specified it, the hedge will exactly replicate the value of the commodity at time T, $S(T)$. The critical assumptions behind this result are those that guarantee that the Markov nature of the process is properly modelled. It is that which insures that the short futures and the long-dated contract differ only in their sensitivity to the underlying spot price.

In the next section we will extend the analysis to the multi-state case in which the spot price is no longer a sufficient statistic for its future development.

Extensions and problems

MULTIPLE STATE VARIABLES

Suppose that we drop the strict Markov assumption and consider a richer process that involves a variety of state variables for which the current spot price is not a sufficient statistic. Let x denote the vector of state variables. Assuming that x follows a vector Markov process, we will posit the dynamics

$$dx = K(\theta - x)\,dt + \Sigma dz$$

where K denotes a diagonal matrix of positive constants, θ is a vector of positive constants, Σ is a diagonal matrix with entries θ_i that are arbitrary functions of x, and dz is a vector of independent Wiener processes. The state vector x exhibits mean-reversion with θ as its long-run equilibrium value. (Notice that this particular specification of the state dynamics is quite general since any linear transformation is equivalent.) For concreteness and without loss of generality we will assume that the spot price

$$S = \Sigma\, x_i$$

With this specification, the value of the contract committing delivery of one unit of the commodity at date T is given be the following generalisations of Theorems 1 and 2.

THEOREM 4 *Following the same pricing assumptions as those of Theorem 1, the current value of an asset paying* $S(T)$ *at time* T *when the spot price follows the multi-state process is given by*

$$P(x) = E\{e^{-rT} S(T) \mid x\}$$
$$= e^{-rT} \Sigma \left[x_i e^{-k_i T} + \theta_i (1 - e^{-k_i T})\right]$$

and the futures price is given by

$$F(x,t) = \Sigma \left[x_i e^{-k_i T} + \theta_i (1 - e^{-k_i T})\right]$$

PROOF A straightforward extension of that for Theorem 1.

Clearly the way to hedge this contract exactly is to hedge each of the state variables. But that is the essence of the problem we face when there are inadequate futures and options markets. In practice it is not simply a question of numbers, which is to say that we can hedge if we merely have more futures contracts traded than there are relevant state variables. While this is true in theory, in practice the available contracts are generally bunched in time and relatively close substitutes. This implies a practical problem of multicollinearity that has implications, among other matters, for position sizes, measurement errors and trading costs in using such contracts to hedge state movements.

Nevertheless, as a matter of theory, if there are m distinctly dated futures contracts, P_j, with $j = 1,\ldots, m$ with associated maturities $T_1 < \ldots < T_m$, then these contracts will span the m state variables. Letting H denote the matrix of delta sensitivities

$$H = \left(\frac{\partial P_j}{\partial x_i}\right) = (e^{-k_i T_j})$$

and if α denotes the replicating portfolio of futures contracts, we have

$$H\alpha = \left(\frac{\partial P}{\partial x_i}\right) = (e^{-(r+k_i)T}) = e^{-(r+k)T}$$

where $e^{-(r+k)T}$ denotes the vector of contract sensitivities to the m underlying state variables. Inverting we can solve for α

$$\alpha = H^{-1} e^{-(r+k)T}$$

The special case of $m = 2$ is probably of most importance and in this case the solution for α is

$$\alpha_1 = [e^{-((r+k_1)T + k_2T_2)} - e^{-((r+k_2)T + k_1T_2)}]/\det$$

and

$$\alpha_2 = [e^{-((r+k_2)T + k_1T_1)} - e^{-((r+k_1)T + k_2T_1)}]/\det$$

where

$$\det = e^{-(k_1T_1 + k_2T_2)} - e^{-(k_2T_1 + k_1T_2)}$$

is the determinant and can be used as a measure of multicollinearity.[4]

The seeming precision of the above solution is misleading. To illustrate the problem, Table 1 displays the solutions for a particular range of parameter values. (To avoid the hedge matrix, H, being singular. the parameters were offset by 0.01.) Letting the interest rate be 7%, $k_1 = 0.5$ and $k_2 = 0.7$, $T_1 = 1$ year, $T_2 = 2$ years and $T = 10$ years produces hedge values of $\alpha_1 = -0.020$ and $\alpha_2 = 0.042$. As a single-state model, using $k_1 = 0.5$ and hedging using the one-year contract, the proper current hedge is 0.0055 contracts. By contrast, changing k_1 to 0.6 and keeping k_2 at 0.7 changes the single-state hedge to 0.0022 while the two-state hedges change to $\alpha_1 = -0.012$ and $\alpha_2 = 0.025$. Thus, a 0.1 (20%) change in the coefficient of mean-reversion causes both the single-state hedge and the two-state hedges to approximately halve in magnitude. Notice, too, that the two-state case differs significantly from the single-state model in the size of the positions. For some parameter values, the individual positions are larger in absolute values by a factor of 10 or more.

If there is no mean-reversion, then the hedge in the single-state case is simply the current discounted value 10 years out, 0.497 (= e^{-1}), as we showed in the first section of the chapter. In general, as the mean-reversion parameter increases, the single hedge declines. This is to be expected since the higher the mean-reversion, the less of a link there is between the current value of the short contract and that of the longer one. The same occurs with the two-state case. As can be seen in Table 1, the entries in the lower right corner are all nearly zero and there is a general tendency for the coefficients to decline in absolute value as both k_1 and k_2 increase.

While the hedges themselves are very sensitive to variations in the estimated parameters and, therefore, to errors in the parameters, it remains possible that the hedge itself could be relatively insensitive. In general, multicollinearity is more of a problem for determining the hedge positions than for the hedge itself. To understand this distinction better, we can look at a limiting case as $|T_m - T_1| \rightarrow 0$. The positions, $\|\alpha\| = \|H^{-1}e^{-(r+k)T}\| \rightarrow \infty$, as H becomes increasingly ill-conditioned, but, the hedge sensitivities remain at $H\alpha = e^{-(r+k)T}$. Consider, then, what happens to the hedge if we err in the estimation of, say, k_1. The true hedge sensitivity for the first state changes as

$$\left(H\frac{\partial \alpha}{\partial k_1}\right)_1 = -Te^{-(r+k_1)T} + \Sigma T_j e^{-k_1 T_j} \alpha_j$$

As $|T_m - T_1| \rightarrow 0$, $T_j - T_1$ for all j, and since the second term in the above equation converges to the first row of H, and $\alpha = H^{-1}e^{-(r+k)T}$, we have the elasticity

$$\eta = \frac{\left(H\frac{\partial \alpha}{\partial k_1}\right)_1}{(H\alpha)_1} - (T_1 - T)$$

Table 1. Table of hedge holdings for different choices of mean-reversion for single- and two-state variables

Single-state variable hedge

k_1	0.000	0.100	0.200	0.300	0.400	0.500	0.600	0.700	0.800	0.900	1.000
Hedge:	0.497	0.202	0.082	0.033	0.014	0.006	0.002	0.001	0.000	0.000	0.000

Two-state variable hedges

Hedge 1:

k_2 \ **k_1**	**0.000**	**0.100**	**0.200**	**0.300**	**0.400**	**0.500**	**0.600**	**0.700**	**0.800**	**0.900**	**1.000**
0.01	−3.799	−2.473	−1.695	−1.216	−0.909	−0.704	−0.559	−0.455	−0.376	−0.316	−0.268
0.101	−2.590	−1.608	−1.052	−0.724	−0.522	−0.391	−0.304	−0.242	−0.197	−0.163	−0.137
0.201	−1.784	−1.053	−0.654	−0.428	−0.294	−0.212	−0.159	−0.123	−0.098	−0.080	−0.066
0.301	−1.287	−0.725	−0.428	−0.266	−0.174	−0.120	−0.086	−0.065	−0.050	−0.040	−0.033
0.401	−0.966	−0.523	−0.295	−0.174	−0.108	−0.071	−0.049	−0.035	−0.026	−0.020	−0.016
0.501	−0.750	−0.393	−0.213	−0.120	−0.071	−0.044	−0.029	−0.020	−0.014	−0.011	−0.008
0.601	−0.598	−0.305	−0.160	−0.086	−0.049	−0.029	−0.018	−0.012	−0.008	−0.006	−0.004
0.701	−0.487	−0.243	−0.124	−0.065	−0.035	−0.020	−0.012	−0.007	−0.005	−0.003	−0.002
0.801	−0.404	−0.198	−0.099	−0.050	−0.026	−0.014	−0.008	−0.005	−0.003	−0.002	−0.001
0.901	−0.339	−0.164	−0.081	−0.040	−0.020	−0.011	−0.006	−0.003	−0.002	−0.001	−0.001
1.01	−0.284	−0.136	−0.066	−0.032	−0.016	−0.008	−0.004	−0.002	−0.001	−0.001	0.000

Hedge 2:

k_2 \ **k_1**	**0.000**	**0.100**	**0.200**	**0.300**	**0.400**	**0.500**	**0.600**	**0.700**	**0.800**	**0.900**	**1.000**
0.01	4.295	2.957	2.170	1.687	1.377	1.169	1.023	0.918	0.839	0.778	0.729
0.101	3.086	2.000	1.385	1.022	0.798	0.654	0.557	0.489	0.439	0.402	0.373
0.201	2.280	1.387	0.899	0.622	0.459	0.359	0.294	0.250	0.220	0.197	0.181
0.301	1.783	1.025	0.623	0.404	0.280	0.206	0.161	0.132	0.112	0.099	0.089
0.401	1.463	0.801	0.460	0.280	0.181	0.126	0.093	0.072	0.059	0.051	0.044
0.501	1.246	0.657	0.360	0.207	0.126	0.082	0.056	0.042	0.033	0.027	0.023
0.601	1.094	0.560	0.295	0.162	0.093	0.057	0.037	0.025	0.019	0.015	0.012
0.701	0.984	0.492	0.252	0.133	0.073	0.042	0.025	0.016	0.011	0.008	0.007
0.801	0.900	0.442	0.221	0.113	0.060	0.033	0.019	0.011	0.007	0.005	0.004
0.901	0.836	0.405	0.199	0.099	0.051	0.027	0.015	0.008	0.005	0.003	0.002
1.01	0.781	0.373	0.180	0.088	0.044	0.023	0.012	0.006	0.004	0.002	0.001

The first line gives the hedge using a one-year contract with a single-state variable as its mean-reversion is changed. The arrays give the range of hedge holdings of a one-year contract and a two-year contract for differing mean-reversion coefficients, k_1 and k_2. The contract to be hedged is a 10-year future and the first contract is a one-year future and the second is a two-year future. The interest rate is 7% per annum.

Thus, while the percentage elasticity of the hedge position with respect to an error on the estimation of k_1 is bounded above as H becomes singular, it can be quite large, magnifying the impact of errors on hedge sensitivity as well as the hedge positions.

If these results are, perhaps, better than might be expected, no such comfort is available for the more significant misspecification error of using a single one-year future to hedge in a world with two-state variables. If the first reversion is measured correctly then it can be hedged correctly. By contrast, using the single hedge of 0.0055 one-year futures from Table 1 produces an exposure to the second factor of $0.0055\, e^{-k(2)} = 0.00274$ compared to the desired exposure of $e^{-(r+k2T)} = 0.00045$, a sixfold difference.

Of course, multicollinearity is only a problem when parameters cannot be measured exactly, and, unfortunately, this is the rule. First, there are the usual errors associated with measuring means; the standard errors only diminish asymptotically with longer time series, which, in turn, raises issue of modelling non-stationarities. Second, each new instrument brings its own idiosyncratic pricing error and multicollinearity magnifies the impact of these errors.

Our inability, or, rather, the imprecision in our attempt to exactly hedge suggests that it might be useful to consider hedges which, while not perfect, may be very good. In the next section we will examine the properties of one class of hedges and analyse the implications of not being able to hedge the residual from the projection on to a single process.

Robust hedges

As we have seen in the second section, perhaps the most significant difficulty with synthetically hedging long-dated contracts is the burden it places on correct modelling. This, in turn, puts a premium on robust or process-free replication techniques, and in this section we will study one such class of hedge procedures.

Consider the problem of hedging a commitment to deliver a single unit of the spot commodity at a time T that extends beyond the limit of the traded futures contracts. We will confine our attention to non-anticipating strategies that involve continually rolling the shortest - an infinitesimal - futures contract (even though we could establish a finite one as we approach the horizon). We will also restrict ourselves to policies that guarantee possession of a unit of the commodity at time T and, we will refer to these policies as "convergent" hedges. Notice that such strategies are not self-financing; indeed, their costs are the costs of acquiring the commodity.

Formally, a convergent hedge is a non-anticipating policy, $\phi(t)$, satisfying

$$\phi(T) = 1$$

for sure, where ϕ may be state-dependent but where the Itô differential, $d\phi$, is well defined. Often we will specialise these policies to the deterministic exponential form

$$\phi(t) = e^{-\delta(T-t)}$$

As we have already seen, with a mean-reverting process such a strategy is equivalent to the optimal (delta) hedge for the forward delivery problem. For now, though, we are interested in more general results and will not assume a particular process for the spot price.

THEOREM 5 *If a convergent hedge is used to hedge a forward commitment to deliver the commodity at a price of* p *at time* T, *and if the current price is* S, *then the discounted profits of the strategy are given by*

$$\Pi(\phi) = e^{-rT}(p - S) - \int_{|0,T|} e^{-rt}\left[(d\phi - r\phi dt)(S_t - S) + \phi_s\sigma^2 dt + \phi b_t dt\right]$$

where b_t is the derivative of the basis at time t evaluated from the spot contract (t = 0).

PROOF Letting $f_{t+dt|t}$ denote the instantaneous futures price, we have

$$P(\phi) = e^{-rT}(p - S_T) + \int_{|0,T|} e^{-rt}\{\phi(S_{t+dt} - \phi_{t+dt|t})\}$$

$$= e^{-rT}(p - S_T) + \int_{|0,T|} e^{-rt}\phi\{dS - b_t dt\}$$

$$= e^{-rT}(p - S_T) + e^{-rT}S_T - \phi(0)S - \int_{[0,T]} e^{-rt}(d\phi - r\phi dt)S_t - \int_{[0,T]} e^{-rt}d\phi dS - \int_{[0,T]} e^{-rt}\phi b_t dt$$

$$= e^{-rT}p - \phi(0)S - \int_{[0,T]} e^{-rt}(d\phi - r\phi dt)(S_t - S) - e^{-rT}S + \phi(0)S - \int_{[0,T]} e^{-rt}\phi_s\sigma^2 dt - \int_{[0,T]} e^{-rt}\phi b_t dt$$

$$= e^{-rT}(p - S) - \int_{[0,T]} e^{-rt}\left[(d\phi - r\phi dt)(S_t - S) + \phi_s\sigma^2 dt + \phi b_t dt\right]$$

Theorem 5 provides a useful decomposition of the profits from the hedge. The first term of the profit is the discounted value of the commitment at the current spot price. The second term integrates two separate effects. The first is the accumulated interest cashflow from continuously rolling the hedge. The hedge is in or out of the money to the extent that the current price differs from the starting price, and it is amortised to the extent that it is growing at a rate faster than it is being discounted.

Another way to understand this term is to imagine maintaining an account whose unit value at any time is given by $S_1 - S$, the difference between the current value of the commodity and its initial price. Since the position at time t is ϕ, $r\phi(S_t - S)\,dt$ is the interest earned on the position. Since the position is changing at the rate, $d\phi$, $-d\phi$ is the rate at which the position is being sold and $-d\phi(S_t - S)$ is the cash generated. The additional term, $d\phi dS$, arises from integration by parts with the stochastic integral formulation. With a stochastic policy, ϕ, at each instant of time, a portion of the change $d\phi$ is certain and a portion is stochastic. That portion that is stochastic is correlated with the local change in the spot price and this produces a locally certain addition to the account of $\phi_s\sigma^2 dt$. Notice that this term only arises if ϕ depends on S.

The second term under the integral is the basis loss. If the market is in contango then the strategy is continually rolled at a loss. To see this, recall that the first term captures the impact of the changing spot price, so the basis term is the gain or loss independent of concurrent spot price changes. Imagine, then, rolling a one-month futures contract with an unchanging spot price in a market with persistent contango. Each month a futures position that was established at a price that exceeded the spot price by the basis is rolled at a loss equal to the last month's basis.

The exponential case is of particular interest because of its tractability and its richness. Letting

$$\phi(t) = e^{-\delta(T-t)}$$

and applying Theorem 5, we have

$$\Pi(\delta) = e^{-rT}(p - S) - e^{-\delta T}\int_{[0,T]} e^{(\delta - r)t}\left[(\delta - r)(S_t - S) + b_t\right]dt$$

(i) "Tailing the Market", $\delta = r$

The strategy of holding a futures position equal to the discounted value of the commitment is well known to participants in the futures market and is called "tailing the market". For this strategy the hedge is exposed only to basis risk

$$\Pi(r) = e^{-rT}(p - S) - e^{-rT}\int_{[0,T]} b_t dt$$

This is generally stochastic and shifts as the slope of the futures curve changes.

(ii) A constant hedge, $\delta = 0$

This case corresponds to maintaining and rolling an unchanging unit futures position. In this case

$$\Pi(0) = e^{-rT}(p - S) + \int_{[0,T]} e^{-rt}\left[r(S_t - S) - b_t\right]dt$$

This strategy can be expected to be riskier than the first to the extent to which the basis does not convey positively with the spot price.

(iii) The spot price follows a mean-reverting process
For a process with mean-reverting drift, we can solve for the basis slope as

$$b_t = k(\theta - S_t)$$

Hence

$$\Pi(\delta) = e^{-rT}(p - S) - e^{-\delta T} \int_{[0,T]} e^{(\delta - r)t}[(\delta - r)(S_t - S) + k(\theta - S_t)]\,dt$$

Setting $\delta = r + k$ we have

$$\begin{aligned}\Pi(r + k) &= e^{-rT}(p - S) - e^{-(r+k)T} \int_{[0,T]} e^{kt}[k(S_t - S) + k(\theta - S_t)]\,dt \\ &= e^{-rT}\{(p - \theta) - e^{-kT}(S - \theta)\} \\ &= e^{-rT}\{p - F(S,T)\} \\ &= e^{-rT}p - P(S,T)\end{aligned}$$

that is fully hedged, ie, riskless.

This hedge locks in the difference between the discounted value of the contract price and the current value of the commitment to receive $S(T)$, and generates a profit or a loss depending on whether the commitment price, p, is greater or less than the long-term futures price, $F(S,T)$. This difference, in turn, depends on the relation among the contract price, p, the long-run equilibrium level, θ, and the current spot price, S. If both p and S exceed the equilibrium level, θ, then a profit is assured.[5] Clearly, any strategy that can achieve a higher profit than $\Pi(r + k)$ must risk a relative loss.

THEOREM 6 *With a mean-reverting process, the maximum riskless profit that can be achieved is given by*

$$\Pi(r + k) = e^{-rT}\{p - F(S,T)\} = e^{-rT}p - P(S,T)$$

PROOF The proof is a bit subtle. We have shown that the $\delta = r + k$ strategy produces a value of S_T at time T - exactly offsetting the commitment to deliver a unit of the commodity at time T. To offer a riskless greater profit, an alternative strategy would have to provide at least a value of S_T at time T and do so at a cost less than $P(S,T)$. But combining the two strategies would provide an arbitrage (which is ruled out by the existence of the martingale measure).

Notice that the argument of the proof is not quite the same as the one which would be invoked if futures markets actually existed out to time T. If that were the case, then we could simply argue that the futures price had to be unique to avoid arbitrage. Here we argue one synthetic strategy cannot dominate another.

(iv) General stochastic price processes
Following the approach used in the earlier section on extensions and problems, if the model has two or more relevant state variables, market limitations or estimation difficulties or simple model misspecification might still lead us to hedge with a single futures contract. As a consequence, there will be a residual volatility, e, which is not hedged. If we knew the actual structure of the dynamic process, then the t period futures hedge that minimises the residual volatility will be the regression coefficient of the contract price change on the futures change:

$$\begin{aligned}\beta &= \mathrm{cov}(dP, dF) / \mathrm{var}(dF) \\ &= e^{-rt}\frac{\sum \sigma_i^2 e^{-k_t(t+T)}}{\sum \sigma_i^2 e^{-2k_t t}}\end{aligned}$$

and the residual volatility of the regression and the hedge will be:

$$\sigma^2(e) = e^{-rT}\sum \sigma_i^2 e^{-2k_t T} - e^{-rT}\frac{(\sum \sigma_i^2 e^{-k_t(t+T)})^2}{\sum \sigma_i^2 e^{-2k_t t}}$$

This generalises the delta hedge in the basic set-up section of this chapter, and, as the maturity of the future $t - 0$, the hedge

$$\beta - e^{-rT} \frac{\sum \sigma_i^2 e^{-k_i T}}{\sum \sigma_i^2}$$

which is the relevant hedge for the short rolled futures we are considering.

Unfortunately, though, since we do not know the actual underlying dynamics of the spot price we approximate it with a mean-reverting structure

$$dS = k(\theta - S)dt + \sigma(\cdot)dz$$

in which $-k$ is the regression coefficient of dS on the spot price, S,

$$-k = \frac{\sigma^2(\sum k_i(\theta_i - x_i), \sum x_i)}{\sigma^2(\sum x_i)}$$

Even if the basis is not mean-reverting, we can still improve the hedge properties by removing that portion of the basis that is mean-reverting. If we regress the basis risk on the spot level:

$$b_t = k(\theta - S_t) + \epsilon_t$$

then case (iii) generalises to:

$$\Pi(r + k) = e^{-rT}\{(p - \theta) - e^{-kT}(S - \theta)\} - e^{-(r+k)T}\int_{|0,T|} e^{kt}\epsilon_t dt$$

This same formula is also appropriate for incorporating errors in the basis process into the residual, ϵ_t.

A special case is where there is no discernible correlation between the basis and the spot price, ie, mean-reversion $k = 0$:

$$\Pi(r + k) = \Pi(r) = e^{-rT}(p - S) - e^{-rT}\int_{|0,T|} \epsilon_t dt$$

The optimality results we have obtained can be generalised to comparisons with a broad class of strategies, and we will conclude with a general theorem that validates our focus on the exponential strategies. This theorem displays an important aspect of their robustness.

LEMMA B *Let* $\phi(t)$ *and* $\psi(t)$ *be two feasible, non-anticipating, convergent strategies. It follows that the profit function is affine in the strategies,*

$$\Pi(\phi) = e^{-rT}(p - S_T) + \int_{|0,T|} e^{-rt}\phi\sigma(\cdot)dz$$

which implies that

$$E\{\Pi(\phi)\} = e^{-rT}(p - E(S_T))$$

and, therefore, the strategies have identical values,

$$E\{P(\phi) - \Pi(\psi)\} = 0$$

PROOF From the proof of Theorem 5. we have

$$\Pi(\phi) = e^{-rT}(p - S_T) + \int_{|0,T|} e^{-rt}\phi\{dS - b_t dt\}$$

For any process, we have that

$$b_t dt = E(S + dS) - S = E(dS)$$

hence

$$\Pi(\phi) = e^{-rT}(p - S_T) + \int_{[0,T]} e^{-rt}\phi\{E(dS) + \sigma(\cdot)dz - b_t dt\}$$

$$= e^{-rT}(p - S_T) + \int_{[0,T]} e^{-rt}\phi\,\sigma(\cdot)dz$$

The remaining results are now immediate.

Lemma B is not surprising from the efficient markets perspective. Since valuation is by the martingale expectation, all strategies that simply take a sequence of futures positions are taking zero value positions at all points of time. Despite its simplicity, though, Lemma B is a powerful tool for deriving some unexpected results. For example, it is now possible to bypass the algebra and conclude immediately that the expectation of all δ strategies is independent of δ. Furthermore, we can establish the following important result.

THEOREM 7 All convergent strategies have identical exposure to residual basis risk, ϵ_t.

PROOF From Lemma B, the difference between any two convergent strategies depends only on $z(t)$.

We can now generalise Theorem 6 to the case where there is an uncorrelated residual basis risk.

THEOREM 8 If $\epsilon(t)$ is uncorrelated with $z(t)$, then the exponential strategy, $\delta = r + k$, has minimum risk among all possible strategies that are uncorrelated with $\epsilon(t)$.

PROOF From Lemma B, if we let ϕ denote the difference between an alternative strategy and the exponential strategy, $\delta = r + k$, then with obvious notation we have

$$E\{\Pi(\delta + \phi) - \Pi(\delta)\} = 0$$

It follows that

$$E\{\Pi(\delta)[\Pi(\delta + \phi) - \Pi(\delta)]\}$$

$$= E\left\{\left[e^{-rT}\{(p - \theta) - e^{-kT}(S - \theta)\} - e^{-(r+k)T}\int_{[0,T]} e^{kt}\epsilon_t dt\right]\left[\int_{[0,T]} e^{-rt}\phi\,\sigma(\cdot)dz\right]\right\}$$

$$= E\left\{\left[e^{-(r+k)T}\int_{[0,T]} e^{kt}\epsilon_t dt\right]\left[\int_{[0,T]} e^{-rt}\phi\,\sigma(\cdot)dz + \right]\right\}$$

$$= 0$$

Hence, $\Pi(\delta + \phi)$ equals $\Pi(\delta)$ plus a mean zero and uncorrelated term, $\Pi(\delta + \phi) - \Pi(\delta)$. This verifies that $\Pi(\delta)$ has minimum variance amongst all such strategies.

In satisfying the conditions of Theorem 8, ϵ_t could have a quite complex dynamic structure. All that is required is that it be intertemporally uncorrelated with the integral of the Brownian path over time. For example, since ϵ_t is the residual from the regression on the current spot price, it is orthogonal to S_t. If it is also independent of past and future S_t and if the volatility depends only on the current spot price, then the conditions of Theorem 8 will be satisfied. Theorem 8 is important because it verifies that one must know something about the stochastic properties of the residual to better the delta hedge. To do so, one must find observable variables in addition to the spot price that can be employed to better explain the basis.

The limitation that the strategy not depend on ϵ_t rules out dynamic strategies that respond reactively to past movements in ϵ_t, ie, we are restricting ourselves to strategies that are path-independent in ϵ_t. Path-dependent strategies can produce a rich menu of terminal profit distributions limited only by the requirement that they hedge the final unit position. But, the motivation behind examining robust strategies is precisely the inability to model the process for ϵ_t. Insofar as we have correctly modelled the stochastic process for the basis (in the martingale pricing measure) – and, equivalently, the drift of the spot price – then ϵ_t is that portion we have not been able to model. This perspective is likely to render the issue of path-dependent strategies moot.

Stacked hedges

In recent series of papers, Culp and Miller (1994a, 1994b) have examined the hedging policies of Metallgesellschaft in the oil markets. Briefly, Metallgesellschaft had committed to the delivery over a period of time, say 10 years, of a fixed amount of oil per month. To hedge this commitment it had engaged in a policy of what Culp and Miller refer to as a stacked hedge. In such a hedge at any moment of time a position is taken in a short futures contract equal to the entire remaining delivery commitment. For example, if the total commitment were to deliver 1 million barrels per month, then when there are eight years remaining on the contracts, $8 \times 12 = 96$ million barrels of short futures would be maintained (rolled as they mature).[6]

THE STACKED HEDGE

For the purpose of analysis we will set aside issues of basis risk or the practicalities of trading such a large position. The stacked hedge may sound complex, but it is simply the sum of a set of individual constant hedges for each delivery month. We have already examined the properties of the constant hedge in the case $\delta = 0$ in the previous section. In what follows we will use the term δ-stacked hedge to refer to a hedge that is composed of the sum of individual hedges each of which increases to its maturity at the rate δ, and we will refer to the constant, $\delta = 0$, hedge as simply a stacked or a constant hedge. Applying the results obtained in the previous section, we obtain the following.

THEOREM 9 Assume that we have to hedge a continuous commitment to deliver a commodity at a price of p and at a unit flow rate over the interval $[0,T]$. If we follow a δ-stacked hedge with δ as the rate of increase in each monthly hedge over time, then the discounted profits on the hedge strategy are given by:

$$\Pi_s(\delta) = ([1 - e^{-rT}]/r)(p - S) - \int_{[0,T]} [(e^{-\delta t} - e^{-\delta T})/\delta] e^{(\delta - r)T} [(\delta - r)(S_t - S) + b_t] \, dt$$

and in the special case of $\delta = 0$, we have the Culp and Miller stacked hedge

$$\Pi_s(0) = ([1 - e^{-rT}]/r)(p - S) + \int_{[0,T]} [T - t] e^{-rt} [r(S_t - S) - b_t] \, dt$$

PROOF The proof follows from integrating over the individual hedge results of Theorem 5. The Culp and Miller stacked hedge follows from letting δ approach 0. Alternatively, the Culp and Miller formula can be obtained by applying the integration by parts approach of Theorem 5 directly to a hedge position of size $T - t$ at time t.

Stacked hedges inherit the characteristics of their component units and we can look at the same special cases as in the previous section.

(i) Tailing the market, $\delta = r$

Again, the hedge has only basis risk and

$$\Pi_s(\delta) = ([1 - e^{-rT}]/r)(p - S) - \int_{[0,T]} [(e^{-rt} - e^{-rT})/r] b_t \, dt$$

(ii) The spot price follows a mean-reverting process

Now we have

$$\Pi_s(\delta) = ([1 - e^{-rT}]/r)(p - S) - \int_{[0,T]} [(e^{-\delta t} - e^{-\delta T})/\delta] e^{(\delta - r)t} [(\delta - r)(S_t - S) + k(\theta - S_t)] \, dt$$

and, setting $\delta = r + k$, we have

$$\begin{aligned}\Pi_s(r + k) &= ([1 - e^{-rT}]/r)(p - S) - \int_{[0,T]} [(e^{-(r+k)t} - e^{-(r+k)T})/(r + k)] e^{kt} [k(\theta - S)] \, dt \\ &= ([1 - e^{-rT}]/r)(p - \theta) + [(\theta - S)/(r + k)] [1 - e^{-(r+k)T}]\end{aligned}$$

which is riskless.

(iii) General stochastic price processes
If the drift and the basis are not simply mean-reverting, then, as we saw in the previous section for the single hedge, we can still make use of any mean-reverting properties of the basis. Regressing the basis on the spot level:

$$b_t = k(\theta - s_t) + \epsilon_t$$

then case (ii) generalises to:

$$\Pi_s(r+k) = ([1 - e^{-rT}]/r)(p - \theta) + [(\theta - S)/(r+k)][1 - e^{-(r+k)T}]$$

$$- \int_{[0,T]} [(e^{-(r+k)t} - e^{-(r+k)T})/(r+k)]\, e^{kt}\, \epsilon_t\, dt$$

We could now apply Theorem 8 to show that, under the conditions of that theorem, the $\delta = r + k$ hedge has minimum risk among all strategies that are uncorrelated with ϵ_t, and, therefore, has less risk than the stacked hedge. We will do so in a more direct fashion in Theorem 11 below.

The argument against the simple stacked hedge is somewhat more robust than might at first appear. From Theorem 9, the volatile component of a stacked hedge comes from the term

$$\int_{[0,T]} [T-t]\, e^{-rt}[r(S_t - S) - b_t]\, dt$$

in which the increase in the spot price is offset by the basis. If these two terms are uncorrelated, or if the basis negatively covaries with the spot price, then the tailing hedge must be less risky, and if these two terms positively covary, then the mean-reverting hedge dominates the stacked hedge.

THEOREM 10 If the basis is uncorrelated or negatively covaries with present and past spot prices, then the tailing hedge is less risky than the stacked hedge.

PROOF It is sufficient to show that the volatility of the tailing hedge is less than the contribution of the basis to the volatility of the stacked hedge. The latter is the volatility of

$$\int_{[0,T]} [T-t]\, e^{-rt}\, b_t\, dt$$

while the volatility of the tailing hedge is the volatility of

$$\int_{[0,T]} [(e^{-rt} - e^{-rT})/r]\, b_t\, dt$$

The result follows from the observation that

$$(e^{rt} - e^{-rT})/r = e^{-rt}(1 - e^{-r(T-t)})/r$$
$$< e^{-rt}(T-t)$$

Normally we would expect a negative relation between the spot price and the basis, ie, when the current spot price spikes upward because of near term conditions, if the long-run price expectations vary more slowly, then the basis will decline and, conversely, it will rise if the spot price falls.

Suppose, on the other hand, that the basis and the spot price are correlated. Then the results of cases (ii) and (iii) apply, and for completeness we will gather these results in a surprisingly strong theorem.

THEOREM 11 The hedge $\delta = r + k$ has minimum risk among all non-anticipating hedges with the same pattern of terminal delivery. This includes, in particular, all exponential hedges and the stacked hedge.

PROOF From Theorem 9, the δ-stacked hedge profit is given by

$$\Pi_s(\delta) = E\{\Pi_s(\delta)\} + \Pi_s(\delta) - E\{\Pi_s(\delta)\}$$

$$= E\{\Pi_s(\delta)\} - \int_{[0,T]} [(e^{-\delta t} - e^{-\delta T})/\delta]\, e^{(\delta - r)t}[(\delta - r)(S_t - m_t) + (b_t - E\{b_t\})]\, dt$$

where, in the mean-reverting case,

$$m_t = E\{S_t\} = \theta + e^{-kt}(S - \theta)$$

and

$$E\{b_t\} = k(\theta - m_t)$$

From Lemma B we know that $E\{\Pi_s(\delta)\}$ is independent of δ and carrying out the computations yields

$$E\{\Pi_s(\delta)\} = ([1 - e^{-rT}]/r)(p - \theta) + [(\theta - S)/(r + k)][1 - e^{-(r+k)T}]$$

Setting $\delta = r + k$, we have

$$\Pi_s(r + k)$$

$$= E\{\Pi_s(\delta)\} - \int_{[0,T]} [(e^{-\delta t} - e^{-\delta T})/\delta]\, e^{(\delta - r)t}[(\delta - r)(S_t - m_t) + (b_t - E\{b_t\})]\, dt$$

$$= E\{\Pi_s(\delta)\} - \int_{[0,T]} [(e^{-\delta t} - e^{-\delta T})/\delta]\, e^{(\delta - r)t}[k(S_t - m_t) + k(\theta - S_t) - k(\theta - m_t) + \epsilon_t]\, dt$$

$$= E\{\Pi_s(\delta)\} - \int_{[0,T]} [(e^{-\delta t} - e^{-\delta T})/\delta]\, e^{(\delta - r)t}\, \epsilon_t\, dt$$

All general strategies with the same pattern of final deliveries (eg, one unit per month) are integrals of individual convergent strategies. Hence, Theorem 7 implies that all such strategies must have identical exposure to residual basis risk, ϵ_t. In particular, the above integral gives the common exposure. (This may seem surprising since it contains the variable δ, but, in fact, some algebra verifies that it is independent of the choice of δ.) Since the $\delta = r + k$ strategy is the unique strategy that is only exposed to ϵ_t, it has minimum exposure among all strategies with the same delivery pattern.

These results verify that the stacked hedge is dominated under the particular assumptions we have made. If the basis risk and the spot price are uncorrelated or negatively covary, then the tailing hedge dominates the stacked hedge, and if there is mean-reversion then the $r + k$ hedge dominates all hedges. (Of course, the tailing hedge is a special case of the $r + k$ hedge when there is no mean-reversion, $k = 0$.) The section below examines some analytical, historical, and simulated results to see how important this dominance is.

Empirical results and simulations

The difficulty with detecting mean-reversion in price series through traditional time series techniques is well known. To quote Dixit and Pindyck (1994, pp.77/8) referring to crude oil prices from 1870 to 1990 in constant dollars: "A cursory look at these figures suggests that these prices are mean-reverting, but that the rate of mean-reversion is very slow. This is indeed confirmed by running unit root tests on the data. Running these tests on the full 120 years of data, one can easily reject the random walk hypothesis: that is, the data confirm that the prices are mean-reverting. However, if one performs unit root tests using data for only the past 30 or 40 years, one fails to reject the random walk hypothesis. This seems to be the case for many other economic variables as well; using 30 or so years of data, it is difficult to statistically distinguish between a random walk and a mean-reverting process."

1.

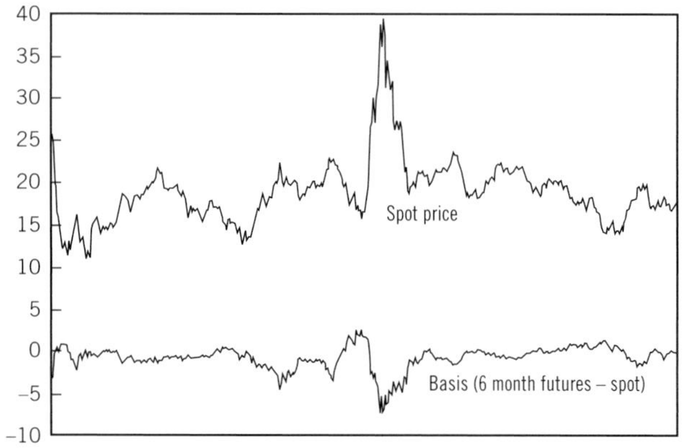

December 30, 1985 to December 30, 1994

But in the futures markets we have a more refined way of examining this issue that goes beyond having to rely solely on the time series properties of the spot price. Figure 1 displays the spot price per barrel and the six-month basis (six-month futures price – spot price) for Nymex contracts weekly over the nine-year period from the end of 1985 to the end of 1994. The chart displays a striking negative correlation between the spot price and the basis. Insofar as the basis is the

Table 2

(a) Crude oil price statistics (weekly, Dec 1985 to Dec 1994)

		Futures											
	Spot	One-month	Two-month	Three-month	Four-month	Five-month	Six-month	Seven-month	Eight-month	Nine-month	Ten-month	Eleven-month	Twelve-month
Mean	19.13	19.11	18.97	18.86	18.77	18.70	18.63	18.58	18.53	18.50	18.50	18.62	18.89
Sigma	3.88	3.85	3.68	3.48	3.30	3.14	3.00	2.88	2.78	2.70	2.64	2.59	2.43

(b) Regression of change in spot price on lagged spot prices

Delta Spot = Spot (t) – Spot (t – 1)

Constant	Spot (t – 1)	Spot (t – 2)	Delta spot	R-square
–0.018			0.005	0.000
			(–0.110)	
0.644	–0.035			0.019
	(–3.010)			
0.662	–0.014	–0.021		0.020
	(–0.312)	(–0.457)		

(c) Regressions of basis on current spot price

	Basis								
Constant	One-month	Two-month	Three-month	Four-month	Five-month	Six-month	Seven-month	Eight-month	R-square
0.152	–0.009								0.037
	(–4.219)								
0.988	–0.060							0.203	
		(–10.932)							
2.019			–0.120						0.335
			(–15.387)						
2.980				–0.175					0.424
				(–18.577)					
3.857					–0.224				0.488
					(–21.156)				
4.629						–0.268			0.536
						(–23.284)			
5.293							–0.306		0.573
							(–25.065)		
5.867								–0.338	0.600
								(–26.518)	

(d) Non-overlapping regressions of spot price change on past basis

Spot change	Constant	Two-month basis	Six-month basis	R-square
Two-month	0.019	0.771		
		(1.097)		0.021
Six-month	0.804		1.464	
			(2.182)	0.219

(t-statistics are reported under coefficient estimates)

expected change in the spot this is strong evidence for mean-reversion. Table 2 reports the results of some simple statistical summary analyses for these series. The table has four parts. It begins with a straightforward time-series variance of the spot and the futures. It is clear that the variance of the spot is significantly higher than that of the futures contracts and that the variance declines as we look at longer maturity futures. This is consistent with a pattern of mean-reversion in which the long-run futures are more stable than the shorter maturities and the spot. Part (b) of the table displays the results of regressing the current spot price on lagged values. (These tests are biased, but the sample size is large enough that the bias should be relatively small.) The results are consistent with those of Dixit and Pindyck (1994). While it is possible to reject the null hypothesis of a random walk, or, more precisely, a martingale in which the expected change in price is zero independent of the current level, the results are not overwhelming.

The third set of tests in part (c) displays the contemporaneous regressions of the basis on the spot price. These results are all highly significant and document a strong negative – ie, mean-reverting – relation between the futures and the basis, confirming the pattern displayed in Figure 1. When spot prices are high, the market goes into backwardation and when they are low it is in contango. It is evident that the basis is predicting that spot prices will revert.

Fama and French (1987, 1988) also observed the negative relation between the basis and the spot price. We are only taking their results one step along and noting that the basis provides a powerful tool for finding and estimating the drift of the spot price relative to traditional time-series approaches. Table 2(d) reports the results of regressing the future change in the spot price on the current basis. The six-month regression is significant, but not the two-month – clearly a testimony to the noisy nature of the data. Needless to say, we are unable to reject the hypothesis that the basis is an unbiased predictor of the future spot price movement.

Perhaps a more pertinent test of our understanding of the movement of prices is an examination of the performance of the hedges we have developed in the previous sections. This is equivalent to testing whether there exist superior trading strategies and it nicely fits the spirit of the efficient market hypothesis. This can be done analytically assuming that the models of the previous sections are valid, but the analytical results are sensitive to misspecification of the underlying process. For greater robustness, the volatilities were estimated by bootstrapping the past observations.

Figure 2 reports the results of bootstrapped simulations of 10,000 paths of the spot price in which historical pairs of the rolling return and the (percentage) spot price change are resampled independently. The sampling period chosen was from June 1983 to July 1995 – the longest period over which data were available – and each constructed path was taken to be 10 years in length. The interest rate was taken to be 7% per year. In each simulation the total amortised terminal costs of acquiring the commodity for continual delivery were calculated from rolling the three-month contract at the end of each month, ie, the initial three-month contract was purchased and sold one month later. The figure displays the distribution of costs for each hedge. The units in this and subsequent simulations were scaled so that 100 million barrels in total were delivered, at the rate of 833,000 barrels per month.

The results display a marked dominance of the tailing hedge over the stacked hedge. The means are about the same. This is the cost of maintaining the hedge and is predominantly negative, but this cost would be offset in both cases by the same profits from the continuing sale of the commodity. (In these simulations we are reporting the total amortised cost of acquiring the commodity including the hedges, but we are not crediting the revenues from the sale of the commodity.) What is most important, though, is that the stacked hedge has a standard deviation of US$891 million over the period versus US$639 million for the tailing hedge. In other words, merely tailing the hedge has lowered the volatility of the terminal cost by nearly 30%.

2.

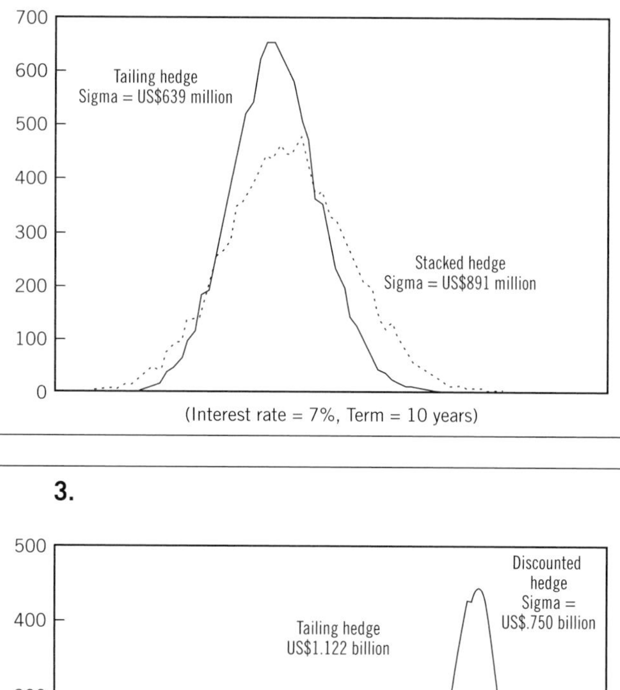

(Interest rate = 7%, Term = 10 years)

3.

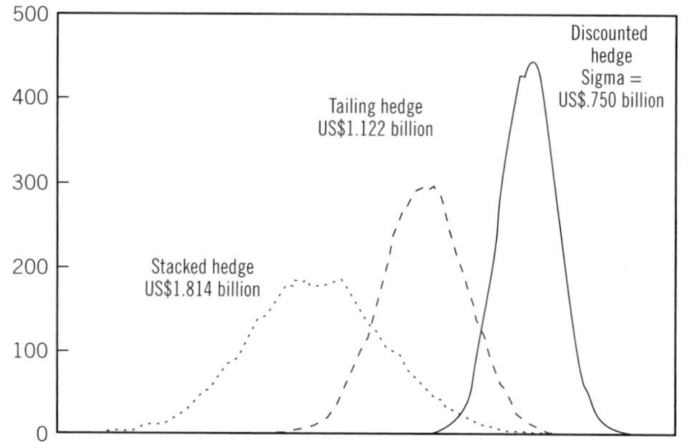

(Interest rate = 7%, Term = 10 years)

Figure 3 repeats the experiment, this time bootstrapping on the residuals from the regressions in Table 2. The data period from January 1987 to September 1991 was chosen because it began after the break-up of OPEC price controls and ended just prior to the establishment of the Metallgesellschaft business. (Experimentation verified that the computed volatilities results are relatively insensitive to the time period chosen.) In each month of the simulation the basis was computed from a random draw from the residuals of the regression of the basis on the prevailing spot price. The change in the spot price was then computed using the residuals from the regression of the subsequent spot price change on the basis (as in Part (d) of Table 2).

The means differ solely because the prices tended to fall over this period, thereby favouring the policies with the smaller positions. As before, the tailing hedge dominated the stacked hedge and at about the same order of magnitude. But because of the presence of mean-reversion in the data, a δ-hedge that discounted the holdings at $\delta = 18\%$ significantly outperformed both. The standard deviation of the δ-hedge was

US$750 million, or less than half of the US$1.814 billion of the stacked hedge and about 30% less than the US$1.122 billion of the tailing hedge. The hedge of $\delta = 18\%$ was chosen by adding the interest rate of 7% to the 12% coefficient in the regression for the three-month basis on the spot price in Table 2 (this rounded to 18%).

It should be noted that these simulations did not account for transactions costs, but one would expect such costs to favour the winning hedges with their smaller positions.

Concluding remarks

We have examined one special type of incompleteness in markets, temporal incompleteness, by looking at the performance of a variety of hedges that might be constructed by rolling over short-term securities so as to replicate the ideal hedge for a long-term commitment.

While, in theory, this is possible under a wide variety of circumstances, in practice our ability to do so is limited by our ability to correctly estimate the underlying stochastic processes that move valuations. This occurs for two principal reasons: first, because the bunching of markets at short maturities raises an issue of multicollinearity; and second, because, to the extent to which it is important to measure the drift of a process, this is done with significant measurement error. This latter problem is exacerbated when the underlying commodity is not an asset in the sense that its convenience yield is significant.

All of this makes it desirable to examine robust hedges, ie, hedges that will do an acceptable job across a variety of model misspecifications. We have introduced one interesting class of such hedges, δ-hedges, in which the hedge position rises over time at the exponential rate δ. These proved to have surprisingly general optimality properties for hedging forward commitments, but the examination of robust hedges for options with inherent non-linearities has yet to begin.

As an example of our analysis, we compared δ-hedges with some alternatives, including the stacked hedge that Culp and Miller (1995) have argued is a viable hedge strategy for the rolling oil delivery commitments of Metallgesellschaft. The δ-hedge class is quite rich and includes, for example, both the stacked hedge and the hedge of "tailing the market", which maintains a position equal in size to the discounted value of the commitment, rather than the full value of the commitment as in the stacked hedge. Simulation studies confirmed the analytic results that tailing the market and other types of δ-hedges significantly dominate the stacked hedge. This dominance is sharpest when δ is chosen to mimic mean-reversion in the underlying spot price.

It would seem that further examination of robust hedges is a deserving topic of study. At both the empirical and the theoretical levels, the problems with hedging are not resolved. We have focused on these issues in the simplest case, that of hedging a fixed future commitment. Even in this simple case, where the only real concern is with δ-hedges and where issues of convexity are less important, the study of robust hedges proves subtle. Needless to say, these issues are much more complex when non-linear commitments such as options are introduced along with the resulting convexity questions.

1 *If there is a risk adjustment to be made it would be interpreted as a beta adjustment term added to the discount rate. This is formally equivalent to subtracting such an adjustment from the drift in the spot price. If the commodity were an asset, then this subtraction would simply leave the risk-free rate,* r, *for the drift, but that would be a fluke in the case when* S *is not an asset price.*

2 *Formally the discount factor* $e^{-rT} = E\{e^{-\int r dt}\}$, *where* E *denotes the martingale expectation and where no restrictions are placed on the choice of interest rate model.*

3 *Modelling inflation would generally push futures prices upwards and bias the long contract towards contango by the addition to the basis of the term:*

$$\theta^* e^{\pi T}(1 - e^{-k^* T})$$

4 *As a mathematical aside, it is interesting to note that the hedge gives rise to what are called cyclical matrices and the particular equation for the hedge portfolio is actually an inverse form of what is called a truncated Laplace transform. This suggests some potential for future work in more carefully refining the nature of such hedges.*

5 *In the special case where the commodity is an asset, ie, where storage is costless, in the martingale measure the basis slope,* $b_t = rS_t$, *hence* $k = -r$ *and setting* $\delta = r + k = 0$, *a constant hedge, produces a riskless profit of* $\Pi(0) = e^{-rT}p - S$.

6 *In addition, the Metallgesellschaft contracts had several so-called "blow-out" options. See Ross (1995) for a detailed discussion.*

BIBLIOGRAPHY

Brennan, M. J., and N. Crew, 1995, "Hedging Long Maturity Commodity Commitments with Short-Dated Futures Contracts", Working paper, UCLA, pp. 13-95; reprinted as Chapter 16 of the present volume.

Cox, J. C., J. E. Ingersoll Jr. and S. A. Ross, 1981, "The Relation Between Forward and Futures Prices", *Journal of Financial Economics* 9(4), pp. 321-46.

Cox, J. C., and S. A. Ross, 1976, "A Survey of Some New Results in Financial Option Pricing Theory", *Journal of Finance* 31(2), pp. 383-401.

Culp, C. C., and M. H. Miller, 1994a, "Risk Management Lessons from Metallgesellschaft", *Journal of Applied Corporate Finance.*

Culp, C. C., and M. H. Miller, 1994b, "Hedging a Flow of Commodity Deliveries with Futures: Lessons from Metallgesellschaft", *Derivatives Review* 1(1).

Dixit, A. K., and R. S. Pindyck, 1994, *Investment Under Uncertainty* (Princeton, NJ: Princeton University Press).

Edwards, F. R., and M. S. Canter, 1995, "The Collapse of Metallgesellschaft: Unhedgable Risks, Poor Hedging Strategy, or Just Bad Luck?", *Journal of Applied Corporate Finance* 8(1), pp. 86-105; reprinted as Chapter 13 of the present volume.

Fama, E., and K. French, 1987, "Commodity Futures Prices: Some Evidence on Forecast Power, Premiums, and the Theory of Storage", *Journal of Business.*

Fama, E., and K. French, 1988, "Business Cycles and the Behaviour of Metals Prices", *Journal of Finance* 42.

Harrison, J. M., and D. M. Kreps, 1979, "Martingales and Arbitrage in Multiperiod Securities Markets", *Journal of Economic Theory* 20, pp. 381-408.

Mello, A. S., and J. E. Parsons, 1994, "Hedging a Flow of Commodity Deliveries with Futures: Lessons from Metallgesellschaft", *Derivatives Quarterly* 1(4), 7(2), pp. 7-15.

Mello, A. S., and J. E. Parsons, 1995, "Maturity Structure of a Hedge Matters: Lessons from the Metallgesellschaft Debacle", *Journal of Applied Corporate Finance* 8(1), pp.106-20; reprinted as Chapter 12 of the present volume.

Neuberger, A., 1995, "How Well can you Hedge Long Term Exposures with Multiple Short Term Futures Contracts?", London Business School IFA working paper 214-195.

Ross, S. A., 1976, "Return, Risk and Arbitrage", In I. Friend and J. L. Bicksler, eds, *Risk and Return in Finance* (Cambridge, Mass: Ballinger).

Ross, S. A., 1978, "A Simple Approach to the Pricing of Risky Assets", *Journal of Business* 51, pp. 453-75.

Ross, S. A., 1995, "Hedging Long Run Commitments: Exercises in Incomplete Market Pricing", Yale School of Management Discussion Paper Series.

20

The Stochastic Behaviour of Commodity Prices: Implications for Valuation and Hedging*

Eduardo S. Schwartz

University of California, Los Angeles

The stochastic behaviour of commodity prices plays a central role in the models for valuing financial contingent claims on the commodity and in the procedures for evaluating investments to extract or produce the commodity. Earlier studies, by assuming that interest rates and convenience yields are constant, allowed for a straightforward extension of the procedures developed for common stock option pricing to the valuation of financial and real commodity contingent claims. The assumption, however, is clearly not very satisfactory since it implies that the volatility of future prices is equal to the volatility of spot prices and that the distribution of future spot prices under the equivalent martingale measure has a variance that increases without bound as the horizon increases. In an equilibrium setting we would expect that, when prices are relatively high, supply will increase since higher-cost producers of the commodity will enter the market, putting a downward pressure on prices. Conversely, when prices are relatively low, supply will decrease since some of the higher-cost producers will exit the market, putting upward pressure on prices. The impact of relative prices on the supply of the commodity will induce mean-reversion on commodity prices.[1]

In this chapter we compare three models of the stochastic behaviour of commodity prices that take into account mean-reversion, in terms of their ability to price existing futures contracts and their implication with respect to the valuation of other financial and real assets. The first model is a simple one-factor model in which the logarithm of the spot price of the commodity is assumed to follow a mean-reverting process of the Ornstein-Uhlenbeck type. The second model we consider is a variation of the two-factor Gibson and Schwartz (1990) model. The second factor in this model is the convenience yield of the commodity and it is assumed to follow a mean-reverting process. Finally, we extend the Gibson and Schwartz model to include stochastic interest rates. In this three-factor model, the instantaneous interest rate is also assumed to follow a mean-reverting process as in Vasicek (1977).

For these three models, closed-form solutions for the prices of futures and forward contracts[2] can be obtained, which greatly simplifies the comparative statics and empirical estimation. In addition, for all three models the logarithm of the futures price is linear in the underlying factors, a property that turns out to be very useful in view of the econometric technique used to estimate the parameters of the models.

**Originally published in the* Journal of Finance *52(3) (1997), pp. 923–73; reproduced with permission of Blackwell Publishers. I thank Richard Roll, Alan Kraus, Ernest Greenwood and Kristian Miltersen for suggestions and Olivier Ledoit, Piet de Jong and Julian Franks for helpful discussions. I especially thank Michael Brennan, not only for his comments on this chapter, but for 25 years of inspiration, advice and friendship. Part of this research was done while I was a visiting scholar at the University of British Columbia during the summer of 1996.*

One of the main difficulties in the empirical implementation of commodity price models is that frequently the factors or state variables of these models are not directly observable. In many cases the spot price of a commodity is so uncertain that the corresponding futures contract closest to maturity is used as a proxy for the spot price. The instantaneous convenience yield is even more difficult to estimate. Futures contracts, however, are traded on several exchanges and their prices are more easily observed.

A tool that is especially well suited to deal with situations in which the state variables are not observable, but are known to be generated by a Markov process, is the state-space form. Once a model has been put in state-space form, the Kalman filter may be applied to estimate the parameters of the model and the time series of the unobservable state variables.

We apply the Kalman filter method to estimate the parameters of the three models for two commercial commodities, copper and oil, and for one precious metal, gold. The analysis reveals strong mean-reversion in the commercial commodity prices but not for the precious metal. Using the estimated parameters, we analyse the implications of the models for the term structure of futures prices and volatilities beyond the observed contracts and for hedging contracts for future delivery.

The "real options" approach to investment under uncertainty (for an excellent recent survey of the literature see Dixit and Pindyck, 1994) emphasises the importance of uncertainty for the value of a project and for determining when the project should be undertaken. The valuation of natural resource investment projects and the rule for determining when it is optimal to invest depend significantly on the stochastic process assumed for the underlying commodity price.[3] We compare the value and the investment rule for simple projects under the different assumptions about the commodity price process implied by the models, using realistic estimated parameters.

The remainder of the chapter is organised as follows. The valuation models are developed in the first section and the second delineates their empirical counterparts. The third section describes the data, and the fourth reports the empirical estimates of the models and a comparison of their relative performance. In the fifth section the implications of the models for the volatility of futures returns are discussed. The sixth section considers futures contracts with longer maturities than the available data, and the seventh the hedging of contracts for future delivery. The eighth section looks at the implications of the models for investment under uncertainty and compares their predictions with two benchmarks: the discounted cashflow criterion and a real option model with no mean-reversion.

Valuation models

In this section we present three models of commodity prices and derive the corresponding formulas for pricing futures contracts in each model. The first model, which is a one-factor model, assumes that the logarithm of the spot price of the commodity follows a mean-reverting process of the Ornstein–Uhlenbeck type. The second model includes a second stochastic factor, the convenience yield, which is mean-reverting and positively correlated with the spot price.[4] The third model extends the second by allowing for stochastic interest rates. The three models are very tractable, since they allow for closed-form solutions for futures prices and for a linear relation between the logarithm of futures prices and the underlying factors. These properties will be extensively used in the empirical work that follows.

MODEL 1

To develop the one-factor model we first assume that the commodity spot price follows the stochastic process[5]

$$dS = \kappa(\mu - \ln S)Sdt + \sigma Sdz \tag{1}$$

Defining $X = \ln S$ and applying Itô's lemma, this implies that the log price can be characterised by an Ornstein–Uhlenbeck stochastic process:

$$dX = \kappa(\alpha - X)dt + \sigma dz \tag{2}$$

$$\alpha = \mu - \frac{\sigma^2}{2\kappa} \tag{3}$$

The magnitude of the speed of adjustment $\kappa > 0$ measures the degree of mean-reversion to the long-run mean log price, α. The second term in equation (2) characterises the volatility of the process, with dz being an increment to a standard Brownian motion.

In this model, the commodity is not an asset in the usual sense[6] and the spot price, or, equivalently, the log of the spot price, plays the role of an underlying state variable on which contingent claims can be written. Under standard assumptions, the dynamics of the Ornstein–Uhlenbeck process under the equivalent martingale measure can be written as[7]

$$dX = \kappa(\alpha^* - X)dt + \sigma dz^* \tag{4}$$

where $\alpha^* = \alpha - \lambda$, λ is the market price of risk (assumed constant)[8] and dz^* is the increment to the Brownian motion under the equivalent martingale measure.

From equation (4), the conditional distribution of X at time T under the equivalent martingale measure is normal with mean and variance

$$E_0[X(T)] = e^{-\kappa T}X(0) + (1 - e^{-\kappa T})\alpha^*$$

$$\mathrm{Var}_0[X(T)] = \frac{\sigma^2}{2\kappa}(1 - e^{-2\kappa T}) \tag{5}$$

Since $X = \ln S$, the spot price of the commodity at time T is lognormally distributed under the martingale measure with these same parameters.

Assuming a constant interest rate, the futures (or forward) price of the commodity with maturity T is the expected price of the commodity at time T under the equivalent martingale measure. Then, from the properties of the lognormal distribution, we have

$$F(S,T) = E[S(T)] = \exp(E_0[X(T)] + \tfrac{1}{2}\mathrm{Var}_0[X(T)]) \tag{6}$$

Then

$$F(S,T) = \exp\left[e^{-\kappa T}\ln S + (1 - e^{-\kappa T})\alpha^* + \frac{\sigma^2}{4\kappa}(1 - e^{-2\kappa T})\right] \tag{7}$$

Or, in log form:

$$\ln F(S,T) = e^{-\kappa T}\ln S + (1 - e^{-\kappa T})\alpha^* + \frac{\sigma^2}{4\kappa}(1 - e^{-2\kappa T}) \tag{8}$$

This last equation is the one used in the empirical tests.

It is easy to verify that equation (7) is the solution of the partial differential equation:

$$\tfrac{1}{2}\sigma^2 S^2 F_{SS} + \kappa(\mu - \lambda - \ln S)SF_S - F_T = 0 \tag{9}$$

with terminal boundary condition $F(S, 0) = S$.

MODEL 2

The two-factor model is based on the one developed by Gibson and Schwartz (1990). The first factor is the spot price of the commodity and the second is the instantaneous convenience yield, δ.[9] These factors are assumed to follow the joint stochastic process

$$dS = (\mu - \delta)S\,dt + \sigma_1 S\,dz_1 \tag{10}$$

$$d\delta = \kappa(\alpha - \delta)\,dt + \sigma_2 dz_2 \tag{11}$$

where the increments to standard Brownian motion are correlated with

$$dz_1 dz_2 = \rho\,dt \tag{12}$$

Equation (10) is a standard process for the commodity price allowing for a stochastic convenience yield, which follows an Ornstein–Uhlenbeck stochastic process described in equation (11). Note that if δ, instead of being stochastic as in equation (11), is a deterministic function of S, $\delta(S) = \kappa \ln S$, Model 2 reduces to Model 1, and if δ is constant it reduces to the model of Brennan and Schwartz (1985).

Defining once again $X = \ln S$ and applying Itô's lemma, the process for the log price can be written as

$$dX = (\mu - \delta - \tfrac{1}{2}\sigma_1^2)dt + \sigma_1 dz_1 \tag{13}$$

In this model the commodity is treated as an asset that pays a stochastic dividend yield δ. Thus, the risk-adjusted drift of the commodity price process will be $r - \delta$. Since convenience yield risk cannot be hedged, the risk-adjusted convenience yield process will have a market price of risk associated with it. The stochastic process for the factors under the equivalent martingale measure can be expressed as[10]

$$dS = (r - \delta)Sdt + \sigma_1 S dz_1^* \tag{14}$$

$$d\delta = [\kappa(\alpha - \delta) - \lambda]dt + \sigma_2 dz_2^* \tag{15}$$

$$dz_1^* dz_2^* = \rho dt \tag{16}$$

where now λ is the market price of convenience yield risk, which is assumed constant. Futures prices must then satisfy the partial differential equation

$$\tfrac{1}{2}\sigma_1^2 S^2 F_{SS} + \sigma_1\sigma_2\rho S F_{S\delta} + \tfrac{1}{2}\sigma_2^2 F_{\delta\delta} + (r - \delta)SF_S + (\kappa(\alpha - \delta) - \lambda)F_\delta - F_T = 0 \tag{17}$$

subject to the terminal boundary condition $F(S, \delta, 0) = S$.

Jamshidian and Fein (1990) and Bjerksund (1991) have shown that the solution to (17) is[11]

$$F(S,\delta,T) = S \exp\left[-\delta \frac{1 - e^{-\kappa T}}{\kappa} + A(T)\right] \tag{18}$$

Or, in log form:

$$\ln F(S,\delta,T) = \ln S - \delta \frac{1 - e^{-\kappa T}}{\kappa} + A(T) \tag{19}$$

where

$$\begin{aligned} A(T) &= \left(r - \hat{\alpha} + \frac{1}{2}\frac{\sigma_2^2}{\kappa^2} - \frac{\sigma_1\sigma_2\rho}{\kappa}\right)T + \frac{1}{4}\sigma_2^2 \frac{1 - e^{-2\kappa T}}{\kappa^3} \\ &\quad + \left(\hat{\alpha}\kappa + \sigma_1\sigma_2\rho - \frac{\sigma_2^2}{\kappa}\right)\frac{1 - e^{-\kappa T}}{\kappa^2} \\ \hat{\alpha} &= \alpha - \frac{\lambda}{\kappa} \end{aligned} \tag{20}$$

MODEL 3

Model 3 is a three-factor model of commodity contingent claims. The stochastic factors or state variables in the model are the spot price of the commodity, the instantaneous convenience yield and the instantaneous interest rate. By assuming a simple mean-reverting process for the interest rate, it is possible to obtain a closed-form solution for futures prices.

Assuming that the instantaneous risk-free interest rate follows an Ornstein–Uhlenbeck stochastic process (as in Vasicek, 1977), Model 2 can easily be extended to a three-factor model. Using (14) and (15), the joint stochastic process for the factors under the equivalent martingale measure can be expressed as

$$dS = (r - \delta)Sdt + \sigma_1 S dz_1^* \tag{21}$$

$$d\delta = \kappa(\hat{\alpha} - \delta)dt + \sigma_2 dz_2^* \tag{22}$$

$$dr = a(m^* - r)dt + \sigma_3 dz_3^* \tag{23}$$

$$dz_1^* dz_2^* = \rho_1 dt, \quad dz_2^* dz_3^* = \rho_2 dt, \quad dz_1^* dz_3^* = \rho_3 dt \tag{24}$$

where a and m^* are, respectively, the speed of adjustment coefficient and the risk-adjusted mean short rate of the interest rate process. Futures prices must then satisfy the partial differential equation

$$\tfrac{1}{2}\sigma_1^2 S^2 F_{SS} + \tfrac{1}{2}\sigma_2^2 F_{\delta\delta} + \tfrac{1}{2}\sigma_3^2 F_{rr} + \sigma_1\sigma_2\rho_1 S F_{S\delta} + \sigma_2\sigma_3\rho_2 F_{\delta r} + \sigma_1\sigma_3\rho_3 S F_{Sr} + (r-\delta)SF_S + \kappa(\hat{\alpha}-\delta)F_\delta + a(m^* - r)F_r - F_T = 0 \quad (25)$$

subject to the terminal boundary condition $F(S, \delta, r, 0) = S$.

The solution to partial differential equation (25) subject to its terminal boundary condition can be shown to be[12]

$$F(S,\delta,r,T) = S \exp\left[\frac{-\delta(1-e^{-\kappa T})}{\kappa} + \frac{r(1-e^{-aT})}{a} + C(T)\right] \quad (26)$$

Or, in log form:

$$\ln F(S,\delta,r,T) = \ln S - \frac{\delta(1-e^{-\kappa T})}{\kappa} + \frac{r(1-e^{-aT})}{a} + C(T) \quad (27)$$

where

$$C(T) = \frac{(\kappa\hat{\alpha} + \sigma_1\sigma_2\rho_1)((1-e^{-\kappa T}) - \kappa T)}{\kappa^2} - \frac{\sigma_2^2(4(1-e^{-\kappa T}) - (1-e^{-2\kappa T}) - 2\kappa T)}{4\kappa^3}$$
$$- \frac{(am^* + \sigma_1\sigma_3\rho_3)((1-e^{-aT}) - aT)}{a^2} - \frac{\sigma_3^2(4(1-e^{-aT}) - (1-e^{-2aT}) - 2aT)}{4a^3}$$
$$+ \sigma_2\sigma_3\rho_2\left(\frac{(1-e^{-\kappa T}) + (1-e^{-aT}) - (1-e^{-(\kappa+a)T})}{\kappa a(\kappa+a)}\right.$$
$$\left. + \frac{\kappa^2(1-e^{-aT}) + a^2(1-e^{-\kappa T}) - \kappa a^2 T - a\kappa^2 T}{\kappa^2 a^2(\kappa+a)}\right) \quad (28)$$

Since in this model interest rates are stochastic, futures prices are not equal to forward prices. With the assumed risk-adjusted stochastic process for the instantaneous interest rate given in equation (23), the present value of a unit discount bond payable at time T when the interest rate is r is given by (see Vasicek, 1977):

$$B(r,T) = \exp\left[-r\frac{1-e^{-aT}}{a} + \frac{m^*((1-e^{-aT}) - aT)}{a} - \frac{\sigma_3^2(4(1-e^{-aT}) - (1-e^{-2aT}) - 2aT)}{4a^3}\right] \quad (29)$$

To obtain the present value of a forward commitment to deliver one unit of the commodity, $P(S, \delta, R, t)$, we need to solve a partial differential equation and boundary conditions identical to equation (25) except that in the right-hand side we have rP instead of zero. The solution to this modified equation is

$$P(S,\delta,r,T) = S \exp\left[\frac{-\delta(1-e^{-\kappa T})}{\kappa} + D(T)\right] \quad (30)$$

where

$$D(T) = \frac{(\kappa\hat{\alpha} + \sigma_1\sigma_2\rho_1)((1-e^{-\kappa T}) - \kappa T)}{\kappa^2} - \frac{\sigma_2^2(4(1-e^{-\kappa T}) - (1-e^{-2\kappa T}) - 2\kappa T)}{4\kappa^3} \quad (31)$$

Given the present value of a forward commitment in equation (30) and the present value of a unit discount bond in equation (29), the forward price implied by Model 3 can be easily obtained by dividing $P(S, \delta, R, t)$ by $B(r, T)$. Note that the present value of a forward commitment in Model 3 is independent of the interest rate, r, and is identical to the corresponding one in Model 2. Forward prices in both models, however, are different.

Empirical models

As mentioned in the introduction, one of the difficulties in the empirical implementation of commodity price models is that frequently the factors or state variables of these models are not directly observable. For some commodities the spot price is hard to obtain, and the futures contract closest to maturity is used as a proxy for the spot price. The problems of estimating the instantaneous convenience yield are even more complex; normally, two futures prices with different maturities are used to compute the convenience yield.[13] The instantaneous interest rate is also not directly observable. Futures contracts, however, are widely traded in several exchanges and their prices are more easily observed.

The state-space form is the appropriate procedure to deal with situations in which the state variables are not observable but are known to be generated by a Markov process. Once a model has been cast in state-space form, the Kalman filter may be applied to estimate the parameters of the model and the time series of the unobservable state variables.

The general state-space form applies to a multivariate time series of observable variables, in this case futures prices for different maturities, related to an unobservable vector of state variables (state vector), in this case the spot price alone or both the spot price and the instantaneous convenience yield, via a *measurement equation*. In our context the measurement equations are obtained from equations (8), (19) and (27) for the one-, two- and three-factor models, respectively, by adding serially and cross-sectionally uncorrelated disturbances with mean zero to take into account bid–ask spreads, price limits, non-simultaneity of the observations, errors in the data, etc. This simple structure for the measurement errors is imposed so that the serial correlation and cross-correlation in the log prices are attributed to the variation of the unobservable state variables. The unobservable state variables are generated via the *transition equation*, which in our context is a discrete-time version of the stochastic process for the state variables: equation (2) for the one-factor model and equations (11) to (13) for the two- and three-factor models.[14] The Kalman filter is a recursive procedure for computing the optimal estimator of the state vector at time t on the basis of the information available at time t, and it enables the estimate of the state vector to be continuously updated as new information becomes available. When the disturbances and the initial state vector are normally distributed the Kalman filter enables the likelihood function to be calculated, which allows for the estimation of any unknown parameters of the model and provides the basis for statistical testing and model specification. For a detailed discussion of state-space models and the Kalman filter see chapter 3 in Harvey (1989).

MODEL 1

From equation (8) the measurement equation can be written as

$$y_t = d_t + Z_t X_t + \varepsilon_t, \qquad t = 1, \ldots, NT$$

where

$$y_t = [\ln F(T_i)], \qquad i = 1, \ldots, N, \qquad N \times 1 \text{ vector of observables}$$

$$d_t = \left[(1 - e^{-\kappa T_i})\alpha^* + \frac{\sigma^2}{4\kappa}(1 - e^{-2kT_i})\right], \qquad i = 1, \ldots, N, \qquad N \times 1 \text{ vector}$$

$$Z_t = \left[e^{-\kappa T_i}\right], \qquad i = 1, \ldots, N, \qquad N \times 1 \text{ vector}$$

ε_t, $N \times 1$ vector of serially uncorrelated disturbances with

$$E(\varepsilon_t) = 0, \qquad Var(\varepsilon_t) = H \tag{32}$$

and from equation (2) the transition equation can be written as[15]

$$X_t = c_t + Q_t X_{t-1} + \eta_t, \qquad t = 1, \ldots, NT$$

where

$$c_t = \kappa\alpha\Delta t \qquad Q_t = 1 - \kappa\Delta t$$

η_t, serially uncorrelated disturbances with

$$E(\eta_t) = 0, \qquad Var(\eta_t) = \sigma^2\Delta t \tag{33}$$

MODEL 2

From equation (19) the measurement equation can be written as:

$$y_t = d_t + Z_t[X_t, \delta_t]' + \varepsilon_t, \qquad t = 1,\ldots, NT$$

where

$$y_t = [\ln F(T_i)], \qquad i = 1,\ldots, N, \qquad N \times 1 \text{ vector of observables}$$

$$d_t = [A(T_i)], \qquad i = 1,\ldots, N, \qquad N \times 1 \text{ vector}$$

$$Z_t = \left[1, -\frac{1 - e^{-\kappa T_i}}{\kappa}\right], \qquad i = 1,\ldots, N, \qquad N \times 2 \text{ matrix}$$

ε_t, $N \times 1$ vector of serially uncorrelated disturbances with

$$E(\varepsilon_t) = 0, \qquad Var(\varepsilon_t) = H \tag{34}$$

and from equations (11) to (13) the transition equation can be written as:

$$[X_t, \delta_t]' = c_t + Q_t[X_{t-1}, \delta_{t-1}]' + \eta_t, \qquad t = 1,\ldots, NT$$

where

$$c_t = \left[\left(\mu - \tfrac{1}{2}\sigma_1^2\right)\Delta t, \kappa\alpha\Delta t\right]', \qquad 2 \times 1 \text{ vector}$$

$$Q_t = \begin{vmatrix} 1 & & -\Delta t \\ 0 & 1 & -\kappa\Delta t \end{vmatrix}$$

η_t, serially uncorrelated disturbances with

$$E(\eta_t) = 0, \qquad Var(\eta_t) = \begin{vmatrix} \sigma_1^2\Delta t & \rho\sigma_1\sigma_2\Delta t \\ \rho\sigma_1\sigma_2\Delta t & \sigma_1^2\Delta t \end{vmatrix} \tag{35}$$

MODEL 3

We estimate a simplified version of Model 3. Ideally, the commodity spot price process, the convenience yield process and the interest rate process should be estimated simultaneously from a time series and cross-section of futures prices and discount bond prices. To simplify the estimation we first estimate the parameters of the interest rate process and then we use Model 3 to estimate the parameters of the spot price and convenience yield processes. We are essentially assuming that the parameters of the interest rate process are not affected by commodity futures prices, which seems to be a reasonable assumption.

Once we have estimated the interest rate process, we have only to estimate the parameters and state variables from the spot price and the convenience yield processes. From equations (27) and (28) the measurement equation is then

$$y_t = d_t + Z_t[X_t, \delta_t]' + \varepsilon_t, \qquad t = 1,\ldots, NT$$

where

$$y_t = [\ln F(T_i)], \qquad i = 1,\ldots, N, \qquad N \times 1 \text{ vector of observables}$$

$$d_t = \left[\frac{r_t(1 - e^{-aT_i})}{a} + C(T_i)\right], \qquad i = 1,\ldots, N, \qquad N \times 1 \text{ vector}$$

$$Z_t = \left[1, -\frac{1 - e^{-\kappa T_i}}{\kappa}\right], \qquad i = 1,\ldots, N, \qquad N \times 2 \text{ matrix}$$

ε_t, $N \times 1$ vector of serially uncorrelated disturbances with

$$E(\varepsilon_t) = 0, \qquad Var(\varepsilon_t) = H \tag{36}$$

Since we are using the Kalman filter to estimate the same state variables as in model 2, the transition equation for this model is also (35).

Table 1. Oil data

Futures contract	Mean price (standard error)	Mean maturity (standard error)
Panel A: January 2, 1985–February 17, 1995: 510 weekly observations		
F1	US$19.99 (4.52)	0.043 (0.024) years
F3	19.65 (4.08)	0.210 (0.025)
F5	19.45 (3.74)	0.377 (0.024)
F7	19.31 (3.51)	0.543 (0.024)
F9	19.21 (3.35)	0.709 (0.025)
Panel B: January 2,1990–February 17, 1995: 259 weekly observations		
F1	US$20.41 (4.13)	0.043 (0.024) years
F3	20.26 (3.54)	0.210 (0.025)
F5	20.09 (3.02)	0.376 (0.025)
F7	19.94 (2.62)	0.543 (0.025)
F9	19.84 (2.32)	0.709 (0.025)
Panel C: January 2, 1990–February 17, 1995: 259 weekly observations		
F1	US$20.41 (4.13)	0.043 (0.024) years
F5	20.09 (3.02)	0.376 (0.025)
F9	19.84 (2.32)	0.709 (0.025)
F13	19.76 (1.95)	1.041 (0.025)
F17	19.76 (1.74)	1.374 (0.025)
Forward maturity	**Mean price (standard error)**	**Mean maturity (standard error)**
Panel D: January 15, 1993–May 16, 1996: 163 weekly observations (Enron data)		
Two months	US$18.16 (1.54)	0.122 (0.024)
Five months	18.00 (1.31)	0.372 (0.024)
Eight months	18.00 (1.23)	0.621 (0.024)
One year	18.05 (1.15)	0.955 (0.024)
$1\frac{1}{2}$ years	18.20 (1.09)	1.457 (0.024)
Two years	18.38 (1.03)	1.955 (0.024)
Three years	18.81 (1.95)	2.955 (0.024)
Five years	19.67 (0.87)	4.955 (0.024)
Seven years	20.34 (0.79)	6.955 (0.024)
Nine years	20.92 (0.71)	8.955 (0.024)

Table 2. Copper data

Futures contract	Mean price (standard error)	Mean maturity (standard error)
Panel A: July 29, 1988–June 13,1995: 347 weekly observations		
F1	110.04 (18.05) cents	0.109 (0.065) years
F3	105.45 (13.54)	0.504 (0.084)
F5	102.42 (10.95)	0.899 (0.065)
F7	100.46 (9.34)	1.299 (0.085)
F9	99.78 (8.79)	1.663 (0.111)

Table 3. Gold data

Futures contract	Mean price (standard error)	Mean maturity (standard error)
Panel A: January 2, 1985–June 13, 1995: 527 weekly observations		
F1	US$379.27 (40.95)	0.084 (0.048) years
F3	386.12 (42.46)	0.417 (0.048)
F6	397.55 (44.96)	0.917 (0.048)
F9	409.95 (47.79)	1.416 (0.048)
F11	418.87 (49.79)	1.749 (0.049)
Panel B: November 21, 1990–June 13, 1995: 230 weekly observations		
F1	US$365.50 (19.57)	0.084 (0.048) years
F3	370.12 (20.56)	0.417 (0.048)
F6	378.02 (22.30)	0.917 (0.048)
F9	386.70 (24.11)	1.413 (0.048)
F11	393.03 (25.32)	1.745 (0.049)
Panel C: November 21, 1990–June 13, 1995: 230 weekly observations		
F1	US$365.50 (19.57)	0.084 (0.048) years
F5	375.31 (21.70)	0.750 (0.048)
F9	386.70 (24.11)	1.413 (0.048)
F13	403.02 (27.05)	2.237 (.0144)
F18	460.85 (33.93)	4.703 (0.145)

Data

The data used to test the models consisted of weekly observations[16] of futures prices for two commercial commodities, oil and copper, and one precious metal, gold. In every case five futures contracts (ie, N = 5) were used in the estimation.[17] For different commodities and different time periods, however, different specific futures contracts had to be used because they vary across commodities and through time for a particular commodity. The interest rate data consisted of yields on three-month Treasury bills. These data were used in the models that require variable interest rates.

The oil data used are presented in Table 1. From January 2, 1985, to February 17, 1995, complete data on the first nine contracts were available, so the first set of tests used contracts F1, F3, F5, F7 and F9 (see Panel A), where F1 is the contract closest to maturity, F2 is the second contract closest to maturity, and so on. Since the contracts have a fixed maturity date, the time-to-maturity changes as time progresses. Figure 1 shows that time-to-maturity remains within a narrow range for each one of the contracts during the whole sample period. The figure is representative of the maturity structure for all the data used in this study. Starting on January 2, 1990, complete data on 17 oil futures contracts were available, extending the maximum maturity of the contracts from an average of 0.71 years to 1.34 years. Longer-maturity contracts are of most interest in this study, since we will be concerned with investment decisions in real assets with much longer maturities. The second set of tests (see Panel C of Table 1) then used contracts F1, F5, F9, F13 and F17. To be able to distinguish whether the possible differences between these two tests were due to the time period used or to the contracts used, a third set of tests was carried out using the contracts of the first set of tests over the period of the second set of tests (Panel B in Table 1).

The high-grade copper futures contract started trading in 1988, so complete data on the first nine contracts were available for the period July 29, 1988, to June 13, 1995 (see Table 2). The only set of tests performed for copper used contracts F1, F3, F5, F7 and F9. In the case of copper, however, the last contract had an average maturity of 1.66 years (contract F17 for oil has an average maturity of only 1.34 years).

The gold data are given in Table 3. Complete data for the first 11 contracts were available for January 2, 1985 to June 13, 1995, so the first set of tests used contracts F1, F3, F6, F9 and F11 (see Panel A). The average maturity of the F11 contracts was 1.75 years. Starting on November 21, 1990, complete data on the first 18 contracts were available, so the second set of tests used contracts F1, F5, F9, F13 and F18, extending the average maturity of the longest contract to 4.70 years (see Panel C). As was done in the case of oil, a third set of tests was performed using the same contracts as in the first tests during the period of the second tests (see Panel B).

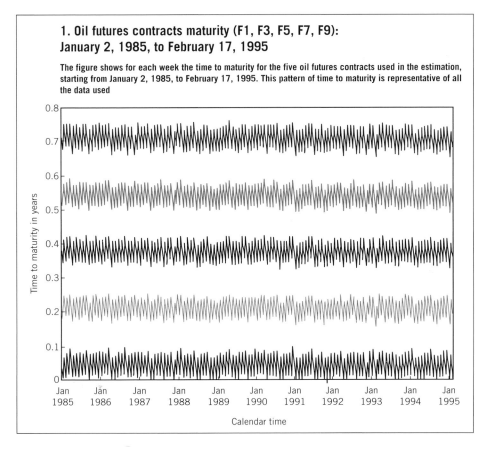

1. Oil futures contracts maturity (F1, F3, F5, F7, F9): January 2, 1985, to February 17, 1995

The figure shows for each week the time to maturity for the five oil futures contracts used in the estimation, starting from January 2, 1985, to February 17, 1995. This pattern of time to maturity is representative of all the data used

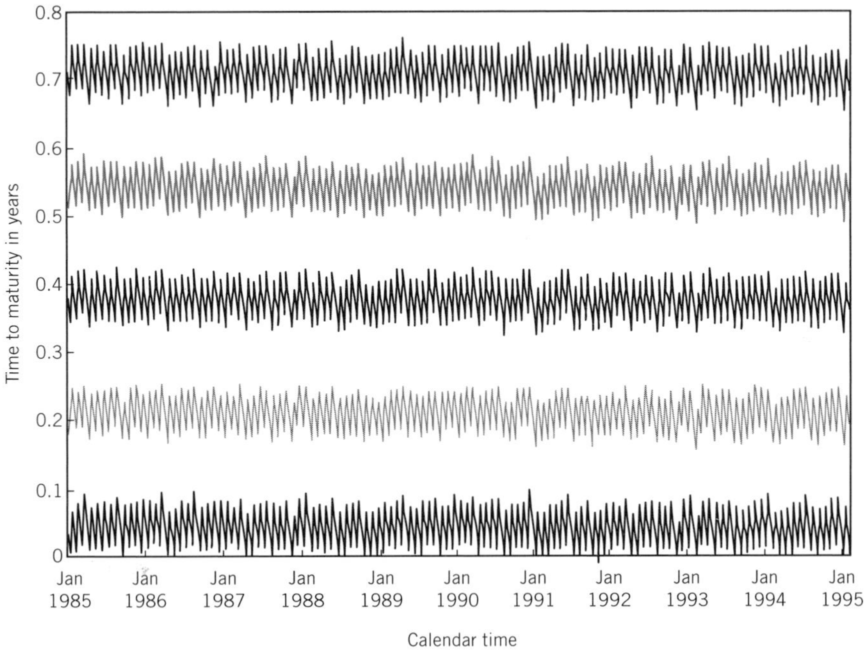

In addition to the publicly available futures data described above, for the purposes of this study Enron Capital and Trade Resources made available some proprietary historical crude oil forward price curves for January 15, 1993, to May 16, 1996. From these data 10 forward prices were used in the estimation, ranging in maturities from two months to nine years (see Panel D of Table 1). The great advantage of these data is the longer maturities of the contracts. The disadvantage is that we do not know exactly how the crude oil forward curves were constructed.

Empirical results

MODEL 1

Table 4 presents the results for the one-factor model applied to the four data sets for oil described in Table 1. In all cases the speed of adjustment coefficient is highly significant and the market price of risk is not significantly different from zero. The main difference between columns 2 and 3, which use the same contracts, is that the later period has much stronger mean-reversion (0.7 as opposed to 0.3 for the whole period). The other parameters are very similar both in magnitude and significance. In all cases, one of the standard deviations of the measurement errors goes to zero. This is a common phenomenon in this type of analysis.

The prediction errors[18] for the first oil data set are shown in Figure 2. Though the average error is quite small (0.0032), the average absolute deviation is 0.033, which is around 1% of the log of the price of the futures contract closest to maturity, reflecting some very large deviations in the figure. Note also that there seems to be some negative autocorrelation of the errors, which could imply the existence of some errors in the data. Figure 3 presents the value of the state variable and the log of the first futures contract for the same data set. Here we can see that the state variable (the log of the spot price) follows closely, but is not identical to, the log of the price of the futures contract closest to maturity (F1).

Comparing now columns 3 and 4 of Table 4, which use the same time period but different futures contracts, we see that the main effect of extending the maturity of the contracts is to reduce the mean-reversion parameter (from 0.7 to 0.4). This could have important implications in the application of this model to long-term oil investment, since in this case the relevant futures contracts would be much longer in maturity. Even though the Enron data cover a different time period (with some overlap), from column 5 we can see that the mean-reversion parameter is even smaller (0.1).

Table 4. One-factor model: oil

Period	January 2, 1985–February 17, 1995	January 2, 1990–February 17, 1995	January 2, 1990–February 17, 1995	January 15, 1993–May 16, 1996
Contracts	**F1, F3, F5, F7, F9**	**F1, F3, F5, F7, F9**	**F1, F5, F9, F13, F17**	**Enron Data**
NOBS	510	259	259	163
κ	0.301 (0.005)	0.694 (0.010)	0.428 (0.008)	0.099 (0.003)
μ	3.093 (0.346)	3.037 (0.228)	2.991 (0.280)	2.857 (0.635)
σ	0.334 (0.005)	0.326 (0.008)	0.257 (0.007)	0.129 (0.007)
λ	–0.242 (0.346)	–0.072 (0.228)	0.002 (0.279)	–0.320 (0.636)
$\xi 1$	0.049 (0.003)	0.045 (0.005)	0.080 (0.006)	0.079 (0.012)
$\xi 2$	0.018 (0.001)	0.017 (0.002)	0.031 (0.004)	0.046 (0.033)
$\xi 3$	0	0	0.010 (0.001)	0.029 (0.025)
$\xi 4$	0.012 (0.002)	0.009 (0.002)	0	0.014 (0.005)
$\xi 5$	0.022 (0.003)	0.015 (0.003)	0.007 (0.001)	0
$\xi 6$				0.007 (0.001)
$\xi 7$				0.018 (0.003)
$\xi 8$				0.031 (0.015)
$\xi 9$				0.035 (0.029)
$\xi 10$				0.035 (0.019)
Log-likelihood function	8130	4369	4345	5146

* (Standard errors in parentheses)
NOBS = number of observations.

Table 5. One-factor model: copper

Period	July 29, 1988–June 13, 1995
Contracts	**F1, F3, F5, F7, F9**
NOBS	347
κ	0.369 (0.009)
μ	4.854 (0.230)
σ	0.233 (0.007)
λ	–0.339 (0.230)
$\xi 1$	0.064 (0.002)
$\xi 2$	0.023 (0.001)
$\xi 3$	0
$\xi 4$	0.015 (0.001)
$\xi 5$	0.021 (0.002)
Log-likelihood function	5482

*(Standard errors in parentheses)
NOBS = number of observations.

Table 5 gives the results of applying the one-factor model to the copper data. These results are similar to those for oil. There is strong and significant mean-reversion (of 0.37) and the market price of risk is positive, but not significantly different from zero.

The one-factor model could not be fitted to the gold data, giving us a first indication that there is no detectable mean-reversion in gold prices for the period considered.

MODEL 2

The risk-free rate of interest, r, which is assumed constant, is a parameter in Model 2. It appears in the measurement equation (23) through $A(T)$ defined in equation (20). For purposes of estimating this two-factor model, we assumed a constant risk-free interest rate of 0.06, which was approximately the average interest rate over the period considered.[19] The risk-free rate enters into the analysis through the risk-adjusted process for the spot price

2. Oil futures prediction errors: Model 1 (January 2, 1985, to February 17, 1995)

The figure shows for each week the Model 1 oil futures prediction errors for the five futures contracts used in the estimation, starting from January 2, 1985, to February 17, 1995

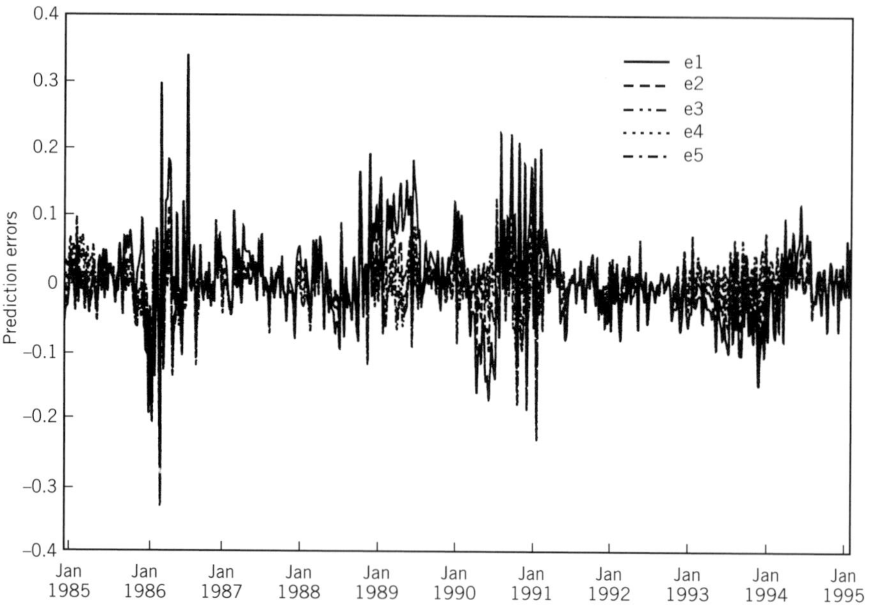

Table 6. Two-factor model: oil

Period	January 2, 1985– February 17, 1995	January 2, 1990– February 17, 1995	January 2, 1990– February 17, 1995	January 15, 1993– May 16, 1996
Contracts	F1, F3, F5, F7, F9	F1, F3, F5, F7, F9	F1, F5, F9, F13, F17	Enron Data
NOBS	510	259	259	163
μ	0.142 (0.125)	0.244 (0.150)	0.238 (0.160)	0.082 (0.120)
κ	1.876 (0.024)	1.829 (0.033)	1.488 (0.027)	1.187 (0.026)
α	0.106 (0.025)	0.184 (0.110)	0.180 (0.126)	0.090 (0.086)
$\sigma 1$	0.393 (0.007)	0.374 (0.011)	0.358 (0.010)	0.212 (0.011)
$\sigma 2$	0.527 (0.015)	0.556 (0.024)	0.426 (0.017)	0.187 (0.012)
ρ	0.766 (0.013)	0.882 (0.013)	0.922 (0.006)	0.845 (0.024)
λ	0.198 (0.166)	0.316 (0.203)	0.291 (0.190)	0.093 (0.101)
$\xi 1$	0.022 (0.001)	0.020 (0.001)	0.043 (0.002)	0.027 (0.001)
$\xi 2$	0.001 (0.001)	0	0.006 (0.001)	0.006 (0.001)
$\xi 3$	0.003 (0.001)	0.004 (0.000)	0.003 (0.000)	0
$\xi 4$	0	0	0	0.002 (0.000)
$\xi 5$	0.005 (0.000)	0.006 (0.000)	0.004 (0.000)	0
$\xi 6$				0.004 (0.000)
$\xi 7$				0.014 (0.003)
$\xi 8$				0.032 (0.015)
$\xi 9$				0.043 (0.036)
$\xi 10$				0.055 (0.039)
Log-likelihood function	10267	5256	5139	6182

* (Standard errors in parentheses)
NOBS = number of observations.

described in equation (14). From this equation it can be seen that any variation in the interest rate through time will be absorbed by variations in the convenience yield. The estimated instantaneous convenience yield will then be a composite of the actual convenience yield and the deviations of the interest rate from 0.06.

Table 6 reports the results of the two-factor model for the four oil data sets. In all cases the speed of adjustment coefficient in the convenience yield equation and the correlation coefficient between the two factors are large and highly significant; the total expected return on the spot commodity, μ, the average convenience yield and the market price of convenience yield risk are positive but not always significant at standard levels. It is interesting to

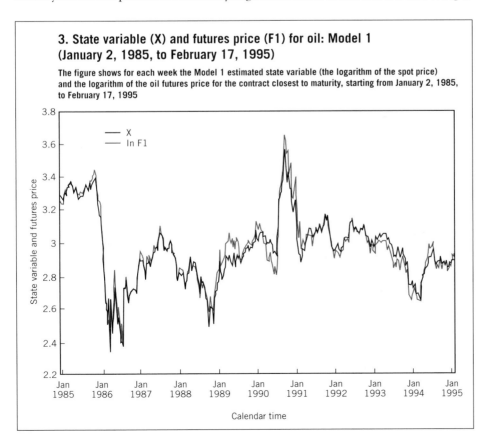

3. State variable (X) and futures price (F1) for oil: Model 1 (January 2, 1985, to February 17, 1995)

The figure shows for each week the Model 1 estimated state variable (the logarithm of the spot price) and the logarithm of the oil futures price for the contract closest to maturity, starting from January 2, 1985, to February 17, 1995

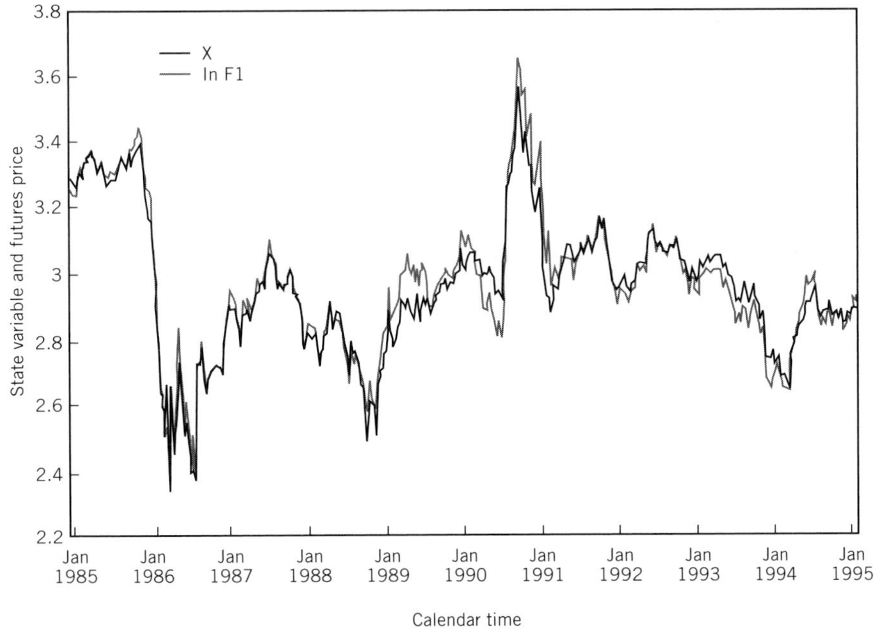

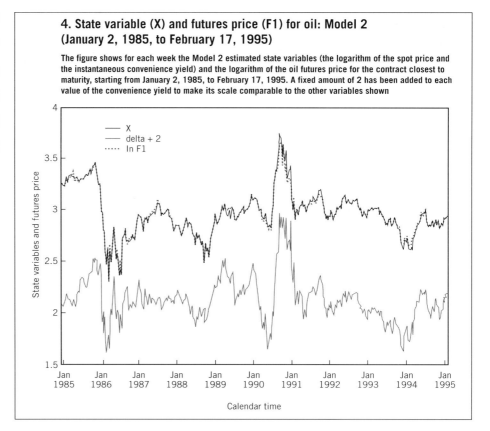

4. State variable (X) and futures price (F1) for oil: Model 2 (January 2, 1985, to February 17, 1995)

The figure shows for each week the Model 2 estimated state variables (the logarithm of the spot price and the instantaneous convenience yield) and the logarithm of the oil futures price for the contract closest to maturity, starting from January 2, 1985, to February 17, 1995. A fixed amount of 2 has been added to each value of the convenience yield to make its scale comparable to the other variables shown

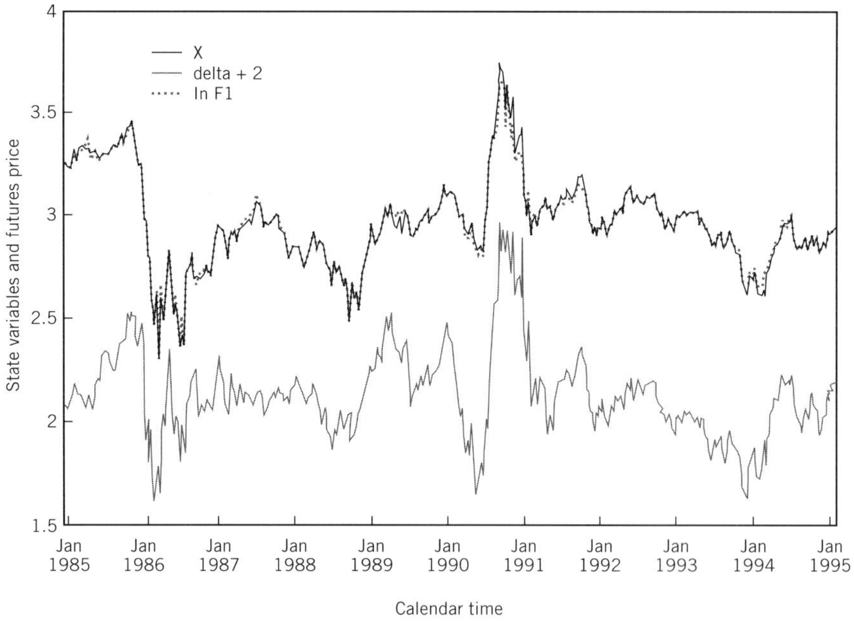

note that the estimations that use longer-term futures have a somewhat lower mean-reversion coefficient (1.2 for the Enron data versus 1.5 for the longer-term data and 1.8 for the shorter-term oil data). Figure 4 shows the two state variables for the first data set, which covers all the sample period,[20] and the log price of the futures contract closest to maturity. The strong correlation between the two state variables (0.77) and the closeness between the log spot price and the log of F1 can be observed from the figure. Figure 5 displays the prediction errors. Both the mean error of 0.0016 and the average absolute deviation of 0.029 are smaller than those in Model 1 (see Figure 2).

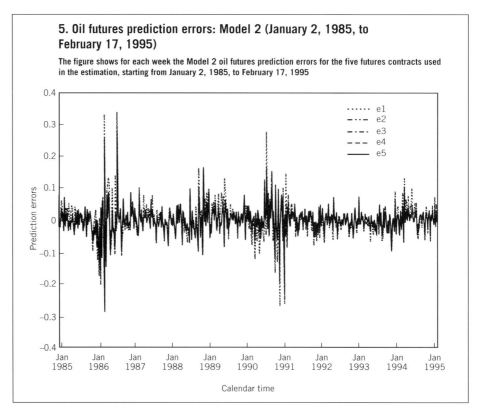

5. Oil futures prediction errors: Model 2 (January 2, 1985, to February 17, 1995)

The figure shows for each week the Model 2 oil futures prediction errors for the five futures contracts used in the estimation, starting from January 2, 1985, to February 17, 1995

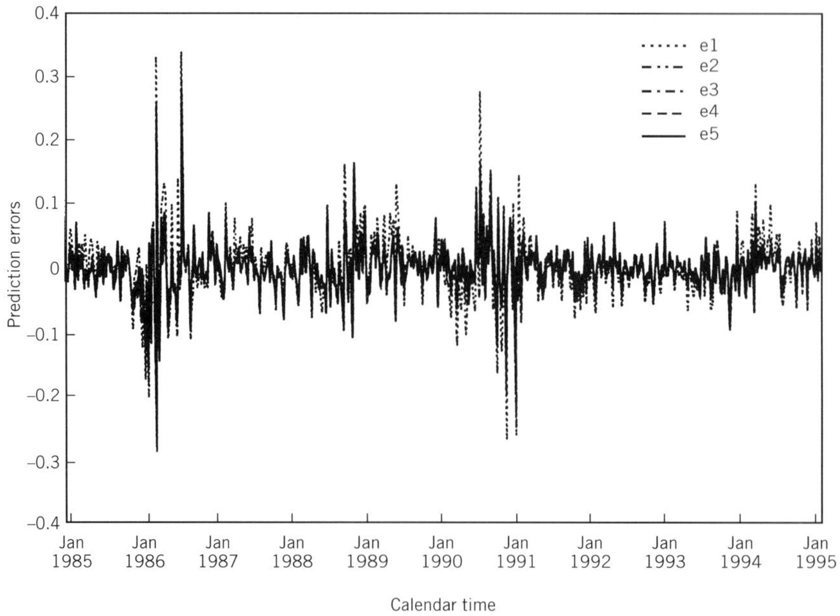

Table 7. Two-factor model: copper

Period	July 29, 1988–June 13, 1995
Contracts	F1, F3, F5, F7, F9
NOBS	347
μ	0.326 (0.110)
κ	1.156 (0.041)
α	0.248 (0.098)
$\sigma 1$	0.274 (0.012)
$\sigma 2$	0.280 (0.017)
ρ	0.818 (0.020)
λ	0.256 (0.114)
$\xi 1$	0.033 (0.001)
$\xi 2$	0.003 (0.001)
$\xi 3$	0.006 (0.000)
$\xi 4$	0.005 (0.000)
$\xi 5$	0.009 (0.001)
Log-likelihood function	6473

* (Standard errors in parentheses)
NOBS = number of observations.

Table 8. Two-factor model: gold

Period	January 2, 1985–June 13, 1995	November 21, 1990–June 13, 1995	November 21, 1990–June 13, 1995
Contracts	F1, F3, F6, F9, F11	F1, F3, F6, F9, F11	F1, F5, F9, F13, F18
NOBS	527	230	230
μ	0.039 (0.044)	0.033 (0.054)	0.030 (0.054)
κ	0.011 (0.008)	0.114 (0.015)	0.298 (0.018)
α	–0.002 (0.322)	0.018 (0.052)	0.019 (0.023)
$\sigma 1$	0.135 (0.003)	0.106 (0.004)	0.107 (0.004)
$\sigma 2$	0.016 (0.001)	0.0124 (0.0007)	0.015 (0.001)
ρ	0.056 (0.034)	0.113 (0.066)	0.250 (0.068)
λ	0.0067 (0.0036)	0.0076 (0.0060)	0.008 (0.007)
$\xi 1$	0.003 (0.000)	0.002 (0.000)	0.004 (0.000)
$\xi 2$	0	0	0
$\xi 3$	0.001 (0.000)	0.001 (0.000)	0.001 (0.001)
$\xi 4$	0	0	0.001 (0.000)
$\xi 5$	0.001 (0.000)	0.001 (0.000)	0.012 (0.001)
Log-likelihood function	14437	6662	5660

* (Standard errors in parentheses)
NOBS = number of observations.

The results for copper, presented in Table 7, also show very strong and significant correlation between the state variables and mean-reversion in the convenience yield. The total expected return on copper, the average convenience yield and the market price of risk are also positive and significant, but not as strongly as the other parameters. Note that the average convenience yield is high (25% per year) because we are estimating instantaneous convenience yields - that is, for futures contracts maturing in the next instant of time.

The results for gold, displayed in Table 8, differ importantly from those for the commercial commodities. The mean-reversion in the convenience yield and the correlation between the state variables are significant only in the later period and of much smaller magnitude, 0.3 and 0.25, respectively, for the longer-term data. The total expected return, average convenience yield and market price of risk are insignificant in all cases. As we shall see when we discuss the three-factor model, even the mean-reversion in the convenience yield becomes insignificant when stochastic interest rates are considered, which suggests that in the two-factor model mean-reversion in convenience yield is proxying for mean-reversion in interest rates (which are assumed constant in this model).

MODEL 3

The parameters for the risk-adjusted interest rate process (23) were obtained using three-month Treasury bill yields. The standard deviation of changes in r, σ_3, for each data set were computed using contemporaneous yields. As reported in Tables 9, 10 and 11, this standard deviation varied from 0.0073 to 0.0096 for different time periods. The speed of adjustment coefficient of the process, a, was assumed to be equal to 0.2, which implies that one-half of any deviation from the average interest rate is expected to be corrected in 3.5 years.[21] The risk-adjusted drift of the process, m^*, was computed so that the infinite-maturity discount yield be 7%. In the Vasicek model this infinite-maturity yield is

$$R(\infty) = m^* - \frac{\sigma_3^2}{2a^2} \qquad (37)$$

The instantaneous correlations between the interest rate process and the process for the log spot price and the convenience yield defined in equation (24) were approximated by the correlations obtained using weekly data between the three-month Treasury bill yield and the values of these state variables obtained from Model 2. The estimated values of these correlations are shown in Tables 9, 10 and 11. Apart from the correlation between the interest rate and the convenience yield for copper (0.12) and gold (0.4), the other correlations were very close to zero.[22]

Tables 9 and 10 present the parameter estimates for Model 3 for oil and copper, respectively.[23] For both oil and copper these results are quite close to those of Model 2. The para-

Table 9. Three-factor model: oil

Period	January 2, 1990–February 17, 1995	January 15, 1993–May 16, 1996
Contracts	F1, F5, F9, F13, F17	Enron Data
NOBS	259	163
μ	0.315 (0.125)	0.008 (0.109)
κ	1.314 (0.027)	0.976 (0.022)
α	0.249 (0.093)	0.038 (0.077)
σ1	0.344 (0.009)	0.196 (0.009)
σ2	0.372 (0.014)	0.145 (0.008)
ρ1	0.915 (0.007)	0.809 (0.027)
λ	0.353 (0.123)	0.013 (0.075)
ξ1	0.045 (0.002)	0.028 (0.001)
ξ2	0.007 (0.001)	0.006 (0.001)
ξ3	0.003 (0.000)	0
ξ4	0	0.002 (0.000)
ξ5	0.004 (0.000)	0.000 (0.001)
ξ6		0.005 (0.000)
ξ7		0.013 (0.002)
ξ8		0.024 (0.008)
ξ9		0.032 (0.014)
ξ10		0.053 (0.023)
Log-likelihood function	5128	6287
σ3	0.0081	0.0073
a	0.2	0.2
R(∞)	0.07	0.07
ρ2	−0.0039	0.0399
ρ3	−0.0293	−0.0057

* (Standard errors in parentheses)
NOBS = number of observations.

Table 10. Three-factor model: copper

Period	July 29, 1988–June 13, 1995
Contracts	F1, F3, F5, F7, F9
NOBS	347
μ	0.332 (0.094)
κ	1.045 (0.030)
α	0.255 (0.078)
σ1	0.266 (0.011)
σ2	0.249 (0.014)
ρ1	0.805 (0.022)
λ	0.243 (0.082)
ξ1	0.032 (0.001)
ξ2	0.004 (0.001)
ξ3	0.005 (0.000)
ξ4	0.005 (0.000)
ξ5	0.007 (0.000)
Log-likelihood function	6520
σ3	0.0096
a	0.2
R(∞)	0.07
ρ2	0.1243
ρ3	0.0964

*(Standard errors in parentheses)
NOBS = number of observations.

Table 11. Three-factor model: gold

Period	November 21, 1990–June 13, 1995
Contracts	F1, F5, F9, F13, F18
NOBS	230
μ	0.023 (0.054)
κ	0.023 (0.023)
α	0.021 (0.189)
σ1	0.106 (0.004)
σ2	0.009 (0.001)
ρ1	0.208 (0.069)
λ	0.002 (0.004)
ξ1	0.003 (0.000)
ξ2	0
ξ3	0.001 (0.000)
ξ4	0.001 (0.000)
ξ5	0.015 (0.001)
Log-likelihood function	5688
σ3	0.0082
a	0.2
R(∞)	0.07
ρ2	−0.4005
ρ3	−0.0260

*(Standard errors in parentheses)
NOBS = number of observations.

meters of the processes for the spot price and convenience yield seem to be robust to the specification of the interest rate process. This does not mean, however, that the value of the futures contract is insensitive to the interest rate used in the computation.

Table 11 reports the parameter estimates of Model 3 for gold. The fact that the mean-reversion in the convenience yield becomes insignificant when stochastic interest rates are included and that the correlation between changes in the interest rate and the convenience yield is so high in absolute terms (− 0.4) suggests that the models are misspecified for gold. Mean-reversion in prices induced by a mean-reverting convenience yield does not seem to hold for gold.

COMPARING THE THREE MODELS

For the purpose of comparing the relative performance of the three models, we will concentrate on three data sets: the long-term oil futures data, the copper futures data and the Enron oil forward data. Figures 6, 7 and 8 illustrate how the three models fit the data for three dates in the sample period. These dates were the first observation in the sample, the last observation in the sample, and an intermediate observation chosen so that futures prices were in contango, since the first and last observations were in backwardation.[24] Figures 6a, 6b and 6c correspond to the long-term oil data, Figures 7a, 7b and 7c to the copper data, and Figures 8a, 8b and 8c to the Enron oil data. From these figures we can observe that Model 1 is very often incapable of adequately describing the data. From equation (7) we can see that when the maturity of the futures contract tends to infinity, in Model 1 the futures price converges to

$$F(S,\infty) = \exp\left[\alpha^* + \frac{\sigma^2}{4\kappa}\right] \tag{38}$$

which is independent of the spot price. For the estimated parameters of Model 1 the infinite-maturity futures prices are US$20.13 for the long-term oil data, US$22.99 dollar for the Enron oil data and 88.08 cents for the copper data. When the spot price is above these infinite-maturity futures prices Model 1 will be in backwardation, and when the spot price is below it will be in contango. This feature does not allow for much flexibility in the term structure of futures prices.

6. Model and market oil futures prices

(a) The figure shows the term structure of oil futures prices for January 2, 1990, the starting date for the long-term oil data, and the term structure implied by the three models. (b) The figure shows the term structure of oil futures prices for December 22, 1993, a date on which oil futures prices were in contango, and the term structure implied by the three models. (c) The figure shows the term structure of oil futures prices for February 17, 1995, the last date for the oil data, and the term structure implied by the three models.

(a) January 2, 1990

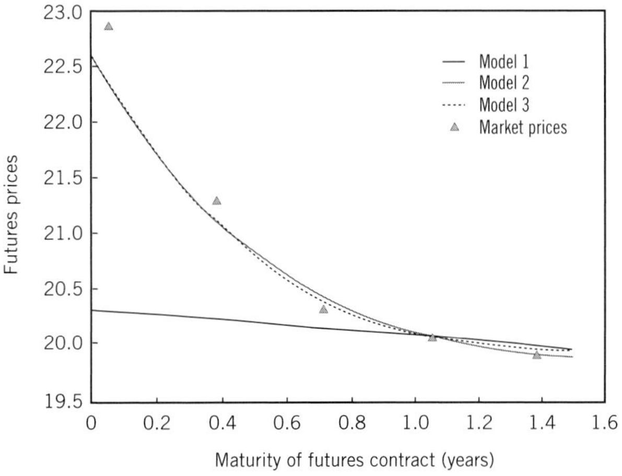

(b) December 22, 1993

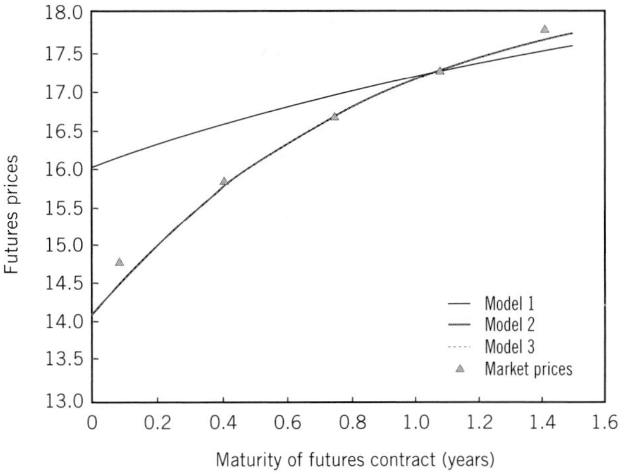

(c) February 17, 1995

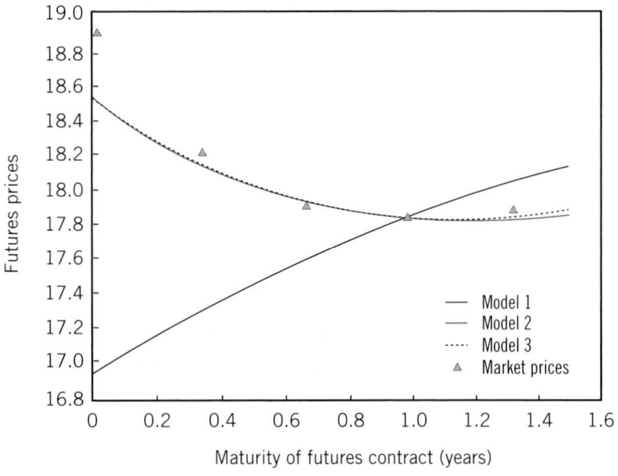

7. Model and market copper futures prices

(a) The figure shows the term structure of copper futures prices for July 29, 1988, the starting date for the copper data, and the term structure implied by the three models. (b) The figure shows the term structure of copper futures prices for July 13, 1993, a date on which copper futures prices were in contango, and the term structure implied by the three models. (c) The figure shows the term structure of copper futures prices for June 13, 1995, the last date for the copper data, and the term structure implied by the three models.

(a) July 29, 1988

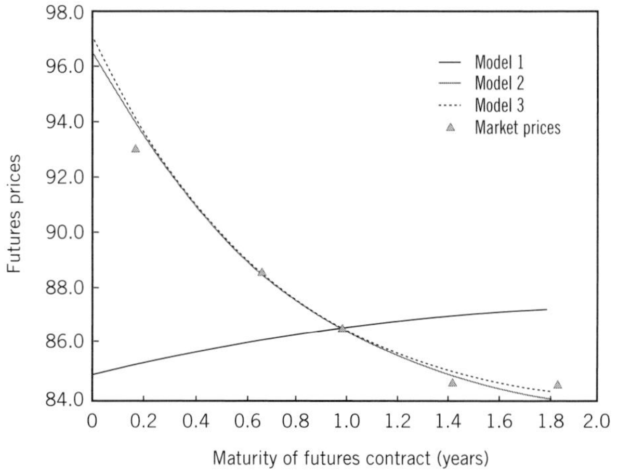

(b) July 13, 1993

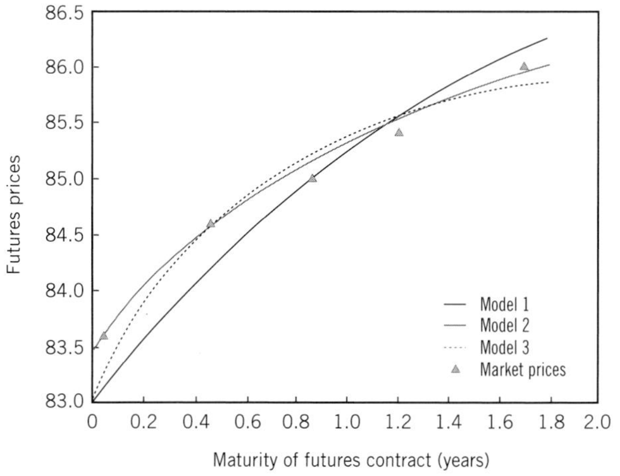

(c) June 13, 1995

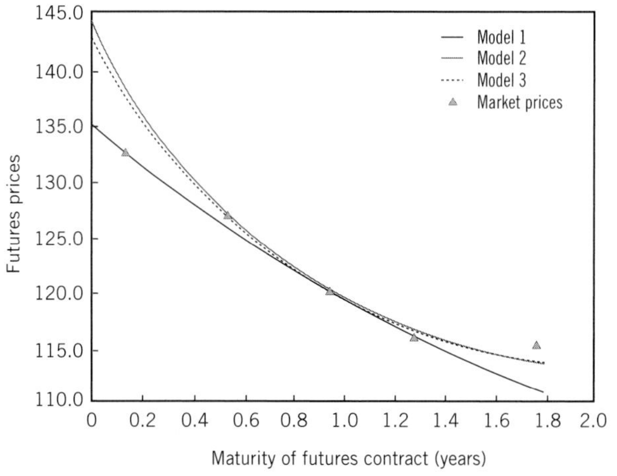

8. Model and market Enron oil futures prices

(a) The figure shows the term structure of oil futures prices for January 15, 1993, the starting date for the Enron oil data, and the term structure implied by the three models. (b) The figure shows the term structure of oil futures prices for February 15, 1994, a date on which Enron oil futures prices were in contango, and the term structure implied by the three models. (c) The figure shows the term structure of oil futures prices for May 16, 1996, the last date for the Enron oil data, and the term structure implied by the three models.

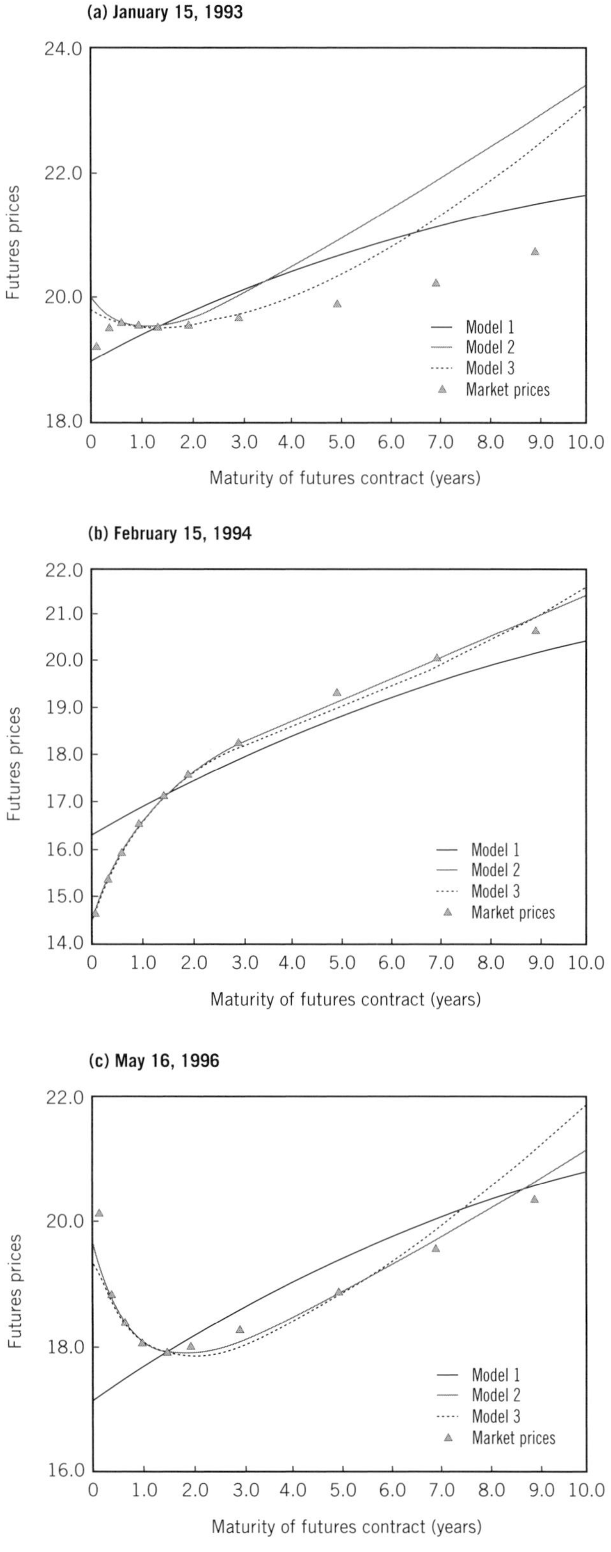

From Figures 6 and 7 we can also observe that the term structure of futures prices implied by Models 2 and 3 for the long-term oil data and the copper data are sometimes indistinguishable and that they are always very close to each other. This holds true for all the in-sample term structures. As we shall see in the section on long-maturity futures contracts, this does not mean that both models have the same implications for futures prices with longer maturities than the observable ones. For the Enron oil data, however, Models 2 and 3 can imply quite different term structures of futures prices, as shown in Figure 8.

The empirical models we have estimated are not nested, so a statistical comparison between them is not straightforward.[25] Model 1 is not nested in Model 2 nor in 3. Even though model 2 is nested in Model 3, we estimate the same number of parameters in both models since in Model 3 we take as exogenous the parameters of the interest rate process. This complicates the interpretation of the value of the likelihood function. To compare the relative performance of the models we performed two types of tests. The first were cross-section tests using all the available futures prices not used in the estimation of the parameters of the models. Recall that only five futures prices (and 10 for the Enron data) were used to estimate the parameters of the models. The second were time-series tests using the last 50 observations in the sample.

In cross-section tests we used the parameters and the value of the state variables estimated over the whole sample period to price at every observation date all the futures contracts that were not used in the estimation. In some sense, this is an out-of-sample test because we are only pricing contracts not used in the estimation. The parameters used, however, have been estimated over the whole sample period, so in strict sense only the last observation is truly out-of-sample. Also, prices of futures contracts are correlated. The procedure, anyhow, should give us an indication of the relative performance of the models. Tables 12, 13 and 14 show the results for the long-term oil, copper and Enron oil data, respectively. For oil we had 12 futures prices not used in the estimation, but for copper we only had four. For the Enron oil data we used 10 - forward prices not used in the estimation. We report the root mean square error (RMSE) and the mean error in monetary terms in Panel A of the tables and as percentages in Panel B for the contracts available and also for all the contracts together. Models 2 and 3 clearly outperform Model 1 in every dimension and for the three data sets. For example, for the oil data the RMSE is 2.7% for Model 1, whereas it is around 1% for Models 2 and 3. The relative performance of Models 2 and 3 is not so clear when we consider only the shorter-maturity futures data: Model 2 outperforms Model 3 for oil, and vice versa for copper. For the futures contracts also the copper data fit all the models better than the oil data. This is possibly due to the fact that the oil data period includes the Gulf War in August, 1990, which had a dramatic impact in the oil

Table 12. Cross-section comparison between Models 1, 2 and 3 out-of-sample oil data January 2, 1990–February 17, 1995

	RMSE			Mean error		
Model contract	**1**	**2**	**3**	**1**	**2**	**3**
Panel A: (in US$)						
F2	1.537	0.538	0.577	0.453	–0.057	–0.032
F3	1.215	0.325	0.363	0.376	–0.019	–0.003
F4	0.952	0.183	0.22	0.3	0.004	0.013
F6	0.55	0.061	0.074	0.163	0.01	0.011
F7	0.41	0.058	0.056	0.108	0.006	0.005
F8	0.296	0.054	0.044	0.063	0	–0.001
F10	0.138	0.045	0.037	0.009	–0.005	–0.006
F11	0.082	0.035	0.03	–0.001	–0.003	–0.004
F12	0.039	0.02	0.019	–0.003	–0.001	–0.002
F14	0.039	0.02	0.019	0.009	0.001	0.001
F15	0.075	0.036	0.034	0.021	0.001	0.001
F16	0.109	0.053	0.051	0.037	0.001	0
All	0.668	0.193	0.21	0.128	–0.005	–0.001
Panel B: In percentage						
F2	6.203	2.574	2.795	1.566	–0.273	–0.188
F3	4.94	1.546	1.737	1.386	–0.091	–0.035
F4	3.92	0.862	1.032	1.159	0.012	0.045
F6	2.369	0.272	0.329	0.671	0.042	0.046
F7	1.814	0.253	0.238	0.45	0.021	0.018
F8	1.35	0.256	0.204	0.268	–0.003	–0.008
F10	0.664	0.218	0.179	0.04	–0.024	–0.03
F11	0.406	0.169	0.146	–0.002	–0.016	–0.02
F12	0.194	0.099	0.089	–0.013	–0.006	–0.008
F14	0.192	0.1	0.093	0.038	0.005	0.005
F15	0.366	0.18	0.171	0.095	0.007	0.006
F16	0.536	0.265	0.257	0.171	0.007	0.004
All	2.74	0.92	1.011	0.486	–0.027	–0.014

markets. For the longer-maturity Enron oil data, however, Model 3 appears as the clear winner: the RMSE is 4.1% for Model 1, 2.6% for Model 2 and 2.2% for Model 3. Note also that, for these data, volatilities are smaller since they does not include the Gulf War period.

A truly out-of-sample time-series test of the models would compute the prediction errors for period $t + 1$ using all the information available up to period t. This would require the estimation of the new parameters of the model at every period t. Instead, we computed an upper and lower bound of these prediction errors in the following manner. First, we computed the prediction errors for the last 50 observations of the sample using the parameters estimated for the whole sample period. This is a lower bound of the error, since we are using the last observations also to estimate the parameters. Second, we estimated the parameters over the period that did not include the last 50 observations and used them to estimate the

Table 13. Cross-section comparison between Models 1, 2 and 3 out-of-sample copper data July 29, 1988 to June 13, 1995

	RMSE			Mean error		
Model contract	**1**	**2**	**3**	**1**	**2**	**3**
Panel A: In cents						
F2	4.617	1.311	1.27	1.75	–0.155	–0.142
F4	1.17	0.548	0.539	0.327	0.116	0.119
F6	1.133	0.616	0.621	–0.194	–0.105	–0.098
F8	1.824	0.534	0.482	0.257	–0.042	–0.064
All	2.612	0.819	0.794	0.535	–0.046	–0.046
Panel B: In percentage						
F2	3.929	1.103	1.073	1.404	–0.151	–0.135
F4	1.063	0.483	0.474	0.284	0.093	0.094
F6	1.064	0.568	0.572	–0.188	–0.102	–0.097
F8	1.78	0.512	0.462	0.213	–0.036	–0.058
All	2.284	0.713	0.692	0.428	–0.049	–0.049

Table 14. Cross-section comparison between Models 1, 2 and 3 out-of-sample Enron oil data, January 15, 1993–May 16, 1996

	RMSE			Mean error		
Model contract	1	2	3	1	2	3
Panel A: In US$						
One month	1.86	0.905	0.942	0.839	0.332	0.427
Four months	0.934	0.179	0.181	0.413	0.05	0.089
Seven months	0.588	0.028	0.028	0.254	0.005	0.012
10 months	0.358	0.034	0.033	0.153	–0.005	–0.014
15 months	0.108	0.033	0.031	0.043	–0.004	–0.013
21 months	0.078	0.046	0.043	–0.027	0.009	0.021
$2\frac{1}{2}$ years	0.245	0.183	0.162	–0.058	0.039	0.093
Four years	0.505	0.493	0.439	0.095	0.185	0.283
Six years	0.713	0.802	0.575	0.191	0.092	0. 135
Eight years	0.756	1.027	0.792	0.221	–0.238	–0.395
All	0.789	0.532	0.459	0.212	0.046	0.064
Panel B: In percentage						
One month	9.428	4.305	4.46	3.958	1.701	2.182
Four months	5.247	0.967	0.987	2.113	0.303	0.506
Seven months	3.347	0.155	0.156	1.335	0.034	0.068
10 months	2.036	0.184	0.181	0.819	–0.034	–0.079
15 months	0.611	0.177	0.172	0.235	–0.03	–0.077
21 months	0.435	0.249	0.242	–0.148	0.057	0.12
$2\frac{1}{2}$ years	1.316	0.962	0.885	–0.31	0.242	0.522
Four years	2.584	0.506	2.257	0.461	0.997	1.483
Six years	3.499	3.925	2.813	0.883	0.47	0.666
Eight years	3.586	4.944	3.827	0.996	–1.154	–1.933
All	4.072	2.582	2.224	1.034	0.259	0.346

prediction errors for the last 50 observations of the sample. This is an upper bound of the error since we did not update the parameters of the models as new data became known. Tables 15, 16 and 17 present the results of these tests for oil, copper and Enron oil data, respectively. Panel A of the tables gives the root mean square errors and the mean errors of the log prices[26] using the in-sample estimation of parameters, whereas Panel B gives the same information but using the out-of-sample parameter estimates. The period over which the parameters are estimated does not make a significant difference in the results, justifying the procedure used. As before, Models 2 and 3 clearly outperform Model 1. Model 3 marginally outperforms Model 2 for the oil and copper data. In the out-of-sample parameter estimation, Model 3 outperforms Model 2 for the Enron oil data, but the reverse occurs for the in-sample parameter estimation.

Table 15. Time-series comparison between Models 1, 2 and 3: last 50 observations of oil data

	RMSE (of log prices)			Mean error (of log prices)		
Model	1	2	3	1	2	3
Panel A: In-sample parameter estimation						
F1	0.0830	0.0538	0.0540	0.0628	0.0291	0.0279
F5	0.0390	0.0240	0.0248	0.0260	0.0049	0.0040
F9	0.0230	0.0195	0.0194	0.0096	0.0003	–0.0007
F13	0.0171	0.0170	0.0170	0.0012	0.0012	0.0001
F17	0.0157	0.0161	0.0160	–0.0033	0.0034	0.0016
All	0.0435	0.0300	0.0299	0.0193	0.0077	0.0066
Panel B: Out-of-sample parameter estimation						
F1	0.0919	0.0551	0.0541	0.0770	0.0315	0.0289
F5	0.0378	0.0249	0.0246	0.0273	0.0045	0.0030
F9	0.0198	0.0195	0.0195	0.0020	–0.0004	–0.0017
F13	0.0210	0.0170	0.0170	–0.0125	0.0014	0.0002
F17	0.0262	0.0166	0.0162	–0.0212	0.0050	0.0028
All	0.0477	0.0303	0.0299	0.0145	0.0084	0.0066

Table 16. Time-series comparison between Models 1, 2 and 3: last 50 observations of copper data

	RMSE (of log prices)			Mean error (of log prices)		
Model	1	2	3	1	2	3
Panel A: In-sample parameter estimation						
F1	0.0453	0.0430	0.0412	0.0046	−0.0253	−0.0232
F3	0.0294	0.0216	0.0217	0.0061	0.0029	0.0024
F5	0.0192	0.0194	0.0190	0.0027	0.0070	0.0062
F7	0.0207	0.0180	0.0180	−0.0000	−0.00126	−0.0016
F9	0.0255	0.0187	0.0186	0.0140	−0.00021	−0.0003
All	0.0296	0.0260	0.0253	0.0055	−0.0034	−0.0033
Panel B: Out-of-sample parameter estimation						
F1	0.0455	0.0467	0.0434	0.0058	−0.0301	−0.0264
F3	0.0295	0.0218	0.0216	0.0068	0.0030	0.0023
F5	0.0193	0.0199	0.0193	0.0031	0.0080	0.0068
F7	0.0207	0.0182	0.0181	0.0001	−0.0013	−0.0015
F9	0.0256	0.0188	0.0188	0.0141	−0.0018	−0.0012
All	0.0297	0.0273	0.0261	0.0060	−0.0044	−0.0040

Volatility of futures returns

When we use a model to value a financial or real asset contingent on a commodity price, we are interested in modelling not only the term structure of futures prices, but also the term structure of volatilities. Each model considered has different implications for the term structure of the volatilities of commodity futures returns. One property that will be common to the three models is that volatilities will be independent of the state variables of each model and will only depend on time-to-maturity of the futures contracts.

Applying Itô's lemma to equation (7) we see that the term structure of proportional futures volatilities in Model 1 is given by

$$\sigma_F^2(T) = \sigma^2 e^{-2\kappa T} \tag{39}$$

A feature of this model is that as the time-to-maturity of the futures contract approaches infinity, the volatility of its price converges to zero.

Table 17. Time-series comparison between Models 1, 2 and 3: last 50 observations of Enron oil data

	RMSE (of log prices)			Mean error (of log prices)		
Model	1	2	3	1	2	3
Panel A: In-sample parameter estimation						
Two months	0.1184	0.0480	0.0522	0.1024	0.0287	0.0340
Five months	0.0646	0.0213	0.0220	0.0563	0.0047	0.0071
Eight months	0.0422	0.0173	0.0173	0.0353	0.0010	0.0019
One year	0.0239	0.0149	0.0149	0.0168	−0.0001	0.0002
$1\frac{1}{2}$ years	0.0129	0.0131	0.0132	−0.0001	0.0006	0.0013
Two years	0.0151	0.0144	0.0152	−0.0075	0.0040	0.0056
Three years	0.0201	0.0155	0.0173	−0.0145	0.0080	0.0101
Five years	0.0270	0.0193	0.0160	−0.0154	0.0103	0.0065
Seven years	0.0280	0.0215	0.0183	−0.0086	0.0085	−0.0077
Nine years	0.0221	0.0177	0.0358	−0.0002	0.0009	−0.0318
All	0.0483	0.0225	0.0251	0.0164	0.0067	0.0027
Panel B: Out-of-sample parameter estimation						
Two months	0.1391	0.0540	0.0622	0.1258	0.0364	0.0450
Five months	0.0810	0.0221	0.0242	0.0744	0.0075	0.0117
Eight months	0.0534	0.0172	0.0172	0.0485	0.0012	0.0021
One year	0.0297	0.0150	0.0149	0.0241	−0.0010	−0.0031
$1\frac{1}{2}$ years	0.0128	0.0131	0.0132	−0.0002	0.0008	−0.0034
Two years	0.0186	0.0157	0.0126	−0.0135	0.0067	0.0017
Three years	0.0319	0.0215	0.0165	−0.0288	0.0163	0.0110
Five years	0.0429	0.0301	0.0225	−0.0360	0.0263	0.0183
Seven years	0.0392	0.0338	0.0196	−0.0274	0.0297	0.0133
Nine years	0.0267	0.0303	0.0142	−0.0131	0.0264	−0.0025
All	0.0594	0.0279	0.0258	0.0154	0.0150	0.0094

9. Volatility of futures returns: Models 1, 2, 3 and market

(a) The figure shows the term structure of oil futures returns and the term structure implied by the three models. (b) The figure shows the term structure of volatilities of copper futures returns and the term structure implied by the three models. (c) The figure shows the term structure of volatilities of oil futures returns and the term structure implied by the three models, using the parameters for the Enron oil data.

(a) Oil

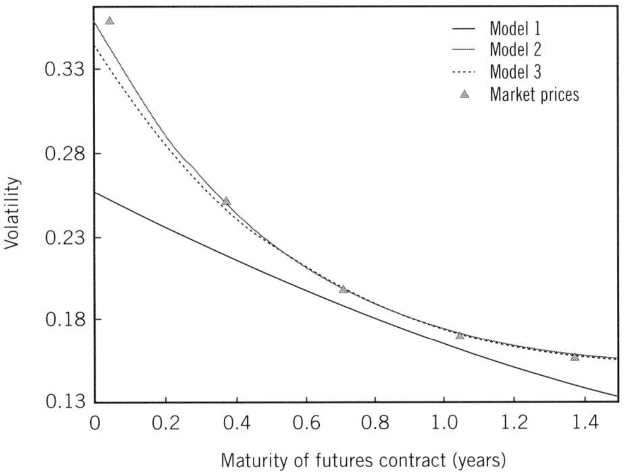

(b) Copper

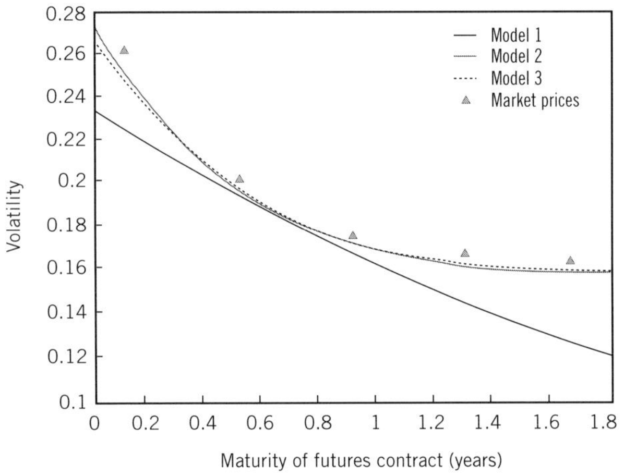

(c) Enron oil

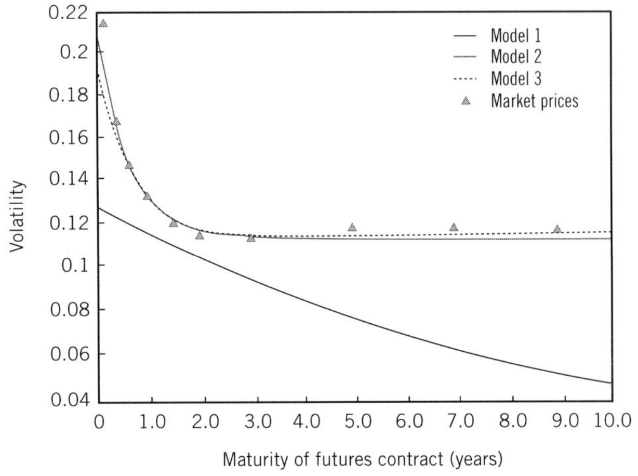

From equation (18) we can obtain the volatility of futures returns in Model 2:

$$\sigma_F^2(T) = \sigma_1^2 + \sigma_2^2 \frac{(1 - e^{-\kappa T})^2}{\kappa^2} - 2\rho\sigma_1\sigma_2 \frac{(1 - e^{-\kappa T})}{\kappa} \tag{40}$$

When time-to-maturity approaches infinity, the volatility of futures returns in this model converges to

$$\sigma_F^2(\infty) = \sigma_1^2 + \frac{\sigma_2^2}{\kappa^2} - \frac{2\rho\sigma_1\sigma_2}{\kappa} \tag{41}$$

Finally, the volatility in Model 3 can be obtained from equation (26):

$$\begin{aligned}\sigma_F^2(T) = {} & \sigma_1^2 + \sigma_2^2 \frac{(1 - e^{-\kappa T})^2}{\kappa^2} \\ & + \sigma_3^2 \frac{(1 - e^{-aT})^2}{a^2} - 2\rho_1\sigma_1\sigma_2 \frac{(1 - e^{-\kappa T})}{\kappa} \\ & + 2\rho_3\sigma_1\sigma_3 \frac{(1 - e^{-aT})}{a} \\ & - 2\rho_2\sigma_2\sigma_3 \frac{(1 - e^{-aT})(1 - e^{-\kappa T})}{a\kappa}\end{aligned} \tag{42}$$

When time-to-maturity approaches infinity this expression converges to

$$\begin{aligned}\sigma_F^2(\infty) = {} & \sigma_1^2 + \frac{\sigma_2^2}{\kappa^2} + \frac{\sigma_3^2}{a^2} \\ & - \frac{2\rho_1\sigma_1\sigma_2}{\kappa} + \frac{2\rho_3\sigma_1\sigma_3}{a} - \frac{2\rho_2\sigma_2\sigma_3}{a\kappa}\end{aligned} \tag{43}$$

Figures 9a, 9b and 9c plot the volatility of futures returns implied by the three models (using equations (39), (40) and (42)) for the oil data, the copper data and the Enron oil data, respectively. The figures also show the actual volatility of futures returns of the contracts used in the estimation of the parameters of the models. It is surprising to see how well Models 2 and 3 fit the volatility of the data. It should be noted that only futures prices were used in the estimation; the volatility of futures returns is not an input in the estimation. The only volatility that enters into the estimation procedure is the volatility of the unobserved state variables. Finally, the figures show that Model 1 implies volatilities that are always smaller than the volatility of the data, with the difference being smaller for mid-maturities and then increasing with increasing maturity of the futures contracts.

Figure 9 also indicates that, for the data considered, Models 2 and 3 imply very similar futures volatilities. The reason for this is that the volatility of the interest rate process in Model 3 (see Table 9) is of an order of magnitude smaller than the volatilities of the other state variables (around 1/25). If we compare equation (42) with (40), we see that the volatility of futures returns in Model 3 converges to the one in Model 2 when the volatility of interest rates goes to zero.

Table 18. Volatilities of futures returns implied by Models 1, 2 and 3

	Oil futures	
Model	**Zero maturity**	**Infinite maturity**
1	0.257	0
2	0.358	0.145
3	0.344	0.146
	Copper futures	
Model	**Zero maturity**	**Infinite maturity**
1	0.233	0
2	0.274	0.159
3	0.266	0.166
	Enron oil forwards	
Model	**Zero maturity**	**Infinite maturity**
1	0.129	0
2	0.212	0.159
3	0.196	0.166

Table 18 reports the limiting volatilities (when time-to-maturity is zero and infinity) for the three models. Note that for the three data sets the volatilities for Model 2 start at a higher level and end at a lower level than for Model 3. The crossover is barely observed in Figure 9.

In summary, Model 1, which has very different implications about the volatility of futures returns as the maturity of the contract increases than Models 2 and 3, is incapable of describing the volatility of the futures data. Models 2 and 3 give similar implications because the volatility of the convenience yield overshadows the volatility of interest rates. This feature has important implications for valuation when the models are used in situations that involve longer-term assets.

Long-maturity futures contracts

The futures contracts available to estimate the parameters of the models discussed in this chapter have maximum maturities that are less than two years. Only the proprietary Enron oil forward curves have longer-term maturities. It is of great interest to find out what are the implications of the models estimated with short-maturity futures contracts with respect to longer-term contracts, since many of the potential applications would involve assets with maturities longer than two years. In the previous section we examined the implications of the models with respect to volatility, and here we look at the implications with respect to price.

Figures 10 and 11 show the futures prices implied by the models for contracts up to 10 years to maturity for the same observations as in Figures 6 and 7, respectively. Here we observe that even though Models 2 and 3 give very similar values in the range of observed contracts, they can diverge substantially as maturity increases. As mentioned in the fourth section (see equation (38)), in Model 1 the futures price converges to a fixed value, so the rate of change in price as maturity increases converges to zero. For the estimated parameters in Models 2 and 3, however, even if initially the term structure of futures prices is decreasing,

10. Long-term model oil futures prices

(a) The figure shows the term structures of oil futures prices for January 2, 1990, by the three models for maturities up to 10 years. (b) The figure shows the term structure of oil futures prices for December 22, 1993, implied by the three models for maturities up to 10 years. (c) The figure shows the term structure of oil futures prices for February 17, 1995, implied by the three models for maturities up to 10 years.

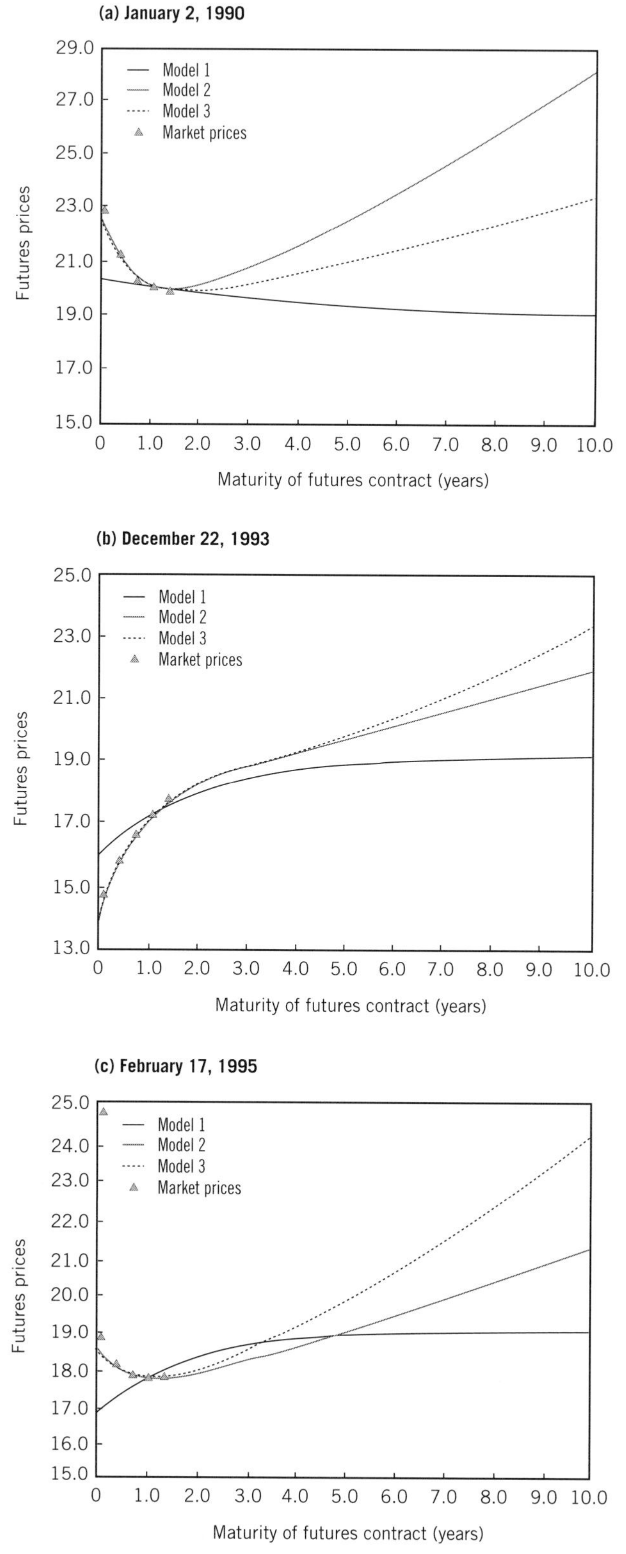

11. Long-term model copper futures prices

(a) The figure shows the term structure of copper futures prices for July 29, 1988, implied by the three models for maturities up to 10 years.
(b) The figure shows the term structure of copper futures prices for July 13, 1993, implied by the three models for maturities up to 10 years.
(c) The figure shows the term structure of copper futures prices for June 13, 1995, implied by the three models for maturities up to 10 years.

(a) July 29, 1988

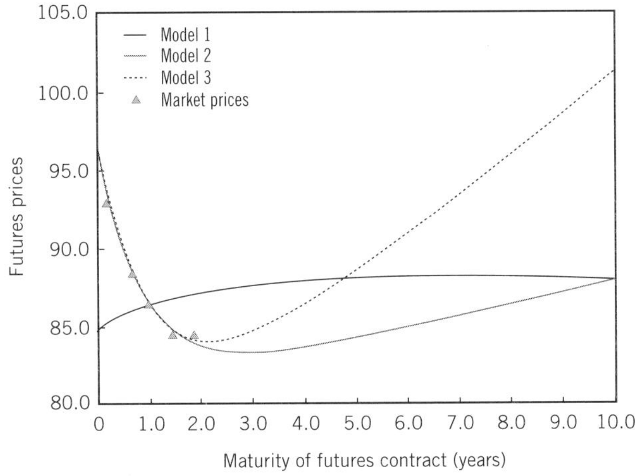

(b) July 13, 1993

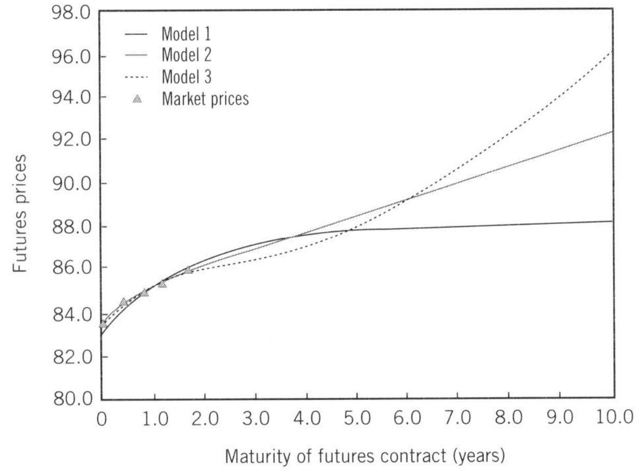

(c) June 13, 1995

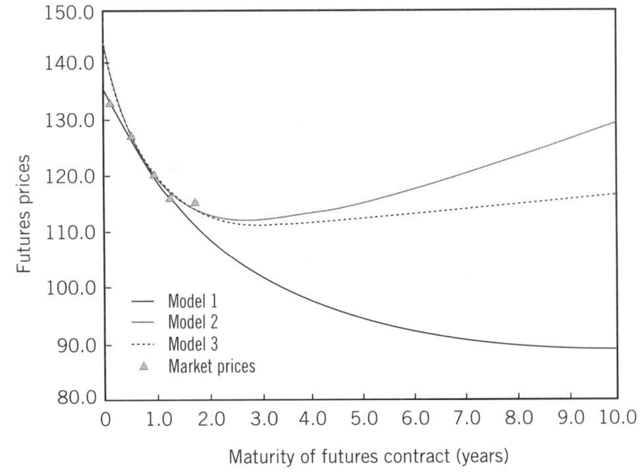

it eventually turns upward. In Models 2 and 3, the rate of change in price as maturity increases can easily be obtained by taking the derivative of the futures price with respect to time-to-maturity, dividing by the price, and taking the limit when time-to-maturity goes to infinity. For both models this "forward cost of carry"[27] converges to a rate that is independent of the initial value of the state variables. In Model 2 this rate is

$$\frac{1}{F}\frac{\partial F}{\partial T}(T \rightarrow \infty) = r - \hat{\alpha} + \frac{\sigma_2^2}{2\kappa^2} - \frac{\rho\sigma_1\sigma_2}{\kappa} \tag{44}$$

which translates, given the estimated parameters, into 2.71% per year for oil futures and 0.85% per year for copper futures. The corresponding rate in Model 3 is

$$\frac{1}{F}\frac{\partial F}{\partial T}(T \rightarrow \infty) = m^* - \hat{\alpha} + \frac{\sigma_2^2}{2\kappa^2} - \frac{\rho_1\sigma_1\sigma_2}{\kappa} + \frac{\sigma_3^2}{2a^2} + \frac{\rho_3\sigma_1\sigma_3}{a} - \frac{\rho_2\sigma_2\sigma_3}{\kappa a} \tag{45}$$

which gives substantially higher values: 4.19% per year for oil futures and 2.70% per year for copper futures. This difference of 1.48% per year for oil futures and 1.95% per year for copper futures can make a big difference for futures prices with 10 years to maturity, as can be observed in the figures.

The infinite-maturity discount bond yield assumed in Model 3 has significant impact on the value to which the forward cost of carry converges. If the model is re-estimated with an infinite maturity discount yield of 6% instead of 7%, there is practically no change in the estimated parameters, but the forward cost of carry converges to 3.56% for oil (instead of 4.19%) and 2.00% for copper (instead of 2.70%). These values are still higher, but much closer to those in Model 2.

Even when the models are estimated with the longer-term Enron oil data, the forward cost of carry converges to a higher value in Model 3 (3.38% per year) than in Model 2 (2.25% per year). When Model 3 is re-estimated assuming an infinite maturity discount bond yield of 6% instead of 7%, the obtained value of 3.03% per year is closer to that in Model 2.

To give some insight into the performance of the models on longer-term data when they are estimated on short-term data, we estimate the parameters of the three models using the first five forward prices of the Enron oil data with maturities of two months to 1.5 years and then analyse how well they price the last five forward contracts with maturities of two to nine years. Table 19 reports the root mean square error, both in dollars and in percentages, for Models 1 and 2 and for two versions of Model 3, one assuming a 7% infinite-maturity discount bond yield and the other a 6%. The table shows that Model 2 always outperforms Model 1, with a RMSE on all contracts of 5.8% versus 7%. Model 3 performs the best when a 6% infinite-maturity discount bond yield is assumed (with a RMSE on all contracts of 3.9%), but performs the worst when a 7% infinite-maturity discount yield is assumed (with

Table 19. Cross-section comparison between Models 1, 2 and 3 out-of-sample Enron oil data January 15, 1993–May 16, 1996

	RMSE (in US$)			
Model	**1**	**2**	**3 (7%)**	**3 (6%)**
Two years	0.35	0.09	0.16	0.20
Three years	0.65	0.29	0.37	0.38
Five years	1.29	0.80	0.96	0.65
Seven years	1.79	1.40	1.93	0.87
Nine years	2.24	2.14	3.27	1.33
All	1.44	1.20	1.76	0.79
	RMSE (in %)			
	1	**2**	**3 (7%)**	**3 (6%)**
Two years	1.91	0.49	0.86	1.12
Three years	3.42	1.45	1.91	1.98
Five years	6.42	3.94	4.89	3.24
Seven years	8.59	6.84	9.53	4.24
Nine years	10.53	10.22	15.68	6.38
All	6.95	5.81	8.54	3.85

a RMSE on all contracts of 8.5%). This confirms the importance of the interest rate process parameters in Model 3 for the valuation of long-term contracts. The main difference between Models 2 and 3 remains the valuation of long-term futures contracts.

Hedging contracts for future delivery

An issue that has received increased attention in the literature[28] is the feasibility of hedging long-term forward commitments in commodities with the existing short-term futures contracts. The three models discussed in this chapter have implications for hedging strategies, which we now briefly discuss.

To properly hedge a forward commitment in a particular commodity, the sensitivity of the present value of the commitment with respect to each one of the underlying factors must equal the sensitivity of the portfolio of futures contracts used to hedge the commitment with respect to the same factors. This implies that the number of futures contracts required for the hedge is equal to the number of factors in the model used. Since Models 1 and 2 assume constant interest rates – and therefore futures prices are equal to forward prices – the present value of the forward commitment per unit of the commodity can simply be obtained by discounting the future (forward) price in equations (7) and (18).[29] For Model 3 the present value of a forward commitment, $P(S, \delta, r, T)$, is given in equation (30).

The number of long positions, w_i, in future contract with maturity t_i required to hedge a forward commitment to deliver one unit of a commodity at time T is then obtained in each of the models by solving the following system of equations.

Model 1 (from equation (7)):

$$w_1 F_S(S, t_1) = e^{-rT} F_S(S, T) \qquad (46)$$

12. Hedging 10-year oil forward commitments with futures contracts

(a) The figure shows the number of one-month oil futures contracts required in Model 1 to hedge a 10-year forward commitment to deliver one barrel of oil, as a function of the current spot price. (b) The figure shows the number of one-month and one-year oil futures contracts required in Model 2 to hedge a 10-year forward commitment to deliver one barrel of oil, as a function of the current instantaneous convenience yield. (c) The figure shows the number of one-month and six-month oil futures contracts and one-year unit discount bonds required in Model 3 to hedge a five-year forward commitment to deliver one barrel of oil, as a function of the current instantaneous interest rate and convenience yield.

(a) Model 1: one-month futures

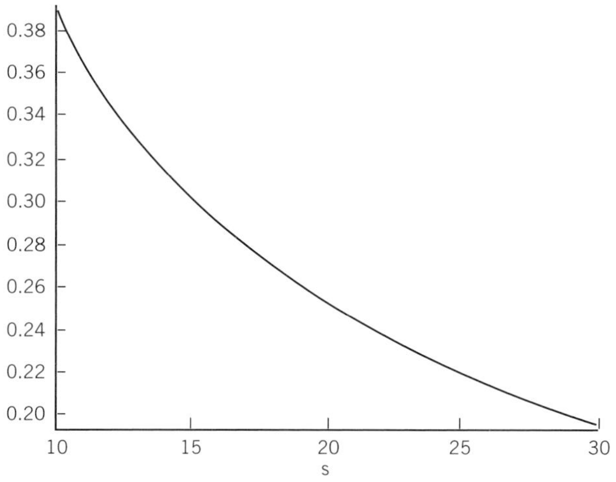

(b) Model 2: one-month and one-year futures

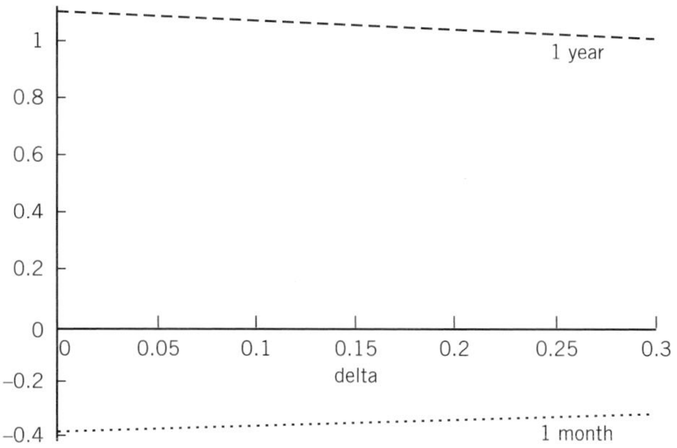

(c) Model 3: one- and six-month futures and one-year discount bond

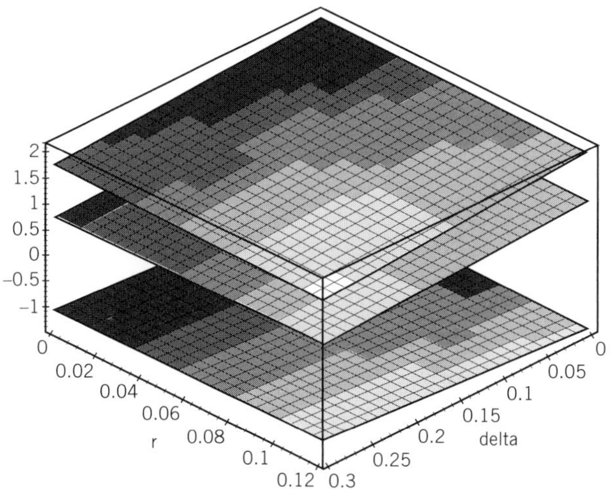

Model 2 (from equation (18)):

$$w_1 F_S(S, \delta, t_1) + w_2 F_S(S, \delta, t_2) = e^{-rT} F_S(S, \delta, T)$$
$$w_1 F_\delta(S, \delta, t_1) + w_2 F_\delta(S, \delta, t_2) = e^{-rT} F_\delta(S, \delta, T) \quad (47)$$

Model 3 (from equations (26) and (30)):[30]

$$w_1 F_S(S, \delta, r, t_1) + w_2 F_S(S, \delta, r, t_2) + w_3 F_S(S, \delta, r, t_3) = P_S(S, \delta, r, T)$$
$$w_1 F_\delta(S, \delta, r, t_1) + w_2 F_\delta(S, \delta, r, t_2) + w_3 F_\delta(S, \delta, r, t_3) = P_\delta(S, \delta, r, T)$$
$$w_1 F_r(S, \delta, r, t_1) + w_2 F_r(S, \delta, r, t_2) + w_3 F_r(S, \delta, r, t_3) = P_r(S, \delta, r, T) \quad (48)$$

Note that in Models 2 and 3 the hedge ratios w_i are independent of the spot price S.

Figure 12 illustrates the positions required to hedge a 10-year forward commitment to deliver one barrel of oil implied by the three models, using the parameter estimates from the Enron data. Panel A presents the number of one-month oil futures contracts required in Model 1 as a function of the spot price. Due to the strong mean-reversion implied by this model, the hedging positions are unreasonably low. For example, for a spot price of US$20 the hedge ratio is only 0.25. Panel B shows the number of one-month futures contracts short and the number of one-year futures contract long required in Model 2 to hedge the 10-year oil forward commitment as a function of the convenience yield. Even though the hedge ratios do not depend on the spot price, we need two futures contracts to hedge the two risk factors in the model.[31] For example, for a convenience yield of 0.10, the hedge ratios are 1.09 long in the one-year contract and 0.34 short in the one-month contract. Finally, Panel C displays the number of six-month futures contracts long (top surface), one-month futures contracts short (bottom surface), and one-year unit discount bonds long (middle surface) required in Model 3 as a function of the convenience yield and the instantaneous interest rate. For example, for a convenience yield of 0.10 and an interest rate of 0.05, the hedge ratios are 1.96 long in the six-month contract, 1.29 short in the one-month contract and 0.94 long in the one-year discount bond. In this case we take positions in the discount bond to hedge against changes in interest rates. Note that in this model, as well as in Model 2, the hedge ratios are not very sensitive to the factors.

Investment under uncertainty

The stochastic behaviour of commodity prices has important implications for the valuation of projects related to the prices of those commodities (mines, oil deposits) and for the determination of the optimal investment rule – ie, the commodity price above which it is optimal to undertake the project immediately. In this section we analyse a simple investment project and evaluate it using the three models developed in this chapter and two other benchmark procedures. The first benchmark is the traditional discounted cashflow (DCF) criterion and the second is a real option approach based on the assumption that commodity prices follow a geometric random walk – that is, neglecting mean-reversion.

The objective of this section is to show that different methods of analysis can give quite different values for an investment project and for the optimal investment rule, even if the assumptions made in each methodology are as realistic as possible. To be able to judge which methodology is superior, however, we would need to apply them to situations in which we have valid transaction prices. The conclusion to a recent article in the *Engineering and Mining Journal* on the capital budgeting methods used by mining companies directly addresses the issue we want to raise:

> The use of DCF techniques to project valuations appears to be the industry standard. One disturbing result of the study, however, is the inability to explain the high premium that market values command over DCF valuations. The well known and used DCF analysis does not allow for placing premium values on projects under consideration. Perhaps the newer techniques such as option pricing methods of valuation may provide more accurate market value results. (Bhappu and Guzman, 1995, page 38.)

We want to analyse a project as simply as possible but retaining the main features that we want to highlight. Consider a copper mine that can produce one ounce of copper at the end of each year for 10 years. Suppose that the initial investment required is K = US$2 and that

Table 20. Investment criteria and project value in mine example

Row	Model	δ	r	NPV = 0	S*	$S_1 = 0.50$	$S_2 = 1.00$	$S_3 = 1.50$
1	DCF	**	0.10	0.73	0.73	–1.40	1.61*	4.61*
2	DCF	**	0.12	0.76	0.76	–1.45	1.29*	4.03*
3	DCF	**	0.15	0.82	0.82	–1.52	0.88*	3.28*
4	Model 0	0.118	0.06	0.89	1.30	0.11	0.99	3.38*
5	Model 1	**	0.06	0.26	0.97	1.23	1.75*	2.52*
6	Model 2	0.10	0.06	0.70	1.12	0.27	2.38	5.94*
7	Model 2	0.25	0.06	0.80	1.20	0.16	1.68	4.68*
8	Model 2	0.40	0.06	0.90	1.32	0.09	1.15	3.58*
9	Model 3	0.10	0.03	0.69	0.96	0.19	2.29*	5.99*
10	Model 3	0.25	0.03	0.79	1.10	0.17	1.42	4.60*
11	Model 3	0.40	0.03	0.90	1.24	0.15	0.83	3.38*
12	Model 3	0.10	0.06	0.66	1.02	0.25	2.55	6.25*
13	Model 3	0.25	0.06	0.75	1.14	0.21	1.69	4.86*
14	Model 3	0.40	0.06	0.86	1.26	0.18	1.05	3.64*
15	Model 3	0.10	0.09	0.62	1.18	0.32	2.81	6.48*
16	Model 3	0.25	0.09	0.71	1.24	0.27	1.96	5.09*
17	Model 3	0.40	0.09	0.82	1.36	0.23	1.29	3.87*

* For copper spot prices above S* it is optimal to invest immediately.
** This model does not use the convenience yield.
DCF = Discounted cashflow.

the unit cost of production is C = US\$0.40 (constant for the 10 years). Assume that, once the investment is done, production will go ahead for the following 10 years; that is, we ignore in this analysis the options to close and open the mine and the option to abandon it[32] and concentrate entirely on the option to invest. The first step in all the procedures we will discuss consists in the determination of the net present value of the project once it has been decided to go ahead with the investment (this is the "boundary condition" of the second step), and the second step consists in the evaluation of the option to invest. The net present value of the project once the investment has been decided is

$$NPV = \sum_{T=1}^{10} P(r,T,\cdot) - C\sum_{T=1}^{10} B(r,T) - K \tag{49}$$

where $P(r,T,\cdot)$ is the present value of the commodity to be received at time T when the interest rate is r (it also depends on the specific factors of a particular model) and, similarly, $B(r,T)$ is the present value of US\$1 (which is equal to $\exp(-rT)$ when the interest rate is constant). It is important to note that the net present value, NPV, in equation (49) will be different for the different approaches since each one of them implies a different present value for the commodity to be received some time in the future (and also for the interest rate in Model 3).

We will first evaluate our simple project using the traditional DCF criterion and the constant convenience yield model of Brennan and Schwartz (1985). Then we will evaluate it using the three models developed and estimated in this chapter. All the results are reported in Table 20, which gives the copper spot price above which it is optimal to invest, S^*, the value of the project for copper spot prices of S_1 = US\$0.50, S_2 = US\$1.00 and S_3 = US\$1.50, and the copper spot price at which the net present value of the project is zero (NPV = 0).

DISCOUNTED CASHFLOW CRITERIA

In this approach the expected net cashflows are discounted at a rate that reflects the risk of these cashflows, so we need to specify the discount rate and the expected futures copper spot prices for the next 10 years. In practice, it is common to assume that spot prices will remain constant or use some industry prediction of future spot prices and use discount rates that vary between 0.10 and 0.15.[33] In rows 1, 2 and 3 of Table 20 we report the results using risk-adjusted discount rates of 0.10, 0.12 and 0.15, respectively, and a flat copper spot price. At a discount rate of 0.12 the net present value is zero for a copper price of US\$0.76 and the value of the mine is US\$1.29 for a copper price of US\$1.00. Note that the value of the project is very sensitive to the discount rate used, almost doubling from US\$0.88 for a discount rate of 0.15 to US\$1.61 for a discount rate of 0.10. There is always a discount rate that gives the same value as the other approaches discussed below but, as we shall see, all option-based methods give spot prices above which it is optimal to invest significantly higher than in the discounted cashflow criterion. The assumption of constant copper spot prices is also quite arbitrary; small deviations from this assumption can give very different project values.

CONSTANT CONVENIENCE YIELD: MODEL 0

In the methods that use the real options approach to valuation, instead of discounting expected cashflows at a risk-adjusted discount rate, certainty-equivalent cashflows are discounted at the risk-free interest rate. For commodities this certainty-equivalent cashflow is related to the forward price of the underlying commodity, which is equal to the futures price if the interest rate is constant. The different models make different assumptions about the stochastic behaviour of commodity prices and therefore imply a different valuation of forward and futures contracts.

In the constant convenience yield model, which we shall call Model 0, the risk-adjusted process for the spot commodity price is assumed to follow a geometric Brownian motion:

$$\frac{dS}{S} = (r - c)\,dt + \sigma\,dz^* \tag{50}$$

where we use c for the convenience yield to distinguish it from δ used in the stochastic convenience yield models. In this model the net present value (49) becomes

$$NPV(S) = S\sum_{T=1}^{10} e^{-cT} - C\sum_{T=1}^{10} e^{-rT} - K = S\beta_1 - \beta_2 \tag{51}$$

and the option to invest, $V(S)$, satisfies the ordinary differential equation

$$\tfrac{1}{2}\sigma^2 S^2 V_{SS} + (r - c)SV_S - rV = 0 \tag{52}$$

subject to the boundary condition

$$V(S) \geq \max[S\beta_1 - \beta_2, 0] \tag{53}$$

The solution to this equation is

$$V(S) = (S^*\beta_1 - \beta_2)\left(\frac{S}{S^*}\right)^d$$

where

$$S^* = \frac{\beta_2 d}{\beta_1(d - 1)}$$

$$d = \frac{1}{2} - \frac{r - c}{\sigma^2} + \sqrt{\left(\frac{1}{2} - \frac{r - c}{\sigma^2}\right)^2 + \frac{2r}{\sigma^2}} \tag{54}$$

S^* is the commodity price above which it is optimal to invest in the project.

Row 4 of Table 20 shows the results for Model 0. The future contract closest to maturity (F_1) is used as a proxy for the spot to compute the standard deviation of the return on the spot copper price ($\sigma = 0.266$) and the convenience yield is computed as the average of the weekly convenience yields calculated from the first (F_1) and the last (F_9) futures contract assuming an interest rate of 0.06 ($c = 0.118$). The critical copper price is US\$1.30, which is, as expected, substantially higher than those obtained using the DCF criterion, and the value of the option to invest when the price of copper is US\$1.00 is US\$0.99; only for a discount rate of 0.15 does the discounted cashflow criterion give a lower value of the project at this price. The reason for this is that with the estimated convenience yield for this period of approximately 0.12 and an interest rate of 0.06, the risk-adjusted drift is close to −0.06, which implies that the term structure of futures prices is declining at a rate of 6% per year.[34]

MEAN-REVERTING SPOT PRICE: MODEL 1

The net present value in Model 1 is obtained from equation (49) by discounting the futures (or forward) prices as given by equation (7). To obtain the value of the investment option, $V(S)$, we need to solve a partial differential equation (PDE) identical to equation (9) except that in the right-hand side we have rV instead of zero (also, if the investment option has infinite maturity, the partial derivative with respect to time-to-maturity disappears). The boundary condition is the maximum of the net present value for this case and zero.

The PDE is solved by numerical methods and the results using the estimated parameters from Table 5 are reported in row 5 of Table 20.[35] Since in this model futures prices converge to US$0.88 with zero volatility whatever the initial copper spot price, the value of the project is less sensitive to the spot price than in any of the other methods discussed and the net present value becomes negative only when the spot price is below US$0.26, the lowest of any other case considered. In spite of this the critical spot price is quite high at US$0.97 since the spot price has a relatively high volatility.

STOCHASTIC CONVENIENCE YIELD: MODEL 2

For this model the NPV in equation (49) depends on both the spot price and the convenience yield, and the present value of one unit of the commodity is obtained by discounting the future (or forward) price given in equation (18). The value of the option to invest, $V(S, \delta)$, satisfies a PDE identical to (17) except that the right-hand side is rV instead of zero.

The corresponding PDE is solved numerically for the estimated parameters in Table 7 and the results are given in rows 6, 7 and 8 of Table 20 for instantaneous convenience yields of 0.10 (a low convenience yield), 0.25 (an average convenience yield),[36] and 0.40 (a high convenience yield), respectively. Since the convenience yield is highly correlated with the spot price and strongly mean-reverting, a low convenience yield indicates that spot prices will tend to go up, so the commodity spot price above which it is optimal to invest is lower and the value of the option to invest higher than when the convenience yield is high, which indicates that spot prices will tend to go down. For comparison with the other models it is best to focus on the case with average convenience yield: the critical spot price of US$1.20 is lower than in Model 0, where mean-reversion is neglected, but higher than Model 1, where mean-reversion seems to be too strong for longer maturities.

STOCHASTIC CONVENIENCE YIELD AND INTEREST RATES: MODEL 3

In Model 3 the NPV of the project equation (49) depends also on the interest rate, in addition to the spot price of the commodity and the convenience yield. The present value of a unit of the commodity deliverable at time T must be computed using equation (30) since now forward prices are not equal to futures prices, and the present value of a unit discount bond must be computed using equation (29). The value of the option to invest, $V(S, \delta, R)$, satisfies a PDE identical to (25) except that the right-hand side is rV instead of zero.

The PDE is solved by numerical methods for the estimated parameters in Table 10 and the results are reported in rows 9–17 of Table 20 for three different values of the convenience yield (0.10, 0.25 and 0.40) and three different interest rates (0.03, 0.06 and 0.09). Copper spot prices that trigger investment and the value of the investment option are very sensitive to the initial value of the convenience yield and interest rate. Note that, for an initial convenience yield of 0.25 and an interest rate of 0.06, the copper spot price that triggers investment is lower than in Model 2 (US$1.14 versus US$1.20) but the value of the investment option is very similar when the spot copper price is US$1.00 (US$1.69 versus US$1.68).

DISCUSSION

To be able to compare the investment implications of the different models we will concentrate on discussion of Model 2, assuming an average initial convenience yield (row 7 of Table 20), and of Model 3, assuming an average initial convenience yield and interest rate (row 13 of Table 20). For the DCF criterion we will assume a risk-adjusted discount rate of 0.12 (row 2 of Table 20). Figure 13 shows, for the different models considered, the net present value of the project once the investment has been decided. The investment will actually be undertaken, however, only when this value is positive for the DCF criterion, or when the investment option is optimally exercised in the other (option) models; this value, then, represents the boundary condition for the investment option problem. From equation (49) and the formulas for forward prices, it is easy to see that in every case except Model 1 the investment value is a linear function of the spot price. The strong mean-

13. Project value implied by different models

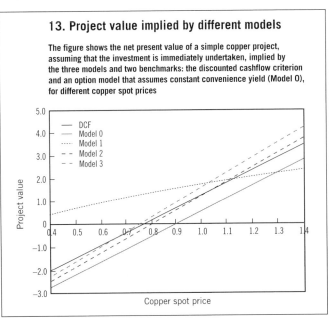

The figure shows the net present value of a simple copper project, assuming that the investment is immediately undertaken, implied by the three models and two benchmarks: the discounted cashflow criterion and an option model that assumes constant convenience yield (Model 0), for different copper spot prices

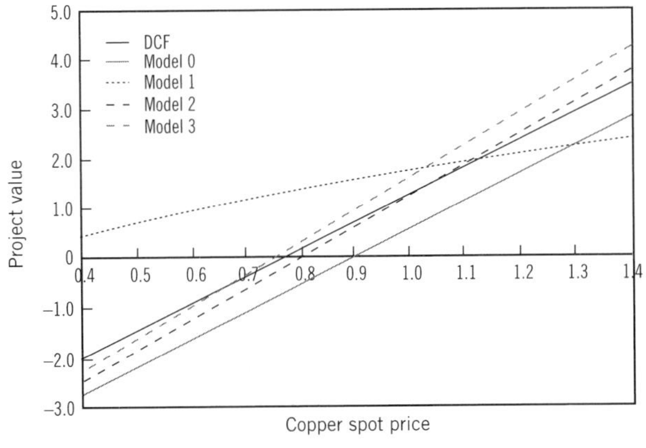

reversion to a fixed price makes the investment value in Model 1 very insensitive to the spot price. The other models give similar values for low spot prices, but their values diverge when the spot price increases, Model 3 giving the highest value, followed by Model 2, the NPV criteria, and finally Model 0. The valuation results for Models 1, 2 and 3 are consistent with the long-term futures prices shown in Figure 11.

When the option element of the investment is considered, the values obtained under the different models will be non-linear functions of the spot price (and also of the other factors in the particular model) and the investment rule will be determined by the optimal exercise of the option. From Table 20 we observe that the NPV criteria give the lowest copper spot price above which it is optimal to invest and Model 0, which does not consider mean-reversion, gives the highest. The three models discussed in this chapter, which take into account mean-reversion, give intermediate copper prices that trigger investment (US$0.97 for Model 1, US$1.20 for Model 2, and US$1.14 for Model 3).

Conclusion

The pricing and hedging of commodity contingent claims and the valuation of natural resource investments depend critically on the assumed stochastic process of the underlying commodity. In this chapter we develop three models that in different ways take into account the mean-reverting nature of commodity prices and estimate them using recent data on oil and copper futures prices.

The major difficulty we encounter in the analysis is that publicly available futures contracts have maturities shorter than two years, whereas many of the assets we wish to price and hedge have maturities much longer than two years. A particular model could fit very well the available short-term futures contracts and do a poor job in predicting longer-term futures prices that are essential for hedging long-term commitments in the commodity or valuing mines or oil deposits. The proprietary oil data provided by Enron has allowed us to gain some insight into this issue.

Each one of the models we consider has implications with respect to the volatility of futures returns and with respect to the behaviour of long-term futures prices. Model 1 implies that the volatility of futures returns will converge to zero and futures prices will converge to a fixed value as maturity increases. Models 2 and 3, however, for the estimated data imply that futures volatility will decrease but converge to a fixed value different from zero and the term structure of futures prices will eventually turn upward and converge to a fixed rate of growth even if initially it is in strong backwardation. The evidence from the Enron oil forward curves imply that these properties are more desirable.

The real options approach to capital budgeting is gaining support both in the academic community and in the practice of finance. The analysis in this chapter suggests that it is very important to consider mean-reversion in prices in evaluation projects. The DCF criterion induces investment too early (ie, when prices are too low), but the real options approach induces investment too late (ie, when prices are too high) when it neglects mean-reversion in prices.

1 *The mean-reverting nature of commodity prices has been considered in a series of recent articles. See, for example, Brennan (1991), Gibson and Schwartz (1990), Cortazar and Schwartz (1994), Bessembinder, Coughenour, Seguin and Smoller (1995) and Ross (1995).*

2 *Since the first two models assume that the interest rate is constant, for these models prices of futures and forward contracts are the same (see Cox, Ingersoll and Ross, 1981).*

3 *See for example Ingersoll and Ross (1992).*

4 *The positive correlation between changes in the spot price and changes in the convenience yield of the commodity is induced by the level of inventories. When inventories of the commodity decrease, the spot price should increase since the commodity is scarce and the convenience yield should also increase since futures prices will not increase as much as the spot price, and vice versa when inventories increase.*

5 *This model is similar to the one proposed by Ross (1995).*

6 *See Ross (1995).*

7 *See for example Bjerksund and Ekern (1995).*

8 *More generally we would expect the market price of risk to be related to the business cycle and to be correlated with the level of inventories.*

9 *The convenience yield can be interpreted as the flow of services accruing to the holder of the spot commodity but not to the owner of a futures contract.*

10 *See Gibson and Schwartz (1990).*

11 *Brennan and Crew (1995) use this formulation in their article.*

12 *This can easily be verified by substitution.*

13 *See for example Gibson and Schwartz (1990).*

14 *As we shall explain later, we estimate a simplified version of Model 3 in which the interest rate process is estimated separately.*

15 *The exact transition equation is:*

$$X_t = \alpha(1 - e^{-\kappa\Delta t}) + e^{-\kappa\Delta t} X_{t-1} + \eta_t$$

Using weekly data, the linear approximation gives the identical parameters estimates up to the fourth significant figure and has been used in all the estimations.

16 *The data obtained from Knight-Ridder Financial consists of daily observations. To approximately transform them into weekly data, every fifth observation from the original data was used in the empirical tests.*

17 *Except for the Enron oil data, where 10 contracts were used in the estimation.*

18 *Also called* innovations *since they represent the new information in the latest observation.*

19 *For the Enron oil data we used an interest rate of 0.05, since in this latter period interest rates were lower.*

20 *A fixed amount of two has been added to each value of the convenience yield to make its scale more comparable with the log of the spot price.*

21 *The mean-reversion coefficient can be obtained by running a regression of changes in interest rate on lagged interest rates. Since there is a lot of measurement error on this parameter, we took an average value.*

22 *Since the correlation between the interest rate process and the commodity spot process is zero, futures prices are equal to forward prices (see Cox, Ingersoll and Ross, 1981); in the estimation we treated the forward prices in the Enron data as futures prices.*

23 *The results for the shorter-maturity data sets are similar. For this reason, in what follows we report only results for the longer-term data.*

24 *The illustrations are representative of the rest of the observations in the sample.*

25 *There are procedures for testing non-nested models. See, for example, Cox (1961, 1962), Atkinson (1970), Pesaran and Deaton (1978) and Davidson and MacKinnon (1981). These procedures, however, are not easily adapted to our framework.*

26 *The reason to deal with log prices comes from their use in the Kalman filter estimation.*

27 *See Cortazar and Schwartz (1994).*

28 *See, for example, Brennan and Crew (1995), Culp and Miller (1994, 1995), Edwards and Canter (1995) and Ross (1995).*

29 *Note that for Model 2 this present value is independent of the interest rate,* r.

30 *Note that in this model the interest risk could be hedged using a bond instead of a third futures contract. This is what we do in the illustration that follows.*

31 *The results here are very similar to those presented for oil in Brennan and Crew (1995).*

32 *For a detailed discussion of these options see Brennan and Schwartz (1985). Since the procedures to evaluate the mine are numerical, it would be trivial to incorporate them in the analysis. We have chosen to leave them out to simplify the analysis and presentation.*

33 *Moyen, Slade and Uppal (1996) report that most firms use a long-run commodity price, that there is a substantial agreement concerning this price, and that the most common hurdle rate used is 15%.*

34 *A more typical long-term convenience yield is 0.06. The example, however, shows the high variability of the convenience yield and its significant impact on valuation.*

35 *For the three cases that involved the numerical solution of the PDE, we assumed that the investment option had a maturity of 10 years.*

36 *The reason this average convenience yield is much larger than the one used in Model 0 is that the former is an instantaneous convenience yield, whereas the latter is a convenience yield obtained between the first and last future contracts available.*

BIBLIOGRAPHY

Atkinson, A. C., 1970, "A Method for Discrimination Between Models", *Journal of the Royal Statistical Society* B32, pp. 323-53.

Bessembinder, H., J. F. Coughenour, P. J. Seguin and M. M. Smoller, 1995, "Mean Reversion in Equilibrium Asset Prices: Evidence from the Futures Term Structure", *Journal of Finance* 50(1), pp. 361-75.

Bhappu, R. R., and J. Guzman, 1995, "Mineral Investment Decision Making: A Study of Mining Company Practices", *Engineering and Mining Journal* 70, pp. 36-8.

Bjerksund, P., 1991, "Contingent Claims Evaluation when the Convenience Yield is Stochastic: Analytical Results", Working paper, Norwegian School of Economics and Business Administration.

Bjerksund, P., and S. Ekern, 1995, "Contingent Claims Evaluation of Mean-Reverting Cashflows in Shipping", in L. Trigeorgis (ed.), *Real Options in Capital Investment: Models, Strategies, and Applications* (Preager).

Brennan, M. J., 1991, "The Price of Convenience and the Valuation of Commodity Contingent Claims", in D. Lund and B. Oksendal (eds), *Stochastic Models and Option Values* (Amsterdam: North-Holland).

Brennan, M. J., and N. Crew, 1995, "Hedging Long Maturity Commodity Commitments with Short-Dated Futures Contracts", Working paper, UCLA. Reprinted as Chapter 16 of the present volume.

Brennan, M. J., and E. S. Schwartz, 1985, "Evaluating Natural Resource Investments", *Journal of Business* 58, pp. 133-55.

Cortazar, G., and E. S. Schwartz, 1994, "The Evaluation of Commodity Contingent Claims", *Journal of Derivatives* 1, pp. 27-39.

Cox, R. C., 1961, "Tests of Separate Families of Hypotheses", in *Proceedings of the Fourth Berkeley Symposium on Mathematical Statistics and Probability*", vol. 1 (University of California Press), pp. 105-23.

Cox, R. C., 1962, "Further Results on Tests of Separate Families of Hypotheses", *Journal of the Royal Statistical Society* B24, pp. 406-24.

Cox, J. C., J. E. Ingersoll and S. A. Ross, 1981, "The Relation Between Forward Prices and Futures Prices", *Journal of Financial Economics* 9, pp. 321-46.

Culp, C. L., and M. H. Miller, 1994, "Hedging a Flow of Commodity Derivatives with Futures: Lessons From Metallgesellschaft", *Derivatives Quarterly* 1, pp. 7-15.

Culp, C. L., and M. H. Miller, 1995, "Metallgesellschaft and the Economics of Synthetic Storage", *Journal of Applied Corporate Finance* 7, pp. 62-76. Reprinted as Chapter 9 of the present volume.

Davidson, R., and J. G. MacKinnon, 1981, "Several Tests for Model Specification in the Presence of Alternative Hypotheses", *Econometrica* 49, pp. 781-93.

Dixit, A. K., and R. S. Pindyck, 1994, *Investment Under Uncertainty* (Princeton University Press).

Edwards, F. R., and M. S. Canter, 1995, "The Collapse of Metallgesellschaft: Unhedgeable Risks, Poor Hedging Strategy, or Just Bad Luck?", *Journal of Applied Corporate Finance* 8(1), pp. 86-105. Reprinted as Chapter 13 of the present volume.

Gibson, R., and E. S. Schwartz, 1990, "Stochastic Convenience Yield and the Pricing of Oil Contingent Claims", *Journal of Finance* 45, pp. 959-76.

Harvey, A. C., 1989, *Forecasting, Structural Time Series Models, and the Kalman Filter* (Cambridge University Press).

Ingersoll, J. E., and S. A. Ross, 1992, "Waiting to Invest: Investment under Uncertainty", *Journal of Business* 65, pp. 1-29.

Jamshidian, F., and M. Fein, 1990, "Closed-form Solutions for Oil Futures and European Options in the Gibson-Schwartz model: A Note", Working paper, Merrill Lynch Capital Markets.

Moyen, N., M. Slade and R. Uppal, 1996, "Valuing Risk and Flexibility: A Comparison of Methods", Working paper, University of British Columbia.

Pesaran, M. H., and A. S. Deaton, 1976, "Testing Non-Nested Non-Linear Regression Models", *Econometrica* 46, pp. 677-94.

Ross, S. A., 1995, "Hedging Long Run Commitments: Exercises in Incomplete Market Pricing", preliminary draft.

Vasicek, O., 1977, "An Equilibrium Characterisation of the Term Structure", *Journal of Financial Economics* 5, pp. 177-88.

Postscript: How the Story Turned Out

Christopher L. Culp and Merton H. Miller
The University of Chicago

Was the MGRM programme so fatally flawed that it was doomed to financial failure before it ever started? That is perhaps still the conventional view in many quarters, but to us the evidence does not support that conclusion. Bollen and Whaley have shown in Chapter 11, for example, that despite the obvious *funding* risks of MGRM's programme, it would have resulted in substantial economic profits for the company in almost any reasonable scenario. In addition, the position that the programme was flawed *from its inception* is hard to sustain if it can be shown that the programme had a positive initial discounted expected net present value (NPV), and we have attempted in Chapters 9 and 10 to demonstrate exactly that.

Our estimates of the value of MGRM's programme have drawn surprisingly little criticism from the academic community. The more common complaint seems to have been that while we may have correctly calculated the *expected* value of MGRM's combined marketing/hedging strategy, we failed to consider the *variance* of the programme.

As evident in many of the essays in this book, variance of either value or cashflows has become the focus of most corporate finance discussions of hedging. Despite the prominent role of variance in any mechanical discussions of how firms hedge, surprisingly little work has been done to substantiate the role of variance at the theoretical level. Classic articles about why risk-averse traders hedge (for example, Johnson in Chapter 1 and Ederington in Chapter 2) imply a variance-minimisation objective. But articles on *corporate* hedging simply argue for the reduction in risk, usually with no specific attention to variance as a source of reduction in the value of the firm. Total variance is treated as a "bad" rather than a "good" virtually by assumption, as in the classic Markowitz investment paradigm. But if the net present-value calculations have been done properly, any negative contributions to a firm's value from variance *should already have been accounted for* in the NPV.

The simplest example of the actual costs supposedly contributed by variance appears in the paper by Mello and Parsons in Chapter 12 of this book. Mello and Parsons presume that cashflow volatility – or, more specifically, increases in volatility that result in decreases in cash – creates costs for a firm through higher external financing costs, as in Myers (1977)* and Froot, Scharfstein and Stein (Chapter 7). To Mello and Parsons, the stack-and-roll approach works fine when prices spike upwards, but price decreases that create variation margin obligations might well put pressure on the firm's short-run borrowing capacity.

Myers (1977) argues that agency costs of external finance are most significant for firms with private information about intangible assets and investment opportunities. Those companies find it more difficult to convey the positive NPVs of their investments to external creditors and consequently face a higher cost of debt. Froot, Scharfstein and Stein suggest that firms plagued with this problem would be well advised to rely as little as possible on external finance and to eliminate their cashflow volatility by hedging.

Yet the Myers and Froot–Scharfstein–Stein analysis adopted by Mello and Parsons and others cannot have applied to MGRM, for a variety of reasons. One is that MGRM's hedged marketing programme was not an *intangible* asset at all; on the contrary, it had a significant positive NPV – easily verifiable by outside calculations – that could have served as ample

* *S. C. Myers (1977), "Determinants of Corporate Borrowing"*, Journal of Financial Economics *3*.

collateral to prospective lenders. True, some *generic* firm following an MGRM-like strategy might have found it difficult to secure external financing quickly after a period of sharply declining oil prices – a company forced into the capital market for liquidity when prices fall could be forced to pay what some might consider "distress costs" for that liquidity, even if the long-run expected NPV of its programme was positive. But external financing costs are all almost totally irrelevant as applied to MGRM. As noted earlier, this company's major shareholders – and creditors – were the two largest banks in Germany and also members of the parent company's supervisory board. MGRM's financing was thus virtually all *internal* from "delegated monitors", and those creditors should have had no trouble seeing the positive NPV of MGRM's programme.

If the NPV of MGRM's hedged marketing programme was positive (as the Bollen–Whaley analysis makes clear), why, then, was it closed down at such great cost? The answer in our opinion lies in one of the hardest problems in all of corporate finance: namely, when is it rational to throw good money after bad? A simple example may help to illustrate the piquancy of this dilemma. Suppose a multinational corporation has a subsidiary in France that is currently incurring net cashflow deficits at the rate of US$1 million per year. The multinational could shut the operation down, but severance pay and other termination expenses required under French law would run to about US$12 million cash, net of after-tax recoveries. Efforts to find a buyer for the subsidiary have not been successful. Suppose that consultants report one of the problems to be inadequate production capacity for some of the plant's products. Additional equipment can be purchased for a current expenditure of about US$4 million and will cut the net cash deficit to about US$500,000 per annum. Suppose the cost of capital is 10% and the planning horizon is 25 years.

The multinational has three options: (1) continue operating at a loss of US$1 million per year; (2) shut down the plant for a current expenditure of US$12 million; or (3) invest US$4 million now to reduce losses to US$500,000 per annum. The NPV of each alternative can be calculated as follows:

$$\mathrm{NPV}_t = \sum_{j=1}^{25} \frac{X_{t+j}}{(1+r)^j} - I_t$$

where r is the firm's cost of capital (10% in our example), X_{t+j} is the net cashflow at time $t + j$, and I_t is the current investment cost (of expansion or shut-down). The NPV of the immediate-shutdown alternative is – US$12,000,000. To maintain the status quo yields a current NPV of – US$9,077,040. And to invest the additional US$4 million today and cut losses to US$500,000 per year thereafter over the 25 years yields a current NPV of – US$8,538,520. Counterintuitive as it may seem, the best option is to invest the additional US$4 million today in plant improvements, even though the French subsidiary is a loss-making operation.

When we have given the French subsidiary example in the classroom, less experienced students faithfully compute the present values and get the right answers. Experienced executives, however, often refuse to do the calculations at all. They say the solution is obvious: shut the plant down and blame the previous management for the loss! MGRM's situation may well have been no different from the example: terminating a swap early is not so different from closing a factory, after all.

Like most major swap dealers, the management board of MG AG – in other words, the board of directors with responsibility for day-to-day operational oversight of the firm and its subsidiaries – sought to limit the firm's exposure to catastrophic bankruptcy risks arising from unhedged spot-price exposure on its delivery obligations. Because MGRM was short its fixed forward commitments, the company sought insulation from financial ruin by using long futures contracts and futures-equivalent swaps. Given the limited range of liquid futures and swaps available, the firm thus went long futures and swaps with maturities ranging from one to three months. For a variety of strategic and organisational reasons discussed in Chapter 9, MGRM chose a one-for-one stack-and-roll hedging strategy, namely long one barrel in futures for every barrel short in forwards, stacked in the short-dated contracts and rolled forward (net of current deliveries) each month.

We know that rolling the stack of short-term futures month by month would indeed have generated the cash (in current-value terms) to insulate MGRM from sudden surges in spot prices. By the same token, a price decline meant a corresponding cash drain for variation margin on the futures. The MGRM marketing subsidiary and the management board of its parent, MG AG, believed that the necessary cash to finance such a margin had been firmly committed by the supervisory board of MG AG. A supervisory board, it will be recalled, is a second type of board of directors in Germany responsible for broad oversight of the management board. In typically German fashion, MG AG's supervisory board represented not only MG's largest stockholders (Deutsche Bank, Dresdner Bank, Daimler-Benz, Allianz Insurance and the Kuwait Investment Authority) but also MGRM's largest *creditors*, again including Deutsche Bank and Dresdner Bank.

In December 1993, after a fairly substantial drop in petroleum product prices during the autumn months and over a billion dollars in variation margin calls, the supervisory board pulled the plug on MGRM. They fired the old management and ordered the immediate liquidation of most of the futures stack - shades of our French subsidiary example.

The decision to liquidate the hedge may have looked safe enough to the supervisory board at the price levels of December 1993 (even though it meant recognising and realising the past losses on the futures contracts), but prices soon began to recover. The profits that MG AG anticipated on its now unhedged forwards threatened to turn into losses. So, in addition to incurring unnecessary costs of hasty liquidation at the end of 1993, the company lost its chance for profits in 1994 and 1995. And to avoid the unhedged spot-price exposure, the company incurred further losses by simply *forgiving* the in-the-money customer contracts rather than closing them out at then current market prices.

In summary, the MGRM disaster occurred because the old MG AG management board *thought* the supervisory board was supporting the activities of MGRM, including the "basis trading" programme set forth in MGRM's 1993 Annual Report, when in fact it was not. Or, alternatively, the supervisory board supported the programme initially but subsequently abandoned MGRM, perhaps in an effort to justify the ousting of the old management board (which the supervisory board seems to have been attempting for some time).

Any post mortem of MGRM has proved difficult because MG AG's lawyers chose to shunt the lawsuits filed by its dismissed former derivatives team off to an arbitration hearing that was closed to the public. Even with the many separate lawsuits in which MG AG ultimately became involved, the settlements invariably had "shut-up" clauses that specified the closure of files to outside inspection. Thus, alas, the full story of MGRM - who did what to whom, when, and why - may never come out.

INDEX

INDEX